The Unity of the Proposition

The Unity of the Proposition

Richard Gaskin

OXFORD
UNIVERSITY PRESS

OXFORD

UNIVERSITY PRESS

Great Clarendon Street, Oxford OX2 6DP

Oxford University Press is a department of the University of Oxford.
It furthers the University's objective of excellence in research, scholarship,
and education by publishing worldwide in

Oxford New York

Auckland Cape Town Dar es Salaam Hong Kong Karachi
Kuala Lumpur Madrid Melbourne Mexico City Nairobi
New Delhi Shanghai Taipei Toronto

With offices in

Argentina Austria Brazil Chile Czech Republic France Greece
Guatemala Hungary Italy Japan Poland Portugal Singapore
South Korea Switzerland Thailand Turkey Ukraine Vietnam

Oxford is a registered trademark of Oxford University Press
in the UK and in certain other countries

Published in the United States
by Oxford University Press Inc., New York

British Library Cataloguing in Publication Data

Data available

Library of Congress Cataloging in Publication Data

Data available

Typeset by Laserwords Private Limited, Chennai, India
Printed in Great Britain
on acid-free paper by
CPI Antony Rowe, Chippenham, Wiltshire

ISBN 978−0−19−923945−0

10 9 8 7 6 5 4 3 2 1

Preface

The problem which, in the Western philosophical tradition, commonly goes under the name 'The Unity of the Proposition' is one with a curious lineage. It is explicitly raised at the end of Plato's *Sophist*, and is implicit in Aristotle's deliberations in the early chapters of *De Interpretatione*, but it is not examined in detail by either philosopher. The problem might be said to lurk just under the surface of Stoic theorizing about reference, and its presence can be detected, occasionally in the foreground but mostly in the background, of medieval treatments of the semantics of the *propositio*. Again, the unity problem can be sensed in the subtext of Leibniz's doctrines of substance and predication, and in Kant's theory of judgement and those of his nineteenth-century successors. But although the problem is to a greater or lesser extent present in earlier texts, it was not until the rise of analytic philosophy in the late nineteenth and early twentieth centuries that the problem both secured clear recognition as an important issue in its own right, and attracted serious attempts at solutions: indeed, it would hardly be an exaggeration to say that the problem furnished the new discipline of analytic philosophy with much of its original rationale. At any rate, we find in the writings of Frege, the early Russell, and the early Wittgenstein not merely an acknowledgement of the depth and difficulty of the problem, but also an urge to tackle it using the newly discovered and sophisticated tools of modern mathematical and philosophical logic.

Frege developed his core notion of the unsaturatedness of the concept specifically in order to solve the problem of unity. Wittgenstein constructed the metaphysics of the *Tractatus* around the notion of logical form, whose purpose, again, was to address the issue of propositional unity. Russell remarked near the beginning of his book on Leibniz, published in 1900: 'That all sound philosophy should begin with an analysis of propositions, is a truth too evident, perhaps, to demand a proof',[1] and he followed his own precept in his seminal work *The Principles of Mathematics*, published in 1903. Ironically, however, not only was the problem of the unity of the proposition deeply implicated in the original rationale of analytic philosophy, but, by presenting the new subject with its first and most basic problem, it also in a sense precipitated that subject's first crisis. For, as Russell remarked in *Principles*, the analysis of

---

[1] [2], p. 8.

a proposition seems inevitably to involve some degree of falsification, since to analyse a proposition into its constituents perforce destroys its unity.[2] This was precisely Bradley's position, the position against which Russell and Moore saw themselves as reacting.[3]

My objective in this book is to solve the problem of propositional unity, in the context of giving as full an account of its background, mainly in the Western tradition, as I judge to be interesting and expedient. But though I make considerable use of historical materials, and draw especially on the writings of Frege, Russell, and Wittgenstein, I should stress that my main aim *is* a systematic one: I have tried to present as full a case as I could devise for my preferred solution to the unity problem. Of course, it goes without saying that it is not possible to ground every part of one's argument. To keep the project within manageable bounds, unargued assumptions have had to be made, including ones that some readers may find objectionable. And I am aware that the linguistic idealism within which I embed the enquiry will raise a few hackles: I attempt some defence of that doctrine in these pages, but a fuller and more adequate treatment must await another occasion. In essaying an account of propositional unity, I do of course incur an obligation to say what propositions—the entities whose unity is up for elucidation—are, and where they are located in the semantic hierarchy, and it is in that context that the topic of linguistic idealism emerges. But to some extent an account of the nature and status of propositions is incidental to an explanation of their unity, and the account of what propositional unity consists in, when I give it, though presented in terms of propositions as I have constructed them, should be readily adaptable to other treatments. In particular, those who favour a Fregean semantical disposition, which locates propositionally structured meanings of declarative sentences (Thoughts[4]) exclusively at the level of sense, and who do not in addition, as I do, locate propositions *in re* at the level of reference as what Thoughts present, ought to find it quite straightforward to apply my account of unity to propositions as they understand them.

The problem of the unity of the proposition intersects with many other issues in metaphysics, in the philosophy of mind, and (most obviously) in the philosophies of language and logic. Donald Davidson remarks:

At one time there was much discussion of what was called the 'unity of the proposition'; it is just this unity that a theory of predication must explain. The philosophy

---

[2] [3], §54. Cf. N. Griffin [4], pp. 160–1; Stevens [1], pp. 237–8; [3], p. 31.
[3] Cf. Küng, p. 24; Candlish [2], pp. 57–8.
[4] I capitalize this word throughout whenever Frege's *Gedanken* are in question.

of language lacks its most important chapter without such a theory; the philosophy of mind is missing a crucial first step if it cannot describe the nature of judgement; and it is woeful if metaphysics cannot say how a substance is related to its attributes.[5]

I touch on some of the wider issues mentioned by Davidson in my study, but my main focus is on the problem as a problem in the philosophy of language. I do not regard that as a genuine curtailment of the domain of investigation because, as I have put it elsewhere, 'the analytic philosophy of language is the context in which our deepest metaphysical and epistemological concerns should be addressed'.[6] As for the other categories Davidson mentions, I have said little about the theory of judgement, except insofar is it has been necessary to do so—it is sometimes necessary, given that, historically speaking, the problem of the unity of the proposition has often been posed in terms of the unity of judgement[7]—because, as I shall explain in due course, the question what unifies mental acts of some particular kind does not, in my view, raise the problem of unity in its deepest form; the same holds for the question what unifies a substance with its attributes.

So far as I know, this book provides a fuller treatment of its topic (at least in its Western manifestation) than has ever been undertaken. Whether or not I succeed in my systematic aim of persuading readers that the solution I offer to the problem of unity is the correct one, I shall certainly have achieved an important subsidiary goal if I manage to convince the philosophical public that the problem of the unity of the proposition is a serious and profound issue which deserves, after long neglect, to be once again the focus of attention. Because the book is long, and contains many detailed discussions of related issues in the philosophy of language, it may be helpful to readers if I here provide a chapter-by-chapter precis of what I take to be the main line of argument. What follows is not intended to be an exhaustive account of the book's contents: there are many important points, both systematic and historical, omitted in the interests of delivering a concise and surveyable conspectus of the whole. But I hope that it will still prove useful in supplying some orientation before the reader plunges into the thickets of the text. (The order of presentation of points in these summaries usually but not always matches the order of their occurrence in the corresponding chapters.)

---

[5] [2], p. 77.   [6] [15], p. 10.
[7] For a representative statement, see e.g. Destutt de Tracy [1], ch. 1, p. 24: 'J'ose affirmer ici qu'aucun grammairien jusqu'à présent n'a connu en quoi consiste précisément l'opération de juger, et que c'est-là la principale cause pour laquelle les meilleurs esprits et les têtes les plus fortes ne nous ont encore donné que de mauvaises théories de langage.'

Chapter 1

The problem of unity is this: what distinguishes a declarative sentence from a mere list of words? (Other kinds of sentence may be presumed, for these purposes, to be conceptually posterior to declaratives.) The tradition has always assumed that declarative sentences are semantically complex, and I argue that this is correct: there would in any case be no issue of unity in respect of absolutely simple entities. Declarative sentences are by definition those that can be true or false. But their meanings—what recent analytic philosophers call propositions—can also be true or false, so that we must ask which of sentences and propositions enjoy metaphysical priority in respect of unity: I argue that propositions do. I outline two senses in which a proposition might be conceived to be the referent of a declarative sentence and connect these with the *suppositio* and *significatio* conceptions of meaning in medieval thought; although the former conception is preferred by Frege and many more recent philosophers, I favour the latter conception, but postpone justification of this choice to Chapter 2. The argument for linguistic idealism, which is the basis of my investigation, is briefly set out, and the chapter concludes with a detailed examination of some of the difficulties that beset Russell in his discussions of propositional unity and related issues between 1903 and 1918: the moral of this historical excursus is that the philosophical problem of propositional unity should not be confused with that of truth: false propositions are just as unified as true ones.

Chapter 2

I introduce the Fregean semantic hierarchy and argue that propositions should be located at the level of reference, as the referents of declarative sentences (the senses of which are Fregean Thoughts). I discuss the semantic hierarchy in some detail, arguing that Frege's assimilation of definite descriptions to proper names was a mistake, and that the entities that Frege called concepts, and rightly located at the level of reference, may be identified with Carnapian intensions. This latter move then enables us to give a more sophisticated account of the nature of propositions at the level of reference. On this more developed account, propositions are functional structures that can be identified with what I call phrase markers *in re*. I argue that there is no objection to construing propositions both as values of unifying functions and as wholes with function and arguments (concept and object, as it might be) as parts. In the remainder of the chapter I consider the viability and status of propositions at the level of reference, answering some objections that have been raised (particularly to the presence of false propositions at that level), and suggesting, in accordance with linguistic idealism, that the world is composed of (true and false) such propositions. As part of this picture, I discharge the debt left over from Chapter I and argue that the *significatio* approach to reference is superior to the *suppositio* approach.

Chapter 3

In this chapter I turn to two important historical accounts of unity that I wish to consider: Frege's and Russell's. These are rather similar accounts in their end effect, and we can abstract here from the differences between them. According to the Frege–Russell story, then, one component of the proposition, the concept, explains the unity of the whole by virtue of what Frege calls its essentially unsaturated nature. I argue that this story fails. Both Frege and Russell succumb to a paradox which vitiates their account of unity. The paradox can indeed be avoided, while remaining within the spirit of their joint account, but only at the cost of refusing to reify concepts, and this manœuvre is in turn obnoxious to a charge of arbitrariness: why are concepts held to be unsaturated (or deprived of entity status), and not objects? I argue that the context principle requires us to regard all components of the proposition as, alike, unsaturated, if any are, and that we have no reason not to treat such components as (unsaturated) objects, their linguistic counterparts being then (unsaturated) names. The only way to make coherent use of Frege's chemical metaphor is to count sentences as saturated, and semantically significant subsentential components as uniformly unsaturated. But, though treating these components as unsaturated objects in our philosophical grammar marks an improvement on Frege's position, we still have the original problem: what distinguishes a sentence from a mere list of (unsaturated) words, and its corresponding proposition from a mere aggregate of (unsaturated) objects?

Chapter 4

Before addressing this question directly, I consider in more detail the charge of arbitrariness that was lodged against Frege's philosophical grammar in Chapter 3. Frege conceives expressions and their referents to be arranged in linguistic and ontological hierarchies with saturated such expressions (referents) located at the zeroth level. (There is also a corresponding hierarchy comprising senses.) But we can construct rival linguistic and ontological hierarchies to Frege's which reverse the positions in the linguistic hierarchy of proper names and monadic concept-expressions, and correspondingly reverse the positions in the ontological hierarchy of their referents. I connect this alternative strategy with the Montague tradition in semantics, and discuss the relevant contributions of Ramsey and Dummett, answering the latter's objections to the viability of the alternative strategy to Frege's (which I call the 'anti-Fregean strategy'). Dummett's qualms are traced to a suspect conception of the relation between language and world, conflicting with the theoretical status of the reference relation and with linguistic idealism. In the remainder of the chapter I provide a detailed discussion of the so-called syntactic priority thesis, distinguishing it from linguistic idealism, and arguing that it is empty.

Chapter 5

Returning to the question left unresolved at the end of Chapter 3, I suggest that a fruitful way forward is to look at artificial languages whose sentences are composed entirely of type-identical names. These cases provide further evidence that concepts and concept-expressions have nothing essentially to do with unity, for the sentences in question are unified in the relevant sense (they can be true or false) but contain no such expressions, and their propositional referents are configurations of entities all of which a Fregean would classify as objects. In general, I argue that no antecedently available ingredient can be what constitutes a proposition as unified, because, to put it compendiously, a mere aggregate can always duplicate the recipe. I introduce the idea of a sentence's logical copula, which is a structural feature common to sentences of ordinary language (which have a grammatical copula) and artificially constructed sentences composed of type-identical names (which do not), and suggest that, trivially, the logical copula does supply the moment of propositional unity—only trivially, because it is simply definitive of the difference between a sentence, however composed (even if composed of type-identical names), and a mere list that the one contains a logical copula which the other lacks. I note that the logical copula's unifying capacity is embodied in a regress that arises when it is nominalized and we try to specify its reference. I look at traditional attitudes to this regress (Bradley's regress), especially Russell's. The chapter concludes with an examination of Russell's and Wittgenstein's attempts to avoid Bradley's regress in their discussions of propositional unity and logical form.

Chapter 6

I argue that the generation of a regress consequent on the specification of the logical copula's reference or referent (these options are distinct and I claim that, for these purposes, we do not need to choose between them) is the solution to the unity problem. Bradley's regress is not vicious, as many have supposed, but an innocent, constituting regress. This solution is a semantic, not a pragmatic, one: I argue that this is just what is wanted. Perhaps unexpectedly, it turns out that there is no ontological midpoint between a fully unified proposition, on the one hand, and sheer disunity, on the other: the referents of complex names turn out, upon analysis, to be propositionally unified, and the 'mere aggregates' that have been serving, from the beginning of the investigation, as the point of contrast with propositions, turn out to consist of sheer objects, with no—even minimal—principle of cohesion. In the general case we may think of the reference or referent of the logical copula as a unifying function applied to the proposition's other components as its arguments. The analysis of that operation of functional application draws down a regress that is in all relevant respects the same as Bradley's regress. It is its generation of the functional application regress which is what the unity of a proposition, in the general case, consists in.

So much, then, by way of summary of the book's contents. Earlier versions of parts of this book have been read to various audiences in the UK and in Germany, and I have benefited from the comments of the participants in these occasions. Otherwise, I have received intellectual stimulation or practical assistance from the following (though the period of gestation has been sufficiently long that they may not all remember it): Allan Bäck, Stewart Candlish, Andrew Chitty, Ron Chrisley, Barry Dainton, Paul Davies, Nick Denyer, Julian Dodd, Jonardon Ganeri, Bob Hale, Daniel Hill, Klaus Jacobi, Ulrike Kleemeier, David Langslow, Michael McGhee, Stephen McLeod, Peter Milne, Michael Morris, Ulrich Nortmann, Francesco Orilia, Claude Panaccio, Pauline Phemister, Graham Priest, Oliver Primavesi, Murali Ramachandran, R. R. Rockingham Gill, Oliver Scholtz, William Stirton, Rainer Stuhlmann-Laeisz, Peter Sullivan, Hermann Weidemann, Alan Weir, Bernhard Weiss, and David Wiggins. I thank all of these most cordially, and any others who should figure in this list but whom I have inadvertently omitted to mention. I am especially grateful to Barry Dainton, Daniel Hill, Stephen McLeod, William Stirton, and the two anonymous readers for the Press, all of whom gave me very useful comments on (part or all of) an advanced draft of the book. At the Press, Victoria Patton and Catherine Berry have been sympathetic and generous editors throughout. At various points in the text I have made use of short extracts from previously published articles of mine, though in all cases the adopted material has been rewritten; but, insofar as any materials from earlier articles appear unchanged in the present work, I am grateful to the

Austrian Ludwig Wittgenstein Society, Basil Blackwell, Taylor & Francis, and Cambridge University Press for permission to reuse them. It remains to add that I alone am responsible for the final product; and to thank my family for their unfailing support and encouragement over the period in which the project has come to fruition.

Contents

4 The Hierarchy of Levels and the Syntactic Priority Thesis   208

When two terms have a relation, is the relation related to each? To answer affirmatively would lead at once to an endless regress; to answer negatively leaves it inexplicable how the relation can in any way belong to the terms. I am entirely unable to solve this difficulty, but I am not convinced that it is insoluble. . . . When a subject has a predicate, is the predicability of the predicate a new predicate of the subject? The question seems to raise precisely the same difficulty. . . To solve this difficulty—if indeed it be soluble—would, I conceive, be the most valuable contribution which a modern philosopher could possibly make to philosophy.

(Russell, 'The Classification of Relations', [16], p. 146.)

1

Truth, Falsity, and Unity

1 Sentences, Lists, and Collections

We start from the traditional and familiar observation that a sentence has a certain unity, distinguishing it from a 'mere list' of words, as it is often put. In virtue of that unity, a sentence manages not merely to mention the things its component words refer to or are about, as a list would do, but to accomplish something in respect of those referents, to 'make a move in the language-game', in Wittgenstein's arresting phrase,[1] or, in an older terminology that has been influential down the ages, to achieve a *perfecta oratio*.[2] The point that a sentence manages to do more than a mere list goes back to a well-known passage in Plato's *Sophist*, where we are told that the sentence 'man understands' reveals something

about the things that are or are becoming or that have been or are going to be, and does not merely name, but achieves something (*perainei ti*), by interweaving (*sumplekôn*) verbs with names. Wherefore we affirm that it says (*legein*) [something] and does not merely name (*onomazein*), and indeed we have bestowed the name *logos* on this combination.[3]

Now a sentence makes not just any old move in the language-game, but a move of a special kind; it is perfect in a distinctive way; it achieves something unprecedented. As Monboddo put it in his treatise on the origin of language,

[I]t is evident, that any number of words, expressing in the most clear and accurate manner the several things they stand for, would convey no meaning at all, if they were not some way or another connected together. For though the bare utterance of the words would let us know that the speaker had the ideas affixed to the words; yet, without some connection of those words, there would be no *speech*, because there

---

[1] [5], I, §49.
[2] See Priscian, *Inst. Gramm.* 17. 3 (Keil ii, pp. 108.16–109.3). Cf. Abelard [2], p. 148.27–8; de Rijk [4], pp. 95–6. On Peter of Spain's use of the terminology, see Prior [3], p. 15.
[3] *Sophist* 262d2–6.

would be neither affirmation nor denial, prayer or command expressed, nor any other operation of the mind.[4]

Of course, contrary to what our author here seems to suggest, lists as well as sentences may have a kind of unity. Some lists indeed have an implied *sentential* unity: a shopping list given by one person to another, for instance, might have the implied structure '[you are to buy the following things:] five red apples, . . .'. But the point in framing a contrast between sentences and 'mere lists' is that a list need not, just as such, have the kind of unity that is distinctive of sentences: a list can indeed be a *mere* list. One might have framed the contrast differently, in terms of the difference between sentences and, for example, sheer unorganized medleys or assemblages of words—collections that are not sufficiently coherent even to merit the label 'list'—and the traditional problem of the unity of the sentence is indeed sometimes posed in such terms. After all, it is not as though just *any* conceivable item we pick to contrast with sentences and their distinctive kind of unity will inevitably have unity of *some* sort: surely we might contrast sentences with medleys of objects (words, as it might be) having, as such—or being conceived in this context to have—*no* kind of unity.

For any such medley, it is doubtless a short step to conceiving it as unified—indeed in calling the item in question a medley, in thinking of *it* as a single *entity* at all, one has presumably already taken that minimal step.[5] For surely any plurality can be unified, and contrariwise: *pluralitas et unitas convertuntur*—or so one would naïvely think. At any rate, we see this two-way process in operation constantly—the unification of plurality and the plurification of unity—and the gracing of a hitherto unassembled collection of objects with the title of unity, or the articulation into discrete parts of what had hitherto counted as an undifferentiated whole, are processes that can be of enduring significance in our lives. To take an obvious case of the former type of transaction: the constellations of the zodiac are, in one sense, wholly artificially assembled. We have, since time immemorial, grouped into these constellations stars which, considered objectively, stand in no significant natural relation to one another, save that of belonging to a common space–time manifold, and in many cases, despite their apparent relative proximity judged by the naked eye from the surface of our planet—as seen from a ship at sea on a clear night, say—are in fact separated by such enormous distances in the plane of the ecliptic that their mutual influence is negligible. To be sure, stellar constellations are perhaps a rather unexciting example of collections of

---

[4] Monboddo, II. i, §1 (vol. ii, p. 16); cf. Hobbes [1], I. ii, §3.

[5] Cf. Frege, letter to Russell of 28 July 1902 ([22], p. 222): 'Indem man von einer Vielheit oder Menge etwas aussagt, behandelt man sie als Gegenstand'.

loosely related entities: after all, their members are physical objects of a broadly similar composition. But we can easily come up with more heterogeneous groupings of objects—for instance, to borrow an example of Husserl's which was criticized by Frege: redness, the Moon, and Napoleon;[6] or, even more miscellaneously, the centre of gravity of the universe, Mont Blanc's snowfields, Shakespeare's *Julius Caesar*, the cardinal number $\beth_\omega$, the sound of middle C-sharp played on a clarinet, the murder of Wallenstein, the mereological sum of my cat Hesperus and the planet Venus, and my current headache.

It would seem that even the most outrageously gerrymandered collection of disparate items still has a unity of a sort, or, as I noted above, if it does not have any natural unity, it surely can, by the slightest of ontological swerves, be invested with a unity—if only the minimal unity accruing to it in virtue of its being that very collection.[7] At least, that is what, as I put it above, one would naïvely suppose. But here the reader may be tempted to object that our slogan 'pluralitas et unitas convertuntur' cannot be granted unrestricted application. As David Lewis remarks, following a long line of commentators, 'we dare not say that whenever there are some things, there is a class of them, because there can be no class of all non-self-members'.[8] Lewis here alludes to what is known as Russell's paradox,[9] which concerns the class of all classes that are not members of themselves, a class which, if it existed, would both have to contain and not contain itself as a member. But I shall for the moment ignore this putative exception to our slogan, and embrace the following permissive collection-formation principle: wherever and whenever there are some things, there is a collection comprising just those things. This principle actually adapts to the case of collections Lewis's own formulation of an unrestricted principle of mereological fusion:[10] he, of course, would not approve of the adaptation, as the passage cited above indicates. But I postpone the question of our principle's status and justification to later in this study (§§63, 79).

A collection's attaining to whatever degree of unity it possesses is, despite the language I employed in the last paragraph of 'investing' the item in question with unity, not a matter of whether anyone ever *thinks* of it as a unified collection or not—nor even whether anyone *can think* of it as unified, unless

---

[6] Husserl [1], p. 74. Frege's objection is driven by his intensionalist approach to classes: [9], pp. 322–3 ([21], pp. 185–6). Cf. Angelelli [1], pp. 97–101. I return to this point in §33 below.

[7] Cf. Lewis [7], pp. 12–13.

[8] [5], p. 8. Cf. Zermelo [2], p. 124; Gödel *apud* Wang [3], p. 260; Wang [2], pp. 310–11.

[9] Some writers call it the Russell–Zermelo paradox in recognition of the fact that, though it was independently discovered and popularized by Russell, in strict chronological terms it had already been formulated by Zermelo: see G. H. Moore, p. 105; Ebbinghaus, pp. 45–7. But I shall continue to use the standard label.

[10] [5], pp. 7, 74, 79–81.

one takes that proviso in a thin, transcendental sense amounting to no genuine constraint on the existence of the relevant collection. For I want no truck with any kind of psychologism (such as Husserl embraces[11]) about the ontological status of arbitrary collections.[12] Nor do I require that a collection be in any substantial sense collectible, let alone collected, by anyone at any time. In espousing realism about collections I follow Gödel:

> Classes and concepts may . . . be conceived as real objects, namely classes as 'pluralities of things' or as structures consisting of a plurality of things and concepts as the properties and relations of things existing independently of our definitions and constructions.[13]

Gödel here adjoins to his realism about classes a parallel realism (as opposed to a conceptualism, or constructivism, or conventionalism) about concepts, 'which, as well as their properties, we can create as little as [we can] the primitive constituents of matter and their properties';[14] and I endorse that too. The realism of my position on collections comes out in the twin facts that (i) I agree with Husserl against Frege that such collections do not require any lawlike and antecedently stateable collecting *principle*, that no entities are so disparate, so ontologically ill-matched, so minimally related to each other, or so many that they cannot form a unified collection; and (ii) I agree with Frege against Husserl, and with Gödel, in rejecting a psychologistic or constructivist account of what unifies collections.

It might be tempting to connect the existence of such arbitrary collections with the thesis that there are more objects than names—that there are uncountably many objects, but only countably many names.[15] But the fact that there exist arbitrary collections, collections with no purely general, conceptual principle of membership, no antecedently formulable concept-expression that collects the relevant objects in a lawlike way, is not significantly related to the fact—if it is one, a matter to which I shall return shortly (§5)—that there are only countably many names. Entailment fails in both directions: (i) concepts, so understood, may collect uncountably many objects; and (ii) countable and even finite collections may be arbitrarily assembled, that is, may be associated with no purely conceptual principle of membership.[16] Presumably the miscellany I mentioned above (the centre of gravity of the universe, etc.) is a case of a finite collection with no general collecting principle: I say 'presumably', because we

---

[11] Husserl deploys the example I have cited in the text in a context where he is arguing for psychologism about collections.

[12] Cf. Black [3], p. 618; Jubien [1], pp. 91–2.   [13] Gödel, ii, p. 128.

[14] Gödel, iii, p. 360. Cf. von Kutschera [2], p. 321; Crocco [2], esp. pp. 188–90. In this Gödel follows Frege, whose concepts (*Begriffe*) are not necessarily 'denoted by expressions of any language we use or understand' (C. Parsons [2], p. 283).

[15] So Muller, p. 421.   [16] Cf. Hale [2], pp. 242–3.

cannot rule out a priori that a future pure or applied science will discover some theoretically or empirically significant kind to which just these objects belong. But it seems unlikely. Note that the fact of their being mentioned together in this book does *not* yield a collecting principle for those objects within the meaning of the act; and in general we may observe that a principle of collection whose specification depends in any essential way on enumerating the elements of the collection—so a specification of what it is to be ϕ along the lines of the schema

$$\phi x \leftrightarrow (x = a) \vee (x = b) \vee \ldots,^{17}-$$

does not count as conceptual in the relevant sense, because it is not purely general (lawlike). The idea of a concept's antecedent availability, in the sense I have just specified, is going to be important for me in due course (especially in §79), and I pause here to draw attention to it and to distinguish it from another idea with which it might be confused, that of recursiveness. Again, entailment fails in both directions: (i) finite collections are recursive but not necessarily collected by an antecedently available concept; and (ii) although, as is familiar, the consequences of any consistent, recursive set of axioms strong enough to prove statements of elementary arithmetic themselves form a non-recursive set,[18] that set, though non-recursive, does have a principle of collection which is antecedently available, in my sense, seeing that we are able to specify precisely the axioms we have in mind, and what it is for a sentence to be a consequence of those axioms.[19]

The key point about the items with which we find ourselves contrasting sentences together with their distinctively sentential kind of unity is that these contrasting items do not, as such (or as conceived in this context), have *sentential* unity. Perhaps they do not (or are not being conceived to) have any kind of unity at all; or perhaps they (are being allowed to) form an at least minimal unity, the sort of unity that accrues to a mere collection, in which nothing unifies the collected items beyond their belonging to just that collection; or perhaps, finally, they (are being conceived to) enjoy some higher degree of unity than that pertaining to a bare collection, such as evincing a principle of ordering, a functional coherence, or a common natural kind. But, whatever the extent of their unity or disunity, the point is that such unity as the relevant items have falls short (or is being conceived in this context to fall short) of the unity enjoyed by sentences. At least, that will be so if the items we are contrasting with sentences are the kind of thing for which the question

---

[17] Cf. Ramsey [2], p. 22.   [18] See e.g. Enderton [2], pp. 234–41.

[19] The same applies to the set of (Gödel numbers of) sentences of first-order logic that are not theorems: Wright [4], p. 400.

of unity arises in the first place. But that will surely be the case: for I take it that only pluralities can be unities. It would be misguided to raise up for comparison with a unified sentence such entities as the Parmenidean sphere, the Leibnizian monad, or the Tractarian simple object: for all such entities, if they are conceivable at all, are supposed to be absolutely *simple*, in which case no question of their *unity* as individual entities can arise.[20] The interesting question is not what distinguishes sentences from these purportedly absolutely simple entities, given that, even waiving the issue of the intelligibility of such supposed simples, the mere fact that sentences are (semantically)[21] complex will serve to make the distinction. Rather, the question we need to address is what distinguishes sentences from other complex linguistic expressions which either lack all unity or have some degree of coherence or order but not enough to constitute them as sentences. So long as the items we select for contrast have at most a degree of unity falling short of full sentential unity (or are not being regarded, in this context, as having that kind of unity), we can sensibly use them to draw the needed contrast—to ask what, when we move from items of this sort to sentences, constitutes the moment of sentential unity. The contrast between a unified sentence and a (mere) list has been the traditional starting point for posing the problem of sentential unity, and so long as it is understood in the way I have indicated, it is in my judgement unobjectionable.

2 Declarative and Other Kinds of Sentence

Sentences can have different kinds of mood—declarative, interrogative, imperative, and so on—but the question 'What does the characteristic unity of a sentence consist in?' has traditionally been posed just in the case of the declarative sentence, that is, the sort of sentence that can be true or false, a definition of Aristotelian provenance.[22] Indeed the logical tradition has concentrated on the declarative sentence in its investigations into semantical questions generally. Sometimes, no doubt, the privileging of the declarative sentence has been applied unthinkingly, or on the basis of a scientistic prejudice in favour of descriptive discourse; but that has by no means always been the case. In his seminal paper 'General Semantics', Lewis mentioned two distinct though closely related strategies for justifying the tradition's partiality for the declarative

---

[20] Contra Meirav, p. 240 n. 27.   [21] See §6 below.

[22] *Int.* 17a2–3. Cf. Sextus, *Adv. Math.* 8. 12: the Stoic definition of the *axiôma*. In the medieval period the Boethian definition of the *propositio* (i.e. the declarative sentence) as *oratio verum falsumve significans* ([2], i, p. 1174, B7–8; cf. Kretzmann, p. 771) was highly influential. Cf. Nuchelmans [1], pp. 123–37; [4], p. 197.

sentence.[23] In the first place, it might be assumed, in the manner of so-called speech-act theories,[24] that if a semantical question could be answered in the case of the declarative sentence, the answer would apply to other types of sentence, which are (on this approach) generated from underlying declarative sentence-radicals by the prefixing of appropriate mood indicators.[25] So, for example, the imperative 'Shut the door!' and the interrogative 'Is the door shut?' would be taken to be generated from the base form 'The door is shut' by the prefixing of operators with the rough meaning 'Make it the case that . . .!' and 'Is it the case that . . .?' respectively. Alternatively, non-declarative sentences might be regarded as generated by a suitable transformational grammar from declarative structures containing appropriate performative components: so 'Shut the door!' and 'Is the door shut?' would be taken to be generated from base structures of the form 'I order you to shut the door' and 'I ask you whether the door is shut' respectively. Strategies of these forms have long been anticipated in the logico-grammatical tradition, for example by Apollonius Dyscolus, Peter Abelard, and Paul of Venice in ancient and medieval times,[26] and by Hobbes and Destutt de Tracy in the early modern period.[27] Note that, here and throughout, I distinguish between mood and force: the former is a semantic notion, the latter a pragmatic one. Of course there are conventional connections between the two, but these connections hold only 'for the most part'. For example, the interrogative mood is conventionally associated with performing the speech act of asking a question, but that connection is not as tight as an entailment, in either direction: one can perform the speech act of asking a question without employing the interrogative mood, and one can employ that mood without performing that speech act.[28]

A third justification is suggested by Davidson. Concerning 'imperatives, interrogatives, sentences which tell us our duties, or what is good, bad, or beautiful', he writes:

Some sentences of these types may be neither true nor false, but all of them are related logically or evidentially to sentences that are true or false, and it is unlikely that the

[23] [1], pp. 37–44. [24] Cf. Searle [1], pp. 22–33, 122–3; [2], pp. 42–4.

[25] The terminology of 'sentence-radicals' derives from Wittgenstein: [5], p. 27; [2], p. 11.

[26] For details see Nuchelmans [1], pp. 102, 148–9, 267–8.

[27] Hobbes [2], I, §6; Destutt de Tracy [1], ii, pp. 47–55: cf. Nuchelmans [5], pp. 126–7, 181. See also Bolzano [2], §22, with Textor [1], pp. 12–13; Frege [17], pp. 60–2 ([21], pp. 344–6), with von Kutschera [1], pp. 73–4; Chomsky [1], pp. 80–1, 106–7; [3], p. 46; Z. Harris, pp. 93, 202–3, 212; Kimball, pp. 121–2.

[28] Mood, so understood, has often been called 'mode' in the tradition (see e.g. J. Harris, I. viii, pp. 140–72), and it is common today to apply the label 'force' to semantic mood (see e.g. Cook and Newson, p. 103), but that usage frequently conceals a confusion between semantics and pragmatics and is best avoided: see further §83 below.

semantics of such sentences can be given without appeal to their relations to sentences for which we know the truth-conditions. This is obvious in the case of imperatives and interrogatives. We understand an imperative if and only if we know under what conditions what it orders or commands is obeyed. The possible answers to a question are sentences related syntactically and semantically to the question, and the answers have a truth-value, even if the questions do not.[29]

All of these justifications seem to me to have something to be said for them. On the assumption that one or other of these strategies can be made good, I will be adhering to the traditional policy of posing the question of unity in respect of specifically declarative sentences, thereby pinning my faith on the supposition that, by some device or other, any satisfactory account of the unity of the declarative sentence will be extendable to non-declaratives. I do not thereby rule out other approaches to unity which take a different kind of 'move in the language-game'—say, questions or commands—to be central, and treat the unity of the declarative sentence as derivative.[30] Perhaps such alternative approaches are possible: if they are, it will be a good question how much of the account I am going to offer can be carried over to these different approaches. But that is a matter I leave to one side.

3 Declarative Sentences and Propositions

In classical Latin, the word 'propositio' meant the major premiss of a syllogism,[31] but in medieval philosophical texts it is used to mean 'declarative sentence', taken to be an item (usually a token) at the level of spoken, written, or mental language, unless this implication is expressly cancelled by the insertion of an appropriate qualification; and this usage persisted into the era of the vernacular, in which (for example) English texts deployed 'proposition' as their standard rendering of 'propositio'. Thus, in Thomas Wilson's *The Rule of Reason* (1551), a proposition is defined as 'a sentence uttered in plain wordes expressly signifying either truth or falshed [= falsehood]'.[32] But in recent decades propositions have usually been taken by analytic philosophers to be the *meanings* of declarative sentences, rather than those (token or type) sentences themselves—or rather to be their *cognitive* meanings, that is, just so much of the meanings of declarative sentences as is relevant to their truth or falsity (compare

---

[29] [2], p. 124. Cf. Wiggins [1], p. 22; Dummett [2], p. 307; Tugendhat [2], pp. 72–6.
[30] Cf. Wittgenstein [5], I, §22.
[31] Cicero, *De Inv.* 1. 62; cf. Quintilian, *Institutio* 5. 14. 5; Kneale and Kneale, pp. 177–8.
[32] Wilson, Biiii. Cf. Watts, II, chs. 1 and 2, pp. 116–48; Kneale and Kneale, p. 299; Prior [3], pp. 16–17.

Wilson's 'in plain wordes').[33] In what follows I shall omit the qualification 'cognitive' when I speak of the meanings of declarative sentences, taking it to be understood. Of course, apart from containing affective elements irrelevant to truth-value, sentences may, and typically will, contain indexical features, which may be implicit rather than explicit.[34] If propositions, thought of as the meanings of declarative sentences, are to be fully determinate, then they must, given the phenomenon of indexicality, be the meanings of declarative sentences whose indexical parameters are treated as semantically fixed.[35]

Note that the meaning of a declarative sentence cannot coherently be identified either with that very type sentence, or with a token of it. This is obvious in the case of token sentences, for, waiving the issue of the extent to which distinct tokenings—that is, (spatio-)temporally located utterances, inscriptions, or entertainings—of *different* type (abstract) sentences can mean the same, it must at least be possible for distinct tokenings of the *same* type sentence, in which any indexical parameters present in that sentence are fixed in the same way, to mean the same. But if distinct token sentences can mean the same, we cannot, on pain of breaching the logic of identity, allow meanings to *be* token sentences. In his 'The Foundations of Mathematics' (1925), Ramsey suggested that propositions, taken to be the meanings of declarative sentences, might be construed as type sentences:[36] but this suggestion is also wide of the mark, and was by implication contradicted by Ramsey himself in his paper 'Universals' (also of 1925), where we are told that 'Socrates is wise' and 'Wisdom is a characteristic of Socrates'—though plainly distinct sentences—'express the same proposition'.[37] And, whatever restrictions we place on the extent to which distinct type sentences can mean the same—a thorny issue which I shall revisit in due course—we must allow for at least the theoretical *possibility* of synonymy between distinct type sentences, say between two distinct sentences of the same or different languages that are identically constructed from pairwise distinct but synonymous components. For it seems to be a general constraint on the very idea of linguistic meaning that distinct linguistic types can in principle mean the same:[38] without this governing idea, it is not clear that there would be anything to call linguistic meaning. But, again, if distinct type sentences can mean the same, we cannot allow meanings to *be* type sentences.

Following Moore in his 1899 article 'The Nature of Judgment',[39] Russell announced in *The Principles of Mathematics* (1903) a new non-linguistic sense of

---

[33] Cf. Quine [4], p. 139.   [34] Cf. Lemmon, pp. 91–2, 101–2.
[35] Cf. Quine [4], p. 139; Künne [1], pp. 198–9.   [36] [2], p. 33; cf. p. 274.
[37] [2], p. 116.   [38] Cf. Haller, p. 83.
[39] See G. E. Moore [2], esp. pp. 4–5. Cf. King [2], p. 505.

the word 'proposition'.[40] When propositions are first introduced in that work, they are defined as 'anything that is true or that is false',[41] but any impression that we have to do with declarative sentences—as the echo of Aristotle might encourage us to believe—is dissipated by Russell's subsequent remark that 'a proposition, unless it happens to be linguistic [i.e. unless it is about words: RG] does not itself contain words: it contains the entities indicated by words'.[42] In his unpublished essay 'On Meaning and Denotation', which his editors date to the latter part of 1903, Russell discusses the proposition *that Arthur Balfour is a nephew of Lord Salisbury*, and indicates that the constituents of the proposition are Arthur Balfour, Lord Salisbury, and the relation of being a nephew.[43] And we might also here recall Russell's famous remark in a letter to Frege written in 1904 to the effect that Mont Blanc is, 'in spite of all its snowfields, a component part of what is really asserted in the *Satz* "Mont Blanc is higher than 4000 metres"'; he adds that what is asserted is the 'object of the thought, and this is in my view a certain complex (an *objektiver Satz*, one might say), in which Mont Blanc itself is a component part'.[44] But the shift to the new usage can hardly be said to have occurred cleanly, and Frege speaks for many readers of Russell's early work when he remarks: 'Often I am in doubt as to whether I ought to understand by the word "proposition" an expression of a thought formed out of audible or visible signs, or a thought.'[45] Ironically enough, though something like the above sense of 'proposition', according to which it refers to what a declarative sentence expresses rather than to the sentence itself, has become firmly embedded in the analytical tradition,[46] Russell soon abandoned it,[47] and Moore may have done so as well.[48] In his 1913 manuscript *Theory of Knowledge*, Russell classifies propositions as linguistic entities,[49] in harmony once again with the medieval tradition, and this usage was (at least officially) maintained in 'The Philosophy of Logical Atomism' of 1918, where we are told that 'a proposition is just

---

[40] An important terminological feature of Russell's revolt from idealism was his substituting (under Moore's influence) the term 'proposition' for 'judgment'. The changeover occurs in Russell's 1899 paper 'The Classification of Relations': Imaguire, pp. 9–12.

[41] [3], §13.   [42] [3], §51.   [43] [18], p. 319 with n. 4.

[44] Letter of 12 Dec. 1904 (Frege [22], pp. 250–1). 'Objektiver Satz' is Russell's rendering of 'proposition' (Hylton [1], p. 171 n. 6).

[45] [16], p. 239 ([21], p. 336).

[46] Perhaps in Frege's rather than Russell's version: see §13 below.

[47] Though not as early as his 1905 paper 'On Denoting', as is sometimes suggested. See here Pelham and Urquhart, pp. 309–13. Indeed, even after Russell had officially espoused (in 1910) the multiple relation theory of judgement, which dispensed with propositions, he nevertheless formulated his principle of acquaintance in terms that seem to presuppose the existence of worldly propositions: [8], p. 32; B. Linsky [2], p. 42.

[48] See [1], pp. 56, 265, with Olson, p. 47 n. 1, and Cartwright [2], p. 127 n. 26.   [49] [9], p. 105.

a symbol' and is 'a sentence in the indicative',[50] and in his *Introduction to Mathematical Philosophy* of 1919, where a proposition is 'a form of words which expresses what is either true or false'.[51] (Thereafter, Russell discarded both these approaches in favour of a form of psychologism about the proposition; but that change takes us beyond the period of Russell's activity of interest to us here.[52])

The shift in our understanding of the location and status of propositions, inaugurated by Moore and Russell, decisive as it was for the course of modern analytic philosophy, was not in fact a new departure in the tradition. Setting aside for the moment Fregean 'judgeable contents' (*beurteilbare Inhalte*),[53] later 'Thoughts' (*Gedanken*), which though chronologically prior to Moorean propositions in their conception were not widely known about until Moore's and Russell's contributions had fixed the tradition, anticipations might reasonably be claimed (to itemize only some of the more prominent and familiar cases) for Stoic *axiômata*,[54] Abelard's *dicta* (and the *enuntiabilia* of some of his contemporaries),[55] Burleigh's *propositiones in re*,[56] Adam Wodeham's *significabilia per complexum* and Gregory of Rimini's *complexe significabilia*,[57] Christian Wolff's *propositiones/Urteile*,[58] Leibniz's *propositiones*,[59] and Bolzano's *Sätze an sich*:[60] these are all propositionally structured entities that can be regarded as the meanings of spoken or written declarative sentences rather than as the sentences themselves, as I shall briefly explain.

Stoic *axiômata* are propositions existing not at the level of spoken and written language, but at the lectical level, which corresponds roughly to the

[50] [13], p. 185. But in §VI 'proposition' is repeatedly used in something like the 1903 sense.
[51] [11], p. 155 (cf. p. 170).   [52] See Stevens [3], pp. 114–19.
[53] The terminology of *Begriffsschrift* and *Grundlagen der Arithmetik*, which gave way to *Gedanken* in Frege's mature writings: see here Olson, p. 67.
[54] See Mates [2], pp. 11–19; Schubert; my [7].
[55] Abelard [1], pp. 365.13–369.36; [2], pp. 157.13–162.36. The most interesting contemporary texts from our point of view are the *Ars Meliduna* and the *Ars Burana*: de Rijk [1], ii/1, ch. 10; ii/2, ch. 5. See Nuchelmans [1], pp. 139–76; de Rijk [2]; de Libera [1]; Panaccio [4], p. 178 nn. 1 and 2.
[56] Burleigh [1], C3. See Pinborg [2]; my [13], §8. Burleigh's idea of the *propositio in re*, composed of worldly things (at least in part), was anticipated in his own writings and in those of his contemporary Richard Campsall by the idea of the *propositio enunciata tantum*, an idea current in England in the early 1300s: see Panaccio [4], pp. 241–8. Even Ockham, in some of his early writings, entertained the idea of a proposition with real components: see Karger [1], pp. 441–4, and [3]; my [12], pp. 232–3; Panaccio [4], pp. 260–1.
[57] Wodeham, d. 1 q. 1 (pp. 180–208); Gregory [1], Prol. q. 1, aa. 1–3 (pp. 1–40). On adherents and opponents of this theory, see Nuchelmans [1], pp. 237–47; [3], pp. 3–140; [4], pp. 197–210; [5], pp. 28–30; Ashworth [1], pp. 37–76; [2], ch. 4. See further de Libera [2]; Karger [2], pp. 188–94; my [13] and [14].
[58] See Wolff, I. III. iv, §§328–31 (pp. 288–9).   [59] See Leibniz [1], vii. 190–3 ([5], pp. 25–37).
[60] See Bolzano [2], esp. §§19–33.

level of Fregean sense.[61] Abelard's *dicta* are supposed to be quasi-entities in the world—states of things (*status rerum*) rather than things in their own right[62]—and the *Ars Burana* explicitly notes that *enuntiabilia* are not among Aristotle's ten categories but are in a category of their own (*praedicamentum enuntiabilium*).[63] One modern commentator speaks of Abelard's *dicta* and the *enuntiabilia* of other twelfth-century texts as anticipating Russellian *facts*:[64] but these early texts are clear that there are false *dicta* and *enuntiabilia* as well as true ones.[65] Burleigh's propositions *in re* are partly in the world (the meanings of the categorematic terms in the governing sentence are *res*), and partly in the mind (the meaning of the relevant copula is a mental concept).[66] Adam Wodeham's *significabilia per complexum* and Gregory of Rimini's *complexe significabilia* are, plausibly, intended to be propositions—or at any rate propositionally structured entities, entities of the form *that a is F, that a has R to b*, etc.—existing wholly in the world.[67] Christian Wolff had a notion of judgements or propositions as the common contents of sentences.[68] It seems evident, too, that Leibniz held propositions, or what he also calls 'complex knowables' (*cognoscibilia complexa*), to be the meanings of declarative sentences, rather than those (token or type) sentences themselves.[69] For in his 'Dialogus de connexione inter res et verba', Leibniz says that truth and falsity attach to possible propositions or possible thoughts.[70] (Alonzo Church has suggested that Leibniz may have had the possible sentences of some particular language in mind;[71] but the suggestion is surely too restrictive, in view of Leibniz's insistence that truth and falsity are common to different languages.) At any rate, that was how Bolzano, who regarded Leibniz's *propositiones* as precursors of his own *Sätze an sich*, read the essay; and it seems clear that Bolzano's *Sätze an sich* are entities at the level of meaning rather than at the level of spoken or written (token or type) sentences.[72] Finally, we should mention that Meinong, more or less contemporaneously

---

[61] See Diogenes Laertius 7. 63; Sextus, *Adv. Math.* 8. 12. Cf. Haller, pp. 83–4, who compares Stoic *lekta* with Bolzano's *Vorstellungen/Sätze an sich* and Frege's *Sinne*.

[62] See e.g. Abelard [2], p. 160.35–6.   [63] See de Rijk [1], ii/2, p. 208.24–30.

[64] De Libera [1].

[65] See e.g. Abelard [2], p. 160.22–36; *Ars Burana*, de Rijk [1], ii/2, p. 208.20–3.

[66] See Pinborg [2]; my [13], §8.

[67] This interpretation is disputed by some commentators: see e.g. Eckermann, p. 77, and Wendland for the view that complexly signifiables are merely intentional objects.

[68] Note esp. §328, p. 288: 'Quod stylo Leibnitiano dicitur calculus differentialis, stylo Newtoniano appellatur methodus fluxionum. Quamobrem si dicas: calculus differentialis inservit tangentibus determinandis, et methodus fluxionum inservit tangentibus determinandis, propositiones eaedem sunt, subiectum in utraque idem.' See here Lenders, pp. 125–6; Nuchelmans [5], pp. 240–1.

[69] [1], vii, pp. 190–3; cf. [1], ii, p. 470; [3], IV. v, §1 ([1], v, p. 377); Nuchelmans [5], pp. 221–2, 232.

[70] [1], vii, p. 190 ([5], p. 28); cf. [3], I. i, §26 ([1], v, p. 79).

[71] Church [7], pp. 7–8; cf. Kneale and Kneale, p. 361.

[72] See [2], §§19–33 (the reference to Leibniz is in §21); cf. Berg, pp. 149–56.

with the advance inaugurated by Moore and Russell, introduced in a series of writings the idea of what he called *objectives*, entities of the form *that a is F, that a has R to b*, etc., to serve as the main objects of propositional attitudes.[73] Russell discussed Meinong's writings in 1904, and approved of objectives.

Hand in hand with the terminological shift initiated by Moore and Russell at the beginning of the twentieth century there went, at least for Russell, a shift in focus with respect to the unity problem. For Russell, the problem of unity was not primarily a problem of *sentential* unity, as it plainly had been for Plato in the *Sophist*, but a problem of the unity of *what sentences mean*. It is useful to compare Russell on this point with Frege and Wittgenstein. For the mature Frege, the problem of sentential or propositional unity posed itself at two levels: at the level of symbolic language, and at the level sense, where we find what he called *Gedanken* (Thoughts), that is, the senses of declarative sentences. The problem did not pose itself, for Frege, at the level of reference: at least, insofar as there was a problem of unity for Frege at the level of reference—and there was indeed such a problem, namely the problem how what he called concepts and objects (the worldly referents of concept-words and proper names respectively) could combine—it was not a problem how something *propositional* in form could emerge as a unified entity, because (at least in his mature work) Frege identified the referents of declarative sentences with unstructured truth-values, propositionally structured meanings (Thoughts) being confined by him, as they had been by Aquinas and most medieval philosophers,[74] to the mental level or level of sense. The contrast with Russell is this: for Russell, we might say, the problem of sentential or propositional unity posed itself primarily at the level of reference—Russell recognized no level of Fregean sense—and only derivatively at the level of symbolic language; for Frege, as we shall see in due course (§25), the problem posed itself primarily at the level of sense, and only derivatively at the level of symbolic language. For the Wittgenstein of the *Tractatus*, in contrast with both Frege and Russell, the problem was primarily a linguistic one and derivatively an ontological one (like Russell, Wittgenstein recognized no level of Fregean sense). Hence he posed the problem in unambiguously linguistic terms: 'The question here is: how does the sentential tie arise' ('Es fragt sich hier, wie kommt der Satzverband zustande').[75] But the nature of the connection between language and the world is such, according to the Tractarian picture theory of meaning, that whatever answer the question attracts at the level of language will have a mirror-image at the level of what language is about.

---

[73] See [1], §2, pp. 381–5; [2], ch. 7.
[74] Aquinas [1], 1a, q. 14, a. 14; [2], q. 2, a. 7; see Nuchelmans [5], pp. 14–16.   [75] [1], §4.221.

If the question of the unity of the sentence is what distinguishes a (declarative) sentence from a mere list of words, the question of the unity of the proposition is what distinguishes a proposition from a mere aggregate of word-meanings.[76] In this study I am going to tackle the problem of unity at the level of the proposition, that is, at the level of what declarative sentences mean. But, given the Fregean division of the intuitive notion of semantic meaning into levels of sense and reference, the question naturally arises for anyone who adopts my approach to the unity problem whether the unity of sentential meanings as these exist at the level of reference has priority over the unity of their meanings as these exist at the level of sense, or vice versa. Since, as I shall explain in due course (§14), I take the level of reference to be the primary level of meaning, and the level of sense to be of essentially secondary importance, my account of unity will be delivered in respect of propositionally structured sentential meanings taken as entities existing at the level of reference (Russellian propositions), rather than in respect of such meanings taken as the senses of declarative sentences (Fregean Thoughts). But since, as I shall argue in the sequel (§14), spoken and written declarative sentences refer to propositions at the level of reference, and do so by dint of expressing Fregean Thoughts, what I say about the unity of the proposition at the level of reference will *eo ipso* yield derivative accounts of the unity of the declarative sentence and of the Fregean Thought. Here and throughout I individuate sentences rhetically, to borrow J. L. Austin's terminology: that is, sentences are individuated not merely phonetically or orthographically, but also in terms of their meanings.[77] In §5 I will explain why I believe that Russell was right to shift the emphasis of the problem of unity from language to what language means, and correlatively why Wittgenstein was wrong to regard the unity of the sentence as prior to the unity of what it expresses. But before addressing that issue it will be helpful to deal with another matter of priority: are the primary bearers of truth-values sentences or propositions?

4 Sentences, Propositions, and Truth-Values

Propositions have been introduced as the meanings of declarative sentences, and declarative sentences have, as I noted above, been defined since Aristotle

---

[76] On the terminology, cf. Russell [3], §135.

[77] Austin [1], p. 93. This approach has a long tradition, having been followed by Aristotle (*Int.* 16b26; cf. Porphyry *apud* Simplicius, *In Cat.*, p. 10.21–3), the Stoics (D. L. 8. 56; Haller, p. 81), Frege (see Rumfitt [1], pp. 600–1), Wittgenstein ([1], §§3.12, 3.3–3.31, 5.473; cf. Conant [1], pp. 25–6 n. 19), and Russell (see B. Linsky [2], pp. 15–16).

to be those sentences which can be true or false. Significantly, propositions themselves can also be true or false. This is guaranteed by grammar, for we say not only

(1)   'Man is a rational animal' is true,

that is,

(2)   The sentence 'man is a rational animal' is true,

but also

(3)   'Man is a rational animal' means that man is a rational animal,

and

(4)   That man is a rational animal is true.

In (3) the meaning of 'Man is a rational animal', which, as we have said, is a proposition, appears to be named by the noun clause 'that man is a rational animal', and in (4) that proposition is said to be true. We find this observation in Abelard,[78] and plausibly it was the starting point for the influential fourteenth-century theory of complexly signifiables,[79] initially propounded around 1330 by Adam Wodeham, and then more thoroughly and influentially by Gregory of Rimini in the mid-1340s. According to this theory the significates of declarative sentences and the objects of propositional attitudes such as assent, dissent, and knowledge are neither spoken nor written sentences, nor mental sentences, nor individuals in the world, but rather worldly, propositionally structured extra-categorial objects specified (in English as well as in Latin) by a that-clause or by an accusative-and-infinitive construction, such as *that man is a rational animal* or *the earth to be round*, as in 'Seneca said that man is a rational animal' or 'Columbus believed the earth to be round'.[80] (Note that the italics here employed are not a device of quotation—for complexly signifiables are indeed worldly entities, not items of spoken, written, or mental language—but of emphasis only. Likewise when I write, as I shall frequently do in this study, of the proposition *that p*—the proposition *that Socrates is wise*, as it might be—the italics are not to be understood as indicating semantic ascent.) These propositionally structured worldly objects were taken by the theory's proponents to be essentially signifiable in language, but adequately signifiable

---

[78] [2], p. 154.4–20: in this passage *propositio* = sentence, and what I am calling a proposition figures as a *dictum*, such as *Socratem currere*. Cf. de Rijk [2], p. 157.

[79] Kretzmann, pp. 774–5.

[80] Cf. Church [2], p. 97. On the case-marking of 'the earth' in 'Columbus believed the earth to be round', see Chomsky [7], p. 58; Cook and Newson, p. 153.

only in a complex way: that is, any non-complex way of signifying them is essentially derivative of—definable in terms of—canonical complex ways; hence their standard name, 'complexly signifiables' (*complexe significabilia*).

If both declarative sentences and propositions can take truth-values, is there any priority? That is, do sentences take truth-values because propositions do, or is it rather that propositions take truth-values because sentences do, or is there no priority? (I assume that the *act of forming a judgement* is not a candidate for priority, despite a respectable tradition to the contrary;[81] for it seems obvious that acts of judgement are describable as true or false only by virtue of having a true or false sentential or propositional *content*.) In answering our question we need to consider both sentence tokens and sentence types. I take tokens first. If we are thinking of sentences as tokens (as medieval philosophers generally did), the question of priority in respect of possession of a truth-value will surely be answered in favour of propositions.[82] As we have said, sentences may, and usually will, contain explicit or implicit indexical features. Now token sentences are constituted as being the very token sentences they are—as being the very phonetic or orthographic patterns they are and as having the very meanings they have—*both* in virtue of tokening the type sentences (with *their* phonetic, orthographic, and semantic properties) that they do token, *and* as a function of the context in which, or in respect of which, they are tokened.[83] ('In respect of which', because sentences do not need to be tokened in a context in order to have their content fixed with respect to that context.[84]) Token declarative sentences express propositions, and the propositions expressed by token sentences exist as bona-fide entities whether or not their corresponding sentences are tokened. But that implies that truth-values attach to propositions as a matter of priority: after all, if a sentence that is tokened on some particular occasion and is, let us say, true in that context had not been tokened there and then, its *propositional content*, as fixed by that context, would still have been true, so that the truth of that content relative to that context cannot depend on the truth of the token sentence, which *ex hypothesi* was not tokened in the counterfactual scenario we are considering; the relationship of dependence must be the other way round.[85] In general, given that the context of tokening

---

[81] The tradition is exemplified by Descartes's claim that 'veritatem proprie vel falsitatem nonnisi in solo intellectu esse posse': *Regulae*, VIII (x, p. 396; cf. Nuchelmans [5], p. 51 n. 64). On the bearing of pragmatic issues on the problem of unity, see §§10 and 85 below.

[82] Künne [1], pp. 277–8.

[83] Cf. Frege [17], p. 64 ([21], pp. 348–9); [26], p. 146; Carl [2], pp. 101–6.

[84] Kaplan [2], p. 546.

[85] For a discussion of this issue, see Gregory of Rimini [1], Prol. q. 1, a. 1 (pp. 8–12). On Abelard's expression of the point (in his terminology: the truth-value of a *propositio* is dependent on that of its *dictum*), see Nuchelmans [1], p. 159.

and circumstances of evaluation may come apart,[86] a sentence which is tokened in or in respect of a particular context and whose content is thereby fixed may have that content evaluated for truth or falsity in respect of a quite different context in which (and in respect of which) it is *ex hypothesi* not tokened and by which its content is not fixed. Thus an utterance by me here and now of, say, 'I do not exist', which has a content that, if evaluated for truth or falsity in respect of the context of utterance, would be false, might have its content, as fixed by that original context, evaluated for truth or falsity in respect of a quite different context, perhaps at another possible world, and found there to be true, there being many possible worlds at which I do not exist.[87]

Let us turn to type sentences. Given the phenomenon of indexicality, type sentences do not, in general, have truth-values just as such; but they acquire them when the parameters introduced by their indexical features are semantically fixed, and the resulting content is evaluated in respect of some context[88]—they acquire them, that is to say, when (i) we consider what proposition is or would be expressed either in or in respect of a particular context if the sentence either were tokened in that context or had its indexical features fixed relative to that context, and (ii) we evaluate the resulting proposition in respect of that or another context.[89] But that is as much as to say that, again, truth-values attach to *propositions* as a matter of priority.[90] Note further that, in individuating sentences rhetically (§3), one both obviates any threat of sentential ambiguity and avails oneself of a relativization of relevant word patterns—patterns which, just as such, may be common to more than one language—to a particular language. Without these presuppositions, it is obvious that mere word patterns, individuated in such a way that they may be common to more than one language or may, within a single language, be semantically ambiguous, cannot attract truth-values.[91] Individuating sentences rhetically simply builds these presuppositions into the identity-conditions of sentences. But that, in effect, contaminates the identity of the type sentence with that of the proposition(s) it does, or would, express in or in respect of relevant contexts. So our opponent on this point in effect confronts a dilemma: either sentences are individuated

---

[86] Kaplan [2], pp. 492–505.

[87] The question which indexical features of a sentence must remain fixed relative to a context, and which can be varied, if *propositions* are to be the contents of declarative sentences in those contexts is a delicate one that we can pass over here: for discussion, see Stalnaker [2], ch. 1, §II; Lewis [6], ch. 2; and esp. King [5], ch. 6. (For the record, I agree with King that time and location go to the identity of propositions, while possible worlds can be varied.)

[88] Cf. Wallace, p. 120; Tugendhat [2], pp. 282–3, 290.

[89] See Barwise and Etchemendy, p. 10; cf. p. 138; Etchemendy, p. 12 n. 1.

[90] Cf. Bealer [1], p. 201.   [91] Cf. Textor [1], p. 38; [2], p. 185.

rhetically or they are not. If they are not, there can be no question of their possessing truth-values; if they are, their ability to possess truth-values is plausibly dependent on a prior ability of the propositions they are capable of expressing to possess truth-values. On these several grounds, then, it seems clear that truth-values attach in the first instance to propositions, and only derivatively to sentences.

5 Sentences, Propositions, and Unity

The problem of the unity of a declarative sentence is: what distinguishes a declarative sentence from a mere list of words? Since the defining characteristic of declarative sentences is their capacity to be true or false, we may re-express the problem of their unity as follows: what *enables* declarative sentences to *be* true or false?[92] The corresponding question in the case of propositions, the meanings of declarative sentences, will be: what distinguishes propositions from mere aggregates of their components, and enables *them* to be true or false? What the components of propositions are, and what propositions themselves are, is an issue that must be addressed in due course, and I shall do so in Chapter 2. But at any rate, whatever the outcome of that investigation, we can specify now, as I have just done, what in quite general terms the unity problem for propositions is. The questions concerning the unity of the declarative sentence and the unity of the proposition are prior questions to the classic question 'What is truth?'. For we are in effect asking: what is truth-or-falsity?[93] That much is obvious. But it turns out—what is perhaps less obvious at first blush, though one might expect it given the result of the previous section—that the question what unifies propositions is also prior, in general, to the question what unifies declarative sentences. There are two preliminary points to note here.

The first is this: as between token and type sentences, type sentences enjoy priority in respect of unity. That is, any given token sentence is unified in virtue of the unity of the type it realizes, and not vice versa: for, as we have said, a token sentence is constituted as being the very sentence it is in virtue of its realizing, in or in respect of a particular context, the type sentence that it does realize. Consider a bunch of words that are tokened in some context, that are of syntactically the right form, and are tokened in the right order, to constitute a sentence. It seems clear that any such group of words may be tokened in some context without actually composing a sentence: whether the

---

[92] Cf. Davidson [2], pp. 86, 120.   [93] Cf. Nuchelmans [5], p. 257.

words do compose a sentence will depend, in the first instance, on features of the context, and in particular on their being tokened with the right intention.[94] But, as I shall explain in more detail below (§85), linguistic intentions cannot themselves constitute the moment of sentential unity in respect of a group of token words: for the intention that turns a bunch of token words into a sentence, on any given occasion of use, is precisely the intention to produce a token sentence of such and such a type, taken as an already unified abstract entity. The unity of a token sentence thus depends asymmetrically on the unity of the type sentence it realizes.

The second preliminary point, and one that will be of fundamental importance in the rest of this study, is this: the criterion for the unity of a type sentence cannot be merely syntactic. For there is a conceptual distinction to be drawn between a bunch of type words, taken just as such—that is, something that in my terminology counts as a *mere list* of type words—and a type sentence *actually composed* of those type words. This is so even if the list comprises type words of the right syntactic form to compose a sentence, and even if the words are ordered, in the list, in the right way to form a sentence. It is important to stress this point at the outset of our investigation, for it is common among philosophers and linguists to assume that the problem of the unity of the sentence can be solved by merely adverting to the fact that a sentence is made up of words which are syntactically of the right form to constitute a sentence and are appropriately ordered, as if there were no distinction to be drawn between a *list* of words of the right (or any) syntactic form and appropriately ordered, on the one hand, and an ordering of such words which *actually is* a sentence, on the other. But there must be such a distinction, at least conceptually speaking: there is a distinction, for example, between a mere list comprising the type words 'Socrates', 'is', and 'wise', arranged in that order—we should not baulk at the inclusion of 'is' in the list, for, as Benjamin Schnieder remarks, 'you cannot deny a verb the possibility of being listed just because it is inflected'[95]—and the type sentence 'Socrates is wise'. The collection of those three type words, ordered or otherwise, has a being just as such, as a list comprising those very linguistic items, in abstraction from any particular type sentence they go to compose. In his polemic against Locke's definition of truth, according to which truth is 'the joining or separating of signs, as the things signified by them do agree or disagree with one another',[96] Leibniz makes an interesting remark. He says: 'But a phrase, e.g. "the wise man", does not make a proposition; yet it involves the joining of two terms. Nor is negation the same as separation; for saying "the man"

[94] Cf. Schnieder [1], p. 244.   [95] [1], p. 246.   [96] Locke, IV. v, §2.

and then after a pause uttering "wise" is not making a denial.'[97] It is not clear whether Leibniz would have said the same if the string in question had been capable of constituting a sentence as opposed to a mere phrase (at least for the affirmative case; obviously denial is not effected by separating words); but my claim is that one *should* say the same, that is, that collocating or concatenating words, of whatever grammatical or syntactic form, is not *sufficient* for achieving a sentence.

Incidentally, lest we become entangled in use–mention embarrassments at this point, it is worth stressing, in connection with the remark of Schnieder's quoted in the last paragraph, that Schnieder means, as I mean, that the collocation of words 'Socrates is wise', including as it does an inflected verb, may *be* a list.[98] Of course a verb may be listed in the less interesting sense that a word *referring to* a verb may feature in a list, as for example in this list: 'Socrates', 'is', 'wise'. But that is not what is in question here. When we ask what distinguishes a sentence from a mere list of words, we mean to ask what distinguishes it from a mere list *comprising words* (referring to things), not: from a mere list comprising *items that refer to words*. The word 'list' is ambiguous as between formal and material senses: we say that a team list, for instance, is made up of the names of the players ('Your name is not on the list'), but also of the players themselves ('You are not on the list'). We move freely between these locutions and no confusion arises: if you ask me 'Am I on the list?' and I reply in the negative, I am not to be understood as leaving open the possibility that, notwithstanding *your* absence from the list, your *name* is on it. In the current context, the claim that a verb may be listed is to be read in the formal sense; in the material sense, what is listed when the word 'is' features (in the formal sense) on a list would be something like predicative being.

Now it is true that a randomly generated bunch of words may, on occasion, produce a string which we *recognize* as a sentence. Schnieder writes further:

> if a friend of mine and I are mindlessly scrabbling down some words on the same sheet of paper, and they happen to be in the order of a well-formed sentence (I write down 'I want', he writes down 'to fly'), then *there is* a sentence inscription on the paper.[99]

What is going on in this sort of case is that we admit the token string of concatenated inscriptions as falling under a given sentential type, relative to a particular language (in this case English). Sometimes we insist that the string be produced by a single agent with the intention to produce a type sentence;[100] sometimes, as in Schnieder's example, we do not impose any such condition.

---

[97] [3], IV. v, §2 ([1], v, p. 377). The tr. is by Remnant and Bennett. [98] Cf. King [5], p. 36.
[99] [1], p. 243. [100] Cf. Searle [1], pp. 16–17; [2], p. 40.

It would even be possible to treat patterns formed by natural events involving no intelligent agent—as it might be, sounds formed by the wind in trees or shapes formed out of pebbles on the beach by waves—as sentences of some language. But it does not follow from these possibilities that the type sentence which, in cases of the sort illustrated by Schnieder's example, we allow a token string of concatenated words to exemplify is simply *conceptually indistinguishable* from an equiform type list. That is, the theoretical distinction between a *type* sentence and a *type* list remains, despite the acknowledged fact that a given *token* string of concatenated words may, taken in itself and considered from a purely formal point of view, be assignable to either category. What *constitutes* the difference—what *allows* us to subordinate a given token string of concatenated symbols to one category (type sentence) rather than to the other (type list)—is precisely what we have to investigate here.

In saying that the criterion for the unity of a type sentence cannot be merely syntactic, I mean that the criterion cannot be a mere matter of superficial linguistic form, given that the superficial linguistic form of a sentence is not, as such, distinct from that of a mere list. This use of the word 'syntax', and the accompanying contrast with semantics, pervades the treatises of logicians and philosophers—it has its origins in model theory[101]—and it is the way I shall employ the word throughout this book. But it must be noted here, in order to avert misunderstanding, that when linguists talk of a sentence's syntax they are typically concerned with one or more levels of *syntactic analysis* in respect of that sentence—as for instance, in the Chomskian 'principles and parameters' approach to syntactic theory, S-structure, D-structure, or LF (originally abbreviations for 'surface structure', 'deep structure', and 'logical form' respectively).[102] If it were objected to me that the difference between a sentence and a list *is* syntactic—in a sense of 'syntactic' drawn from linguistic theory and differing from the typical philosopher's usage—and that syntactic analysis of suitably regimented sentential structures reveals that difference, as displayed in (for example) the distinct phrase-marker syntactic trees generated, I would reply that this is a merely verbal point. Of course, on *that* conception of syntax, it is indeed open to us to say that sentences enjoy internal syntactic relations lacked by mere lists: for certainly, a phrase marker appropriate to a sentence (at some level of syntactic analysis) will look quite different from one

---

[101] Cf. Etchemendy, ch. 1.

[102] See e.g. Chomsky [2], pp. 128–47; [6], pp. 143–5; [7], ch. 1; Poole, pp. 168–70; Carnie, pp. 359–64; Cook and Newson, pp. 177–83. In some more recent approaches, the identifications of S-structure with surface structure and D-structure with deep structure have been abandoned, while often the original labels are retained as terms of art for successor notions (see Chomsky [5], pp. 81–2; [6], p. 148; Cook and Newson, p. 61).

appropriate to a list. But this just means that the syntactic tree generated by a sentence at some level of analysis will have a suitably annotated sentential structure occupying its root node and dominating all other nodes, whereas the tree generated by a list will not.[103] So, for instance, if we suppose that semantic properties attach to LF regimentations of input sequences of words, rather than directly to those sequences themselves, we can apparently simply exploit the fact that sentences and lists are differently represented at the level of LF to 'account for' the unity of the sentence and its corresponding proposition.[104] But obviously this simply pushes the question one stage back: what *is* it for us, confronting a bunch of words that might prima facie be analysed either as a sentence or as a list, to apply the one kind of syntactic analysis rather than the other—to associate the words with one kind of representation at the level of LF, say, rather than with another kind? In pursuing this question—which will, for me, turn out to have a semantical answer—it is plainly not a solution to have one's attention directed to intrasentential relations at some level of syntactic analysis, but rather a placeholder for a solution. For our question precisely is: in virtue of what are those intrasentential syntactic relations in place at the relevant level of syntactic analysis? (It is all too easy to misconstrue a mere placeholder for the solution to the problem of unity as the solution itself; we will need to avoid this snare again when, in particular, we come to deploy the important idea of a sentence's *logical copula* in Chapters 5 and 6.)

As I have mentioned, it is commonly assumed that the concatenation or ordering of grammatically congruent expressions provides the solution to the unity problem,[105] and that despite the fact that the insufficiency of a sheer concatenation of grammatically congruent expressions to unify those expressions so as to guarantee more than list status was clearly enunciated by Aristotle in his *De Interpretatione*, one of the founding texts of the Western philosophical tradition, where he remarks that the expressions 'two-footed', 'land', and 'animal' are not unified (into a definition of 'man') merely by being said together.[106] There are two reasons why concatenation cannot play the unifying role that has been foisted on it. First, concatenation is an operation which is common to sentences and lists. Peter Long writes that

whereas it would be absurd to suggest that a notation is possible in which, although there are names and predicates, a proposition [i.e. sentence] does not result from

[103] On trees in linguistic theory, see Partee *et al.*, pp. 439–53.   [104] So King [5], ch. 2.
[105] See e.g. Simons [6], p. 85; Sainsbury [3], pp. 142–3, but on p. 145 Sainsbury recognizes that a mere appeal to the idea of ordering relevant items in the 'right' way does not solve the problem of unity.
[106] *Int.* 17a14.

attaching a predicate to a name, there is no absurdity in the idea of a notation in which, although there are names, a proposition does not result from attaching a name to a name. Indeed, our notation is one such![107]

The first part of this claim is incorrect: a predicate can be 'attached' to a name so as to form a mere list—unless we do not count it as an *attaching* if a sentence does not result; but then attaching will not be the syntactic operation of concatenating. There is nothing wrong with reserving the label 'attaching' for an operation which actually produces a sentence; but any such stipulation only throws the question one stage back: what *is* it to attach a predicate to a name? Given, now, that sentences may be orthographically and phonetically indistinguishable from lists, it follows that appeal to the idea of a suitable concatenation of grammatically congruent elements does not suffice to distinguish sentences from mere lists. Secondly, our concern, as I have stressed, is with the unity of type sentences and the question what distinguishes them from type lists, for the unity of token sentences is conceptually posterior to that of type sentences. Type sentences are abstract objects, so that peculiar features of token sentences which might be thought to play a role in unifying them—and in particular the spatial or temporal concatenation of grammatically congruent token words—fall away as irrelevant to our problem. There is, to be sure, an abstract conjugate of concatenation, recoverable as it were from the spatial and temporal relations that join token words: namely, order. But, again, the difficulty is that order is—or can be—common to sentences and lists and so cannot be the principle of distinction between them.

The trite assumption that the problem of unity can be solved by merely adverting to the fact that a sentence is composed of words which are syntactically of the right form to compose one, and which are concatenated (in general: ordered) in an appropriate way, may be briefly illustrated from the semantic tradition. Plato tells us that neither a succession of names, such as 'lion stag horse', nor a succession of verbs, such as 'walks runs sleeps', yields a sentence; to arrive at a sentence, in the simplest case, we need—and the implication is that it will suffice—to take one of each, as in the sample sentence he offers, 'man understands' (§1). Abelard remarks that in order to obtain a complete sentence (*perfecta oratio*) it is not sufficient for a word referring to, say, whiteness or running to be juxtaposed to 'man': if we want to form a sentence we need—and again the implication is that it will suffice—to juxtapose a verb.[108] We will see this position replicated, in essentials, in many more recent discussions of the problem of unity, especially those of Frege and Russell. And

[107] Long, p. 96.   [108] [2], p. 149.11–16. Cf. de Rijk [4], pp. 94–8; Jacobi [4], p. 144.

it is the position implied in the following contemporary account of the origin of the problem of unity:

It is an inclination to think of all words as names—as expressing a sense which determines an entity as referent, the semantic role of a word being to stand for its referent—that gives rise to the problem of sentential unity. For of course we know that not *any* old combination of words will constitute a significant sentence.[109]

Likewise, the late scholastic philosopher Domingo de Soto tells us that

we agree . . . that the predicate is united of itself to the subject. For the unity [of the proposition] in the mind is not like the way a thread unites two pieces of cloth: but rather two [mental] concepts are united by grammatical congruence. It is extraordinary that [my opponents] concede that form is united of itself to matter, and accident to subject [i.e. substance], but deny that the predicate [of a sentence] is united [of itself] to the subject. We reply, therefore, that just as the [phrase] 'white man' is formed by joining in a congruent way adjective and substantive, so too is the unity of the [sc. mental proposition] 'Peter loves' constituted in the mind.[110]

Examples of this attitude might be multiplied from historical and contemporary texts.

For our purposes, the point is that the suggestion in the excerpts I have quoted that what secures sentential unity is merely a matter of the appropriate syntactic organization of grammatically congruent words—as it might be, the mere concatenation of proper name and finite verb—is, as we have seen, mistaken. The appropriate syntactic arrangement of grammatically congruent component words is no doubt a *necessary* condition for sentential unity,[111] although we shall see later (Chapter 5) that it is not necessary for a sentence to be composed of words, such as names and verbs, performing *distinct* syntactic roles: we can find (or construct) languages or fragments of languages containing sentences composed exclusively of (for example) syntactically co-congruent names, without detriment to the unity of those sentences in the relevant sense.[112] Still, one might say, even in such degenerate cases there *is* a requirement of grammatical congruence, albeit one that is met trivially. Be that as it may, the fact remains that the arrangement of grammatically congruent bits is not *sufficient* for sentential unity: for the mere arrangement—in any

---

[109] Carruthers, p. 70. Cf. Palmer, pp. 5, 63.   [110] De Soto, fo. 20rb.

[111] Cf. Carnie, pp. 443–4. The use of the word 'congruence' in this context derives from the 'congruitas' of medieval grammarians: see e.g. Pinborg [1], pp. 52–5. Pinborg discusses Martin of Dacia's treatise on modes of signification, which concludes with the words (p. 115.5–9): 'Ex iam dictis patet quod perfectio praesupponit congruitatem, quia perfectio requirit principia congruitatis et super illa addit propria principia, et ideo principia perfectionis praesupponunt principia congruitatis, et ita perfectio congruitatem praesupponit.'

[112] Cf. Potter [1], pp. 21–2; Gibson, pp. 9–10.

order, including the 'right' order—of words which are syntactically fitted up
to form a sentence does not of itself guarantee that the words so assembled
do indeed constitute a sentence, as opposed to a mere list. There must be
something—some component or structuring principle, as we might at this stage
non-committally put it—beyond mere order and grammatical congruence,
beyond the kind of arranging of suitable words that can be duplicated by mere
lists, which constitutes a bunch of type words as a type sentence. So far as
our immediate purposes are concerned, we are now in a position to return
to the question of priority in respect of the unity of the sentence and the
unity of the proposition. The first preliminary point told us that we should be
addressing this question with the type sentence in mind, not the token sentence,
while the second preliminary point insists that the unity of the type sentence
cannot be constituted by its having any particular syntax—at least, not by
that alone.

Bearing these points in mind, the answer we should give to the priority question is, it seems to me, that the unity of the type sentence will be constituted,
in general, by an asymmetrical relation of dependence on the prior unity of
the proposition.[113] That is because any syntactically well-formed type sentence
will both itself be unified and will, when its indexical features are semantically
fixed, express a unified proposition; and there can be no restrictions in advance
on what counts as an acceptable syntax—an arrangement of words unified in
the right way—for the purpose of constituting a linguistic entity capable of
bearing a truth-value. Declarative sentences are by definition sentences that
can be true or false: they therefore have essentially *semantic* identity-criteria,
and there can accordingly be no purely *syntactic* surrogate—understanding
'syntactic' in the philosopher's sense—for those criteria. (Of course, for any
given well-defined natural or artificial language, that is, one whose parameters
can be effectively enumerated, its well-formed formulae can also be effectively
enumerated, so that in this restricted context well-formedness counts as a
purely syntactic notion: but the point is that well-formedness ceases to be a
purely syntactic notion when we *lift* that restriction.) We may gather up all
actual and possible type sentences—that is, sentences of possible languages as
well as of actual languages, for all well-formed sentences of an actual language
count as actual (type) sentences, even if they are never tokened[114]—expressive
(when their indexical parameters are appropriately fixed) of a given proposition, and treat them as members of an equivalence class, collected by

---

[113] Contrast Davidson: 'We cannot solve the problem of predication by speculating about the unity
of the proposition if by "proposition" we have in mind the sense or meaning of a sentence' ([2],
p. 143). The 'problem of predication' is the problem of the unity of the proposition (p. 77).

[114] Cf. King [5], p. 46.

a suitable synonymy relation.[115] What *collects* this class—what determines its membership—is the identity and unity of the expressed proposition; its unity is therefore constitutive of the several unities of the collected sentences.[116] Hence, though a proposition is unified if and only if it is expressed by a unified declarative sentence whose indexical parameters are appropriately fixed—thus far no asymmetry emerges—what *determines* whether a purported declarative sentence has an acceptable syntax and is sententially unified is just whether it is a member of a class of synonymous sentences expressive of some given unified proposition. Propositions are accordingly prior to sentences, in respect of their unity, in the fifth sense of priority identified by Aristotle in his discussion of the senses of 'prior' in the *Categories*,[117] namely priority in the order of explanation for two things that 'reciprocate in respect of the entailment of existence'.

As we have noted, sentences expressive of a given proposition include merely possible sentences (sentences of merely possible languages) as well as actual ones. Given this point, one consideration that might be advanced in favour of the relative priority of propositional to sentential unity seems in fact to lack suasive force. This consideration is the claim that there are *more* propositions than sentences.[118] It is often stated or implied that words form a denumerable totality;[119] and certainly, if the words of a given language form a denumerable totality, it is easy to show, assuming that sentences are finite strings of words, that the sentences of that language do so too (and conversely).[120] Further, there is undoubtedly a case to be made to the effect that propositions are non-denumerable, at least when they are conceived (as I shall argue in the next chapter they should be conceived) along the lines of Russell's 1903 theory, namely as abstract entities at the level of reference containing abstract and concrete objects and properties. For objects include the real numbers, and so are, by Cantor's theorem, non-denumerable; indeed, they include not only the real numbers, but all sets of real numbers, sets of sets of real numbers, and so on. But there must be at least as many propositions as there are objects.[121] (There are paradoxes lurking here, in particular the so-called

---

[115] We must include possible as well as actual sentences in the range of sentences correlated with a given proposition (cf. Langendoen and Postal, pp. 128–9): Chomsky's suggestion that 'the variety of [sc. empirical] languages provides an upper bound on the richness and specificity of the properties that [the theorist] may assign to universal grammar' ([5], p. 153; cf. [8], p. 70) is hardly plausible. That the number of actual and possible natural languages is infinite admits, given certain reasonable ancillary assumptions, of formal proof: Langendoen and Postal, pp. 140–2.

[116] Cf. Tugendhat [2], pp. 283–4.   [117] *Cat.* 14b9–23.

[118] See e.g. Textor [1], pp. 27–8, 38–9; Berg, pp. 151–2.

[119] See e.g. Church [6], p. 20 n. 50; Quine [5], p. 113; [11], pp. 247–8; Putnam [1], p. 327; Chomsky [6], pp. 239–40.

[120] See e.g. Kleene, pp. 4–5; Church [6], p. 239 n. 416; Bridge, p. 71; Enderton [2], pp. 6–7.

[121] Cf. Russell [3], §348.

Russell–Myhill paradox: I return to the point in §63.) If the proposed contrast between sentences and propositions were correct, according to which there are 'more' propositions than sentences, an account of unity that focused on the sentence might be thought to 'miss out' some (indeed most) propositions.

But there are three objections to this line of thinking. First, we must ask whether the words of a given language do in fact form a denumerable totality. For the words of any *actual* language—language in empirical use—the claim is quite plausible, though it has not passed unchallenged.[122] But when we widen our purview to include *possible* as well as actual languages, it may be that words will form non-denumerable totalities, if objects in general are being permitted to form a non-denumerable totality. For perhaps we can think of objects as supplying the means to constitute their own names.[123] Secondly, the line of thinking presupposes that all sentences are of finite length: but this assumption is surely false. In a discussion of the size of natural languages, D. Terence Langendoen and Paul Postal contend persuasively that

objects having all the defining conditions of sentencehood in an NL [natural language] *are* sentences of that NL. Therefore *any* restriction, finite or transfinite, on the length of NL sentences yields a framework unable to describe infinitely many well-formed sentences in every NL.[124]

It has generally been held that while there is no *finite* upper bound on sentence size, $\aleph_0$, the smallest transfinite cardinal, *is* such a bound.[125] But if Langendoen and Postal are right, there is no upper bound, finite or transfinite, on sentence size. Their argument depends on the claim that natural languages are closed under the operation of co-ordinate compounding;[126] from this it follows in the first instance that 'an NL can be identified with no fixed set of sentences at all, no matter how great its cardinality';[127] and from that lemma, in turn, follows the thesis that natural-language sentences are subject to no upper bound on their size, finite or transfinite. The argument presupposes a—by my lights, unexceptionable—platonism about abstract objects such as languages and sentences.[128] Thirdly, and most importantly, even if the suggested contrast between propositions and sentences, in point of denumerability, held when possible as well as actual sentences were taken into account, it would still not

---

[122] See e.g. Bonevac, pp. 235–6. [123] Cf. Hodges [2], p. 36.
[124] Langendoen and Postal, p. 43. [125] See e.g. Z. Harris, pp. 10, 205.
[126] This closure principle is analogous to the power set axiom: Langendoen and Postal, p. 61.
[127] Ibid., p. 59.
[128] Cf. ibid., pp. 104–12; Boolos, pp. 128–9. Languages learnable by finite creatures like ourselves will be generated from a finite base. This means that transfinitely long sentences, and even finitely long sentences involving more than *n* constructive operations, for some suitably large *n*, will contain lexical or structural repetition: Z. Harris, pp. 129–30.

follow that an account of unity should have to focus on the proposition rather than the sentence: for it is not as though one is seeking to give an account of the unity of *all* sentences and *all* propositions taken as simultaneously given totalities, in which case the fact, if it is one, that there are more propositions than sentences might indeed matter; rather, one is aiming to give an account of the unity of *any* (that is, an arbitrary) sentence, and correspondingly of *any* (an arbitrary) proposition, so that the question of the comparative total numbers of sentences and propositions is surely immaterial. It seems safer, then, not to rely on comparative cardinality considerations in staking the claim that propositions are prior, in respect of unity, to sentences, and I accordingly do not do so. My argument for the priority of propositions is that what determines whether a purported declarative sentence has an acceptable syntax and so is unified is whether it is a member of a class of synonymous sentences expressive of some given unified proposition.

This is, I think, the correct *metaphysical* answer to the priority question, but I stress that proviso because there is an *epistemological* sense in which the reverse answer to the priority question would be correct. The two answers are diametrically opposed, but when they are relativized to their respective points of view, they are seen to be compatible with one another. The reason for this diversity is that, although a type declarative sentence is *constituted* as a unity by its expressing a unified proposition when its indexical parameters are semantically fixed (the metaphysical priority of the unified proposition), we can in practice *identify* unified propositions only as the meanings of given unified type declarative sentences whose parameters are so fixed (the epistemological priority of the unified sentence). Our epistemic position is that we start with a number of empirical languages in which we can identify meaningful declarative sentences as those linguistic items capable of being true or false. These sentences express propositions. (That is just another way of saying that they are meaningful.) Further, I have accepted (§3) that it is a constraint on the idea of linguistic meaning that distinct declarative sentences (of the same language, or of different languages) may express the same proposition.[129] (That is just another way of saying that distinct such sentences can mean the same.) Once we have that structure in place, we can see that an epistemological priority attaches to the unity of the type declarative

---

[129] Cf. Dummett [10], pp. 11, 17–18. The possibility of synonymy between sentences of different languages, which I here presuppose, is by no means uncontroversial: it would be rejected by anyone who took a particular kind of holistic approach to sentence meaning, or who counted etymology as relevant to meaning. The *loci classici* for this latter position are Plato's *Cratylus* and Horne Tooke's *Diversions of Purley* (e.g. II, ch. 4: ii, pp. 121, 208): see Funke, pp. 109–14; Aarsleff [1], pp. 105–6, 242, 250; [2], pp. 486–7.

sentence, for our sole means of identifying a particular unified proposition goes via a prior identification of a type declarative sentence that expresses the given proposition and that is already certified as unified; but, compatibly with this, a metaphysical priority attaches to the unity of the proposition, seeing that we cannot impose, a priori, any limits on the range of grammatically acceptable sentences, whether of actual or of possible languages, capable of expressing any given proposition.

6 Unity and Complexity

In asking what distinguishes a sentence from a mere list of words, or a proposition from a mere aggregate of word-meanings, I am supposing that a sentence does indeed contain more than one word, and a proposition more than one word-meaning. Plato also made this assumption,[130] and Aristotle maintained Plato's approach, telling us that 'falsehood and truth arise in connection with composition and division', and so a fortiori in connection with syntactic and semantic *complexity*.[131] In view of the fact that it is possible to construct one-word declarative sentences this might seem a problematic assumption. Yet, in spite of this rather obvious reservation that one might have, the Aristotelian confidence that truth and falsity require complexity has been endorsed on virtually all sides. The view was standard (though not quite universal) in medieval discussions of truth.[132] Locke tells us that 'truth or falsehood being never without some affirmation or negation, express or tacit, it is not to be found but where signs are joined or separated, according to the agreement or disagreement of the things they stand for'.[133] The view was shared by Frege,[134] and by Moore, who stated in 1899 concerning propositions and their components ('concepts'), that

a proposition is nothing other than a complex concept. The difference between a concept and a proposition, in virtue of which the latter alone can be called true or false, would seem to lie merely in the simplicity of the former. A proposition is a synthesis of concepts.[135]

[130] *Sophist* 262d3–6.
[131] *Int.* 16a12–13. See also *Cat.* 2a4–10, 13b10–12; *DA* 432a10–11; *Met.* 1027b18–22. Cf. Prior [3], pp. 13–14; Panaccio [4], pp. 44–5.
[132] See Panaccio [4], pp. 232, 292–5. In the mental language tradition, against the standard view (of e.g. Ockham and Buridan) that mental propositions are complex (having, in the basic case, the structure: subject + copula + predicate), Gregory of Rimini, and following him Peter of Ailly, argued that they are simple: see Ashworth [2], ch. 6, pp. 73–5.
[133] II. xxxii, §19. Cf. Condillac, II. iii, §31.   [134] [26], pp. 18–19; cf. Dummett [3], pp. 294–6.
[135] [2], p. 5.

Russell too noted, in 1908, that 'propositions are essentially complex',[136] and in 1918, after he had moved over to regarding propositions as linguistic, he still thought that 'a proposition . . . is a complex symbol in the sense that it has parts which are also symbols'.[137] In his *Notebooks* Wittgenstein remarked that 'the sentence (*Satz*) is a picture of a state of affairs only insofar as it is logically articulated', and he added that 'a simple—unarticulated—sign can be neither true nor false'.[138]

Does the problem of unity arise for one-word sentences, and if so what does it look like? As a matter of fact there was a lively debate in the late medieval period concerning the status of such apparently simple, 'feature-placing'[139] declarative sentences as 'pluit' ('it is raining'), 'tonat' ('there is thunder'), etc., and on the question whether such sentences could be reduced to articulated sentences containing more than one word.[140] A prominent opponent of the reductive strategy was Domingo de Soto, who argued that when rustics hear the word 'pluit' they do not, in forming a mental proposition, articulate the one-word spoken sentence into something like 'Natura pluit' ('Nature rains'), but have a simple conception of its meaning corresponding to the simplicity of the sentence itself.[141] This view was echoed much later (and more influentially) by Adam Smith, who in his *Considerations Concerning the First Formation of Languages* (1761) attacked the suggestion that 'pluit' abbreviates 'pluvia pluit' ('the rain rains'),[142] and who contrasted the 'perfect simplicity and unity' of impersonal verbs with the artificiality and imperfection of constructions involving personal verbs:

> Everybody must observe how much more simplicity there is in the natural expression, *pluit*, than in the more artificial expressions, *imber decidit, the rain falls*; or *tempestas est pluvia, the weather is rainy*. In these last two expressions, the simple event, or matter of fact, is artificially split and divided in the one, into two; in the other, into three parts. . . . The first verbs, therefore, perhaps even the first words, made use of in the beginnings of language, would in all probability be such impersonal verbs.[143]

Against Smith's admittedly rather quaint view, we are told in a standard modern text on Latin syntax that the fact that impersonal verbs such as 'pluit' have no person-ending except the third-person singular

---

[136] [13], p. 76. Cf. Burge [2], p. 133.   [137] [13], p. 185.

[138] [6], entry for 3 Oct. 1914, p. 8, taken up into [1] at §4.032.

[139] I borrow Strawson's terminology: [1], p. 202; [2], pp. 36–9.

[140] See Nuchelmans [1], pp. 95–6, 113; [6], p. 39; Ashworth [2], ch. 5, pp. 66–71. Cf. Simplicius, *In Cat.* p. 43.23–5; Strawson [1], pp. 202–9.

[141] De Soto, fo. 20[rb].   [142] Smith, §30, p. 217 n. See the editor's note ad loc.

[143] Smith, §28, p. 216. Cf. Funke, pp. 24–7; Land, pp. 80–7; Nuchelmans [5], pp. 167–8.

does not mean that they have no 'subject', for the activity denoted by the third-personal verbal inflexion must be performed by someone or something, even if the speaker does not know what it is. . . . [T]he subject may be assumed to be the noun implied in the root of the verb. With those impersonal verbs of active form which denote the activities of natural phenomena, such as *tonat* ('it thunders'); *pluit* ('it rains'); *ningit* ('it snows'); *vesperascit* ('the shades of evening fall'); etc., the subjects are 'thunder', 'rain', 'snow', 'evening', etc.[144]

Now the suggestion that such one-word, feature-placing sentences might be, as they perhaps appear, semantically simple does indeed seem to me erroneous. But I do not think that the quoted account, though it may be correct as a matter of etymology, points us in the right direction when it comes to saying why the semantics of such words must be complex.

Consider first-person one-word Latin sentences, such as 'lego' ('I read'), where the first-person subject is indicated by inflecting the verb rather than by inserting a separate word (though a personal pronoun—in this case it would be 'ego'—can be inserted as well). Boethius, agreeing with Aristotle that truth and falsity arise in connection with composition and division (and so essentially involve semantic complexity), took the view that, in effect, 'lego' has a deep structure that can be brought to the surface by transforming it into the equivalent but articulated form 'ego lego'.[145] Although neither he nor Aristotle attempted to justify the claim that truth and falsity require semantic complexity, we can make good the deficiency. That such superficially simple forms as 'lego' are semantically structured is indicated by their role in *inference*. For there will be many inferences, involving the word 'lego', the validity of which will trade on the fact that an account of the semantics of that word must discern a structuring of more than one element in its semantic make-up. That observation indirectly vindicates the Aristotelian claim, because of the constitutive connection between logical validity on the one hand and truth and falsity on the other: for an inference is defined to be logically valid just if no interpretation of its non-logical constants renders all of its premises true and the conclusion false.

Impersonal verbs work in inference in an entirely similar way to personal verbs like 'lego'. For example, a feature-placing sentence such as 'pluit' will mean not simply that it is raining, but—if the feature in question is genuinely to be *placed*—that it is raining *here and now*.[146] That the sentence has this deep

144 Woodcock, p. 166. The view is an old one in the grammatical tradition: see J. Harris, p. 175 n., referring to Apollonius Dyscolus (III, §188: Uhlig II ii/iii, pp. 431.1–432.6) and Priscian (*Inst. Gramm.* 18, §56: Keil II, pp. 231.21–232.5).
145 [1], II. i, §1, pp. 47.31–48.6.   146 Cf. Strawson [1], p. 215.

structure is indicated by the fact that we (and de Soto's Latinate rustics) want to be able to use it in such inference patterns as (translated):

It is raining;

If it is raining, then it is not dry;

Hence it is not dry.

This inference considered as a type is formally valid, but on any actual occasion of employment the validity and usefulness of (a tokening of) an argument of that type will depend on the circumstance that the deployment of the argument takes place over a sufficiently short period of time and in a sufficiently stable location. A substantial lapse of time or change of location between the utterances or inscriptions (or, in general, entertainings) of the premisses and the conclusion can affect the *validity* of the token argument (for given a sufficient dislocation of time or place tokenings of the first two premisses could be true and a tokening of the conclusion false), and a similar hiatus between the utterance or inscription (entertaining) of the antecedent and the consequent of the conditional in the second premiss can affect the truth-value of that premiss, so detracting from the *usefulness* of the argument as a whole. We can spell all this out by inserting explicit place and time indexicals:

It is raining here and now;

If it is raining here and now, then it is not dry here and now;

Hence it is not dry here and now.

The point is that the validity and usefulness of any given tokening of the argument require the references of the indexicals to be fixed to the same place and time.[147]

It follows that while a language may certainly contain one-word sentences, insofar as these sentences are capable of figuring in inferences they will be semantically subordinated to articulated propositions, in the sense that the account of what those sentences mean will discern a structuring of more than one element—just as many elements, in fact, as are required to make sense of their role in inference. Now this way of putting the matter might

---

[147] If we attempted to secure co-reference of the indexicals by inserting further premisses explicitly stating that relevant token indexicals are co-referential—for of course their mere inclusion in the argument does not guarantee that—we should find ourselves launched on a regress, since we should require yet further premisses to secure the co-reference of the new indexicals with the originals, and so on. This point will be of relevance in Ch. 6 (§82).

superficially seem to support the main claim of the preceding section, namely that the unity of sentences is asymmetrically dependent on a metaphysically prior propositional unity. But, though that claim is not undermined by the argument of the present section, as far as the issue of sentential and propositional complexity is concerned the metaphysical dependence relation can be seen to run in the opposite direction: that is, the complexity of propositions is an artefact of the complexity of sentences, not vice versa. The point is crucially connected with the definition of declarative sentences as those sentences that can be true or false. For it is essential to such items of language as are capable of bearing truth-values that they can figure in inference (as premisses or conclusions). And, in the first instance, inferential relations connect *sentences*, not *propositions*; validity is a property of, and semantic and syntactic consequence are relations on, sentences.[148] Hence the argument I have mounted in the present section yields, in the first instance, the subordination of one-word sentences capable of figuring in inference to articulated, many-word sentences. That is what is really meant by saying that one-word sentences are semantically subordinated to articulated propositions: the complexity of the propositions to which these sentences are subordinated has to be thought of as constituted by the complexity of the sentences that canonically or most completely express them.[149] (A proposition will be as highly structured as the most highly structured sentence in the relevant synonymy class represents it as being: the more structure we can *represent* a proposition as having, the more structure it *has*.) There is no inconsistency between this metaphysical dependence relation and the different metaphysical dependence relation embodied in the main claim of the previous section. Propositions are *complex* in virtue of being expressed canonically or completely by complex sentences; but the *unity* of those complex sentences in turn depends asymmetrically on the unity of the complex propositions they express.

7   Reference and Supposition

So far propositions have been defined to be the meanings of declarative sentences. The intuitive notion of meaning has not been subjected to further analysis. But it is time to remedy this lack. I approach the question of the unity of the proposition from within the semantic tradition which, in modern times, derives from Frege, but which was inaugurated by Aristotle: in this tradition

---

[148] See my [4], §6; contra Frege [26], p. 195.   [149] Cf. Hale [4], p. 188.

we articulate the relation between language and the world into a hierarchy comprising three orders or levels. In the Fregean picture there is a level of symbolic language at the top of the hierarchy, an intermediate level of sense, and a worldly level of reference at the bottom. The items of language that are housed at the top of the hierarchy are conceived as types, and the levels of sense and reference correspond to two distinct components of the intuitive notion of meaning. The medieval tradition represented the upper tiers of the hierarchy rather differently: the linguistic items at the top were usually thought of as spoken or written linguistic tokens rather than types, and the intermediate level as a level of mental language, whose elements were again normally thought of as tokens. On either conception, the intermediate level acts as a link between symbolic language on the one hand and a worldly realm of reference on the other. Reference is thus the relation that in some way connects language to the world. But what exactly is this relation? What is it for an item of language to *refer to* something in the world? There are, broadly speaking, two strategies in the tradition for elucidating the notion of reference.[150]

According to one strategy, 'the theory of reference is a theory of the manner of determination of the truth-value of any sentence in accordance with its composition'.[151] On this approach, reference is in effect what medieval philosophers called *suppositio*:[152] according to this conception, the referent of a linguistic expression is that feature or aspect of it which determines the *truth* of those (true) sentences in which it occurs. Supposition theory is a contextualist doctrine in the sense that it has to do not with the references of words taken in isolation from sentential contexts, but with the way the references of individual words affect the semantics of sentences in which they occur, and in particular with the way in which different kinds of reference determine the *truth* of various kinds of sentence.[153] This emerges especially clearly from those parts of supposition theory that anticipate modern quantification theory. Without going too far into the details, we can illustrate this point briefly from

---

[150] But it is common for philosophers to discuss reference without attempting to elucidate the notion at all. For example, Sainsbury tells us at the beginning of his [5] that he is not going to 'prejudge' the question what reference is, but rather let a view 'emerge over the course of the book' (p. 1). This unhelpful policy precipitates disaster in ch. 3, where Sainsbury argues for his main claim, that there can be intelligible but empty referring expressions. How can such issues be decided if we do not know what reference is? On p. 93 it is confidently affirmed that 'the analogues of knowing the referent of a name are knowing which things a predicate applies to and knowing which truth-value a sentence possesses'. Again, how can we be sure that these are the right analogues, when we have not been told what the referent of a name *is*?

[151] Dummett [3], p. 479.

[152] See e.g. Spade [2], p. 192; Panaccio [4], pp. 257, 311, 313; Scott, intro. to Buridan, [2], pp. 29–42; and in general on the history of supposition theory, see Arnold.

[153] Cf. Panaccio [1], p. 268.

the writings of one of the theory's clearest and most influential exponents. William of Ockham tells us that the term 'man' stands in personal determinate supposition in the sentence 'a man is an animal', and what this means is that we can 'descend' from the sentence 'a man is an animal' to the disjunction 'this man is an animal, or that man is an animal etc.', and we can 'ascend' from any of the particular sentences 'this man is an animal', 'that man is an animal' etc., to the main sentence; again, the term 'man' is said to stand in personal confused distributive mobile supposition in the sentence 'every man is an animal', and what this means is that we can 'descend' from the sentence 'every man is an animal' to the conjunction 'this man is an animal and that man is an animal, etc.', but we cannot 'ascend' from any of the particular sentences of the form 'this man is an animal', 'that man is an animal', etc. to the main sentence.[154] (These are Ockham's analyses of existential and universal quantification; evidently they, like Wittgenstein's analyses in the *Tractatus*, are given in terms of 'long disjunctions' and 'long conjunctions' respectively.[155]) Even from this brief illustration it is clear that we are here concerned not with properties enjoyed by terms as such, in abstraction from the sentential contexts in which they occur, but with properties of terms as they occur in sentential contexts, and in particular with the way they determine the various sentences in which they occur to be true. This is the force of Ockham's version of the context principle, according to which a term has supposition only in the context of a sentence.[156]

In the case of simple categorical sentences—that is, unmodalized, quantifier-free non-composite declarative sentences of the form 'a is F',[157] where 'a' is a proper name and 'F' a monadic general term[158]—Ockham subscribed to the so-called identity theory of predication, according to which such a sentence is true just if what the subject supposits for is identical with what (or with one of the things which)[159] the predicate supposits for,[160] where a term is

---

[154] [1], I, §70.   [155] Cf. Kleene, pp. 177–9.   [156] [1], I, §63, p. 193.

[157] Throughout this book, ordinary quotation marks will double as marks of quasi-quotation.

[158] See Whately, II. ii. 1, p. 75.

[159] The parenthesis is necessary, otherwise if 'This is red' and 'That is red' were both true (in some context), by the transitivity of identity we would have 'This = that'. See here Sinisi [1].

[160] [1], II, §2, pp. 249–50; [3], III, §12, p. 250. On the identity and inference theories of predication, see Pinborg [3], p. 53; Malcolm; Perler, pp. 80–2; my [5]; Leppin, pp. 102–3, 141. In the early modern period one of the clearest statements of the identity theory was given by Hobbes: [1], I. iii, §§2, 7–10, 16, and I. iv, §8; [2], I, §4; cf. Nuchelmans [5], pp. 128–30. See also the passage from John Sergeant cited by Wilson, pp. 97–8; and De Morgan, p. 50. The identity theory was still adhered to by Geach in his [1] (p. 478), but a few years later he thought it 'logically worthless' ([2], p. 252). It is the 'two name' theory which he went on to attack influentially in his [3]. Frege, incidentally, repudiates the identity theory ([11], p. 442; [21], p. 200; cf. Angelelli [1], p. 95) as do Mill and Johnson (see Prior [3], pp. 85–8). In spite of its dubious credentials, the theory has recently been revived by Armstrong ([6]).

taken to supposit for what it is verified of:[161] hence a sentence of the form 'a is F' is true just if 'That is a' and 'That is F' are both verified when the references of the demonstratives are fixed to the same object. (This definition evidently sets up a circle[162] or, better, a regress; but the regress seems to me an innocent, constituting regress of the sort I discuss in §82 below.) Of course, as a nominalist (or conceptualist) Ockham is quite happy to embrace the implication of this doctrine that general terms refer to their instances.[163] But the key point is, here again, that the type of supposition which a word has in any given sentential context is governed by the requirement that it have just the right kind of supposition in that context to render the sentence in which it occurs true. Thus, for example, in the sentence 'Man is an animal', 'man' has personal supposition, and so refers to its instances, because it is real men—as opposed to either mental entities or spoken and written linguistic signs—who, in virtue of being animals, render that sentence true; in 'Man is a word', by contrast, 'man' is held to have material supposition (that is, to refer to the spoken or written sign 'man'), because in this context *that* is the kind of supposition which will render the sentence true. No room is made for the possibility that the sentence 'Man is a word' might be *false* because 'man' has *personal* supposition in that context: indeed, supposition theory is unable, in general, to accommodate meaningful falsity—it is, we might say, not primarily in the business of doing so—for it is a theory of what makes sentences true, when they are true, and not of what gives them meaning, regardless of truth-value. The supposition of a term is fixed, as the early logic text *Dialectica Monacensis* tells us—and this constraint pervades later expositions of the theory in the medieval period—'according to the requirement that the expression [in which the term occurs] be true' (*secundum exigentiam veritatis in locutione*).[164] On this approach to reference, then, it coincides with satisfaction.

---

[161] [1], I, §§33, 63. Cf. Buridan [2], §3, p. 50 (see my [5], p. 93).

[162] Cf. my [5], pp. 92–3, where I quote Peter of Ailly's charge to this effect.

[163] [1], I, §4, p. 15; §10, pp. 35–8; §17, p. 60; §21, p. 70; §33, p. 96; §43, pp. 123–4. Cf. Descartes, *Principles*, I, §59 (viiiA, pp. 27–8); Hobbes [1], I. ii, §9. On Ockham see Panaccio [1], pp. 280–5. There is a distinction to be drawn between the way an 'absolute' term (such as 'animal') refers to the entities in its extension and the way a 'connotative' term (such as 'white') does so: cf. Mill, I. ii, §5. (The distinction has generated considerable controversy in the exegesis of Ockham: see Spade [1]; Adams, pp. 319–27; my [12]; Panaccio [5], ch. 4.) I shall return to Ockham's theory of reference for general terms in §17.

[164] De Rijk [1], ii/2, p. 608. Here one might also mention the commonly expressed principle that 'the subjects [of sentences] are such as [i.e. have the kind of supposition that] their predicates permit' (*talia sunt subiecta, qualia permiserint praedicata*): see Spade [2], p. 193; my [5], §5. Noteworthy too in this connection is the doctrine of *restrictio* and *ampliatio*, according to which the domain of discourse can be contracted or extended, in the semantic analysis of a given sentence, in whatever way is necessary to render the sentence true: thus e.g. a future-tensed statement about men will have its domain of

Contemporary adherents of what is in essence a continuation of the supposition strategy include Quine and Davidson, for both of whom satisfaction
is, as Davidson puts it, 'a generalized form of reference'.[165] To some extent
it is also Frege's strategy. Frege's semantical approach is non-extensionalist
insofar as he does not identify the referent of what he calls a concept-word
(a predicative general term) with the objects that satisfy it, as Quine and
Davidson do and as is quite standard in contemporary semantics in respect
of both natural and artificial languages,[166] but rather with what he calls a
concept. But he does not consistently take the opportunity provided by
this semantical disposition to allow particular pairs of concept-words satisfied
by the same objects (as it might be, 'is renate' and 'is cordate') to refer
to distinct concepts: sometimes he does adopt an intensionalist reading of
concepts, but elsewhere it is clear that he thinks of them along extensionalist lines, according to which concepts are identical provided only that they
have the same extension.[167] On an extensionalist approach, the referent of
an expression is that in virtue of whose identity linguistic expressions can be
intersubstituted *salva veritate* in referentially transparent contexts,[168] or more
generally it is, as David Bell puts it, 'a property which an expression must
possess if that expression is to be *truth-valuable*', or again 'that property of
an expression which enables it to participate in valid deductive inference
within the predicate calculus with identity'.[169] It is the 'conceptual content'
(*begrifflicher Inhalt*) of the *Begriffsschrift*, about which we are told that it is
content relevant to inferential properties.[170] These formulations need to be
extended, or glossed, so as to make it clear that they apply to subsentential
expressions as well as to sentences: in the case of subsentential expressions, it
would be more perspicuous to say that the reference of any such expression
is the contribution it makes towards determining the inferential properties of
sentences.[171]

---

discourse enlarged to include men who are going to exist as well as currently existing men (the latter
being the default personal supposition of 'man'), so as to obviate the relevant sentence's being rendered
false or truth-valueless for failure of reference. See Scott's intro. to Buridan's [2], pp. 33–4.

[165] Davidson [2], p. 30. Cf. [1], pp. 216–17, 223, 229; Quine [3], §§19–22; Carnap [3], §29.

[166] See e.g. Geach [3], p. 46; Martin, pp. 99–100; Wallace; Kimball, pp. 112–13; Kripke [2], p. 328;
Partee *et al.*, pp. 142–3, 231–2; Bostock [2], pp. 74–90; Hodges [2], p. 43; Priest [1], p. 200; Sainsbury
[5], p. 93 (quoted above, n. 150); Hale [4], p. 201.

[167] For the intensionalist approach, see [3], §68 n. For the extensionalist approach, see [9], p. 320
([21], p. 184); [26], pp. 132–4. Frege is often wrongly taken to have had an exclusively extensionalist
understanding of concepts: see e.g. von Kutschera [1], p. 78; Cocchiarella [2], p. 58; Crocco [1], p. 23;
[2], p. 180. For a modern exposition of the intensionalist approach, see Zalta [1], esp. chs. 2 and 3.

[168] Cf. Bell [1], pp. 24–5; [2], p. 191; [4], p. 41; Brandom [1], p. 279.

[169] [1], p. 42; [2], p. 193; cf. McDowell [6], p. 56.

[170] Frege [1], p. x; §3, pp. 2–3. Cf. Grossmann [1], pp. 13–14.   [171] Cf. Dummett [3], p. 479.

As far as proper names are concerned, adopting the *suppositio* approach to reference—construing reference as satisfaction—fits with a descriptivist rather than a *de re* construal of sense. It is definitive of the idea of the *de re* sense of a proper name that (i) a name's having a referent is essential to its having a sense—and so essential to there being anything that counts as understanding that name; (ii) its having the very referent it has is essential to that name's having the very sense it has; and (iii) the understander, in grasping a *de re* sense, thereby cognizes the object which is the name's referent.[172] Grasping the *de re* sense of an appropriate name is a matter of thinking of the name's referent in some particular, non-descriptive way; hence its reference, as well as sense, is correlative with understanding. By contrast, if one opts for a descriptivist approach to the senses of proper names,[173] there will, as in the case of the approach to general terms which identifies their referents with their extensions, be a clear respect in which, while the senses of relevant expressions are correlative with understanding,[174] their references—objects satisfying descriptions in the case of names, extensions in the case of general terms—will not be. Now on the *suppositio* approach to meaning the referent of any expression will be, as we have said, that aspect of the expression which is relevant to determining the inferential properties of sentences the expression goes to compose. Plainly there is no guarantee, on this approach, that the understander of an expression will know what its referent is; so there can be no requirement that the understander think of its referent as a condition of understanding the expression.[175] Such a dislocation between reference and understanding is exactly what descriptivism about the senses of proper names provides.

Davidson attributes the general conception of reference we are currently considering to Tarski, and it is familiar that Tarski has been the inspiration for Davidson's sustained and influential attempts to elucidate the notion of meaning both by constructing (fragments of) axiomatized theories of meaning for natural languages, and more importantly by adumbrating what would be involved in constructing such theories. But one can agree with Davidson in his contention that the study of such theories is capable of shedding light on meaning, and one can even follow him in his further proposal that

---

[172] On the notion of *de re* sense see Evans [1], ch. 1; McDowell [3], Essays 8–10, and [6]; Davies, esp. ch. 5; Strawson [6], p. 48; Brandom [2], pp. 547–52; Sainsbury [5], pp. 83–5.

[173] This approach includes Dummett's construal of understanding a proper name as a matter of having a criterion by which we can identify an object as its referent (see also Chomsky [5], p. 42; and Tugendhat [2], pp. 359, 478–9, who follows Dummett). Any such criterion will, when expressed, take the form of a definite description: see e.g. [4], p. 87; [10], pp. 46, 74. Descriptive readings of Fregean sense are all too common: e.g. Bealer [1], pp. 159, 164; [4], pp. 19, 40–1; Zalta [1], pp. 164–5, and [2]; Sainsbury [5], pp. 92–4.

[174] Cf. Hylton [2], pp. 124–5.   [175] Cf. Church [4], p. 101.

theories of meaning should take the form of theories of truth—theories, that is, whose theorems state the truth-conditions of object-language sentences in some suitably chosen metalanguage (possibly the same language as the object-language)—without being thereby compelled to endorse any particular strategy for assigning semantic values to subsentential expressions. Semantic values are assigned to subsentential expressions under the overall constraint that the assignment should enable the theorist to derive *correct* meaning-specifications for complete sentences; and that constraint does not, just as such, dictate any particular way of making the assignments.[176] It surely ought to be possible to adopt a strategy deriving truth-conditions for complete sentences from clauses for subsentential expressions that work by assigning, as the semantic values of general terms, not *satisfying objects* (or sequences of objects, the complication being required to deal with polyadic terms), but rather *satisfaction conditions*. On this approach the referent of a general term 'F' would be not a set of satisfying objects (or satisfying sequences of objects), but an abstract condition which any given object(s) would have to satisfy in order to count as being (an) *F*. Such an alternative strategy would actually seem to harmonize better—at least for the purposes of constructing a theory of meaning for *natural* languages—with the way Tarski and Davidson treat sentences, for their approach envisages the derivation not of sentences' truth-*values* as the semantic values determining (and in this case coinciding with) sentence meanings, but of their truth-*conditions*. The motivation for adopting such an alternative strategy would be to connect, in a way that the *suppositio* strategy does not, reference with understanding.

8 Reference and Signification

That brings us to the second strategy for making sense of the relation of reference. According to this approach, reference equates to what medieval philosophers called *significatio*: that is, the reference of a linguistic expression is what grounds *understanding*.[177] Now medieval philosophers typically subscribed to a causal and atomistic account of this grounding relation;[178] but it is familiar

---

[176] Cf. McGinn, ch. 3.

[177] Spade [2], pp. 188–9. See e.g. Abelard [1], pp. 307.28–308.1, discussed by Jacobi [2]. The main source for this approach was (Boethius' translation of) a passage in Aristotle's *Int.* (16b19–21), which I quote and discuss in §26 below.

[178] This conception of signification goes back to Augustine and Boethius, and is explicitly followed by Ockham in [1], I, §1 (pp. 8–9), and by Buridan in [2], ch. 1 (p. 22). See Panaccio [2], pp. 67–70 (on Ockham). For the post-medieval continuation of the doctrine, see Ashworth [1], pp. 39–40 with e.g. de Soto, fos. 2rb–3vb, and Fonseca, I, §8.

from the philosophy of the later Wittgenstein, and the literature this has spawned, that causal accounts are not competent to construct the essential normativity of meaning and understanding.[179] That is, we require of the notion of signification (reference), if it is to be genuinely correlative with linguistic understanding, that it characterize not what the understander actually *does* think of—what he or she is, as a matter of fact, *caused* to think of—when entertaining a linguistic expression, but rather what he or she *ought to* think of in order to count as understanding that expression.

As a rule, the causal account was supplemented in medieval accounts of signification (and we find this too in Descartes)[180] by a story locating a relation of *similitude* between mental concepts and suitable worldly entities. (The account applied in the first instance to singular thought, and was then generalized by appeal to the notion of abstraction.[181]) The notion that a mental image 'resembles' something in the 'external' world plausibly goes back, at least for medieval thinkers, to Plato's description of the demiurge's creative activity in the *Timaeus*.[182] But for reasons that we also owe to the later Wittgenstein, this approach to mental representation has to be rejected as well: it does not make sense to suppose that mental images look (sound etc.) like worldly entities, for mental images do not present an *appearance* (as it were to an inner homunculus) at all: we *have* mental images; we do not *perceive* them. Claude Panaccio has suggested that the notion of *resemblance* between mental images (or acts) and worldly things might be glossed in terms of a structural isomorphism,[183] and the idea, while perhaps too modern for Ockham, is certainly one we find in Descartes and Leibniz.[184] But the appeal to isomorphism still invites us to conceive of mental images (acts) inappropriately, in photographic or similar terms. And the relation between the propositional content of mental images and the propositionality of (bits of) the world is one of identity, not merely of resemblance or isomorphism.[185]

If we adopt the *significatio* approach to reference, as I shall be doing in this study, a more satisfactory construal of the reference relation than the atomistic

---

[179] See Kripke [4], esp. pp. 22–37.   [180] Nuchelmans [5], p. 44.

[181] On Ockham, a prime exponent of this approach, see Arnold, pp. 124–5; Panaccio [4], pp. 273–5. In his mature thought Ockham abandoned the so-called *fictum* theory of his early writings in favour of a mental-act theory (see here Nuchelmans [5], pp. 26–8; Karger [1], pp. 445–51; [2], pp. 173–9; Panaccio [4], pp. 258–64), but he continued to maintain the idea of resemblance between semantically significant mental acts and relevant worldly entities.

[182] Nuchelmans [5], pp. 23–4, 37.   [183] [4], pp. 275, 315–16.

[184] See Nuchelmans [5], pp. 37, 215–18. In his essay 'Quid sit idea', Leibniz remarks: 'patet non esse necessarium ut id quod exprimit simile sit rei expressae, modo habitudinum quaedam analogia servetur' ([1], vii, p. 264; [5], p. 64).

[185] See my [15], ch. 6, and Ch. 2 below.

causal-cum-similitude one will be the following: the object of reference of an expression is just that thing which an adequate theory of meaning for the language in question specifies as what understanders need to think of, and what it suffices for them to think of (so long as they think of the relevant object *as* the meaning of the relevant item of language),[186] in order to count as understanding the expression in question. Or, to put it in Russellian terms: the object of reference of an expression is just that thing (concrete or abstract)[187] which it is necessary and sufficient for an understander to be acquainted with in order to count as understanding the expression in question.[188] The requirement that the notion of reference be embedded within the idea of a theory of meaning cancels the atomism of the medieval approach to *significatio*, because a theory of meaning, on the view I endorse and shall examine more closely in the next section, privileges the complete sentence as the primary unit of semantic meaning, subsentential items and their references being derivative, and essentially theoretical, posits required to account for the semantic properties of whole sentences. As Michael Dummett puts it, sentences are prior to words in the order of explanation: that is, as *theorists* we explain what words are in terms of their role in forming sentences. This does not conflict with an opposing priority in what Dummett calls the order of recognition: that is, as *speakers* we understand sentences on the basis of a prior understanding of their component words.[189]

This definition of reference obviously invites the larger question: what sorts and strengths of epistemic connection between understander and object of reference are required to constitute a genuine relation of acquaintance? My view is that we should insist on a fairly strong connection, one that requires the subject to be able to distinguish an object of acquaintance (thought of as the referent of a given linguistic expression) not indeed from *all* other things,[190] but from all other *contextually relevant* things. In the particular case of sentences, if truth-values are what declarative sentences refer to (as Frege believed), then we should demand that an understander know whether a sentence is true or false in order to count as understanding it. (Of course, on Frege's own approach to reference—which, as we have seen, is a *suppositio* approach—it would by

[186] Grandy, p. 403.

[187] Geach rejects the Russellian view that we can have direct acquaintance with universals ([6], p. 47), but he does so on the basis of a rejection of the empiricist doctrine that our acquaintance with universals is achieved by a process of abstraction, which leaves open the possibility that our acquaintance with them might be otherwise grounded.

[188] Russell [13], p. 56; [8], p. 32; cf. too [5], p. 209. Contrary to what Russell implies in 'On Denoting' ([13], p. 55), the principle of acquaintance does not have anything essentially to do with the theory of descriptions: Hylton [2], p. 207; Cartwright [3], p. 922.

[189] Dummett [2], p. 4. See further §56 below.   [190] So Evans [1], p. 89.

no means follow that the understander of a sentence need be acquainted with its truth-value in the sense of knowing whether the sentence is true or false: for, on that approach, the level of *sense* is supposed to encode everything that is necessary and sufficient for understanding.[191]) I also take a realist epistemology for granted, according to which the objects of our acquaintance include not only abstract objects and universals, but also the ordinary concrete individuals, animate and inanimate, among which we pass our lives, rather than sense-data (and perhaps Cartesian selves), as Russell wanted. Though broader than Russell's own notion of acquaintance[192]—at least when he came to see the doctrine as having principal (or even exclusive) application to sense-data and Cartesian selves[193]—my understanding of acquaintance is also weaker, for Russell eventually espoused a doctrine of total epistemic transparency for objects of acquaintance—hence the restriction of acquaintance to items that he felt could meet that demand—in the sense that anything figuring as an object of acquaintance must be something which the subject, in effect, knows infallibly.[194] Any such Cartesian understanding of the acquaintance relation is no part of my picture. For me, aside from a handful of degenerate and uninteresting exceptions, fallibility infects one's knowledge of all one's mental states, including such paradigmatically 'inner' experiences as seeing an after-image and feeling pain.[195]

9 Linguistic Idealism and Empirical Realism

There are two approaches to the Aristotelian and Fregean semantic hierarchy which both demand to be recognized, but which may seem to be in conflict with one another: the perspective of linguistic idealism and the perspective of empirical realism. According to the first of these perspectives, sense and refer-ence are essentially *derived* notions. Intelligible symbolic language is the given, and the senses and referents of items of symbolic language are theoretically derived posits, precipitated by a correct account of the meaningfulness of those

---

[191] Evans takes himself to be in part interpreting Frege when he tells us that he has 'felt able to grasp the nettle—to suppose that in understanding a sentence one *would*, in one way, be thinking of its truth-value' ([1], p. 17 n. 17). In what way? McDowell has a suggestion on that score, which I shall consider in §14 below. In fact, however, on my reading of Frege, it is a misinterpretation to impute to him the view that the understander of a sentence is obliged to think, in any way at all, of its truth-value: for on Frege's *suppositio* approach to reference, everything the understander 'has to think about' is accommodated at the level of sense, and the level of reference simply has no role to play in grounding linguistic understanding.

[192] Cf. B. Linsky [1], pp. 195–7.   [193] Cf. Hylton [2], pp. 39–40.

[194] See here again McDowell [3], Essays 8–11; Potter [1], p. 121.   [195] See my [15], pp. 79–89.

items: put otherwise, the levels of sense and reference are transcendentally deduced by the semantic theorist as required for a correct theoretical understanding of the meaningfulness of symbolic language. Even before that, the phenomenon of creative language use forces us to find structure and compositionality in language, and in order to model this aspect of language we need to discern fundamental components of meaningful language—the basic building blocks out of which everything else is constructed.[196] Having done that, we proceed to assign semantic values (referents) to the components of language we have discerned and to their combinations. In pursuing this bipartite strategy we will be able to show how the meanings of complex linguistic structures (in the first instance, sentences) are functionally dependent on the semantic values we assign to relatively simple components. We might put the perspective of linguistic idealism by saying that sentences are the primary datum, and that theoretically posited entities are derived in two directions, horizontally and vertically: horizontally (that is, at the level of symbolic language), we derive the notion of semantically significant parts of sentences (words, phrases, clauses); vertically (descending the semantic hierarchy), we derive the referents of sentences and of their semantically significant parts. It is obvious that this account of the theoretical provenance of the notion of reference appeals to the idea of reference as signification, rather than to that of reference as supposition. Having established the basic framework in which semantic significance is modelled in terms of relations between linguistic items and their *referents*, we need in addition to posit a notion of *sense*: that is because we need (at least in some contexts) a notion of the particular *way* in which a piece of discourse presents its subject matter; in these contexts we must accommodate the idea not merely of *what* an understander needs to think of in order to count as understanding a given linguistic expression, but also of *how* he or she needs to think of that entity.[197]

The linguistic idealism of this approach now needs to be coordinated with an empirical realism. Suppose we ask: 'how can we be assured that our thinking latches onto the world at all?'[198] The answer to this question has two parts. First, given that from a theoretical point of view the most fundamental unit of discourse is the sentence, and that subsentential components are theoretically derived posits, we would expect the basic connection between language and the world to be established at the level of the sentence. Indeed it is: for it is in the fact that declarative sentences are bearers of *truth-values* that the primary

---

[196] Creativity has been a persistent theme of Chomsky's writings: see e.g. [6], pp. 221–2.

[197] See here my [15], ch. 6, §2, for a fuller treatment of the approach summarized in this paragraph.

[198] Sullivan [5], p. 99.

connection between language and the world is set up. The truth-values of sentences are not in general up to us, so that any risk that our linguistic idealism might topple over into an objectionably strong form of idealism is averted at this initial point, and in a way that is not compromised by our insistence on the theoretical status of the reference relation. Secondly, though objects, taken collectively, exist as a transcendentally deduced necessary condition of the meaningfulness of language, it remains the case that, taken individually, their existence may be, and usually is, independent of the existence of any particular empirical language or family of languages, or even of *all* empirical languages: for an object's existence is dependent only on the *possibility* of its being referred to in some language or other.

Given, now, that the metaphysical perspective I invoke to justify my approach to the unity problem involves a form of realism, as well as of linguistic idealism, it ought to follow that the question of propositional unity is as much an ontological as a linguistic one. And it does follow: for like Russell and unlike Frege I locate propositions at the level of reference, corresponding to declarative sentences at the level of symbolic language, though unlike Russell but like Frege I also insert an intermediate level of sense into the hierarchy, so that Russellian propositions are conceived to be presented by declarative sentences in quite specific ways, that is, by means of appropriately structured Fregean Thoughts. Moreover, I identify the level of reference, so construed, with the world: objects of discourse turn out to be worldly entities, whether concrete or abstract, individual or universal, and worldly entities are, in turn, essentially objects of discourse. These points, which I here simply set out dogmatically, will be revisited and defended in later chapters, especially Chapter 2, where I shall also explain why I favour the *significatio* approach to reference.

But in the remainder of this chapter I want to examine a number of difficulties that ensnared Russell when he tackled the problem of propositional unity in the early twentieth century. As I have said (§5), the question what constitutes the unities of declarative sentence and proposition is prior to the question 'What is truth?'; for we are in effect asking after the nature not of truth, but of truth-or-falsity. It follows that it is a constraint on any solution to the problem of unity that it apply to meaningful false sentences and propositions as well as to meaningful true ones: any purported solution to the problem of unity which ends up stating, or implying, that only true sentences and propositions are unified can be rejected without further ado. As we shall now see, however, some of Russell's discussions of the unity problem in the period 1903–18 breached the above constraint in interesting ways: setting out how this came about will both help fix the significance of the constraint in our minds and focus our attention on a number of texts and issues that will be important later in this study.

10 Russell on Truth, Falsity, and Unity (I): 1903

An early indication of a difficulty that was to occupy Russell intermittently throughout the first two decades of the last century comes in *The Principles of Mathematics*. According to the account of the proposition contained therein, as I have mentioned (§3), a proposition consists not of words or senses, but of 'the entities indicated by words',[199] which Russell calls 'terms'. 'Terms', we are told, are

whatever may be an object of thought, or may occur in any true or false proposition, or can be counted as *one*. . . . A man, a moment, a number, a class, a relation, a chimaera, or anything else that can be mentioned, is sure to be a term; and to deny that such and such a thing is a term must always be false.[200]

For Russell, before he developed the type theory which was given its first detailed presentation in his paper 'Mathematical Logic as Based on the Theory of Types' (1908)—an appendix to *Principles* contains a sketch of a type theory for classes, but it hardly influences the main text—and later incorporated into *Principia Mathematica* (1910), all entities are, in effect, of the same ontological type.[201] As I have noted, Russell derived his 1903 treatment of propositions as containing worldly entities from Moore, though he also indicated that he thought there were important differences between his (Russell's) terms and Moore's concepts.[202] One difference would be the following. Moore thinks that 'in the end, the concept turns out to be the only substantive or subject, and no one concept either more or less an adjective than any other',[203] whereas Russell argues that 'terms which are concepts differ from those which are not. . . in virtue of the fact that, in certain true or false propositions, they occur in a manner which is different in an indefinable way from the manner in which subjects or terms of relations occur'.[204] I shall return to Russell's distinction between things and concepts in Chapter 3, where I discuss Russell's 1903 solution to the unity problem. Here I wish to focus not on the solution itself, but on a preliminary point.

---

[199] [3], §51.

[200] [3], §47; cf. §427, and [16], p. 143. See also Strawson [1], ch. 8, e.g. p. 240: 'There is nothing of which we can speak which cannot appear as a logical subject'.

[201] Cf. Cocchiarella [1], pp. 7, 20–1; Stevens [2], pp. 31–2.   [202] [3], §47, p. 44 n.

[203] [2], p. 18.   [204] [3], §49. Cf. Imaguire, p. 149.

At the stage where the issue of propositional unity obtrudes, Russell is discussing whether, and if so in what sense, a verb—or its referent, but as we have noted in connection with a complaint of Frege's (§3), Russell tends to neglect this distinction—can be made a logical subject.[205] His official position (against Frege, as he notes[206]) is that it is contradictory to deny that any entity can be made a logical subject, because in stating that a given entity cannot be made a logical subject, we thereby make it one. Russell continues:

> If we ask: What is asserted in the proposition 'Caesar died'? the answer must be 'the death of Caesar is asserted'. In that case, it would seem, it is the death of Caesar which is true or false; and yet neither truth nor falsity belongs to a mere logical subject. The answer seems to be that the death of Caesar has an external relation to truth or falsehood (as the case may be), whereas 'Caesar died' in some way or other contains its own truth or falsehood as an element. But if this is the correct analysis, it is difficult to see how 'Caesar died' differs from 'the truth of Caesar's death' in the case where it is true, or 'the falsehood of Caesar's death' in the other case. Yet it is quite plain that the latter, at any rate, is never equivalent to 'Caesar died'. There appears to be an ultimate notion of assertion, given by the verb, which is lost as soon as we substitute a verbal noun, and is lost when the proposition in question is made the subject of some other proposition. This does not depend upon grammatical form: for if I say 'Caesar died is a proposition', I do not assert that Caesar did die, and an element which is present in 'Caesar died' has disappeared. Thus the contradiction which was to have been avoided, of an entity which cannot be made a logical subject, appears to have here become inevitable. This difficulty, which seems to be inherent in the very nature of truth and falsehood, is one with which I do not know how to deal satisfactorily.[207]

The problem that concerns Russell in the wider context from which this passage is drawn is, as I have indicated, the question what distinguishes a proposition, which is constitutively true or false, from a 'logical subject'—that is, the referent of any kind of name—which is not either true or false. In particular, he focuses on what distinguishes a proposition from (i) the propositional concept (as he subsequently calls it[208]) formed from it, and (ii) the reification of that proposition formed by making it the logical subject of another proposition.

But once we are clear that this is the nature of Russell's real concern, we can see that his claim that 'if I say "*Caesar died* is a proposition", I do not assert that Caesar did die, and an element which is present in "Caesar died" has disappeared' is wrong. The feature of the proposition—or as we should say, sentence—'Caesar died' which concerns (or ought to concern) us in a

---

[205] This is the problem that leads Frege into the 'paradox of the concept *horse*', which I shall discuss, in connection with both Frege and Russell, in Ch. 3.
[206] [3], §475.   [207] [3], §52; cf. §38.   [208] [3], §55. Cf. N. Griffin [4], p. 169.

context where the issue of unity is at stake is its *declarative* status—that is, its ability to be true or false—not whether anyone at any time *asserts* it. And that declarative status does not disappear when we make the sentence 'Caesar died' the grammatical subject of another sentence, so turning its corresponding proposition into the logical subject of another proposition. Moreover, it is not intrinsic to the sentence 'Caesar died' that anyone at any time assert it: the presence in that sentence of a copula has—contrary to a venerable, but mistaken, tradition[209]—nothing to do with the force, assertoric or other, with which that sentence may, on any given occasion, be expressed. And whether anyone does assert that sentence is (semantically speaking) a purely adventitious feature of it, not an element that 'disappears' from the sentence when it is made the grammatical subject of another sentence (and its corresponding proposition made the logical subject of another proposition). So Russell's claim is mistaken: there is no relevant—no *semantic*—attribute of 'Caesar died' which 'disappears' when that sentence is embedded in larger sentential contexts. Russell should not have brought extraneous pragmatic considerations to bear in a context where we are exclusively concerned with semantics.

Elsewhere, Russell distinguishes between a 'psychological' conception of assertion and a 'logical' one,[210] and it might look as though this terminological policy were meant to accommodate the distinction between the pragmatic notion of a sentence's being put forward on some occasion with assertoric force, and the semantic notion of a sentence's having declarative status. But if that was the intention behind the distinction, it misfires for the following reason: while we may plausibly identify Russell's 'psychological' assertion with the pragmatic notion I have specified, any attempted identification of 'logical' assertion with the contrasting semantic notion fails. For it turns out that, while both true and false propositions (sentences) may be asserted in the 'psychological' sense, according to Russell only true propositions (sentences) are asserted in the 'logical' sense.[211] (Something similar was held by Frege.[212]) It is possible that this restriction is hinted at in the passage I have quoted, at the point where Russell says:

it is difficult to see how 'Caesar died' differs from 'the truth of Caesar's death' *in the case where it is true*, or 'the falsehood of Caesar's death' in the other case. Yet it is quite plain that the latter, at any rate, is never equivalent to 'Caesar died'. (My emphasis)

Actually, the suggestion contained in this excerpt is mistaken: the equivalence, if it obtains, between 'Caesar died' and 'the truth of Caesar's death' does

---

[209] Still alive in e.g. Anderson, at pp. 21–2.
[210] See [3], §§38, 43, 135, 478.   [211] [3], §§52, 478.
[212] See his letter to Jourdain of (about) Jan. 1914 ([22], p. 127); Bell [1], p. 91.

not depend upon the assumption that 'Caesar died' is true. By contrast, as Russell notes, 'the falsehood of Caesar's death' is never equivalent to 'Caesar died'—*not even if it is false that Caesar died*. In other words, we can have a redundancy theory of truth, but not of falsity: truth is, in that sense, *prior to* falsity. But it by no means follows from this observation that a true sentence or proposition is, in any sense, more *unified* than a false one, and if that is what Russell meant to imply with his strange doctrine that only true propositions are 'logically' asserted—and what else could be meant?—he was wrong. The idea of 'logical' assertion is entirely bogus.

Russell's question was whether 'Caesar died' enjoys some unity lacked by '(the truth of) Caesar's death' (and 'the truth of the truth of Caesar's death' etc.), and if so what that difference consists in. On the basis of the points I have made, we can say that this question should be addressed without having recourse either to pragmatic considerations or to the particular truth-values of any given sentences or propositions. But, as we shall now see, confusion on both these points—a feeling that unity is peculiarly proprietary to judged ('psychologically asserted') propositions, and that true ('logically asserted') propositions are somehow more unified than false ones—plagued Russell's examination of the issue of propositional unity, and of truth and falsity, over the next fifteen years.[213]

11 Russell on Truth, Falsity, and Unity (II): 1910–13

Russell's renewed attack in his 1910 paper 'On the Nature of Truth and Falsehood' on the problem of propositional unity was characterized by a rejection of the existence of what, using Meinongian terminology, he called 'false objectives', that is, entities such as *that Charles I died in his bed*.[214] Such entities—false complexly signifiables, or false propositions *in re*—had in one respect been allowed for in the 1903 theory, according to which 'true and false propositions alike are in some sense entities, and are in some sense capable of being logical subjects',[215] though the doctrine that only true propositions are 'logically asserted' threatened to compromise any such even-handed approach to the unity, and hence reality, of both true and false propositions. At any rate, however equivocal Russell's 1903 position may have been, he now

---

[213] On some historical antecedents of these mistakes, see my [6], pp. 145–9; [13], pp. 200–5.

[214] See here N. Griffin [2], p. 134; B. Linsky [1], pp. 198–9; Weiss, pp. 263–5; Hylton [2], pp. 46–7; Davidson [2], p. 106. These authors all take the rejection of false objectives to be the main motivation for the new account, and I follow that view here; for a contrasting approach, see Stevens [2], pp. 30–6.

[215] [3], §52. Cf. Ricketts [4], p. 104; Imaguire, pp. 51–4.

(in 1910) held the existence of false worldly propositions to be 'in itself almost incredible'.[216] In his 1904 critique of Meinong he had written:

It may be said—and this is, I believe, the correct view—that there is no problem at all in truth and falsehood; that some propositions are true and some false, just as some roses are red and some white. . . . What is truth, and what falsehood, we must merely apprehend, for both seem incapable of analysis.[217]

But his new position is that the postulation of false objectives 'leaves the difference between truth and falsehood quite inexplicable', and 'ultimate and unanalysable, whereas it seems obvious that the difference between truth and falsehood must be explicable by reference to *fact*';[218] and in the introduction to the first edition of *Principia Mathematica* we are told that, in the case of perceptual judgements, 'when we judge "*a* has the relation *R* to *b*", our judgment is said to be *true* when there is a complex "*a*-in-the-relation-*R*-to-*b*", and is said to be *false* when this is not the case'.[219]

This was an expression of the correspondence theory of truth: the thesis that whereas something corresponds to a true judgement,[220] namely a fact or complex on the ground, nothing corresponds to a false one. Whereas in the earlier theory facts just were true objectives, the new theory seemed to require Russell to draw an ontological distinction between worldly complexes (facts), on the one hand, and true intentional contents of judgements (objectives), on the other—these entities presumably becoming respectively the worldly and intentional relata of the correspondence relation. At least, that is what one would expect, but Russell's version of the correspondence theory is of an unusual and perplexing variety, for he continued to suppose that objectives, if they exist, must be worldly entities. But he also wished to avoid having to treat truth and falsehood differently by postulating the existence of true but not false objectives, his reason for rejecting such a differential treatment being that we would then be enabled, absurdly as he thought, 'to discover the truth or falsehood of a judgment merely by examining the intrinsic nature of the judgment'.[221] Actually, his proffering this reason evinces Russell's notoriously unreliable memory: for given, as we have seen, that the propositions of the 1903 theory were officially held to be composed (in the normal case) of worldly objects, rather than of linguistic signs or mental intentions, there ought

[216] [6], p. 152. Cf. [9], p. 109: 'It seems plain that a false proposition is not itself an actual entity'.
[217] [15], pp. 75–6.   [218] [6], p. 152; [9], p. 153. Cf. N. Griffin [4], pp. 168–9.
[219] Whitehead and Russell, i, p. 43.
[220] I adopt Russell's new terminology, but the claim can obviously be made independently of his chosen truth-bearers. (In 1918 Russell moved from talk of judgement to talk of belief.)
[221] [6], p. 153. Cf. [13], p. 187.

to be nothing absurd, on that theory, in supposing that we should discover
the truth or falsehood of a judgement by inspecting the judged proposition.
On the contrary, that is exactly what you would expect the search for truth
to involve, since such a procedure cannot be distinguished from inspecting
reality.[222] So the dialectical position is thoroughly confused. Russell's refusal
to treat true and false objectives differently only *makes sense* if objectives are
taken to be worldly as opposed to intentional entities; for if they were merely
intentional entities, one would not think that inspection of them could suffice
for discovering the truth about the world. But his criticism of the move he
refuses only *bites* on the presupposition that objectives are being taken to be
intentional as opposed to worldly entities; for if they were worldly entities,
it would be entirely reasonable to suppose that one could discover the truth
about the world by inspecting them.

In another respect, too, the abandonment of the earlier position was a
wrong turning. In his critique of Meinong, Russell had cogently identified
facts with true propositions, and he had offered a debunking explanation
of our undeniable inclination to treat true propositions as in some sense
ontologically privileged: we have a natural but erroneous tendency to attach
special importance to facts we can *perceive*.[223] Russell's decision to resile
from the position on propositions which he had taken up in 1903–4 was
highly regrettable. But, however inadequate his reasons, the fact was that
Russell now (in 1910) felt he had to reject the view that judgement is a
relation of a thinking subject to a single entity—an objective, true or false;
instead, he treated judgement as a multiple relation of that subject to each
of the constituents of the judgement (that is, to each of the referents of its
categorematic terms).[224] Russell laid some stress on the point that the subject
is connected to those constituents by a *single multiple relation*, and not (or not
merely) by a plurality of dual relations to each of the constituents. The reason
for his insistence on this point was that he needed something to supply unity to
the act of judgement, now that he was denying that the judging subject enjoys
a single relation to a single, unified proposition. That unifying element was
supplied by the judging subject. The unity of the erstwhile proposition was

---

[222] Candlish [1], §2; [2], p. 59. It might be objected that Russell's point may be that it would be
absurd to suppose we could discover the truth or falsity of a judgement by checking to see whether it
is a dyadic or multiple-relation judgement—true if the former, false if the latter (Hanks [2], p. 126).
But that checking process, in turn, cannot be distinguished, on the 1903 view of propositions, from
inspecting reality, since the logical form of the judgement depends on the existence or otherwise of the
objective which is the judgement's intentional object.

[223] [15], pp. 75–6.

[224] [6], pp. 153–9; Whitehead and Russell, i, pp. 43–4. The 1910 position grew out of earlier
published materials, esp. [4]: see N. Griffin [4], p. 174; Hylton [2], p. 47 n. 11.

thus dismantled at the level of the *content* of the judgement and reconstituted in the mental *activity* of the judging subject, this activity being held to unite elements that, taken in themselves, were unconnected.

Russell's 1910 theory was intended, at least in part, to provide a solution to the problem of false judgement, namely the problem that in doing away with false objectives there no longer seemed to be anything for false judgements to be *of*. But the new theory can also be read as an attempt to keep the issue of the unity of the proposition separate from that of propositional truth or falsity. For, on the new theory, what makes a judgement true is now officially separated from what unifies it. When I judge that *A* loves *B*, the subordinate relation 'love' appears not as a relation unifying the proposition *that A loves B*, but as a constituent of the judgement on a level with *A* and *B*. Or we can say, to borrow Russell's earlier terminology,[225] that the relation appears not as a 'relation actually relating', but as a 'relation in itself'; in Frege's terminology (which I will explore in Chapter 3), the relation appears as a saturated object rather than as an unsaturated concept.[226] The task of unifying the proposition *that A loves B* is removed from the (now subordinate) relation figuring in it and transferred to the judging subject. And the subordinate relation, which, now that the unifying function has been removed from it, is left to discharge the role of propositional constituent, is assigned a further role, namely that of a truth-maker. The relation 'love' has, then, to perform two tasks in the judgement that *A* loves *B*: (i) as part of the judged proposition it is an entity on all fours with the constituents *A* and *B*, making no special contribution towards the unity of the judged proposition, judgemental unity being now effected not by any propositional constituent but by the judging subject; (ii) as truth-maker, the relation 'love', when the judgement is true, *actually does* relate *A* and *B* on the ground.[227]

I have tried to restate the theory as neutrally as possible, but it is hard to do so without thereby drawing attention to its incoherence. One respect in which it is incoherent, which subsequently became clear to Russell himself, concerns a point I have ignored in my exposition, namely the role the theory accords to the *direction* of a relation. There is obviously a difference between *A*'s loving *B* and *B*'s loving *A*, and correspondingly between my judgement that *A* loves *B* and my judgement that *B* loves *A*. This directionality must, as Russell already realized in 1910,[228] be incorporated not (or not only) into the act of judgement, but (also) into the judged relation itself: the constituent 'love' must, as he put it, have a 'sense'. But, as Russell quickly came to see, it is impossible for a relation

[225] [3], §54. I quote this passage in §29.   [226] Cf. Candlish [2], p. 62.
[227] [6], p. 155.   [228] [6], p. 158.

to have sense or direction without thereby unifying its terms; conversely, if the judged relation really is, as the multiple relation theory requires, a 'relation in itself', not a 'relating actually relating', then it cannot intelligibly be thought of as having a 'sense'.[229] Russell's response to this difficulty, integrated into the account of judgement offered in *The Problems of Philosophy* of 1912,[230] was to transfer the function of providing 'sense' wholly to the act of judgement, thus effectively going back on his previous insight that directionality must be part of the judged relation. This move was not only implausible in itself; it also highlighted what should have been obvious all along, namely that the duality of function assigned to the subordinate relation figuring in the *content* of the judgement—a duality which is indeed accentuated by the complete transfer of 'sense' away from that content to the judging act—cannot stand. The reason for this is that incompatible commitments are being foisted on the subordinate relation: on the one hand it is supposed to be a universal entity on all fours with the other components of the judgement—a 'relation in itself';[231] on the other hand, in the case where the judgement is true, the subordinate relation also figures as a particular 'relation actually relating'—which must have 'sense'.

Russell quickly came to regard the 1912 manœuvre as inadequate, but the adjustment which he made in his 1913 manuscript *Theory of Knowledge* merely consisted in adding an extra component to the act of judgement. Russell now thought it inadequate simply to locate directionality in the act of judgement: for while that might suffice to impose unity on judgements involving *non-symmetrical* relations, it could not suffice to impose unity on judgements involving *symmetrical* relations, such as the relation of similarity. In this latter case the judger must (to take, as Russell does, the case of dyadic relational propositions) additionally bring to bear 'the general form of dual complexes', which Russell conveys in the expressions 'something has some relation to something', and 'something and something have a certain relation'.[232] Presumably the idea is that, although in the case of any non-symmetrical *n*-place relation too the judger must bring to bear the general form of *n*-place complexes, that is automatically achieved in imposing directionality on the relevant relation, so that here the judger has only one task to accomplish, not two. (Russell has an ingenious account of what it is for a subject to make a judgement involving a non-symmetrical relation: but we can disregard the details here.[233])

---

[229] See here N. Griffin [1], p. 220; [2], p. 135; Geach [6], pp. 51–2; Candlish [1], §3; [2], p. 68; Stevens [2], pp. 37–8.

[230] [8], p. 73.   [231] Cf. N. Griffin [1], pp. 215–16.   [232] [9], pp. 114, 116.

[233] See [9], pp. 144–8; Hochberg [2], p. 219; [5], pp. 203–7; N. Griffin [2], pp. 137–8.

This manœuvre, however, aside from creating its own difficulties,[234] fails to address what is surely the fundamental awkwardness in Russell's account of judgement, namely that the unifying ingredient present at the level of the *act* of judgement is absent at the level of *what* is judged (the content of the judgement). And Russell now tells us that this unifying ingredient is also missing as an ingredient of extra-mental reality: 'in an actual complex, the general form is not presupposed'.[235] That is, the general form of *n*-place complexes, while *exemplified* by an actual complex on the ground, is not a *constituent* of it, as it is of an act of judgement.[236] This point serves to bring out what was anyway implicit in the earlier account, namely that Russell is in effect working with *two* unifying ingredients: something that unifies an act of judgement (the general form of *n*-place complexes), and something that unifies complexes (facts) on the ground (the 'relation actually relating'). In between these we have the fragmented content of the judgement, containing as one of its components the 'relation in itself'. But on this three-tier approach no tier is isomorphic to any other: the act of judgement and the complex on the ground are unified by virtue of completely different things (respectively, the general form of *n*-place complexes, and the 'relation actually relating'), while the content of the judgement is not a unity at all.[237]

12   Russell on Truth, Falsity, and Unity (III): 1918

Already in *Theory of Knowledge* Russell had expressed doubt about the multiple relation theory of judgement, since it gives us no indication how to handle simple generalizations over propositions.[238] But, quite apart from that point, it is clear from what we have said that the multiple relation theory of judgement is inadequate even to deal with the contexts for which it was designed: the judged relation cannot figure merely as a 'relation in itself' in the judgement, as the theory proposes; rather, it has to figure as a 'relation actually relating'. At last, in his 1918 lectures 'The Philosophy of Logical Atomism', Russell came to see this point. Since, however, he continued to treat the 'relation actually relating' as the truth-maker of the proposition, the result was open incoherence:

Suppose I take '*A* believes that *B* loves *C*'. 'Othello believes that Desdemona loves Cassio.' There you have a false belief. You have this odd state of affairs that the verb

---

[234] See Hylton [2], pp. 20–4; N. Griffin [1], §II. I discuss some of these difficulties in §71.
[235] [9], p. 116; cf. [6], p. 158.   [236] Cf. Hochberg [8], p. 13; Candlish [2], p. 73.
[237] For further criticisms of the 1913 account, see Pears [2]; Candlish [2], pp. 87–8.
[238] [9], p. 155; cf. Ricketts [4], p. 121 n. 50.

'loves' occurs in that proposition and seems to occur as relating Desdemona to Cassio whereas in fact it does not do so, but yet it does occur as a verb, it does occur in the sort of way that a verb should do. I mean that when *A* believes that *B* loves *C*, you have to have a verb in the place where 'loves' occurs. You cannot put a substantive in its place. Therefore it is clear that the subordinate verb (i.e., the verb other than believing) is functioning as a verb, and seems to be relating two terms, but as a matter of fact does not [do so] when a judgment happens to be false.[239]

And Russell immured himself further by imposing on any solution the following two unattractive constraints:

The *first* is the impossibility of treating the proposition believed as an independent entity, entering as a unit into the occurrence of the belief, and the *other* is the impossibility of putting the subordinate verb on a level with its terms as an object term in the belief.[240]

But these constraints must be rejected in any adequate account of judgement and propositional unity: the first constraint has to be rejected because to treat the subordinate proposition as a unity is a precondition of making sense of judgement as being what it manifestly is: it is a *propositional* attitude, an attitude to entities that occur as unities *outside* propositional-attitude contexts; the second constraint has to be rejected as a consequence of our rejecting the first.

   It follows that, unwinding, we are forced back to a recognition of the existence of false objectives: there must, after all, be such things as *that Charles I died in his bed*, figuring both as objects of propositional attitudes and as propositions *in re*. Russell's difficulties have stemmed fundamentally from his failure to make a sharp separation between (i) whatever it is that unifies a proposition, regardless whether that proposition be judged or not, and regardless of its truth-value, and (ii) whatever it is (if anything) that determines whether the relevant proposition is true or false. The confusion was certainly abetted, and perhaps in some measure instigated, by his reliance on the notion of 'a relation actually relating'. For this phrase is fatally ambiguous between the two roles that Russell has tried, incoherently, to combine: the relation as unifier, and the relation as truth-maker.[241]

   That part of the explanation for the confusion is that Russell was indeed stumbling over the word 'actual' is suggested by the passage in *Theory of Knowledge* leading up to his introduction of the idea that the subject must (in the case of dyadic relational judgements) bring to bear 'the general form of dual complexes':

What is the proof that we must understand the 'form' before we can understand the proposition? I held formerly that the objects alone sufficed, and that the 'sense' of

---

[239] [13], p. 225.   [240] [13], p. 226.   [241] Cf. Sainsbury [1], pp. 21–2; Stevens [3], p. 130.

the relation of understanding would put them in the right order;[242] this, however, no longer seems to me to be the case. Suppose we wish to understand 'A and B are similar'. It is essential that our thought should, as is said, 'unite' or 'synthesize' the two terms and the relation; but we cannot *actually* 'unite' them, since either A and B are similar, in which case they are already united, or they are dissimilar, in which case no amount of thinking can force them to become united.[243]

The relation actually relating cannot after all, it seems, *be* the relation actually relating, because it is not inevitably a relation *actually* relating. That looks incoherent, but the apparent stumbling-block is an illusion: had Russell seen that the essential point is that the relation as unifier cannot *also* be a truth-maker, because we have to allow for the possibility that the proposition in question is false (and that, in any case, we need no truth-maker, a claim I will substantiate in the next chapter), no spectre of incoherence would have arisen.

I will return in later chapters to examine these and further aspects of Russell's 1903–18 treatments of the nature of the proposition and the question of its unity. For the moment the moral of my brief excursus through those treatments is that three issues have to be kept clearly separate: the unity of the proposition, the truth-value of a proposition, and the act of asserting or judging a proposition to be true. An account of the first of these issues should not stray into the terrains set aside for accounts of the second and third issues: for a unified proposition can be false, and need not figure in assertoric mode or in an act of judgement.

---

[242] 'Put them in the right order' means here, despite appearances, not *supply direction* to them—in this context, as is clear, we have to do with an account which must be adequate for *symmetrical* relations, as well as non-symmetrical ones—but simply *unify* them: see Hylton [1], pp. 344–5; Candlish [2], pp. 69–70.

[243] [9], p. 116.

2

Sense, Reference, and Propositions

13 Russellian Propositions, Fregean Thoughts, and Facts

In the first chapter propositions were simply, and vaguely, introduced as the meanings of declarative sentences. We have noted from our preliminary examination of the early Russell's discussions concerning the nature and unity of the proposition that whatever account we give concerning propositional *unity* must be adequate for false as well as true propositions, and unjudged as well as judged ones; and we have further seen that the only usable materials Russell delivers towards an account of the *nature* of the proposition are contained in his discussion of the problem of propositional unity in *The Principles of Mathematics*, since his subsequent accounts fragmented the judged proposition, so destroying its unity.

In the modern literature on reference, it is customary to identify what are called 'Russellian propositions' with ordered *n*-tuples of objects and properties (including relations).[1] To take a simple example, the Russellian proposition corresponding to the sentence 'Socrates is wise' would be the ordered pair <Socrates, wisdom>, which can be represented (using the familiar Kuratowski technique) by the set {{Socrates}, {Socrates, wisdom}}.[2] Russell himself does not explicitly identify his propositions with such set-theoretic

---

[1] For an elementary summary of a common position, see Neale [2], §2. (Neale aims to characterize only true Russellian propositions—'facts'—but the account can easily be generalized.) Cf. Almog; Donaho, §7; Barwise and Etchemendy, pp. 27–8; B. Linsky [2], pp. 123–4; Schiffer, ch. 1. Note also McDowell [3], Essays 9 and 10. 'Russellian propositions' were introduced into the modern literature by Kaplan ([2], pp. 494–6).

[2] Kuratowski, p. 171. For discussion of this technique, see e.g. Enderton [1], pp. 35–6; Potter [2], pp. 63–5.

constructions,³ and there are indeed difficulties in the way of this or any set-theoretic reconstruction of Russellian propositions so far as the exegesis of Russell's 1903 position is concerned: for there is an issue in *Principles* about the relative definitional priority of sets and what Russell calls propositional functions.⁴ In due course I shall consider in more detail how Russellian propositions, construed as suitable constructions out of worldly entities (objects and properties, including relations), should be understood. For the moment, however, we can work with the following rough characterization: Russellian propositions are meanings of declarative sentences, and contain as literal constituents the worldly entities—centrally objects and properties (including relations)—introduced by the semantically significant parts of those sentences. On this approach, then, propositions are abstract objects, similar in this regard to (type) sentences.

If Russellian propositions exhausted the meanings of declarative sentences, it would follow that where 'Hesperus' and 'Phosophorus' are co-referring names, the sentences 'Hesperus is bright' and 'Phosphorus is bright' would not present different propositions; and this was indeed a position maintained in essentials by Russell throughout the period from 1903 to 1918.⁵ The Russellian view may be contrasted with a Fregean view, according to which a 'third realm'—the realm of (objective) sense (*Sinn*), distinct on the one hand from the realm of (objective) reference (*Bedeutung*) and on the other from the realm of (subjective) ideas (*Vorstellungen*)—must be admitted to our metaphysical economy, in order to register the fact that when items of symbolic language present entities in the world, they present those worldly entities not barely, but in some particular way, which is (or at any rate may be) of semantic and epistemological significance.⁶ In his mature philosophy Frege located propositionally structured meanings of declarative sentences, entities which (as we have noted) he called *Gedanken* (Thoughts), at the level of sense: their constituents were then appropriately conceived as senses, rather than the objects presented by those senses. Fregean Thoughts, so conceived, presented not propositionally structured but simple entities in the realm of reference, namely truth-values. In contrast to both Frege and the early Russell, the early Wittgenstein held that declarative sentences do not name anything at all, either truth-values or complexes. So we are told in his 1913 *Notes*

³ Ricketts [4], p. 103 n. 7.   ⁴ See §33 below.   ⁵ See e.g. [13], p. 245.
⁶ Cf. Bolzano's view that *Sätze an sich* are composed of *Vorstellungen an sich*, or objective ideas, rather than the things they are about: [2], §48; cf. Kneale and Kneale, p. 363.

on Logic: 'Frege said "propositions [i.e. *Sätze*, (declarative) sentences] are names"; Russell said "propositions correspond to complexes". Both are false; and especially false is the statement "propositions are names of complexes" '.[7] (By the time of 'The Philosophy of Logical Atomism', Russell, under Wittgenstein's influence, agreed.[8])

If we ask where *facts* are located in the metaphysical economy, assuming with Frege that facts are identical with true propositionally structured meanings of declarative sentences,[9] we will receive different answers depending on whether we adopt a Russellian or a Fregean position: as we have seen, the Russell of 1903–4 identified facts with true propositions as he understood them, which are not only composed of worldly entities, but are themselves denizens of the world,[10] and a modern follower of Russell will be well advised to identify facts with true Russellian propositions, understood along the lines I have (in a preliminary way) expounded; at least, I shall argue in this chapter that a correspondence theory of truth must be rejected, which leaves identity as the most plausible candidate to constitute the relation between facts and true propositions.[11] That Russellian propositions are abstract objects presents no bar to the identification: a cat is a concrete object, and so is a mat, but it does not follow—and it is not true—that the fact that the cat sat on the mat is also concrete. And, given my identification below of the world with all the true and false propositions at the level of reference, there will be good reason to say (§24) that the world, though containing concrete as well as abstract objects, is itself essentially abstract.

By contrast with Russell, Frege in his mature writings identified facts with true Fregean Thoughts, which are inhabitants of Frege's 'third realm'.[12] The general framework also makes available a hybrid position, not claimed by either of these historical figures. This is the position I endorse. In this mixed position we combine a tripartite approach to semantics in the style of Frege, recognizing distinct levels comprising items of symbolic language, sense, and reference, with a Russellian approach to propositions (and facts), locating these, identified with 'Russellian propositions', not at the level of sense but at the level of reference, as the referents of declarative sentences (facts being true such propositions); the level of sense will then contain propositionally structured items that we may as well for the sake of a label continue to call Fregean Thoughts, these being not propositions as such but rather propositionally

---

[7] [6], p. 97; cf. [1], §3.143. Note that, although declarative sentences are not names, their *Bedeutungen* are nevertheless facts ([6], p. 112). Cf. Simons [7], p. 206.

[8] [13], pp. 187–8.   [9] [17], p. 74 ([21], p. 359).   [10] Candlish [2], p. 114.

[11] Cf. Fitch, p. 100.

[12] [17], p. 74 ([21], pp. 358–9); Currie [1], p. 155. Cf. Dodd and Hornsby.

structured senses of declarative sentences (propositionally structured modes of presentation of Russellian propositions).

It is probably true to say that most philosophers nowadays find the idea that propositions might be, or contain, worldly entities a counterintuitive one, and so prefer Frege's position to either Russell's or (insofar as it is ever considered) the hybrid position I have just sketched. As Leonard Linsky puts it, commenting on the passage from Russell's 1904 letter to Frege that I quoted in §3, where Russell tells Frege that Mont Blanc itself is ('in spite of all its snowfields') part of the proposition *that Mont Blanc is higher than 4,000 metres*: 'For a contemporary reader, propositions (if allowed at all) are abstract entities whose constituents are nothing so concrete as a snow-capped mountain.'[13] But the suggestion that propositions, being abstract, cannot contain concrete objects is a strange non sequitur. Many philosophers feel no corresponding qualm about recognizing the existence of sets,[14] that is of abstract objects with a membership range including both concrete and abstract objects, as a typical Russellian proposition would be constituted. (In pure set theory we construct the universe of sets from the empty set, but there is an argument, based on considerations having to do with the applicability of set theory, for including ordinary objects at the ground level of the cumulative hierarchy.[15]) And some philosophers, particularly nominalists, are willing to countenance the identification of type sentences, which are after all abstract objects, with sets of token sentences, which a nominalist would classify as concrete objects. So for anyone who accepts set theory in its standard modern form, or who is attracted by the reduction of types to sets of tokens, there can be no difficulty in principle about the Russellian conception of propositions as potentially composed of both concrete and abstract objects. In my view it is a mistake to assign propositionally structured meanings of sentences exclusively to the level of sense in the semantic hierarchy; I shall now explain why I endorse what I have called the hybrid position.

14 The Location of Propositions

Propositionally structured meanings of declarative sentences cannot, once a distinction between sense and reference is on the table, be located exclusively

---

[13] [1], p. 626. See also Searle [1], p. 114; Hylton [2], p. 88 n. 3. Correspondingly, Russell's 1903–4 belief in the indefinability of truth and falsehood, which I quoted above (§11) and shall be defending below (§24), is described by Hylton as 'evidently absurd' ([2], p. 19).

[14] Pelham and Urquhart, p. 311.

[15] This consideration moved Zermelo: [4], pp. 38, 45; Ebbinghaus, p. 190 n. 183.

on the sense side of the sense–reference divide, on pain of failure to introduce a sense–reference distinction in contexts where we need it, not only for sub-sentential components, but also for complete sentences themselves. Dummett's claim (made on Frege's behalf) that 'when we grasp a proposition, it is not given to us in one way rather than another; anything given to us in a different way would be a different proposition (if it were a proposition at all)'[16] is false. If propositions are conceived initially as the meanings of declarative sentences, it is surely evident that we can grasp such meanings in different ways (cf. §3): the proposition (to put it schematically) *that a is F* may be given to us in different ways (for example, in different languages), and this rather elementary fact ought to have alerted Frege (and Dummett) to the need to recognize that there must be propositionally structured entities (though not the same ones, of course) on both sides of the sense–reference divide.

Further, if we insisted on housing all propositionally structured sentential meanings at the level of sense, we should disable ourselves from ever treating any of them extensionally. But there will be many contexts in which we want to do just that. For example, while we may for some purposes wish to say that the propositionally structured entity *that Hesperus is Phosphorus* is a different such entity from the propositionally structured entity *that Hesperus is Hesperus* (here identifying the entities in question with Fregean Thoughts)—if, for example, we are trying to convey what the ancient Babylonians discovered without trivializing their discovery—in other contexts we may have no interest in distinguishing between the propositionally structured entities *that Hesperus is a planet* and *that Phosphorus is a planet*.[17] This will be so in situations, for example, where one is reporting a speaker's attitude and where nothing turns, either for the speaker or for the reporter's audience, on retaining the particular words used by that speaker. And it is not *generally* the case that fair reportage demands that one retain the same words as those used by the subject of one's report: the conditions under which fair reportage demands that one retain exactly the same words, or even a consistent translation scheme, are in fact quite specialized. In many contexts the (schematic) assertion *that a is F* can be fairly reported as the assertion *that b is F*—assuming that *a* is *b*—if, for instance, the reporter's audience is familiar with the name '*b*' but not with the name '*a*', and if replacing the name used by the speaker with the name familiar to the audience would not convey misleading implications about the speaker's attitudes to relevant entities. In cases like these, though what the speaker actually said was (schematically) '*a is F*', he or she can be reported as having expressed the *proposition that b is F*, even though the relevant (schematic)

---

[16] [9], p. 155.   [17] Cf. Zalta [1], pp. 166–72.

sentences express distinct (schematic) Fregean Thoughts.[18] That shows that we need an extensional notion of the proposition—that is, that we need to discern propositions obtaining at the level of reference—as well as a notion of propositionally structured entities (Fregean Thoughts) obtaining at the level of sense.[19] Dummett is quite wrong to say that semantics 'has no need to operate with the concept of a proposition'.[20]

The situation is even clearer in the (widespread) cases where we communicate using proper names with which we (speaker and hearer) associate distinct Fregean senses. A case in which speaker and hearer are not aware that they associate quite different, but co-referential, senses with a common name will illustrate the point best. Consider, then, the Polish politician and musician Paderewski.[21] Here we surely want to say that the proposition (and fact) *that Paderewski* [thought of as a musician] *is talented* is the same proposition (fact) as the proposition (fact) *that Paderewski* [the very same man, but now thought of as a politician] *is talented* (again identifying facts with true propositions). It would be right, for instance, for someone who, let us say, thinks of Paderewski exclusively as a musician, overhearing someone else who, let us say, thinks of Paderewski exclusively as a politician and who utters the sentence 'Paderewski is talented', to report this latter person as having said *that Paderewski is talented*, even though the two actors in this scenario associate quite different senses with the proper name 'Paderewski'.

In the example I have just given we have to do with a quite general truth about proper names, the fact that, as Gareth Evans puts it, 'the single main requirement for understanding a use of a proper name is that one think of the referent',[22] and hence that proper names may figure in successful communicative episodes even though speaker and hearer think of the relevant referent in quite different ways. These ways may be sufficiently different to generate distinct Fregean senses, where distinctness of sense is governed by a principle which Frege expresses many times,[23] and which Evans calls the intuitive criterion of difference:[24] according to this criterion, sentences differ in sense if someone can, without irrationality, take different cognitive

---

[18] Cf. Kneale and Kneale, pp. 609–10; J. Moore [2], §3; Soames, p. 218.

[19] Modal contexts provide a further illustration of this point: see Forbes, ch. 5. Forbes conceives of the referents of declarative sentences as what he calls 'states of affairs', which are in all essentials identical with what I am characterizing as (true) Russellian propositions (cf. Grossmann [1]). Forbes argues, however, that this latter characterization is a misnomer, since things in the world cannot literally be *propositions*: cf. B. Smith, pp. 49–50. I reject this claim, as well as a restriction of what is in the world to just the true Russellian propositions, below. See also my [15], ch. 6, on the issue of locating propositions at the level of reference.

[20] [10], p. 17.   [21] Kripke [3].   [22] [1], p. 400.

[23] See e.g. [22], p. 128.   [24] [1], pp. 18–19.

attitudes to them—accepting or rejecting one but not the other. (The 'if' of this definition cannot be strengthened to an 'if and only if': this point will be important below: §67.) Where such sentences differ only in point of replacement of a single expression occurring in one by a congruent but distinct expression in the other, the difference in sense of the sentences as wholes will be accounted for by positing a difference in sense in respect of these distinct expressions. The distinct expressions in question need not be phonologically or morphologically distinct. Thus, in the 'Paderewski' example cited above, different senses may be associated with the proper name 'Paderewski', thus in effect generating the presence in the language of two distinct though phonologically and morphologically identical names. This phenomenon may arise even within a single person's linguistic repertoire. That is because a subject may, without irrationality, deny that Paderewski (thought of in one way) is the same man as Paderewski (thought of in another way)—perhaps as a consequence of having been introduced to Paderewski in quite distinct contexts—and may come to realize, perhaps with a flash of illumination, that Paderewski (thought of in one way) *is* Paderewski (thought of in another way).

But, for the purposes of semantics, we do not want to cut senses as finely as may be necessary to meet the demands set by the intuitive criterion of difference: no one charged with the task of constructing a systematic theory of meaning for a language would wish to incorporate multiple clauses for a name such as 'Paderewski', corresponding to the multifarious ways in which speakers of the language in question think of that man. Epistemologically speaking, then, Fregean sense may play a role which is semantically without significance. That does not mean that there is no place for a purely semantic conception of sense, but any such conception will, at least in the case of proper names, be a relatively thin notion, no more than what one might call the internal accusative of the reference relation: for a proper name to have sense, in this sense of 'sense', is just for it—that very name—to have a referent. For in having *a referent* the name necessarily has *reference*—where this latter word has its full force as a verbal noun, and is not a synonym of 'referent'—and, on the semantic conception of sense, there is no distinction to be drawn between a proper name's having sense and its having *reference* (verbal noun), notwithstanding the clear distinction that obtains between its having sense and its having a *referent*. (The distinction I intend here is the theoretical distinction between *what it is* to have a sense and *what it is* to have a referent. I do not mean to imply that it is possible for an expression to *have* a sense but not a referent, or vice versa: on the contrary, as we shall see in more detail shortly, that is not possible.) A proper name's sense is its *mode of presentation* of its referent, where modes of presentation are understood in the austere, or modest, way captured in such clauses as

'Hesperus' refers to Hesperus.

Nothing more than this—no richer specification of the sense of the name 'Hesperus'—is either required or warranted if we are seeking to give an account of the semantics (as opposed to the epistemology) of proper names.[25]

Traditionally, so-called singular-proposition theorists have erred in locating propositionally structured meanings of declarative sentences exclusively at the level of *reference*. This strategy fails because it does not yield a sufficiently fine-grained semantics in many contexts,[26] and such theorists have sometimes recognized the need to compensate elsewhere in their theory for the coarseness of Russellian propositions located at the level of reference.[27] I have argued, in effect, that to respond to the inadequacy of this approach by locating propositionally structured meanings of declarative sentences exclusively at the level of *sense* would be an overreaction. In some contexts, certainly, fineness of grain is wanted in the individuation of propositionally structured entities; but in other contexts what is required is rather coarseness of grain, including, sometimes, the coarsest possible grain, compatibly with retaining propositional structure, namely in cases where sense plays *no* role in establishing criteria of fair reportage.[28] To cater for these contexts, we need to make room for propositionally structured entities at the level of reference as well as at the level of sense. Plausibly, then, we need to conceive not only of Fregean Thoughts as propositionally structured, but of what Fregean Thoughts present in the realm of reference as propositionally structured too: the items figuring at the level of sense will naturally be composed of senses, that is, of modes of presentation of (centrally) objects and properties (including relations); those figuring at the level of reference will naturally be composed of the corresponding individual and universal entities themselves, and hence will coincide with what I am calling 'Russellian propositions'.

In general terms, we can think of my argument as proceeding along the following lines. There are two conceptions of sense, an epistemological and a semantic one. To conceive sense epistemologically is to conceive

[25] See further McDowell [3], Essay 8; my [4]. The relative austerity of sense, in its semantic manifestation, affects expressions of other linguistic types than proper names—all expressions, in fact, to which the sense–reference distinction may intelligibly be applied, and these certainly include what Frege calls concept-words. I return to this point in Ch. 3 below.
[26] See Bealer [5], pp. 2–3, 9–10.
[27] Thus Salmon introduces 'guises', Bealer 'non-Platonic modes of presentation' ([4]), and Zalta 'abstract constituents' ([2], pp. 460–1).
[28] See here again my [4], §4; [15], pp. 211–15.

it as governed by the intuitive criterion of difference; to conceive sense semantically is to conceive it as a by-product of reference. But whichever of these conceptions we select (and we may, for different purposes, select sometimes the one conception and sometimes the other), we find that we are obliged to recognize the existence of propositions at the level of reference. If we select an epistemological conception of sense, then, in addition to a level of meaning (namely, sense) at which sentential meanings are individuated *finely* in accordance with the intuitive criterion, we will, I have argued, need to recognize a level of meaning (reference) at which propositionally structured entities are individuated *coarsely*. If we select the semantic conception of sense, then sense and reference are, as it were, too closely involved in one another to differ in point of whether they are propositionally structured or not: on the austere, semantic approach to sense, if an entity at the level of sense is propositionally structured then its referent must be propositionally structured too, for otherwise it is impossible to see how one could specify the sense of a linguistic expression *in* specifying its referent, as the austere conception of sense requires. For it is not as though, on Frege's model of sentential reference according to which declarative sentences refer to truth-values, in specifying the truth-value of a sentence one would be specifying its sense; and the argument can be generalized to any other non-propositionally structured candidate for referential status in respect of declarative sentences.

As I have just indicated, the semantics I am recommending involves a departure from Frege's own picture of what corresponds to Thoughts in the realm of reference, namely truth-values. In some passages Frege simply asserts that declarative sentences refer to truth-values without offering an argument.[29] Where an argument is given, it can be difficult to reconstruct its drift; but as I understand him Frege has essentially two reasons for making truth-values the referents of declarative sentences. The first is that our 'striving for truth' requires that we identify the referents of declarative sentences with truth-values.[30] The second reason is that, under intersubstitution of co-referential parts of a sentence, while the Fregean Thought introduced by the sentence may change, its truth-value will not;[31] and, as Frege remarks in 'Über Sinn und Bedeutung',

what, apart from the truth-value, could be found which (i) belongs quite generally to every sentence for which the reference (*Bedeutung*) of the parts comes into consideration,

---

[29] See e.g. his letter to Russell of 21 May 1903 ([22], p. 240).

[30] See e.g. [6], pp. 33–4 ([21], p. 149); cf. Gabriel; Davidson [2], p. 133.

[31] See e.g. Frege's letter to Russell of 28 Dec. 1902 ([22], pp. 234–7). Cf. Dummett [2], p. 182; Simons [6], p. 79; Bell [4], p. 41; Künne [2], p. 132; Weiner [1], pp. 96–7.

and which (ii) remains unaltered when intersubstitutions of the specified kind [that is, of co-referential parts of the sentences] are undertaken?[32]

It is significant that here Frege is taking the reference of at least some subsentential expressions to be already fixed: one might then ask how that is supposed to square with his understanding of reference as, in Bell's phrase, 'that property of an expression which enables it to participate in valid deductive inference within the predicate calculus with identity'.[33] Which comes first for Frege: the reference of sentences or the reference of their components? The answer seems to be, as Dummett says,[34] that Frege takes the reference of (at least some) *proper names* for granted, as something pre-theoretically given: that then, so Frege on this interpretation supposes, enables us to fix the references of *sentences* (in which those names occur) in accordance with the principle quoted above from 'Über Sinn und Bedeutung', and from there we can proceed to fix the references of other subsentential expressions in accordance with the principle formulated by Bell.

But if this is an accurate reconstruction of Frege's position, it must be said that the two arguments I have identified to the effect that sentences refer to truth-values are inadequate. The first is insufficient because the supporting consideration is not precise enough to dictate any particular semantical strategy for declarative sentences. It is of course correct that our semantics must in some significant way register the central role played by the notion of truth in our lives and linguistic practices; but it by no means follows that the recognition of that role must proceed by establishing truth-values as the referents of sentences. Surely we might claim, in the spirit of Davidson (recall the passage of his I quoted in §2), that in keying our analysis of unity to propositions, that is, to the referents of linguistic items (declarative sentences) which can possess truth-values as a matter of their very essence, we are taking full account of the Fregean insistence on the semantic centrality of truth. And once Russellian propositions are on the scene as candidates for referential status, Frege's second reason for taking truth-values to be the referents of sentences (the insensitivity of truth-values to intersubstitution of co-referential parts of sentences) is also exposed as inadequate, because it is equally the case that the Russellian proposition introduced by a given declarative sentence, being an extensional entity, will not change under intersubstitution of co-referential parts of that sentence.[35] Moreover, if, following the conception of *Bedeutung* formulated by Bell, we take the referents of declarative sentences to be truth-values on the basis of the fact that the truth-values of compound sentences

[32] [6], p. 35 ([21], p. 150).   [33] [2], p. 193.
[34] [2], pp. 198–203.   [35] Cf. Angelelli [1], pp. 57–8; Thiel, p. 93.

are determined by the truth-values of their component sentences, we thereby ignore non-truth-functional modes of sentential composition, to which this principle of determination does not, in general, apply (I shall return to this shortly). And it is obvious that the intersubstitution of component sentences referring to the same Russellian proposition will leave the truth-values of compound sentences unaffected no less than does the intersubstitution (in extensional contexts) of component sentences with the same truth-value.

The most important point by my lights is that, given that we are employing reference as our central semantic notion, according to which the referent of an expression is just what an adequate theory of meaning for the language in question will specify as what an understander needs to think of, and what it suffices for him or her to think of (presupposing, in each case, that the understander thinks of the referent *as* the referent of the relevant linguistic item), in order to count as understanding the expression, it follows that it will not be an option to select truth-values as the referents of sentences. This is not because we reject the referential approach to the semantics of sentences *tout court*, perhaps on the basis that 'pre-theoretically, we have no commitment to—and can indeed make very little of—the idea that a sentence stands for anything'.[36] For on my approach, and indeed on any reasonable understanding of the reference relation, 'referring to' or 'standing for' is an essentially *theoretical* relation, so that any pre-theoretical intuitions we might have on the subject are of no consequence, and Frege's helping himself to a *pre*-theoretical conception of the reference of proper names, assuming that he does indeed do so, is unacceptable. After all, if we were to rely on our pre-theoretical intuitions, we would have to say that *no* words or items of language—neither proper names nor anything else—*stand for* anything in the world: for no linguistic items *go proxy for* anything in the world, which is what, literally, 'standing for' means (standing for is standing *in* for). I shall return to this important issue in §53. For now the point we need is that it is not an option to select truth-values as referents of sentences, on my approach to the reference relation, but that is not because sentences do not refer at all: it is rather because there is a better candidate for the job. It is not an option to select truth-values to discharge this function because it is, in general, neither necessary nor sufficient for the understanding of a sentence that one know its truth-value. That it is not necessary is obvious. The reason why it is not sufficient has to do with the principle of compositionality: we must conceive the object of the understander's acquaintance at the level of reference that corresponds to sentences at the level of symbolic language as being *composed of*

---

[36] Sullivan [1], p. 91. Cf. Bell [1], pp. 53–4.

other entities at the level of reference (in the simplest case, of an object and a monadic property). Frege's preferred candidate for what a sentence refers to is too crude to do justice to this important principle, for sentences with the same truth-value may express propositions composed of distinct objects and properties. The entities that we, as theorists, discern at the level of reference corresponding to declarative sentences at the level of symbolic language must be as finely individuated as the principle of compositionality requires: only entities that, like Russellian propositions, are by definition composed of the entities at the level of reference corresponding to all the semantically significant parts of declarative sentences can meet this requirement.[37]

Recall (§8) that I am assuming that in order to count in this context as thinking of a truth-value one must know which truth-value it is that one is thinking of. This assumption underlies Church's approach to reference:

The sense of a sentence may be described as that which is grasped when one understands the sentence, or as that which sentences in different languages must have in common in order to be correct translations each of the other. As in the case of names generally, it is possible to grasp the sense of a sentence without therefore necessarily having knowledge of its denotation (truth-value) otherwise than as determined by this sense. In particular, though the sense is grasped, it may sometimes remain unknown whether the denotation is truth.[38]

In a number of respects this passage is unsatisfactory. Setting aside the underlying *suppositio* approach to reference, which I reject, I think Church is wrong to suggest that the truth-value of a sentence is *determined* by its sense. At least in the case of contingencies, a sentence's truth-value is a quite distinct feature of it.[39] Still, despite its shortcomings, the quoted passage is right in assuming that if grasping its truth-value *were* part of understanding a sentence, the understander would have to *know which* truth-value he or she thereby cognized, in the demanding sense of knowing whether the sentence in question was true or false. Actually, it does not help Frege's cause to drop the assumption, as John McDowell implies in a discussion of Evans. For even *without* the presumption that one knows which truth-value it is that one is thinking of in understanding a sentence (in the demanding sense I have specified), cognizing the truth-value to which, on Frege's (and Evans's) conception, a given sentence refers is *still* neither necessary nor sufficient for understanding that sentence. McDowell

---

[37] Cf. Sullivan [2], §4; Potter [1], p. 111.   [38] [6], pp. 25–6.

[39] Subsequently, in the face of undecided sentences such as Goldbach's conjecture, Church seems to modify his position so as to make the sense of a sentence fix *how* rather than *what* it denotes ([6], p. 54 with n. 122). And no one who thought, with Aristotle (see my [2], esp. ch. 12), that statements about future contingencies lack truth-values could suppose that in understanding these statements one was in any sense thinking of their truth-values.

contrives to suggest otherwise when he says that 'in entertaining the *Sinn* of the sentence ["Kant wrote three Critiques"], one is thinking of the truth-value as the truth-value thereof that Kant wrote three Critiques'.[40] But why should one insist that the understander of a sentence think of a truth-value even in this diluted sense? On this highly attenuated approach to 'thinking of a truth-value'—in which one can count as thinking of a truth-value (the True, as it might be) in connection with a particular sentence even if one does not know whether the relevant sentence is true or false (one thinks of it under a description, such as 'the truth-value of this sentence, whichever it is')—the truth-value itself drops out of consideration as irrelevant: there seems no reason to insist that the understander think of that truth-value, in grasping the sense of the relevant sentence, as opposed to any other object (or nothing at all).

I noted above that the principle of compositionality supplies an important argument for identifying the referents of declarative sentences with Russellian propositions: this consideration applies, too, when we take complex sentences into account—sentences with sentences as semantically significant proper parts. For many complex sentential contexts involve non-truth-functional combinations of component sentences, and in such contexts the truth-values of component sentences will be insufficient to determine even the truth-value, let alone the meaning (in the sense of what an understander needs to be acquainted with), of the complex whole. Nothing short of propositionally structured entities recapitulating in their manner of composition the way their governing sentences are composed will be competent to constitute inputs from which the meanings of complex sentences can reasonably be regarded as having been constructed. Frege's doctrine of indirect senses goes some way towards rectifying the deficit in his main theory, but not far enough: for although the *Bedeutung* of a sentence in an indirect context is its sense, and so something with sufficient structure to give a viable model of meaning in the sense of what engages with understanding, the overall *Bedeutung* of the sentential context in which it is embedded is again, and disastrously, an unstructured truth-value. So notwithstanding the fact that, on Frege's approach, the *Bedeutung* of what replaces '*p*' in contexts of the form 'Peter believes that *p*' is sufficiently structured to yield a viable model of meaning, the *Bedeutung* of the whole sentence is not. It follows that the propositional entity that we identify with the referent of a declarative sentence must not only *contain* the referents of the semantically significant parts of that sentence (as Russellian propositions have been defined to do); it must also *structure* those elements in a way that mirrors the way in which the corresponding sentence is built up out of its constituents

---

[40] [6], p. 53 n. 18.

(as Russellian propositions have not so far been defined to do, but I shall address this point below: §18). Only so will acquaintance with that referential entity be adequate for understanding the relevant sentence.

15 Proper Names, Concept-Expressions, and Definite Descriptions

Frege's own picture of the composition, at the levels of symbolic language, sense, and reference, of a simple categorical sentence—that is, of a declarative sentence that is not hypothetical (not complex) and not modal—was conveniently sketched by him in a letter to Husserl of 24 May 1891 (see Figure 2.1).[41] (In the diagram the vertical arrows represent semantical relations, the single horizontal arrow a non-semantical relation.) I have already remarked that Frege's reasons for taking truth-values to be the referents of declarative sentences are inconclusive: as far as the considerations he adduced go, we may as well take Russellian propositions to be the referents of sentences. Given further that, as I have argued, we require an extensional conception of propositions as worldly entities, as well as a conception of propositionally structured entities housed at the level of sense (Fregean Thoughts), it follows that we must locate Russellian propositions in Frege's diagram as referents of declarative sentences; the principle of compositionality for reference then forces us to jettison Frege's candidate for sentential referents, truth-values, in favour of entities composed in some appropriate way of the other referential entities in the picture, namely objects and concepts (which, for present purposes, can

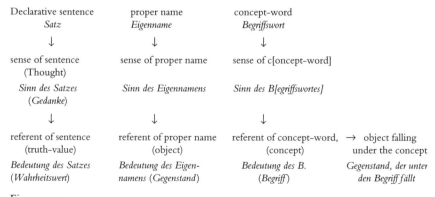

Figure 2.1

<hr />

[41] [22], pp. 94–8.

be identified with properties),[42] that is, in favour of the Russellian propositions we have anyway been required to locate in the diagram. The supplanting of truth-values by Russellian propositions is not a trivial change since, as I have noted, there is a tension between Frege's preferred candidate for the referents of sentences and mine: sentences with the same truth-value may express distinct Russellian propositions. But there is a way of softening the clash between Frege's candidate for the referents of sentences and mine.

To see what is required we need to ask why Frege draws the column for the sense and reference of concept-words in the way he does. In particular, why does Frege not treat the object (presumably we should say: object or objects) satisfying a concept-word as its referent? For though, as I have noted (§7), Frege's treatment of the reference of concept-words is—at least sometimes—extensional, he does not *identify* the referents of concept-words with their extensions, as we have seen Davidson do, and as is standard in modern semantics. The reason, as Frege explains to Husserl in the same letter, is that a concept-word may be empty—it may be the case that nothing satisfies the corresponding concept—without its ceasing to be scientifically useful.[43] Indeed, our very ability to claim of certain concept-expressions—'is a witch', say—that they are empty *depends* upon their having reference: otherwise nothing truth-evaluable would be expressed by our form of words; the sentence 'There are no witches' would be truth-valueless. (Or, to put it in my terms, that sentence, in lacking a referent, would be meaningless.) Frege himself makes this point about necessarily unsatisfiable concept-expressions such as 'is not identical with itself' and 'is a fraction smaller than 1 and so constituted that no fraction smaller than 1 is greater than it'.[44] Hence, in the case of concept-words—or, in general, concept-expressions, whether simple or complex—we need to draw a distinction between reference and satisfaction: that a meaningful concept-expression must have reference (refer to a concept) is just truistic, given the conception of reference we are working with, but it by no means follows that it must be satisfied by any object(s).

It is plausible that no such distinction is either required or admissible in the case of at least some proper names, which we may term proper names in the strict sense. In the case of strict proper names referent and satisfier

---

[42] For Frege, of course, there is a significant difference between a concept and a property (i.e. the referent of a nominalization like 'wisdom'), though they are both entities at the level of reference: concepts are unsaturated whereas properties are not. For the time being I ignore this difference; I shall return to it in the next chapter.

[43] Cf. [26], p. 133; Bell [1], pp. 41–2. There is a further important difference: concepts are unsaturated (see n. 42), but extensions are objects, and so saturated ([26], p. 129). Cf. Bell [2], p. 192; Tiles, p. 149; Dummett [3], p. 172.

[44] [3], §74; cf. §94.

coincide: that is, the object that the understander has to cognize in order to count as understanding the name coincides with the object satisfying the name, that is, to which the name can be truly applied in identifying sentences of the form 'That is *a*'. Words which purport to be strict proper names but which are empty—have no referent/satisfier—*eo ipso* lack a sense, and sentences in which such names are used (as opposed to mentioned) have no sense either.[45] In the case of such names, negative existential sentences like 'It is not the case that *a* exists' can be false (if *a* exists) but not true: if there is no relevant object '*a* exists' is senseless, and so renders any larger sentence in which it is embedded senseless, and thereby truth-valueless.[46] The sense of a strict proper name is accordingly *de re* in the ways I have identified (§7): grasping a *de re* sense involves thinking of the object which is the referent (satisfier) of the name; correspondingly the kind of sense a strict proper name has is essentially object-involving (satisfier-involving)—that is, a given *de re* sense necessarily presents the referent (satisfier) it does present, and would not exist in the absence of that referent (satisfier). (This does not mean that such sentences as 'Santa Claus does not exist' and 'Vulcan does not exist' are senseless, for in these and many similar cases the names are not strict but abbreviate definite descriptions: I return to this point shortly.)

Frege's category of proper names did not exactly coincide with what I am calling strict such names. For in the first place this category included definite descriptions; and, secondly, given Frege's *suppositio* approach to reference, he was obliged, as I argued in §7, to construe the semantics even of those items within the category that we (and he) would call genuine proper names (such as his own name) descriptively. But now definite descriptions may, as Russell observed in 'On Denoting',[47] be empty (that is, lack a satisfier) without forfeiting meaning; hence they may be empty without forfeiting either sense or reference, once the intuitive notion of meaning has been subdivided into these further species (as it was not by Russell himself). Indeed Russell had recognized this well before he introduced his theory of descriptions: in his 1903 theory of denoting concepts it was fully allowed that denoting phrases might be meaningful but empty in the sense of indicating (in my terminology: referring to) a denoting concept that fails to denote (be satisfied by) anything.[48] And there is a very clear expression of the point in connection with empty definite descriptions in a paper written in 1905 but before 'On Denoting'.[49] (Accommodating empty descriptions cannot therefore have been

---

[45] Cf. Rumfitt [3], p. 206.   [46] *Pace* Bostock [2], p. 358; see here McDowell [3], Essay 9.
[47] [13], pp. 46–7.   [48] [3], §73; N. Griffin [5], pp. 48–9.
[49] [18], p. 487. Cf. p. 318; [14], p. 64; Potter [1], pp. 123–5.

what motivated Russell to move from the 1903 theory of denoting concepts to the 1905 theory of descriptions, as was for many years assumed, the story having been encouraged by Russell himself.[50] The mistake has been corrected only relatively recently.[51]) In the *Grundlagen* Frege implicitly denied that such expressions might be both meaningful and empty, saying of the expression 'the largest proper fraction' that it has no content (*Inhalt*) and is senseless (*sinnlos*), because though purporting to designate a definite object it does not do so.[52] But he is surely wrong on this point: for one way in which we may register that no unique largest proper fraction exists is by saying 'There is no such thing as *the* largest proper fraction', stressing the definite article, so that the offending phrase must have meaning. The remark I have just reported was made before Frege had hit on his distinction between sense and reference: after he drew that distinction, he preferred to say that such phrases as 'the celestial body most distant from the Earth' and 'the least rapidly convergent series' have—in the former case conjecturally, in the latter demonstrably—sense but no reference.[53]

Now it is a matter of controversy exactly how the distinctive semantics of definite descriptions should be characterized,[54] and Russell himself thought that for some purposes definite descriptions of the form 'the F', when proper (that is, when there is exactly one F), may be treated as proper names.[55] But it should be uncontroversial that there are at least some 'pure' definite descriptions (or perhaps uses thereof) for which the slogan that applies to *de re* sense—'no object [i.e. no *satisfying* object], no Thought'—fails. Plausibly, the examples of definite descriptions given in the previous paragraph ('the largest proper fraction', 'the celestial body most distant from the Earth', 'the least rapidly convergent series') are cases in point: these descriptions, though empty (as we are supposing), are perfectly meaningful, and go transparently into sentences expressing Thoughts. Of course, there is no way things could be such that the statement that the least rapidly convergent series is F (where 'F' holds place for some suitable mathematical concept-expression) is true. But

---

[50] See e.g. [11], pp. 170–1, where the argument that indefinite descriptions are incomplete symbols turns on the existence of empty such descriptions. It is clear from the way Russell introduces the topic of definite descriptions on p. 172 that he regards this argument as establishing the incompleteness of definite descriptions also.

[51] See here Hylton [2], pp. 95–6, 128 n. 11, 200–1; L. Linsky [1], p. 632; Makin, esp. chs. 1 and 2; N. Griffin [5], pp. 46–57; Levine [1]; Stevens [3], pp. 43–9; Candlish [2], ch. 5.

[52] [3], §74 n. Cf. §97 on 'the square root of −1', with Frege's subsequent remarks on this section in his letter to Husserl of 24 May 1891: [22], p. 96.

[53] [6], p. 28 ([21], p. 145). Cf. Thiel, pp. 87–8.

[54] For a standard account see e.g. Neale [1]; contrast Ramachandran.

[55] Whitehead and Russell, i, pp. 179–80 (*14.15, *14.16, *14.18). Cf. B. Linsky [3], pp. 385–6; Zalta [1], pp. 78–81.

that is because the layout of mathematical reality affords no object satisfying the description, not because the descriptive phrase lacks either sense or a referent.[56] And equally, there *is* a way things could be such that the judgement that the least rapidly convergent series does not exist is true—for things even are that way—showing that the phrase as such *does* have both a sense and referent.[57] Hence our *general* account of the semantics of definite descriptions must distinguish between reference and satisfaction: that a meaningful definite description must, like any other semantically significant linguistic item, have reference is just (on the conception of reference I am presupposing: reference as signification) truistic; but whether a definite description is satisfied by anything (and, if so, by what) is of no concern to the theorist of meaning. So when Church writes 'that "the number of planets" denotes the number nine is a fact as much of astronomy as it is of the semantics of the English language, and can be described only as belonging to a discipline broad enough to include both semantics and astronomy',[58] we should reply that, on the contrary, if there is indeed such a fact as that 'the number of planets' denotes a particular number—that is, is satisfied by it: for it clearly does refer to (signify) that number—it can at best be an astronomical, not a semantical, fact; and there is no such portmanteau discipline as Church postulates.

But if Frege's excessively broad category of proper names is narrowed so as to exclude such descriptions—and presumably also those ordinary proper names that are introduced or interpreted to abbreviate pure descriptions, such as 'Vulcan',[59] and fictional names as these occur in 'discourse about the fiction' (where they abbreviate definite descriptions that spell out the fictional attributes of the character in question)[60]—but include strict proper names, then the 'proper name' column of the Fregean diagram can be sustained.[61] Of course, a name may be introduced as an abbreviation of a definite description; alternatively, it may be introduced with a purported *de re* sense, but, in the absence of a suitable object, the name must either be discarded as senseless or, if its intelligibility is to be saved, interpreted as

---

[56] Similar remarks apply to Rumfitt's example ([3], p. 208) of 'the set of non-self-membered sets' and its paradoxical congeners: see further §§63, 84 below.

[57] McDowell seems to evince the same confusion as Frege on this point at [6], p. 61.

[58] [4], p. 105.   [59] Cf. Zalta [1], p. 124.

[60] Within the scope of the fiction, by contrast, many names will be strict proper names, for *within the fiction* it is usually fictionally supposed that relevant names are ordinary proper names, and such names typically are strict. When we use the name 'Brutus' to talk about a central character of *Julius Caesar*, we use it as an abbreviated definite description (compiled from what Shakespeare tells us); but when, in the drama, Caesar says 'Doth not Brutus bootless kneel?', he is represented as using the name as a strict proper name of whose referent he has an essentially *de re* cognitive grasp. See helpfully on these issues Currie [3].

[61] Cf. Russell [18], p. 285; Cartwright [2], p. 120.

abbreviating a description. Since, as I am stressing, the meaningfulness of any such abbreviating description is indifferent to the existence or otherwise of a satisfying object, the name can successfully figure in acts of communication, even if some (or all) of its users are under an illusion concerning the kind of sense it has: in such a situation the interpreter is certainly not obliged to relinquish its intelligibility.[62]

It should be emphasized that, if we do amend Frege's doctrine in the suggested way, then in the resulting position the principle that sense *determines* reference, that is, that a sense necessarily presents a referent—alternatively: that if a purported linguistic expression fails to have reference, it has no sense either—holds for proper names strictly so called as for all other linguistic expressions (including those, such as the logical constants, which refer to functions). A further important point is this: on this conception of sense, it is a *direct* route to the referent; the fact that a sense presents its referent *in some particular way* does not derogate from that directness, for it is not as though an object could be presented in just no way at all.[63] Russell was wrong to think that if reference is mediated by sense that will render the route to the referent epistemically indirect.[64] It is equally wrong to suppose that to think of an object in some particular way (under a Fregean sense) is necessarily to think of it descriptively, so that the object itself cannot figure in the proposition one grasps, and that, conversely, if an object does figure in one's thought, it must do so in a way that is unmediated by a Fregean sense. Unfortunately these errors are widespread.[65]

It might be confusing to say that all semantically significant expressions have *de re* senses (have senses that essentially involve the presentation of a *res*), given that that characterization is normally reserved for expressions that refer to *individuals*, as opposed to properties or (Fregean) concepts, but we can at any rate say that all semantically significant linguistic expressions have senses that are essentially *referent-involving* in a way that parallels the essentially referent-involving *de re* senses of strict proper names. Hence the distinctive characteristic of a strict proper name is not that its sense essentially involves the presentation of a real referent—and something like that is what is typically meant by that terminology in the literature—for that feature is (truistically) common to all semantically significant expressions. Rather, when we say that a proper name has *de re* sense we mean, as I explained above, that its referent and satisfying

---

[62] This is implied by Sainsbury: [4], p. 215.   [63] See Evans [1], p. 62; my [15], pp. 214–15.
[64] See his letter to Frege of 12 Dec. 1904: Frege [22], p. 251; cf. Hylton [2], pp. 124–8; Candlish [2], pp. 54–5.
[65] See e.g. Kaplan [2], pp. 483–8; Cartwright [3], p. 923; Tugendhat [2], pp. 147–8; Dummett [4], p. 306.

object coincide. For a definite description, by contrast, whose referent is a complex conceptual entity,[66] there will (except perhaps in a few degenerate cases) be a necessary divergence between referent and satisfying object (if any). On this approach it would be quite wrong to say that satisfaction is a form of reference. Satisfaction is almost universally assumed to be a semantical relation, since in model theory it plays a role analogous to reference;[67] but if by 'semantics' we mean to invoke those properties and relations that engage significantly with linguistic understanding, then satisfaction does not count as a semantical relation.

Like the terminology of *de re* sense, the distinction between general and singular terms can be misleading: it is objectionable if it is taken to imply that the satisfaction and referring (naming) relations are as it were points on the same scale, distinguished not qualitatively (semantically) but only in respect of the number of objects on the world end of the relations.[68] This was the line taken influentially in the Port-Royal *Logic*, in which singular propositions were grouped with universal propositions rather than with particular propositions, because 'they have a singular subject which is necessarily taken throughout its entire extension', and 'it makes no difference to the universality of a proposition whether the subject's extension is large or small, provided that whatever it is, it is taken completely throughout'.[69] But this, as the Kneales rightly remark, is an 'unhappy dodge',[70] for in any sense in which concept-expressions can be called general terms, only singular definite descriptions, not strict proper names, are singular terms.[71] Ignacio Angelelli well remarks:

The so-called 'common' name 'man' has nothing to do *immediately* with the individuals falling under *man*; it has only a *mediate* relation [to them], but one of the relations of this relative product is *not* a semantic one.[72]

That is, 'man' has an immediate and semantic relation (reference) to a property or concept, and a mediate and non-semantic relation (satisfaction) to the individuals falling under it. As Mill noted: 'When mankind fixed the meaning of the word wise, they were not thinking of Socrates.'[73] When Socrates was given his name, by contrast, fixing the meaning of 'Socrates' was exactly what

---

[66] It is what Grossmann calls a 'structure': see [2] (cf. [1], p. 233).
[67] See e.g. Rumfitt [4], p. 93.   [68] Cf. Hochberg [1], pp. 462–6.
[69] Arnauld and Nicole [1], II, ch. 3; [2], p. 84. On the influence of this text, see Kneale and Kneale, p. 305 (on Wallis), and p. 323 (on Leibniz). Cf. Hutcheson [2], I, ch. 3 ([3], p. 15).
[70] Kneale and Kneale, p. 319.   [71] Künne [1], pp. 20–2.
[72] [1], pp. 71–2. Cf. Frege [9], p. 326 ([21], p. 188). See also Frege [2], pp. 49–50 ([25], p. 92); [11], p. 454 ([21], p. 209); [15], p. 308 ([21], p. 294); Grossmann [1], p. 51.
[73] Mill, I. v, §2; cf. Prior [3], pp. 70–1.

those who were naming him were engaged in doing. The mistake was started by Aristotle, who held that the general term differs from the proper name merely by virtue of being predicable of many.[74]

Given the principle of compositionality for reference, the distinction I have drawn between the semantics of definite descriptions and the semantics of strict proper names is just what one would expect: for strict proper names are semantically simple, whereas definite descriptions are semantically complex phrases constructed out of concept-expressions and the description operator. It is therefore unsurprising that the distinction between reference and satisfaction which, as Frege saw,[75] is mandatory for the semantics of concept-expressions should, as he unfortunately failed to see, apply in consequence to the semantics of definite descriptions. As Russell nicely put it in his 1903 manuscript 'On Meaning and Denotation':

When we make a statement about Arthur Balfour, he himself forms part of the object before our minds, i.e. of the proposition stated. If we say, for instance, 'Arthur Balfour advocates retaliation', that expresses a thought which has for its object a complex containing as a constituent the man himself; no one who does not know what is the designation of the name 'Arthur Balfour' can understand what we *mean*: the object of our thought cannot, by our statement, be communicated to him. But when we say 'the present Prime Minister of England believes in retaliation', it is possible for a person to understand completely what we mean without his knowing that Mr. Arthur Balfour is Prime Minister, and indeed without his ever having heard of Mr. Arthur Balfour.[76]

And he later adds: 'It is thus plain that there is a sense in which Mr. Arthur Balfour is not a constituent' of the proposition (expressed by) 'the present prime minister of England favours retaliation';[77] it is the denoting concept indicated by the denoting phrase 'the present prime minister of England' that is the constituent of the relevant proposition.[78]

In my terms, both the strict proper name 'Arthur Balfour' and the definite description 'the present Prime Minister of England' are—like every semantically significant linguistic expression—essentially referent-involving, but whereas the referent of the name is the man Arthur Balfour,[79] the referent of the description is a complex conceptual entity composed of the referent

---

[74] See e.g. *Int.* 17a39–b1. For further development of the error in supposition theory (in particular the coordinating of *suppositio discreta* and *confusa*), see Arnold, pp. 67–70, 98, 107, 111–12, 132.

[75] But I suggest below (§17) that his reason for making the distinction was not the right one.

[76] [18], pp. 315–16.   [77] [18], p. 327.   [78] Cf. N. Griffin [5], p. 54.

[79] That is, assuming that 'Arthur Balfour' is a strict proper name, as it no doubt was for Russell when he wrote the passage, even if it is not for us now: for us mere consumers of the name, standing in a relation of semantic deference to its producers, the name is descriptive (the relevant descriptions identifying, perhaps recursively, the right producing group). For the terminology here, see Evans [1], ch. 11.

of the description operator 'the' and the complex conceptual referent of the expression 'present Prime Minister of England'; it is this complex entity (what Russell calls the denoting concept), not the man Arthur Balfour, that is the constituent of the proposition expressed by 'The present prime minister of England advocates retaliation'. So the description can, unlike the name, be understood by someone who is not acquainted with Balfour. Russell expresses some discomfiture with 'the strange consequence that we may know a proposition about a man, without knowing that it is about him, and without even having ever heard of him'.[80] But the feeling of strangeness is a trick of the terminology: Russell is here using 'about' in a deviant way, to introduce a relation (satisfaction) that, as I have said, is in fact *non*-semantic; still less is it a *logical* relation, as Russell thinks.[81] If instead we talked of cognizing an abstract content satisfied by *NN*, without the cognizer's knowing or having heard of *NN*, no feeling of strangeness would arise.

As Russell observed, all ordinary mathematical functional expressions are of definite-description form.[82] For example, the statement that $\sin \pi = 0$ is the statement that the object satisfying the definite description 'the sine of π' equals zero. Now this fact, contrary to what some commentators suppose, does not oblige us to take the referent of a description such as '$\sin \pi$' to coincide with its satisfier. There is no justification for Peter Hylton's claim that such descriptions 'have a semantically significant complexity which is not (in general) reflected in the object to which they refer'.[83] It is true that the complexity of functors need not be reflected in the *value* of the corresponding function for a given argument—though it *may* be so reflected, a point that will be of some importance to us below (§19). But it is a mistake to conflate, as Hylton does, the value of a function for a given argument with the referent of the expression formed by applying the corresponding functor to a name of that argument. On the conception of reference as signification, referent and value for expressions of the schematic form '$\phi^n(a_1 \ldots a_n)$' are not, in general, the same entities.

It follows that we do not want to say, with Frege, that '$(2 + 3 \times 1^2)$' is a *name* of the number 5,[84] or that '$2 + 3$' and '5', though differing in sense, *designate* (*bezeichnen*, i.e. *bedeuten*)[85] the same number,[86] nor do we want to say with

---

[80] [18], p. 317.   [81] [18], pp. 317–18; [3] §56; cf. Stevens [3], p. 44.

[82] [13], p. 92; Whitehead and Russell, i, pp. 31, 232 (*30). Cf. Bostock [2], p. 342.

[83] [2], p. 132.

[84] [10], i, §1; cf. [12], pp. 17, 28–9 ([21], pp. 251, 258–9), and [15], p. 399 ([21], p. 314), where '2^4' and '4^2' are said to have the same *Bedeutung*.

[85] On the synonymy of these terms, see [15], p. 298 ([21], p. 285).

[86] [26], p. 243; cf. [14], pp. 657–8 ([21], p. 274); Kneale and Kneale, p. 495.

Church that 'the author of Waverley' is a *name* of Scott,[87] nor with P. T. Geach
that the description 'the (positive) square root of 25' *refers to* the number 5,[88]
nor with Dummett that 'the victor at Austerlitz' *refers to* Napoleon.[89] Saying
these things would have the consequence, given the conception of reference
I am working with, that in order to understand such phrases as 'the author
of Waverley', 'the (positive) square root of 25', and 'the victor at Austerlitz',
one would have to think of Scott, the number 5, and Napoleon respectively:
but one can obviously understand those descriptions without, as we say,
knowing who the author of Waverley *was*, what the (positive) square root of
25 *is*, or who the victor at Austerlitz *was*. This is simply an extension of the
parallel point one must make concerning the concept-expressions 'authored
Waverley', 'is a square root of 25', and 'was victorious at Austerlitz'—that
we can understand these concept-expressions (grasp the concepts they refer
to) without knowing which objects (if any) fall under them—and it is a pity
that Frege, who so perceptively recognized that concept-expressions refer to
concepts, not the objects (if any) in their extension, should have failed to
draw the consequences for definite descriptions. Frege's taking a functional
expression such as 'sin π' (which has the form of a definite description) to *refer
to* its value was not, as Peter Simons suggests,[90] an 'achievement' on his part,
but a catastrophic error.

Frege's curious blindness to the fact that, given that the referent of a
concept-expression is a concept, not its satisfying objects (if any), it follows
(assuming an obvious compositionality principle) that the referent of a definite
description should also be a conceptual entity, not its satisfying object (if any),
is replicated at the level of functions and their values. In his 1904 essay 'Was
ist eine Funktion?', having told us, in line with what we have seen so far,
that 'of the expressions "sin 0", "sin 1", "sin 2", each refers to (*bedeutet*)
a particular number',[91] Frege goes on to remark that, when we read the
equation '$y = f(x)$' as 'y is a function of x', we 'confuse the function with
its value for an argument'.[92] Just so: but it would seem that, on Frege's view,
as soon as we select a particular argument-name, and affix to it a particular
functor, we arrive at a name not of the corresponding function as applied
to the corresponding argument but of the value of that function for that
argument; and indeed he speaks in the same passage as though completing
a function with a number brings it about that the completed function *itself*

---

[87] [6], p. 5. At p. 16 n. 41 Church suggests that a plural description such as 'the square roots of 25' is
a common name of its values: cf. Oliver and Smiley [3], pp. 1055–6.
[88] [2], pp. 260–1; cf. Oliver and Smiley [3], pp. 1049.   [89] [7], p. 269.
[90] [6], p. 76 (point 2).   [91] [14], p. 663 ([21], p. 278).
[92] [14], p. 665 ([21], p. 280). Cf. [16], p. 265 ([21], p. 341).

becomes—not, as the Geach and Black translation has it, *yields* (which suggests the production of something *else*)—the number that is its value for the relevant argument.[93]

Notice that, if we follow my recommendation and distinguish between reference and satisfaction in the case of definite descriptions, we must specify the truth-conditions of sentences of the form 'the *F* is *G*' (under which I include identity statements of the forms 'the *F* is the *G*' and '*a* is the *F*' as a special case) in terms not of the *referent* of the description, but of its *satisfier*: that is, 'the *F* is *G*' will be true just if the unique object satisfying the description 'the *F*' is *G*. For, to take an identity statement of the form '*a* is the *F*', we do not want to say, absurdly, that 'Socrates is Xanthippe's husband' is true just if Socrates is identical with the complex conceptual *referent* of 'Xanthippe's husband',[94] but rather that this sentence is true just if Socrates is identical with the *satisfier* of that complex referent. Similarly, '7 + 5 = 12' will be true just in case the satisfier (not: referent) of the description 'the sum of 7 and 5' also satisfies the property of being identical with 12.[95] All this will seem surprising to anyone brought up in the *suppositio* school of reference; but on the *significatio* approach, which I shall defend towards the end of this chapter, there is no reason to expect that, in general, reference will engage significantly with truth-conditions.

Russell makes the same point in terms of his pre-1903 theory of denoting concepts: 'any proposition about sin *x*, e.g. $\sin^2 x + \cos^2 x = 1$, is false as regards the meanings [= the referents, in my terminology], and holds only of the numbers which the meanings denote'.[96] For in the theory of denoting concepts (which included the referents of definite and indefinite descriptions, and quantifier-phrases), Russell distinguished between a denoting concept and what it denotes, telling us that although the proposition (expressed by) 'I met a man' contains the denoting concept *a man*, it denotes a *particular* man, 'some actual biped denoted by the concept, . . . an actual man with a tailor and a bank-account or a public house and a drunken wife'.[97] Maybe Hylton is right to suggest that one of the purposes of 'On Denoting' was 'to analyse phrases which appear to be complex referring expressions [sc. referring to their satisfiers] in a way that makes them out not to be'.[98] But if that was indeed in Russell's mind, he was muddled. For, according to the ousted theory of denoting concepts, a denoting phrase such as 'the victor at Austerlitz' does not *refer to* Napoleon: a proposition containing the corresponding denoting

[93] [14], p. 665 ([21], p. 280): 'Wird eine Funktion durch eine Zahl zu einer Zahl *ergänzt*, . . .'.
[94] Cf. Ricketts [5], p. 231.
[95] Cf. Cresswell, pp. 11–15. But Cresswell thinks that '7 + 5' also *refers to* 12.
[96] [18], p. 331.   [97] [3], §§51, 56.   [98] [2], p. 130.

concept does not *eo ipso contain* Napoleon. The phrase refers to—and the corresponding proposition contains—a denoting concept, which then may or may not denote or be about (in the non-semantic sense that, as noted above, caused Russell some discomfiture) someone or something.

A further suggestion of Hylton's seems to me definitely wrong.[99] Hylton argues that an alternative strategy for Russell, in order to handle the complexity of denoting phrases without accepting complex referents for them, would have been to introduce a level of sense. But the point of introducing a level of sense into our semantics is to accommodate different ways in which entities at the level of reference may be presented by items of symbolic language, or may be thought about by language users; it has nothing to do with securing necessary degrees of fineness of grain in our modelling of semantic complexity at the level of reference. The mistake of supposing that complexity at the level of reference is a semantic competitor to the notion of sense, or equivalently that absence of structure at the level of reference may be compensated for by its presence at the level of sense, is quite common.[100]

As is familiar, the 1905 theory treated definite descriptions as 'incomplete symbols' lacking semantic integrity. Hence, despite the difference of terminology, my application of the distinction between (in my terms) reference and satisfaction in respect of definite descriptions is much closer to Russell's 1903 theory of denoting concepts than it is to the 1905 theory of definite descriptions. (But of course I also insert a level of sense, absent from Russell's semantic hierarchy.) Here it is noteworthy that if, in our analysis of definite descriptions, we avoid what Evans memorably called 'the butchering of surface structure in which Russell so perversely delighted',[101] the point that I insisted on above, namely that we must specify the truth-conditions of sentences of the form 'the F is G' in terms not of the *referent* of the description, but of its *satisfier*, will bring down an infinite regress. For we will not now say, as the Russell of 1905 had it, that 'the F is G' is true just if *there is a unique object* satisfying the description 'the F', and that object is G, but will say rather, as the Russell of 1903 would have preferred and as I put it above, that 'the F is G' is true just if *the unique object* satisfying the description 'the F' is G. Here the analysans itself contains a definite description. So in specifying *its* truth-conditions we will have to say, along similar lines to our treatment of the original analysandum, that 'the unique object satisfying the description "the F" is G' is true just if the unique object satisfying the description 'the unique object satisfying the description

[99] [2], pp. 128–34.
[100] See e.g. Grossmann [1]; Church [4], p. 110 n. 14; [10], esp. pp. 164–5; Cresswell, pp. 26–31, 69–92; N. Griffin [5], p. 44 n. 29; Ricketts [5], p. 231; and Goldfarb [2], p. 197.
[101] [1], p. 57.

"the F" ' is G, and so on into a regress. I shall discuss the significance of this point in Chapter 6.

16 Concept-Expressions and Carnapian Intensions

Frege's separation, in the case of concept-expressions, of the question of reference from that of satisfaction is convenient when one comes to consider modal discourse, something in which Frege himself took no interest, indeed excluded from the remit of logic.[102] For one wishes to say that concept-expressions that have the same extension in the actual world, but distinct extensions in other possible worlds, have different references. But there is nothing to prevent us from identifying the referents at least of semantically simple concept-expressions (concept-words) with what, following Lewis in his 'General Semantics', we may call their Carnapian intensions, that is, with functions from possible worlds and times to sets of objects, such that the function keyed to a given concept-expression maps each world/time pair to the set of objects satisfying the concept-expression in that world at that time.[103] There are several points that need to be stressed in connection with this identification.

First, Lewis employs a more general notion of Carnapian intension than I do, as involving (in the case of concepts) functions from indices to sets, where indices are determined by eight co-ordinates: a possible-world co-ordinate, a time co-ordinate, a place co-ordinate, a speaker co-ordinate, an audience co-ordinate, an indicated-objects co-ordinate, a previous-discourse co-ordinate, and an assignment-of-variables co-ordinate.[104] Actually, Lewis does not have a consistent position on this matter: sometimes he implies that the above is not a complete list of co-ordinates;[105] but elsewhere he even suggests that a single possible-world co-ordinate will suffice.[106] Mostly I shall assume that the relevant domains comprise possible worlds and times; occasionally I shall abstract from the latter.

Secondly, the items to be identified with Carnapian intensions are indeed the *referents* of semantically simple concept-expressions, not their *senses*: for two distinct concept-expressions may present the same Carnapian intension in different ways (e.g. 'is a lapwing'/'is a peewit'; 'is a groundhog'/'is a

---

[102] [1], §4; Kneale and Kneale, p. 480; Kreiser, p. 209.
[103] Lewis [1], §III. Cf. Carnap [3], ch. 1; Dowty *et al.*, p. 137; Stalnaker [1], pp. 79–80; Soames, p. 225.
[104] [1], pp. 7–8 and appendix.   [105] [6], p. 30.   [106] [7], pp. 13–18 (cf. [2], p. 175).

woodchuck'). It is a familiar point that it would be fatal to identify the senses of (strict) *proper names* with Carnapian intensions—functions from possible worlds and times to objects—given that all co-referential such names would end up expressing the same sense,[107] and a precisely analogous point holds for *concept-expressions*. Despite the seeming obviousness of the parallel, many philosophers and linguists (especially those working in the tradition of Montague grammar) identify properties, construed as Carnapian intensions, with the senses of concept-expressions, in effect conflating Frege with Carnap.[108] This disastrous identification was instigated not by Carnap himself but by Russell when, in the appendix on Frege included in *Principles*, he commented that 'The distinction [sc. of Frege's] between meaning (*Sinn*) and indication (*Bedeutung*) is roughly, though not exactly, equivalent to my distinction between a concept as such and what the concept denotes'.[109] And it was helped on its way by Church, who remarked,[110] concerning the distinct constants '$-1/(2\pi)$' and '$(1 - 4 + 1)/4\pi$', that 'a plausible case might be made out for supposing that the two constants have the same sense, on some such ground as that the equation between them expresses a necessary proposition or is true on logical grounds alone or the like', though he rightly noted that Frege 'would regard these two constants as having different senses'. But the conflation—which, *pace* Russell, is not even roughly along the right lines—fails to accommodate the fact that we need a sense–reference distinction for concept-expressions as much as we do for proper names: Davidson is quite wrong to suggest that the inclusion in our semantic theory of referents for concept-expressions in addition to sense and extension is a wheel turning idly.[111] In fact, if there is a redundancy here, it is the notion of a concept-expression's extension that is the rogue element, as Frege in effect saw when, in his letter to Husserl (§15), he inserted a dog-leg into the semantics for concept-expressions, using a horizontal arrow (representing a non-semantical relation) for the connection between a concept and its satisfying object(s), rather than a vertical arrow. Not that we should say that there *is* a redundancy: it is surely rather the case that we have to do with two different areas of concern, namely intensions and extensions.

---

[107] Cf. von Kutschera [1], pp. 83–4. We may of course identify the *referents* of proper names with such functions, but in the case of strict proper names the identification would be pointless (cf. Lewis [2], p. 251), since the function would be constant: a strict proper name refers to the same object at all indices where that object exists (cf. Soames, p. 225).

[108] Carnap [3], §§14, 29. See e.g. Dowty *et al.*, pp. 145–9, 160–1; Küng, p. 40. The accusation that this approach confuses Frege with Carnap is a criticism directed by Evans ([1], p. 63) against Kaplan. For the confusion, see Kaplan [1], p. 717.

[109] [3], §476. Cf. Crocco [2], p. 181 n. 34.   [110] [6], p. 14 n. 37. Cf. [3], pp. 4–5.

[111] [2], pp. 139, 142–3. So too Bell [1], p. 78.

At any rate, we cannot manage without a sense–reference distinction for concept-expressions: for it is obvious (though the point is widely ducked) that exactly the same considerations as compel that distinction in the case of proper names also compel it in the case of concept-expressions—indeed compel it for *all* linguistic expressions.[112] The property (concept)[113] of being a lapwing is the same property as the property of being a peewit—the Carnapian intensions of the concept-expressions 'is a lapwing' and 'is a peewit' are one and the same—but those concept-expressions differ in 'semantic' sense (§14) in virtue of the difference in linguistic expression used to refer to the relevant property, and they may differ in 'epistemological' sense inasmuch as they may be keyed to distinct ways of thinking about the property in question—ways that are distinct by the intuitive criterion of difference. Hence the sense of a concept-expression cannot be identified with its Carnapian intension without eliding the phenomena that, as Frege was the first to see clearly, require our semantic theory to include a level of description marking distinct modes of presentation of a concept or property. The failure in (for example) the Montague tradition to incorporate a proper understanding of Fregean sense generates difficulties for its treatment of strict proper names—for such proper names are rigid designators in the sense that they refer to the same objects at all indices where the relevant objects exist—as well as difficulties for its treatment of concept-expressions, which are rigid designators, in the same sense, of concepts or properties. This is what one would expect: for in the case both of strict proper names and of concept-expressions, co-referring expressions have the same Carnapian intension, and so inconveniently turn out to have the same sense if senses are being identified with Carnapian intensions.

Thirdly, it is crucial that the identification proceed only in respect of semantically *simple* concept-expressions, for it is possible for *complex* concept-expressions which have distinct references—because they are composed of items having distinct references—to enjoy the same Carnapian intensions. In Kit Fine's terminology, the procedure is structuralist at a global level, and empirical at the local level:[114] to apply the empirical criterion at the global level would be too crude in the manner indicated. Globally, the identity-conditions of complex concepts are structuralist, or hyperintensional: two such concepts are identical just if they are composed of the same bits in the

---

[112] Künne ([1], pp. 212–15) appears to think that abstract general terms cannot give rise to Fregean informativeness problems, but I see no reason to exempt them (cf. Bealer [4], p. 55 n. 47). Abstract objects can present different 'semantic' and 'epistemological' aspects to cognizers as readily as do concrete objects like planets.

[113] Recall (n. 42) that for the moment I am not distinguishing concepts and properties.

[114] [1], pp. 57–62.

same ways.[115] But at the atomic level sameness of bits is settled by empirical criteria: for atomic parts of complex concepts count as the same just if they are identical Carnapian intensions. An old example, much exploited by Leibniz, who introduced the modern terminology of extension and intension,[116] will illustrate the point: 'triangular' and 'trilateral' are satisfied by the same objects in respect of any given world/time pair; but the concepts they refer to are distinct, given that they are have corresponding semantically significant components ('-angular' and '-lateral') which are not co-referential.[117] That is, what it takes to *understand* 'trilateral' is distinct from what it takes to understand 'triangular': it is a consequence of the notion of reference I favour that we are forced to say that these words introduce distinct concepts or properties.[118] Since our general account of the reference of semantically complex expressions will exploit the notion of a recursive construction from semantically simple components and suitable modes of combination, any referential difference between two simple words will generate a referential difference between the complex expressions they go to compose.[119]

Fourthly, the identification of concepts or properties with suitable Carnapian intensions is not, as such, a nominalistic move. The identification of concepts with functions from possible worlds and times (and perhaps other indices) to sets of objects imports sets of various kinds into our ontology: these include (i) the sets of objects (actual and merely possible) that compose the ranges of the relevant functions; (ii) non-actual possible worlds, which are most naturally identified with sets of truth-value-tagged sentences; and (iii) functions, which, though it is plausible that they should not literally be *identified* with sets of ordered *n*-tuples,[120] can at any rate in some contexts and for some purposes be *proxied* by suitable such sets. Rather than claiming that the identification of concepts with Carnapian intensions shows how to 'analyse out' universals, where the various species of sets (including those going proxy for functions) invoked by the analysis supposedly offer us a less mysterious ontology than one containing universals, it seems to me more plausible to say that the

---

[115] See e.g. Cresswell, p. 72; Menzel; Lewis [8], p. 3.

[116] See [3], IV. xvii, §8 ([1], V, p. 469). On the background of the terminology in the Port-Royal *Logic* see Kneale and Kneale, pp. 318–19; Hamacher-Hermes, pp. 43–8.

[117] Cf. Leibniz's notes on a letter from des Bosses of 12 Dec. 1712 ([1], ii, p. 471; [1], vii, p. 236); Nuchelmans [5], pp. 223–7.

[118] Hence I do not think the laissez-faire policy favoured by Lewis at [3], p. 55, is an option. Similarly, Church's notion of synonymous isomorphism ([5], p. 67) is not sufficiently fine-grained for our purposes.

[119] See further on this point Hobbes [1], I. i, §3 (with the editors' remarks on pp. 126–7); Bolzano [2], §§25–6; Carnap [3], §14; Lewis [1], p. 20; Putnam [2], pp. 26–7; Donaho, p. 49.

[120] I return to this important point in §§33 and 88 below.

analysis tells us what universals really are, not necessarily by reducing them to sets—at least, not if one wishes, as I do, to preserve some ontological distance between functions and sets—but by drawing constitutive connections between one sort of abstract object (universals, identified with functions) and another sort (sets).[121]

17 Carnapian Intensions and Understanding

The reason that Frege gives to Husserl in his letter (§15) for not treating the objects satisfying a concept-expression as its referent is inadequate. The fact that a concept-expression may be empty without that expression's ceasing to be scientifically useful is of course correct, and important, but it cannot do more than indicate that in such cases it is not an option to say that the concept-expression has *no* referent: the point does not show that, where a concept-expression *is* satisfied by one or more objects, those objects are not the referent of the expression. We might satisfy Frege's demand that scientifically useful concept-expressions always be assigned a referent by finding some appropriate object—say, the empty set[122]—to serve as the referent of empty such expressions, while maintaining that non-empty concept-expressions refer to the objects satisfying them.[123] The objection to *this* (nominalist) position—which, so far as its treatment of non-empty concept-expressions goes, certainly was, as we have seen (§7), the one adopted by Ockham,[124] has been standard in both recent and not so recent semantic theory, and is imputed by Frege to Husserl[125]—is that it renders impossible a satisfactory semantics, not for *empty* concept-expressions, but for *non-empty* concept-expressions, since it is subject to a certain vicious circularity.[126]

---

[121] Bealer objects to the identification of properties (and propositions: see §18 below) with functions (or with sets) on the score of unnaturalness: e.g. [1], pp. 46, 90; [2], p. 1; [4], pp. 20–2. The charge is well answered by J. Moore [1], pp. 254–5. Bealer further objects that the identification does nothing to solve Mates's problem (see Mates [1]). But Mates's problem, like Frege's puzzle (of which it is a special case), can only be solved by appealing to a level of sense: as I in effect claimed in §15, in response to Hylton, no degree of hyperintensionality in individuating reference-level entities obviates the need to recognize a level of sense.

[122] Cf. Lewis [5], p. 11.

[123] This is in effect Frege's strategy for dealing with empty definite descriptions: [10], I, §11.

[124] We have to do here with the first sense of signification defined by Ockham at [1], I, §33. The Ockhamist approach is followed by Hobbes: [1], I. ii, §9.

[125] [22], pp. 94–8.

[126] On the usual interpretation of it, Leśniewski's Ontology would be subject to a similar difficulty: see Trentman [2]; Sinisi [1] and [2]; Lejewski, p. 17; Henry, pp. 16–18; Küng, ch. 8. This interpretation is challenged by Simons: [4] and [8], pp. 19, 142–3.

For suppose that the referent of the concept-expression 'is green' is all the green objects. That means (given the conception of reference we are working with) that in order to understand this concept-expression an understander needs to be acquainted with those objects, and needs to think of them—and think of them *as* green—when entertaining that concept-expression. But that in turn means that the understander's grasp of that concept-expression will consist in knowledge of the truth-values of a (presumably infinite) number of sentences of the form '*a* is green' (where we may suppose that '*a*' holds place for a suitable name or demonstrative expression, referring to the sort of object that can be coloured). Quite apart from the surely excessive demand thereby placed on understanders, the requirement subjects the understander to an intolerable epistemic bind, for it is plausible that, in order to know whether a sentence of the form '*a* is green' is true, one must first understand it. A vicious circularity ensues. Of course, there must be *some* connection between understanding a simple observational concept-expression such as 'is green' and identifying particular objects as green. Plausibly, to understand that concept-expression is to have (at least) the ability to settle the truth of sentences of the form '*a* is green'—and, equally, '*a* is not green'[127]—in favourable viewing conditions. But having that ability falls well short of knowing, in advance of giving consideration to any particular sentence of that form, which objects are green. The position which Frege is attacking, and which was indeed Ockham's, is thus untenable, though not for the reason Frege gave.

We must be careful in our handling of the charge of vicious circularity. For it is important to note that (a version of) the circularity here in question both obtains and is *not* vicious in the case of analytic truths (falsehoods), where it *is* a condition of understanding such statements that one know that they are true (false). Further, in the case of understanding strict proper names, it is a condition on grasping such a name that one know the truth-value of statements of the form 'This is *a*', where '*a*' is the name in question and 'this' demonstrates a (contextually relevant) candidate referent: so an argument of the form offered in the previous paragraph would prove too much if it were run on analytic truths or an example involving a strict proper name instead of a concept-expression.[128] In both these cases (grasp of analytic truths, grasp of the meanings of proper names), knowledge of meaning is dependent on knowledge

---

[127] Cf. Adam Smith, §7, p. 207; Wittgenstein [5], p. 32 ([2], p. 14), and I, §429.

[128] Note (cf. §15 above) that it is crucial to this point that in the case of a sentence like 'This is *a*', where '*a*' is a strict proper name, the demonstrative expression purports to refer to the *referent* of '*a*', whereas in the case of sentences like '*a* is green' or 'this is green', the subject-term normally purports to refer not to the referent of 'is green'—the concept or property of being green—but to an object *satisfying* that concept or property.

of the truth-values of appropriate statements that make use of the term or terms whose meaning is just what is in question: yet the consequent circularity is clearly innocent. So it would be wrong to argue that the circularity we have identified is vicious quite generally.[129] The fact is that the argument I offered in the previous paragraph cannot be generalized beyond the particular type of example used: our grasp of an empirical concept-expression like 'is green' cannot consist in an acquaintance with the objects in its extension (acquaintance with all the green objects as such), for that would have a devastating effect on the integrity of the synthetic statements in which such concept-expressions occur, and on the very possibility of a posteriori knowledge: in effect, it would render empirical investigation, broadly construed, impossible.

As far as the charge of vicious circularity goes, the Ockhamist position can be remedied if, instead of identifying the referent of a non-empty concept-expression with just the objects satisfying it, we identify that referent with the *set* of such objects.[130] The move from the concrete (at least in the case of objects satisfying concept-expressions like 'is green') to the abstract obviates the circularity problem, because there is no obligation to construe acquaintance with a set as requiring acquaintance with its members (together with the knowledge that they are its members). Instead, it is open to us to say that it suffices for acquaintance with a set of objects that one have knowledge of the *membership condition* of that set—so moving from an extensional constraint on the content of the relevant state of acquaintance to an intensional one[131]—an achievement which we can, in turn, identify with the state of understanding the concept-expression in question, a state which, as we have seen, involves (in part) having the ability, in favourable circumstances, to settle whether a given object is a member of the corresponding set or not. Being acquainted with the set of green objects is not, on this account, identical with having the ability, in favourable conditions, to settle whether a given object is green or not, but it might plausibly be taken to be sufficient for being so acquainted that one have that ability. (There is no prospect here of a more informative specification of the membership condition, which is that an object is a member of the set if and only if it is green. But that is no objection to the account.) Having this general ability is not constituted by knowledge of the truth of any relevant synthetic statements; which is the result we require to avoid the circularity problem.

---

[129] Contra Carruthers, pp. 63–5.

[130] This is a standard approach in the Montague tradition: see e.g. Dowty *et al.*, p. 144; Partee [1], p. 54. Note that identifying the referent of a concept-expression like 'is green' with the *set* of green objects is conceptually distinct from identifying that referent with all the green objects (i.e. with the members of the set): McGinn, pp. 66–7. See §79 below.

[131] Cf. Hale [2], p. 188; Tiles, pp. 38–9.

But of course we cannot rest content with an identification of the concept that the concept-expression 'is green' refers to with the set of green things. For one thing, we need to take into account a point that was noted by Burleigh, in opposition to an Ockhamist account.[132] Green things are constantly coming into and going out of existence, but the concept-expression 'is green' is not at the same time undergoing a change of meaning: hence we cannot identify the meaning (referent) of that concept-expression with the set of green objects at any given time. Strictly, Burleigh's point would be met by extending the membership of the set of green objects to include all objects which ever have been, are, and ever will be green.[133] But this adjustment does not go far enough to resolve two residual problems.

One problem is that the adjustment does not take account of modal discourse. Since sets necessarily have the members they have, a statement such as 'That wall might have been painted green', said of a wall which is painted white and remains so throughout the period of its existence, would come out false, whereas it ought (in normal circumstances) to be true. The other problem is that, although we have allowed that knowledge of the membership condition of a set is sufficient for acquaintance with that set, it would be quite implausible to hold that such knowledge is also necessary. For we must allow that someone who knows *de re* which things are members of the set in question, rather than having cognizance of an antecedently given condition (§1) that the members satisfy—there may, after all, be no such condition, as in the case of the miscellany I constructed in §1 (the centre of gravity of the universe, . . .), or so we presumed—is acquainted with the set. But then it might be held that it is at least in principle possible for someone to be acquainted with the set of green things—even when this is taken to contain all objects that are at any time green—without knowing that they are green, that is, without realizing that their satisfying *that* condition is exactly what makes them members of this set, and so without genuinely understanding the concept-expression 'is green'. For suppose it were to turn out that the §1 miscellany, contrary to our presumption, fell under a purely general concept after all: we could hardly require that anyone acquainted with the set know that condition, since as a matter of fact we *do not* demand as much. It follows that in order to understand the concept-expression 'is green' it is not sufficient to be acquainted with the set of (any or all of) the objects that actually are

---

[132] [2], p. 9.7–16.

[133] As Ockham does in defining the second sense of signification at [1], I, §33. Cf. Russell's 1903 theory of denoting, according to which, in assertions about a man, some man, any man etc., 'the whole human race is involved in my assertion: if any man who ever existed or will exist had not existed or been going to exist, the purport of my proposition would have been different' ([3], §62).

(at any time) green. It is, of course, *necessary* to be acquainted with that set in order to understand the concept-expression 'is green': for we have allowed that knowledge of the membership condition of the set suffices for acquaintance with it, and we have also identified knowledge of that membership condition with understanding the concept-expression in question. Perhaps it will help if I map out the relations between the various notions in play. Taking '→' to represent, as usual, 'suffices for' or 'has as a necessary condition', and '←' for its converse, we have the following:

> understanding the concept-expression 'is green' ↔ knowing the membership condition of the set of green things → being able to settle, in favourable conditions, which objects are green → acquaintance with the set of green things ← having *de re* acquaintance with all the green things.

From this it is immediately clear, given that none of the one-way implications can be strengthened to biconditionals, that being acquainted with the set of green things is not sufficient, and that having *de re* acquaintance with all the green things is not necessary, for understanding the concept-expression 'is green'.

We simultaneously solve both the problems mooted in the last paragraph if we adopt the strategy I have already recommended, and identify simple Fregean concepts with what I have been calling their Carnapian intensions. That strategy yields the right result for modal discourse, and it also delivers something acquaintance with which we may plausibly take to be necessary *and* sufficient for understanding corresponding concept-expressions. It might seem here as if an analogue of the second problem threatened the proposed identification: could one not imagine a subject acquainted *de re*, so to speak, with the Carnapian intension of 'is green'—that is, acquainted with the mapping from possible worlds and times to sets of objects—and acquainted with it *as* the Carnapian intension of 'is green', but ignorant of the meaning of 'is green', in the sense that he or she would have no substantial sense of what all these objects had in common? No: the worry underestimates the epistemic achievement of being genuinely acquainted '*de re*' with the Carnapian intension of 'is green'. The point is that acquaintance with a mapping from possible worlds to sets of objects (we can abstract from time and other indices here) would require acquaintance with the relevant possible worlds themselves, and that in turn would require one to know (of all worlds other than the actual world, which we can presumably identify ostensively) which sentences are true (and false) at any given such world; for, as I have suggested (§16), that is plausibly how non-actual possible worlds are individuated. Hence one could not be merely acquainted '*de re*' with the Carnapian intension of 'is green' without knowing, in the case of worlds other than the actual world, which things were green in those worlds, and that would in turn require one to think of the green objects in those worlds *as* green (as satisfying the schema '*a* is green').

But one might now wonder whether a recurrence of the vicious circularity problem that plagued Ockham's semantics could undermine the possibility of acquaintance with the Carnapian intension of 'is green': would not such acquaintance have to embrace knowledge of which sentences (and, in particular, which sentences of the form '*a* is green') were true? No. As I observed in passing above, one can (and presumably must) identify the actual world ostensively, not in terms of lists of truth-value-tagged sentences. In fact, quite apart from the circularity problem, it would be impossible to have an understanding of 'is green' based on knowledge of (i) which objects were (in fact) green in the actual world and (ii) truth-values of sentences of the form '*a* is green' in respect of non-actual possible worlds, for that would destroy the univocity of the concept-expression 'is green': it would have one meaning in its application to the actual world, where it would refer to the objects which are in fact green, and another in its application to non-actual possible worlds, where it would refer to a function mapping those worlds to sets of objects—just the objects satisfying the schema '*a* is green' in those worlds (again I abstract from time and other indices). Knowledge of the meaning of the expression 'is green' would, on this basis, be *de re* (in the sense of requiring acquaintance with the objects in its extension) in respect of the actual world but not in respect of non-actual worlds; but that entails that 'is green' would have meant something different (understanding it would have required a different ability) had some other world been actual, which contradicts the univocity of the expression.

If we are to preserve the univocity of the concept-expression 'is green', we must insist that acquaintance with the Carnapian intension of 'is green' is constituted by knowledge of the membership condition of this intension; that intension can for these purposes be represented by a set, comprising ordered pairs of world/time pairs and objects. The achievement of knowing the membership condition of the relevant intension, I argued in the last paragraph but one, is not distinct (as we saw it *was* distinct in the case of the simple set of green objects) from having '*de re*' acquaintance with the relevant set (representing the intension). Since knowledge of the membership condition of this set (representing the mapping from world/time pairs and other indices to green objects) is tantamount to knowledge of the membership condition of the set of objects constituting the range of the mapping—that is, the set of actual and possible green objects—and since knowledge of the membership condition of the set of actual and possible green objects is, as I have suggested, equivalent to understanding the concept-expression which collects the set of actual and possible green objects, we have it that acquaintance with the Carnapian intension of 'is green' is equivalent to understanding the concept-expression 'is green'. So while we may agree that one cannot simply identify the referent of 'is green' with the set of (actual) green objects, it would be going too far to say with Colin McGinn that 'set theory is . . . not the right format for stating semantic truths'.[134] The problem with the rejected identification is not that the referent is identified with (or represented by) a set, but that the set chosen is the wrong one. Indeed, McGinn himself thinks (following Frege) that properties are functions from objects to truth-values and, as I have indicated (§16), though a simple *identification* of functions with sets is objectionable on metaphysical grounds, in some contexts and for some purposes there is no question but that functions can be *represented* by sets. But again, selecting McGinn's favoured candidates to serve as proxies for properties involves alighting on the wrong things: for if sets of (actual) green objects are too crude to figure as the referent of 'is green'—and we have seen that they are—sets representing functions from those objects to truth-values will be too crude for exactly the same reasons.[135]

18 Carnapian Intensions and Russellian Propositions

The proposed identification of concepts with Carnapian intensions enables us to arrive at a more sophisticated treatment of Russellian propositions. Once we have suitable Carnapian intensions in place as the referents of semantically simple concept-expressions—as what simple concepts or properties *are*—we can construe the referents of simple categorical sentences as suitable constructions of objects and concepts or properties, so understood. To deal with the general case—and in particular the case of sentences involving complex concept-expressions—it seems best to say that a Russellian proposition is to be identified with the objects, simple concepts or properties, and structures of

---

[134] McGinn, p. 68. Cf. Cocchiarella [2], pp. 69–70.

[135] Barwise and Etchemendy go too far in the opposite direction from McGinn. Having identified properties with simple sets, they acknowledge that 'the same set could not have had different members, though the same property could well have applied to different things' (p. 129). However, they continue, 'all this means is that, had the world been different, the same property would have had a different set-theoretic counterpart, not that the modelling technique is faulty' (pp. 129–30). But the univocity of concept-expressions across possible worlds ensures that corresponding properties are not varied merely in virtue of a variation in *extensions*, without prejudice to the fact that concept-expressions can of course vary in their *meanings* across models, i.e. from one structure of possible worlds to another.

composition given by the phrase marker which specifies how the governing sentence is built up.[136] That phrase marker I conceive in functional terms.[137] In pursuing here the phrase-structure approach to grammar, I do not necessarily mean to rule out alternatives, such as the so-called 'word grammar' or dependency theory, provided these alternatives replicate the functional nature of the phrase-structure approach. That functionality will be crucial to my account of unity.

Now the identification of Russellian propositions with the structures given by their governing sentences' phrase markers allows us to make finer grained distinctions among propositions than the mere appeal to the notion of a Carnapian intension would enable us to do: for on any natural application of that notion to sentences taken as unarticulated wholes, logically equivalent sentences (and so all tautologies, for example) would emerge with the same Carnapian intension,[138] whereas what we want to be in a position to say is that sentences that are differently constructed out of the same lexical components, or identically constructed out of different lexical components, or differently constructed out of different lexical components, will normally (though not invariably: see §§21 and 67 below) have distinct referents matching the semantic differences between their basic lexical components and/or the way these are put together. We want to be able to say, in general, that pairs of sentences which, taken as unarticulated wholes, share the same Carnapian intension, such as 'The shape in the diagram is a circle'/'The shape in the diagram is a locus of co-planar points equidistant from a given point on the same plane', or 'She fasted for a fortnight'/'She fasted for fourteen days', have distinct referents matching the distinctness of their lexical components and/or syntactic structure.[139] So the identity-conditions of Russellian propositions must, like those of complex concepts (§16), be structuralist or hyperintensional. The view one commonly encounters, and which derives not only from Carnap but more immediately from Kripke's semantics for modal logic,[140] that propositions are sets of possible worlds or functions from possible worlds (and perhaps other indices) to truth-values[141] is simply too crude to do justice to the

---

[136] Cf. Pelham and Urquhart, pp. 313–17; Dummett [9], pp. 158–9. Here I presuppose that phrase-structure analyses of (disambiguated) sentences are unique: cf. Chomsky [1], pp. 26–32, 87 n. 2. The assumption is one of temporary convenience only, and I relax it in Ch. 6.

[137] Cf. Wittgenstein [1], §§3.318, 4.24, 5.47.

[138] Lewis [1], p. 8; Bealer [4], p. 20; Pelham and Urquhart, p. 318.

[139] Cf. Kaplan [2], pp. 494–5; Zalta [1], pp. 3–9, 58, 78–81; King [1], pp. 526–30; [5], pp. 54–5.

[140] Kripke [1], pp. 65–7; cf. King [4], pp. 564–5.

[141] See e.g. Stalnaker [1]; Cresswell, pp. 4, 100; Lewis [2], p. 163 (though cf. p. 176); [6], p. 37; Sainsbury [2], p. 137; Carpenter, p. 19. On Montague, see Cocchiarella [2], pp. 48–50; on Cresswell, see King [5], pp. 111–20.

semantical facts, if only because it assimilates all logical and mathematical truths to a single proposition.[142] The strategy of identifying simple concepts with Carnapian intensions cannot be generalized to semantically more complex entities.

Once again, it is important to stress that the complex structured entities that we are identifying with Russellian propositions are the *referents* of declarative sentences, not their *senses*: the sentences 'Lapwings are in decline' and 'Peewits are in decline' express the same Russellian proposition at the level of reference, since they are identically constructed save for their employment of distinct concept-expressions which nevertheless have the same referent (Carnapian intension). But though they express the same Russellian proposition they do so in different 'semantical' ways (§14), and may be keyed to distinct 'epistemological' ways of thinking about the proposition expressed (ibid.); that is, they are fitted up to express distinct Fregean Thoughts. Note that in 'General Semantics' Lewis (i) appears simply to *identify* what he calls meanings with 'semantically interpreted phrase markers minus their terminal nodes' (the terminal nodes being the lexical entries, words or morphemes that are arbitrary labels of these intensions), that is, 'finite ordered trees having at each node a category and an appropriate intension',[143] and he (ii) makes no room, alongside Carnapian intensions and meanings—both items that, by my lights, inhabit the level of reference—for Fregean senses. On both of these points my approach differs. (i) For me, the phrase markers by which Russellian propositions are, as I put it above, 'given' (that is, referred to), are *linguistic representations* of meanings and not those meanings themselves: the latter are not pieces of symbolic language but worldly entities structured in the way specified by the corresponding phrase marker. We might call these structured, worldly entities 'phrase markers *in re*'. (ii) As I have made clear, I recognize different 'semantical' and 'epistemological' ways of referring to and thinking about entities at the level of reference.

That, then, is the way in which we can mitigate the inconcinnity between Frege's candidate for the referents of declarative sentences and mine (§15). Frege made truth-values the referents of declarative sentences, and one of his motivations for so doing was, as we saw (ibid.), the desire to do justice in our semantic theory to the 'striving for truth' which is such a vital feature of our lives and linguistic practices. I countered that we could take sufficient cognizance of that feature, whose centrality in our lives I freely accept, by making Russellian

---

[142] Cf. Soames, pp. 197–202; Menzel, pp. 61–3.

[143] [1], p. 14; cf. Pelham and Urquhart, pp. 315–16. On categorial grammar, see Wood; Carpenter, ch. 4.

propositions the referents of declarative sentences, for although at that stage we had not yet developed any very sophisticated understanding of the nature of Russellian propositions, we could at least say that they are the meanings of declarative sentences, and that it is constitutive of such sentences, and of their propositionally structured meanings (§4), that they are capable of taking a truth-value. Now, however, we are able to draw a closer connection between Russellian propositions and truth-values, as follows. For simplicity I consider the case of a proposition referred to by a simple categorical sentence: each such proposition is composed of an object and a simple concept, and since concepts are, on the approach I have been considering, to be identified with mappings from possible worlds and times (and any other indices that we need to include) to objects, it follows that a Russellian proposition, conceived as constructed out of an object and a concept, determines a function from those objects and concepts to truth-values. The function is such (again I focus on the simplest case) that its value is determined as true just in case the object is in the range of the function with which we are identifying the concept for the appropriate indices. Note here that the points made in §17 concerning acquaintance with the Carnapian intension of 'is green'—in particular the point that being acquainted with the Carnapian intension of 'is green' does not require one to know which objects are green—also ensure that acquaintance with this function will not require the understander of its corresponding sentence to know the truth-value of a Russellian proposition, which would be in breach of the constraint established in Chapter I.

I have identified Russellian propositions with phrase markers *in re*, which are abstract trees. This is a more sophisticated move than the crude identification of Russellian propositions with ordered *n*-tuples that I mentioned at the beginning of this chapter; but an objection that is sometimes raised against the latter identification would, if successful, also work against the identification I have proposed. This is the familiar 'Benacerraf' objection, which states that we cannot coherently identify objects such as numbers or propositions with abstract mathematical entities such as sets or trees if there are several distinct but equally good abstract candidates to serve as the target relata of the identification.[144] For if there is more than one candidate set with which to identify the number three, say, and if there is no principled basis on which to make the choice among at least some rival candidates, given that arithmetic can be adequately reconstructed whichever of these candidates we select, assuming suitable further choices in each case, surely that shows,

[144] For discussion, see Benacerraf's original paper, Hale [2], ch. 8; J. Moore [1]; Jubien [2], §I; Potter [2], pp. 64–5, 150; King [5], pp. 7–9, 47, 63–4.

so runs the objection, that the number three *is not* a set. *Any* progression of the right kind can model the natural numbers; so no one of them can *be* the numbers. But whatever force the 'Benacerraf' point may have in its application to the attempted identification of numbers with sets,[145] I do not think it should be regarded as carrying weight in the present context, where we are concerned with the nature of propositions and the question of their unity. Here it seems plausible that if we can give an account of that unity in respect of *some* theoretically adequate abstract reconstruction of propositions, we will have done all that is required to meet the challenge of elucidating propositional unity. It would be prudent to concede that the constraints I have argued to be operative in determining the identity-conditions and ontological status of propositions may make viable more than one abstract reconstruction of them; moreover, it is likely that the reconstruction I favour is itself indeterminate in various respects, permitting more than one way of filling out the characterization. Perhaps indeed any account of the nature of abstract objects like propositions will be obliged to leave some details unfixed; but I do not see this as being, in itself, a matter for embarrassment. If my account of the nature of the proposition does turn out to be just one among other, equally good such accounts, then the upshot will be not that my explanation of propositional unity is thereby invalidated, but that its validity will be local to the particular reconstruction offered, and that in order to give the preferred solution wider application it will need to be subjected to a further process of abstraction.

The 'Benacerraf' objection is by no means the only difficulty to have been raised in respect of the identification of propositions with abstract structures such as mathematical trees. I conclude this section with an examination of a modal argument that has been offered by George Bealer against what he calls the 'propositional-complex theory'—the identification of propositions with ordered sets, sequences, abstract trees, or mereological sums.[146] The argument is directed explicitly against the identification of propositions with ordered sets; but, like the 'Benacerraf' objection, it would, if successful, net not only the identification of Russellian propositions with ordered *n*-tuples, but also their identification with what I am calling phrase markers *in re*. The argument proceeds as follows. We are asked to accept the following 'intuitively true sentence':

> Every x is such that, necessarily, for every y, either it is possible that $x = y$ or it is impossible that $x = y$.

---

[145] For some cogent doubts on this score, see Wright [1], §xv.

[146] [3], pp. 21–3, 28–9; [4], pp. 22–3.

Bealer symbolizes this as

(1) $\forall x \,\square\, \forall y(\text{Possible } [x = y] \vee \text{Impossible } [x = y])$,

where '$[x = y]$' is a name of the proposition that x is identical to y. By the propositional-complex theory, (1) is equivalent to:

(2) $\forall x \,\square\, \forall y(\text{Possible } <x, \text{identity}, y> \vee \text{Impossible } <x, \text{identity}, y>)$.

Bealer then splits the argument into two branches according as '$<x$, identity, $y>$' is construed as having narrow scope or wide scope. But we can ignore the wide-scope option, because it is clear that that expression either has anyway, or can be treated as having, narrow scope: for either it is a strict proper name referring to a proposition, in which case it has narrow scope *de jure*, or (as I would prefer) it is a definite description *necessarily* satisfied by the relevant proposition, in which case scope distinctions play no role in its semantics, and it may as well be treated as having narrow scope. On the assumption that the expression in question has narrow scope, Bealer now suggests that (2) implies

(3) $\forall x \,\square\, \forall y \exists v(v = <x, \text{identity}, y>)$.

But this in turn implies, by the principle that, necessarily, a set (or tree, etc.) exists only if its members (constituents) exist:

(4) $\forall x \,\square\, \exists v(v = x)$,

which states that everything necessarily exists, 'a manifest falsehood'.

But unfortunately this argument rests on an equivocation. Putting the matter in terms of the standard method of interpreting the modal operators as quantifiers over possible worlds, the argument works by deriving the existence, at all possible worlds, of a certain proposition. It then follows that this proposition's constituents exist at every possible world. Since the proposition in question in effect contains an arbitrary actual object as one of its constituents, it follows finally that all objects x belonging to the actual world exist at all possible worlds. How we respond to the argument depends on exactly how we settle the identity-conditions of propositions in the current context. Suppose first that we insist, naturally enough, that a proposition exists at a world w if, and only if, its constituents exist at w. In that case it will not in general be true that, for any actual object a, a given proposition containing a will exist at all possible worlds: plainly that proposition will only exist at worlds where a exists. On this approach (1), and the 'intuitively true sentence' it formalizes, will be false. Suppose, alternatively, that a proposition exists at a world w so long as each of its constituents exists at some world (not necessarily the same world) accessible to w.[147] In that case, assuming a background logic of S5, (1) can count as true, but (3) will not entail (4), since the proposition that x is identical with y may exist at a world, on this view, without x's existing at that world: we cannot, therefore, conclude from (3) that x is a necessary existent. The most we can conclude is

(5) $\forall x \, \Box \, \Diamond \, \exists v (v = x)$, i.e. $\forall x \, \exists v (v = x)$.

But (5) is harmless.

19 Russellian Propositions and Functionality

I have said that Russellian propositions are composed (in the simplest case) of an object and a simple concept, and that brings us back to the question of their adequate representation. What tells against the ordered-pair style of representation mentioned in §13 is surely the point that, though an entity such as <Socrates, wisdom> is no doubt a unity of some sort, the sheer ordering of the elements Socrates and wisdom does not as such seem to import the kind of togetherness that is characteristic of the proposition *that Socrates is wise*.[148] What appears to be missing from the representation is something signalling the presence of a function that takes Socrates and wisdom as its arguments and delivers the unified proposition *that Socrates is wise* as its value, thereby making the difference between the mere aggregate of Socrates and wisdom on the one hand and that unified proposition on the other.[149] Hence we need a representation along the lines of u(Socrates, wisdom), where u is the unifying function in question. (In the general case, a phrase marker *in re* thought of as a functional structure can itself be conceived as the value of a unifying function.[150]) But here there might seem to be a clash between the proposed functional model and the principle of compositionality for reference, which I have accepted (§14). Can Russellian propositions, conceived as values of appropriate unifying functions, be simultaneously taken to be constructed out of the arguments to those functions (and perhaps the functions themselves) as parts composing a whole? The question beckons us into a familiar area of difficulty in the exegesis of Frege, one which has

---

[147] I take it that this is Bealer's own view: [3], p. 29.   [148] Cf. Hylton [2], p. 134.

[149] Cf. Frege [1], §2. Frege seems to have envisaged a unifying role for the horizontal in *Begriffsschrift*: Carl [2], pp. 54–5.

[150] Cf. Dever, p. 636.

been a battleground involving Dummett, Geach, and others, the issue being to what extent Frege regarded concept-expressions, their senses, and their referents (concepts) as functions, and in what sense, if any, he sought to combine a functional model of sentential or propositional complexity with a part–whole model.[151] At least so far as concerns the level of reference, which is what principally interests us here, it is uncontroversial that Frege did adopt a functional approach, regarding concepts as functions from objects to truth-values,[152] and he also, in one passage (in 'Über Sinn und Bedeutung'), suggested that truth-values, as referents of sentences, are wholes composed of parts (objects and concepts), though he later seems to have retracted that view.[153]

It has been urged by Dummett and others that the suggestion which Frege briefly entertained and later abandoned—that truth-values are wholes composed of the objects and concepts on which they are functionally dependent—was an egregious error: for how can the value of a function for an argument be a *whole composed* of the argument and the function?[154] In making this claim, Dummett is influenced by the thought that, 'given only the value of a function for some argument, it is not possible to recover the function or the argument'—as Kenneth Olson nicely puts it, functions 'pass away without a trace, leaving only their "value" behind'[155]—whereas, in the case of a whole comprising parts, 'we naturally suppose that [such a whole] is uniquely analysable into its ultimate constituents, and that the parts of [this whole] may be discerned by scrutiny of it'; accordingly, insofar as we conceive the referent of a whole as a function of the referents of its parts, Dummett avers that we should '*never* say that the reference of the part is part of the reference of the whole'.[156] In Dummett's view, the part–whole model and the functional model are mutually exclusive: according to his reading of Frege, the former model applies at the level of sense, the latter at the level of reference. (Geach in effect agrees that the models are mutually exclusive, but takes Frege to favour a functional model at the level of sense as well as at the level of reference.) At the level of sense, Dummett claims, we must already know the sense of a concept-expression in order to grasp a Thought of which it is a component,

---

[151] See Geach [8], pp. 149–50; [9], pp. 443–5; Dummett [2], pp. 293–4; [3], pp. 249–53, 264–70; [4], pp. 190–8; Rumfitt [1], pp. 610–12; Sullivan [1].

[152] See esp. [5]. The treatment of concepts as functions was anticipated at [1], §9, though the idea there seems to be that they are functions to possible states of affairs: cf. Burge [2], p. 100; Currie [1], p. 153.

[153] [6], p. 35 ([21], p. 150). For the later repudiation of this view, see [26], p. 275; [27], p. 20. Cf. Dummett [2], pp. 159–60; [3], pp. 172, 265–6, 272; [9], p. 157; Currie [1], pp. 154–5.

[154] See the passages of Dummett cited in the previous note; Bell [1], p. 51; Beaney, p. 165.

[155] Olson, p. 81.   [156] [4], p. 190.

'whereas we must be able to identify the value of a function in advance of knowing that it is the value of that function'.[157]

Now I have already indicated that we are concerned in this context with the level of reference, not the level of sense. Dummett's epistemological argument against the applicability of a functional model to the level of sense is nevertheless of prima-facie relevance to my concerns because for me the level of reference *is* a level of understanding—indeed it is the *fundamental* level of understanding (though one that does not render the level of sense superfluous). Translated into my terms, the claim will be that the grasping of a concept (which is what understanding a concept-expression consists in) is prior to, and cannot be construed in terms of, the grasping of Russellian propositions which that concept goes to compose: in order to understand a sentence (grasp the corresponding Russellian proposition), one must *already* understand its constituent concept-expressions (grasp the corresponding concepts). This is a claim that I can simply accept, for I am not construing Russellian propositions as values of the functions with which I am identifying concepts (rather, concepts are mappings from appropriate indices to objects), but as values of special unifying functions, which take objects and concepts as arguments or, in the general case, as functional structures given by appropriate phrase markers (as phrase markers *in re*). (Of course, Dummett's claim can be repeated in respect of one's grasp of the relevant unifying functions or functional structures, but in this case it seems obviously to lack plausibility: why should one suppose that in order to grasp a unified proposition one must have *already* grasped the functional structure which, given the relevant arguments, produces that proposition as its value? Grasping that functional structure, in its application to the relevant arguments, *is* grasping the unified proposition.[158]) Again, insofar as the objection to Frege's fleeting suggestion that we might combine a functional with a part–whole model at the level of reference turns on the implausibility of construing *truth-values*, which certainly appear to be simple entities, as wholes composed of objectual and conceptual parts, it does not touch my position, which is that *Russellian propositions*, not truth-values, are the referents of declarative sentences; for Russellian propositions are quite evidently composite entities. But, when we have factored out these two points, relevant to Frege's semantical disposition but irrelevant to mine, the core of Dummett's objection to Frege remains as a threat to my position, namely: how can Russellian propositions be *both* wholes composed of parts *and* values of

---

[157] [4], p. 190; cf. [2], pp. 293–4; [3], pp. 251–3; 267–9; [4], pp. 26–7, 87–8; King [5], pp. 11–12.
[158] On the bearing of Dummett's argument on Frege's semantics, see Sullivan's cogent criticisms: [1], pp. 101–6.

functions taking those parts as arguments? Is it not, quite generally, incoherent to try to combine these two models in the proposed way?

No. The considerations raised by Dummett against combining functional and part–whole models are, in the case under current scrutiny, ineffective. Of course it is true that, if we are given the value of a function as an *unstructured* entity—we are given the number 4, say, and given it as an unstructured entity—and told to recover the argument(s) and function of which (we are told) it is the value, there is no unique way of carrying out the task: the argument might be 2 and the function squaring, but there are infinitely many equally good alternative answers.[159] The same point would apply to the case where we are given the value of a function as a structured entity, but told that that structure is *irrelevant* to the task of recovering argument and function. But what about the case where we are given the value of a function as a structured entity and told that the structure *determines* how we are to recover function and argument? In other words, what is to stop us conceiving of a whole that is given to us as such—given in such a way that we can discern its (unique) parts and their structuring—as arising from the application of a function that, by virtue of operating on those parts (the function itself being conceived as a part), unifies them into the whole we have before us? The case of the natural numbers is particularly pertinent in this regard, because here we have a privileged or canonical means of representation, in terms of zero and the successor function. If the number 4 is represented recursively as '$s(s(s(s(o))))$', we can recover the argument(s) and function(s) from the value, and there is a clear sense in which that value is actually *composed* of the argument(s) and function(s) yielding it.[160] Accordingly, while we would not deduce from the fact that $2 = 5 - 3$ that 5 and 3 are parts of 2, it makes good sense to say, and it is true, that 1 is part of 2: we may say that the number 1 *generates* the number 2, whereas 5 and 3 do not.[161] Hence the number 2, *in se*, is not unstructured, though it can be *given* in an unstructured way—and is so given when it is presented as the referent of the Arabic numeral '2', though not when it is presented as the referent of the Roman numeral 'II'.

In the case of propositions, the early Russell regarded the proposition *that Socrates is wise* as the value of the propositional function $\lambda x(x$ is wise$)$[162] for the argument Socrates, and he held that this proposition actually contains Socrates as a part,[163] though he noted that it is not characteristic of functions in

---

[159] Olson, p. 77.   [160] Olson, pp. 78–9. Cf. Oliver [1], p. 91 (the 'functional model').

[161] Fine [1], p. 52.

[162] I substitute Church's more convenient lambda notation ([6], pp. 19–22) for Russell's device of capping abstracted variables.

[163] [3], §§338, 482. Cf. Hylton [2], pp. 132–3, 142–4; B. Linsky [2], p. 77.

general that the value contains the argument as a part.[164] Here again we have a canonical means of representing the proposition in question, enabling us to recover function and argument from the value: there is, as one commentator has put it, a 'lack of space between the intrinsic nature of a proposition or propositional function and the manner in which it is represented'.[165] Ramsey too noted that the meanings of (expressions for) propositional functions are 'derived from the meanings of the propositions which are their values';[166] and in the *Tractatus* Wittgenstein regarded sentences as the values of sentential functions that are clearly meant to be linguistic counterparts of Russell's propositional functions.[167] Russell did not maintain the implied intensionality of this approach to propositions and propositional functions uniformly during the period running from 1903 to 1918, for he did not always believe in the existence of both propositions and propositional functions as bona-fide worldly entities: in *Principles* propositional functions are officially not treated as entities, whereas propositions are; in *Principia* it seems to be the other way round.[168] Actually the position in *Principia* is more complicated, for (i) Whitehead and Russell quantify over propositions as though they were genuine entities;[169] (ii) the Vicious Circle Principle (the principle that whatever involves all of a collection must not itself be one of the collection) requires a propositional function asymmetrically to presuppose the range of propositions constituting its values;[170] and (iii) propositional functions are never acknowledged as basic entities, and it is indeed implied at one point that they are not basic,[171] though the first numbered sentence to employ the cap abstraction notation appears to assume that the notation has already been defined.[172] By 1913, as I have noted (§3), Russell had (at least officially) moved to a linguistic construal of propositions, and his later view of propositional functions also took them to be linguistic.[173] Some commentators argue that propositional functions were conceived to be linguistic items even as early as the first edition of *Principia*;[174] but, without getting embroiled in the detail of this

---

[164] [18], pp. 86, 331. Cf. Levine [2], p. 212.   [165] Goldfarb [1], p. 33; cf. p. 31.

[166] [2], p. 37.   [167] [1], §5.501; Hylton [2], p. 141.

[168] See Cocchiarella [1], pp. 196–200. The substitutional theory, which Russell adopted in 1906, also refuses to accord entity status to propositional functions, while continuing to regard propositions and their constituents as entities: see Hylton [2], pp. 83–107; Pelham and Urquhart, pp. 311–22; Potter [1], pp. 130–1.

[169] Whitehead and Russell, i, pp. 41–3; cf. i, p. 185 (*14.3). See Hylton [2], pp. 102–3; B. Linsky [2], p. 58.

[170] Whitehead and Russell, i, p. 39; B. Linsky [2], pp. 23–4.   [171] Whitehead and Russell, i, p. 51.

[172] Ibid. p. 133 (*9.131). See here again Hylton [2], pp. 106–7.

[173] See [11], pp. 155–6; [13], p. 230; [14], pp. 53, 62; Cocchiarella [1], pp. 193–4, 212; B. Linsky [2], pp. 127–31.

[174] So Stevens [3], pp. 81–9.

debate, I think we may safely say that, whenever and to the extent that, during the period of his activity which interests us here (roughly the first two decades of the twentieth century), Russell accepted the existence either of propositions or of propositional functions as real (worldly) entities, he construed them intensionally.[175] The intensional approach was finally abandoned in the introduction to the second edition of *Principia* (1925), where Russell substituted an extensional approach, constituted by his acceptance of every statement of the form:

$$\forall x(Fx \leftrightarrow Gx) \rightarrow (H(\lambda x(Fx)) \leftrightarrow H(\lambda x(Gx))).^{[176]}$$

Note that the intensionality of worldly propositions, if that doctrine is being maintained, is perfectly compatible with the extensionality of certain positions within a given such proposition: for example, in the proposition *that Socrates is wise* one of the constituents is Socrates—the man himself (assuming that 'Socrates' functions in the corresponding sentence as a strict proper name). There is no tension here, for the property of wisdom is, for Russell, an intensional entity (though it would be anachronistic to identify it with a Carnapian intension along the lines of §16 above), and intensionality in any part of a proposition suffices for the intensionality of the whole.[177] But the key point we need here is that, while in many cases it is true that there is no backward road from the value of a function to the function itself and its argument(s), in the specific case of values of functions that admit of a canonical, structural-descriptive representation, such as numbers and propositions, there can indeed be such a route back.[178] As Peter Sullivan puts it: 'I do not understand [a property or concept] on the basis of a *prior* conception of the propositions that are its values. Rather, it is true *both* that I understand it *as* having these values, *and* that I understand those values *as* its values.'[179]

Although the early Russell treated the entity Socrates both as argument to the propositional function $\lambda x(x$ is wise$)$ and as part of the proposition *that Socrates is wise*, he did not, in spite of its recoverability from that proposition, take the propositional function $\lambda x(x$ is wise$)$ to be part of the proposition that is its value for Socrates as argument, and his main reason for this differential approach to argument and function as candidate constituents of the value—apart from his tendency, already noted, to treat the propositional function as a non-entity—was that the propositional function contains a

---

[175] See e.g. [3], §§485–6, 500; Whitehead and Russell, i, pp. 14–15, 23, 26; Russell [11], pp. 183–4; L. Linsky [1], p. 637; Urquhart, p. 294; Tiles, pp. 159, 164.

[176] Whitehead and Russell, i, p. xxxix; appendix C.   [177] Cf. Cartwright [3], pp. 919–20.

[178] Hylton [2], pp. 132–3.   [179] [3], p. 118.

variable as a worldly entity, whereas the proposition does not.[180] Actually, this would have been a poor piece of reasoning for Russell to put forward after 1905: for the theory of descriptions has it that a sentence involving a description will express a collection of worldly propositions containing worldly—and, after the adoption of type theory, typed—variables.[181] Accordingly, since the Russell of 1905 and thereafter cannot, so long as he continues to admit either worldly propositions or propositional functions, strictly avoid, as constituents of such propositions and propositional functions, worldly variables to which nothing directly corresponds at the level of syntax,[182] it seems that he might as well allow the (worldly) propositional function $\lambda x(x$ is wise) to be part of the (worldly) proposition *that Socrates is wise*.

Frege, by contrast with Russell, rejected the view that variables are real (worldly) entities.[183] But, if we abstract from that point, it seems that nothing would prevent him from analysing Thoughts and, if he could be brought to accept their status as referents of declarative sentences in place of truth-values, Russellian propositions, as being composed, respectively, of both the senses of names and the senses of concept-expressions, and of both objects and concepts, where in each pairing the latter entities (the senses of concept-expressions, concepts) are to be conceived as functions applied to the former entities (senses of names, objects) as arguments, with their respective outputs (Thoughts, Russellian propositions) as values.[184] Alternatively, to revert to the understanding of Russellian propositions suggested at the beginning of this section, we could conceive such propositions to be composed of (in the simplest case) object and concept as arguments to an appropriate unifying function, or (in the general case), the functional structures of phrase markers *in re*. It seems to me, then, that on this issue we can indeed say, while maintaining a functional model of propositional complexity, that the referent of a part is part of the referent of the whole.

Let me summarize the results of this section. At the level of sense, nothing stands in the way of our applying a functional model (whether or not Frege

---

[180] [18], pp. 96, 99, 130, 138; Whitehead and Russell, i, pp. 54–5; cf. p. 39. See Hylton [2], pp. 132–3; Levine [2], pp. 209–10; B. Linsky [2], p. 122; Crocco [2], p. 182.

[181] Cf. Potter [1], pp. 127, 168–9. Contrast Stevens [3], pp. 102–5.

[182] Russell admitted this to be a difficulty with the 1905 theory: Hylton [1], pp. 255–6.

[183] [26], p. 269.

[184] Hence, on this view, grasping a Thought as a whole composed of semantically significant parts and understanding its inferential connections are not two different activities, as Dummett supposes, correlating the activities with what he calls analysis and decomposition respectively (see below, §64), but rather two aspects of the same activity: see Levine [2], p. 214; Brandom [1], pp. 256–7; Sullivan [1], p. 107 n. 12. (This reading of Frege dovetails neatly with Brandom's inferentialist approach to linguistic understanding in his [2].)

intended to do so) alongside a part–whole model. At the level of reference, Frege took concepts to be functions from objects to truth-values, and I have suggested that if he had been persuaded to substitute Russellian propositions as the values of these functions, nothing would have prevented his applying a part–whole model, as well as the assumed functional model, at that level. Russell did combine functional and part–whole models at the level of reference, but while he granted the argument of a propositional function to be part of the propositional value, impelled by his refusal to accept real (worldly) variables as constituents of propositions, he denied that title to the propositional functions themselves. I have proposed yet another disposition, according to which a Russellian proposition is taken to be the value of a special unifying function applied to (in the simplest case) an object and a concept, the latter being construed as a Carnapian intension (a function from appropriate indices to objects), rather than as a function from objects to truth-values along Fregean lines; in the general case we may identify Russellian propositions with what I have called phrase markers *in re*. Further, given the possibility of canonical representations of Russellian propositions, I have argued that nothing stands in the way of our acknowledging appropriate arguments and functions (objects, concepts, and unifying functions) to be literal constituents of the Russellian propositions they go to compose.

20 A Revised Semantic Map

If we follow my recommended way of construing Russellian propositions, the revised diagram of the relations between the levels of symbolic language, sense and reference, for the case of the simple categorical sentence, will look like Figure 2.2. A simple categorical sentence and its corresponding proposition are determined to be true in respect of a given world at a given time just in case the object referred to by the proper name is a member of the set of

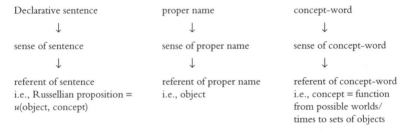

Figure 2.2

objects to which the function from possible worlds and times to sets of objects with which we identify the concept referred to by the concept-word maps the relevant world and time; otherwise it is false.

It is worth observing that there is a good sense in which the items in the lower levels of this map determine items at higher levels. Thus, for example, objects (the referents of proper names) determine equivalence classes of proper names, the relevant equivalence relation being 'x has the same referent as y', where the variables range over (actual and possible) proper names. And objects also determine equivalence classes of senses of names—that is, equivalence classes of senses in the *semantic* sense of 'sense' (§14)—the relevant equivalence relation being 's presents the same object as t', where the variables range over (actual and possible) senses of names. Similarly, senses of names (in the semantic sense of 'sense') determine equivalence classes of (actual and possible) names. Is any closer relation than one of determination in the offing? Can items at lower levels simply be *identified* with suitable equivalence classes composed of items at higher levels?

In fact there is an epistemological reason why we cannot countenance the identifications of objects with sets of senses or names, though an identification of senses with suitable sets of names can go through. (I shall continue to take the middle column of the revised diagram as my example, though the argument is generalizable to all three columns.) Grasping a sense S is a matter of being acquainted with the object presented by S, call it O, in some particular way. Suppose now we identify O with a suitable equivalence class of senses, Σ. That means that being acquainted with O will be tantamount to being acquainted with Σ. Being acquainted with Σ will consist in knowing its membership condition (there cannot be *de re* acquaintance with Σ for a finite subject of thought, since it may contain infinitely many members). That in turn will be tantamount to knowing that a given sense s is in Σ just in case it presents Σ. But here we have a vicious circularity, because there is no way into this equation for a subject of thought. To find out whether s presents Σ you first have to know what set Σ is, but to find that out you need to ascertain whether s is in Σ or not, and to find *that* out you need to ascertain whether s presents Σ.

Now one can construct a precisely parallel argument for the case of a purported identification of senses with suitable equivalence classes of names, but here I think it is possible to escape from the epistemic bind. The method I propose trades crucially on the fact that senses are not at the lowest level in the semantic hierarchy: that is why the tactic works in this case, but would not work to save an identification of objects with sets composed of items higher up in the semantic table. Understanding a name is a matter of grasping its sense. Suppose now we identify that sense with a suitable equivalence class of names. Understanding a name will then be tantamount to being acquainted with the relevant set. But instead of saying that acquaintance with a suitable set of names requires knowledge of the membership condition of that set (which would take us into a vicious circle), we can exploit the fact that names present *objects*, which we are *not* identifying with sets of senses, and say that acquaintance with the relevant set of names is tantamount to acquaintance with the relevant object (in some particular way). There is, then, a reasonable construal of senses (in the 'semantic' sense) according to which they are linguistic entities: at least, they can be identified with suitable *sets* of linguistic expressions (items of symbolic language). But objects (and other entities at the level of reference) remain stubbornly distinct both from entities at the level of sense and from items of symbolic language. Hence the structures with which I identified Russellian propositions in §18 (in the general case, phrase markers *in re*) are to be strictly distinguished from symbolic representations of those propositions (or the senses thereof). The empirical realism I have accepted as a constraint on our semantics, alongside linguistic idealism (§9), accordingly remains intact.

The thesis that referents determine suitable equivalence classes of senses generates no clash with the traditional doctrine, which I have accepted (§15), that sense determines reference but not vice versa or, as it is sometimes put, that there is no backward road from reference to sense. For the meaning of that traditional doctrine is that *individual* senses determine *individual* referents, but not vice versa or, equivalently, that there is no backward road from an individual referent to any given individual sense, that is, that a referent does not on its own determine any particular way in which it can be given. The determination by referents of suitable sets of senses does indeed yield a respect in which reference determines sense; but there is no clash with the traditional doctrine because the determination of sense by reference operates at a more general level than the reverse determination embodied in the traditional doctrine: an individual referent determines not any particular sense, but *all* its corresponding senses (including all *possible* senses).

21 Sentences as Referring Expressions

It is natural to object to any position, such as Frege's or mine, which envisages referents for declarative sentences—whether truth-values as Frege wanted, or Russellian propositions as I would prefer—on the basis that if such sentences refer to entities, of whatever sort, they must be intersubstitutable (at least in transparent and non-reduplicative contexts) with any co-referential names of those entities *salva veritate*. The operative principle here derives from Leibniz: 'Those things are the same of which one may be substituted into the place of the other, such as triangle and trilateral'.[185] But, so the objection continues, declarative sentences ('Socrates is wise') and canonical names of Russellian propositions ('That Socrates is wise', 'Socrates's being wise'), or of truth-values ('the True', 'the False') are plainly not so intersubstitutable: indeed they are not even intersubstitutable *salva congruitate*, let alone *salva veritate*. An objection along these lines has recently been propounded by Ian Rumfitt and others,[186] though the point is an old one, having been raised against the theory of complexly signifiables, which likewise envisaged that non-congruous linguistic expressions (sentences and their nominalizations) might signify the same complexly signifiable *in re*.[187] Rumfitt argues that co-reference or co-designation entails intersubstitutability *salva veritate* (at least in some contexts), remarking that to cut the notion of co-designation off from that of intersubstitutability in what he calls semantically 'central' contexts 'would surely be to deprive the relevant notion of an important conceptual anchor'.[188]

But I have already provided the notion of reference or designation with its conceptual anchor—the referent of an expression of symbolic language is what the understander needs to think of, and what it suffices for him or her to think of (so long as the understander thinks of the relevant entity *as* the referent of the expression), in order to count as understanding that expression—and nothing follows from this characterization about intersubstitutability: all that follows is that if two items of language are co-referential then the understander of them should, by virtue of his or her understanding, think of the same thing. Intersubstitutability (in some contexts) *salva veritate* we may regard as a function of co-referentiality *and* appropriate syntactic category, not merely of the former. Declarative sentences, such as 'Socrates is wise', and purportedly co-referential names, such as 'that Socrates is wise' (or, as Frege would have said, 'the True'), which belong to different syntactic categories will fail to be intersubstitutable (*salva congruitate* and so, a fortiori, *salva veritate*) for just that reason—namely

---

[185] [1], vii, p. 219: 'Eadem sunt quorum unum in alterius locum substitui potest, ut Triangulum et Trilaterum'. Leibniz excepts reduplicative contexts, which involve restrictions on key terms using 'quatenus', 'inquantum' ('insofar as'), *vel sim.*, from the scope of the principle: cf. Nuchelmans [5], pp. 227–31; Angelelli [2], p. 155.

[186] Rumfitt [2]. Cf. Black [2], pp. 229–30; Geach [7], pp. 189–93; Searle [1], p. 102.

[187] See Ashworth [2], ch. 4, pp. 98–9. In outline, the response to the objection that I favour was anticipated by several medieval and post-medieval philosophers, including Abelard ([1], pp. 369–70), André de Neufchâteau (fos. cxxxvi–cxxxviii), and Gervase Waim (fos. iii–iv).

[188] [2], p. 71. Wright agrees: [1], p. 20; [3], p. 73. Cf. Carnap [1], §159.

that the syntactic categories are different—and not because, after all, they are not co-referential.[189] Intersubstitutability in transparent contexts *salva veritate* (and so *salva congruitate*) is, plausibly, not a *sufficient* condition for co-reference (for 'triangular' and 'trilateral' are so intersubstitutable, as Leibniz notes, but they are not co-referential); and I am unaware of any good reason to insist on making it a *necessary* condition. No doubt an ad hominem argument can be mounted against Frege here, on the basis that, as an adherent of the *suppositio* approach to reference, he took intersubstitutability to be necessary and sufficient for co-reference;[190] but I do not see that the objection I have here considered can be mounted against an approach, such as mine, which denies that connection.

On my approach, declarative sentences and their nominalizations—as it might be, 'Socrates is wise' and 'Socrates's being wise' or 'that Socrates is wise' (or an appropriate phrase marker)—are all names referring to the same Russellian proposition.[191] In use, with appropriate force indicators, they may do more than merely name, of course: for example, it is a convention that a declarative sentence may be used on its own, without modification, to make an assertion; it may also be used to ask a question or express doubt, at least when uttered with a suitable intonation, and so on. Nominalizations may also be used to make assertions, ask questions, and so on, but normally more verbal context is required. For example, we can append 'obtains' or 'is the case' to 'that Socrates is wise', and then assert (or perform other linguistic acts with) the result. It is, then, quite wrong to say, as one commentator has, that ' "Socrates is mortal" is a formula, and in using it to make an assertion, we are not committed to the existence of a proposition'.[192] We are indeed committed to the existence of the corresponding proposition when we use that sentence to make an assertion. Partly that is because in making an assertion we commit ourselves to the truth of what we say, and truth, as we have seen, attaches in the first instance to propositions. But there is a deeper point here: whenever and however we use its corresponding sentence, we are committed to a proposition's existence—though not necessarily to its truth, as Ernst Tugendhat confusedly supposes in representing the view (which he opposes) that declarative sentences refer to propositions.[193] For the

---

[189] Cf. King [3]; Oliver [4]; Schnieder [2]; Schiffer, pp. 92–5. But insofar as the purported cases of co-referential, non-congruous expressions advanced by these authors depend on taking definite descriptions to refer to their satisfiers they seem to me incorrect.

[190] Geach [7], p. 227; Searle [1], p. 97; Bell [3], p. 184; [4], p. 41; Weiner [1], pp. 96, 106.

[191] So too Cresswell, pp. 37, 102.   [192] Landini, p. 252.

[193] [2], pp. 61, 156–7. Tugendhat's main opposition to Russellian propositions seems to be based on the point that our access to them is essentially mediated by language (ibid., pp. 63–4). As Carl puts

use (as opposed to mention) of any sentence, in any context, pragmatically presupposes the meaningfulness of that very sentence; but the corresponding Russellian proposition *is* that sentence's meaning.[194]

A further argument, which is explicitly directed against Frege but which, if it worked, would also undermine my position on sentential reference—and would indeed represent a challenge to any view that accorded referents, of whatever sort, to sentences—is offered by Sullivan:

Suppose a function $h(\xi)$, applicable to people, which yields the True, the False, or the father of the argument according as the argument lived wholly before, wholly after, or contemporaneously with Bernard Shaw. What is the sense of 'h(John Lennon)'? Here an a posteriori investigation is needed to determine the reference of the expression. But I cannot conceive of this investigation as 'advancing from a thought to a truth-value' since, until I reach the reference, I do not know whether it is a truth-value I am advancing towards, nor therefore whether it is a thought I am advancing from.[195]

But, so the line of argument goes, it must be intrinsic to a Thought that anyone who grasps it grasps it *as* a Thought: there is no room for a position according to which an expression can be grasped by someone who does not yet know whether it expresses a Thought, because it is not yet known whether it refers to a truth-value or not. One feature of Sullivan's argument against which we can immediately raise a cavil is his use of the word 'reference'. For, as we have seen (§15), the referent of a functor, applied to an argument-expression, is not, in general, the same as the value of this composite expression: hence, while an a posteriori investigation is indeed needed to determine the *value* of 'h(John Lennon)', given the definition of the function, the *referent* of this expression is a semantic construct quite independent of its value, and is automatically grasped by anyone who understands the expression, whether or not the value is known, for *that is what understanding the expression is* (at least in part). But even waiving this point, and meeting Sullivan's argument on its own terms, it cannot be the case that there is *nothing* more to something's being a Thought than its presenting a truth-value (Frege's preference) or a proposition (my preference), as Sullivan's argument presupposes in his opponent's position: for, as we have noted, 'the True' presumably has a sense that presents a truth-value, but Frege would obviously not be willing to concede that it expressed a Thought; and, on my approach to sentential reference, 'that proposition' might with suitable

it: 'There is no knowledge of the reference of a sentence without grasping its Thought' ([2], p. 156). It is true that our grasp of Russellian propositions is essentially mediated by language, at least in a transcendental sense. But a linguistic idealist will say the same about our cognitive access to *any* object: recall §9, and see further §§40 and 53 below.

[194] Notwithstanding Cartwright [1], p. 50.   [195] [2], p. 479; cf. Potter [1], p. 106.

contextualization refer to the proposition *that Socrates is wise*, but it does not express the Thought *that Socrates is wise*. So while it is of the very nature of a Thought that it presents, as Frege would have it, a truth-value, or, as I would prefer, a proposition, it cannot suffice to mark out an entity at the level of sense *as* a Thought that it presents a truth-value (proposition), since other, non-propositionally structured entities may do so as well. Entities at the level of sense are not merely individuated in terms of what they present in the realm of reference, but have formal or structural conditions on their identity as well.

22 False Propositions at the Level of Reference

Propositions figuring at the level of reference can, as I have stressed, be either true or false. As we have seen (§11), the false ones will be what Russell, using Meinongian terminology, called 'false objectives': they include entities like *that Charles I died in his bed* (viewed extensionally). As we have also seen (§11), it was Russell's subsequent horror of false propositions *in re* that led him to abandon the theory of propositions set out in *The Principles of Mathematics* of 1903, and adopt the multiple relation theory of judgement that we find in his writings between 1910 and 1913. In spite of the notorious difficulties of his later approach, some of which were rehearsed in the previous chapter, and which surely constitute good evidence that the attempt to avoid positing 'false objectives' was a wrong turning, there has been a marked tendency among recent writers to concur with the view Russell expressed in 1913 when he wrote that 'it is very difficult to believe that there are objective falsehoods, which would subsist and form part of the universe even if there were no such thing as thought or mind'.[196]

For example Geach, though he is critical of the multiple relation theory of judgement, approves of the abandonment of false objectives, remarking that

Russell seems to me to be certainly right in denying that the meaning of a sentence expressing James's judgment is a complex object (or 'objective', as Meinong would call it) with which James is acquainted. Here we need to bring into play that 'sense of reality' to which Russell rightly attaches importance in logical investigations; we ought to find it incredible on the face of it that if James believes something false, then there is in the nature of things a falsehood that James contemplates and, in his judgment, accepts.[197]

It is curious how philosophical intuitions differ: I should have thought that, on the face of it, what Geach finds incredible is no more than common sense.

---

[196] [9], p. 153. Cf. Prior [3], pp. 24–6.   [197] [6], p. 48.

SENSE, REFERENCE, AND PROPOSITIONS I I I

Still, it is clear that Geach is by no means alone in harbouring a distrust of false objectives. Fine says that 'there is hardly any temptation to regard falsehoods as in the world';[198] Thomas Baldwin objects that false propositions, conceived as occupying the level of reference, would 'need to have, so to speak, all the substance of actual states of affairs, but just to lack their actuality';[199] and Julian Dodd calls the positing of what he calls 'objective non-facts' a 'crass example of metaphysical extremism'.[200] But let us keep our heads here. The sense in which false propositions at the level of reference can be said to *have* the substance of actual states of affairs is just this: they are really existent abstract entities composed of other (abstract and concrete) entities. The sense in which false propositions *lack* the actuality of actual states of affairs is just this: while the components of false propositions are real enough, those components are not, as it happens, related in the way in which, in the proposition in question, they are said to be related. True propositions at the level of reference are facts; but there is certainly no call to invoke the paradoxical-sounding label 'false facts' to characterize false propositions at the level of reference.[201]

Bernard Linsky, diagnosing Russell's post-1910 aversion to false propositions *in re*, remarks that, on the view to be rejected, while a proposition binds its components together to form a unity, that unity is not yet one which, just as such, constitutes a fact (for the proposition may not be true): 'One would need something to hold *a*, *R*, and *b* together, and then something else about the way they are held together that would make the proposition that *aRb* true'.[202] The 'something' binding *a*, *R*, and *b* together to form a unity is certainly logically prior to, and so distinct from, the 'something else' in virtue of which the proposition is true, in the case where it is true; but Linsky is wrong to imply that the 'something else' concerns 'the way they [*a*, *R*, and *b*] are held together'. The diagnosis indeed captures what went awry in Russell's thinking: he was beset by a compulsion to believe that a proposition could not be unified without *eo ipso* being rendered true,[203] and, unable to overcome that unfortunate tendency in his thinking, was forced to abandon the attempt to explain its unity. But we should be clear that there is no obligation to suppose that what makes a proposition *in re* true or false has anything at all to do with the way its components are put together. As we shall see in more detail in the remainder of this chapter, there is no prospect of giving a philosophical analysis of truth and falsity at the level of the real proposition: there is simply nothing of a general and metaphysical nature—nothing internal to the proposition,

---

[198] [1], p. 53.   [199] [2], p. 46.   [200] [1], p. 163.
[201] As do e.g. B. Linsky [2], p. 47, and Stevens [3], p. 129.   [202] [2], p. 48.
[203] Recall the passage from [9], p. 116, quoted near the end of §12.

and nothing external to it either—that *makes* a real proposition, as such, true or false.

If, as I have claimed, we are obliged by semantical considerations to modify the Fregean picture so as to house Russellian propositions at the level of reference as well as Fregean Thoughts at the level of sense, we cannot avoid positing extensional entities corresponding to those false Fregean Thoughts and false declarative sentences that obtain at the levels of sense and symbolic language respectively. For the argument rehearsed in §14 to the referential status of appropriate propositionally structured entities was utterly neutral on the question of truth-value. Why should it be thought that the sheer availability of false as well as true Fregean Thoughts obtaining at the level of sense creates difficulties for the project of colonizing the referential level with propositional entities corresponding to Fregean Thoughts? To the question whether false propositions at the level of reference are as real as true ones, the answer must be affirmative: after all, the constituents of false propositions at the level of reference are, as I have noted, just as real as the constituents of true propositions at the level of reference, for it is not possible to refer to objects and properties that are not there to be referred to. And these constituents must be unified in a false proposition as they are in a true one: for a false proposition is no less unified than a true one. False propositions at the level of reference differ from true ones at that level neither in point of unity nor in their ontological status: the only difference is that their constituents are *being said* (by the proposition) to be related in a way in which they are not related.

It is crucial here not to be misled by superficial rhetoric or frightened by homilies on the Tragicall History of the Life and Death of Dr Meinong. Russell reminisces:

> Time was when I thought there were propositions, but it does not seem to me very plausible to say that in addition to facts there are also these curious shadowy things going about such as 'That today is Wednesday' when in fact it is Tuesday.[204]

Obviously false propositions do not 'go about'; but that is entirely beside the point. True propositions (facts) do not 'go about' either:[205] propositions may have concrete constituents but they are themselves abstract objects, whether false or true, and so do not 'go about' the world any more than do numbers or sets—or indeed the world itself which, as I shall shortly explain (§24), though it contains concrete objects (as well as abstract ones), is, by virtue of its identity with (all the true and false) propositions, essentially abstract. Setting

---

[204] [13], p. 223. On Meinong, see Grossmann [1], p. 203, and esp. Zalta [1], pp. 115–23.
[205] Cf. B. Linsky [2], p. 46.

aside Russell's misplaced qualm, it might be said that the claim that false propositions are as real as true ones confronts the following difficulty. If the level of reference consists of false propositions as well as true ones, if, at that level, there are non-facts in just as good a sense as there are facts, how can we account for what is *distinctive* about truth, or factuality, and how can we justify thinking of truth, or factuality, as metaphysically privileged in the sense that it is (in some sense) *better* than falsity? Saying that facts *obtain*, whereas non-facts do not, is saying no more than that some propositions, at the level of reference, are true, and others are not, and saying this much does not, so it might be objected against me, either tell us what really distinguishes truth from falsity, or why truth is peculiarly important to us. I think the charge that the picture I am offering tells us neither what truth is nor what is special about it should simply be accepted. But accepting the charge does nothing to undermine the picture, for we should seek satisfaction on these issues elsewhere. The picture is (so I claim) forced on us by semantical considerations, and it is a consequence of the picture that some propositions at the level of reference may be false just as others are true; but there is no obligation on us, merely in virtue of offering this picture, to address all puzzles that arise in connection with the distinction between truth and falsity.

Having said that, however, it might be advisable for me to indicate (albeit in a provisional and partial way) how I envisage responses to the above queries proceeding. What is distinctive of truth—what marks it off from falsity—is just that the concept-expression 'is true' conforms to the disquotation schema, whereas the concept-expression 'is false' does not. What makes truth special is not merely that it has a certain normative character—that, as Russell put it in his 1904 critique of Meinong, there is 'an ultimate ethical proposition' to the effect that 'it is good to believe true propositions, and bad to believe false ones'[206]—but also that there is a transcendental requirement on language users to give systematic doxastic preference to true propositions over false ones, both because it is only possible to learn a language if the learner is exposed to (salient) truths,[207] and because, as Davidson has made familiar, it is only possible to interpret other speakers if the interpreter makes the assumption that they intend, by and large, to utter truths.[208]

But even if the reader is satisfied by these inchoate remarks, I do not suppose that all reservations one might feel about the semantical picture I am offering will have been laid to rest. In particular, doubts may have surfaced concerning

---

[206] [15], p. 76.

[207] And the attempt to expose the learner to salient falsehoods would be self-defeating: Wittgenstein [1], §4.062.

[208] See Davidson [1], *passim*; McDowell [3], pp. 3–9; Hornsby, pp. 12–14.

the statement made several paragraphs back that the constituent objects and properties of false propositions at the level of reference are *said by the proposition in question* to be related in a way in which they are not related. How, someone might complain, can propositions at the level of reference (whether true or false) both be *worldly* entities—as they must be if they really exist at the level of reference—and also *say* something?

23 The World's Own Language

For it is tempting to object to the doctrine that the realm of reference contains propositions on the ground that it commits us to an intolerable transcendental realism. According to this objection, what is wrong with the doctrine is that it forces us (in an image of McDowell's, adapted from Richard Rorty) to 'picture objects as speaking to us in the world's own language'.[209] We might give substance to the objection as follows. Suppose that, following the opening claim of the *Tractatus*, we conceive of the world as being everything that is the case. One way of putting Wittgenstein's idea would be to say that the world is (in the first instance) propositional, and is (in the first instance) composed specifically of *true* propositions.[210] Now in the context of the Fregean distinction between sense and reference it is natural to ask whether propositionally structured meanings of declarative sentences are to be conceived as located in the realm of sense or in the realm of reference. Here we cannot, I have argued, be satisfied with a Fregean position, according to which such propositionally structured entities, and so facts (which are just true such entities),[211] are held to occupy exclusively the realm of sense. I have suggested that there are propositionally structured entities not merely in the realm of sense, where they take the form of Fregean Thoughts (the true ones being facts in a Fregean sense), but also distinct such entities, namely Russellian propositions (the true ones being facts in a Russellian sense), located in the realm of reference. The Wittgensteinian aphorism that the world is everything that is the case might then seem to present us with a choice: either we

[209] See McDowell [2], p. 470.

[210] 'In the first instance', because it need be no part of this position to deny that there are objects and properties in the world: but they get into the world by virtue of their figuring in (true) propositions (cf. Johnston, pp. 244–6). I accept the restriction to true propositions as a temporary convenience; but I shall relax it in due course.

[211] Fine has suggested (following others) that facts cannot be identified with true propositions on the basis that they have different modal properties: [1], pp. 46–7. But his argument depends on an equivocation: facts do indeed have different modal properties from propositions as such, but not from true propositions.

identify the world with the (Fregean) facts inhabiting the realm of sense, or we identify it with the (Russellian) facts inhabiting the realm of reference. And this apparent choice might then take on the appearance of an intolerable dilemma. For either way, it might be claimed, we are compelled to conceive the world as composed of what are essentially linguistic items, namely true propositionally structured entities, whether these are construed as senses (Fregean Thoughts) on the first horn of the dilemma, or as referents (Russellian propositions) on the second horn.

But we are now in a position to see that the dilemma is a chimerical one. We do not need to choose between the options offered; and in fact we cannot ultimately do so, because selecting one option amounts to selecting both, so that the appearance of our having a choice is illusory. If we identify the world with the Fregean facts inhabiting the realm of sense, we find ourselves—given that the realm of sense *presents* the realm of reference—having to recognize the corresponding entities in the realm of reference as in some good sense part of the world's furniture. If, on the other hand, we identify the world with the Russellian facts inhabiting the realm of reference, we find—given that entities at the level of reference systematically determine items at the level of sense collected under suitable equivalence relations (§20)—that our initial identification of the world with entities at the level of reference necessarily imports into our ontology appropriate corresponding items at the level of sense. In other words, the realms of sense and reference come together as a package: there is no having the one without the other. Seeing this point gives us the materials we need to answer the charge that the semantical picture I have been defending commits us, absurdly, to thinking of objects as 'speaking to us in the world's own language'. We should accept the image, but reject the imputation of absurdity. It is no more absurd to say that objects speak to us in their, or the world's, own language than it is to say that actions speak louder than words or that someone's facial expression can speak volumes about her state of mind. In these latter cases, after all, we do not stop to ask in which language actions speak to us, or in which language the volumes that facial expressions speak are written. What saves the image of objects' speaking to us in the world's own language from absurdity is that it is not to be read in a transcendentally realistic way, as the objector was in effect supposing.

We can orient ourselves here by contrasting the semantical doctrine I am recommending with the correspondence theory of truth, on one standard conception of it. According to that theory, the world is taken to be composed of entities, namely facts, which are not in any sense linguistic, but which nevertheless correspond to things that are linguistic, namely propositions, or at least to some of them (the true ones). Crispin Wright, for instance, argues that 'there is no alternative but to think of the truth of a proposition as conferred upon it, in the general case, by its relations [sc. of correspondence] to non-propositional reality'.[212] He suggests further that, in the general case, propositions are 'made true when they are true by, inter alia, non-propositional matters'.[213] His definition of the correspondence theory of truth is: 'Correspondence theory holds that truth is a relational characteristic whose terms are respectively propositions . . . and *non-propositional items*—facts, or states of affairs—in an independent world'.[214] In a similar vein, D. M. Armstrong tells us that

The Redundancy Theory gives us a true account of the semantics of the truth predicate, but it stays at the level of truths. At a deeper, ontological, level the Correspondence Theory tells us that, since truths require a truth-maker, there is something in the world that corresponds to a true proposition. The correspondent and the truth-maker are the same thing.[215]

Armstrong's remark that the redundancy theory 'stays at the level of truths' suggests that he does not appreciate the significance of disquotation: for there is nothing trivial or superficial, as Armstrong implies, in what is conveyed by instances of the disquotational schema, which on the contrary states, when instantiated, 'eminently learnable and forgettable' facts about the relations between a bunch of (English, or German, or . . .) words and a bit of the world.[216]

Against Armstrong's assumption that ontology is 'deeper' than semantics one naturally wishes to object that if the philosophy of the twentieth century, and in particular of the later Wittgenstein, has taught us anything, it is surely that this traditional view is back to front. Armstrong's meditations in the book from which this quotation is taken, as well as elsewhere in his writings, well illustrate the vacuity of metaphysical speculation when it is conducted outside the framework of a mature philosophy of language, with no guide except 'what one is inclined to say'.[217] Take an example: disjunctive universals. Armstrong writes: 'consider an *a* that has property *P* but lacks [property] *Q*, while *b* has *Q* but lacks *P*. Is it not a joke to say that they have $(P \vee Q)$ in common?'[218] Without guidance from a philosophical semantics, conceived as driving ontological questions, I see no way of answering Armstrong's (rhetorical) question. With that guidance, the answer is simple: disjunctive or other combinations of universals are no more problematic than the base universals themselves, for we employ disjunctive concept-expressions of arbitrary complexity in true

---

[212] [2], p. 223.   [213] Ibid., p. 224.   [214] Ibid., p. 206.
[215] [5], p. 128.   [216] Evans and McDowell, p. xi.
[217] See e.g. his [6] for an especially egregious case of this vacuity.
[218] [3], p. 197; cf. [1], p. 20; Mellor, pp. 109–10; Fine [1], pp. 63–7.

sentences, as well as syntactically simple, but semantically complex such expressions ('sibling').[219]

There was a general trend towards the end of the twentieth century to divorce ontology from language,[220] and, apart from Armstrong, one of the principal exponents of this trend has been D. H. Mellor. Mellor takes the realist line that objects and properties are independent of word-meanings. What does this mean? If it just means that the existence and identity of, say, the planet Mars is independent of the existence and use of any particular empirical name, such as 'Mars', then that is a realism we ought all to endorse, and I have already committed myself to it (§9). But it is clear that Mellor means more than that empirical realism: he wishes to assert a deeper independence—that of objects and properties from language as such, not just from historically conditioned empirical languages. He writes:

There is . . . no such property as being red, i.e. no property that all red things share. No one property gives our predicate 'red' its sense in even the minimal sense of fixing its extension, let alone in any more substantial sense of fixing its connotations and hence our concept of red. . . . [I]t is the similarity of [a collection of] sensations that makes us call all the different things that cause them red.[221]

Here we see the natural alliance between a transcendental realism like Mellor's, which as we have noted asserts the independence of objects and properties from language as such, and a substantial empiricism, which tries to recover common meanings, and the possibility therefore of communication (and so of language), on the basis of similarity of sensations, perforce understood as having a semantical content available to us in advance of the presence on the scene of language as such. But the idea is incoherent, for the claim that sensations might have a semantical content in advance of the presence on the scene of language as such in effect invests sensations with a semantical content in advance of existence of anything that could *have* (or confer) a semantics. Typically empiricists try to avoid this incoherence by positing a brute, pre-semantical similarity of red objects to one another—in respect of colour, one has of necessity to add, and the need for such a gloss already refutes Mellor's anti-realism about the property of being red[222]—but the posited similarity is a philosophers' myth. For the suppositious brute similarities cannot be envisaged without helping ourselves to content in a way that requires language to be already available to characterize it, at least as a sheer possibility (transcendentally), if not in actuality.[223]

---

[219] Strawson [2], p. 108.   [220] Cf. MacBride [5], p. 95.
[221] Mellor, p. 111.   [222] See here Jackson; Künne [1], pp. 128–37.
[223] See McDowell [1], esp. Lecture 1; and my [15], pp. 89–93.

The substantial empiricism we find in an approach such as Mellor's is transcendentally realistic in the sense that reality is supposed not to be constituted in any sense by our language, but nevertheless magically fitted up to match that language in relevant ways. The picture I am offering is not transcendentally realistic, for I deny that reality is not in any sense linguistic. Reality *is* linguistic—though it does not consist of *symbolic* language—in just the sense that it is essentially expressible (though not necessarily expressed) in symbolic language. The position I recommend is, rather, transcendentally idealistic, not in Kant's sense, but in the sense that the existence of the world is conceived as a necessary condition of the meaningfulness of symbolic language. More precisely, the existence of Russellian propositions at the level of reference is conceived as a necessary condition of the meaningfulness of our language. Not only is it a necessary condition: it is also a sufficient condition. For, as we have seen (§20), entities at the level of reference determine suitable sets of items at the level of ('semantical') sense, and those sets can in turn actually be identified with suitable sets of (meaningful) linguistic items. It is in this sense that the propositions in question are linguistic; but they are also non-linguistic in the sense that they are entities at the level of reference, not at the level of sense (let alone at the level of symbolic language itself), and, as we have seen (§20), there is no prospect of a reduction of the level of reference to the levels of sense or symbolic language. The reader may have noticed that in the course of my discussion in this section I have moved from speaking narrowly of facts (true propositions) to speaking broadly of propositions (false as well as true) at the level of reference. That coheres with what I was saying about the level of reference before I introduced the Wittgensteinian aphorism at the beginning of this section. For to follow Wittgenstein in restricting the world to everything that is the case is to tell only half the story. The whole truth is that the world comprises *both* everything that is the case *and* everything that is not the case.[224] It might be objected here that, if we assume bivalence, then the true propositions determine the false ones (and vice versa), so that it is otiose to identify the world with *both* true and false propositions. But the point is that the world is all the propositions that there are: the fact (if it is one) that, within that class, some members jointly determine others (jointly) is, from this point of view, purely adventitious.

My position represents the radicalization of a tendency clearly discernible in the Platonic and Aristotelian semantic traditions. Gabriel Nuchelmans

---

[224] But note that Wittgenstein does call everything that is the case and everything that is not the case 'reality' (*die Wirklichkeit*): [1], §2.06. And at §2.063, inconsistently with §§1–1.13, 2, 2.04, and 2.06, he even identifies 'the total reality' (*die gesamte Wirklichkeit*) with the world. See here Stenius [1], pp. 50–2; J. Griffin, pp. 36–8.

has drawn attention to what he calls the *lingualization* of thought in that tradition,[225] that is, the representation of the intermediate level in the semantic hierarchy—the level of sense, or the mental level as the case may be—as linguistically structured. The notion of mental language was one that could trace its origins to Augustine and the Aristotelian commentators[226]—ultimately to Plato's idea of thought as internal speech[227]—and that reached its apogee in Ockham's philosophy, for whom it is clear that mental language has a determinate and describable grammatical structure.[228] But, following in the footsteps of the theory of complexly signifiables, as I understand that (§3), I envisage the lingualization not merely of the level of sense but of the level of reference too, and so, in effect (as I shall shortly explain), of the world. Better, the position involves not so much the *lingualization* of the world, but—to borrow a term applied by Nuchelmans to Wodeham's semantic theory[229]—its *propositionalization*. Indeed, given that Ockham surely goes beyond plausibility in transferring the syntactic structures of symbolic language to the mental level, we should posit the propositionalization of the levels of sense and reference, and hence of the world, *rather than* their lingualization, since the latter label could suggest something like Ockham's excessively literalistic approach: for the world has propositional, but not syntactic, structure.[230]

24 Signification and Supposition Revisited

The reasons I gave in the previous section for rejecting a correspondence theory of truth now provide the basis for a justification of the approach to reference that I am adopting in this study: reference as *signification*, rather than as *supposition*. It might be thought, given that the lowest level in my semantic hierarchy is a 'level of signification', that a further, still lower level—a 'level of supposition'—would be required to ground the distribution of truth-values among the propositions housed at my level of reference. The objection might be put in this way: my level of reference is really a further level of *sense*, so that an additional level, one that (so the objector would say) is genuinely of *reference*, needs to be supplied. But against this, if entities in the world, existing at the supposed ultimate level, are genuinely to be capable of grounding the truth of true Russellian propositions existing at the level of reference, and by their

---

[225] [1], p. 19.

[226] Esp. Porphyry, Ammonius, and Boethius: see Panaccio [4], pp. 123, 130–1, 205, 210–11.

[227] *Theaetetus* 189e4–190a6; *Sophist* 263e3–6.

[228] See Panaccio [3], pp. 136–8; [4], *passim*; and my [12], pp. 230–3.

[229] [2], p. 184.   [230] Cf. my [15], p. 229.

absence of accounting for the falsity of false such propositions existing at that level, then the entities in question will need to be propositionally structured, and essentially so; Geach's contention that an object *a* might, taken in itself, be that in virtue of which the proposition *that a is F* is true (supposing that it is true) is plainly wrong.[231] For 'Socrates is wise' cannot be rendered true by Socrates considered just as such (or by wisdom considered just as such), since Socrates considered just as such is neither wise nor foolish (and wisdom considered just as such is not instantiated by Socrates or by anyone else): the only plausible candidates for the purported ultimate-level truth-makers are obtaining states of affairs or true complexly signifiables, that is, true (or obtaining) entities of the schematic form (in the simplest case) *that a is F.*

   This point applies to essential as well as accidental properties; and it holds even when the sentence to be verified is of the minimally contentful form '*a* exists', where '*a*' is a strict proper name.[232] Even in this case, what verifies the sentence, if it is true, is not the object *a* considered just as such, but *a*'s existence, or the fact (if it is one) *that a exists.*[233] But such worldly entities—*that Socrates is wise, that a exists,* and so on—purportedly existing at an ultimately real level, below any level that is still a level of signification (as my level of reference is), are in point of fact not distinct from the very propositions at the level of reference whose truth they purport to ground: for there is no principle of distinction between these worldly entities and Russellian propositions. Armstrong writes:

We are asking what in the world will ensure, make true, underlie, serve as the ontological ground for, the truth that *a* is *F.* The obvious candidate seems to be the state of affairs of *a*'s being *F.* In this state of affairs (fact, circumstance) *a* and *F* are brought together.[234]

The natural response to this is to say that the state of affairs of *a*'s being *F just is* the truth that *a* is *F*: what is the difference between them supposed to be, by dint of which the one could underlie or ground the other? Armstrong himself cannot keep the two supposed relata cleanly apart: having asked 'What is the truth-maker for the true statements that *a* is not *G* and *b* is not *F*?', he continues, 'Could the truth-maker for *a*'s not being *G* be provided for by. . .?'[235] So *a*'s not being such-and-such turns up on both sides of the bogus truth-making relation.[236]

[231] [2], p. 261.   [232] Cf. Russell [13], p. 182.
[233] *Pace* Mulligan *et al.*, pp. 300–3; Stevens [3], p. 139.
[234] [5], p. 116. Cf. Mulligan *et al.*, p. 297; Grossmann [1], p. 206.   [235] [5], p. 134.
[236] Even more glaringly so in the following: 'What is needed is something in the world which ensures that *a* is *F*, some truth-maker or ontological ground for *a*'s being *F.* What can this be except the state of affairs of *a*'s being *F*?': [3], p. 190.

To reply that one relatum (the state of affairs) is a worldly entity while the other relatum (the truth) is in the mind, or is a product of language, or something of the sort, simply reinvites the question: what difference is *that*? Why should being 'in the mind' or being 'a product of language' prevent an entity from being worldly, in the fullest sense of the term? Mental life is not located in our heads, but rather—insofar as it makes sense to speak of a location for mind at all (which is perhaps not very far)—'takes place where our lives take place', as McDowell puts it.[237] The fact that propositions and states of affairs are keyed to different locutions in English—we typically speak of propositions as being true or false, whereas we say that states of affairs obtain or fail to obtain[238]—seems to me to cut no philosophical ice at all, at least, not just as such, not unless the difference in usage can be independently shown to be keyed to a philosophically significant difference (the difference in usage does not itself show that). And what are the worldly truth-makers of true *negative* atomic propositions?[239] Perhaps the set of all positive atomic facts?[240] But for this to serve, we need, as Russell pointed out in 1918, the additional, non-atomic proviso that the set in question indeed contains *all* positive atomic facts;[241] and that addition is obviously just a dressed-up version of the proposition that any given true negative atomic fact is *not* in the set. What is the truth-maker for *this* proposition? If at this point we try positing a negative state of affairs, then my reply is as before: this is just bogus duplication. We already have true negative atomic propositions, and these are *already* negative states of affairs.

My argument against truth-makers overlaps with Dodd's.[242] But I differ from him in locating propositionally structured entities at the level of reference as well as (distinct such entities) at the level of sense. Dodd seems to me to go too far in denying the existence of states of affairs: there is no reason to embrace such an extreme view—we do, after all, make apparent reference to (obtaining and non-obtaining) states of affairs in true sentences—so long as we do not try to prise them apart from propositions at the level of reference. The point is not that it is *unnecessary* to posit (obtaining) states of affairs as truth-makers, as Dodd thinks, but that these states of affairs turn out to be identical with the things they are supposed to be making true. Reifying *how things are* is by no

---

[237] McDowell [3], p. 281.   [238] See Mulligan *et al.*, pp. 295–6.
[239] Cf. Stevens [3], pp. 130–6.   [240] So Hochberg [7], pp. 179–80; Armstrong [5], pp. 196–201.
[241] [13], p. 236; Urmson, pp. 62–3; Olson, p. 86 n. 12; Stevens [3], pp. 137–8. Hochberg suggests ([4], pp. 272–9) that there is a way to circumvent Russell's insistence that general facts are additional to atomic facts. For in being given a variable one is thereby given its domain of variability (the Cantorian 'domain principle': see §77), and one thereby 'has' all the objects, without needing to be told explicitly that they are all the objects. But that just pushes the 'extra premiss' back into the specification of the domain of variability—which must be specified, if the variable is to be of determinate meaning.
[242] See his [2] and [3].

means problematic; but the resultant states of affairs are just true propositions. Dodd makes a revealing mistake when he writes that a belief to the effect that *a* and *b* instantiate the universal *R* 'commits us only to *a*, *b*, and *R*, not to a state of affairs'.[243] That cannot be right, for those objects—*a*, *b*, and *R*—taken as a mere aggregate do not even amount to the false (but unified!) proposition *that aRb*, let alone the true proposition *that aRb* (= the obtaining state of affairs consisting of *a*'s having *R* to *b*). Again, Dodd writes that 'if the ball is red at *t*, why should we think that we are ontologically committed to anything but the ball, redness, and *t*?'[244] But that will not do: the mere existence of the (possibly false) proposition *that the ball is red at t* commits us to more than the existence of that aggregate. If the proposition is, in addition, *true*, the more we are committed to by our belief is the existence not of a truth-*maker* but of the *truth itself.*

It will not help here to respond to these difficulties by specifying the worldly object in virtue of which 'Socrates is wise' is true not as 'Socrates considered just as such' but as 'wise Socrates'.[245] For wise Socrates—that worldly object—*is* structured in the way that a complexly signifiable is structured, or at any rate *involves* an entity structured in that way, namely the entity *that Socrates is wise*: any ontological level at which such a thing as wise Socrates comes into view is one that already contains propositional structures of the sort *that Socrates is wise*. Or if we say that wise Socrates is simple—is in effect Socrates taken just as such—then we will have the untoward upshot that a simple entity has to serve as truth-maker for all manner of complex and logically independent sentences: but how can logically independent sentences have the same truth-maker?[246] Similarly, it will not help to specify the worldly object in virtue of which 'Socrates exists' (where 'Socrates' is a strict proper name) is true as existing Socrates, for the same reason. The regrettable trend among many English speakers to replace the gerund in certain constructions with a participle—the tendency to say things like 'He is opposed to me doing that' (where the accusative form 'me' indicates that 'doing' is a participle) instead of 'He is opposed to my doing that' (where the possessive form 'my' indicates that 'doing' is a gerund)—illustrates this point well. For the fact that this development is possible at all shows that the participial construction is actually *heard* by these speakers to have the force of a gerund. Indeed in some languages the use of the participle instead of the gerund in such constructions is quite standard.[247]

---

[243] [2], p. 155.   [244] [3], p. 81; cf. p. 74.
[245] So Davidson [2], p. 144.   [246] Cf. Vallicella [1], p. 237; Hochberg [9], p. 39.
[247] The *ab urbe condita* construction in classical Latin would be a case in point: when Horace says that 'Hector (having been) removed handed over Troy to the Greeks' ('Ademptus Hector

Dummett has rightly inveighed against the current tendency to submerge the gerund–participle distinction in English;[248] but, returning to our main line of argument, it seems to me that he is himself prone to fall into the very way of thinking about the relation between language and reality which I am here concerned to rebut. Consider this passage:

> The fact that a bird is perched on a bough of the ash tree is surely a different fact from the fact that a starling is perched on a bough of the tree, since one may know the one and not the other—unless, indeed, facts are not what we know (nor propositions what we believe). Hence neither can be the same fact as that a bird is perched on a bough of the tree; and yet, given that all these *are* facts, and that the same bough of the same tree is involved in each, what different complexes existing in the world, and containing bird, tree, and bough as components, can constitute these three different facts?[249]

Dummett here assumes that, on the view he is attacking, there must be supposed to be a single chunk of non-propositional reality making all three propositions he mentions true; since, however, the propositions are logically distinct, there would have to be three such chunks—which is absurd. But the absurdity resides in Dummett's own conception of what a worldly complex would have to be like. There is no such non-propositional reality to render a given proposition is true. Propositions are themselves already at the lowest ontological level: *they are* worldly complexes.

Dummett's sample propositions are infelicitously expressed for the purpose in hand, since no individual bird or tree is a component of the proposition that *the* bird is F or of the proposition that *a* tree is F: definite descriptions do not, as we have seen, refer to the objects (if any) that satisfy them, and the same applies to indefinite descriptions. But suppose we consider propositions to the effect that

> *that* bird is perched on *that* bough of *that* ash tree,
> *that* starling is perched on *that* bough of *that* tree, and
> *that* bird is perched on *that* bough of *that* tree,

and assume that the demonstratives are appropriately fixed, so that we are referring to just one bird, bough, and tree throughout: in that case we do indeed have three different, though logically related (truth-value-linked)

---

tradidit. . .Pergama Grais': *Odes* 2, iv, 10–12) he means not that *Hector* handed over Troy to the Greeks, but that *his having been removed* did so; when Tacitus says that 'Caesar (having been) killed seemed to some the worst, to others the best of deeds' ('[cum] occisus dictator Caesar aliis pessimum, aliis pulcherrimum facinus videretur': *Ann.* 1. 8. 6), he means that *Caesar's having been killed* seemed to some the worst, etc.

[248] [5], p. 195 n. 11; [6], pp. 31–5.   [249] [10], p. 7.

propositions, each containing the bird, the bough, and the tree in question. But there is no single or multiple piece of brute reality underlying these propositions and making them true (assuming that they are true). The whole idea of a non-propositional underlying reality is fantastical. So when Dummett subsequently writes that 'Propositions are not objects discovered in external reality, either material or immaterial; they are entities abstracted from the practice of using language in which all human beings engage',[250] I reply that the contrast is a false one: propositions are *both* objects discovered in external reality *and* abstractions. Or rather: they are both objects in reality (not 'external' reality: for, as I made clear above, I do not accept the traditional division between what is external to mind and what is internal) and abstractions (from sentences).[251] And it is irrelevant whether these objects are discovered, known, or even knowable. The world is *composed* of propositions and is *itself*, it is plausible to suppose, abstract.[252]

To seek to peel off worldly states of affairs from the Russellian propositions housed at my level of reference and locate those states of affairs at an ontologically lower level in the semantic hierarchy than the propositions whose truth their existence allegedly grounds is not only futile but even self-defeating. For the grounding can only work if the correspondence between the resultant states of affairs and the original propositions is perfect—that is, if the entities grounding the truth of propositions of the form *that a is F* (to stay with this simple case) are themselves of exactly that form. But then, as both Moore and Frege saw, what we have linking purported worldly entities of the form *that a is F* (facts) and true propositions of the same form is a relation of identity, not one of mere correspondence.[253] Putting this point together with the argument of the previous section, we might say that I am offering my opponent a dilemma. Either the worldly facts which are said to correspond to true propositions at my level of reference are propositionally structured entities or they are not. If they are not, there can be no question of correspondence with propositions; if they are, there is no structure which they can intelligibly have other than (in the simplest case) the (schematic) form *that a is F*, in which case the relation they enjoy with true propositions is one of identity, not of mere correspondence. Either way, the correspondence theorist is wrong to think that, as Russell puts it in a passage I have already partially quoted (§11), 'the difference between truth and falsehood must

---

[250] Ibid., p. 11.   [251] For another version of Dummett's false contrast, see Hudson, p. 138.
[252] Cf. Zalta [1], pp. 61–2, 70.
[253] G. E. Moore [2], pp. 20–1; Frege [17], pp. 59–60 ([21], pp. 342–4). See my [15], ch. 6, §§1 and 4, and cf. McDowell [4], p. 137 with n. 21; Davidson [2], p. 126; Candlish [2], pp. 100–1.

be explicable by reference to *fact*, i.e. to what is actually in the universe whatever we may see fit to believe'.[254] The difference between truth and falsehood *just is* the difference between fact and (propositionally structured) non-fact; it is not *explained* by it.

At the level of reference, some propositions are true and some are false; and there is no general underpinning of this distinction at some purportedly more fundamental level of reality. As Stewart Candlish puts it (characterizing Russell's 1903 position), 'truth is an unanalysable property possessed by the true propositions and lacked by the false ones'.[255] And we might recall Russell's 1904 remark (quoted in §11) that 'some propositions are true and some false, just as some roses are red and some white'.[256] For semantic purposes we need a notion of reference as signification, as what grounds understanding; more precisely, given an intuitive notion of linguistic understanding, we need to *articulate* that notion into distinct levels of sense and reference—levels encoding *what* is understood, when an item of symbolic language is understood (reference), and *how* it is understood (sense)—and the argument I gave earlier in this chapter (§14) showed that we need to cast Russellian propositions as the referents of declarative sentences. The argument I have just given shows that we do not need, and cannot make sense of, a 'level of supposition' existing below a referential 'level of signification'; that is, we should reject the idea of a further, supposedly ultimately real, level purportedly grounding the distribution of truth-values among propositions at the level of reference. We can and should make do with a notion of reference as signification: the alternative notion of reference as supposition, as what grounds the distribution of truth-values among propositions, can and should simply be jettisoned.

That does not mean that the truth of true propositions is inexplicable on a case-by-case basis. It is the attempt to explain the truth of true propositions in general and *simpliciter* that I have repudiated. Of course, in the case of any particular true proposition, such as the proposition *that it is raining today*, or the proposition *that Caesar overcame the Nervii*, there will often be entirely legitimate ways to explain that proposition's truth, in terms of causal processes,

---

[254] [9], p. 153.

[255] [2], p. 101. Cf. Ricketts [5], p. 230. Candlish and others call this position 'primitivism'; elsewhere, following Wright, I have used the label 'instrinsicism' ([15], pp. 220–4). Candlish remarks that 'primitivism has generally been thought so implausible that almost no one else [apart from Russell in 1903–4] has ever been able to take it seriously' ([2], p. 101), and for a recent rejection of it (apart from Wright's in his [2]), see Read, pp. 325–6. I am trying to revive the doctrine, which I believe to be correct.

[256] [15], pp. 75–6. Russell was following Moore: [2], p. 5.

perhaps, or the realizing of human intentions in behaviour.[257] Or, to take
Russell's 1904 example recalled above, there will be case-by-case explanations
for the redness of this rose and the whiteness of that one. What there will not
and cannot be is an explanation of a peculiarly metaphysical kind, in terms
of ontologically more fundamental entities, whether objects, facts, or states of
affairs—an explanation seeking to give a perfectly general account of what the
truth of true propositions, regardless of content, consists in. When asking why
a given proposition is true, we may seek a 'dynamic answer from the scientists',
but not a 'static answer from the logicians'.[258] As far as the metaphysics of
truth (or of falsity) is concerned, a true (or false) proposition at the level of
reference is already at the deepest level to which, metaphysically speaking, we
can penetrate.[259]

If concepts are conceived, with Frege, as the (universal) referents of concept-
expressions, and properties are conceived, with many modern metaphysicians,
as (universal) components of states of affairs, it will surely follow from our
identification of (obtaining or non-obtaining) states of affairs with (true or
false) propositions at the level of reference that no significant metaphysical
distinction can be made between concepts and properties. Of course the
expressions 'concept' and 'property' engage with different locutions: we talk,
for instance, of the exemplification or instantiation of properties but not of
concepts, and when we say that someone possesses a concept (that of courage,
for example) we mean that the concept is grasped (that the subject knows
what courage is), whereas to possess a property (such as that of courage) is
to exemplify it (to be courageous).[260] But, like the difference between the
ways we talk about states of affairs (as obtaining or not) and propositions (as
being true or not), this distinction seems to me to be of no philosophical
significance. It is mere stylistic variation, just as, though 'almost' and 'nearly'
are as close to being synonyms as any two English words, they are not simply
interchangeable *salva proprietate*: for instance, the final lines of Philip Larkin's
poem 'An Arundel Tomb'—'The stone fidelity/They hardly meant has come
to be/Their final blazon, and to prove/Our almost-instinct almost true:/What
will survive of us is love'[261]—would not work with 'nearly' substituted for
'almost', for while 'almost' can be commandeered to serve as an adjective, 'our
nearly-instinct' would be much more difficult. I remain unimpressed, then,
by arguments for the distinctness of states of affairs and propositions, on the
one hand, and properties and concepts, on the other, based on considerations

---

[257] Cf. Vallicella [3], pp. 33–4.   [258] Pears [1], p. 36.   [259] Cf. Zalta [1], p. 57.
[260] Cf. Strawson [4], p. 404; Schnieder [1], p. 226.   [261] Larkin, p. 111.

of linguistic propriety. Nevertheless, in a context such as the present one where Frege's views are of paramount importance, we cannot simply assume an identity of properties and concepts, since he took these entities to differ in point of saturatedness and unsaturatedness. That distinction forms the main topic of the next chapter.

3

Frege and Russell on Unity

25 Saturatedness and Unsaturatedness

In the revised semantic map for the simple categorical sentence offered in the previous chapter (§20), the concepts that are referred to by the concept-words contained in such sentences were assimilated to functions from possible worlds and times to sets of objects. Though the detail of this approach is not Fregean, the general proposal to treat concepts as functions is: for, as we have seen (§19), in his mature thought Frege assimilated concepts to functions from (in the basic case) objects to truth-values. Frege's solution to the problem of unity was to draw a fundamental distinction between object and concept (function). Crucial to this distinction is the claim that concepts (in general: functions) are not objects. They are not a special kind of object; they are *not* objects. Of course, since Frege did not in his mature philosophy recognize propositions as entities at the level of reference composed in some way of objects and concepts, he did not offer his radical distinction between objects and concepts as a purported solution to the problem of the unity of the *proposition*, where this is taken to be an entity at the level of reference. But it is a good question what Frege thought his distinction between object and concept (as opposed to parallel distinctions at the levels of sense and symbolic language) achieved *at the level of reference*, given that in his mature reflections he recognized no complex entity at that level—except that, as we have noted (§19), he did fleetingly (and implausibly) take truth-values to be complex—whose unity has to be explained in terms of the distinction. In what follows I shall for convenience, in order to be able to talk about a Fregean solution to the problem of the unity of the proposition, taken as an entity at the level of reference, treat the fundamental distinction that Frege drew between object and concept at the level of reference as, in effect, and in spite of his official mature doctrine, meant to subserve an account of the unity of propositions housed at that level. Of course at the levels of sense and symbolic language there is no comparable problem, for both the declarative sentence and the Thought which is its sense are undoubtedly, for Frege, complex objects.[1]

The distinction between object and concept is adduced by Frege in *Die Grundlagen der Arithmetik* (1884), where it is set up as one of the three guiding principles of the work,[2] and appealed to at a number of points (especially in part IV, which contains the definition of number), but it does not receive extensive attention until the writings of his mature period, inaugurated by the essays *Funktion und Begriff* (1891), 'Über Sinn und Bedeutung' (1892), and 'Über Begriff und Gegenstand' (1892). In his mature thought Frege divided expressions into *saturated* or *complete* expressions on the one hand, and *unsaturated* or *incomplete* expressions on the other: expressions of the former kind include proper names (*Eigennamen*), in Frege's broad sense, which comprise not only what I have called strict proper names, but also definite descriptions; those of the latter kind consist of what Frege called concept-words (*Begriffswörter*) and relation-words (*Beziehungswörter*); I shall continue to replace the term 'concept-words' with 'concept-expressions' when it is necessary to cover semantically complex such items. Each type of discourse will, at least when employed in the service of science, introduce its own peculiar kind of *Bedeutung*—respectively object and concept—which will be correspondingly complete (object) or incomplete (concept).[3] (Similar distinctions are found in part IV of Husserl's *Logische Untersuchungen*, but I shall concentrate on Frege's version of the doctrine.[4])

After Frege drew his celebrated distinction between sense (*Sinn*) and reference (*Bedeutung*), first explicitly promulgated in his lecture *Funktion und Begriff*, though it is implicit both in the *Begriffsschrift* and in the *Grundlagen*,[5] this picture had naturally to be extended, by admitting complete and incomplete senses corresponding to the complete and incomplete items at the levels of language and world. In fact, it might be said that it was only with the extension of the complete–incomplete distinction to the case of the senses of linguistic expressions that, in Frege's view, the true nature of his distinction could be understood. For Frege thinks that senses are the *primary* bearers of these characterizations,[6] which are then transferred from the level of sense to the level of reference, on the one hand, and to the level of symbolic language, on the other, so that the characterizations as applied to the levels of reference

---

[1] But, as I have noted (§19), it is controversial in these cases to what extent Frege thought of concept-expressions and their senses as functions: see here Sullivan [1], p. 92.

[2] [3], p. x.   [3] See also [26], p. 129.

[4] Cf. Armstrong's notion of universals as unsaturated state-of-affairs types: [5], pp. 28–9.

[5] [1], §8; [3], §67; cf. Angelelli [1], pp. 39–42.

[6] Cf. Simons [3], p. 74; Wright [1], p. 22; Sullivan [1], p. 102.

and of symbolic language are essentially derivative. The point (at least so far as symbolic language is concerned[7]) is clearly made by Frege in his late essay 'Gedankengefüge'. He is explaining the use of the conjunction 'and' to link two sentences. The word 'and', we are told,

requires for its saturation a preceding and a succeeding declarative sentence (*Satz*). What corresponds to 'and' in the realm of sense must also be doubly unsaturated: in becoming saturated by thoughts it combines these thoughts together. The collection of letters 'and' is, of course, regarded as a mere thing, as little unsaturated as any other thing. It can be called 'unsaturated' in respect of its use as a sign to express a sense, inasmuch as it can, in this regard, have the intended sense only when positioned between two sentences. Its purpose as a sign requires completion by a preceding and a succeeding declarative sentence. It is really in the realm of sense that the unsaturatedness arises, and it is transferred from there to the sign.[8]

The point, so far as it goes, is well taken. That is, we can agree that the spoken or written sign 'and' is as complete an object as anything else.[9] There is no difficulty in referring to it using a proper name: that is exactly what placing the sign in inverted commas achieves, and no paradox, such as ensues upon the attempt to refer to concepts by means of a proper name—the notorious paradox of the concept *horse*, which will exercise us below (§28)—arises when we do so.[10] Even if we strive to make clear in the sign the sense in which it is incomplete, by writing '--- and . . .', the dashes and dots indicating the places where sentences are to be inserted,[11] we still have a symbolic entity of a sort for which no problem of naming arises: there is no paradox of the sign '--- and . . .' any more than there is a paradox of the sign 'and'. If we call the sign 'and' unsaturated rather than saturated, as (assuming that we are deploying the distinction at all) it is admittedly convenient to do, that can only be by virtue of the fact that it expresses an unsaturated sense. Frege's position is thus that the distinction between the saturatedness and unsaturatedness, or completeness and incompleteness, of *senses* has priority over, and determines, a parallel distinction drawn at the level of symbolic language: in calling signs unsaturated, we mean that they express an unsaturated sense. Whether Frege is right about this is a question that will turn out to be otiose, for I shall be rejecting the distinction, as applied to the subsentential level, between the saturated and the unsaturated.

---

[7] On the level of reference, cf. [26], p. 209.

[8] [19], p. 39 ([21], p. 381); cf. [18], p. 155 ([21], p. 375).   [9] Cf. Simons [3], pp. 84–8.

[10] In his [7] Frege notoriously opined otherwise: I discuss this in §31.

[11] Of course 'and' may link subsentential expressions as well as sentences. On 'Fregean' and 'Tarskian' strategies for dealing with this point, see Davies, ch. 6; Evans [2], pp. 80–7; and my [9], pp. 206–7.

26 The Copula as *Secundum Adiacens* and as *Tertium Adiacens*

There is no doubt that Frege regarded the distinction between saturatedness and unsaturatedness at the level of sense as subserving an account of the unity of the Thought.[12] As he remarks in 'Über Begriff und Gegenstand', in a passage I shall discuss below (§27), 'not all parts of a Thought can be complete; at least one must be in some way unsaturated or predicative, otherwise they would not stick together'.[13] At the level of reference, given that I am proceeding *as if* Frege maintained a doctrine of propositionally structured referents for declarative sentences, the Fregean will want to say that the unsaturatedness of the concept—its yearning for completion—is just what guarantees the unity of the proposition. The point is perhaps made most clearly by Frege in his posthumously published review of Schoenflies's 'Über die logischen Paradoxien der Mengenlehre'. I shall pick up the story at a point before the problem of unity is mentioned: that will provide a useful summary of Frege's understanding of the complete–incomplete distinction, as well as introducing an aspect of the topic which will exercise us greatly below, namely the role of the copula:

In the signs, a proper name (*nomen proprium*) corresponds to an object, a concept-word or concept-sign (*nomen appellativum*) to a concept.[14] We can analyse a sentence such as 'Two is a prime number' into two essentially different components: into 'Two' and 'is a prime number'. The former appears complete, the latter in need of supplementation, unsaturated. 'Two'—at least in this sentence—is a proper name, and its referent (*Bedeutung*) is an object, which one can also designate with greater prolixity with the words 'the number two'. The object, too, appears as a completed whole, whereas the predicative component has something unsaturated in its reference (*Bedeutung*). We count the copula 'is' as belonging to this part of the sentence. But there is usually something combined with it that we must here disregard: assertoric force. We can of course express a Thought (*Gedanke*) without asserting it to be true. Really, the Thought is the same, whether we merely express it or whether we put it forward as true as well. Consequently assertoric force, which is often connected with the copula or else with the grammatical predicate, does not belong to the expression of the Thought, and that is why we may here disregard it.

The predicative component of our sentence which we have described in this way also has reference. We call it a concept-word or *nomen appellativum*, even though it is not

---

[12] Cf. Matilal and Sen, p. 82; Imaguire, p. 176; Stevens [3], pp. 18–19.

[13] See also [19], pp. 36–7 ([21], pp. 378–9); cf. Carl [1], p. 42; Bell [1], pp. 13–14; Dummett [3], p. 265; Beaney, p. 164.

[14] On the scholastic terminology, see helpfully Angelelli [1], pp. 70–1 with n. 186, where he adduces Fonseca's remark to the effect that 'nomina communia vocari apud grammaticos appellativa, singularia vero propria' (I. xxvi).

customary to include the copula in this. Just as it itself appears unsaturated, so also there corresponds to it something unsaturated in the realm of referents: we call this a concept. This unsaturatedness of one of the components is necessary, since otherwise the parts do not stick together. Of course two complete wholes can stand in a relation to one another; but then this relation is a third element—and one that is doubly unsaturated! In the case of a concept we can also call its unsaturatedness its predicative nature.[15]

The problem of the unity of the proposition arises, so Frege thinks, when we find ourselves splitting the sentence into components all of which are conceived as having reference on the model of proper name and bearer. It then becomes impossible to see how the sentence can succeed in *saying* anything, as opposed to merely listing the referents of its component words. In order to preserve unity we must—so Frege thinks, and his view, in one form or another, has found wide acceptance in the analytical tradition—insist on the uniquely unsaturated nature of one sentential component. Which component should that be? Frege's answer in the above passage is that it is the *concept-word*—generalizing, we would say: concept-expression, whether simple (as a concept-word is), or composite—and he does not appear to distinguish this from the grammatical predicate of (presumably) a simple categorical sentence. (I conjecture that Frege must have the simple categorical sentence in mind, for he would not deny that concept-words can figure in complex sentences in roles other than that of grammatical predicate of the whole sentence.[16])

Frege notes in the above passage that his inclusion of the copula in the concept-word is unusual, and indeed before Frege's time a prominent view had been that the copula is (to put it in Frege's terms) the bearer of unsaturatedness par excellence, and hence that the responsibility for the unity of the sentence resides in the copula alone. According to the Kantian position, for example, the copula 'is employed to distinguish the objective unity of given representations from the subjective'.[17] These representations may, Kant supposes, be combined in a merely subjective unity, as happens when they are linked by a law of association of the general form 'When I experience representations of such-and-such a sort, I also experience representations of such-and-such another sort'. This kind of subjective association of representations does not amount, in Kant's view, to a judgement, in which a property is objectively ascribed

---

[15] [26], pp. 191–2. I have used the translation given at Frege [23], p. 177, as the basis for my own but altered it fairly extensively. With this passage compare Frege's remarks at [13], pp. 371–2 ([21], pp. 269–70).

[16] But Frege's view is that, even where a concept-expression does not function as the grammatical predicate of a whole sentence, it still functions *predicatively*: e.g. the sentence 'All mammals have red blood' is, we are told ([7], pp. 197–8; [21], pp. 171–2), equivalent to 'Everything that is a mammal has red blood'.

[17] Kant, B142.

to a thing. But given that such a subjective association is possible at all, it follows that, when an objective judgement is achieved, it is formed on the basis of already available representations—representations whose identity is not constituted by their figuring in judgements constructed on their basis. Hence the Kantian analysis of a simple categorical judgement sees it as composed of three things: two representations, each of these being, to put it in Fregean terms, saturated, and a copula, linking the two representations in an objective judgement. For Kant, as for the medieval tradition on which he relies, the linking of representations is a mental act.[18]

The Kantian analysis of the copula is of course thoroughly traditional: it goes back initially to the standard medieval regimentation of the copulative 'est' as a *tertium adiacens*,[19] and ultimately to Aristotle, who wrote that in a sentence like 'a man is just' the copulative 'is' is 'predicated additionally as a third thing'.[20] Aristotle stressed the equivalence of 'a man walks' and 'a man is walking',[21] an equivalence which was taken by the majority of medieval thinkers to point towards the *tertium adiacens* analysis of the copula, in the sense that the *tertium adiacens* regimentation of the simple categorical sentence was assumed to represent its fundamental logical form. In the case of sentences where the copula does not figure as a separate word but is absorbed into the inflection of the main verb, the analysis in question holds that it will be possible to re-express such sentences in canonical form; and for the medieval tradition what this meant, in turn, was that any simple categorical sentence of spoken or written language, whether already in canonical form or not, was correlated with a canonically formed mental sentence revealing its deep structure, that is, a mental sentence in which a mental copula figured as a *tertium adiacens*.[22] The reducibility of sentences of the form 'a man walks' to sentences of the form 'a man is walking' was, as I have said, accepted by most medieval thinkers, though towards the end of the Middle Ages it came under fire from the humanists Juan Luis Vives and Lorenzo Valla, as well as from a number of late scholastic thinkers, including Domingo de Soto.[23] But this equivalence was not the only aspect of Aristotelian thought that seemed to favour the *tertium adiacens* approach to the copula.

In his discussion of verbs in chapter 3 of *De Interpretatione* Aristotle wrote (I offer a translation-cum-paraphrase):

(i) Verbs when spoken just by themselves are names and signify something, for the speaker brings his thought to a stop and the hearer comes to rest, (ii) but

---

[18] Cf. Hylton [2], p. 13. On Burleigh and Ockham, see Gelber; Karger [3]; and my [13].
[19] See e.g. Burleigh [2], iii, pp. 54–9. On the history of this conception, and the correlative analysis of the existential 'est' as a *secundum adiacens*, see Nuchelmans [3], pp. 39–50; [6].
[20] *Int.* 19b19–20.   [21] *Int.* 21b9–10; *Met.* 1017a27–30.
[22] See Jacobi [1], pp. 168–71; Nuchelmans [6], pp. 23–35.   [23] Nuchelmans [6], pp. 35–41.

they do not [sc. when uttered on their own] yet signify whether [anything] *is* [what is signified by the verb]. (iii) For [a verb] is not a sign of the being or not-being of the thing [signified by it][24]—(iv) not even if you should mention 'being' all on its own. (v) For it [i.e. the word 'being'] is [on its own] nothing, but consignifies some composite, which cannot be thought about without the [other] components.[25]

On my interpretation of this vexed passage, Aristotle is saying in (i) that verbs are like names in the sense that they refer to (Fregean) objects. They do not, as he makes clear in (ii) and (iii), have predicative import just as such. This is even true, he points out in (iv), of the copula itself: if you say 'is' (in the sense of 'is *F*', for some *F*), you have not yet effected a predication; you have not yet said *that anything is (F)*. Have you nevertheless succeeded in mentioning being? Certainly (i) might suggest so; but in (v) Aristotle restricts the generality of the claim in (i), for he remarks there, on my interpretation, that the copula all on its own is 'nothing', in which case if you just utter it on its own you will presumably not have succeeded in mentioning being, or anything else. Rather, we are told, the copula *consignifies* a certain composite 'which cannot be thought about without the [other] components': this I take to mean that the copula only signifies *together with* suitable components, and that when it is put together with them the whole compound expression signifies something complex. The apparent tension between (i) and (v) on the status of the copula is heightened by the observation that it cannot, on Aristotle's view, be quite right to say that the copulative 'is' has *no* significance on its own, for after all it is a verb, and as such shares the peculiarity of all verbs, namely that, in Aristotle's phrase, it consignifies a time.[26]

We can, I believe, make sense of Aristotle's pronouncements on the copula if we read them as an inchoate expression of a view which was to be echoed in some medieval discussions of the *tertium adiacens* analysis of the copula,[27] but which achieved its zenith in the position outlined in the *Logic* and *Grammar* of the Port-Royal, as well as in Arnold Geulincx's contemporary *Logica*.[28] In the Port-Royal treatment of verbs, Arnauld and his co-authors teased out the copulative component of verbs from the rest of their semantic content, including tense and person, treating the separated copula as encapsulating the

---

[24] At 16b22, following Weidemann, I read: *ou gar tou* [transmitted text: *to*] *einai ê mê einai sêmeion esti tou pragmatos*.

[25] *Int.* 16b19–25.   [26] *Int.* 16b6.

[27] See e.g. Abelard [2], I. iii, pp. 129.6–142.20, with de Rijk [4], pp. 116–23.

[28] Arnauld and Nicole [1], II. ii, pp. 100–5; Arnauld and Lancelot, II. xiii, pp. 65–70. Cf. Geulincx [1], I. i, §1, pp. 176–7; Nuchelmans [5], pp. 75–7, 108, 240; [6], pp. 35, 45.

essence of the verb—as (to borrow William of Sherwood's phrase) the *radix omnium verborum*:[29]

It is indubitable that if a word such as 'is' had been invented that always indicated an affirmation without any difference of person or tense, so that a difference in person were indicated only by nouns and pronouns, and a difference in tense by adverbs, it would not cease to be a true verb.[30]

What is essential to the verb is its ability to unify elements into an 'affirmation' (by which our authors mean a positive declarative sentence):[31] that is the only function discharged by verbs that cannot be hived off to words of other types, such as nouns, pronouns, and adverbs. (The later development of tense logic, which depends on just such a strategy of separating the tense of a verb from the rest of its semantic content, is thus nicely anticipated by our text.[32])

If we read Aristotle's text in the light of the subsequent course of Aristotelian philosophy, or at least of this part of it, we might take him to be saying something along the following lines. For convenience let us call a verb or verb-phrase that includes the copula (e.g. 'is wise', 'runs'), a *full verb*, and a verb or verb-phrase from which the copula has been stripped ('wise', 'run', where this latter is understood to be an uninflected core to which inflections, including the null inflection, are superadded) a *verb radical*.[33] A full verb might then be said to be composed of a verb radical together with the copula (inflection). The verb radical is the part which, on its own, has semantic content and so resembles a name; the copula has no semantic content on its own. Full verbs do not on their own effect a predication: they could only do so (so we may take Aristotle to be implying) if one of their components effected predication on its own. Now in general a move of this shape would be fallacious—it would commit the fallacy of supposing that a whole cannot be composed of parts unless the parts have the same properties as the whole (which is not only not necessarily true of whole–part composites but is indeed necessarily not true of them)—but in the particular case under consideration Aristotle may not be guilty of fallacy: for in view of the proposed composition of the full verb it might be reasonable to suppose that, given that it is obvious

---

[29] [1], p. 71. Cf. Nuchelmans [5], p. 76.

[30] Arnauld and Nicole [1], p. 104 (= Arnauld and Lancelot, p. 69). I have used Buroker's translation ([2], p. 81). See further Condillac, II. I, §98, p. 86; J. Harris, i, p. 90; Priestley, iv, p. 56; Monboddo, II. i, §13 (vol. ii, pp. 167–8); Whately, II. i, §2, p. 71; Strawson [1], pp. 164–6; Nuchelmans [5], pp. 167, 207–8; Prior [1], p. 105, and [3], pp. 49–50.

[31] But it is possible that an irrelevant pragmatic element of assertoric force is distorting our authors' conception of affirmation: see Nuchelmans [5], pp. 84–5, 97–8. This contamination may also be present in a parallel passage in Geulincx [1], I. i, §1, pp. 176–7.

[32] Cf. Geach [1], pp. 464–5.

[33] Aristotle calls 'white' (*leukos*) a verb: *Int.* 16a15; cf. 20a31–2, 20b1–2; Bäck, pp. 116–24.

that the *verb radical* cannot on its own effect a predication (since it is a name), the whole composed of verb radical and copula can only effect a predication if the *copula* does. But, perhaps surprisingly, it turns out in Aristotle's view that the copula cannot on its own effect a predication either. This is because a predication is brought about by the copula—and it is indeed the copula that is responsible for effecting a predication—only when it is embedded in a suitable context.[34]

However this may stand as an interpretation of Aristotle's text, it ought to be clear at any rate that the passage I have quoted can be read so as to give succour to the very view Frege wishes to oppose, namely that the simple categorical sentence is decomposable into two names, one of which will be a verb radical (and at least one of which will mention something general), the two names being linked by a copula whose job is to effect, in context, the unity of the sentence. There is a lucid statement of this view in Mill's *Logic*, one that Frege must have known, since he was familiar with that work:

A proposition . . . is a portion of discourse in which a predicate is affirmed or denied of a subject. A predicate and a subject are all that is necessarily required to make up a proposition: but as we cannot conclude from merely seeing two names put together, that they are a predicate and a subject, that is, that one of them is intended to be affirmed or denied of the other, it is necessary that there should be some mode or form of indicating that such is the intention; some sign to distinguish a predication from any other kind of discourse. This is sometimes done by a slight alteration of one of the words, called an *inflection*; as when we say, Fire burns; the change of the second word from *burn* to *burns* showing that we mean to affirm the predicate burn of the subject fire. But this function is more commonly fulfilled by the word *is*, when an affirmation is intended, *is not*, when a negation; or by some other part of the verb *to be*. The word which thus serves the purpose of a sign of predication is called . . . the *copula*.[35]

On this traditional approach, the two names linked by the copula are (to put it in Frege's terms) saturated, and so have a fully determinate reference. The copula, on the other hand, is not a name and has no reference. It does not have significance but consignificance, in the sense explained. (That presumably entails that it will not receive a meaning-specification in a suitable semantic theory for the language in question.) It is, in Frege's own phrase, mere propositional form without content ('die bloße Form der Aussage ohne Inhalt').[36] As Sullivan puts it (he is glossing the *Tractatus*, but the characterization has general application to the Aristotelian tradition),

---

[34] With my interpretation of *Int.* 16b19–25, cf. the interpretation offered by Albert the Great in the passage quoted by Zimmermann, p. 287 n. 16.

[35] Mill, I. iv, §1. Cf. Hobbes [1], I. iii, §2.

[36] [26], p. 71. Cf. [7], p. 194 ([21], p. 168); [11], p. 442 ([21], p. 200); Russell [11], p. 200.

'the role of the copula in a proposition is not to be the representative of anything, but to indicate how its representing elements are therein combined'.[37]

This last point, namely a coincidence between the Aristotelian position (as I am interpreting it, in the light of the precisification propounded by Arnauld and his co-authors) and Frege's on the nature of the copula, may seem to be a surprising turn, given that I have so far been casting these views in opposition to one another. What observing the Aristotelian's and Frege's agreement on this point helps to do is highlight where the real divergence between them lies. The difference between Frege's approach and that of the *tertium adiacens* school of thought is not that, in offering a tripartite analysis of the simple categorical sentence the *tertium adiacens* school automatically attributes an independent semantic significance to the copula which Frege's bipartite analysis avoids: in fact, as we have just seen, on at least one possible interpretation of Aristotle's key text the copula has *no* independent significance. Rather, the difference between the two approaches is just that while the *tertium adiacens* school distinguishes, within the full verb, between a semantically significant verb radical and a copulative component (which, on Aristotle's view, at least has consignification) responsible for sentential unity, Frege refuses to decompose the full verb (the concept-expression) in this way. For Frege, it is the *full verb* (the concept-expression) taken as a whole, and not merely part of it, that is unsaturated, and so responsible for the unity of the sentence.

We have observed that most medieval thinkers preferred the *tertium adiacens* (tripartite) to the *secundum adiacens* (bipartite) analysis of the simple categorical sentence. But Frege was anticipated in his preferential treatment of the full verb (the concept-expression) by a few medieval philosophers, including Abelard[38] and the late scholastics Antonius Coronel[39] and Domingo de Soto.[40] These semantical schismatics, in conscious opposition to the clear orthodoxy prevailing among their contemporaries which backed the *tertium adiacens* strategy, regarded the *secundum adiacens* analysis of a sentence like 'a man is walking' (that is, 'a man walks') as logically fundamental: in effect they read the

---

[37] [5], p. 101. Cf. Siderits [3], pp. 12–13.

[38] See e.g. [1], pp. 348.28–349.31; [2], pp. 138.5–140.29. But Abelard does not consistently anticipate Frege: see Tweedale, pp. 282–304; Jacobi [1], [3], and [4], p. 148; de Rijk [3], and his introduction to Abelard's [2], pp. xli–xlvii; Marenbon, p. 41 n. 21.

[39] Coronel, fo. 10: 'Dico quod in ista propositione "Homo est animal" in mente non sunt nisi due noticie, noticia hominis, et hoc totum "est animal" [sc. quod] subordinatur uni simplici noticie supponens pro animali, et significat aliqualiter quia unit se ipsam cum subiecto.' See in this connection Nuchelmans [6], p. 40.

[40] See here Nuchelmans [5], pp. 89–90; [6], p. 39; and recall the passage quoted in §5.

Aristotelian equivalence between tripartite and bipartite forms of the simple categorical sentence in the reverse direction from the one favoured by most of their contemporaries. According to their rival analysis, simple categorical spoken and written sentences in tripartite form break down, at the level of deep structure (that is, at the level of mental language), into a subject, on the one hand, and a full verb incorporating the verb radical and the copula ('is-walking', 'is-wise'), on the other, after the model of such explicitly bipartite structures as 'homo ambulat' ('a man walks') and 'Socrates currit' ('Socrates runs'), whose real logical form was taken to coincide with their surface grammar.[41] Abelard indeed anticipated Frege and Russell in a further respect, since he regarded the verb as responsible for unity, telling us that completeness of sense (*perfectio sensus*) depends principally on verbs.[42] (So too Adam Smith: 'Verbs must necessarily have been coeval with the very first attempts towards the formation of language. No affirmation can be expressed without the assistance of some verb'.[43]) Similarly, a number of early modern philosophers and grammarians reacted against the *tertium adiacens* approach of the Port-Royal by reviving the *secundum adiacens* approach.[44] For example, Destutt de Tracy attacked the tripartite theory in the guise of Condillac's version of the identity theory of predication, remarking that identity judgements are a species of judgements in general, not vice versa,[45] and that in the proposition *that x is x* the first term is *x* and the second *being x*, the latter distinct from *x*.[46] As the cases of Abelard, Frege, and Russell illustrate, the thesis that the verb is responsible for propositional unity goes well with the bipartite analysis of the simple categorical sentence, and Destutt de Tracy provides a nice statement of this mutually commodious partnership in his *Grammaire*.[47]

27 Frege and the Copula

It is clear from what we have said so far that, in refusing to separate the copula from the concept-expression, Frege was bypassing a number of alternative

---

[41] See Jacobi [1], pp. 171–4; [3], p. 166.   [42] Abelard [2], II. i, p. 149.20; cf. de Rijk [4], p. 99.

[43] A. Smith, §27, p. 215. Cf. Monboddo, I. i, §1 (vol. i, p. 5): 'No language ever existed, or can be conceived, consisting only of the expression of individuals, or what is commonly called *proper names*.' The rebuttal of this widely held view will be important to my project.

[44] Nuchelmans [5], pp. 88–90 (Du Marsais), 94–5 (Beauzée), 184–5 (Destutt de Tracy).

[45] [2], I, p. 156. Cf. Condillac, I. ii, §69, p. 27.   [46] [2], I, pp. 159–60 n. 1.

[47] [1], ch. 2, p. 47: 'Il n'y a point de proposition sans verbe exprimé ou sous-entendu. Quelle que soit la nature de ce mot, . . . il est certain que c'est lui seul qui constitue la proposition, et determine le sens de celle dans laquelle il entre.'

strategies.[48] Take the simple categorical sentence 'Socrates is wise'. Instead of pursuing Frege's policy, one might

(i) follow the *tertium adiacens* strategy in the version of it we have seen so far—namely the version which reached its apogee in the Port-Royal *Logic* and *Grammar*, and which I have tentatively read back into Aristotle himself—and separate the copula from the rest of the full verb, so permitting the remaining expression (the verb radical, 'wise') to count as saturated, but refuse to accord the copula ('is') any independent significance, the copula then counting as a syncategorematic term.[49]

Alternatively, one might

(ii) follow a different *tertium adiacens* strategy and separate the copula from the full verb, so, again, permitting the remaining verb radical to count as saturated, but instead accord the copula independent significance (normally existential import), the copula then counting, qua significative (not merely consignificative) expression, as a categorematic term.[50]

This strategy is subjected to withering criticism by Mill in his *Logic* shortly after the passage quoted above:

Many volumes might be filled with the frivolous speculations concerning the nature of Being... which have arisen from overlooking [the] double meaning of the words *to be*; from supposing that when it signifies *to exist*, and when it signifies to *be* some specified thing, as to *be* a man, to *be* Socrates, to *be* seen or spoken of, to *be* a phantom, even to *be* a nonentity, it must still, at bottom, answer to the same idea,... The fog which rose from this narrow spot diffused itself at an early period over the whole surface of metaphysics.[51]

Here one naturally recalls Russell's equally intemperate claim that, while the 'is' of 'Socrates is human' expresses predication, 'the *is* of "Socrates is a man" expresses identity. It is a disgrace to the human race that it has chosen to employ the same word "is" for these two entirely different ideas.'[52] The first

[48] Cf. Dufour, pp. 61–2.
[49] For this strategy, see e.g. de Rijk [1], ii/2, at pp. 605–6; Burleigh [2], III (pp. 54–6).
[50] For this strategy, see e.g. William of Sherwood [1], pp. 70–1: cf. Kretzmann at Sherwood [2], p. 92 n. 14); Nuchelmans [6], pp. 18–20. Bäck argues that we should interpret Aristotle as adhering to an 'aspect theory of predication', which is in effect (ii). A clear statement of this second strategy is also given by de Soto, fo. 20rb–va: cf. Nuchelmans [5], pp. 89–90.
[51] Mill, I. iv, §1.
[52] [11], p. 172. Actually, of course, 'Socrates is a man' is no more an identity statement than 'Socrates is human'.

two strategies envisage a tripartite analysis of the simple categorical sentence;[53] the third and fourth strategies are bipartite. Here we might

(iii) follow a strategy implied by Leibniz in his essay 'Difficultates Quaedam Logicae', namely separate the copula from the full verb, collapse the proper name 'Socrates' and verb radical 'wise' into a single complex notion, and reclassify the separated copula as a categorematic *secundum adiacens* ('Wise-Socrates is (a being)', i.e. 'Wise-Socrates exists').[54]

Finally, we might

(iv) follow a strategy suggested by some of Ramsey's remarks in his paper 'Universals', which I shall discuss in due course, and divide the sentence into two components, taking the proper name together with the copula ('Socrates is') on the one hand, and the verb radical ('wise') on the other, regarding the former as unsaturated and the latter as saturated.[55]

In (iv), one refuses to recognize the copula as a separate component, but instead of attaching it to the verb one attaches it to the proper name of our sample sentence. On this approach, the sentence 'Socrates is wise' would be analysed as composed not of a saturated proper name ('Socrates'), with correspondingly saturated sense and reference, and an unsaturated concept-expression ('is wise'), with correspondingly unsaturated sense and reference, but rather as composed of the unsaturated name-plus-copula complex 'Socrates is' and the saturated verb radical 'wise' (with, again, correspondingly unsaturated and saturated senses and references respectively). The third and fourth strategies would perhaps have seemed to Frege so strange as hardly to merit serious attention;[56] at any rate, I do not know of any passage in which he subjects them to serious consideration. He appears to assume that the only viable alternative to a tripartite analysis (that is, to (i) or (ii)) is his own version of the bipartite one. But in fact, as we shall see shortly, the availability of alternative bipartite analyses to Frege's own analysis will be of critical importance in assessing the merits of Frege's proposed analysis of the simple categorical sentence.

So much, for the moment, on the alternative bipartite strategies. What of the alternative tripartite ones?[57] It is a good question why Frege gives (i) such

---

[53] On (i) and (ii) in general see Jacobi [1], pp. 168–9.

[54] [1], vii, pp. 211–17 ([2], pp. 115–21; [5], pp. 179–201). See Kneale and Kneale, pp. 338–9. Leibniz does not use singular examples in 'Difficultates', but cf. Ch. 2 n. 69.

[55] Cf. Kemmerling [1], pp. 11–14.   [56] Cf. Strawson [2], p. 65.

[57] For a modern application of a tripartite strategy, see Bealer [1], ch. 4.

short shrift in his writings, in view of his concurrence with it on the nature of
the copula, taken on its own, and also in view of the difficulties he is plunged
into (§28) by his doctrine of the essentially unsaturated nature of the concept.
In the case of (ii), at any rate, we do get from Frege a reason for his rejection of
it: he thinks that it is an idle shuffle. In one place, indeed, he seems initially to
countenance something like (ii), apparently contemplating the possibility that
the copula might be taken to designate a relation—that of subsumption. But
the apparent concession is immediately withdrawn:

> In the sentence 'Two is a prime' we find a relation designated: that of subsumption . . .
> This . . . creates the impression that the relation of subsumption is a third element
> supervenient upon the object and the concept. This is not the case: rather the
> unsaturatedness of the concept brings it about that the object, in effecting the saturation,
> engages immediately with the concept, without the need of any special cement. Object
> and concept are fundamentally made for each other, and in subsumption we have their
> fundamental union (*ihre ursprüngliche Verbindung*).[58]

Frege makes it clear here that he is opposed to finding an independent
significance for the copula, that of designating the relation of subsumption:
but what exactly does he suppose is wrong with doing so? That question
is answered for us in an extended passage at the end of 'Über Begriff und
Gegenstand'.

In the context where this passage occurs, Frege has been discussing the
paradox (which I shall examine shortly) arising from our apparent ability to
refer to concepts, which on Frege's official line are unsaturated, using proper
names, which are saturated, and in particular by using proper names of the
form 'the concept *F*'. He moots the possibility of avoiding this paradox by
adopting something along the lines of (ii) above, and replies:

> Anyone who imagines that the difficulty of the paradox is herein circumvented is
> very much mistaken. It is only postponed. For not all parts of a Thought can be
> complete; at least one must be in some way unsaturated or predicative, otherwise
> they would not stick together. So, for example, the sense of the word complex 'the
> number 2' does not stick to that of the expression 'the concept *prime number*' without
> some cement. We apply such a cement in the sentence 'the number 2 falls under
> the concept *prime number*'. It is contained in the words 'falls under', which require
> completion in two respects—by a subject and an accusative—and it is only by virtue
> of this unsaturatedness of their sense that they are capable of serving as a link. We do
> not get a complete sense—we do not get a Thought—until they are completed in this
> twofold respect. Suppose now I say of such words or word complexes that they refer

[58] [26], p. 193. (I have adapted the translation from [23], p. 178.) Cf. Geach [7], p. 221; [10], p. 182.
See too Frege's letter to Marty of 29 Aug. 1882, at [22], p. 164 (the relevant part is quoted by Dummett
at [5], p. 90); and Dummett [2], pp. 174–6.

to a relation. Well, now we have the same difficulty in the case of the relation as the one we wanted to avoid in the case of the concept. For we do not, with the words 'the relation of an object's falling under a concept', designate any relation, but rather an object, and the three proper names 'the number 2', 'the concept *prime number*', and 'the relation of an object's falling under a concept' remain every bit as aloof from one another as do the first two on their own: however we put them together, we do not get a sentence. Hence we readily perceive that while the difficulty which lies in the unsaturatedness of a Thought-component may be postponed, it may not avoided.[59]

Frege's response to (in effect) strategy (ii) is that it is futile if the proposal is merely to shift the burden of unsaturatedness from the sense of the concept-word onto another component of the Thought.[60] But unsaturatedness must be located somewhere, otherwise we sacrifice the unity of the Thought. If we seek to evade the difficulties attaching to the unsaturatedness of concepts by treating them as saturated items we will in effect be launched on a regress. We will have to find a further conceptual component in the Thought to be the bearer of unsaturatedness: this, at the initial stage, might be the relation of subsumption. But, given that we are attempting to respond to the difficulties inherent in Frege's claim that concepts are unsaturated precisely by jettisoning that claim in favour of the saturatedness of concepts, we will find that the newly discerned relation of subsumption, being a conceptual item, is not unsaturated after all, but saturated. If we then repeat the routine of searching for something unsaturated to cement the (now three) saturated components of the original Thought, we will clearly bring down a regress.[61]

Frege's strategy for the avoidance of the regress is to insist on the unique status of the original concept—its unsaturatedness—before the regress can get off the ground: on this line we do not even move to the first stage of appealing to a relation of subsumption.[62] In making this move Frege has been followed by a number of more recent philosophers, including P. F. Strawson. In one place where he discusses this issue, Strawson warns us of the risk of regress if we reify the relation of exemplification.[63] He then remarks that the unifying function in a sentence must be discharged by the verb or verb-phrase. (We have seen that this approach to unity goes naturally with the bipartite analysis of the simple

[59] [7], p. 205 ([21], pp. 177–8). Cf. [13], pp. 371–2 ([21], pp. 269–70).
[60] Davidson agrees: [2], pp. 93–4, 146–7, 156. So too, in effect, Burge: [2], p. 293 n. 16.
[61] Cf. Siderits [3], p. 16; Larson and Segal, pp. 139–40. In this paragraph I have moved between different levels of the semantic hierarchy, but that is faithful to Frege's own style: the passage I have cited concentrates on the levels of sense and symbolic language, but the problem to which it is a response is stated in terms of the level of reference. As far as the saturated–unsaturated distinction goes, we have an isomorphism between the three levels.
[62] Cf. Olson, pp. 48–9. On a similar bipartite approach in the Russell of 1898, see Imaguire, p. 127.
[63] [6], pp. 18, 21. Cf. [1], pp. 167–76.

sentence.) He allows that the verb-phrase 'cannot perform the combining function without an attendant or juxtaposed expression to combine with. The grappling machinery needs something to grapple.' But Strawson is nevertheless sure that 'we locate that machinery on the side of the verb-phrase rather than that of the noun-phrase'.[64] We shall examine the credentials of this confidence later in this chapter. Before that I want to look at a notorious difficulty accruing to Frege's doctrine of the unsaturatedness of the concept-expression.

28 The Paradox of the Concept *Horse*

This difficulty concerns Frege's strategy of attaching the copula to the concept-expression, and it cannot be convincingly answered on his behalf without substantially amending his doctrine. This is the problem I have already mentioned a couple of times, and which was acknowledged by Frege himself in 'Über Begriff und Gegenstand' and elsewhere: it is generally known as the paradox of the concept *horse*.[65] By driving such a sharp wedge between proper names (in his broad sense) and concept-expressions, and correspondingly between their respective senses and between their respective referents, Frege thinks to ensure that (to put it in my terms) the proposition does not degenerate into a mere aggregate,[66] but the price he pays is that concepts, not being objects, cannot be referred to by means of proper names. For proper names necessarily reify their referents. But the awkward fact is that we seem to be able quite satisfactorily to refer to concepts: Frege himself does so on numerous occasions, as when (to pick a case at random) he tells us that 'the largest meaningful part of "$a > 0$" is the predicate part [i.e. "> 0"] and its meaning (*Bedeutung*) is the concept (*Begriff*) of positive number'.[67] In the face of this linguistic practice, Frege is forced to say that the forms of words in which we apparently achieve these referential feats are systematically misleading. The proper name 'the concept *horse*' necessarily refers not to a concept, but to an object—an object which in some sense 'goes proxy for' the concept.[68] (Which objects go proxy for concepts? Perhaps extensions of concept-expressions? This is suggested by a remark of Frege's in a critique of Kerry that he did not publish.[69] Of

---

[64] [6], p. 25.

[65] Frege emphasizes the word 'horse' in the phrase 'the concept *horse*' in order to mark the paradoxicality, as he sees it, of the attempt to refer to concepts; it is not a form of quotation: [7], p. 197 ([21], p. 171). I adopt his convention merely out of deference: as we shall see (§30), there is a perfectly good, non-paradoxical understanding of that phrase.

[66] Cf. Wright [1], p. 20.   [67] [15], p. 400 ([21], p. 315).   [68] [7], p. 197 ([21], p. 171).

[69] [26], p. 116 n. See Thiel, pp. 68–73; Angelelli [1], p. 171; Burge [2], pp. 283–4.

course, if the suggestion is right, Frege will be immediately encumbered with the difficulties which, as we saw in Chapter 2, plague Ockham's semantics. Frege subsequently repudiated the suggestion that objects might go proxy for concepts,[70] and in his later writings, as a consequence of the discovery of Russell's paradox, he abjured his earlier view that 'the concept F' introduces an object.[71]) A concept can only strictly be referred to by an appropriate concept-expression, such as 'is a horse', as that occurs in a particular sentence.[72] Hence Frege is forced to say that the concept *horse* is not a concept.[73] That, as Kerry had pointed out in the publications to which Frege's 'Über Begriff und Gegenstand' was a response,[74] is an intolerable conclusion.[75]

The problem arises, so Frege tells us, because 'the concept *horse*', being a proper name in his broad sense (which includes definite descriptions, as we now call them) necessarily refers to an object, not a concept. Now recall (§15) that it is important to draw a semantical distinction (which Frege failed to draw) between definite descriptions and proper names strictly so called. As we have seen, Frege's broad category of proper names is too broad. Frege was wrong to assimilate definite descriptions semantically to strict proper names, because whereas the latter refer to their bearers, and moreover leave no room for a distinction between reference and satisfaction—the satisfier (bearer) of a strict proper name *is* its referent—definite descriptions, like the concept-expressions out of which they are composed, import precisely such a distinction, so that while their referents will be complex conceptual entities—those abstract entities with which the understander must be acquainted in order to count as understanding the linguistic description in question—their satisfiers, by contrast, will be those objects (if any) of which the relevant descriptions are true. The distinction between reference and satisfaction that, as Frege was the first to see clearly, is mandatory in the case of concept-expressions, must be carried over to the case of definite descriptions. In the light of this semantic distinction, it is natural to ask: is 'the concept *horse*' a strict proper name or a definite description? However, though in itself the question is an interesting one, and in other contexts might be important, it turns out that in the present context nothing substantial turns on answering it. (For what it is worth, I would be inclined to give the former answer, whereas Davidson, it seems, favours the latter.[76]) Let us see why this is so.

[70] [26], p. 130; cf. Kemmerling [2], p. 46 n. 8.
[71] See [26], pp. 288–9. Cf. C. Parsons [1], p. 275; Burge [2], p. 294.
[72] See [13], p. 372 n. ([21], p. 270 n. 5). Cf. [2], p. 50 ([25], pp. 92–3); Currie [1], p. 152.
[73] [7], pp. 196–7 ([21], pp. 170–1).   [74] Angelelli [1], p. 185 n. 86.
[75] Cf. Wright [1], p. 16, and [3].   [76] Davidson [2], p. 134. So too Grossmann [1], pp. 53–4.

If 'the concept *horse*' is a strict proper name (like 'the Mersey' or 'the Sun'), then the problem confronting Frege is that its referent is an object—a saturated entity—not a concept. Frege himself conceived the problem in exactly these terms. But the situation is not materially altered for Frege if we construe 'the concept *horse*' as a definite description (meaning 'the concept referred to by the predicate "... is a horse"'). Of course, if we construed 'the concept *horse*' in this way, although it would be true that the *referent* of that expression was a complex conceptual entity and also, paradoxically, an object (because we might pick it out using an expression like '*that* concept'), the paradox thereby generated would not be exactly *Frege's* paradox. Frege's paradox is that the *satisfier* of this description (if that is what it is) is both a concept and an object. Note that, in the case of linguistic expressions that have both a referent and a distinct satisfier, both referent and satisfier must be saturated, since *any* referent, and *any* satisfier, is necessarily an object, in Frege's terms, and so saturated. If, then, we decide that 'the concept *horse*' is a definite description, we will say: both its referent and its satisfier are saturated. But, as we saw in §15, the *truth-conditions* of a sentence like 'The concept *horse* is not a concept', which expresses Frege's paradox, will be such that the sentence is determined to be true just in case the *satisfier* (not: the *referent*) of the definite description (if that is what it is) in subject position satisfies the concept-expression figuring in the sentence as its grammatical predicate. The satisfier of any linguistic expression is necessarily an object; but it is plausible that the satisfier (if any) of a purported definite description of the specific form 'the concept...' must *also* be a concept, which precipitates a paradox. Since nothing turns on which approach we adopt, I shall assume that 'the concept *horse*' is a strict proper name, not a definite description.

Having dealt with this complication, if only to set it aside, it is time to ask: is the paradox avoidable in any way? Geach tries to rectify Frege's position (as least as that is set out in 'Über Begriff und Gegenstand'), which he regards as basically sound, by stipulating that 'the concept *horse*' is to stand neither for a concept nor for an object, but should be treated as an incomplete symbol, along the lines of Russell's 1905 treatment of definite descriptions.[77] So no reference is recognized as attaching to the phrase 'the concept *horse*' just as such, but the whole context 'The concept *horse* is realized' (or: 'The concept *horse* applies to Xanthos') is analysed as 'Something is a horse' ('Xanthos is a horse'). Or consider an example of Graham Priest's: 'Phar Lap falls under the concept *horse*'.[78] Since *falling under* is a relation between an object and a concept, this sentence is, on Frege's showing, false, even if Phar Lap is a horse: for 'the

---

[77] [7], pp. 220–1, 229–30; cf. [1], pp. 472–3; [2], p. 259; [4], pp. 77–80.   [78] [1], pp. 181–2.

concept *horse*' refers to an object, not a concept. But the offending sentence can be harmlessly paraphrased as 'Phar Lap is a horse'. Geach now suggests that 'sentences not exponible in some such innocent way (e.g., "The concept *man* is timeless") may be regarded as nonsensical';[79] and again, 'Sentences from which "the concept Man" cannot be . . . eliminated, like "The concept Man is an abstract entity", may well be treated as meaningless; *vile damnum*'.[80] Unfortunately the loss of such non-exponible sentences is not so cheap after all, for, on Geach's own showing, the sentence 'The concept *horse* is neither a concept nor an object', not being exponible, will come out nonsensical, but on Geach's treatment of the semantics of 'the concept *horse*' it surely ought to be true. Similarly with 'The concept *horse* was considered by Frege'.[81] That ought to be true, but how does Geach propose to paraphrase it? Did Frege perhaps contemplate individual horses (Xanthos, Balios, Podarge, . . .), or what all horses have in common—the universal equinity? Obviously these suggestions fail. In fact, on either Frege's original approach or Geach's suggested revision of it, the fundamental division in Frege's philosophy between concepts and objects threatens to collapse. The division is expressed by saying, for example, 'No concept is an object', as I said at the beginning of this chapter: but on Frege's and Geach's showing this sentence either fails to express a proposition at all, or expresses a (necessarily) false one, since in order to say what it is trying to say it has to reify concepts, something that, in Frege's view, cannot be done.[82] Alternatively, it has to admit a variable ranging over both objects and concepts, which, again, Frege disallows.[83] (A similar difficulty confronts Russellian type theory. For type restrictions require us to ban variables ranging over more than one type: but then the restrictions themselves cannot be stated, for we precisely need to employ promiscuous variables to state them.[84])

Our response to Geach's proposal gives us the means to deal with a related suggestion made by Richard Mendelsohn. Mendelsohn attempts to circumvent the paradox by construing 'ξ is a concept' as a special functor referring to the second-order existential quantifier. (In terms of the Fregean hierarchy of levels, which I shall explore in the next chapter, it would be a third-level expression.[85]) One might object to Mendelsohn's proposal on the basis that the sentence 'the concept *horse* is a concept' would not come out false, as

---

[79] [7], p. 221.   [80] [7], p. 230; cf. [4], p. 79.   [81] Priest [1], p. 182.

[82] Cf. Mendelsohn, pp. 80–1; Dummett [3], p. 240; T. Parsons [2], p. 451.

[83] Ricketts [3], pp. 179–80. Cf. Noonan, pp. 163–4.

[84] See e.g. Russell [3], §492; Gödel, ii, p. 138; Black [1], p. 117; Hylton [2], pp. 91–2, 104–5; Bostock [1], p. 113; Weir, pp. 76–7; Potter [1], pp. 144–6; Menzel, pp. 66, 79.

[85] Mendelsohn, p. 80. A similar strategy is pursued by T. Parsons [2], pp. 452–4, 459–63. Cf. Frege's remarks in his letter to Russell of 28 July 1902 ([22], p. 224; cf. p. 218).

Frege thinks it should, but rather ill formed, for its subject term 'the concept *horse*' is a proper name, and so cannot be fitted into a slot which, if 'ξ is a concept' refers to the second-order existential quantifier, must be reserved for a first-order quantifier.[86] But Mendelsohn can deal with this objection, at least in part: he tells us that, 'logically, "the concept *horse*" is no more serving as an *Eigenname* in ["The concept *horse* exists"] than is "the number 2" in ["The number 2 exists"]'.[87] Hence the nominal appearance of the phrase 'the concept *horse*' will disappear in our formalization of (for example) 'the concept *horse* is a concept': on Mendelsohn's proposal, this sentence emerges as

$$\exists\phi\forall x(\phi(x) \leftrightarrow \text{Horse}(x)).$$

This is certainly well formed: unfortunately it is also trivially true, whereas Frege thought, as we noted, that 'the concept *horse* is a concept' is false. Waiving that inconvenience, whose status as a point against Mendelsohn is admittedly unclear, the most pressing problem with his proposal is not, as the objection in effect supposed, that 'the concept *horse*' *cannot* be treated as an incomplete symbol. As with Geach's similar proposal, the problem is that the strategy does not go far enough:[88] it may work in a few individual cases, but it provides us with no general way of capturing the meaningfulness of a whole range of statements about concepts that, on Frege's own showing, ought to be true—and are indeed fundamental to his philosophy of language—such as 'the concept *horse* is an abstract entity', 'the concept *horse* is not an object', 'every concept is unsaturated', 'a concept is a function whose value is a truth-value'.[89] These and similar sentences are *not* exponible along the lines suggested by Geach and Mendelsohn. So the proposal that the paradox can be circumvented by treating expressions of the form 'the concept . . .' as incomplete symbols fails.

The upshot of these considerations is that the paradox must be regarded as no mere quirk of language, without theoretical significance, as Frege evidently hoped, but as a serious setback to his account of unity.[90] Angelelli, having rightly remarked that 'there is no way out of the paradox, if one wishes to stay *within* Frege's system', adds that Frege's plea to the reader to grant him a pinch of salt 'indicates that we should take into account what we *mean* and not what we *say*. Is this perhaps the simplest way out?'[91] The answer to the question is

---

[86] So Kleemeier, p. 232 n. 1.   [87] Mendelsohn, p. 80.

[88] These remarks apply also to Dummett's rather similar strategy for avoiding the paradox at [2], pp. 211–22, and to Kemmerling's in his [2]. See further §30 below.

[89] See here again Priest [1], pp. 182–3, from whom I have drawn the latter two examples.

[90] See Frege [7], p. 204 ([21], p. 177); [13], p. 372 ([21], pp. 269–70); [14], p. 665 ([21], pp. 279–80); [26], pp. 288–9. Cf. Resnik [1], pp. 337–9; [4], pp. 94–5.

[91] [1], p. 188, n. 140.

that it is not a way out at all: if we cannot say it, we cannot mean it either. Angelelli writes further:

'The relation *instantiation* is not the name of instantiation—is not the name of what we *mean* by saying 'instantiation'. For, again, 'instantiation' (if taken as a saturated name) would fail to designate a relation. The name of instantiation is '$\phi(\xi)$'. This is strikingly similar to the scholastic theory of modes, which are for inherence what second intentions are for predication.[92]

Our suspicions are naturally aroused by the (perfectly apposite) comparison with modes: for modes are supposed not to be things, but that very statement is of course self-refuting.[93] Similarly, Angelelli's claim that 'the name of instantiation is "$\phi(\xi)$"' is, given that we are not allowed to use the word 'instantiation' to name instantiation, self-refuting: it is like saying 'concepts are not objects'. In the same place Angelelli refers us to an analogy given by Frege for the saturated–unsaturated distinction, according to which, when we divide a line in two at a particular point, the segment including the point of division may be compared to a saturated argument, while the segment with its end point missing may be compared to an unsaturated function.[94] But the analogy fails, for the 'incomplete' line segment is, ontologically speaking, just as finished an object as the 'complete' segment: we have no more difficulty in referring to open intervals, as objects, than we do to closed intervals.

29 Russell on Unity and the Paradox

Frege's paradox is replicated in a part of Russell's *The Principles of Mathematics* which we have already looked at (§10), namely the crucial fourth chapter, 'Proper Names, Adjectives, and Verbs'. It is in this chapter that Russell addresses the issue of propositional unity. We have seen (§10) that Russell held propositions to be composed of what he called terms, and that he divided terms into things and concepts. Things are terms 'indicated by proper names'; concepts are terms 'indicated by all other words', and in particular by adjectives or verbs.[95] Now Russellian concepts are like Fregean concepts at least to the extent that they are (to put it in Fregean terminology) unsaturated entities and, as such, supposedly responsible for the unity of the proposition.[96] But there

---

[92] [1], p. 178, incorporating n. 155 and substituting 'instantiation' for Angelelli's expression 'UF' (= 'das Fallen eines Einzelnen unter einen Begriff': p. 7). On modes, Angelelli has in mind Suarez, VII. i, §§17–19. Cf. also Hobbes [1], I. iii, §3.

[93] Cf. my [15], p. 150.   [94] Frege [5], p. 7 ([21], pp. 128–9); cf. Davidson [2], p. 132.

[95] [3], §48.   [96] Cf. Palmer, p. 20; Imaguire, pp. 160, 176.

is a noteworthy difference between Fregean and Russellian concepts, and this emerges when we ask whether, in view of the fact that Russellian concepts are, like Fregean concepts, unsaturated, the attempt to refer to one of them by means of a proper name necessarily misfires. Frege's answer to this question, as we have seen, is affirmative: for the attempt to refer to a concept by means of a proper name necessarily nets an object instead (if it nets anything), so that even an expression like 'the concept *horse*', which ought to refer to a concept, in fact refers to (at best) an object. But Russell's answer to our question is negative.

For Russell contends that concepts must be 'capable of being made into a logical subject';[97] and by this he clearly means that they must be capable of being made into logical subjects without relinquishing their status as concepts. He has two arguments for his claim, one to deal with concepts which are (indicated by) adjectives, and another to accommodate concepts which are (indicated by) verbs. First, he argues that if '*one* as adjective' differed from '1 as term', then in that very statement '*one* as adjective has been made into a term [i.e. logical subject]', so that the thesis cannot be stated without self-contradiction.[98] Secondly, he contends that 'If we say "*kills* does not mean the same as *to kill*" we have already made *kills* a subject, and we cannot say that the concept expressed by the word *kills* cannot be made a subject.'[99] These arguments are unsuccessful. The first fails because, as Frege would insist, Russell has not managed to refer to a concept in using the phrase '*one* as adjective': if he means to refer to the conceptual referent of the concept-expression 'ξ is one', he can only do so by putting that concept-expression into a sentence in which it is used (not mentioned); the concept cannot be got at outside the sentential context by means of a sheer designating expression, which in this case necessarily misses its target.[100] The second argument fails because Russell's sample sentence is either nonsense or else means: 'kills' does not mean the same as 'to kill'. But that sentence is not about concepts: it is about words.

These deficiencies of his account notwithstanding, Russell attempts to accommodate both aspects of the concept he purports to have identified—the concept's unsaturatedness and its capacity to function as a 'logical subject'—with a curious doctrine of the 'twofold nature' of the concept.[101] As far as concepts as adjectives (which Russell also calls predicates) are concerned, we are told that '*human* and *humanity* denote precisely the same concept,

[97] [3], §52. Cf. Hylton [2], pp. 89–91; Stevens [3], pp. 23–6.
[98] [3], §49. Cf. his letter to Frege of 24 June 1902 (Frege [22], p. 216).   [99] [3], §52.
[100] See Frege [13], p. 372 n. ([21], p. 270), where he comments on Russell's [3], §49.
[101] On this doctrine and its background in Russell's pre-1903 writings, see N. Griffin [4], esp. pp. 162–4, 179–80.

these words being employed respectively according to the kind of relation in which this concept stands to the other constituents of a proposition in which it occurs',[102] so that in 'Humanity belongs to Socrates' the common concept figures as logical subject, whereas in 'Socrates is human' it figures as adjective or predicate.[103] As for verbs, the doctrine of the 'twofold nature of the verb' is introduced in the context of a discussion of the way analysis destroys the unity of the sentence '*A* differs from *B*'. This comes in §54, of which I quote the whole, since it is a key text containing a number of important ideas that will feature prominently later in this study:[104]

> The twofold nature of the verb, as actual verb and as verbal noun, may be expressed, if all verbs are held to be relations, as the difference between a relation in itself and a relation actually relating. Consider, for example, the proposition '*A* differs from *B*'. The constituents of this proposition, if we analyse it, appear to be only *A*, difference, *B*. Yet these constituents, thus placed side by side, do not reconstitute the proposition. The difference which occurs in the proposition actually relates *A* and *B*, whereas the difference after analysis is a notion which has no connection with *A* and *B*. It may be said that we ought, in the analysis, to mention the relations which difference has to *A* and *B*, relations which are expressed by *is* and *from* when we say '*A* is different from *B*'. These relations consist in the fact that *A* is referent and *B* relatum with respect to difference.[105] But '*A*, referent, difference, relatum, *B*' is still merely a list of terms, not a proposition. A proposition, in fact, is essentially a unity, and when analysis has destroyed the unity, no enumeration of constituents will restore the proposition. The verb, when used as a verb, embodies the unity of the proposition, and is thus distinguishable from the verb considered as a term, though I do not know how to give a clear account of the precise nature of the distinction.[106]

Note that the view mentioned in passing at the beginning of this passage, namely that all verbs are relations, is one that Russell has just tentatively endorsed ('the true logical verb in a proposition may be always regarded as asserting a relation').[107] Given the conclusion of the passage, which asserts that the verb is, when used as a verb, responsible for the unity of the proposition,[108] that implies that responsibility for unity is ultimately shouldered by relations.[109] It is also an implication of what is said here that, as Russell recognizes, 'one

---

[102] [3], §46.   [103] [3], §48. Cf. Ricketts [4], p. 103.

[104] On this text see Hylton [2], pp. 15–16.

[105] The referent is the source of the relation, the relatum its target: see n. 151 below.

[106] Cf. [3], §§55, 81, 135–6, 138, 439; Meinong [1], §15, p. 432; Davidson [2], p. 84.

[107] [3], §53. Cf. the passage from the Port-Royal *Logic* and *Grammar* quoted above (§26); Bolzano [2], §§127, 132–44.

[108] With the conclusion of the passage cf. his unpublished paper 'The Nature of Truth', [18], p. 503: 'Verbs seem to be used to express just that particular kind of complexity which propositions have and other complexes do not have. But I do not know how to describe this kind of complexity.'

[109] Cf. L. Linsky [1], p. 627.

verb, and one only, must occur as verb in every proposition',[110] since every proposition must be unified, and cannot be unified twice.

One point which emerges from the passage I have quoted, and which is of immediate relevance to our concerns, is this: the passage surely indicates that the difference I identified above between Fregean and Russellian concepts is in fact quite superficial. The difference between Frege's and Russell's treatments of concepts might indeed *seem* to point to a substantial doctrinal disparity: for Russell continues to count a concept that has been made into a 'logical subject' as a *concept*, unlike Frege, who would classify it as an *object* (if anything); and indeed in the appendix to *Principles* Russell criticizes Frege on just this point.[111] But in reality the difference amounts to very little. This is because it is clear that Russell no longer regards a concept that has been made into a 'logical subject' as (in Frege's terminology) *unsaturated*—as capable of performing a *unifying* function in the proposition in which it occurs. And that robs the apparent difference in their treatments of the concept of philosophical significance. In the above passage, the thesis of the unanalysability of the 'relation actually relating' is Russell's version of Frege's doctrine of the unsaturatedness of the concept. The relation actually relating, when made into a 'logical subject', ceases to be a relation actually relating and becomes a relation in itself: it does indeed remain a relation and a concept, but it is no longer performing the office that is proprietary to it *as* a relation and a concept; it is no longer unifying.

In contradistinction to concepts, which, as we have seen, Russell in *Principles* thinks have to be capable of being made into logical subjects, Russell regarded propositional functions in that work as *incapable* of being treated as logical subjects, in spite of the arguments we have rehearsed above. This is in order to avoid 'the Contradiction' (Russell's paradox),[112] as well as the difficulty that if propositional functions are individuals there will be more values of the propositional function 'the self-identity of x' than there are individuals.[113] Hence we are told in *Principles* that 'the ϕ in ϕx is not a separate and distinguishable entity: it lives in the propositions of the form ϕx, and cannot survive analysis',[114] and in the introduction to the second edition of *Principia* it is remarked that

whereas a is a constituent of $f!a$ [i.e. an elementary function in a],[115] f is not; thus the matrix $\phi!x$ [i.e. the elementary propositional function $\phi(x)$] has the peculiarity that,

---

[110] [3], §55. Cf. his letter to Moore of 1 Dec. 1898: I quote the relevant passage in §86.

[111] [3], §483. But Russell's discussion of Frege in §§481 and 483 in particular, where he seems to interpret Frege as holding that 'the concept F' is the name of a name, is vitiated by misunderstanding: see Angelelli [1], p. 189 n. 145.

[112] [3], §85.   [113] See [3], §499. Cf. Cocchiarella [1], pp. 199–200.   [114] [3], §85.

[115] Whitehead and Russell, i, p. xxviii.

when a value is assigned to x, this value is a constituent of the result, but when a value is assigned to ϕ, this value is absorbed in the resulting proposition, and completely disappears.[116]

Russell was 'highly doubtful' whether this view does not lead to contradiction, though he comforts himself with the thought that it does not precipitate *the* Contradiction.[117] In fact, of course, it is clear that the view does lead to contradiction, at least by Russell's lights, for his argument that concepts in general must be capable of being made into logical subjects, on pain of contradiction, carries over without let or hindrance to the case of propositional functions. In any event, in *Principles* propositional functions are much closer to Fregean *Begriffe* than are Russellian 'concepts', and Russell indeed noted in his appendix on Frege that 'the word *Begriff* is used by Frege to mean nearly the same thing as *propositional function*'.[118]

Now although, as we have seen (§§11–12), Russell was later to get into entanglements over the phrase 'relation actually relating', confusing the relation actually relating taken as unifier with the relation actually relating taken as truth-maker, the ambiguity that gives rise to those difficulties seems to be absent from the discussion from which the long passage quoted above is drawn, where the 'relation actually relating' figures unequivocally as propositional unifier, and is distinguished as such from the 'relation in itself'. So too Strawson, in agreement with the Frege–Russell ascription of the responsibility for sentential unity to the verb or verb-phrase, remarks on the 'double function' of such expressions—the function of 'introducing' a concept, and the function of unifying the expressed proposition.[119] But the pessimism Russell evinces at the end of the passage I have quoted, and which is not shared by Strawson,[120] is well placed: for the moral of Frege's paradox is indeed that nothing can play both the roles which Russell and Strawson assign to verbs.[121]

And unfortunately Russell cannot, in the end, avoid the paradox. That is indeed what we should expect, given that the difference between his treatment of the concept and Frege's is, as I have urged, entirely superficial. If the difference between them on this point really is so slight, we should expect the difficulties that beset Frege to encumber Russell too; and they do. The paradox is not hard to find: it is lurking in, for example, Russell's use of the phrase 'the relation actually relating'. What does this phrase refer to? (Or: what

---

[116] Whitehead and Russell, i, p. xxx. Cf. Russell [15], p. 137.   [117] [3], §85.
[118] [3], §481; cf. Cocchiarella [1], pp. 68–9; Pelham and Urquhart, pp. 313–14.
[119] [1], pp. 140, 146, 151; [3], p. 293; [6], pp. 26–8. Similarly Hochberg [2], pp. 222, 234–5.
[120] See [1], pp. 167–73; [5], p. 11.   [121] Cf. Ryle, i, p. 187.

is it satisfied by?)[122] Suppose I want to talk about the relation actually relating in the proposition expressed by the sentence '*A* differs from *B*': how can I do that? Well, it cannot be done. In making the attempt, as I just did, I necessarily turn the thing I want to talk about into a relation in itself. The thing remains a relation and a concept (herein lies the divergence from Frege), but it is no longer functioning as a relation actually relating, that is, as an unsaturated entity (which is why the divergence is merely superficial). The paradox of the concept *horse* emerges in Russell's doctrine of the necessary inadequacy of analysis—the fact that whatever is responsible for the unity of the proposition cannot be identified and labelled as such in an inventory of the proposition's constituents. We have not yet expressed Russell's version of the paradox in a recognizably paradoxical form, but it is easy to do that: Russell is obliged to say that the relation actually relating (in, for example, the proposition expressed by the sentence '*A* differs from *B*') is not a relation actually relating. That is every bit as intolerable a state of affairs as the alleged circumstance that the concept *horse* is not a concept.

30 An Unsuccessful Attempt to Avoid the Paradox

The paradox in Frege's version of it—the upshot that the concept *horse* is not a concept—cannot be circumvented by replacing expressions like 'the concept *horse*' with circumlocutions like 'what the concept-word "horse" refers to', as Frege at one point envisages:

The expression 'the reference (*Bedeutung*) of the concept-word *A*' is really one we should reject, because the definite article in front of 'reference' indicates an object and negates the predicative nature of the concept. It would at least be an improvement to talk about 'what the concept-word *A* refers to (*bedeutet*)', for this can at any rate be used predicatively: 'Jesus is what the concept-word "human being" (*Mensch*) refers to' in the sense of 'Jesus is a human being'.[123]

Frege's idea here seems to be that the circumlocution avoids attracting the paradox in virtue of having a purely predicative form, that is, by having a form that fits it to *say something of* an object rather than *refer to* an object. But in this he is plainly mistaken: for if '*E*' is a proper name in Frege's broad sense then a noun-phrase of the form 'what the expression "*E*" refers to' will equally be a proper name. And in the present case '*E*' indeed is a proper name in

---

[122] Recall the discussion of §28 above on the question whether 'the concept *horse*' is a strict proper name or a definite description. Parallel remarks apply to 'the relation actually relating'.

[123] [26], p. 133. Cf. Geach [4], p. 156.

that sense, since it goes proxy for expressions like 'the concept *human being*' or 'the concept *horse*' which, being strict proper names (or perhaps definite descriptions), are proper names in Frege's broad sense; so too, therefore, are the relevant circumlocutions.

If, now, we try to rectify the situation by incorporating the copula into the circumlocution, while we no doubt obtain something unsaturated ('is what the concept-word "horse" refers to'), we do not obtain anything that can be used to circumvent the paradox. This point is overlooked by Frege in the above passage, which in effect cheats: we are first told that 'what the concept-word *A* refers to (*bedeutet*)' is predicative in nature, but when Frege gives us an example of such a phrase functioning predicatively, we find that the copula has been smuggled into it ('Jesus *is* what the concept-word "human being" refers to'): the linguistic item which was introduced to enable us to circumvent the paradox ('what the concept-word *A* refers to') is not the same as the item which figures predicatively in sentences of the form '*X* is what the concept-word *A* refers to' (namely, 'is what the concept-word *A* refers to').[124] But it will not do to prefix or delete the copula *ad libitum*, without proper book-keeping, on the ground that, as Dummett puts it, 'for Frege, the copula is a mere grammatical device, with no content'.[125] Dummett is right, as we have seen (§26), that Frege regards the copula as a mere device for indicating the form of a declarative sentence.[126] There may be some sense in which a truth lies behind Frege's position: at any rate, I shall in due course be suggesting that, although what I shall call the *logical* copula does indeed have sense (and therefore reference), the kind of sense (and reference) it has differs in a radical way from the kinds of sense (and reference) enjoyed by all other words. But Frege's position on the *grammatical* copula cannot be admitted if it is intended to imply that that copula has no semantical significance at all—or even if it merely implies that the copula is a degenerate case of a meaningful expression, that, as Geach puts it, 'the "is" operator is like adding zero or multiplying by one'.[127] I suggested above (§26), and will argue in detail below (§66), that Frege's conception of predication, and hence of unsaturatedness, is a grammatical rather than logical one: it follows that, on Frege's own showing, the grammatical copula has the capacity to render an expression unsaturated. This modification has the most fundamental effect on the reference of the expression so modified that Frege's semantics recognizes, and it is simply not an option for Frege then

---

[124] Cf. Davidson [2], p. 135 n. 17.

[125] [2], p. 214. Frege's cavalier approach to the copula again emerges at [3], §70.

[126] Cf. [26], p. 189: 'Der sprachliche Ausdruck für die Eigentümlichkeit des Gedankens ist die Copula oder die Personalendung des Verbums.'

[127] [10], p. 182.

to say that the difference between saturated and unsaturated expressions is *merely* grammatical—as though the one sort of expression might have the same kind of sense and reference as the other. This latter thesis would undermine the whole point of the doctrine of unsaturatedness, which is to subserve an account of unity: for saturated and unsaturated entities at the levels of sense and reference would no longer engage with one another in the right way, and in a way isomorphic to the way saturated and unsaturated expressions engage with one another at the level of symbolic language, to yield Frege's account of the unities of sentence and proposition.

Evans once remarked that Frege's toleration of Thoughts without truth-values represented 'the great fault-line in Frege's mature philosophy of lang-uage'.[128] But there was, unfortunately, more than one such fault-line in Frege's mature philosophy of language, and another is constituted by his occasional tendency to blur the distinction between phrases like '(a) horse' and '(a) human being'—expressions that it would be quite natural to call 'concept-expressions'—on the one hand, and phrases like 'is a horse' and 'is a human being' on the other, which may be called predicative in the sense indicated, namely that they are fitted to *say something of* an object rather than *refer to* an object. What we might call Frege's official position, as set out in the passage from the Schoenflies review quoted above in §26, and reiterated in a letter to Linke written in 1919,[129] is that the copula belongs with the concept-expression. In practice he sometimes abandons this position, as we have seen.[130] But this insouciance will not do.[131] For either the copula is being counted as part of a linguistic expression or it is not. If it is included, then it may certainly be held to render the phrases to which it is attached unsaturated, in the sense that there is no specifying the reference of such an expression by means of a proper name: but in that case, the unsaturated expression 'is a horse' can at best be said to mean the same as 'is what the concept-word "horse" refers to', and not the same as the truncated 'what the concept-word "horse" refers to'. And then if Frege's paradox attaches to a given form of words, such as 'is a horse', it will arise afresh for any adequate circumlocution of that form of words, such as 'is what the concept-word "horse" refers to'.

Frege's tendency to employ the term 'concept-word' indifferently as a name either of expressions like '(a) horse' or of expressions like 'is a horse' was thus an unhappy one. The natural move, as I have suggested, would have been

---

[128] [1], p. 24.   [129] [22], p. 154.

[130] See also [7], pp. 194, 198 ([21], pp. 168–9, 172), where 'a planet' and 'nothing other than Venus' are given as examples of concept-expressions, and we are told that 'all', 'any', 'no', and 'some' are sometimes prefixed to concept-expressions. Cf. T. Parsons [2], p. 458.

[131] Contra MacBride [6], pp. 441, 462–3.

to reserve the label 'concept-word'—in general, 'concept-expression'—for general terms like '(a) horse', thereby distinguishing these from predicative expressions incorporating the copula, such as 'is a horse'. The paradox would then have been entirely avoided, for the concept *horse* could have figured as a genuine object, the referent of the unambiguously saturated concept-expression '(a) horse'. Unsaturatedness would have been confined to the predicative expression 'is a horse'. And, since there is no grammatically correct way of referring to any purported referent of this expression by means of a proper name, no paradox would have arisen. The paradox which embarrassed Frege depended for its impact on the fact that the relevant self-contradictory claim—the concept *horse* is not a concept—is grammatically well formed. But since expressions like 'the concept *is a horse*' or 'the object *is a horse*' are nonsense, no relevant grammatically well-formed paradox can be constructed in respect of any purported referents of genuinely predicative expressions.[132]

31 The Paradox and the Level of Language

Given that the saturated–unsaturated distinction arises for Frege in the first instance in the realm of sense, and is transferred from there to the levels of symbolic language and of reference (§25), we should expect the paradox of the concept *horse* to arise in the first instance at the level of sense. The paradox does indeed arise at the level of sense: 'The sense of "is a horse" is unsaturated' ought, on Frege's showing, to be both true and false. Or, to put the point in terms closer to the paradox as it arises in the realm of reference, if we employ '[sense]' to mean an unsaturated sense, the paradox takes the form of Frege's having to say that

The [sense] of 'is a horse' is not a [sense]

is both true and false. But while we can perhaps suppose that this is the original form of the paradox, and that it is then read over from the level of sense to the level of reference, there is a difficulty about conceiving a parallel transfer to the level of symbolic language. For if we do not seek to specify the senses or referents of the critical linguistic expressions, but remain at the

---

[132] With the argument of this paragraph, cf. Wiggins [3]. MacBride ([6], pp. 464–5) criticizes Wiggins on the basis that the failure of intersubstitutability of two expressions (as it might be, 'is a horse' and 'a horse') does not show that these expressions are not co-referential (cf. Oliver [4], p. 180). I have agreed with that: §21. But the point here is that (as we also noted in §21) *Frege* took intersubstitutability to be necessary for co-reference.

level of symbolic language, no paradox arises: there is no paradox of the concept-expression 'is a horse'. (A structurally similar point applies to Russellian type theory.[133])

Frege at one point in his essay 'Über Begriff und Gegenstand' tries to deny this. The relevant passage reads:

A similar [awkwardness of language to that precipitated by the paradox of the concept *horse*] arises when we say in connection with the sentence 'This rose is red': the grammatical predicate 'is red' belongs to the subject 'this rose'. Here the words 'the grammatical predicate "is red"' are not a grammatical predicate but a subject. In expressly calling it a predicate, we deprive it of this property.[134]

Here again we find the identification, which we have already noted (§26), of a concept-expression with the grammatical predicate of a sentence. Now a grammatical predicate is an object. That is because it is a linguistic item and, as we have seen (§25), any item of symbolic language, no matter how riddled with slots for further expressions, is an object. We cannot, Frege in effect observes, by means of a proper name refer to a grammatical predicate in a sentence in which that very (token) name occurs *as grammatical predicate*. For the act of reference by means of a proper name necessarily reifies its referent, whereas the attempt to deploy the relevant word(s) as a predicate necessarily removes that referent from the domain of objects. This point is no doubt correct, but it is irrelevant to the saturated–unsaturated distinction: for it is true quite generally that no linguistic expression can simultaneously be used transparently (to refer to its customary referent) and autonymously (to refer to itself), as would be required, in the suggested example, of a grammatical predicate; the impossibility of combining these roles in a single utterance or inscription is not peculiar to grammatical predicates.

The mistake has arisen as a result of a confusion between mention and use. Frege is confounding the referents of grammatical predicates, for which the paradox does arise, with those predicates themselves, for which it does not. For the sentence

The grammatical predicate 'is red' is not a predicate

is quite straightforwardly false, and not paradoxically both true and false, in contradistinction to its counterparts in the realms of reference and sense—

The concept red is not a concept,
The [sense] of 'is red' is not a [sense]—

[133] Black [1], p. 119; Küng, p. 79.   [134] [7], p. 197 n. 8 ([21], pp. 170–1 n. 8).

which clearly have to be false, but are also, on Frege's approach, true. If we search for something true to correspond to these paradoxical statements at the level of symbolic language, what we come up with is

'The grammatical predicate "is red"' is not a predicate,

which, while certainly true, is not at all paradoxical, for the subject phrase ('The grammatical predicate "is red"') does not purport to be a grammatical predicate; 'is red', on the other hand, both purports to be and is a grammatical predicate.[135]

Mendelsohn tries to defend Frege on the basis that 'if the analogy between predicates and concepts is to hold rigorously, then just as a concept is a function, so too the predicate that denotes it would have to be a function'.[136] A similar strategy has long been advocated by Geach.[137] This approach has the consequence that a predicate cannot be identified with a word or string of words, for words (and strings of words) are straightforwardly (in Frege's terms) objects, not functions. But even when we construe predicates as expressions containing their argument-places essentially, these being rigorously annotated, such expressions remain, for Frege, objects rather than functions.[138] Geach is right that an annotated predicate like 'ξ is a horse', taken as abstracted from a sentence like 'Xanthos is a horse', is not a *quotable part of that sentence*;[139] but it is still—*pace* Geach[140]—*quotable*, and, as such, an object, not a function in any sense that would given rise to Frege's paradox.[141]

It is true, of course, that a given annotated predicate cannot simply be identified with the linguistic expression we use to express it, for although 'ξ from bondage will deliver ξ' (abstracted from 'Cassius from bondage will deliver Cassius') is a different linguistic expression from 'ζ from bondage will deliver ζ', because they contain different symbols, they count as the same annotated predicate, since the difference in Greek letters used to annotate these expressions does not signify a difference in predicate. But the fact that annotated predicates, so understood, have different identity-conditions from the linguistic expressions we use to convey them does not prevent us from quoting and referring to them, so long as we make clear what we are talking

---

[135]   See Dummett [1], p. 75; Stevens [3], pp. 29–30.

[136]   Mendelsohn, p. 81. Cf. Angelelli [1], p. 174; Bell [1], p. 40.

[137]   See [4], pp. 143–7; [7], pp. 224–5; [9], pp. 440–5. But note that Geach's use of 'predicate' is not uniform: at [3], p. 23, a predicate is held to be a linguistic entity.

[138]   Such predicates are closely related to what Dummett calls complex predicates: see §64.

[139]   [4], p. 143; cf. Hale [1], p. 285; Noonan, pp. 157–8.   [140]   [4], p. 147.

[141]   In his letter to Russell of 29 June 1902 Frege clearly implies ([22], pp. 218–19) that this is his view: for he suggests replacing the illicit expression 'ξ ist eine Funktion' with the—by implication, acceptable—variant locution 'ξ ist ein Funktionsname'.

about—that, for instance, in mentioning the expression 'ξ is a horse' we mean the predicate abstracted from a sentence (say, 'Xanthos is a horse'), and not the linguistic expression formed from the fourteenth letter of the Greek alphabet concatenated with the English expression 'is a horse'. Again, when we treat an expression like '$\lambda x(\frac{1}{2}(e^x - e^{-x}))$' as the name of a function, the function-name is not to be identified with that particular linguistic expression, for the expression '$\lambda x(\frac{1}{2}(e^x - e^{-x}))$' not only refers to the same function as does any transform of that formula in which new variables have been substituted for old (avoiding 'clash of variables'), such as '$\lambda y(\frac{1}{2}(e^y - e^{-y}))$'; it is even the case that, as Church notes,[142] these two expressions have the same sense—they are in fact the *same* functional expression.[143] So the function name is a *pattern* displayed by that expression, not a linguistic expression. Annotated predicates, in general, can be treated as patterns occurring in sentences that are similar in certain respects: though such patterns cannot be *identified* with the linguistic expressions we use to pick them out, they can nonetheless *be* referred to by means of these expressions, and are accordingly objects.[144]

32 Reforming Frege's Treatment of Concept-Expressions

Given Frege's careless assimilation of concept-expressions to grammatical predicates, he can only extricate himself from his difficulties at the level of reference by insisting that there is no way of *referring* to the unsaturated entity allegedly introduced by a concept-expression or grammatical predicate—and I shall continue, for convenience and in deference to Frege, to call these unsaturated referents 'concepts'[145]—other than by *using* the relevant concept-expression (or a synonym) in a sentence.[146] Concepts cannot be, as it were, first metamorphosed[147] into objects and then referred to in that manifestation: any attempt to turn the trick by employing the prefix 'the concept...'

---

[142] [6], p. 20 n. 52; cf. p. 40 n. 96; [4], p. 103.   [143] Cf. Thiel, p. 47 n. 1; Bridge, pp. 29–30, 59.

[144] Cf. Simons [5], p. 201; [6], p. 84.

[145] Frege was departing from ancient tradition in so labelling items at the level of reference 'concepts': see here Tugendhat [2], pp. 190–1. Traditionally, the items that philosophers had called 'concepts' were treated as entities existing at the level of sense, or at the mental as opposed to the worldly level. The terminological issue can be settled either way, so long as one recognizes the existence of universal entities at the level of reference available to structure objects at that level: see here my [15], ch. 5. (Note that Frege is himself not entirely consistent in his terminology, occasionally using 'concept' to mean the sense of a concept-expression: see e.g. [26], p. 273, with Künne [2], pp. 130, 137.)

[146] See the passages listed in n. 72 above. Cf. Palmer, pp. 39–40; Conant [2], p. 434 n. 39.

[147] Frege [7], p. 197 ([21], p. 171); letter to Russell of 28 July 1902 ([22], p. 224).

automatically undermines the attempted reference. In one of the passages where the metaphor of metamorphosis occurs, Frege immediately replaces it with what he regards as a more precise expression: the concept must be *represented by* an object (I noted the occurrence of this locution in §28).[148] But this revised formulation still employs a reifying manner of speaking that must, in strictness, be banned (and that in addition raises the problem we touched on earlier: which objects represent concepts?). Reference to concepts, as one might be tempted to put it, can only be achieved by stealth: by indicating the referent without trying to specify what sort of referent it is (whether saturated or unsaturated); by showing, but not saying (to draw on a Wittgensteinian distinction), that one is referring to the appropriate concept. Hence Frege must stop talking about the concept *horse*, for this form of words is (by his own lights) just nonsense, even—or perhaps we should say especially—in the claim that the concept *horse* is an object. Instead he must confine himself to talking of the *linguistic expression* 'is a horse', which, as we have seen (§31), is a perfectly good object. For given that no paradox arises at the level of language, there ought in principle to be no problem about applying a distinction between *Sinn* and *Bedeutung* to concept-expressions (or grammatical predicates), as Frege wished to do, provided we understand that the referents of such expressions cannot be specified by means of a proper name. I shall call the position resulting from this adjustment to Frege's official doctrine his 'reformed' position.

This description of Frege's reformed position now needs to be deepened; it also needs to be corrected, for, as the reader may have noticed, some of the locutions I have been employing to characterize it are mired in just the same paradoxical implications as the terms used by the historical Frege. Let us ask first how the reformed Frege specifies the meaning of concept-expressions (where these latter are not distinguished from grammatical predicates). Given that this feigned scion of Frege insists on the essentially predicative nature of concepts, and admits no means of referring to them other than by dint of the use in sentential contexts of appropriate concept-expressions, he will, in setting up meaning-specifications for the basic concept-words of a language, countenance only those specifications that respect this point. Thus a homophonic meaning-specification for the concept-word '(is) wise', say, might take the form

(1) $\forall x(x$ satisfies 'is wise' iff x is wise),

rather than a form which introduces concepts as objects, such as

(2) $\forall x(x$ satisfies 'is wise' iff x instantiates wisdom).

---

[148] [7], p. 197 ([21], p. 171).

The reformed Frege can concede the *truth* of (2); but he would insist that it does not give the *meaning* of the concept-word '(is) wise'.

In (1), the connection between language and world has indeed been set up; only, while the items on the language end of the relation are objects, what we find on the world end of the relation are, according to the reformed Frege's position, not objects. Now this last sentence is itself not paradox-free, because it is a consequence of the paradox not merely that one cannot specify, by means of any proper name (in Frege's broad sense), what concept-expressions refer to, but also that one cannot specify what it is that one cannot refer to, because any such specification would be indirectly reifying: hence the phrase 'what we find on the world end of the reference relation (for concept-expressions)', which I used above, is strictly speaking illicit. To keep ourselves unsullied by paradox, we have to remain at the linguistic level in our referential language, and say that the linguistic item 'is wise' does not refer to an object, but has its meaning determined in the way indicated in (1).

It follows that we need to respect the grammatical distinction between the terms 'reference' and 'referent':[149] concept-expressions have *reference*, but not (as I put it incautiously in my initial characterization of the reformed Fregean position) *referents*. A concept-expression could only have a referent if it were possible to refer to that referent using a demonstrative expression or proper name. Having reference, on the other hand, is another matter. A clause like (1) *indicates the reference* of the concept-expression 'is wise' without introducing any referent; or, we might say, it specifies *what that reference is* without specifying a referent. It might be thought that the paradox we are trying to avoid still clings to the emphasized formulations of the previous sentence; but that thought would be based on a misunderstanding of the grammar, in the present context, of phrases like 'indicate the reference of "is wise"', and 'specify what the reference of "is wise" is'. The relevant grammatical distinction is between a dependent clause governed by a relative pronoun and one governed by an interrogative pronoun: in particular, between the relative 'what' and the interrogative 'what'.[150] The distinction is more clearly marked in classical Latin, for example, than it is in either English or German, for classical Latin signals which grammatical construction is in question by employing the indicative mood of the dependent verb in the case of the relative, and the subjunctive mood in the case of the interrogative. As I am using it, the phrase 'to specify the reference of a concept-expression (grammatical predicate)' means *indicare quid significet* [subjunctive] *praedicatum*; 'to specify the referent of a concept-expression (grammatical predicate)', on the other hand, means *indicare (id) quod*

---

[149] See here McDowell [3], Essay 8, §3.   [150] Cf. Austin [2], pp. 96–7; Künne [1], p. 203.

significat [indicative] *praedicatum*. The second of these versions, if employed to disambiguate the phrase 'what a concept-expression refers to', implies that the concept-expression refers to an object, one that could in principle be referred to by means of a demonstrative expression or proper name. The first formulation does not carry this implication, and it is the one that the reformed Frege must insist on if his position is to be free of paradox. The relative 'what' can be distinguished from the interrogative 'what' by virtue of its being meaningfully replaceable by 'that which': it is equivalent to *id quod* (+ indicative) rather than to *quid* (+ subjunctive). Hence arises the paradoxicality, exploited in the previous paragraph, of the noun-phrase 'what we find on the world end of the reference relation for concept-expressions', for this phrase is tantamount to 'that which we find on the world end of the reference relation for concept-expressions'.

Frege himself, it is worth noting in passing, was poorly equipped to make the required distinction between having reference and having a referent. Of course there is no difficulty in making the distinction in modern philosophical German, which has taken over and naturalized the English terms. But there was no ordinary noun in the German of Frege's day corresponding to 'Referent' as it is used in modern philosophical German.[151] Frege felt the need of such a term, and accordingly commandeered the word 'Bedeutung' to perform this function. This was a linguistically unnatural move, for 'Bedeutung' in German corresponds exactly to 'reference' in English in the following sense: there is no necessary implication in the case of the ordinary employment of either word that what has reference (*Bedeutung*) also has a referent. Given this regrettable decision on Frege's part, he could have distinguished between a word that has both reference and a referent, on the one hand, and a word that merely has reference, on the other, only by saying of the former that it has an objectual meaning (*dass ihm eine gegenständliche Bedeutung zukommt*) and of the latter that it is (merely) meaningful (*dass es bedeutungsvoll ist*), or in other words that it is *not meaningless*.[152] But this way round with the terminology, though possible, is rather imprecise, and it would have been much better if Frege had used the word 'Bedeutung' in the sense of 'reference', and had introduced another word to function as a technical term corresponding to our 'referent'. That would have enabled him to say that concept-expressions do indeed have reference

---

[151] The words 'referent' (English) and 'Referent' (German), when used of the target of the reference relation rather than its source, are etymologically wrong (cf. Russell [3], §§28, §54, 94; Whitehead and Russell, i, p. 33). But the usage has become established and I follow it.

[152] Cf. Frege's remarks on the concept-expression 'is a square number' in his letter to Russell of 28 July 1902 ([22], p. 224; cf. p. 219): we are told that, though it falsifies matters to speak of the *Bedeutung* of this concept-expression, it is for all that not *bedeutungslos*.

(*Bedeutung*), but do not refer to any *thing*, that is, they have no referent, where the test of what it is to have a referent is the ability to refer to something that can also be picked out by a strict proper name or demonstrative expression. As it was, Frege simply applied the *Sinn*–*Bedeutung* complex univocally to the cases of proper names and concept-expressions, thereby bringing down upon himself the paradox of the concept *horse*.[153]

Let us be clear how radical a departure from the historical Frege the reformed Fregean position is: if we cannot talk about the referent of a concept-expression, we cannot talk about *concepts* at all, for talk of concepts is not reformulable in an acceptable way.[154] Concepts are things; they can be referred to by means of proper names and demonstrative expressions (if need be, just 'that concept' will serve), and so cannot be tolerated by the reformed Frege. Hence also the suggestion that an object might represent (that is, do duty or go proxy for) a concept is ultimately unacceptable. At least, if we allow it through this will be the only case where it is not possible to specify *what* (relative pronoun!) the representative object is doing duty or going proxy *for*. The reformed Frege must abandon the univocity of the distinction between *Sinn* and *Bedeutung*: as applied to concept-expressions this is merely (as we might put it) a sense–reference distinction, but as applied to proper names it yields in addition a sense–referent distinction, where the distinction between having a reference and having a referent is to be glossed in the manner I have indicated. Proper names refer, and they refer to objects; concept-expressions also refer, but they do not refer to concepts (still less to objects): rather, we must say that they refer not *to* any conceptual *thing* but *in* a conceptual *way*. The reference of concept-expressions is *adverbial* rather than *nominal*; or, to invoke another traditional grammatical distinction, we might say that for the reformed Frege concept-expressions are *syncategorematic* rather than *categorematic*.[155]

Syncategorematic expressions do not, on their own, have (in Ockham's formulation) 'a finite and definite signification',[156] but bring it about, when constructed with suitable categorematic terms (which do have such a signification) that the whole word-complex has a determinate meaning.[157] Syncategorematic expressions signify *aliqualiter* rather than *aliquid*; or, to put it in alternative terms sometimes employed in the tradition, they signify *per modum affectus*

---

[153] Like the unreformed Frege, Husserl allows categorematic expressions to refer to incomplete 'things': [2], iv, §8, pp. 313–14.

[154] Cf. Fisk [1], pp. 60–1.   [155] Cf. Marcus, p. 116.

[156] [1], I, §4. Cf. [2], I. i, §1, p. 378.39–47.

[157] For modern treatments of the syncategorematic, see Thomason at Montague, p. 5; Dowty *et al.*, p. 141; Marciszewski, p. 8; Heim and Kratzer, p. 98. On earlier treatments, see Pinborg [1], pp. 30–4; Nuchelmans [1], pp. 51, 96–7, 124, 140–1; [5], pp. 100–5.

rather than *per modum conceptus*.[158] In his influential 1751 treatise *Hermes*, James Harris tells us that words may be divided into 'principals' and 'accessories', the former being 'significant by themselves', the latter 'significant by relation'.[159] If concept-expressions were construed as syncategorematic, they would count, in Russellian terms, as 'incomplete symbols', which Russell defines, in line with the tradition, as symbols having no meaning in isolation, but only in certain contexts.[160] The suggestion has been made that the claim that concept-expressions are syncategorematic was anticipated in the Thomistic tradition, especially in the writings of Aquinas himself and in those of the late medieval logician Vincent Ferrer.[161] There is also a hint of it in the Port-Royal *Grammar*'s claim that, while nouns and pronouns designate objects of thought, verbs indicate the manner of our thinking about objects.[162] And the view has also been widely attributed, with some justification, to Quine.[163]

Quine himself attributes this view to Frege (and to Wittgenstein),[164] and there are indeed several passages in which the historical Frege might seem to express himself in terms approaching those of the figure I am calling the reformed Frege: for example in the *Grundlagen* we are told that if we remove the phrases 'the Earth' and 'the Moon' from the sentence 'The Earth has a greater mass than the Moon' we are left with a 'relational concept' (*Beziehungsbegriff*) — better, a relational concept-*expression* — which, in Austin's translation, 'taken by itself has no sense any more than a simple concept [i.e. a simple concept-*word*] has'.[165] But does Frege really mean here that the concept-expression 'is more massive than' has *no* sense, taken as an integral unit in abstraction from a sentence? In his translation, Austin glosses the phrase 'no sense' as 'no [assertible] sense': if the gloss is right, Frege would be saying that that concept-expression does not have a *propositional* sense, which would be compatible with its having a *non-propositional* sense. Again, Tyler Burge has suggested that in the passage from the Schoenflies review I quoted above in §26, Frege treats 'falls under' as syncategorematic;[166] but this interpretation seems to me unwarranted by the text. Burge also suggests that Frege took the same line on 'the concept *F*'. It is true, as we have noted (§28), that in some of his later writings Frege rejected his earlier view that phrases of the form 'the concept *F*' refer to objects (going proxy for concepts), without reverting to the intuitive view that they refer to concepts: but this fact does not show that

[158] Nuchelmans [5], pp. 100–5, 119.   [159] J. Harris, i, ch. 3, pp. 27–31.
[160] Whitehead and Russell, i, p. 66.
[161] See here Geach [2]; Trentman [1], [2], and intro. to Ferrer's *Tractatus*, pp. 29–30.
[162] Arnauld and Lancelot, II, ch. 1 (pp. 23–5); cf. Nuchelmans [5], pp. 73–4.
[163] Gochet, p. 61; Davidson [2], p. 188. See Quine [1], p. 704; Goodman and Quine, p. 105.
[164] [8], p. 164.   [165] [3], §70.   [166] [2], p. 294.

Frege came to regard such phrases as syncategorematic; the evidence suggests rather that he regarded them as (perhaps unavoidable but) strictly illegitimate expressions. So I do not think that the historical Frege ever turned into the reformed Frege.

33 Concepts and Functions

The historical Frege assimilated concepts to functions in the mathematical sense, as I have said (§25), but it is hard to see how this identification can help him with the unity problem. There are two points that need to be made here. First, in order to conceive of concepts as incomplete entities, in a way which (on Frege's approach) engages with the problem of the unity of the proposition, it is not necessary to think of those concepts in functional terms: one might think of them simply as universals with slots for further entities.[167] Secondly, on its own the identification of concepts with functions hardly delivers the special status of concepts as incomplete entities. If, as I have suggested, Frege's notion of unsaturatedness or incompleteness was devised precisely to engage with the problem of unity (of the proposition, of the Thought), then one would expect incompleteness to attach in the first instance to concepts, and then, in virtue of an identification of concepts with functions, to be read over from concepts to functions.[168] Even if we judge (as I shall) that Frege's solution to the problem of unity fails, that order of events is at least comprehensible, whereas if we insist that, for Frege, incompleteness attaches in the first instance to functions, and then, in virtue of the identification of concepts with functions, is read over from functions to concepts, we face the mystery how a property, namely incompleteness, whose role is to engage with a quite general problem affecting the signification of language in all its forms, should be found in its original and fundamental manifestation in a small corner of the linguistic terrain, namely mathematical discourse, rather than in meaningful discourse as such, whatever its subject matter.

Here I am in disagreement with Dummett and Geach, both of whom think that the mathematical analogy is enough to establish the special ontological status of concepts, that, as Dummett puts it, 'the functional conception of concepts . . . provides *the* correct account of their incompleteness'.[169] But the Dummett–Geach approach is wrong not only exegetically, since it fails to

---

[167] Siderits [3], p. 11.   [168] See Cocchiarella [1], pp. 71–2.
[169] Dummett [3], p. 175; cf. Geach [2], pp. 258–9; [6], p. 39; [8], pp. 149–50; [4], pp. 79–80. See also Carruthers, p. 51; Currie [1], p. 153; Stevens [1], p. 234; Land, pp. 179–80.

do justice to the connection in Frege's thinking between the notion of incompleteness and the unity problem, but also from a systematic point of view. Explaining the supposed incompleteness of concepts in terms of an alleged prior incompleteness attaching to functions surely inverts the natural direction of explanation. If the incomplete status of concepts is in any sense *sub judice*—and it is—that of functions must equally be so. For it is hardly as though someone who questioned the incompleteness of concepts could simply be directed to the case of functions as an uncontroversial illustration of the kind of thing being alleged to hold of concepts. If anything, the incompleteness of functions is surely a more problematic idea than that of concepts. Not only that; the strategy also seems curiously irrelevant. Mathematicians routinely identify functions with suitable sets, and sets are objects. For these practitioners there would be no paradox of the function *sine*, correlative to Frege's paradox of the concept *horse*, as on Frege's showing there should be if the unsaturatedness of concepts were underwritten by their status as functions; and there would be no need, or scope, for a reformation of these practitioners' understanding of functors and their referents along the lines of the reformed Frege.

Now my position, as I have indicated (§16), is that functions are not literally *identical* with sets; at best they can in some contexts and for some purposes be *proxied* by suitable set-theoretical constructions.[170] So I cannot simply counter that functions, being sets, just *are* objects. But the ease with which we represent functions as sets for technical purposes at least suggests, though admittedly it does not prove, that the functions we are so representing are indeed already *objects*, if not necessarily the very kind of objects that are being adduced to stand in for them. It is plausibly an ontological parity of that kind between functions and suitable sets that explains our willingness to allow for technical purposes mathematical functions *in extenso* to be identified, in the simplest kind of case, with sets of single-valued ordered pairs comprising abscissa and ordinate, or ordered n-tuples comprising a single value (the nth term) preceded by $n - 1$ arguments, so in effect identifying a function with its graph.[171] Thus we have no difficulty treating $\sin 2\theta$ and $2\sin\theta\cos\theta$ as the same function of θ.[172] This development was indeed anticipated by Frege himself, in his notion of the value-range (*Wertverlauf*) of a function: for two functions have the same value-range just if they have the same graph, and

[170]   Cf. Barwise and Etchemendy, pp. 19, 62, 176; Potter [2], pp. 256–7.

[171]   Hausdorff was the first (ch. 2, §1) to identify functions with sets of ordered pairs (cf. Felgner [2]), though his definition of an ordered pair has been superseded by the Kuratowski definition (§13). Cf. von Neumann, pp. 221–2; Church [6], pp. 15–16; Kanamori, pp. 290–1.

[172]   Cf. Church [8], p. 409.

in his commitment (at least sometimes) to an extensional understanding of functions.[173]

I insert the proviso that an extensional understanding of functions is found only sometimes in his work, because there are passages in which Frege seems to embrace an intensional conception of functions (recall a similar ambivalence that we noted in the case of concepts: §7): for example, in the passage from *Funktion und Begriff* where two functions are said to have the same value-range just if they have the same graph, we are expressly told that in the case of the equation '$x^2 - 4x = x(x - 4)$', though the value-ranges of the two functions are identical, the functions themselves are not; and in a footnote at the same place he remarks that functions in his sense are logically prior to their value-ranges.[174] Elsewhere, it is true, an extensional approach is found.[175] But Frege's extensional view of functions, insofar as he held it, is further compromised by the fact that his understanding of classes was uniformly intensional, in the sense that the existence of a class was held to depend on the antecedent availability (in the sense of §1) of a concept collecting that class. As he put it:

The class . . . is something derived, whereas in the concept—as I understand the word—we have something primitive. . . .We can only determine a class by giving the properties which an object must have in order to belong to the class. But these properties are the attributes (*Merkmale*) of a concept. We define a concept, and pass over from it to the class.[176]

In fact, in Frege's philosophy extensionality and intensionality are intertwined in a way he never satisfactorily resolved: concepts are (monadic) functions, functions are (at least sometimes) taken to be extensional entities, but classes, which are the most natural extensional candidate for (monadic) functions to be identified with, though they have extensional identity-conditions, are held by Frege to be intensional entities in the above sense.

Unlike Frege, who treated the general notion of function as primitive and defined *n*-adic concepts ($n \in \{1, 2, 3, \ldots\}$) in functional terms, the Russell of *Principles* took the specific notion of a propositional function to be primitive

[173] [5], p. 9 ([21], pp. 129–30); Letter to Russell, 3 Aug. 1902 ([22], p. 225); [10], I, §3; II, §146. On the question to what extent Frege thought of value-ranges in set-theoretic terms, see Kneale and Kneale, pp. 501–2; Angelelli [1], pp. 205–23; Dummett [3], pp. 172–3; Burge [2], pp. 118–19, 292 n. 19.

[174] [5], p. 10 n. 5 ([21], p. 130 n. 5). See also his letter to Peano (*c*.1894), [22], p. 177; [11], p. 455 ([21], p. 210); [16], p. 251 ([21], p. 339); [22], p. 287 n. 71 (with Burge [2], pp. 123–4).

[175] [9], p. 320 ([21], pp. 183–4); [26], p. 128. See Russell [3], §485, pp. 512–13; Burge [2], p. 289 n. 15; Kreiser, p. 190; Olson, p. 68; Tiles, p. 144; Simons [6].

[176] [16], pp. 251–2 ([21], pp. 339–40). Cf. [4], pp. 96–7 ([21], pp. 104–5); [8], p. 270 ([21], p. 164); [9], pp. 322–3 ([21], pp. 185–6); [10], II, §147; [11], pp. 451–5 ([21], pp. 206–10; cf. Russell [3], §484); [26], p. 199; Tiles, pp. 146–7, 150; Hintikka and Sandu, pp. 298–303.

with respect to functions in general—in effect this amounted to taking as primitive the idea of *n*-adic concepts or properties—and defined the general notion of function in terms of it.[177] (The primitive status of propositional functions with respect to functions in general held notwithstanding the fact that, officially in *Principles*, they did not count as entities.) Whatever Frege's view of the origin of incompleteness, whether in the concept (as I have suggested) or in the function (as Dummett and Geach want), for Russell it is quite clear that the incompleteness of the concept (to put it in Fregean terms) is prior to and explanatory of the incompleteness of the function. Functions are treated as correlations between series,[178] and as such they are polyadic concepts or relations.[179] Now Russell held relations to be intensional entities;[180] correspondingly, his conception of propositional functions was, as I noted when I discussed the way in which the values of propositional functions, when canonically specified, contain arguments to the function as integral parts (§19), an intensional one (at least until the second edition of *Principia*). Classes, on the other hand, were held by Russell in *Principles*, at least officially, to be extensional entities.[181] Indeed Russellian classes in *Principles* not only conform to the axiom of extensionality (as we would say); they also accommodate a distinction between what Russell calls the class as many and the class as one. Classes as many are characterized as classes whose 'component terms, though they have some kind of unity, have less than is required for a whole. They have, in fact, just so much unity as is required to make them many, and not enough to prevent them from remaining many'.[182] In *Principles* Russell refuses to identify the class as many with the class as one; his belief in the separate integrity of the class as many leads, in the main text, to the extrusion from his ontology of the null class (which Frege, motivated by his intensional conception of classes, accepted),[183] and to the identification (which Frege rejected)[184] of singletons with their members.[185] Later, when Russell had stopped talking about the class as many, and indeed had ceased to regard classes as primitive components of our ontology, he readmitted the null class and singletons:[186] indeed the Preface

---

[177] See [3], §482; [18], pp. 332–3; cf. [15], p. 261; Prior [3], pp. 97–8; Cocchiarella [1], p. 71; Hylton [2], pp. 141–4.

[178] On the background to this conception, see Crocco [2], pp. 178–9.

[179] [3], §255. Cf. Cresswell, p. 11.   [180] Kanamori, p. 290.

[181] [3], §§69, 486; cf. [11], pp. 183–4. 'At least officially', because there are tensions which we will come to shortly, and again in §79 below.

[182] [3], §70.

[183] Frege [9], p. 322 ([21], p. 185); [11], p. 451 ([21], pp. 206–7); [10], I, p. 3; II, §150; cf. Hintikka and Sandu, p. 301.

[184] Frege [11], pp. 444–6 ([21], pp. 201–2); [10], I, p. 3. Cf. Thiel, p. 68.

[185] On both these cases, see Russell [3], §69; L. Linksy [1], pp. 630–5.   [186] [11], pp. 23, 183.

to the 1903 edition of *Principles*, the appendix on Frege, and even the main text show signs of an inchoate change of heart on the status of the null class and singletons.[187] (There are obviously difficulties with Russell's notion of the class as many, at least as he expounds it, but Geach's claim that the idea is 'radically incoherent'[188] is surely mistaken.[189] I shall return to the idea in §79, where it will be important.)

The combination of Russell's intensional approach to propositional functions with his extensional approach to classes led to a tension in *Principles* rather like the one I have diagnosed in Frege:[190] for in that work Russell both took propositional functions to be reducible to classes of the propositions that are their values,[191] and took classes to be definable in terms of propositional functions.[192] In *Principles* Russell is haunted by his recent discovery of 'the Contradiction', and by Cantor's proof that the power set of any set A is strictly larger than A.[193] Uncertain how best to respond to these developments—which are of course closely related: Russell's paradox can be regarded as an application of Cantor's theorem in the case where the relevant mapping takes concepts to their extensions,[194] and indeed Russell states that he discovered the paradox through working on Cantor's proof[195]—he asserts both that the axiom that 'the class as one is to be found wherever there is a class as many . . . appears to have been the source of the contradiction',[196] and that Cantor's theorem forces us 'to deny that propositional concepts [i.e. propositional functions] are individuals'.[197] After *Principles*, Russell abandoned his belief in the integrity not only of the class as one, but even of the class as many; eventually, having tried a number of byways and indirect crooked paths,[198] he adopted the so-called 'no class' theory familiar from *Principia*,[199] namely the view that any statement about a class is eliminable in favour of statements about one or more (extensionally equivalent) propositional functions, these being officially (if not always in practice) held to be irreducible individual entities in their own right.[200]

[187] [3], p. xxi, §§106, 488. Cf. Kanamori, pp. 282–5.   [188] [7], p. 225.
[189] Cf. Oliver and Smiley [2], pp. 648–50; [3], pp. 1039–41, 1062.
[190] See Cocchiarella [1], p. 29; B. Linsky [3], pp. 376–7, 387.
[191] See e.g. [3], §85, quoted above (§29).   [192] See e.g. [3], §489.
[193] Cf. Russell [11], pp. 85–6; Kleene, p. 15; Potter [2], p. 158.
[194] See Potter [1], p. 114; Stevens [3], p. 66.
[195] Letter to Frege of 24 June 1902 (Frege [22], pp. 215–16); [11], p. 136; [14], p. 58.
[196] [3], §104; cf. Cocchiarella [1], pp. 80–1.   [197] [3], §499; cf. Cocchiarella [1], p. 33.
[198] Including the substitutional theory, in which there are no classes or relations, and no propositional functions either (their place being taken by specially constructed matrices which also do duty for classes). See further Pelham and Urquhart, pp. 311–13; Potter [1], pp. 130–1; Stevens [3], pp. 49–64.
[199] Whitehead and Russell, i, pp. 66–84 (esp. p. 72 n.), 190 (*20.01). Cf. Russell [11], pp. 183–4; [13], pp. 265–6.
[200] Ramsey [2], p. 63; Pelham and Urquhart, p. 310; Cocchiarella [1], pp. 28–9, 46, 69.

34 The Reformed Frege: Refinements and Objections

I return to a consideration of the reformed Frege. The position we reached in §32 is not materially altered when we make the requisite adjustment to Frege's treatment of the definite article consequent on Russell's discovery that the semantics of definite descriptions are distinct from those of genuine referring expressions. Here we need to recall some points made earlier (§§8, 15). As we have seen, Frege recognized that the semantical properties of concept-words are importantly different from those of proper names—that, in the case of concept-words, a non-semantic step is required to take us from language to satisfying objects—but he unfortunately did not allow this insight to feed into his treatment of (what we now call, following Russell) definite descriptions. In the *Grundlagen*, for instance, he tells us that while a concept-word is not the name of thing, if it is prefixed with the definite article or a demonstrative adjective the resulting expression becomes the name of a thing.[201] This, of course, on the conception of reference with which I am working, has the unacceptable consequence that in order to understand a definite description one would be required to cognize the object(s), if any, satisfying it. It was one of Russell's achievements to realize that the referent of a definite description (to put it in my terminology) cannot in general be identified with what he called its denotation, or, to put it in terms shorn of technicality, that one cannot be required to think of the object(s), if any, satisfying a definite description if one is to count as understanding it.

Making this adjustment has the consequence that Frege's broad category of proper names is, as we have said, too broad: it groups together items that function in quite different ways and have very different kinds of referent. If we use 'reference' as a term of art to signify what (interrogative pronoun), and 'referent' as a term of art to signify what (relative pronoun), the understander needs to be acquainted with in order to count as understanding an expression, it follows, given Russell's discovery, that we must distinguish within Frege's broad category of proper names between, on the one hand, those expressions for which there is available a distinction between reference and satisfaction such that the referent of the expression is not, in general, identical with the object(s), if any, satisfying it, and, on the other, those expressions for which the notion of satisfaction, if applicable at all, has to be applied in such a way that the satisfier(s) of a given expression must be deemed to coincide with its referent(s). In the

---

[201] [3], §51.

former category fall at least some ('pure') uses of definite descriptions, some proper names (those abbreviating 'pure' definite descriptions) and also noun-phrases such as 'what the expression E refers to'; in the latter category fall most indexical expressions, and what I have called strict proper names.[202]

However, even after we have made these necessary adjustments to our understanding of the semantics of what the historical Frege called proper names, the basic thesis on which the reformed Frege must rest—namely that proper names (in the historical Frege's broad sense) are categorematic expressions, whereas concept-expressions are syncategorematic—remains unaffected. For the referents of all expressions in Frege's broad category of proper names are *objects*; or, to put the point without pleonasm, all these expressions *have* referents. Those referents do not form a uniform group: in the case of many uses of demonstrative expressions and most ordinary proper names, the referent will be a spatio-temporal object, such as a building or a person, whereas in the case of definite descriptions like 'the fastest runner in the world' or noun-phrases like 'what we need to complete the puzzle', the referent will be a complex non-spatial, non-temporal entity—what we might call a non-Fregean concept ('non-Fregean' because it is saturated—it is a complex universal—and hence reference to it imports no paradox)—distinct from the further object or objects (often spatio-temporal), if any, which satisfy it. But, to repeat, even after we have made this adjustment to Frege's treatment of proper names, it remains true of all items in Frege's broad category of proper names that they *have referents*: that continues to distinguish them from the items in the category of concept-expressions, as these are construed by the figure I am calling the reformed Frege. For the reformed Frege, concept-expressions will have *satisfiers*, and these satisfiers will of course be objects, but there is no automatic implication from an expression's having an objectual satisfier to its having a referent, and for the reformed Frege concept-expressions indeed have objectual satisfiers, but do not have referents.

Can all our meaning-theoretic commerce with concept-expressions be handled in the manner of clauses like

(1) $\forall x(x$ satisfies 'is wise' iff x is wise),

rather than clauses like

(2) $\forall x(x$ satisfies 'is wise' iff x instantiates wisdom)?

---

[202] Note that in the case of indexical expressions, alongside Fregean sense, which is variable across contexts of use, we will need to recognize an aspect of their meaning which is constant across such contexts, namely a function from indices to (*de re*) senses. See here Kaplan [2], pp. 505–6, who calls this aspect of meaning 'character'. But this point can be set aside in the present context.

The question is often considered in connection with the ontological status of abstract objects. Can a sentence like 'Courage is a virtue' be analysed, in the manner of (1), so that the apparent reference to the abstract object courage is eliminated? If so, there is a question what the ontological significance of the analysis is: which of analysans and analysandum should we take as our guide to ontology?[203] But these latter questions, though important, are not immediately relevant here. Here the point needed by the reformed Frege is just that all *concept-expressions* can be handled in the manner of (1). And this point is surely correct. It is irrelevant in this context to consider whether names apparently referring to abstract objects can be reduced to concept-expressions (and then supplied with meaning-specifications in the manner of (1)). As far as the reformed Frege is concerned, it might be impossible to carry out any such reduction. (And the same applies to the historical Frege;[204] for we know that he was no enemy of abstract objects.) The semantic point would remain: the meaning-specifications of concept-expressions are to be handled in the manner of (1) and not (2).

It might be objected here that if talk of referents for concept-expressions is eschewed, it will be impossible to supply a specification of identity-conditions for whatever corresponds to them in the realm of reference.[205] And if we cannot supply such conditions, there will be no distinguishing between the reference of 'is wise' and that of 'is a horse'. In fact, however, reflection on (1) does suggest a way of supplying identity-conditions for what (interrogative pronoun!) corresponds to concept-expressions in the realm of reference, without finding referents to play this role: as a first approximation we might try saying that the concept-expressions 'F' and 'G' have the same reference just in case $\forall x(Fx \leftrightarrow Gx)$.[206] As it stands this will not quite do, for it carries the upshot that extensionally equivalent concept-expressions (such as 'is renate' and 'is cordate') will turn out to be synonymous. We can rule out such cases by modalizing the analysis: we now say that the concept-expressions 'F' and 'G' have the same reference just in case it is necessary that $\forall x(Fx \leftrightarrow Gx)$. 'Is renate' is now no longer presented by the analysis as synonymous with 'is cordate', because it is possible for some renate animal not to be cordate. That still leaves a problem of necessarily co-extensive concept-expressions, such as 'triangular' and 'trilateral'. I have already indicated how to deal with this sort of case (§16): we have to appeal to a distinction between semantically simple and semantically complex expressions, discerned according to some empirically adequate theory

---

[203] Cf. Wright [1], pp. 31–2; Hale [2], p. 25.
[204] On this point I am in disagreement with Geach [10], p. 183, and Hale [4], pp. 177–8.
[205] So Stevens [1], p. 235; cf. his [3], pp. 28–9.
[206] Cf. Wright [1], pp. 15–16, 55.

of meaning for the language in question. With this distinction in place, we must emend our specification of identity-conditions so that it only applies to semantically simple expressions (basic words). This will have the consequence that semantically simple, necessarily co-extensive concept-expressions have the same reference, but that consequence is just as it should be. As is fitting, our specification of identity-conditions for the reference of concept-expressions treats 'having the same reference as' as distinct from 'having the same referent as': there is no implication that two expressions can have the same reference only if they have referents.

Can Frege's position, reformed along the suggested lines, work? A standard objection to it is that it cannot cope with second-order quantification. As Dummett puts it, 'if second-level quantification is admitted as intelligible, then the assertion that there is something for which "( ) is a horse" stands can scarcely be questioned'.[207] If we cannot talk about concepts using (in Frege's broad sense) proper names—if there are strictly speaking no such things as concepts—then we cannot quantify over them: for example, it will not follow from the fact that Socrates is wise and Plato is not that there is something that Socrates is and Plato is not—to wit, wise. The inability to quantify over concepts surely represents an unacceptable loss of expressive power for any natural language.[208] What Frege's paradox shows, according to this line of thought, is that one cannot both talk about concepts (in a sense that admits of quantification over them) and continue to insist (to put it paradoxically) on their essentially unsaturated nature, or rather (to put it in paradox-free terms), to continue to insist that concept-expressions have an unsaturated reference. One of these commitments has to be jettisoned. If we wish, as we surely do, to talk about concepts (in the above sense), that is, to talk about whatever it is that concept-expressions refer to, then those concept-expressions must have referents, not merely references, otherwise there will be no subject matter for our language to be about—nothing for our quantifiers to range over. So, at any rate, the objector claims.

It is natural to reply to this objection that a shift from objectual or referential quantification to substitutional quantification would remedy this lack:[209] for from the truth of 'Socrates is wise' and the falsity of 'Plato is wise' it does follow that there is a concept-expression (namely, 'ξ is wise') such that substitution of 'Socrates' into its argument-place yields a truth, and substitution of 'Plato' yields a falsehood. We have in effect already conceded the thrust of this reply in observing (§31) that no paradox arises if we remain at the level of language:

---

[207] [3], p. 480. Cf. Dudman; Wiggins [3], p. 132; MacBride [6], p. 440.
[208] Wiggins [3], pp. 136–8.   [209] Stevenson, p. 219; cf. MacBride [6], p. 442–7.

for it follows from that observation that the substitutional formulations must be free of paradoxical implications. But, the objector will counter, remaining at the level of language is not a posture that can be indefinitely sustained. At some point we shall have to allow that language is connected to the world by some suitable semantics, and at that point the equivalence of the two versions of the above argument will become plain.[210] After all, the substitutional formulations themselves employ apparently objectual quantification over linguistic expressions: as I put it above, '. . . there is a concept-expression (namely, "ξ is wise"), such that . . .'.[211] Instead of saying that the paradox is not genuine because we can always shift from the ontological to the linguistic level, where it does not arise, one might as well say that the fact that we can always shift from the linguistic to the ontological level, where the paradox does arise, shows that it is genuine. Hence, the objector concludes, the clash between the reformed Frege's strategy and our commitment, in second-order objectual quantification, to the existence of concepts, cannot be avoided by side-stepping into a substitutional interpretation of the quantifiers, but must be resolved at the ontological level.

How should we adjudicate here between the objection and the reply? It is true enough, as the objector insists, that we are interested in *interpreted* languages, not in languages as merely formal objects of investigation; and it is also plausible that our understanding of what substitutional quantification is depends asymmetrically on a prior understanding of *objectual* quantification (over linguistic expressions). But does it follow from these points that our interpretation of the quantifiers must in every case be objectual? We saw in the previous section that it is feasible for the reformed Frege to handle the semantics of concept-expressions without having to give meaning-specifications of an explicitly reifying nature. That is, the reformed Frege can specify semantics for such expressions without having to recognize the existence of corresponding concepts. On this approach, it need not be denied that we are entitled to employ objectual modes of speech, as I did in the example given above ('there is something that Socrates is and Plato is not—to wit, wise'), but such modes of speech would have to be understood as—strictly speaking, ontologically misleading—shorthand for the more cumbersome but accurate substitutional locutions.

Our brief examination of the semantic strategy to which the reformed Frege is committed in the case of concept-expressions surely gives aid and comfort to the reply at least to this extent: there need be no qualm that,

---

[210] Cf. Dummett [2], p. 526; Orenstein; Wallace, pp. 128–31; Baldwin [1], §1.
[211] Cf. C. Parsons [2], pp. 69–70. I comment on this fact below (§77).

merely in virtue of our adopting a substitutional rather than an objectual interpretation of a range of quantifiers in a range of uses, we are reneging on the semantic obligation—the obligation, that is, to set up connections between language and the world—or denying the essentially derivative status of the method of substitutional quantification. For, as far as the first of these points goes, the semantic obligation was met by the reformed Frege in the case of concept-expressions without finding referents for them. The point insisted on by the reformed Frege was just that, in meeting this obligation to specify the reference of concept-expressions, we can deal in clauses like (1), which does not introduce objects, rather than (2), which does.[212] Surely an extension of this substitutional strategy to the case of the second-order quantifiers will work equally well. On the second point, the essentially derivative status of the method of substitutional quantification need not be ignored by the reply, since (here we exploit the objector's own claim) the substitutional status of the relevant second-order quantifiers may be taken to depend theoretically on the availability of first-order objectual quantification.

But when the position is set out in these terms it becomes hard to overlook a certain rather suspicious arbitrariness in it.[213] Recall the alternative strategies bypassed by Frege in his search for an unsaturated component in the simple categorical sentence 'Socrates is wise' (§27). We saw that Frege expressly rejected the tripartite strategies (i) and (ii), and I speculated that he may (if he considered the matter) or might (if he did not) have found the bipartite strategies (iii) and (iv) too bizarre to merit serious attention. Strategy (iv) involved, we recall, dividing a simple categorical sentence such as 'Socrates is wise' into two components, the proper name together with the copula ('Socrates is') on the one hand, and the verb radical ('wise') on the other, regarding the former as unsaturated and the latter as saturated. Now (iv) is in some sense the mirror-image of Frege's own strategy: it might be called the 'anti-Fregean' strategy. It is therefore interesting at this juncture to compare its credentials with those of the historical and (especially) the reformed Fregean strategies. What, then, can be said on behalf of the anti-Fregean strategy? Surely that it has no worse a claim to provide a model for a semantics than the strategy Frege chose instead. For Frege's selection of the concept-expression—whether this is construed in Frege's preferred way, as incorporating the copula, or construed in the alternative way I recommended earlier (§30), as stripped of the copula—to be the carrier of unsaturatedness in

---

[212] Cf. MacBride [6], p. 427–32.

[213] The charge of arbitrariness also attaches to Tugendhat's position ([2], esp. pp. 190–6), and to Searle's ([1], pp. 97–119), both of which somewhat resemble that of the reformed Frege.

the sentence 'Socrates is wise' seems arbitrary: if there has to be unsaturatedness somewhere in that sentence, there is surely no more reason to attach it to the concept-expression, leaving the proper name to function as a complete expression, than vice versa.[214]

35 Frege, Russell, and the Anti-Fregean Strategy

Indeed this very point was inchoately recognized by Frege himself in §9 of his *Begriffsschrift*, where we are told, quite generally, that

If in an expression, whose content does not need to be judgeable, a simple or compound sign occurs in one or more places, and if we think of it as being replaceable at all or some of these places by another sign (but everywhere replaceable by the same sign), then we call the part of the expression that remains unchanged thereby the expression's function, the replaceable part its argument.[215]

Slightly before this passage, we had been informed that the distinction between function and argument 'has nothing to do with the conceptual content (*begrifflicher Inhalt*), but is just a matter of the way we view [that content]'.[216] These remarks seem to imply that *any* part of a sentence can be treated as argument (and so, for Frege, as saturated), and the remaining part as function (and so, for Frege, as unsaturated). This must indeed have been the way in which Wittgenstein read the passage, as we may gather from the Tractarian claim that every variable can be conceived as a propositional variable, including the variable name (which implies that variables may *also* be substituted for *non*-nominal parts of the sentence).[217]

We might expect to encounter a similar impartiality in Russell's *Principles*. For, as we have seen (§29), we are told there that '*human* and *humanity* denote precisely the same concept',[218] and this claim, together with the central doctrine of that work, which we have also already noted, that 'a proposition, unless it happens to be linguistic [i.e. unless it is about words] does not itself contain words: it contains the entities indicated by words',[219] suggests that, though we can indeed distinguish at the level of symbolic language between the *sentences* 'Socrates is human', 'Socrates has humanity', and 'Humanity belongs to Socrates', at the level of the expressed *proposition* no distinction (or at any rate no distinction keyed to the grammatical distinction between the adjective 'human' and the noun 'humanity') is to be found. That is the conclusion that

---

[214] Cf. Black [2], p. 231; MacBride [6], p. 434–5.   [215] [1], p. 16. Cf. Weiner [1], pp. 72–6.
[216] [1], p. 15. Cf. Dummett [3], p. 282.   [217] [1], §§3.314–15.   [218] [3], §46.
[219] [3], §51.

we expect Russell to draw, and that he ought to draw, given his premises; yet, strikingly, he does not do so. In spite of the fact that we are assured that '*human* and *humanity*... only differ grammatically',[220] and that *human*, as it occurs in the proposition (expressed by)[221] 'Socrates is human' is identical with *humanity*, as that occurs in the proposition (expressed by) 'Socrates has humanity'[222]—implying that no interesting ontological difference is marked by the grammatical difference between the words 'human' and 'humanity'—Russell nevertheless maintains that there is only one subject–predicate analysis of the proposition (expressed by) 'Socrates is human'—in Fregean terms, this means that there is only one argument–function analysis of that proposition—and that the proposition (expressed by) 'Humanity belongs to Socrates', though equivalent to the proposition (expressed by) 'Socrates is human', is a distinct proposition.[223] So, despite a passing flirtation with the thought that (in effect) grammar may not be a good guide to ontology, Russell at least in this case maintains that it is, following his official doctrine that grammatical distinctions are, in general, sound indicators of philosophically important differences.[224]

Somewhat similarly, returning now to Frege, it must be doubted to what extent the view quoted from the *Begriffsschrift* really represents Frege's considered position. It is conspicuous that the immediate illustrations of the quoted principle that Frege gives in the same section of the *Begriffsschrift* (§9) all follow traditional grammar, in the sense that only proper names, in Frege's broad sense, are shown to occur as (capable of introducing) arguments, and only concept-expressions as (capable of introducing) functions. Frege puts his point by saying that in the conceptual content expressed by a sentence like 'Hydrogen is lighter than carbon dioxide' we may regard 'hydrogen' as the argument and 'is lighter than carbon dioxide' as the function, or we may alternatively regard 'carbon dioxide' as the argument and 'is heavier than hydrogen' as the function; but he does not say—what the quoted principle would appear to allow—that given the same sentence we may regard 'is lighter than carbon dioxide' as the argument and 'hydrogen' as the function.[225] (Strictly, 'hydrogen' would be not a function but the name of a function; but I am going along with Frege's earlier mode of expression in the passage in question, to be replaced in his post-1890 writings by a rigorous distinction between functions and their

---

[220] [3], §48.

[221] I insert parenthetical glosses, here and below, to indicate how we would nowadays prefer to put Russell's points.

[222] [3], §57.   [223] [3], §48.

[224] [3], §46; see L. Linsky [1], pp. 624–5. But cf. Russell [3], §72.

[225] Cf. Frege [3], §70; Russell [3], §96.

names.[226]) Similarly, in the important letter to Marty (?) of August 1882, Frege remarks concerning the inequality 3 > 2 that one can regard 2 as the subject, instead of 3,[227] and that one can even treat 3-and-2 as a complex subject, in which case the predicate becomes the relation of greater to smaller. But he does not say that this relation, either on its own or with one of its argument-places filled, can be regarded as the subject, and that either or both of 3 and 2 can be treated as the predicate.[228]

Actually, although it seems to be Frege's practice in his examples to allow only concept-expressions to be (capable of introducing) functions, it would be going too far to say that, in his examples, only proper names, in his broad sense, are (capable of introducing) arguments. For, still in §9 of the *Begriffsschrift*, Frege tells us that, appearances notwithstanding, in the sentences 'The number 20 can be represented as the sum of four squares' and 'Every positive integer can be represented as the sum of four squares', we do not have to do with a common function, namely 'can be represented as the sum of four squares', and two different arguments, 'the number 20' and 'every positive integer' respectively: the reason for this—to put it in terms of Frege's hierarchy of levels, which I shall explore in the next chapter, and again falling in with Frege's linguistic way of talking about functions and arguments—is that whereas 'the number 20' is a proper name, and so (in conformity with appearances) features as argument to the function 'can be represented as the sum of four squares' in the first of the above sentences, 'every positive integer' is a second-level function, taking as its argument the (first-level) function 'can be represented as the sum of four squares' in the second of our sentences.[229] So, depending on context, concept-expressions *may* introduce arguments, not just functions. But the crucial point for our purposes here is that it looks as though Frege thinks that, once the sentential context is given, the analysis is fixed[230]—that is, it is *determinate* whether a concept-expression as it figures in

---

[226] Cf. Thiel, p. 47; Angelelli [1], p. 153 with n. 22; Resnik [1], p. 337; Olson, p. 73. For the later terminological strategy, see e.g. the opening section of [10] with Stevenson, p. 211.

[227] [22], p. 164. Hence, in parallel with the *Begriffsschrift* example, the predicate would be not '3 is greater than . . .' but '. . . is smaller than 3': I comment on this point in §67 below.

[228] Cf. [13], p. 372 ([21], p. 270 n. 4): 'Was man sprachlich als Subjekt anzusehen habe, ist durch die Form des Satzes bestimmt. Anders liegt die Sache für die logische Betrachtungsweise. Wir können den Satz "8 = 2³" zerlegen entweder in "8" und "ist die dritte Potenz von 2", oder in "2" und "ist etwas, dessen dritte Potenz 8 ist", oder in "3" und "ist etwas, womit 2 potenziert 8 ergibt".' Here again, the examples are narrower than the initial principle: there is no suggestion that, in practice, we might take '=' to be the logical subject of the sample sentence.

[229] Frege says that they are not 'Begriffe gleichen Ranges' ([1], p. 17), so anticipating his doctrine of levels (*Stufen*), which first officially appears in the *Grundlagen* (§53): cf. [9], p. 328 ([21], p. 189); Angelelli [1], p. 179; Grossmann [1], pp. 26–7, 56.

[230] Cf. Stevenson, p. 208.

a given sentence introduces an argument or a function—an impression which is surely confirmed by his explanation of the analysis of the second sentence: for he tells us that 'the expression "every positive integer", does not, like "the number 20", of itself yield a self-standing idea (*selbständige Vorstellung*), but only acquires a sense from the context of a sentence'.[231] And, as far as proper names are concerned, Frege does not in practice even accord them the possibility, depending on context, of introducing functions: in his examples they invariably introduce arguments.

Still, despite the bias of the examples, we do have further statements of the neutral official view I quoted above. There is, for instance, the sentence in §9 that Russell picked up on in his fateful letter to Frege of 16 June 1902, the letter in which he informed Frege of 'the Contradiction': in this sentence Frege tells us that, as well as having the possibility of varying the argument of a conceptual content while holding the function fixed, we also have the option of holding the argument fixed and varying the function.[232] And in §10 we are told that in the sign '$\Phi(A)$' we can treat either component as introducing an argument and the other as introducing a function. Of course, these statements are not in themselves incompatible with the picture that has been emerging so far from our examination of Frege's examples: for his point may be that, in '$\Phi(A)$', the concept-expression 'Φ' can count as introducing an argument rather than a function not in *atomic* sentences but in *higher-order* predications, such as the second-level predication '$\forall x(\Phi x)$', in which the 'Φ' position is open to quantification in a statement of (what would in Fregean terms be) a third-level predication, such as '$\exists F \forall x(Fx)$'.[233] But against this there is a difficult paragraph in §9 which seems to be saying that in simple sentences of the form *Fa, Rab*, etc., the function–argument analysis can be applied arbitrarily, but that the analysis becomes fixed as soon as quantification is involved.[234] Finally, however things may be with artificial languages, there remains the question whether Frege held the application of function–argument interpretations of sentences of natural language to be arbitrary.

In the *Begriffsschrift*, then, we have a tension between the seeming generality and impartiality of the principle quoted above, apparently reaffirmed in §§9–10, and the fact that in his examples Frege treats proper names in his broad sense, such as 'the number 20', as fitted, in virtue of their 'yielding a self-standing idea', for the role of (introducing an) argument only: he does not appear to envisage the possibility that such expressions might serve as (names of) functions. And,

---

[231] [1], p. 17. Cf. Geach [4], p. 135.   [232] [1], p. 17.   [233] Cf. Currie [2], p. 291.
[234] 'Für uns haben die verschiedenen Weisen,...', p. 17. On the meaning of this paragraph, see Currie [2], pp. 287–90. My reading of it agrees with Sullivan's: [1], p. 107 n. 9.

however we should read the *Begriffsschrift*, there can be no doubt that in Frege's later writings this position becomes a piece of unvarying dogma. We are told in the introduction to the *Grundlagen* that it is one of its guiding rules to keep in mind the distinction between concept and object,[235] and although the technical distinction between concept and object is only elucidated by Frege in publications subsequent to the *Grundlagen*, it is plausible that, even at this stage, he envisaged a good deal of the later development of the distinction, including in particular the division of subsentential expressions into saturated or complete expressions on the one hand, and unsaturated or incomplete expressions on the other.[236] And it is a mark of Frege's mature thought—or so I shall argue in Chapter 5—that the object–concept dichotomy is not treated by him as a purely *logical* distinction, as some commentators suggest,[237] and as some of his present-day epigoni would have liked, but is assumed to line up neatly with traditional *grammatical* categories, so that proper names are held to fall absolutely—not relative to a specific analysis—on the saturated or complete side of the above division, and correspondingly concept-expressions are held to fall, again absolutely, on the unsaturated or incomplete side of the division.

36 The Anti-Fregean Strategy: The Case of Names

But the claimed semantic independence of the proper name 'the number 20', as against the alleged contextual dependency of the second-level quantificational expression 'every positive integer' (and presumably also of first-level concept-expressions like 'can be represented as the sum of four squares'),[238] cannot be permitted to stand. After all, a name cannot *on its own* express a complete sense. Frege's dignifying of proper names with the label 'complete' therefore seems unmotivated.[239] A bare utterance of 'the number 20' no more makes a 'move

---

[235] [3], p. x.

[236] Cf. Wright [1], p. 7. Resnik argues ([2] and [3]; cf. Angelelli [1], pp. 154–8, 236) that the saturated–unsaturated distinction, which is not mentioned *expressis verbis* in the *Grundlagen*, should not be read back into it. But although Frege does not use the words 'saturated' and 'unsaturated' in the *Grundlagen*, the distinction itself figures prominently (see e.g. §70), so that it seems rather artificial to stand on the terminological point. Further—and this point is surely decisive—Frege's use of the language of (un)saturatedness antedates the *Grundlagen*: we find it in the letter to Marty, where he explains the *Begriffsschrift*. Cf. Beaney, p. 164; Currie [2], p. 295; Olson, p. 73.

[237] See e.g. Ricketts [2], §III; Kemmerling [1]; Goldfarb [2].

[238] As far as *Begriffsschrift* is concerned, the issue is whether first-level concept-expressions yield a 'self-standing idea': Currie argues ([2], p. 289) that in 1879 Frege held that they did. Perhaps; but in the letter to Marty of 1882 the mature view is already firmly in place: [22], p. 164.

[239] Cf. Carl [1]; Grossmann [1], p. 25.

in the language-game' than does one of 'can be represented as the sum of four squares': it requires completion (perhaps implicit, to be gathered from the context) by a concept-expression. This point is denied by Geach, who writes:

An act of naming is of course not an assertion; it may be correct or incorrect, but not, strictly speaking, true or false; it does, however, 'express a complete thought', as grammarians say about sentences—it has a sort of independent sense. Naturally the sense of a name used this way is not independent of the language, or of the situation that makes such use appropriate; but it is independent of any verbal context expressed or understood—it is not like the sense of a fragmentary expression that answers a spoken or unspoken question.[240]

But how can an act of naming be correct or incorrect, if it is independent of any verbal context, expressed *or understood*? What would make a bare utterance or inscription of 'Socrates' correct or incorrect? It seems that there is no possibility of answering this question unless we can supply a suitable sentential context, reconstructed from express or tacit verbal features of the occasion of utterance or inscription, into which the name 'Socrates', as uttered or inscribed on that occasion, slots. In fact Geach seems to concede this very point in the above passage when he allows that the sense of a name 'is not independent. . . of the situation that makes [its] use appropriate'. If you ask 'Who is coming to the symposium?' and I respond with the word 'Socrates', my reply can be eked out from the context so as to yield the declarative sentence 'Socrates is coming to the symposium', and the truth or falsity of this sentence is what makes my more laconic utterance correct or incorrect. Elsewhere, indeed, Geach agrees that such one-word answers to questions do abbreviate sentences, but he claims that the following are independent uses of names: 'nouns in the vocative case used as greetings; labels stuck on things, e.g. "poison" on a bottle or the name-labels sometimes worn at conferences; ejaculations like "Wolf!" and "Fire!"'.[241] But it is surely obvious that these uses also abbreviate sentences.

Actually, the 'correct'–'incorrect' dichotomy, employed by Geach above, is too restrictive: this becomes clear when we consider examples in which a name is uttered on its own, but not in response to a question. Jeremy Bentham made this point:

Looking at my son, whose name is John,—I say to him, John,—he hears me,—what is it that he understands by this? The import, the full import, belonging to one or other of these two phrases. [Namely:] My desire is that you *attend*, (*viz.* to what more I am about to say,) or, my desire is that you come, i.e. come near to the place at which I am sitting.[242]

---

[240] [1], p. 462.   [241] [3], p. 26. Contrast Russell [13], p. 183.
[242] Bentham, vi, §1, p. 322.

To cover this sort of case, we need to speak not of the correctness or incorrectness of the utterance of a name, but perhaps of its appropriateness or inappropriateness. But the general point is indifferent to this refinement, and it is that if a sentential reconstruction cannot in principle be carried out, it is hard to see how the sheer utterance or inscription of a name could be correct or appropriate, as it must be if it is to count as a genuine 'move in the language-game'.[243]

A different argument for the relative completeness of proper names is offered by Strawson.[244] The idea is that understanding a proper name involves knowing some empirical fact which suffices to identify the referent, whereas understanding a concept-expression involves no such knowledge, but rather involves merely 'knowing the language'.[245] In view of this difference, we are told, proper names 'carry a weight of fact in introducing their terms [= referents]', and so have 'a completeness, a self-sufficiency, which [concept-expressions] lack'.[246] But this is quite unconvincing. In both cases (proper names, concept-expressions) the understander needs to be able to identify *what* is being referred to: there may be empirical differences between the ways in which we characteristically become acquainted with individuals and the ways in which we cognize concepts or universals—there surely are such differences—but it is hard to see how that fact alone can, as Strawson wants, bear the weight of Frege's metaphor in its purportedly differential application to proper names and concept-expressions. And that his procedure is back to front is evidenced by Strawson's extraordinary conclusion that 'begot N' and 'is identical with N', which the Fregean would classify as unsaturated expressions, have the same kind of completeness as the proper name 'N', because they presuppose the same kind of identificatory empirical fact.[247] That concession surely constitutes a *reductio ad absurdum* of the whole strategy.[248]

The context-dependency of the use of names is a point on which Wittgenstein insisted both in the *Tractatus* and in the *Philosophical Investigations*.[249]

---

[243] Cf. Kleemeier, pp. 111–14.   [244] [1], pp. 180–98, supplemented by pp. 198–213.

[245] [1], p. 186.   [246] [1], p. 187; cf. p. 243.   [247] [1], p. 242.

[248] Strawson's position is a throwback to one that was quite common in the 18th cent., when a number of authors tried to ground grammatical congruences ontologically. For example, James Harris tells us that 'all Quantities, and Qualities co-alesce immediately with their Substances. Thus 'tis we say, a *fierce Lion, a vast Mountain*; and from *this Natural Concord of Subject and Accident*, arises *the Grammatical Concord of Substantive and Adjective*. . . . THOSE PARTS OF SPEECH UNITE OF THEMSELVES IN GRAMMAR, WHOSE ORIGINAL ARCHETYPES UNITE OF THEMSELVES IN NATURE' (II. iii, pp. 262–4). See also Adam Smith, §14, p. 211; Monboddo, II. iii. 1 (vol. ii, pp. 342–3); Leonard, pp. 28–30; Aarsleff [2], pp. 480–1.

[249] [1], §§3.3, 3.314 (note that this latter text is preceded by a statement of the context principle); [5], i, §49. For a nice statement of the kind of view that Wittgenstein attacks in the early sections of [5], see A. Smith, §1, pp. 203–4.

Admittedly, in his later writings Wittgenstein deploys the point in an objectionable way, since he seems to regard the impulse to treat all words as names of objects (so allowing a wide variety of different kinds of object into one's ontology) as tantamount to an attempt to specify the meanings of words as if words were metaphysically prior to sentences.[250] In doing so he falls victim to a nominalist prejudice, but there is nothing inherently nominalistic in what is, in effect (as Wittgenstein himself observes), merely an insistence on Frege's own context principle, a point to which I shall return in the next section. A similar confusion is found in Ernst Tugendhat's *Vorlesungen*. On the one hand Tugendhat is quite happy to concede that the context principle applies to names.[251] And he allows that what Wittgenstein calls 'the model of object and designation' (*das Muster von Gegenstand und Bezeichnung*)[252] and what he calls the 'object-theoretical conception' (*die gegenstandstheoretische Auffassung*) of reference is compatible with the Wittgensteinian insistence on meaning as use.[253] But, like Wittgenstein, Tugendhat seems to confuse the 'object-theoretical conception' of reference, as such, with an excessively empiricistic reconstruction of that conception, according to which understanding is taken to consist in having a mental image.[254] He likes to insist that, insofar as we admit propositions, Fregean Thoughts, and states of affairs as objects that can be designated by appropriate linguistic expressions, we must not forget that our only access to them is through language,[255] as though it were an inherent claim of the 'object-theoretical conception' of reference, from which it must be purged, that we have a non- or pre-linguistic access to other sorts of object. In fact, however, the view that our access to reality is essentially and everywhere linguistic can coexist perfectly well with the 'model of object and designation', which has nothing, as such, to do with either empiricism or nominalism. For it is not this model that imports the mistaken empiricist idea of understanding as having a mental image; rather, as Frege well remarks, we tend to slip into that mistaken idea when we forget the context principle.[256]

Peter Long has suggested that in the *Tractatus* Wittgenstein incorporates at the level of symbolic language a version of Frege's saturated–unsaturated distinction, according to which concept-expressions, including relational expressions, are not names of objects, but are indices of relations among signs. Thus in the (written) sentence '*A* is next to *B*', what symbolizes the relation of proximity

[250] See here Wright [1], p. 47; my [3]. The later Wittgenstein's suspicion of grammar is anticipated by Frege in one of his last writings: [26], pp. 288–9, where we are told that the philosopher's remit is a 'Kampf mit der Sprache'; cf. von Kutschera [1], pp. 137–8.
[251] [2], pp. 353, 366–7.   [252] [5], i, §293.   [253] [2], p. 207.
[254] [2], pp. 86–7, 178–80, 198, 201–7, 246, 349, 353, 476–7.   [255] [2], pp. 63–4, 280, 343, 351.
[256] [3], p. x, §§60, 106; cf. Thiel, pp. 126–7.

between *A* and *B* is the fact that '*A*' is written to the left, and '*B*' to the right, of the sign 'next to':[257]

For it is only when combined with other signs of suitable type that ['next to'] stands for a relation. We cannot name a relation by writing down 'next to' alone, but must write down such a proposition as '*A* is next to *B*'. . . . What expresses, symbolizes, a relation is not an expression.[258]

But, setting aside the exegetical issue for the moment, as far as the systematic point goes we must reply that in any sense in which concept-expressions are indices of sign-relations, the same may be said of proper names.[259] In any sense in which we cannot name a relation by simply uttering or writing down the words 'next to', in just the same sense we cannot name a person by simply uttering or writing down 'Socrates'.

37 Disquotation and Propositional Form

In more detail, criticism of the reformed Frege's strategy on the basis of a comparison with the anti-Fregean strategy looks like this. Suppose we have to give a fragment of a theory of meaning sufficient to generate a meaning-specification for the sentence 'Socrates is wise'. The reformed Frege will insist on a clause like

(3)   'Socrates' refers to Socrates

for the proper name 'Socrates', a clause like

(1) $\forall x(x$ satisfies 'is wise' iff x is wise)

for the concept-expression 'is wise', and a compositional clause specifying, in general terms, the meanings of simple sentences formed by combining names with concept-expressions. But what reason do we have to prefer this strategy over one that operates with the clauses

(4)   'wise' refers to wisdom
(5) $\forall F(F$ satisfies 'Socrates (is)' iff Socrates has F)

together with a suitable combinatorial axiom?[260] On this approach, 'wise' is treated as a name with a referent (wisdom). 'Socrates (is)', on the other hand,

---

[257] Long, p. 92. A similar account is found in Stenius [1], p. 134.
[258] Long, p. 95.   [259] Cf. T. Parsons [1], pp. 243–4.
[260] Cf. Grossmann [2], p. 29; Bergmann [1], pp. 45–6; MacBride [4], pp. 596–9.

is treated as a concept-expression with a reference (specified by (5)) but no referent. It is the bearer of unsaturatedness, on this strategy, in the sentence 'Socrates is wise'. The difference between the reformed Frege's way of dealing with 'Socrates is wise' and the anti-Fregean way might be expressed by saying that, whereas for Frege there would be a paradox of the concept *(is) wise*, if we were obliged to recognize such a thing (as the reformed Frege insists we are not, going beyond the historical Frege in precisely this regard), but no paradox of the object Socrates, for the anti-Fregean strategy there would be a paradox of the object or concept to which 'Socrates (is)' refers, if we were obliged to recognize such a thing (as, on this approach, we are not), but no paradox of the object to which 'wise' refers.

Note that the metalanguage of the specifications (4) and (5) is one which, although it is being used to convey the purport of the anti-Fregean strategy, itself conforms to a Fregean grammar in a sense I shall explain shortly. So (4) and (5) are, as it were, heterophonic meaning-specifications. If we tried to supply homophonic specifications—specifications in a metalanguage whose grammar also conformed to the anti-Fregean strategy—we should have to write something like

(6) 'wise' refers to wise

and

(7) $\forall F(F$ satisfies 'Socrates (is)' iff Socrates (is) $F)$,

where the quantified variable ranges over objects of the sort introduced in (6). These clauses would make sense if the metalanguage were an imaginary language itself constructed on the grammatical principles of the anti-Fregean strategy, but they are nonsense as sentences of English, because, as I have said, English contains an internalized Fregean grammar.[261] What it means, in the present context, for a language to contain an internalized grammar of some particular kind (Fregean or anti-Fregean) is this: the operation of disquotation takes one in a well-formed way from a linguistic expression to its referent. Hence English contains an internalized Fregean grammar, because in English disquotation takes us in a well-formed way from a proper name like 'Socrates' to its referent, but not from a concept-expression like '(is) wise' to its referent: as a fragment of English, (3) is well formed and true, but (6) is nonsense. Since I am characterizing the anti-Fregean strategy in English, I am forced to give heterophonic rather than homophonic meaning-specifications of 'Socrates' and 'wise', as these are understood by that strategy, but that is just an instance of

---

[261] Cf. MacBride [6], pp. 437–8.

the general and unproblematic fact that, if I am giving a theory of meaning for one language which is designed to be comprehensible to monolingual speakers of a different language, I am forced to give a heterophonic such theory with this different language as the metalanguage.

No doubt Frege was consciously or subconsciously impressed, in drawing and applying the saturated–unsaturated distinction in the way he did, by the facts about disquotation rehearsed above. But it may also be that he was led to ignore the possibility of a semantics along the lines of the anti-Fregean strategy by reflection on the following grammatical fact. To obtain a declarative sentence using the concept-expression 'is wise', we must (in the basic case) deploy a proper name in front of it. Now this fact about the correct positioning of a proper name relative to a concept-expression in a well-formed simple categorical sentence might seem to be determined by the concept-expression rather than by the name. Perhaps it is the case that, as Dummett puts it, the concept-expression

has, as it were, a hook in one particular place (usually in the front) to which something must be attached if it is to occur in a sentence: whereas, although admittedly the proper name does not by itself constitute a sentence, we cannot visualize it as having a hook in any particular place which must be attached to something if a sentence is to be formed; the proper name may occur at the beginning, at the end, or in the middle of the sentence.[262]

The fact—if it is a fact—that concept-expressions determine the relative position of proper names in a well-formed simple categorical sentence, rather than vice versa, might encourage the thought that proper names and their referents are in some sense peculiarly 'complete' or 'saturated'; but the thought is, as Dummett goes on to concede shortly after the quoted passage, an entirely superficial one, having no depth beyond the level of mere object-language syntax: for it does not force metalinguistic meaning-specifications along the lines of (1) and (3), as opposed to (4) and (5) (or, if available, (6) and (7)).[263]

Perhaps Frege was also impressed by a point that Strawson has tried to make precise, namely the claim that the concept-expression is more closely associated with propositional form, or perhaps declarative mood (or assertoric force), than is the proper name.[264] As Strawson puts it, borrowing from

---

[262] [2], p. 63; cf. Carl [1], p. 46.

[263] I have been careful in this paragraph to restrict the scope of my point to the issue of *positionality*: the question whether the fact (if it is one) that it is *concept-expressions* that determine the relative position of proper names in a well-formed simple categorical sentence, rather than vice versa, has theoretical significance. An entirely separate issue (though it is possible that Dummett has both issues in mind in the passage quoted) concerns the *number of occurrences* of proper names and of concept-expressions in sentences: but this takes us from the simple categorical sentence to sentences involving polyadic predication, a topic that I reserve to the next chapter.

[264] [1], pp. 149–53.

W. E. Johnson,[265] 'the expression "is wise" not only introduces being wise, it also carries the assertive or propositional tie'.[266] But again this attempt to distinguish the concept-expression from the proper name comes to nothing. Obviously the concept-expression is no more closely associated with either declarative mood or assertoric force than is the proper name, for a given concept-expression, such as 'is wise', may, like a given proper name, such as 'Socrates', go into non-declarative sentences and sentences employed on any given occasion with non-assertoric force (such as 'Is it the case that Socrates is wise?', 'Let it be the case that Socrates is wise!', used in the obvious way) as readily as it does into declaratives and sentences employed with assertoric force. Strawson is obliged to concede this point, and accordingly weakens his proposal to the suggestion that concept-expressions are peculiarly fitted to introduce *propositional form*, where the latter means something like the indicative core of a sentence to which mood-indicators are conceived as being prefixed. But if concept-expressions can be said to introduce propositional form in this sense, so too can proper names, for on the speech-act approach to the semantic analysis of sentences that this version of the proposal presupposes (recall §2), a proper name will feature, in the first instance, in the indicative core which that analysis discerns in any given sentence of natural language, prior to the application to it of a mood-indicator, and prior to that sentence's employment on some occasion with any particular kind of force.[267]

We may conclude that, at least in respect of the considerations so far adduced, nothing can be made of Frege's differential application of his saturated–unsaturated distinction to proper names and concept-expressions. And that is, in one sense, exactly what you would expect: for the deep fact hereabouts is surely that proper names are made to go with concept-expressions just as much as concept-expressions are made to go with proper names (or with other concept-expressions), for both proper names and concept-expressions are fundamentally made to go into the *sentence*, which must accordingly enjoy some kind of conceptual priority over its parts. Hence if the chemical metaphor of which Frege is so fond has any application in this domain at all, it ought to apply *uniformly* to proper names and concept-expressions. In effect this point is an application of Frege's own context principle, broadly construed. The general point here was already well conveyed by Bentham in his *Essay on Language*, who noted, in an anticipation of Frege's chemical metaphor, that 'words may

---

[265] Johnson, i, pp. 10–13.   [266] [1], p. 151.

[267] So, in this sense of 'proposition', Strawson is wrong to say that 'the name "Socrates" might be completed into *any* kind of remark, not necessarily a proposition; but the expression "is wise" demands a certain kind of completion, namely completion into a proposition or propositional clause' ([1], p. 153). The first part of this claim is incorrect.

be considered as the result of a sort of analysis,—a chemico-logical process, for which, till at a comparatively much later period than that which gave birth to propositions, the powers of the mind were not ripe'.[268] And, in a splendid tour de force, Bentham rebukes those obscurantists who, slavishly following in the footsteps of the author of the *Categories*, treated of the semantics of terms before the semantics of propositions, as though the former were conceptually prior to the latter, instead of—as the context principle assures us is rather the case[269]—vice versa:

These terms [sc. of the Aristotelians] are accordingly spoken of as possessing of themselves an original and independent signification, as having existence before anything of the nature of a proposition came to be in existence:—as if finding these terms endowed, each of them, somehow or other, with a signification of its own, at a subsequent period some ingenious persons took them in hand, and formed them into propositions. But the truth is, that in the first place came propositions, and that out of these propositions, by abstraction and analysis, terms possessed, each of them, of an independent import, were formed.[270]

Despite its having been mentioned (twice) by Quine in his most famous essay,[271] Bentham's key role in the reorientation of modern semantics away from its historic fixation with the subsentential and towards an acknowledgement of the sentence as the fundamental vehicle of meaning is still perhaps not as widely appreciated as it deserves to be. Indeed, in one form or another the context principle has been around for a very long time (recall Ockham's version in §7), and by no means sprang uniquely and unheralded from the head of Frege: but it is his version of the principle that is most familiar and it is the one I shall concentrate on here.[272]

38 The Context Principle

Frege's version of the context principle, which he states in a number of places in the *Grundlagen*, says that it is only in the context of a sentence that words

---

[268] Bentham, vi, §1, p. 322. Cf. p. 321: 'Every man who speaks, speaks in propositions, . . . —terms taken by themselves are the work of abstraction, the produce of a refined analysis:—ages after ages must have elapsed before any such analysis was ever made.'

[269] Cf. Bell [1], pp. 2–5.

[270] Bentham, vi, §1, pp. 322–3. Cf. Priestley, iv, pp. 55–6: 'As the sole use of speech is mutual information, men would never have occasion to name any object but to affirm something concerning it: their first efforts in speech therefore would be to form a proposition'. Contra Locke, I. ii, §23.

[271] [2], pp. 39, 42. Cf. [8], pp. 68–70.

[272] On the context principle in 18th- and early 19th-cent. thought, see Land, pp. 124, 165–9; on Abelard, see Jacobi [2].

mean something (that is, are meaningful),[273] which we can here take to mean that 'if we understand how a word contributes to the meaning of sentences in which it occurs, there is nothing further about its meaning that has been left unsaid'.[274] Sentences are conceptually prior to words in the sense that words are a theoretical abstraction from sentences; the account of what a word is and what it is for makes essential reference to its role in a sentence.[275] I think we must agree with Dummett and Wright that the principle is not to be identified simply with a principle of contextual definition.[276] It has even been suggested that the failed attempts in the *Grundlagen* to specify contextual definitions of directions and numbers indicate—and were intended by Frege to indicate—how *not* to apply the context principle in these cases.[277] Certainly the independence of the context principle in the *Grundlagen* from any principle of contextual definition is clear from the fact that, though Frege rejects the contextual definitions of natural number he discusses, at the end of that work he leaves the context principle standing.[278]

In one of the passages in which he mentions it, Frege shows himself well aware of the point that the context principle applies to proper names as much as it does to concept-expressions.[279] That makes the differential application of his favourite chemical metaphor to subsentential expressions like 'Socrates' and 'is wise', as they figure in our sample sentence 'Socrates is wise', all the more puzzling, and as far as I can see it is best explained on the hypothesis that, distracted by surface grammar, he mistook the metaphysical import of what is in fact a merely syntactic difference between proper names and concept-expressions, proceeding to concoct a spurious independence for names like 'Socrates' that concept-expressions like 'is wise' supposedly lack.[280] In fact the syntactic difference is less impressive, on closer inspection,

---

[273] Frege [3], §62; cf. p. x, §§46, 60; 106; [26], pp. 18–19, 273; Wright [1], ch. 1, esp. §vii.

[274] Potter [1], p. 78.   [275] See my [15], ch. 6; cf. §§9 above and 53 below.

[276] Dummett [1], pp. 38–40; Wright [1], pp. 8–9. Cf. Thiel, pp. 125–6.

[277] Kleemeier, pp. 181–8; contrast Stuhlmann-Laeisz, pp. 99–101.

[278] [3], §106; cf. Potter [1], p. 78.   [279] [3], §60. Cf. Kleemeier, p. 36.

[280] Here I am assuming a continuity in Frege's thought that some writers have questioned: Resnik suggests not only, as I have noted (n. 236), that the saturated–unsaturated distinction should not be read back into the *Grundlagen*, where it is not explicitly mentioned, but that Frege abandoned the context principle after the *Grundlagen*; in Resnik's view the context principle is Frege's *Grundlagen* solution to the problem of the unity of the proposition, the saturated–unsaturated distinction his later solution. I have already (ibid.) warned against making too much of the absence in the *Grundlagen* of an explicit mention of the saturated–unsaturated distinction. As regards the context principle, it is perhaps true that Frege does not affirm it explicitly after the *Grundlagen* (though one or two passages come quite close: see here Sluga [2], p. 268, referring to Frege [26], p. 273); but nor does he repudiate it. The principle is not incompatible with attributing sense and reference to sentential components, as Resnik claims ([2], pp. 361–2; [3], pp. 46–9). Even Frege's later assimilation of sentences to names of truth-values does not in itself conflict with the context principle, as Dummett supposes ([2], pp. 7,

than it might at first sight appear (or have seemed to Frege) to be. Frege's
semantics recognizes sentences constructed from different levels of a linguistic
hierarchy. The details and viability of the Fregean linguistic hierarchy will
occupy us in the next chapter: here we just need the following relatively
simple point.

The Fregean linguistic hierarchy allows us to construct an item from the
lowest level, level 0, with an item from the next level up, level 1: the example
we have been operating with, 'Socrates is wise', is thus constructed, for Frege in
effect assigns a proper name like 'Socrates' to level 0 and a concept-expression
like 'is wise' to level 1. But the hierarchy also permits other constructions,
for example the combination of the first-level concept-expression 'is wise'
with a second-level concept-expression such as the (so-called first-order)
quantifier 'someone', to yield 'someone is wise'. It is indeed one of Frege's
most trumpeted achievements that he classified expressions like 'someone' as
(second-level) *concept-expressions*, rather than as peculiar sorts of name. Now
if 'someone' is a concept-expression, it ought to be unsaturated. But then
it is natural to ask: (i) how can 'someone' be unsaturated, given that, at
least for present purposes, it has exactly the same *surface grammar* as saturated
expressions like 'Socrates' (that is, it can be prefixed to Fregean first-level
concept-expressions to yield grammatically well-formed monadic declarative
sentences); and (ii) how is it possible, in the case of a sentence like 'someone
is wise', to construct a saturated item (a sentence) out of two *unsaturated*
components, given that, in the basic case (the case of 'Socrates is wise')
that was achieved by constructing an unsaturated component with a *saturated*
one?[281] Frege's repeated insistence that in the former case we should speak
of a concept's falling *within* another concept, whereas in the latter we should
speak of an object's falling *under* a concept,[282] does nothing to remove the
puzzlement, but merely serves to highlight the awkward fact that he apparently
recognizes two quite distinct metaphorical models of unity. But how *can* the
metaphor permit two such distinct models?[283]

196, 644–5; [3], p. 295; [4], p. 82; cf. Potter [1], p. 110), or with the theoretical priority of the
sentence over its parts: that emerges in the fact that, as Burge notes ([2], pp. 109–15; cf. Sullivan [4],
p. 72), for Frege the judgement stroke can only be prefixed to the horizontal—i.e. to the name of a
truth-value—not to just any name.

[281] Simons claims ([3], p. 81) that Frege's view is that in a quantified sentence such as 'All *A*s are
B' the parts are not unsaturated, but that seems to me a misinterpretation. See e.g. [13], p. 373 ([21],
pp. 270–1), where it is clearly stated that in the sentence 'es gibt etwas, was eine Primzahl ist' the two
parts 'es gibt etwas, was' and 'eine Primzahl ist' are both unsaturated concept-expressions.
[282] [7], p. 201 ([21], p. 174); [13], p. 373 ([21], pp. 270–1); letters to Marty, 29 Aug. 1882 ([22],
p. 164), and Husserl, 30 Oct. 1906 ([22], p. 103); cf. Angelelli [1], p. 94; Bell [1], pp. 33–6.
[283] Cf. L. Linsky [2], p. 265; Siderits [3], p. 31; MacBride [4], pp. 607–8.

Frege seems to have thought that constructions involving first- and second-level concept-expressions are somehow parasitic on constructions involving proper names and first-level concept-expressions:[284] but, again, it is obscure how this point, whatever its merits (an issue I postpone to the next chapter), can help us understand his application of the metaphor of saturatedness and unsaturatedness. It has been suggested that the function–argument analysis was not taken by Frege to apply to (the meanings of) sentences composed exclusively of higher-level expressions.[285] If that were correct, it would provide a further argument (cf. §33) against the legitimacy of taking that analysis to yield a general account of unity. It seems to me, however, more plausible to interpret Frege as having held that the analysis continues to apply to (the meanings of) sentences when these are composed exclusively of higher-level expressions,[286] the difficulty for Frege then consisting in the possibility of applying the analysis to sentences in two essentially different ways. For the argument to a function may be either saturated (if its name belongs to the zeroth level of the hierarchy) or unsaturated (if its name belongs to a higher level). Reflection on this antinomy ought to have alerted Frege to the fact that the grammar of proper names like 'Socrates', which may (so I am speculating) have encouraged him to regard them as peculiarly saturated, was from a philosophical point of view much more superficial than he was supposing.

What the context principle shows is that there is no warrant for Frege's differential treatment of names and concept-expressions; it is simply not acceptable to claim, as we have seen Frege do, that the proper name 'the number 20' yields by itself a 'self-standing idea',[287] or, as Russell did, that a proper name 'has a meaning by itself, without the need of any context'.[288] Even Carnap's more modest claim that proper names have 'at least a relatively self-standing *Bedeutung*' goes too far.[289] Equally, of course, there is no warrant for the opposite differential treatment favoured by the anti-Fregean strategy, though here it is interesting to note that, if any differentiation among subsentential expressions in point of saturatedness or unsaturatedness is to be maintained, the anti-Fregean can appeal, against the Dummettian intuition aired in the previous section, to the fact that, whereas the notion of an empty concept—a concept under which no object falls—is a perfectly coherent one, and indeed, as we have noted (§15), plays an essential role in science, the correlative notion of an empty object—an object falling under no concept—is incoherent.[290] But, in

[284] [26], p. 192.   [285] Siderits [3], p. 31.
[286] See esp. the passage from [13], p. 373 ([21], p. 271) which I quote in Ch. 4 n. 35 below.
[287] [1], §9.   [288] Whitehead and Russell, i, p. 66.   [289] [1], §27.
[290] Kleemeier, p. 209.

reality, neither the Fregean intuition that I rejected at the end of the previous section, nor this anti-Fregean intuition, serves its purpose. The whole tactic of differentiating between subsentential components in point of saturatedness or unsaturatedness is undermined by the context principle.[291] For if there is any decent notion of unsaturatedness in the offing, the context principle is going to assure us that *all* words (that is, all basic lexical components of the sentence discerned by some suitable semantic theory) are, as far as the saturated–unsaturated distinction is concerned, on a par with one another: whatever we say, we must say the same for them all.

That is not necessarily going to undermine the very basis of the distinction between the saturated and the unsaturated. It would undermine that distinction if we could not, even in principle, point to anything saturated (or unsaturated), to contrast with the unsaturated (saturated) items we purported to have isolated. In that case we would be left with nothing but words, rules of their combination, and their meanings—their meanings being just the ontological precipitate of what any adequate semantic theory tells us someone has to know in order to count as understanding the relevant segment of language. But we can point to sentences themselves as candidates for items to contrast with words in point of saturatedness or unsaturatedness. The context principle surely yields a relevant asymmetry between sentences on the one hand and their semantically significant lexical components on the other: for only the former can 'make a move in the language-game' (say something true or false); the role of the latter is to contribute to the making of this move, but not themselves to make it. We may then register this asymmetry by calling sentences complete or saturated, and semantically significant subsentential lexical components unsaturated or incomplete. In the former part of our claim we follow Frege; in the latter part we depart from Frege inasmuch as we refuse to recognize any relevant distinction in point of unsaturatedness among semantically significant subsentential lexical components. Here we rather find our inspiration in Ramsey, who remarked (putting the point in ontological terms): 'In a sense, it might be urged, all objects are incomplete; they cannot occur in facts except in conjunction with other objects, and they contain the forms of propositions of which they are constituents.'[292] The same point

---

[291] Cf. ibid., pp. 207–26, making the point in ontological terms; I make it here in linguistic terms, but I shall employ an ontological mode of expression in due course. The ontological point is that, in any sense in which it is true that a concept is unsaturated 'indem er etwas fordert, was unter ihn falle' (Frege's letter to Marty, 29 Aug. 1882: [22], p. 164), it is equally true that an object demands a concept under which to fall.

[292] [2], p. 115. Cf. ibid., pp. 121–2, referring us to Wittgenstein [1], §2.0122; Hintikka and Hintikka, p. 42; MacBride [1], p. 34; [4], p. 606; Candlish [2], p. 52; Johnston, p. 243.

about semantically significant subsentential lexical components could be put by saying that there is no place for a distinction between categorematic and syncategorematic such expressions. They are *all* syncategorematic: for all such subsentential expressions exhibit the context-dependency that is proprietary to the syncategorematic.

39 Prābhākara Semantics and the Related Designation Theory

The thesis that all words are syncategorematic is one that was championed by the Prābhākara school of classical Indian thought. On this approach, the context principle is in effect interpreted as saying that words have 'related designation' in the sense that their '*designative* power extends to a designatum *plus* possible linkages with others [i.e. other words]. The word *means* the related item.'[293] In particular, the Prābhākaras insisted that names no more have a saturated meaning than other words: names may be associated with particular concrete objects, but those objects are not, just as such, what the names mean.[294] So far this agrees with the position I have defended. But there are two important ways in which, it seems to me, the Prābhākara position goes wrong in its elucidation of the context principle.

First, B. K. Matilal and P. K. Sen attribute to the Prābhākaras a distinction between an *ontological* domain, which contains just the objects themselves, without linkages, and a *semantic* domain, which contains what they call 'epistemic' objects, that is, objects with linkages.[295] But such a separation of metaphysics from semantics is, as I argued in Chapter 2, a mistake: the 'epistemic' objects *are* the objects themselves. We can have no conception of objects other than those that are accessible through language, and these objects come endowed with linkages to other objects and to properties. Secondly, the Prābhākara school seems to have held that the reference or designation of a word, in context, is affected by the other words in that sentence. This is an extreme version of the context principle, which we have met in connection with the medieval identity theory of predication, and associated doctrines, and which we will meet again in the next chapter. For reasons that were explored in Chapter 2, and to which I will return in the next chapter, the position is unacceptable, because, in effect, the understander is debarred from gaining entry to the sentence. If the rest of a sentence has to be understood before any given part of it can be understood, the sentence cannot be understood on the basis of a grasp of the meanings of its parts and the way they are put together. But we must respect the principle of compositionality at least to that extent, if the understanding of novel sentences is to be explanatorily perspicuous.[296] The linkages carried by words and their referents cannot be *individual* in nature—they cannot be linkages to individual words and their referents as these words occur in a *given* sentence or proposition—but must be *general*, in the sense that words and their referents carry slots for words or objects of a certain general kind.

According to Mark Siderits, the Prābhākaras addressed this difficulty (which was known as the 'mutual locus' objection) by introducing an asymmetry into the way we understand sentences: we process the semantics of some bits of the sentence before other bits, and those bits that are processed first count as, in effect, relatively unsaturated. The idea is that the parts processed earlier generate 'expectancies' that are satisfied by the parts processed later; but the latter do not in turn (at least, not in this context) generate 'expectancies' requiring to be satisfied by the former. Siderits denies that this asymmetry is a mere variant of the Fregean one: the Prābhākara asymmetry 'is not semantic but rather an artefact of processing'.[297] The point seems to be that, as I hinted a moment ago, the Prābhākara analysis is, unlike the Fregean one, context-sensitive. Frege classifies whole syntactic word-groups as saturated or unsaturated, whereas on the Prābhākara approach, a given type of word may count as relatively unsaturated in one sentential context and relatively saturated in another.[298] Or rather, this is what Siderits takes to be the 'best version' of the related designation theory: for he concedes that, in practice, the Prābhākaras tend, like Frege, to treat the verb as being unsaturated in an absolute sense.[299] But, as Siderits rightly says, it is not inherent in the related designation theory as such that it be slanted in the Fregean way:[300] it is perfectly open to supporters of that theory to relativize to sentential context the roles of (relative) (un)saturatedness in the way indicated. And I agree that this is indeed the best version of the theory. Siderits further connects the 'best version' of the theory with a liberated application of the function–argument framework to sentential semantics;[301] and this too strikes me as a fruitful way forward. The idea is that, in the context of a particular sentential analysis, the relatively unsaturated parts of the sentence, and their referents, would count as functional expression and function respectively, while the relatively saturated parts would count as argument expressions and arguments respectively.

---

[296] For this objection, see Siderits [3], pp. 47–50.   [297] Ibid., p. 50.   [298] Ibid., pp. 52, 60.
[299] Ibid., p. 56 n. 31.   [300] Ibid., pp. 56–8.   [301] Ibid., p. 57.

Now Siderits implies, if I understand him correctly, that there are no limits on the extent to which we can distribute these distinct functional roles within a sentence;[302] and that is indeed quite a natural assumption to make (one that I have myself made in the past).[303] It now seems to me mistaken, however, and in the next chapter I shall explain where I think the limits must be drawn. But the basic point remains intact, which is that (to return to the terms in which I have been discussing the unity issue), as between Fregean and anti-Fregean strategies of analysing a simple categorical sentence like 'Socrates is wise', there is no principled way of making a choice; the moral of the context principle is that all semantically significant subsentential lexical expressions are (in Fregean terms) unsaturated or (in more traditional terminology) syncategorematic. If it is right that a proposition must be subjected to a function–argument analysis, there is (or may be) no unique way of carrying out the distribution of roles. As I shall argue in the next chapter, though there are limits on the flexibility of arrangements, a syntactic hierarchy admits of more than one way of assigning expressions (and their referents) to its levels.

40 'For that is Not a *Word* which is Not the *Name* of a Thing'[304]

The picture I have presented so far has to be made slightly more complicated—though not in such a way as to compromise the even-handed approach to subsentential components I am recommending—in order to take account of the fact that sentences may themselves figure as components of larger sentential units, as when they are joined by connectives like 'and' or prefixed by operators like 'it is necessary that'. Frege himself treated sentences as absolutely saturated, in line with his treatment of proper names, so that sentences, like names, remain saturated when they figure as parts of larger wholes.[305] But, in line with our revision of Frege's doctrine of the saturatedness of proper names, it seems to me that a due respect for the context principle requires us to treat sentential components of larger sentences as being just as unsaturated as the components to which they are attached, such as 'and' and 'it is necessary that'. It follows that the saturatedness of a sentence cannot be taken to be absolute, but rather obtains relative to its *subsentential* components. In relation to its components 'Socrates' and 'is wise', the sentence 'Socrates is wise' counts as saturated; but

---

[302] Ibid., p. 60.   [303] See my [8], criticized by Denyer in his [2].

[304] Horne Tooke, II, ch. 6 (vol. ii, p. 435).

[305] Cf. Frege [18], p. 155 ([21], p. 375); [19], p. 37 ([21], pp. 378–9).

in relation to the sentence 'It is possible that Socrates is wise', say, it counts as unsaturated. The saturated or unsaturated status of the sentence is, then, subject to a relativity to linguistic context; but the contrast with subsentential expressions survives this observation, for their status as unsaturated expressions is not thus relative to context. In their case we can continue to maintain that the label 'unsaturated' applies, if to any such components, then to all, and does so absolutely, regardless of context.

That does not yet, perhaps, quite amount to saying that to know the meaning of a word is to be acquainted with an *object* (concrete or abstract), and that correlatively all words are *names*, but it will be a good question why we should resist taking this further step. For if *all* words (primitive semantically significant subsentential lexical components) are uniformly unsaturated, it seems that we may as well say that they are all names referring to objects. At least, we shall have to say either that all words are names referring to objects or that none are, and it is obscure what the point of selecting this latter option could be: the notions of name and object would in that case be deprived of application. And I see nothing to be gained by indulging in the tactic favoured by some commentators of saying that concept-expressions merely 'express' or 'affirm' rather than 'name'.[306] The 'further step' of saying that all words are names was, in effect, taken by Wittgenstein in the *Tractatus*.[307] There is also a sense in which the position was anticipated in the medieval period by the *Modistae*,[308] though, as Jan Pinborg aptly remarks,[309] the modist grammarians had not yet discovered Kant's Copernican turn. Perhaps more to the point for our purposes, medieval thought had not yet discovered the linguistic turn, so that the modist position was never put in the right context—namely the thesis of linguistic idealism that the world is precipitated by language. (It is quite wrong to cast Ockham in the role of a medieval exponent of the linguistic turn,[310] as a reading of his various polemics against realism about universals, which are evidently ontology- not syntax-driven, shows.[311])

For Wittgenstein, of course, the thesis that all words are names is applied at, and not before, the *final stage of analysis*: there are plenty of linguistic expressions which, in the ordinary sense, count as words of natural language but which, in the process of analysis, are alleged to disappear and so do not count, ultimately, as names. In particular, we are told that it is the 'fundamental

---

[306] So Russell [18], p. 320; Bealer [1], pp. 110, 159–60; [4], p. 41; Künne [1], p. 274; Etchemendy, pp. 44, 57.

[307] Cf. Simons [3], p. 91.   [308] See here Pinborg [1], pp. 46–51, 122–3; Haller, p. 107.

[309] Pinborg [1], p. 49 n. 95.

[310] So e.g. Leppin, pp. 103, 110, 280–1. For the right view, see Eckermann, p. 14.

[311] See e.g. [1], I, ch. 51, p. 171.240–7.

thought' of the *Tractatus* that the *logical constants* are not names—that is, that they will disappear on analysis.[312] Russell was influenced by this idea in the second edition of *Principles*, where he rescinded the first edition's claim that logical constants are names.[313] He appealed to the context principle in order to be entitled to say that logical constants can be meaningful *without* being names. But this is back to front: for the whole point of the context principle is that it gives us a reason to say that all words *are* names—we have no basis on which to accord this title to some but not other semantically significant subsentential lexical components. So when Russell writes, in justification of the new policy, that although it is not the case that every word has a meaning, 'what is true is that the word contributes to the meaning of the sentence in which it occurs: but that is a very different matter',[314] we may counter that it is *not* a very different matter: it is exactly the same matter. Similarly, when Priest attempts to justify nominalism in mathematics by saying that 'mathematical objects are irrelevant to mathematics . . . since if all were destroyed mathematics would be unaffected (as long as we continue to practise it in the same way)',[315] the natural reply is that, in *that* sense, objects are irrelevant to *any* domain of discourse: in any sense in which one can coherently suppose that a linguistic practice might continue to exist in the absence of its proprietary objects of discourse, mathematics is not distinguished from any other linguistic practice. For, as we have said, objects are theoretical posits (§9), internal to the linguistic practice in which they are (interpreted by the theorist as being) referred to, so that if there is any sense in which the posits of one domain of discourse are dispensable, then we may say the same of the posits of any other such domain. In fact, however, it does *not* make sense to suppose that a linguistic practice might continue to exist in the absence of its objects if by that we mean to debar the theorist even from the *option* of interpreting the practice to involve reference to worldly objects. For that would be to suppose, absurdly, that the practice in question could continue to exist in the absence of its interpretable signs. The position I am repudiating is encapsulated in Quine's assertion that the 'occurrence of a word in a meaningful sentence gives [us] no presumption that the word designates anything':[316] on the contrary, the lesson of the context principle is that the presumption that a word designates (refers) is grounded precisely and only in the possibility of its occurring in meaningful sentences.

Perhaps supposing that I follow Wittgenstein in his 'fundamental thought', Schnieder speculates that I do not regard 'logical connectives or interjections,

[312] [1], §§4.0312, 5.441.
[313] [3], pp. xiii–xiv, xx, §71. Cf. Potter [1], pp. 126, 140; Imaguire, p. 180; Candlish [2], p. 115.
[314] [3], p. xiv.   [315] [2], p. 280; cf. pp. 148–51.   [316] [7], p. 164.

such as "unfortunately"' as having reference.[317] This is indeed a view we find expressed often enough in the tradition. It is well conveyed by Destutt de Tracy, for example. Commenting on the words 'le', 'de', 'courageux', and 'vivement', he states:

> These are not real signs, but really fragments of signs. . . . They are a kind of cement, if I may be allowed the comparison, which on being applied to a pebble changes its form and dimensions, or, by joining it to others, makes various aggregates (blocs) of which it is an essential part: but this cement is not itself an assemblage of pebbles.[318]

The view in question goes back to a sentence in Aristotle's *Poetics*,[319] and was read into *De Interpretatione* by Apollonius Dyscolus.[320] It was echoed by a number of early modern philosophers, including Locke,[321] Harris,[322] and Monboddo:[323] their endorsement of the Aristotelian view was, in turn, bitterly attacked by Horne Tooke who, affirming all words to be names, satirized the metaphors commonly adduced to describe the linguistic role of conjunctions and prepositions, such as the claim that conjunctions 'are not themselves any parts of language, but only such *accessories* as *salt* is to meat, . . . or that they are *pegs* and *nails* and *nerves* and *joints*, and *ligaments* and *glue*, and *pitch* and *lime*, and *mortar* and so forth'.[324] But the view that Horne Tooke thought to dismiss so summarily will not go away.[325] Tugendhat tells us that it would be 'absurd' to regard the connective 'and' as a name;[326] Quine says that 'there is no such thing as *up*' and that the word 'up' is not a name of anything,[327] and in his lectures on logical atomism Russell warns us not to 'look about the real world for an object which you can call "or", and say, "Now, look at this. This is 'or' "'.[328]

Why should it be held problematic to treat 'and', 'up', 'or', and 'unfortunately'—which incidentally is an adverb, not an interjection, at least not if interjections have 'nothing to do with speech' but are 'the miserable refuge of the speechless', as Horne Tooke put it in his best embellished manner[329]—as names, and so as possessing sense and reference? Obviously if 'or' refers to an object, that object is not going to be a concrete object such as one might

---

[317] [1], p. 248.   [318] [1], ch. 2, pp. 42–3. Cf. Horne Tooke, I, ch. 9 (vol. i, pp. 296–7).

[319] *Poet.* 1457a4–6.   [320] *Fragmenta*, Uhlig II ii/iii, p. 31.26–36; cf. Matthews, p. 31.

[321] Locke, III. vii, §2 (p. 472). Cf. Aarsleff [2], p. 486.   [322] J. Harris, II. ii, p. 238; iii, p. 261.

[323] Monboddo, II. i, §15 (vol. ii, pp. 188–9). Cf. Funke, pp. 76–7.

[324] Horne Tooke, I, ch. 7 (vol. i, pp. 140–2). Cf. I, ch. 9 (vol. i, pp. 276–7, 287–8, 304).

[325] No doubt in part because *The Diversions of Purley*, forthright and original as it is, contains so much etymological nonsense—though its central claim that conjunctions, prepositions, and indeed all parts of speech are really derived from nouns and verbs no longer seems so outlandish: cf. Deutscher, pp. 231–5—that its influence on semantic theory has been negligible. Cf. Quine [8], p. 68.

[326] [2], p. 291. Cf. pp. 308, 501.   [327] [1], p. 703.

[328] [13], pp. 209–10. Cf. the passage from p. 223 quoted above, §22.

[329] Horne Tooke, I, ch. 5 (vol. i, p. 59).

bump into while 'looking around the world', as Russell so disingenuously suggests. (It is a tired nominalistic ploy to represent the realist's abstract objects as would-be concrete objects.) And inconsistently too: for in *The Problems of Philosophy*, Russell had been quite happy to affirm that in the sentence 'I am in my room' the word 'in' refers to

a relation which holds between me and my room. This relation is something, although we cannot say that it exists *in the same sense* in which I and my room exist. The relation 'in' is something which we can think about and understand, for, if we could not understand it, we could not understand the sentence 'I am in my room'.[330]

Again, to the extent that a rejection of the nominal status of the logical constants (to focus on that case) rests on the Tractarian doctrine of analysis—incorporating the picture theory of meaning and the claims that all sentences are truth-functions of elementary sentences, that an ultimate and absolute analysis of the sentences of ordinary language is possible, and that the final stage of analysis yields elementary sentences made up of names of simple objects, which do not include properties and relations (I shall return to these points in Chapter 5)—one need have no qualms about maintaining the thesis that all words, not excluding the logical constants, are names. But there are other, perhaps more colourable objections to this thesis.

One might be worried by a point made by Church, when he notes that if we treat the logical connectives as names, we will in effect need an application function to apply (the referents of) the connectives to (the referents of) their operands.[331] If, now, the application function is itself regarded as a pebble rather than as cement, to borrow Destutt de Tracy's image, we evidently have the beginnings of a regress. This regress will actually turn out (in Chapter 6) to be not only innocent, but even the key to the solution of the problem of unity; I say no more about it here. Alternatively or in addition, one might be impressed by an argument of Mark Sainsbury's, who states in connection with words like 'or', 'in', 'very', and 'unfortunately', as well as modal and temporal expressions, that

It is not that it is impossible to find entities to correspond to such expressions, as shown by the Montague grammar tradition. The point is that these entities unpick the Russellian connection between acquaintance and the constituents of propositions.[332]

Why so? Apparently because these expressions take us too far from the 'perceptual paradigm'. But (i) it is not clear why the case of perception should be held to be paradigmatic for the relation of acquaintance; and (ii) even

[330] [8], pp. 50–1. Cf. MacBride [6], pp. 426–7. [331] [6], pp. 34–5. Cf. p. 41 n. 100 (on Curry).
[332] [5], p. 62.

perception must involve acquaintance with universals, on pain of reducing the perceptual episode to a brute confrontation with things-in-themselves, so that if the thought is that perception has individuals as its exclusive objects of acquaintance, that thought is mistaken. I see no good reason to construe the acquaintance relation in such a way as to make difficulties for the idea that an understander might be acquainted with the referents of 'up', 'or', 'unfortunately', and the rest.

Ramsey, despite his helpful suggestion that all objects should be regarded as incomplete (§38), rejects the (by my lights, correlative) thesis that all words are names, arguing that ' "not" cannot be a name (for if it were, not–not-*p* would have to be about the object not and so different in meaning from "*p*"), but must function in a radically different fashion'.[333] A further consideration that moved Wittgenstein to reject the (ultimate) nominal status of the logical constants was the fact of their interdefinability.[334] But, as to the first argument, why, supposing that 'not–not-*p*' and '*p*' are mutually entailing, should we conclude that they have to mean the same? On the contrary, even if they express what I shall (in §67) call 'intuitively similar Thoughts' (Thoughts to which the understander cannot rationally take different cognitive attitudes), the principle of compositionality gives us an excellent reason to deny that they *mean* the same—express the same Fregean Thought, or refer to the same Russellian propositions. As to the further consideration, how exactly is the interdefinability of a group of terms supposed to show that they are not nominal? The idea is presumably that if we can get by with (say) the logical constants '¬' and ' ∨', defining '&' in terms of them, this shows that there is no conjunction *in re*. But it shows nothing of the sort: all it shows is that, if there are real objects *not, or,* and *and,* they are interestingly related to one another. 'Not' is actually a surprising choice for the opponents of the thesis that all words are names to pick on, for in this case it is easy to state the referent: it is the function given by the familiar truth-table (it is, as it were, a truth-table *in re*: recall §18).[335] Further to my comment above on Russell's inconsistency in this matter, it is interesting to observe that, shortly after seeking to dissuade us from looking around the world for an object to serve as the referent of 'or', Russell is prepared to contemplate the possibility that there are negative facts, which would commit him to the existence of an object referred to by 'not'.[336] And if 'there is no such thing as *up*', as Quine assures us, how can we truly reply 'up' to the question 'Which way did he go?'? Of course nominalists will protest that what Quine means is better put by saying, not that there is no such

---

[333] [2], p. 147; cf. Wittgenstein [1], §§5.44; Russell [10], pp. 212–13.   [334] [1], §5.441.
[335] Cf. Church [6], p. 36.   [336] [13], p. 211; cf. Candlish [2], pp. 120–4.

thing as *up*, but that there is no such *thing* as up. But up is the way he went (the direction he took); and ways (directions) are things.

In the branch of logic Leśniewski devised and called 'protothetic' the truth-functions are objects in the Quinean sense that they have variables ranging over them and are subject to quantification.[337] And there seems no obvious reason why we should not apply the sense–reference distinction to sentential expressions containing unbound variables, and so referring to propositional functions in Russell's sense: indeed the applicability of Frege's informativeness problem to cases involving such expressions surely obliges us so to do.[338] Those who resist this extension generally do so on the basis that something more is achieved by 'genuine' names than by pronouns, conjunctions, and so on. But faced with the context principle they are embarrassed to say what that something more is. Ramsey once asked:

Can we put the problem of philosophy thus? Let us write out all we think; then part of this will contain meaningless terms only there to unify/connect the rest. i. e. some is there on its own account, the rest for the sake of the first. Which is that first, and how far does it extend?[339]

To this my response is that the context principle forces us to say that it extends all the way: the part supposedly containing meaningless terms only there 'for the sake of the rest' is empty; the class of meaningful (referring) terms *is* the class of terms.

In the *Tractatus*, Wittgenstein remarks that the logical constants, unlike signs for genuine relations, need to be accompanied by marks of punctuation (in order to obviate scope ambiguities); he concludes from this that the logical constants are themselves mere marks of punctuation and, as such, do not refer.[340] No one will believe, he confidently affirms, that the brackets have a *selbständige Bedeutung*. But why not? It is true that brackets are generally regarded as syncategorematic, on the basis that they organize or associate categorematic signs rather than discharge a referential function themselves: they are taken to be *Hilfszeichen* rather than *Zeichen*.[341] But, once one has rejected, as we have, the purported subsentential-level distinction between the syncategorematic and the categorematic as an incoherence—at least we have rejected that distinction in respect of subsentential lexical items, but the ground on which we did so (the context principle) seems to apply equally to such non-lexical parts of syntax as the punctuation signs—there seems to be no good reason to deny full nominal status,

---

[337] See e.g. Słupecki, p. 56; Church [6], pp. 152–3.   [338] Cf. Church [4], p. 102 with n. 10.
[339] [3], p. 34.   [340] [1], §§5.461–4611. Cf. Conant [2], p. 445 n. 82.
[341] So Quine [1], p. 704; Church [6], p. 32.

together with a referential role, to brackets and other marks of punctuation. Why should the fact that their job is to organize and associate mean that they are non-referential? Why should discharging the one function (arranging) exclude discharging the other (referring)? I see no reason why we cannot say that punctuation marks refer to organizations of the referents of other signs.

No doubt it will be objected that, if punctuation marks are names, the sense–reference distinction must have application in their case, and that such an application is hardly intuitive. In fact, however, there is no difficulty here: for we can surely acknowledge the existence of alternative *ways* of referring to the same arrangements of referents. So when it is said that, according to Wittgenstein's Tractarian position, 'parentheses function not by having a sense themselves, but rather by indicating how other senses should be combined',[342] we can reply that indicating how other senses should be combined *is* the kind of sense parentheses have. Indeed we might say that, on Wittgenstein's own terms, any sign that plays a semantically significant role in the symbolism has reference: here we appeal to the Tractarian idea that 'the discussion of what it is for a name to function in a certain way in a symbolism *is* a discussion of what it is for it to have a reference'.[343] There simply is no well-motivated distinction between *Zeichen* and *Hilfszeichen*: just as all words are syncategorematic, so all *Zeichen* are *Hilfszeichen*. It is plausible, then, that nominal status, and with it the full panoply of the sense–reference distinction, should be applied to all semantically significant features of the sentence, even those that have no lexical or morphological realization at the level of surface structure. This point will be important when we come to examine the semantics of the logical copula. But for the moment we can continue to focus on the case of lexical components of the sentence (words).

41 The Impartial Strategy

Monboddo reports, with approval, Ammonius's statement that

it was the doctrine both of Plato and Aristotle, that the parts of speech were two, the *noun* and the *verb*; the first denoting substances, the other the properties of substances: and indeed there can nothing exist in nature, but *things*, and their qualities. So whatever more parts of speech we make, they can only be subdivisions of the members of this grand division.[344]

---

[342] Hylton [2], p. 152.   [343] Winch, p. 10. Cf. Wittgenstein [1], §3.328.
[344] Monboddo, II, ch. 3 (vol. ii, pp. 31–2 n.), citing Ammonius, *In De Int.* p. 40.24–30.

The position I have advanced in the previous section can be represented as a radicalization of this view, which was still held, in its essentials, by Frege, Russell, and many of their modern disciples. That is, my philosophical grammar comprises not two parts of speech, the noun and the verb, but one, the name; correspondingly, my ontology contains not two basic categories, thing and quality, but one, the category of thing. Of course, classifying all words as names in our *philosophical* grammar does not relieve us of the obligation to distinguish different congruence classes of words in the context of an *empirical* grammar: that is, there is no question of submerging the different combinatorial properties enjoyed by actual words of empirical languages. Hence I shall continue to speak of proper names and concept-expressions. But, for me, these different labels no longer signal a distinction, in any philosophically pregnant sense, between items that are names and items that are not names, but rather between different congruence classes of names (words).

To make this philosophical approach explicit in the metalanguage we need to adopt meaning-specifications which give objectual referents for all semantically significant subsentential lexical components (together with suitable combinatorial axioms). We may call this metalinguistic strategy the 'impartial' strategy. In the case where the metalanguage is English, and seeing, as I have noted, that English has an internalized Fregean grammar, the impartial strategy requires us to give meaning-specifications that a Fregean would recognize as supplying objectual referents for the component words of the object-language. If, for example, we wish to give a fragment of a semantic theory for the sentence 'Socrates is wise' in English, we can write, as before,

'Socrates' refers to Socrates,

but our clause for 'is wise' will now take the form

'is wise' refers to wisdom

together with a general combinatorial axiom, such as

$$\forall \alpha \forall \Pi (\alpha^* \Pi \text{ means that } \mathit{Ref}(\alpha) \text{ instantiates } \mathit{Ref}(\Pi))$$

where small Greek letters range over proper names, capital Greek letters range over monadic concept-expressions, '$\mathit{Ref}(\gamma)$' refers to the referent of γ, and the star symbolizes concatenation. (Alternatively, the quantifiers may be interpreted substitutionally.) In operating with these clauses we represent the proper name 'Socrates' and the concept-expression 'is wise', together with their respective referents, as being no different from each other in point of saturatedness or unsaturatedness, and hence (given that we are reserving the label 'saturated' for sentences) as being uniformly unsaturated. We not only represent them as unsaturated but also as referring to objects, which accordingly also count as unsaturated.

If all words are names referring to objects, all quantifiers can in effect be treated as referential or objectual quantifiers, binding name positions: so the objection to the reformed Frege mooted in §34 on the basis of considerations relating to second-order quantification has in effect, and by a rather indirect route, been vindicated. That on the impartial strategy we should end up saying—in apparently perverse defiance of Frege—that objects (now taken to be the referents of all semantically significant subsentential lexical components) are *un*saturated need not disturb us. That claim is just the ontological image of the context principle.

42 *Secundum* and *Tertium Adiacens*, Matter and Form

In retrospect, it seems that it should have been obvious all along that if the sentence counts as saturated in the sense that it can 'make a move in the language-game', and if in the particular case of the declarative sentence this ability is in turn constituted by its capacity to be true or false, the extension of the label 'saturated' to any *subsentential* component is really quite unconscionable. For clearly—truistically—no subsentential component can be true or false, so that to label any such component, as well as the sentence, 'saturated', is to introduce an intolerable equivocation into our philosophical semantics. In this respect Plato perhaps saw more clearly than Abelard, Destutt de Tracy, Adam Smith, Monboddo, Frege, Russell, Strawson, and numerous others who have wished to give the verb or verb-phrase a privileged status in constituting the unity of the sentence. As the passage from the *Sophist* quoted in §1 shows, Plato was aware that the sentence has a special unity, lacked by its components, for the sentence 'man understands', he tells us, 'does not merely name, but achieves something, by interweaving verbs with names'. But, unlike these other philosophers, Plato does not give a differential account of the contributions of the various kinds of subsentential component to sentential unity. He notes that neither a succession of *names* nor a succession of *verbs* yields a sentence (§5); for that you need (in the simplest case) one item of each sort.[345] Aristotle follows him in this, and although he thinks that 'every apophantic *logos* [declarative sentence] must be constructed out of a verb',[346]

---

[345] Cf. Davidson [2], pp. 80–1.   [346] *Int.* 17a9–10. Cf. Russell [3], §55.

as well as a noun, he also makes a move in the right direction by classing verbs as 'in themselves' names (§26).

Interestingly, there is implicit in some of Aristotle's writings an analogy, one that achieves greater explicitness in the medieval tradition (particularly in the writings of Aquinas),[347] was picked up in the Port-Royal *Grammar*[348] and in later vernacular logic texts,[349] and is even found in Husserl,[350] between the way a simple categorical sentence is composed of proper name and concept-expression (to continue with Frege's terminology), on the one hand, and the composition of reality out of matter and form, on the other. (The analogy is, in Aristotle's case, made available by the fact that the Greek word *hupokeimenon* can mean either the subject of a sentence or the matter of an individual substance.[351]) Both the *secundum adiacens* and the *tertium adiacens* schools availed themselves of this analogy, but they applied it differently. In the *secundum adiacens* approach the matter of the simple categorical sentence 'Socrates is wise' was the name 'Socrates', the form the concept-expression 'is wise'; in the *tertium adiacens* tradition, by contrast, the name 'Socrates' and verb radical 'wise' were regarded as the matter of the sentence, while the copula was taken to be its form.[352] (Geulincx even suggested that the extremes of a simple categorical sentence might be regarded as its body, and the pure verb—the copula—as its soul![353])

The *tertium adiacens* application of the matter–form analogy seems to me defensible, and I shall explain below (§74) how I think it can be defended. But the differential treatment of subsentential components suggested by the way the *secundum adiacens* approach deploys the analogy between the composition of the simple categorical sentence and the matter–form composition of reality is as much a casualty of the foregoing reflections as was the distinction between categorematic and syncategorematic subsentential expressions, and indeed for much the same reason: making the concept-expression form-like as opposed to matter-like is, in effect, to assimilate it to the category of the syncategorematic. In reality, of course, the matter–form analysis of individual substances cannot

[347] See here Zimmermann, pp. 293–4; Michon, p. 309; Nuchelmans [5], p. 15; Geach [1] and [2]. In the former of these pieces, Geach refers us (p. 465) to Aquinas's claim that 'praedicata tenentur formaliter, et subiecta materialiter' ([1], Ia, q. 13, a. 12; cf. Ia, q. 85, a. 5).

[348] Arnauld and Lancelot, II, ch. 1, pp. 23–5; cf. Nuchelmans [5], pp. 73–4; Land, p. 78.

[349] See e.g. Watts, ii, ch. 1, p. 117. Cf. Prior [3], p. 49.   [350] [2], iv, §10.

[351] For the former, see *Cat.* 1b10–24; for the latter, *Met.* 983a29–30, 1022a17–19, 1024a9 etc. (see the index in Ross, s.v. *hulê*). On a similar ambiguity in Leibniz, see McGuire, p. 217.

[352] Nuchelmans [6], pp. 33, 37–8. Ferrer provides a good example of the former approach (see Nuchelmans, [6], p. 37), Buridan of the latter, in his [3], at p. 33.17–28 (where 'Non enim loquitur' should presumably be corrected to 'Nos enim loquimur').

[353] [1], I. i, §1, p. 177; Nuchelmans [5], p. 106.

sustain a differential ontological treatment of the purported components. For one cannot encounter either uninformed matter or unenmattered form: that is to say, the matter–form distinction is a purely theoretical construct. Both matter and form are ontologically dependent on the complete entity from which they are theoretically abstracted.[354] Somewhat similarly, we can say that, since neither a proper name on its own nor a concept-expression on its own is able to 'make a move in the language-game'—for, as we have agreed, both these subsentential components are governed by the context principle—the distinction between proper names and concept-expressions is an essentially theoretical one, undertaken by the semanticist who is in the business of producing a systematic theory of meaning for a language.

That Frege indeed meant to suggest, by calling the concept-expression unsaturated, that it is peculiarly responsible for the unity of the sentence (with a corresponding division of labour at the levels of sense and reference) is a clear implication not only of the long passage from 'Über Begriff und Gegenstand' that I quoted in §27, where he talks of unsaturated expressions as providing a special 'cement' to stick proper names together, but also from the fact, noted in §38, that he admits unified sentences formed not merely from the construction of an unsaturated expression with a *saturated* one, but also from the construction of an unsaturated expression with another *unsaturated* one. (It might be thought that the context principle presented an impediment to this line of interpretation, given that Frege tells us in several places that the unsaturated senses of concept-expressions are derived from the complete Thought, not vice versa.[355] But in one of those places he goes on to say that in order for the expression of the Thought to be decomposable, it must already be articulated.[356])

But, quite apart from the paradoxical implications of Frege's doctrine of the peculiarly unsaturated nature of the concept, the doctrine flies in the face of his own context principle by refusing to accord parity, in point of (un)saturatedness, to all subsentential expressions. The reformed Frege, who avoids paradox by repudiating reified concepts, still flouts the context principle in essentially the same way as the historical Frege did: the historical Frege told us that concept-words, unlike proper names, have unsaturated referents; the reformed Frege tells us that concept-words, unlike proper names, do not have referents at all. But a proper respect for the context principle requires us, I have argued, to treat all words, including concept-words, as names. We

---

[354] Cf. Trentman [1], pp. 54–5.
[355] So Hylton [2], p. 15 n. 6. See Frege [22], p. 164; [26], pp. 18–19, 273.
[356] [26], pp. 18–19: I here adjust Frege's wording to reflect his mature terminology.

can regard words, as well as their senses and referents (objects), as uniformly (and absolutely) unsaturated, by contrast with the (relatively) saturated status of sentences, along with their senses (Thoughts) and referents (propositions). (In some respects this is a Tractarian position,[357] though one supplemented by Frege's sense–reference distinction, and one which does not commit us to the more dubious assertions of that work.) This move does not resurrect the paradox of the concept *horse*: for that unsaturated object is now in the same boat as everything else. But nor—contra, perhaps, what the Prābhākara school held[358]—does it solve the problem of unity. For it is not as though we can invoke the context principle to outlaw lists: words are essentially made for sentences—that is what the context principle says, and it is what is meant by calling words unsaturated—but they may, for all that, occur in mere lists. What is the principle of distinction between a bunch of unsaturated words (with correspondingly unsaturated senses and referents) as they occur in a mere list, and those same words arranged in a sentence capable of expressing a Thought and referring to a proposition? Extending the label 'unsaturated' (or 'syncategorematic') to all semantically significant subsentential lexical expressions, important though it be to undertake this revision of our Aristotelian and Fregean inheritance, does not in itself help us answer this question.

[357] Cf. Siderits [3], pp. 59–60.
[358] See here Matilal and Sen, p. 90; Siderits [2], pp. 269–70, 290–2; [3], pp. 39–44.

4

The Hierarchy of Levels and the Syntactic Priority Thesis

43 Fregean and Anti-Fregean Strategies

We can make the objection to Frege that we have been considering more precise by locating our discussion explicitly within the terms of the familiar hierarchy of levels generated by Frege's philosophical grammar.[1] The construction of the hierarchy starts from Frege's distinction between saturated and unsaturated expressions. Besides the hierarchy of levels for expressions of symbolic language we have two corresponding hierarchies: a hierarchy of the senses of these expressions and a hierarchy of their references, or, where appropriate, referents. Abstracting from considerations relating to Fregean sense, I shall here concentrate on the hierarchies obtaining at the levels of language and reference: these I shall call the linguistic and ontological hierarchies respectively.[2] Saturated expressions are allocated to the lowest level of the linguistic hierarchy, level 0; the higher levels are then populated with unsaturated expressions of various kinds, according to the following principle: an unsaturated expression of level $n + 1$ is formed from a saturated expression by omission of an expression of level n.[3] If we omit more than one expression, the resulting expression will be of a level one greater than the number of the highest-level expression omitted. Frege himself did not recognize expressions above the third level, but nothing in the principles governing the formation of levels limits the linguistic hierarchy to any finite degree of development.[4]

---

[1] Dummett [2], ch. 3; cf. Frege [10], I, §23. See also Whitehead and Russell, i, p. 48; Tarski [1], pp. 338–9 ([2], p. 218); Resnik [1], pp. 330–1; von Kutschera [1], p. 94.

[2] The hierarchies in question here are of course quite distinct from the semantic hierarchy which was discussed in Ch. 2: that was a hierarchy of (three) *semantic levels* (spoken and written discourse, sense, and reference); here we have to do with (potentially infinite) linguistic and ontological hierarchies of *types of expression* and their references or referents.

[3] Cf. Dummett [2], p. 44.   [4] Van Heijenoort [2], p. 96; Dummett [2], p. 48; [3], p. 289.

What results from this procedure is in essence, as commentators have often observed, a simple theory of types.[5] Because of the close connection between functions and *Wertverläufe*, already noted (§33), from a purely formal perspective Frege's hierarchy of levels comes within an ace of mimicking Russell's hierarchy of classes. And indeed in an early statement of the simple theory of types that we find in a letter to Frege, Russell explicitly mentioned Frege's hierarchy of levels as inspiring his own theory.[6] But there are significant conceptual differences between the Fregean hierarchies and, say, the simple theory of types for classes sketched by Russell in *The Principles of Mathematics*.[7] For example, in Frege's hierarchies, zeroth-level entities are saturated and higher-level entities unsaturated—indeed, as I implied at the start of this section, the Fregean hierarchies might be said to be *generated* by the saturated–unsaturated distinction;[8] hence, as Graham Stevens remarks,[9] Frege's hierarchies are intimately involved with his solution to the unity problem—whereas in Russell's simple theory of types for classes, all entities in a hierarchy are alike saturated.[10] Again, in Russell's simple theory the relations between entities (whether classes or propositional functions) of level n and level $n + 1$ are uniform; by contrast, Frege, as we have noted (§38), is careful to insist that while zeroth-level objects *fall under* first-level concepts, first- or second-level concepts *fall within* second- and third-level concepts. For Frege does not think of higher-level entities as *concepts with extensions*, on the model of first-level concepts, but as *operators*, which may be iterated and commuted.[11] (In his reply to Russell's letter Frege rejected the proffered strategy for dealing with 'the Contradiction', which involved extending type theory to embrace *Wertverläufe* as well as functions,[12] just as he had rejected Schröder's hierarchy of classes.[13] But without a simple type theory for classes Frege's hierarchy of levels is powerless to block Russell's paradox in respect of *Wertverläufe* or classes.[14])

Still, abstracting from these differences, the Fregean hierarchies are certainly closer to a simple theory of types than to the so-called ramified theory which Russell subsequently adopted. According to the ramified theory, 'if the highest

---

[5] Kneale and Kneale, p. 666; Sluga [1], pp. 196–9; Angelelli [1], p. 182; Dummett [2], p. 50; Bostock [1], pp. 94–5; Chihara, pp. 22–8; Cocchiarella [1], pp. 89–90; Urquhart, pp. 286–7.

[6] Letter of 8 Aug. 1902 (Frege [22], p. 226); Sluga [1], p. 206; Church [8].

[7] [3], §104 and appendix B.   [8] Cf. Gödel, ii, p. 136; Crocco [2], p. 173.

[9] [3], p. 19.

[10] See here Church [8], pp. 409–10; Cocchiarella [1], pp. 91, 99–100; Urquhart, p. 287. The same applies to the type hierarchy discussed by Bostock at [1], pp. 97–102.

[11] Cocchiarella [1], pp. 157–60.   [12] Cf. von Kutschera [1], pp. 134–6.

[13] Sluga [1], pp. 203–9; Church [8], p. 410. Of course, Frege rejected Schröder's hierarchy of classes at a stage (1895) when the set-theoretical antinomies were generally unknown.

[14] Cf. Carnap [2], §38.

order of variable occurring in a function, whether as argument or as apparent variable, is a function of the nth order, then the function in which it occurs is of the $n + 1$th order'.[15] The ramified theory of types thus permits an *apparent* (bound) variable to affect the order (that is, level) of an expression, whereas on the approach I am presupposing to the Fregean linguistic hierarchy the level of an expression is determined exclusively by the levels of the omitted expressions—that is, by the levels of the *free* variables—as in the simple theory of types, regardless of the construction of the sentential frame (the functor), and so regardless of the presence of any bound variables in that frame.[16] (There are intimate connections between the ramified theory and the doctrine that propositions and propositional functions are intensional entities.[17] On the one hand,[18] the status of propositional functions as intensional entities was demanded by the ramified theory of types. And, on the other hand,[19] the ramified theory was deployed to block antinomies arising from the assumption that propositions are intensional entities—antinomies which indeed surface at the very end of *Principles*.[20])

Now Frege, as we have seen, recognized two kinds of saturated expression: proper names (in his broad sense) and sentences. Since the latter include complex sentences in which operations are performed on simple sentences, the linguistic hierarchy will include sentential connectives and operators. But for present purposes we may, like Frege himself,[21] ignore the hierarchy generated by the operations performed upon sentences themselves, and concentrate on the hierarchy generated in respect of subsentential expressions that are constructed with other subsentential expressions, not with sentences. (In what follows I shall understand the phrase 'subsentential expression' in this sense.) With the allocation of *sentences* to the zeroth level of the linguistic hierarchy there can, I suggest, be no quarrel: however we construct the hierarchy for subsentential expressions, we must start from the saturatedness, relative to these expressions, of sentences. That is just a consequence (or a way of expressing the point) of the context principle. But what is the motivation for locating *proper names* at the zeroth level? Certainly, (first-level) concept-expressions such as 'is wise' take a proper name to yield a saturated sentence; but so far that looks like

---

[15] Whitehead and Russell, i, p. 53.

[16] On the ramified theory, see Gödel, ii, pp. 136–8; Kleene, pp. 44–5; Fraenkel, Bar-Hillel, and Levy, pp. 171–5; C. Parsons [1], p. 269; Tiles, pp. 163–74; Sullivan [3], pp. 109–10; Grattan-Guinness, pp. 396–7; Potter [1], pp. 139–44; Giaquinto, pp. 87–90, 105–6.

[17] See above §§19, 33; Goldfarb [1], pp. 30–4.

[18] See Hylton [2], pp. 134–6; Potter [1], pp. 154–5.

[19] See L. Linksy [1], pp. 636–42; Sullivan [3], p. 110.

[20] See §63 below; B. Linsky [2], pp. 63–4, 93 n. 7; Sullivan [6], pp. 49–51.

[21] Cf. Dummett [2], p. 38.

a symmetrical relation. Why not locate proper names like 'Socrates' at the first level, and the concept-expressions like 'is wise' which, on Frege's approach, count as first-level expressions at the zeroth level instead?

The question simply reposes the dilemma broached in the previous chapter. On an antithetical approach to Frege's (what I called the anti-Fregean strategy), such concept-expressions would count as saturated, proper names as unsaturated. The claim lodged in the previous chapter, expressed now in terms of the linguistic hierarchy of levels, was that there is no principled way of adjudicating between the rival pretensions of the Fregean hierarchy and the anti-Fregean hierarchy to provide a satisfactory philosophical semantics of our language. The anti-Fregean strategy, as I characterized that for the simple categorical sentence 'Socrates is wise', reversed the orientation of Frege's chemical metaphor as that applied to the proper name and concept-expression of this sentence: the proper name was to count as unsaturated and the concept-expression as saturated. That meant, in turn, that the clauses in an appropriate theory of meaning for this strategy specified a referent for a concept-expression like 'is wise', and a reference—but not a referent—for a proper name like 'Socrates'. When I discussed the anti-Fregean strategy and compared it with the alternatives, including Frege's own, I restricted the scope of the discussion to sentences like 'Socrates is wise', that is, to simple categorical sentences involving only monadic concept-expressions. The reason for this restriction was to convey the basic point to the reader—the arbitrariness of Frege's way of applying his metaphor of saturatedness and unsaturatedness to subsentential components—without unduly complicating the story. But it is time to introduce a complication. For we must ask how the anti-Fregean strategy deals with relational concept-expressions.

44 The Anti-Fregean Strategy and Relations (I)

The first level of Frege's linguistic hierarchy contains not only monadic concept-expressions like 'is wise', but also polyadic concept-expressions like 'loves'. (Frege restricts his use of the terms 'concept-word' and 'concept' to monadic expressions and entities; polyadic conceptual entities he calls *Beziehungen*, 'relations'. As I deploy the terms, here and elsewhere, concepts and their corresponding concept-expressions can be polyadic.) We may call expressions of the former sort 'primary monadic concept-expressions'; by extension we can call expressions of the second sort 'primary polyadic concept-expressions'. At the ontological level we have, correspondingly, primary monadic and polyadic concepts or properties. (The epithet 'primary' is simply intended to remind us that these expressions go to Frege's first level.[22]) The anti-Fregean linguistic hierarchy locates primary monadic concept-expressions at its zeroth level; but does it also locate primary polyadic concept-expressions there? In the course of a brief but illuminating discussion of a possible reparsing of the Fregean linguistic hierarchy, Wright makes the suggestion that whenever, on a Fregean analysis, two individuals a and b are related by a relation R, there ought, on a strategy purporting to reassign Frege's primary monadic concept-expressions to the most basic level of its linguistic hierarchy and his proper names to the next level up—that is, there ought, on what I am calling the 'anti-Fregean' strategy—to be a relation linking the new first-level properties (as they would in effect be) corresponding to a and b, and he takes it that this relation will belong to a *different* level in the ontological hierarchy from primary monadic concepts, now assigned (in effect) to the zeroth level of that hierarchy.[23] Presumably the idea is that if relations link first-level properties they must be second-level entities. Wright does not spell out the details of his suggestion, but it is worth pausing to work out exactly where the anti-Fregean strategy sends primary polyadic concept-expressions and concepts (properties). It will emerge that Wright is correct in his supposition that the anti-Fregean strategy does not locate such expressions and their references at the zeroth levels of the linguistic and ontological hierarchies respectively, though if my elaboration of the details below is correct, that will be because it locates them not at the *second* level of each of its hierarchies, but at the *third* level.

Let us take as an example of a sentence involving a polyadic concept-expression 'Plato loves Socrates'. We may represent this sentence schematically as '$R<a, b>$'. The Fregean strategy assigns 'R' to the first level of its linguistic hierarchy and 'a' and 'b' to the zeroth level. The anti-Fregean strategy assigns primary monadic concept-expressions to the zeroth level of its linguistic hierarchy, but it will not, according to Wright's suggestion, assign primary polyadic concept-expressions like 'R' (and of course those of higher adicity) to that level. The reason he gives is, in effect, that if we tried to assign primary polyadic concept-expressions to the zeroth level, we should have to operate with complex first-level expressions constructed—but, crucially, not recursively constructed—out of other first-level expressions. For

---

[22] Geach calls these expressions 'first-order' ([1], pp. 469–70), and some recent writers follow this convention (e.g. Stirton [2]), but there is a terminological trap in this area that needs to be avoided, and is better avoided if we adopt the policy I am following: for it is useful to reserve the phrase 'first-order' for 'first-order logic' and the 'first-order quantifiers', the latter being (in Fregean terms) second-level concept-expressions. (Correspondingly, the second-order quantifiers are third-level concept-expressions.)

[23] See here Wright [1], pp. 33–5. 'In effect' (here and below), because Wright's numbering of the levels of the anti-Fregean hierarchy differs from mine (he deletes the zeroth level).

example, 'Plato loves Socrates' would be parsed on the anti-Fregean strategy as 'Loving is <Plato-Socrates>-instantiated'. Here the first-level expression 'is <Plato-Socrates>-instantiated' would be semantically primitive, not constructed recursively from the first-level expressions 'is Plato-instantiated' and 'is Socrates-instantiated'. But, as Wright notes, that entails that we would need an infinite number of primitive first-level expressions—for there is no limit on the number of expressions of the form 'is $<a_1 - \ldots - a_n>$-instantiated' generable from a finite stock of names—which conflicts with the plausible requirement placed on a theory of meaning for a learnable language that it have a finite base.

The attempt to locate primary polyadic concept-expressions at the zeroth level of the anti-Fregean linguistic hierarchy accordingly fails, because it wrongly treats items like 'is <Plato-Socrates>-instantiated' as semantic atoms. Since the suggested analysis in effect reduces polyadic to monadic concept-expressions, we may express our objection to it by saying that polyadic concept-expressions cannot, within the constraints set by the project of constructing a finitistic theory of meaning, be so reduced: to put it in ontological terms, relations are, as Russell argued,[24] not in general eliminable from our ontology in favour of monadic properties. (Attempts to 'analyse out' relations have to compensate elsewhere, for example by introducing 'relational properties',[25] which, though superficially monadic, are deeply relational, as any adequate semantic analysis will reveal.[26]) Indeed Russell argued in his 1899 paper 'The Classification of Relations' that predication is inherently relational, which would make attempts to reduce relational sentences to monadic predications futile.[27] (Russell here saw himself as reversing the traditional error of construing all predication to be of ultimately monadic form.[28]) But suppose one tried to locate primary polyadic concept-expressions at the zeroth level without seeking to analyse away their polyadicity. Could this be made to work? No, for two reasons. In the first place, we should fail to account for the fact that proper names as they figure in relational expressions are essentially *ordered*: if 'Plato loves Socrates' is analysed along the lines of 'Loving is Plato-instantiated and is Socrates-instantiated', we deprive ourselves of the resources to distinguish between 'Plato loves Socrates' and

---

[24] See [16], pp. 136–46; [2], chs. 2 and 10; [3], p. xxiii, chs. 26 and 51; [18], p. 495; [8], pp. 51–2; [10], p. 59; [13], pp. 333–6; [14], p. 49; Küng, pp. 25–9; Horstmann, ch. 3; Wilson; Imaguire, ch. 2; Candlish [2], pp. 128–40.

[25] See Fisk [2], pp. 145–6.

[26] Cf. Hochberg [5], p. 194. On the appeal to relations implicit in the Kuratowski method of representing ordered pairs (§13), see Hochberg [2], pp. 231–3; [3].

[27] [16], pp. 143–5; cf. [3], §216. The idea that predication is a relation will recur below (§76).

[28] [3], §212; [13], p. 207. For the error, see e.g. Hutcheson [2], ii. 1 ([3], p. 23).

'Socrates loves Plato'.[29] Secondly, we should incur an objection that has been put forward by a number of commentators, but is particularly prominent in the writings of Geach. In order to state and discuss this objection, we need to take cognizance of a distinction I have so far played down, namely the distinction between subject and predicate.

45 Interlude: The Subject–Predicate Distinction

The reason why I have so far largely passed over the distinction between subject and predicate in my discussion, except where it has been absolutely necessary to mention it (this has principally been in exegetical contexts), is that much of what needs to be said about the Fregean analysis of the sentence into saturated and unsaturated components can best be cast in terms of the distinction between proper name and concept-expression. We have of course already noted (§§26 and 31) that Frege himself has a tendency (in which he is by no means alone[30]) to identify the concept-expression of a simple categorical sentence with that sentence's grammatical predicate. But it makes for clarity if we keep the logico-syntactic distinction between proper name and concept-expression rigorously separate from the functional distinction between subject and predicate. (These distinctions correspond to Geach's distinctions between what he calls, respectively, the logical categories of name and predicable and the logical roles of subject and predicate.[31]) And the *precise* functional distinction between subject and predicate which I need at this point in my argumentation is one that we have not had the resources to define until now. For unlike the traditional distinction between grammatical subject and grammatical predicate, the distinction between subject and predicate that we need here is constitutively defined in terms of the levels of a linguistic hierarchy.

The intuitive idea behind the traditional functional distinction between grammatical subject and predicate is that the grammatical subject of a sentence (or clause) tells us what the subject matter of that sentence (or clause) is—it tells us what the sentence (or clause) is about—while the grammatical predicate makes some kind of statement concerning that subject matter.[32] We can arrive at a formulation of the rather different functional distinction I require here by laying it down that the general and correlative notions of subject and predicate

---

[29] In effect this first reason why relations cannot be located at the zeroth level coincides with Russell's main reason for insisting on the ineliminability of relations, namely that relations are required to characterize order: see here Russell [3], §94; Wilson, p. 291.

[30] See e.g. Tugendhat [2], p. 130.   [31] See e.g. [10], pp. 174–6.

[32] See e.g. Geach [3], pp. 23–4; Searle [1], p. 119; Siderits [3], p. 15; Hale [4], p. 191.

are to be defined as follows: for any analysis of a sentence or subsentential clause that splits the analysandum into an expression of level n constructed with an expression of level $n + 1$, the subject of the sentence or clause is to be identified with the former expression and the predicate with the latter.[33] (This definition leaves open the possibility that more than one subject–predicate analysis of a given sentence or clause may be available, a point that is of some importance to us.) In order to avoid confusion with the traditional distinction between the *grammatical* subject and predicate of a sentence (or clause), I shall call a sentence's (or clause's) subject and predicate as I have just defined them its *analytical* subject and predicate. Analytical subject and predicate by no means coincide, in general, with grammatical subject and predicate: for example, in the sentence 'Something hit me on the head', 'something' is the sentence's grammatical subject and 'hit me on the head' its grammatical predicate: Boole tells us that, in the sentence 'All fixed stars are suns', 'the term "All fixed stars" would be called the *subject*, and "suns" the *predicate*'.[34] But if, following Frege, we treat 'something' as a first-order quantifier (which is a second-level expression in the Fregean linguistic hierarchy), we will classify it as our sentence's analytical predicate, and 'hit me on the head' as its analytical subject.[35] (In *Principles* Russell finds himself betwixt and between grammatical and analytical analyses of sentences like 'Any a is a b': on the one hand, his theory of denoting concepts pushes him in the direction of treating 'any a' as a unit, and as the subject of this sentence, but under the influence of Frege he also wants to analyse the sentence along the lines of '$\forall x(x$ is an $a \rightarrow x$ is a $b)$', the position he goes on to adopt in 'On Denoting'.[36])

It may be remarked in passing that it is not entirely clear what the *point* of the traditional distinction between subject and predicate is, since, though purportedly a functional distinction, insofar as it is well conceived at all it seems to do no more than mimic the grammatical distinction between noun-phrases and verb-phrases,[37] most obviously so, perhaps, in Russell's generalization of 'subject' in his *Introduction to Mathematical Philosophy* to incorporate grammatical objects (and presumably agents, etc.).[38] Certainly the intuitive definition I mentioned above, according to which the subject of a sentence tells us what

---

[33] Cf. Stirton [2], pp. 196–7.   [34] Boole, IV, §9 (p. 59); cf. Angelelli [3], p. 73.

[35] See Frege [11], pp. 435, 441 n. ([21], pp. 194, 198–9), where he attacks Schröder for treating 'einige Menschen' as subject in 'Einige Menschen sind klug'; cf. [13], p. 373 ([21], p. 271), where we are told that, in the sentences 'es gibt etwas, was eine Primzahl ist' and 'es gibt etwas, was eine Quadratwurzel aus 4 ist', we recognize 'einen gemeinsamen Bestandteil "es gibt etwas, was", der die eigentliche Aussage enthält, während die nicht gemeinsamen Bestandteile trotz ihrer prädikativen, ungesättigten Natur eine Rolle spielen, die der des Subjekts in anderen Fällen analog ist'. See further [26], p. 61; Angelelli [1], p. 95; Bell [1], p. 36; Künne [1], p. 184; Kemmerling [2], pp. 51–2.

[36] See Beaney, p. 135; Oliver [3], p. 154.   [37] Cf. Chomsky [2], pp. 68–74; Strawson [6], p. 87.

[38] [11], pp. 141–2.

the sentence is 'about', seems incompetent to deliver a usable criterion for subjecthood: for though in some contexts the sentence 'Socrates is wise' may be said to be about Socrates, in other contexts it will be about wisdom—or even predicative being.[39] The sentence *as such* (considered apart from context) does not seem to be 'about' Socrates rather than wisdom or being, and the sentence *in use* may be about any or all of these.[40] Purely syntactic attempts at drawing the distinction seem to fare little better.[41] Surprisingly, in spite of its evident theoretical inadequacy, the intuitive distinction between subject and predicate continues to find a place in the latest textbooks.[42] But I shall not pause to pursue this issue. We are now in a position to return the question whether it is possible to locate primary polyadic concept-expressions at the zeroth level of a linguistic hierarchy without seeking to analyse away their polyadicity, and to state the second objection to any such move.

46 The Anti-Fregean Strategy and Relations (II)

Frege observed that if we wish to negate such quantified sentences as 'Some numbers are prime' or 'All bodies are heavy', we must place the negation sign before 'some' and 'all' respectively, indicating that 'these words must be counted in with the predicative part of the sentence as far as their sense is concerned'.[43] And Geach has argued that while there is no logically significant distinction to be made between negating a sentence and negating its main predicate, there is such a distinction between negating a sentence and negating its constituent names: conflating these latter two negation operations leads to inconsistency.[44] For suppose that '$\neg a$' is the negation of 'a', and can be inter-substituted with 'a' in all contexts *salva congruitate*; and suppose also that '$(\neg a)F$' is a predication contradicting 'aF', that is, that we have the equivalence:

$$(\neg a)F \leftrightarrow \neg(aF).$$

[39] See Chomsky [2], p. 163; Künne [1], p. 22.

[40] Cf. Strawson [1], pp. 144–5; Dummett [3], pp. 288–9. Note also Frege [1], §3: 'Wenn man sagt: "Subjekt ist der Begriff, von dem das Urteil handelt", so passt dies auch auf das Objekt'.

[41] J. Harris, having told us that 'Every Proposition consists of a *Subject*, and a *Predicate*' (ii, ch. 1, p. 230), adds: 'In *English* these are distinguished by their Position, the Subject standing *first*, the Predicate *last*', which is, in general, false, as he would have realized had he called to mind the opening of Pope's 'Ode on Solitude', which must have been well known to him.

[42] See e.g. Larson and Segal, pp. 124–5; Bostock [2], p. 74; Carnie, pp. 201, 213.

[43] [11], p. 441 n. ([21], p. 198). Cf. [18], p. 150 ([21], p. 369): 'Wir sind gewohnt anzunehmen, das Verneinen erstrecke sich auf den ganzen Gedanken, wenn sich das "nicht" mit dem Verbum des Prädikats verbindet'. Cf. also [18], pp. 154–5 ([21], p. 374).

[44] [8], pp. 143–6; cf. [3], pp. 32–3; [7], pp. 45–6, 70–1. See also Hale [1], pp. 286–7; Strawson [6], pp. 4–8, 19–21, 25–6.

Then, Geach argues, if we interpret 'ξF' as the predicate '$\xi R\xi$', we have the equivalence:

(1) $\quad (\neg a)R(\neg a) \leftrightarrow \neg(aRa)$.

If we interpret 'ξF' as the predicate 'ξRa', we have the equivalence:

(2) $\quad (\neg a)Ra \leftrightarrow \neg(aRa)$.

Finally, if we interpret 'ξF' as '$(\neg a)R\xi$', we have the equivalence:

(3) $\quad (\neg a)R(\neg a) \leftrightarrow \neg((\neg a)Ra)$.

But, though the three interpretations were consistent, the three resulting equivalences form an inconsistent triad, for (1) and (2) imply

$$(\neg a)R(\neg a) \leftrightarrow (\neg a)Ra,$$

which plainly contradicts (3).

In fact it is clear that, contrary to what Geach himself supposes, this proof does not favour any particular analysis of a sentence like 'Raleigh smokes', to borrow Geach's own example: it does not adjudicate against treating 'smokes' as a zeroth-level expression therein and 'Raleigh' as a first-level expression. For the proof tells us nothing about the correct functional analysis of sentences in which proper names are constructed with primary *monadic* concept-expressions. That is what we should expect and is entirely in line with the even-handed approach I have been adopting towards the Fregean and anti-Fregean strategies' treatments of such sentences. What the proof does succeed in showing is that the negation of any syntactic component of a sentence that occurs *more than once* in that sentence cannot consistently be identified with a global negation operator attaching to the sentence as a whole. But this point has nothing in particular to do with proper names and concept-expressions. Indeed, as Fraser MacBride has shown, we can replicate Geach's argument with multiply occurring predicates in place of multiply occurring proper names: if we consider molecular contexts such as 'Fa & Fa' and extract therefrom the complex name 'Φa & Φa', we can then use this expression to derive an inconsistent triad, starting from the equivalence '$(\neg F)a \leftrightarrow \neg(Fa)$', by following a series of moves entirely parallel to those used in Geach's proof.[45]

The proof does not, then, show what Geach takes it to show; but it does show something interesting for our purposes, namely that we cannot

[45] MacBride [3], pp. 80–5. Cf. Grimm, pp. 138–42; Nemirov, pp. 207–8; M. C. Bradley [2], pp. 20–3.

intelligibly locate genuinely polyadic concept-expressions at the zeroth level of a linguistic hierarchy. For adopting that disposition would be tantamount to regarding the proper names filling the argument-places of any given such concept-expression—these names being consequently located at the first level—as collectively constituting the *analytical predicate* of the relevant sentence. And that would lead directly to the inconsistency to which Geach draws our attention. Geach's point is correctly put not in terms of proper names—which are not constitutively associated with any particular level of a linguistic hierarchy—but in terms of the population of the levels of such a hierarchy: the claim, when rephrased in an acceptable form, is that the expression of *highest level* in a sentence, as discerned by some appropriate analysis of the sentence into subsentential components allocated to the levels of a linguistic hierarchy, is such that its negation cannot be distinguished from the negation of the sentence *as a whole*.[46] This claim is true of the Fregean hierarchy. (In the version of the proof mentioned at the end of the preceding paragraph, the name 'a' as it multiply occurs in '$\Phi a \ \& \ \Phi a$' in effect counts as, in Fregean terms, a second-level predicate, and as, in my terms, the analytical predicate of sentences in which that complex name is held to be present. That is why we cannot consistently operate with the equivalence '$(\neg F)a \leftrightarrow \neg(Fa)$', in which negating the (Fregean) first-level concept-expression of the sentence 'Fa' is equated with attaching a global negation operator to the whole sentence.[47]) Accepting the claim in full generality does not, as Geach supposes, undermine the anti-Fregean strategy's reversal of the Fregean disposition of proper names and primary monadic concept-expressions; but it does follow that if we pursue the anti-Fregean strategy we must, on pain of inconsistency, look elsewhere in the linguistic hierarchy than the zeroth level for somewhere to put primary polyadic concept-expressions.[48]

Let us go back to our schematic representation of a relation: '$R<a, b>$'. If we follow Wright's suggestion that (in effect) we should, on the anti-Fregean strategy, assign 'a' and 'b' to the first level of the linguistic hierarchy and 'R' to the second level, we must recognize 'a' and 'b' as containing argument-places for zeroth-level expressions. Let us then write these in, thus: $a(x), b(y)$. In a closed formula these variables must be bound, and we might, initially, conceive of the concept-expression 'R' as binding them, so that an

[46] Cf. Geach [11], pp. 128–30; Simons [3], p. 88; Carpenter, pp. 90–2.
[47] See here again MacBride [3], pp. 83–4.
[48] In a previous publication ([8]) I assumed that there was no objection to the anti-Fregean strategy's locating polyadic concept-expressions like 'loves' at its zeroth level and assigning special concept-expressions like 'Plato-Socrates' to its first level. The present treatment supersedes that discussion.

explicit anti-Fregean-strategy formalization of the Fregean '$R<a, b>$' would, according to this initial thought, have to look like this:

$$R_{x,y} (<a(x), b(y)>).$$

Reverting to our example, 'Plato loves Socrates' would then be regimented thus:

(4) $\text{Loves}_{x,y} (<\text{Plato}(x), \text{Socrates}(y)>).$

What does (4) mean? Of course it means that Plato loves Socrates. But *how* does it come to mean that? It does so by introducing a second-level concept-expression binding zeroth-level variables. These variables, which we are obliged to write into the argument-places of our first-level expressions 'Plato ( )' and 'Socrates ( )', range over the references of Frege's primary monadic concept-expressions, which on the anti-Fregean strategy count as basic, saturated objects (and so as referents, not merely references). From a Fregean perspective these objects will be (regimented as) primary monadic concepts (properties), and will include such entities as wisdom, humanity, and so on. Hence a statement that, on the Fregean analysis, contains no monadic concept-expression and so is not about the referent of any such expression, has been regimented by the anti-Fregean strategy, pursuant to Wright's suggestion, in such a way that it is about the referents (as they would be) of primary such expressions.

Now if Wright's suggestion is correct, it ought to be possible to frame a natural-language sentence—however stilted—expressing the thought that Plato loves Socrates, but doing so in terms of the monadic concepts (properties) that, on the anti-Fregean strategy, Plato and Socrates might be conceived to instantiate, entities such as wisdom, humanity, etc. What, then, is there to say about these and other such entities which can represent the statement that Plato loves Socrates? As far as I can see the cleanest method that is guaranteed to duplicate our statement, while confining its explicit subject matter to the referents of primary monadic concept-expressions, is to restrict the ranges of the variables bound by $R_{x,y}$ to sets of essential and individuative concepts (properties), so that (4) would say: the concepts (properties) making up the individual essence that is Plato-instantiated ('Platonity') are love-related to the concepts (properties) making up the individual essence that is Socrates-instantiated ('Socrateity').[49] Understanders could be said to be acquainted with

---

[49] For the terminology, cf. Boethius [1], II, p. 137.7. The formation of words like 'Socrateity' and 'Platonity' ('Socrateitas', 'Platonitas') goes back to Cicero (see *Ad Fam.* 3. 7. 5; cf. Hobbes [1], I. iii, §3), but he would have used 'Socrateitas' to mean 'the (outstanding) qualities of a Socrates': i.e. for Cicero

a given one of these sets by virtue of knowing its membership condition, and they can have that knowledge insofar as they are able to individuate the object whose essential and individuative concepts (properties) compose the set in question.

It follows that, if we are to achieve full perspicuity in our analysis of the anti-Fregean strategy's parsing of 'Plato loves Socrates', (4) should be replaced by a formalization quantifying explicitly over individual essences. For this I suggest:

(5)   Loves $[<\iota x(\text{Plato}(x)), \iota y(\text{Socrates}(y))>]$,

where 'ι' is the description operator. In (5) the variables 'x' and 'y' are to be understood as ranging over zeroth-level individual essences, corresponding to special monadic concepts (properties) which would be located by Frege at the first level of his ontological hierarchy. These concepts (properties) are individuated, on the anti-Fregean strategy, by specifying which first-level (in the anti-Fregean sense) concept-expression they uniquely satisfy, just as from a Fregean perspective an artificially constructed concept-expression like 'Socratizes' (which something satisfies just if it is identical with Socrates) is given meaning by specifying the unique zeroth-level object (in the Fregean sense) which satisfies it. In (5) 'Plato(x)' and 'Socrates(y)' are first-level concept-expressions, as we should expect on the anti-Fregean strategy, and 'ι' is a second-level concept-expression. Accordingly, given the restriction on the range of the variables 'x' and 'y', the expressions '$\iota x(\text{Plato}(x))$' and '$\iota y(\text{Socrates}(y))$' stand for the (zeroth-level) properties Platonity and Socrateity respectively, and it is these that are taken by the anti-Fregean strategy, on my interpretation of it, to be the relata in polyadic sentences such as 'Plato loves Socrates'.[50] It follows that the relation 'loves' is itself a third-level concept-expression, since it is formed from a sentence by omitting two second-level expressions, namely two expressions of the form '$\iota x(\phi(x))$'.

It turns out, then, that Wright's suggestion that (in my terminology) the anti-Fregean strategy will accommodate primary polyadic concept-expressions at a different level from primary monadic concept-expressions is correct, though his additional insinuation that this is because primary polyadic concept-expressions are taken by the anti-Fregean strategy to stand for relations linking

the property of Socrateity would not be, as it is for me, individuative of the man Socrates, but could be had by anyone sufficiently like Socrates in relevant respects, as in the figure of speech antonomasia ('Some mute inglorious Milton').

[50] Cf. Simons's strategy at [1], pp. 165–6.

first-level concepts or properties (and so are themselves second-level expressions) has apparently turned out to be incorrect. At any rate, according to the most plausible version of the anti-Fregean strategy's treatment of primary polyadic concept-expressions that I am able to construct, those expressions will go to the anti-Fregean strategy's third level, and not either to its second level, as Wright implies, nor to its zeroth level, where primary monadic concept-expressions are housed. Of course, it might be said in Wright's support that, although the relational expression 'loves', considered just as such, belongs to the third level of the anti-Fregean's linguistic hierarchy, its regimented transform, in which it will in practice be recognized by that strategy, namely 'the —izer loves the . . . izer',

$$\text{Loves}\, (<\iota x(-(x)), \iota y(\ldots (y))>),$$

is a second-level expression. (For recall that in the Fregean hierarchy the level of an expression is determined solely by the nature of its free variables, and not, as in Russell's ramified type theory, also by the nature of its bound variables.) Be that as it may, the key point for my purposes is that, as we toggle between Fregean and anti-Fregean strategies, the level occupied in the linguistic hierarchy by primary polyadic concept-expressions remains invariantly *non-zero*. This point of philosophical syntax embodies the fact that polyadic concept-expressions are semantically non-basic.

47 The Reality of Relations

It would be wrong to suppose that this fact about polyadic concept-expressions carries any idealistic implications for relations; equally, it does not imply (and it is not true) that relational facts must supervene on non-relational facts, as has been commonly argued or assumed in the tradition, perhaps most famously by Leibniz, whose thinking on relations was hobbled by his definition of truth—*praedicatum inest subiecto*—which takes no account of relations.[51] But it may perhaps be offered as a partial diagnosis of a recurrent tendency in the semantic tradition to downgrade the ontological status of relations—to regard them as mere *entia rationis*,[52] having, in Locke's words, 'no other reality but

[51] See Kneale and Kneale, pp. 326–7, 329–30, 333; Mugnai, ch. 3. Vallicella argues ([3], pp. 11–12), following Bradley, that relational facts must be ontologically grounded in a non-relational 'condition external to them'. Consistently enough, he claims that 'the grounding "relation" is not strictly a relation' (p. 27). But then what is it?

[52] Cf. Leibniz [3], II. xxv, §1 ([1], v, p. 210): 'Les relations et les ordres ont quelque chose de l'estre de raison, quoyqu' ils ayent leur fondement dans les choses; car on peut dire que leur réalité, comme

what they have in the Minds of Men',[53] and, concomitantly, in Russell's words, to 'suppose relational propositions less ultimate than . . . subject–predicate propositions'.[54] (Adam Smith remarked that 'a relation is, in itself, a more metaphysical object than a quality.'[55]) It is of course a mistake to say, as Davidson does,[56] that Aristotle (and Plato) did not have the concept of a relation. But it is nonetheless undeniable that, for Aristotle, the dependence of relations on other accidents makes the category of relation the least real of the categories.[57] Interestingly, despite the Aristotelian doctrine and its widespread acceptance in the tradition (especially by nominalists), realism about relations has managed to field some notable defenders, including Plotinus,[58] Simplicius,[59] Aquinas,[60] and Scotus,[61] and in modern times—apart from Russell, as I have noted (§44), and Frege, whom I shall discuss directly—Bolzano,[62] De Morgan,[63] Peirce,[64] and McTaggart,[65] to mention only some of the more prominent figures.[66]

As far as Frege is concerned, the point is not that he *argued* for the reality of relations, as Russell did, for so far as I am aware he did not—nor, unlike De Morgan and Peirce, did he develop a logic of relations[67]—but that his logical practice, not only in the *Begriffsschrift* and *Grundgesetze* but also in his philosophical essays, simply *presupposed* their reality; and this has had the effect of demystifying relations in the analytical tradition. By treating relations as ordinary functions, differing from what he called concepts only in the number of their argument-places, Frege not only rendered a proper formalization of polyadic logic at last viable; he also finessed the tendency in the tradition to regard relations as somehow uncanny or merely ideal. For Frege, polyadicity differs in degree, but not in metaphysical kind, from monadicity, and it was this impartiality that, in the context of the contributions of (among others) De Morgan, Peirce, and Russell, enabled

celle des vérités éternelles et des possibilités, vient de la supreme raison'; letter to des Bosses of 21 Apr. 1714 ([1], ii. 486). See Mugnai, esp. chs. 2, 3, 6, and 7.

[53] Locke, II. xxx, §4. Cf. Hutcheson [1], i, ch. 5, §4 ([3], p. 107); Monboddo, II, ch. 9 (vol. ii, p. 95).

[54] Russell [3], §27. Cf. his [2], §10, for cogent criticism of Leibniz [1], vii, p. 401.

[55] A. Smith, §12, p. 209.   [56] [2], p. 104.   [57] *Met.* 1088a15–b13; cf. *EN* 1096a21–2.

[58] *Enneads* 6. 1. 6–9.   [59] *In Cat.*, p. 169.1–30.   [60] [1], Ia, q. 13, a. 7.

[61] *Ordinatio*, II, d. 1, qq. 4–5 (vii, esp. pp. 96–115). Though Aquinas and Scotus are realists to the extent that they deny that relations are the work of the mind, they nevertheless embrace the 'weaker reality' (*ens deminutum*) doctrine of relations as supervenient on accidents, which in turn supervene on substance: see Mugnai, pp. 27–9; Krempel, p. 193; Henninger, esp. §6.

[62] [2], §80 n. 2; see Kneale and Kneale, p. 364.   [63] See Grattan-Guinness, pp. 32–4.

[64] See Nidditch, pp. 50–2; Grattan-Guinness, pp. 145–7.   [65] McTaggart, §§78–82.

[66] See Wilson, p. 299. On the history of philosophical attitudes to the question of the reality of relations, see helpfully Weinberg, pp. 61–119, and Mugnai, ch. 1.

[67] Cf. Grattan-Guinness, p. 181.

formal logic to overcome its historic obsession with monadicity—an obsession that had shackled Aristotle, Leibniz, Kant, and Boole, compromising the generality of their systems.[68] Logicism, too, played a crucial role in the domestication of relations: for the reduction of arithmetic to logic required a definition of number in logical terms, and here Frege (and Dedekind) saw that relations were indispensable, since the idea of a progression, which is essentially a relational structure, lies at the heart of the concept of ordinal number.[69]

Dummett no doubt goes too far (in one direction) when he claims that the functional approach to relations is a *sine qua non* if they are to be rendered intelligible at all:[70] after all, as we have just observed, realism about relations did not lack for supporters before Frege's functional approach to concepts was conceived. And Michael Potter perhaps goes too far (in another direction) when he suggests that, because polyadic logic forces the introduction of explicit variables in a way in which monadic logic does not, Aristotelian and Kantian monadic logic 'is a logic of inclusion of concepts thought of quite independently of any possibility of their application to objects',[71] as though polyadic concepts were tied down to a real world of objects while monadic concepts somehow floated free of any such dependence. That cannot be right, for it is intrinsic to concepts, whether monadic or polyadic, that objects fall under them. Potter acknowledges that this is Frege's position;[72] but the point is surely correct irrespective of Frege's particular understanding of concepts. (Of course it is possible to develop variable-free logics along the lines explored by Quine,[73] for example; but the availability of that option obviously does not show that concepts sit more loosely to objects than we had thought—only that their close relationship to objects can be implicit in the symbolism, rather than explicit.)

48 Polyadicity, Monadicity, and Identity

It is worth noting in this context that there is no simple correlation between the syntactic and semantic differences separating monadic and polyadic concept-expressions which I have been rehearsing in this chapter, on the one hand, and the well-known model- and proof-theoretic differences between monadic and polyadic logic, on the other. These latter differences include the fact that the

---

[68] See here Kneale and Kneale, p. 445; von Kutschera [1], pp. 18, 40–1.
[69] Kneale and Kneale, pp. 455–73. Cf. Simons [11], pp. 261–2.
[70] [3], pp. 175–6. Recall my criticism of Dummett in §33.
[71] [1], p. 64. Cf. Quine [6], pp. 281–2.   [72] [1], p. 67.   [73] [8], pp. 164–72; [11], §xxiii.

first-order pure monadic predicate calculus—the (classical) logic of formulae whose only non-logical symbols are monadic concept-expression letters, and which does not contain identity—is decidable,[74] while the first-order polyadic predicate calculus is, in general, not decidable.[75] But it turns out that the first-order monadic calculus *with identity* is decidable, and indeed that it remains decidable even if stripped of all non-logical symbols apart from an expression for identity.[76] Hence it is not the introduction into first-order languages of just any polyadic concept-expressions that precipitates undecidability, but the introduction (in general) of polyadic concept-expressions *other than* '=', standardly interpreted.[77] It is true that, in view of its special status, the symbol expressing identity is often treated, for metalogical purposes, as a logical symbol.[78] This is in large part a legacy of logicism, which, at least in some versions (such as Frege's) construed identity as a logical relation.[79] Of course, as is familiar, Frege somewhat queered the pitch for logicism by treating a whole raft of phenomena, including identity, subsumption, the relation of equinumerosity, the subordination of concepts, and the extensions of concepts as being of a peculiarly logical nature.[80] Insofar as the issue is not a merely verbal one, there is a case to be made for regarding identity as just one relation among others, enjoying no special relationship with the phenomenon of entailment, which is the subject matter of the science of logic.[81] But in any event, even if we insisted on regarding identity as a definitively logical relation, that would still not in any sense derogate from its genuinely relational status.

Unsurprisingly, identity has always been problematic for empiricists. Locke, for example, tells us that

there can be no Relation, but betwixt two Things, considered as two Things. There must always be in relation two Ideas, or Things, either in themselves really separate, or considered as distinct, and then a ground or occasion for their comparison.[82]

---

[74] Bernays and Schönfinkel, §§1 and 2; Church [6], p. 293; Quine [11], §xvii. If a monadic wff ϕ is valid, then it is valid in all domains with at most 2^k elements, where k is the number of monadic concept-expressions in ϕ: Bridge, pp. 36–7.

[75] See e.g. Quine [11], §xx, based on Church [1]; Fraenkel *et al.*, p. 315.

[76] See e.g. Boolos and Jeffrey, chs. 22 and 25; Bostock [2], pp. 325–31.

[77] Boolos and Jeffrey, p. 251. For other exclusions, see Quine [6], p. 282.

[78] See e.g. Boolos and Jeffrey, p. 97; Boolos, p. 54; Carpenter, p. 76; Hodges [2], p. 66; Enderton [2], pp. 161–2.

[79] Cf. Kneale and Kneale, pp. 619–20; Tiles, p. 169.

[80] [15], p. 428 ([21], p. 322); Potter [1], pp. 94, 98; in his [2], Potter regards class abstraction as a peculiarly logical operation: pp. 299–316. In Bealer's [1], identity, predication, and necessary equivalence are all treated as purely logical relations.

[81] Cf. Kneale and Kneale, p. 742; Etchemendy, esp. ch. 8.

[82] Locke, II. xxv, §6 (p. 321). So too Monboddo, II, ch. 9 (vol. ii, p. 95).

Similarly, in a number of his early writings Russell argued that relations always involve distinct relata, a view that naturally required him to reject identity as a genuine relation: for example, in 'The Classification of Relations' he contended that diversity 'is a relation which may always be asserted, whenever any other relation may be asserted' and that 'there can be no relation without at least two terms [i.e. objects: RG]';[83] and this view survived in *Principles*, where we are told that 'even where the relation asserted is identity, there must be *two* identical terms [i.e. objects], which are therefore not quite identical'.[84] So a claim of identity is always false, a result which surely constitutes a *reductio* of the position. (It cannot be a constraint on the meaningfulness of a sentence of some general kind that it be always false.[85]) Oddly enough, empiricism about identity is a view one meets quite commonly: for instance, Guido Küng claims that 'a reflexive relation... is not a real relation, but rather a relation of reason based on the conceptual duplication of an entity that in reality is a single entity'.[86] And Wittgenstein's Tractarian polemic against identity is familiar.[87] It naturally goes without saying that in any situation in which a reflexive relation holds of an entity, we have to do with a single entity, but why should that mean that the relation (which the entity has to itself) is not real? Why should a relation that holds between two or more entities be *more real* than one that holds between a thing and itself? (Try answering this question without simply repeating the datum that the one scenario contains two or more entities, the other only one.) It is time to set aside empiricist and logicist qualms and affirm that the identity relation is no whit less genuinely relational than any other (than any certifiedly non-logical) relation, and accordingly that it, along with its associated dyadic concept-expression, must receive the same general treatment in the construction of linguistic and ontological hierarchies for a natural language as all other relations together with their associated concept-expressions.[88]

---

[83] [16], p. 141. Cf. [1], §208.   [84] [3], §198.   [85] Cf. my [11], pp. 205–6.
[86] Küng, p. 165.   [87] See Marion, §2.
[88] Fisk writes ([2], p. 150): 'To say that Cicero is the same thing as himself is to say that Cicero is a unity'. But being a unity and being self-identical are quite distinct properties, given that, as we have seen (§1), an absolutely simple entity, though self-identical, would not count as a unity. The opposite mistake is made by Hochberg, who suggests ([6], pp. 70–1; cf. [5], pp. 194–7) that we cannot even construct monadic properties of e.g. self-identity and self-exemplification from relations such as identity and exemplification, the monadic properties so constructed then differing from their dyadic bases in that they are satisfied by single objects instead of pairs of objects. Of course we can, though we should not forget that the constructions are essentially derivative of more basic relational materials, and so in no sense pave the way for a 'reduction' of relations to monadic properties.

49 The Anti-Fregean Strategy and Montague Grammar

The anti-Fregean strategy is following a variant of an approach to the syntax and semantics of proper names familiar from the tradition of Montague grammar, which develops the basic Fregean idea that expressions of a language and their referents can be assigned to levels of a linguistic and ontological hierarchy respectively. As well as assigning linguistic expressions and their referents to the levels of appropriate hierarchies, expressions and their referents are divided into syntactic and semantic types, which encode their categorial and combinatorial properties. There are two basic kinds of syntactic type, t and e, having semantic types t and e respectively.[89] More complex syntactic types, and their corresponding semantic types, are built up on the basis of these. The ontological hierarchy, to start with that, is constructed as follows. The semantic types t and e are the types of truth-values and basic entities (whatever these latter are) respectively. They belong *ex officio* to the zeroth level of the hierarchy. At the first level we have monadic properties of the type $<e, t>$: that is, functions from basic entities to truth-values. At the second level of the hierarchy we have, for example, properties of the type $<<e, t>, t>$, that is, functions from first-level monadic properties to truth-values, and at the third level we have, for example, properties of the type $<<<e, t>, t>, <e, t>>$, that is, functions from second-level properties to first-level properties. Note that this method of specifying semantic types, according to which they are represented as binary types, that is, as functions from a single argument (to a single value), has the advantage that it encodes which level of the ontological hierarchy the relevant type belongs to: this is determined by counting the number of initial consecutive left-hand angle brackets in the expression for the semantic type in question.[90]

Corresponding to these semantic types we have various syntactic types. Montague assigns sentences to the syntactic type t. The syntactic type e, which corresponds to the semantic type e of basic entities, is, significantly for our purposes, empty. To the syntactic type corresponding to the semantic type $<e, t>$ Montague assigns common nouns (CN) and intransitive verbs (IV); to the syntactic type corresponding to the semantic type $<<e, t>, t>$ are assigned

---

[89] In what follows I omit considerations of intensionality, which complicate the presentation of Montague types but are irrelevant to our purposes here.

[90] Cf. van Heijenoort [2], p. 96. This treatment is standard in the Montague tradition, and depends on the method, pioneered by Schönfinkel, of converting functions of more than one argument into functions of a single argument; cf. Frege [10], I, §36, with van Heijenoort [2], p. 95. See Carpenter, pp. 64–9; Heim and Kratzer, pp. 29–31.

terms, that is, noun-phrases (NP), a broad type including proper names, individual variables and quantifier-expressions like 'something' and 'every man'; to the syntactic type corresponding to the semantic type $<<<e, t>, t>$, $<e, t>>$ are assigned transitive verbs (TV).

Montague's reason for, in his later work, assigning proper names to the second level of his linguistic hierarchy rather than the zeroth level was his desire to give a uniform grammar of proper names and other noun-phrases with which proper names are syntactically congruent, such as the unary first-order quantifiers.[91] In so doing he emptied the syntactic type e of its occupants. But he left the semantic type e, housing basic entities, in place. This is an anomaly crying out for simplification: why not simply get rid of the semantic type e, along with its empty syntactic congener, leaving as basic syntactic categories the categories of common nouns and intransitive verbs (what I have been calling primary monadic concept-expressions), alongside t, and renumber the levels correspondingly?[92] At the semantic level corresponding to these we will continue to have t (the type of truth-values), but now we will require in addition a primitive way of representing the semantic type of the now basic primary monadic concept-expressions: I will call these m; they occupy the new zeroth level. Working up the hierarchy, the semantic type of noun-phrases will be $<m, t>$, that of the description operator I employed in reconstructing anti-Fregean primary polyadic concept-expressions (I will dub it 'SDD') will be $<<m, t>, <m, t>>$, and that of primary polyadic concept-expressions (basic transitive verbs) in contexts such as 'Plato loves Socrates' will be

$$<<<m, t>, <m, t>>, <<<m, t>, <m, t>>, <<m, t>, <<m, t>, t>>>>.$$

That is, such expressions are functions from SDDs to (functions from SDDs to (functions from NPs to (functions from NPs to truth-values))). As can be

---

[91] See here Thomason's introduction to Montague, pp. 57–63; Dowty *et al.*, pp. 106–8, 183–4; Carpenter, pp. 85–6. Montague was moved by the thought that, as his editor puts it, 'in English syntax . . . quantifier phrases and proper nouns behave in much the same way; it is difficult to find instances in which replacement of the one kind of expression by the other affects grammaticality' (p. 59). The thought is perhaps more controversial than Montague allowed (see here Oliver [3]), though the principal point on which proper names and quantifier-phrases are sometimes said to differ, namely that the latter cannot stand in the vocative case (cf. Dummett [2], p. 58) strikes me as incorrect. For consider the following (in suitable contexts): 'Answer the question—anyone!', 'Come here everyone!', 'Help me someone!'; readers of Virgil will recall Dido's remarkable invocation (of Hannibal, though she does not know this), 'exoriare aliquis . . .!' (*Aen.* 4. 625). At any rate, I hope we can agree that noun-phrases and quantifier-phrases are syntactically congruent over a wide range of uses, and for the purposes of this exposition we may take these to be theoretically central.

[92] Cf. Lewis [1], pp. 32–3; Dowty *et al.*, pp. 188–9.

confirmed from examining the notation of the syntactic and semantic type, in which the initial left-hand angle brackets are nested to a depth of three, primary polyadic concept-expressions emerge in this treatment as third-level expressions. Apart from the abolition of the semantic type *e* along with its syntactic congener, the only departure from Montague envisaged by my elaboration of the anti-Fregean strategy is the decision to regard proper names as picking out sets of essential properties, whereas Montague regarded such expressions as picking out 'individual sublimations', that is, sets comprising all the properties (non-essential as well as essential) of an individual.[93] But for our purposes this difference is insignificant.

In a grammar strictly in the style of Montague, transitive verbs are, as we saw above, third-level expressions: the reason why they count, both in a strictly Montague-style grammar and on what I am calling the anti-Fregean strategy, as expressions of the third level, in spite of the fact that my anti-Fregean strategy abolishes the denizens of Montague's zeroth level and promotes those of his first level to zeroth-level status, is that the anti-Fregean strategy compensates for its abolition of Montague's zeroth-level individuals by introducing a special second-level description operator (SDD) whose variables range over specially constructed sets of primary monadic properties, which are the new zeroth-level basic individuals. (The SDD is of the form 'the —izer', yielding on completion items like 'the Socratizer' and 'the Platonizer'.) The anti-Fregean strategy is in a clear sense a radicalization of Montague: Montague departs from a Fregean strategy to the extent of reassigning proper names to the second level of the linguistic hierarchy, but he leaves the ontological hierarchy undisturbed. The anti-Fregean strategy, as I have expounded it, pushes this development further, by reassigning the entities in the zeroth level of Montague's ontological hierarchy to the old second level and so (after renumbering) to the new first level, and creating at the new second level special 'essential sublimations' of these entities for contexts that demand them, in particular, for the analysis of sentences involving polyadic predication.

50 Fregean and Anti-Fregean Strategies: Further Comparison

On the anti-Fregean strategy a relation like 'loves' as it figures in the sentence 'Plato loves Socrates' turns out to link second-level entities like Platonity and

---

[93] See here Dowty *et al.*, pp. 180, 193–4, 220–1; Cann, pp. 172–4.

Socrateity. This might seem a rather odd feature of that strategy, but in fact it can to some extent be paralleled in the Fregean strategy. Consider the fact that we want to be able to say things about (for example) being wise just as such. That is, we want to be able to say not only that Socrates is wise but also that it is (say) better in general to be wise than to be foolish, or that being wise is a virtue. Here we seem to be aiming to say something about the referent of the concept-expression 'is wise'. But, as we have seen, on a (reformed) Fregean approach we cannot talk directly about any such referent, because that expression has no referent: it merely has reference. Hence, in order to say what we want to say, we need to find some circumlocution. The formulations I offered above were an attempt in that direction: they worked by constructing the gerunds 'to be wise' and 'being wise', and these are now for a Fregean no longer first-level, but zeroth-level expressions: 'being wise', for example, refers to the comprehension scheme

$$\lambda P \ \Box \ \forall x(Px \leftrightarrow x \text{ is wise}),$$

that is, to the property which, necessarily, everything has if and only if it is wise.[94] (Here it is essential that 'wise' is semantically simple: §16.) The same may be said of abstract nouns like 'wisdom'. The role played in the Fregean hierarchy by these items is not unlike the role played by expressions referring to zeroth-level individual essences, such as 'Platonity' and 'Socrateity', in our characterization of the anti-Fregean strategy.

In view of this, we should not regard as problematic the fact that, if we try to give a semantics for English in a metalanguage which adopts the semantics of the anti-Fregean strategy, we will have to discern a systematic syntactic ambiguity in proper names: 'Socrates', for example, will be classified by that strategy as a first-level expression in monadic sentences such as 'Socrates is wise', but as a second-level expression (referring to Socrateity) in polyadic sentences such as 'Plato loves Socrates'. This ambiguity would certainly be a problem for the anti-Fregean strategy if it could draw no systematic connection between the two different grammars of 'Socrates': but that is not the case. For, as we have seen, 'Socrates' the second-level concept-expression (referring to Socrateity) is *constructed* using the second-level description operator and the first-level concept-expression 'Socrates'. Hence, though the machinery for dealing with proper names has to be more complicated in such a metalanguage than it would be in a metalanguage which adopted a Fregean grammar, that is no objection to the anti-Fregean strategy. It is simply the mirror-image of the fact that, in specifying the grammar of a language which, while translating

---

[94] Cf. Lewis, [7], p. 18.

'wisdom is better than folly' homophonically, translated 'Socrates is wise' along the lines of 'wisdom Socratizes', a Fregean metalinguistic strategy would be forced to treat 'wisdom' as grammatically ambiguous, as between a name ('wisdom') and a concept-expression ('is wise').

Is it a point against the anti-Fregean strategy that it assigns unary quantifier-phrases like 'someone' and 'no one', as these occur in sentences like 'someone is wise', to the same level as it assigns 'Socrates' in 'Socrates is wise'? After all, do we not get into well-documented difficulties when we treat such quantifier-expressions as proper names?[95] No. The traditional difficulties which arise when we treat quantifier-phrases as proper names arise not from the mere attempt to treat them as *names*, but from the attempt to treat them as names of the wrong sort.[96] So for example, if one thought of 'no one' as a name of exactly the same sort as 'Socrates', one would be puzzled by sentences like 'no one is wise', which might seem to require us to locate an object that, like Socrates, is (if the sentence is true) wise, but has the mysterious property of being a non-person. Similarly, one might be puzzled by 'nothing is a round square' if one thought of it as requiring one to find an object, concrete or abstract, designated by 'nothing', which (if the sentence is true) is a round square. But these are phantom worries, which have nothing to do, just as such, with the classification of quantifier-phrases as names and their referents as objects.[97] Such expressions can be regarded as names of objects, but complex conceptual objects, not concrete individuals like Socrates or abstract spatial entities like squares. (As Russell rightly remarked: 'It is plain that there is such a concept as *nothing*, and that in some sense nothing is something'.[98]) We can regard 'no one' as referring to a property of properties, and properties, on my approach (§40), are a species of object. Broadly speaking, then, the difference between 'Socrates' and 'no one', in the sentences 'Socrates is wise' and 'no one is wise', is that 'Socrates' refers to a person, whereas 'no one' refers to a complex conceptual entity.[99] But that is not a reason to assign these expressions to different levels of a linguistic hierarchy, because a linguistic hierarchy is not

---

[95] See e.g. Geach [1], pp. 478–9; [3], ch. 1; [7], pp. 220–1. Church speaks of 'the logically irregular feature of English grammar by which "somebody" is construed as a substantive': [6], p. 45 n. 105.

[96] See here Lewis [1], pp. 35–7.

[97] Strawson's illicit admixture of metaphysical considerations in his philosophical grammar (§37) leads him to reject words like 'something' and 'nothing' as grammatical subjects on the basis that they do not 'introduce a term' (i.e. refer to an object): [1], pp. 147, 158.

[98] [3], §73.

[99] Recall that reference is keyed to understanding, satisfaction to truth-conditions: 'someone is wise' is true just in case there is a satisfying object that is wise (not: just in case the complex concept referred to by 'someone' is wise). The same, *mutatis mutandis*, goes for 'no one is wise' (= 'it is not the case that someone is wise').

concerned with questions of ontological classification insofar as these do not affect questions of syntactic construction and congruence.

51 Ramsey on the Subject–Predicate Distinction

One might think that Frege's way of constructing the hierarchy of levels could be vindicated by exploiting a point made by Ramsey in his paper 'Universals'. Ramsey's avowed aim in that paper is to cast doubt on the putative metaphysical gulf between individuals and universals, and he does so, in part, by questioning the logical significance of the subject–predicate distinction. The section of the paper I am concerned with here comes after an argument, discussion of which I postpone to the next chapter (§68), that composite sentences cannot be analysed as having one or more subject–predicate forms correlated with the existence of one or more complex universals *in re*. Having disposed to his satisfaction of the existence of complex universals (wrongly, as I shall argue), Ramsey goes on to consider the viability of the subject–predicate distinction as applied to atomic (simple categorical) sentences.

In the course of pursuing this latter objective Ramsey fair-mindedly attempts to ascertain the motivation for the position he is attacking, namely the Russellian (and Fregean) view that proper names and their meanings are complete, whereas concept-expressions and their meanings are incomplete.[100] Here Ramsey suggests, on his opponents' behalf, that we may discern, among occurrences of a concept-word like 'wise' and of a proper name like 'Socrates', the following difference between the ways they figure in sentential contexts: whereas 'Socrates' determines only one range of significance, namely those in which it occurs in any way at all in a sentence, 'wise' determines two such ranges, namely a wider range in which it occurs in any way at all in a sentence, and a narrower range in which it occurs 'as a predicate', as Ramsey puts it, in an atomic sentence. In its narrower range of significance, 'wise' occurs in contexts which we may schematize as 'ξ is wise'; as an example of 'wise' in its wider range of significance, Ramsey offers the non-atomic sentence 'Neither Socrates nor Plato is wise'.[101] He remarks, still speaking on his opponents' behalf:

This is obviously the explanation of the difference we feel between Socrates and wise which Mr Russell expresses by saying that with wise you have to bring in the form of a proposition.[102] Since all expressions must be completed to form a proposition, it was previously hard to understand how wise could be more incomplete than Socrates.

---

[100] Ramsey [2], p. 121.   [101] Ibid., p. 124.
[102] I quote the passage Ramsey is alluding to in §69 below.

Now we can see that the reason for this is that whereas with 'Socrates' we only have the idea of completing it in any manner into a proposition, with 'wise' we have not only this but also an idea of completing it in a special way, giving us not merely any proposition in which wise occurs but also one in which it occurs in a particular way, which we may call its occurrence as predicate, as in 'Socrates is wise'.[103]

What should we make of this attempt to motivate the Russellian gloss on the distinction between proper names and concept-expressions in such a way as to vindicate the purported logical significance of the subject–predicate distinction?

The first point to note is that, as Ramsey's example of 'wise' in its wider range of significance suggests, and as he anyway expressly tells us,[104] the distinction between wider and narrower ranges of significance is intended to be a distinction between two logically related phenomena: for contexts in which 'wise' occurs in its wider range of significance are constructed truth-functionally from contexts in which it occurs in its narrower range of significance. (Ramsey is here following the approach to composite sentences adopted in the *Tractatus*, and given eloquent expression in his paper 'The Foundations of Mathematics'.[105]) Hence we can (*modulo* the assumption that all sentential complexity is truth-functional) accommodate all contexts in which 'wise' occurs in terms of its 'narrower' range of significance, that is, by discerning in such contexts the presence of a predicate which we can represent as 'ξ is wise'. A suggestion made by Simons that the distinction Ramsey is driving at approximates to Frege's between different levels of a linguistic hierarchy—the point being that while zeroth-level expressions only engage with expressions of the first level, first-level expressions can engage with either zeroth- or second-level expressions—misses the mark.[106] Simons's example of 'wise' in its allegedly wider range of significance, namely 'Somebody is wise and somebody is not wise', *does* involve the first and second levels of the Fregean linguistic hierarchy, but *Ramsey's* example ('Neither Socrates nor Plato is wise') involves its zeroth and first levels.

Ramsey's truth-functionalist approach to the distinction between wider and narrower ranges of significance might just so far look like something that actually strengthens the case for a radical distinction between 'Socrates' and 'wise' along the lines of his Russellian suggestion; but Ramsey rejects this, and with it the motivation for the distinction he had provisionally offered Russell. Both in the main text of 'Universals' (1925) and again in a sequel to it (1926),[107]

---

[103] Ibid., pp. 124–5. 　[104] Ibid., p. 127.
[105] Cf. ibid., pp. 75–8. 　[106] [9], p. 155.
[107] [1]. The relevant part is excerpted at [2], pp. 135–7.

Ramsey repudiates the attempt to distinguish between 'Socrates' and 'wise' on the basis of the alleged failure of 'Socrates' to introduce a narrower range of predications comparable to the one introduced by 'wise'. The ground of his rejection is, as he puts it in the sequel, that 'it can be shown to be theoretically possible to make a similar narrower range for Socrates'.[108] Ramsey has in mind the possibility of defining a range of what he called qualities—in effect, simple monadic properties—that can then be used to delimit a 'narrower' range of significance for 'Socrates', in which it figures in sentences of the form 'Socrates is q', where 'q' denotes just such a quality.[109] And again, although he does not expressly say so this time, it seems reasonable to assume that, for Ramsey as for the Wittgenstein of the *Tractatus*, all contexts in which 'Socrates' occurs in its wider range of significance will be constructible truth-functionally from basic predications of the form 'Socrates is q', where q is a simple quality.[110]

Ramsey's Wittgensteinian confidence that all complex sentences can be represented as truth-functions of simple or atomic sentences, though it was shared by Russell in the introduction to the second edition of *Principia* (in the introduction to the first edition, Russell had admitted such non-truth-functional combinations as 'A believes that p'),[111] is one to which few philosophers would now subscribe. The same applies, presumably, to his assumption that expressions for relations will disappear on analysis (again, as we shall see in the next chapter, this assumption is derived from the *Tractatus*). Actually, it is clear from the sequel to 'Universals' that Ramsey was uncertain on the question to what extent relations may be eliminable, for he there contemplates the possibility that atomic sentences might turn out to be of the forms $R_1(x)$, $R_2(x, y)$, $R_3(x, y, z)$, etc. (The subscripts indicate adicity; elsewhere in this study I use superscripts for that purpose.) In that case, Ramsey says, the question would arise whether we might be able to apply the *Principia* method of distinguishing the class of proper names and individual variables from the class of terms for properties and relations. The *Principia* method is, as Ramsey construes it, to define proper names as terms that can occur in atomic sentences containing any number of terms, whereas an n-termed relational expression ($n \in \{1, 2, 3, \ldots\}$) can only occur in an atomic sentence if it has $n + 1$ terms.[112] In modern terminology, proper names are held to be multigrade—that is, they have variable adicity—at the atomic

[108] [2], p. 136. Cf. Hale [4], pp. 184–5.   [109] [2], pp. 125–32, 136.
[110] I owe this point to Peter Sullivan.   [111] See here Potter [1], pp. 139, 195–8.
[112] See Ramsey [2], pp. 133, 135; Whitehead and Russell, i, pp. xix–xx, 44. Cf. Russell [11], pp. 141–2; Strawson [6], pp. 4, 31; Hochberg [2], pp. 229–30. On the accuracy of Ramsey's gloss, see MacBride [5], p. 97 n. 13.

level, whereas predicates (including relational expressions) are unigrade—that is, have a determinate and fixed adicity—at that level.[113]

But Russell's surmise that relational expressions at the atomic level will all turn out to be unigrade cannot be justified. Setting aside the fact that he himself introduced a (presumably basic) multigrade relation in his multiple relation theory of judgement,[114] it is obvious that natural language provides plenty of examples of multigrade concept-expressions, and it would be mere prejudice to insist that, at the atomic level, such expressions must disappear in favour of exclusively unigrade ones.[115] It could be the case, rather, that at the atomic level (if, absolutely speaking, there is such a thing) all concept-expressions are multigrade, like proper names: that is no less plausible than Russell's speculation. Of course, one might argue that proper names and concept-expressions can be distinguished at the level of ordinary language by dint of the fact that, at that level, proper names are *all* multigrade, whereas concept-expressions, as a congruence class, presumably include at least *some* unigrade examples.[116] I shall address this issue in full generality below (§61). Here the important point to make is that, at the atomic level, which is what Russell and Ramsey are principally interested in, we cannot exclude the possibility that concept-expressions will turn out to be uniformly multigrade, like proper names; nor indeed can we exclude the possibility that proper names will turn out at that level to be unigrade, or at least to comprise both multigrade and unigrade examples, as ordinary concept-expressions of English do.[117] If there is an absolute atomic level at a conjectural end-point of analysis, we will not know what it looks like until we get there, if we ever do. (Ramsey made this point in 'Universals', but he went back on it in the sequel.[118])

Distinct from Russell's claim, and not to be confused with it, is the supposed principle that a proper name or individual variable may, unlike a concept-expression, occur more than once in an atomic sentence, and that in a relational sentence the occurrences of proper names may be interchanged with one another *salva congruitate* whereas proper names may not be so interchanged with relational expressions.[119] Against this, MacBride contends that higher-order sentences of the form '$R(<F, G>)$' are also atomic, and that since these sentences contain no names of individuals the above principle cannot be

[113] Cf. Armstrong [5], p. 85. The terminology derives from Leonard and Goodman, p. 50. For an excellent study of multigrade predication, see Oliver and Smiley [2].

[114] MacBride [4], pp. 588–9; B. Linsky [2], p. 124.

[115] See here MacBride [4], pp. 574–95; [5], p. 103.

[116] See here Hochberg [10], p. 204. Oliver and Smiley argue that virtually all concept-expressions in English which can take singular terms as arguments are multigrade: [2], p. 612.

[117] See MacBride [5], pp. 98–9.   [118] Cf. also Wittgenstein [1], §5.553.

[119] Cf. Russell [13], pp. 286–7; MacBride [1], p. 33.

THE HIERARCHY OF LEVELS

considered a priori.[120] And certainly, if we define atomicity in terms of the absence of quantifiers and connectives,[121] '$R(<F, G>)$' will count as atomic. But suppose we define an atomic formula as one containing no subformulae (except itself).[122] The two definitions of atomicity coincide over first-order languages, but over higher-order languages they may come apart.[123] Plausibly, we have here a case in point. For, as we have seen (§46), we must discern the tacit presence of zeroth-level variables within the scope of the first-level predicates F and G, in which case '$R(<F, G>)$' will implicitly contain the subformulae '$F(x)$' and '$G(x)$'.[124]

Now MacBride's main point is that we cannot take atomicity for granted in this context; and that is surely correct. But, waiving for the moment the fact that we do not know how the adicities of expressions at an absolute atomic level, if there is indeed such a level, will turn out, it can be responded that these higher-order sentences are distinguishable from 'genuine' atomic sentences by virtue of the fact that the predicates 'F' and 'G' (and 'R'), assuming these to be schematic predicates keyed to a natural language like English, belong to a syntactic class that includes at least some unigrade expressions, whereas for the genuinely atomic 'Rab' the proper names belong to a syntactic class whose constituent expressions are uniformly multigrade. The enunciated principle is connected with the fact that, as we have seen, according to either a Fregean or an anti-Fregean philosophical grammar, relational expressions must be located higher in the linguistic hierarchy than proper names: whereas proper names can coherently be assigned to the lowest level of a linguistic hierarchy, relational expressions cannot; but, as we saw, that fact has no implications for the relative locations in a linguistic hierarchy of proper names and primary monadic concept-expressions, and so does not force us to locate proper names at the zeroth level of our linguistic hierarchy.[125]

In spite of the inadequacy of Ramsey's own response to the suggestion he moots on Russell's behalf, I believe that his rejection of the purported asymmetry between 'Socrates' and 'wise' is correct. For we can accommodate all contexts in which 'Socrates' occurs by discerning in these contexts the presence of a narrower-range concept-expression that can be represented as '(Φ) Socrates', which has a single argument-place to be filled by an expression of suitable type. That is, the proper name 'Socrates' has, just like the concept-expression 'wise', a determinate syntax. By the syntax of expressions we may understand the congruence relations implied by categorial designations

---

[120] [1], pp. 35–6.   [121] So e.g. Enderton [2], pp. 74–5.
[122] So Bridge, p. 18; Bostock [2], p. 51; cf. Russell [14], p. 165.   [123] Bridge, p. 28.
[124] Cf. Kleene, pp. 155–6; Cocchiarella [2], p. 61.   [125] Cf. MacBride [2], pp. 190–1.

of them at phrase-marker nodes. (In the case of the anti-Fregean strategy's understanding of 'Socrates', it may be more perspicuous, as we observed in §50, to discern a grammatical ambiguity between two distinct, but semantically systematically related, words, parallel to the distinction recognized by the Fregean strategy between 'wise' and 'wisdom'.) In other words, insofar as a distinction between narrower and wider ranges of significance for 'wise' is in the offing, we can draw a similar distinction for 'Socrates', although in neither case do we thereby undertake a commitment to construe all sentences in which the relevant words occur in their wider ranges of significance as *truth-functions* of contexts in which they occur in their narrower ranges of significance. In my terms, the point can be put by saying that the anti-Fregean first-level (as distinct from the anti-Fregean second-level) concept-expression '(Φ) Socrates' determines the required narrower range of significance in respect of primary monadic concept-expressions.

It seems, then, that the point which Ramsey sought to deploy on Russell's behalf fails to establish a relevant difference between 'Socrates' and 'wise', such as might warrant constructing the linguistic hierarchy in the way Frege favoured rather than in the anti-Fregean way. As far as the phenomenon of congruence is concerned, we may as well assign 'wise' to the zeroth level, and 'Socrates' (in one of its ranges of use) to the first level. In other words, the Fregean version of the hierarchy receives no special endorsement from the point Ramsey deployed on Russell's behalf over its anti-Fregean rival, which reverses the relative positions in the hierarchy of proper names like 'Socrates' (in some of their uses) and concept-expressions like 'wise'. The phenomenon of congruence guarantees that, when expressions are regimented so as to introduce a 'narrower' range of significance, they carry argument-places to be filled by other expressions of determinate categories, however completing and completed expressions are disposed within a linguistic hierarchy (however the categories are annotated); and all contexts in which expressions occur significantly may be theoretically accommodated by recognizing just their 'narrower' range of significance. And the key point for us here is that the phenomenon of congruence does not dictate a unique assignment of expressions to the levels of a linguistic hierarchy.

52   Dummett's Attack on the Anti-Fregean Strategy

The anti-Fregean regimentation of the proper name 'Socrates' (in some of its uses) as '(Φ) Socrates', where 'Φ' holds place for an expression that the anti-Fregean would classify as a zeroth-level concept-expression, will be read by the Fregean as, in effect, assigning the name 'Socrates' to the second level of the (Fregean) linguistic hierarchy. For '(Φ) Socrates' is plainly not a saturated expression. It is what I called in §31 an 'annotated' predicate, and is what Dummett calls a 'complex' predicate: that is, it is an expression formed from a sentence by the omission of one or more expressions, the resulting gaps then being suitably annotated to indicate the number and type of omitted expressions. I shall discuss the significance of these predicates in the next chapter. Here we just need to observe that an expression like '(Φ) Socrates' is constructed in an entirely parallel way to expressions that the Fregean acknowledges to be second-level expressions, such as the so-called first-order quantifiers.[126] In general, it is standard practice in formal, Fregean treatments of natural-language semantics to recognize the phenomenon of type-raising, according to which an expression of category X located at level n of a linguistic hierarchy can be 'raised' to a homonymous expression of category $Y/(Y/X)$ and level $n+2$; correspondingly, any entity of type a and level n of an ontological hierarchy can be 'raised' to an entity of type $<<a, b>, b>$ and level $n+2$, where b is any type.[127] The equivalence

$$\lambda \Phi((\Phi) \text{ Socrates})(\text{wise}) \leftrightarrow \text{Socrates is wise}$$

is immediate in standard semantic theory by the so-called β-reduction rule of λ-conversion.[128]

Now supporters of the Fregean hierarchy typically concede that proper names can sometimes and for some purposes be regimented as expressions located at Frege's second level instead of at his zeroth level. But they nonetheless contend that the preferential allocation of proper names to, in the first instance, the zeroth level is not thereby superseded, and hence that the Fregean way of determining the location of proper names in the linguistic hierarchy—the claim that proper names are *basic* to the hierarchy—is fixed. Barbara Partee, for instance, writes:

The claim that proper names are basically of type e and derivatively of type $<<e, t>, t>$ hardly needs defence, and there is almost as much tradition (though more controversy) behind the treatment of singular definite descriptions as entity-denoting expressions.[129]

I have already rejected the traditional approach to definite descriptions (§15); here we are concerned with the claim which, according to Partee, hardly

---

[126] Cf. Bostock [1], p. 96: 'Types which are next but one to one another will always have the same range of significance.' Cf. p. 102

[127] On the principles of type-raising, see Lewis [1], pp. 32–3; Partee and Rooth; Carpenter, pp. 100–1, 146–7, 182–3.

[128] For details see e.g. Carpenter, pp. 50, 83, 103–4.   [129] [2], p. 206.

needs defence. On the contrary, one might retort, as one of the key features of Frege's semantics, the claim stands, par excellence, in need of defence. Let us then look at a well-known and influential attempt to defend it.

Like other Fregeans, Dummett accepts that, for certain inferential purposes, we may wish to regiment proper names in such a way as to allocate them to the second level of the linguistic hierarchy.[130] But he holds that this allocation is essentially both derivative and degenerate: it is derivative in that it depends on a prior location of (unregimented) proper names at the zeroth level; and it is degenerate in that it 'involves the most trivial kind of second-level concept'.[131] 'On Ramsey's conception', he writes—that is, on what I am calling the 'anti-Fregean' strategy, or on a conception that was indifferent between Fregean and anti-Fregean strategies[132]—

> there would be no genuine difference between [Frege's] objects and [his] second-level qualities: the supposed difference would correspond merely to the shift in perspective involved in passing from taking, e.g., 'Socrates is wise' to be saying something about Socrates to taking it as saying something about being wise. But, unless the distinction is maintained, it is impossible to recognize the correctness of the Aristotelian thesis that an object has no contrary: we should be unable to understand generalization over objects, as opposed to generalization over all the things that might be true of a first-level quality. A little reflection on such a state of affairs shows it to be impossible: we should be unable to explain, not merely generality, but the truth-conditions even of the most basic atomic statements. For these, the conception of a proper name as standing for an object about which we are asserting that the predicate is true of it is inescapable, whatever may be the case for the extension of this notion to other contexts. It is true that, when our language reaches a certain degree of complexity, we may want to admit the notion of such a second-level predicate as '(Φ) Socrates': but we could not explain the conditions under which a sentence which resulted from putting a first-level predicate in the argument-place of this second-level predicate was true or false unless we already understood those conditions via the construal of that same sentence as resulting from putting the name 'Socrates', viewed as standing for an object, in the argument-place of the first-level predicate.[133]

The passage is rhetorically imposing, but its ultimate probative force is rather modest: the unwary reader gains the impression that several weighty reasons for the central claim are being offered, but in reality the argument is indefinitely deferred.[134] The final clause indeed purports, at last, to deliver the *coup de grâce* to Ramsey; in fact, however, it contains nothing but sheer assertion,

---

[130] [2], pp. 65–6. Cf. Bostock [1], pp. 83–6.   [131] [3], p. 288.
[132] Cf. Siderits [3], p. 19 n. 11.
[133] [2], pp. 66–7. Cf. [3], pp. 288–91; [4], pp. 197–8; Geach [1], pp. 474–5; Strawson [2], ch. 3; Sullivan [1], p. 100.
[134] Cf. MacBride [3], pp. 71–6; Siderits [3], p. 22; Hale [4], pp. 193–5.

the motivation for which remains obscure. It is true, of course, that if the zeroth level of the linguistic hierarchy is treated as basic, the first level as coming next, and so on up through the sequence of natural numbers, it then automatically follows that sentences constructed from first- and second-level concept-expressions, however these categories are constituted, cannot be semantically or epistemologically primary: our understanding of them must depend asymmetrically on a prior understanding of sentences constructed from zeroth- and first-level expressions, however these categories are constituted. But this point is just a truism, following merely from the meaning of the terms 'zeroth level', 'first level', etc., as these apply to hierarchies of the sort under consideration. It is clear, however, that Dummett, like Frege, is after more than that truism: he wants to lodge a substantial claim about the *composition* of the various levels, however these are indexed, and he holds in particular that proper names like 'Socrates' must be allocated to the most basic level of our linguistic hierarchy and concept-expressions like 'is wise' to the next level up, and so on. And it is that claim which we have so far seen no reason to accept.

At this juncture it will be well to call to mind exactly what is at stake. A claim of the form 'Proper names are basic to the linguistic hierarchy' cannot be assessed, just as such, until we know what proper names are. I suppose someone *might* use the phrase 'proper name' in a logical rather than a grammatical sense to apply to *whatever* gets assigned to the zeroth level of a linguistic hierarchy, in which case the claim will be a trivial one. In order to avoid this triviality, we must continue to use 'proper name' not as a synonym for 'zeroth-level expression', but to refer to grammatically recognized proper names which are also semantically simple,[135] of which 'Socrates' is serving as our paradigm example. (In fact, of course, it is highly unlikely that the name of a remote historical person like Socrates is, for us now, free of descriptive elements:[136] but I am abstracting from that point in this study.) We have considered a fragment of an anti-Fregean grammar which in the first instance assigns Frege's primary monadic concept-expressions to the zeroth level of its linguistic hierarchy, instead of to the first level, and makes its remaining dispositions consequentially upon this initial choice. As we have seen, under this transformation the congruence of different types of expression would be unaffected. Proper names such as 'Socrates' would still be constructed with concept-expressions like 'is wise', and their corresponding senses and references (where applicable: referents) would still engage with one another

[135] i.e. which do not abbreviate definite descriptions, and are not descriptive names in the sense of Evans's 'Julius' ([1], ch. 2); note that these two options are distinct.
[136] Cf. Ch. 2 n. 79.

in the appropriate way, in spite of the different assignments of syntactic type yielded by the anti-Fregean's strategy for a sentence like 'Socrates is wise'.[137] In a sense nothing has changed, though from a theoretical point of view we can say that the anti-Fregean strategy reverses the priority of 'Socrates' and 'is wise' in the linguistic hierarchy and, correspondingly, the priority of their references in the ontological hierarchy. But is anything lost or distorted by this transformation?[138]

Dummett claims, in effect, that the anti-Fregean strategy lacks explanatory perspicuity. But it is hard to see the force of this claim. The two different ways of classifying the data are surely just syntactic and semantic doublets. In other words, neither of the rival strategies enjoys an absolute advantage over the other: as far as our paradigm sentence 'Socrates is wise' is concerned, the only absolute constraints on our grammar, so long as our linguistic hierarchy continues to be constructed on the principles laid down at the beginning of this chapter, are (i) the requirement that 'Socrates' and 'is wise', as they figure in this sentence, be assigned to *different* levels of the linguistic hierarchy (with corresponding dispositions of their references in the ontological hierarchy), and (ii) the requirement that these expressions, as they figure in this sentence, be assigned to the *zeroth and first* levels of the linguistic hierarchy (with corresponding assignments in the ontological hierarchy). And those absolutes are respected by both the rival strategies, though they assign the relevant expressions oppositely to the zeroth and first levels. Dummett agrees that for the purposes of some inferences we may need to appeal to an alternative analysis to Frege's, one locating proper names at a higher level than Frege's first-level concept-expressions. But he denies that we *otherwise* need to make this appeal, so that if as a matter of fact a language does not contain resources for engaging in higher-level predication, there can be no reason to appeal to the anti-Fregean analysis in dealing with its (uniformly atomic) sentences. This claim can only rest on the supposition that, quite apart from the question of modelling inference patterns, there is some significant theoretical advantage enjoyed by the Fregean strategy over the anti-Fregean strategy. But what is that advantage supposed to be? The two approaches are surely just using variant but equipollent notations to calibrate the same facts.

---

[137] Hence, incidentally, it would be wrong to say that construing numbers as second-level concepts blocks the notorious 'Julius Caesar' problem—the problem of providing identity-conditions for numbers that settle whether Julius Caesar is a number—on the basis that 'the question whether Julius Caesar is a number now cannot even be posed because it is ungrammatical' (Potter [1], p. 71). If Julius Caesar is himself a second-level concept, the problem returns.

[138] Cf. MacBride [4], p. 602.

53 Linguistic Idealism Revisited

Dummett's charge against what I am calling the anti-Fregean strategy—namely that it lacks explanatory perspicuity—is connected with his repeated insistence that the doctrine of reference as it applies to ordinary proper names contains two ingredients: the conception of reference as semantic role, and the identification of the referent of a proper name with its bearer.[139] The connection is this: just as, in Dummett's view, the location of proper names at the second level of the linguistic hierarchy, though justifiable in some contexts and for some purposes, is an essentially secondary move, dependent on a prior allocation of these names to the zeroth level, so also, in his view, the identification of the referent of a proper name with its bearer plays a foundational part in any conception we may go on to form of the reference of a proper name as its semantic role. (Dummett's worry about names of abstract objects is that, as applied to their case, the relative priority of the two conceptions of reference is reversed, that names of abstract objects count as having bearers by virtue of their having semantic role, rather than vice versa.) But these reflections represent a serious departure from the spirit of the context principle: in particular, there is no warrant for Dummett's inclusion of the second ingredient in his characterization of our conception of the meanings of ordinary proper names—the idea of reference as constituted by the name–bearer relation—which purports to supplement (and indeed determine) the former ingredient—the idea of reference as semantic role—but fails to do so. Rather, as I noted in §9, application to a proper name (ordinary or otherwise) of the distinctively theoretical notion of reference precisely tells us what the bearer (referent) of that name *is*: we have no *pre-theoretical* insight into what a proper name (or any linguistic expression) refers to. Pre-theoretically a word *has* no referent: a proper name's bearer is what theory tells us its referent is.

Dummett claims that 'it is precisely because the expressions we use have . . . extra-linguistic correlates that we succeed in talking about the real world, and in saying things about it which are true or false in virtue of how things are in that world'.[140] But though, as we have noted (§14), this approach has some plausibility as a reading of Frege, from a systematic point of view, as we have also noted (§§9, 38), it gets matters back to front. It is not because our expressions have referents that we succeed in saying things that are true

---

[139] See e.g. [2], pp. 180–6, 190–1, 199–203, 210, 223–6; [3], p. 243; [4], pp. 84–5.

[140] [2], p. 198. Cf. [4], p. 38: 'It cannot be necessary, for every singular term, to secure it a reference by equating its referent with that of some other term: there must be terms whose referentiality is autonomous'. Dummett notes (p. 39) that the view he rejects is a consequence of the context principle.

or false: rather, it is because we succeed in saying things that are true or false that the expressions we use have referents. For this is the whole point of the context principle: in the beginning was the *sentence*—true or false—and words, together with their senses and referents, are posited with a view to gaining an essentially theoretical understanding of how sentences mean, how they are interrelated, and how on the basis of our linguistic training we are able to understand new sentences.[141] The existence of objects is thus fallout from the existence of language: 'Who knows the names, knows the things'.[142] This brings us close to the outlook of the *Tractatus*, where, in Potter's words, '"Object" is . . . a technical term, referring to whatever it is that our language presupposes in order that it should be significant.'[143] Elsewhere Potter remarks *in propria persona* that 'the ultimate point of language is to say things about the world',[144] a view that would be (has been) supported by many philosophers; but by my lights it would be better to say that the ultimate point of the world is to model the meaningfulness of language.[145] Language is not grounded in an extra-linguistic world, as Dummett wants;[146] the grounding relation runs in the opposite direction. But the resulting linguistic idealism is tempered by an empirical realism to the extent that the *original* connection between language and the world is secured at the point of the truth and falsity of *sentences*, not at the subsentential level, and we do not, in general, determine those truth-values, which are, as we have seen (§24), in a metaphysical sense ungrounded.[147]

It follows that Dummett's discussions of whether it is permissible to extend what he calls the name–bearer prototype[148] to concept-expressions or to nominal abstract expressions like the cardinal numerals get off on entirely the wrong foot, for the relation between a proper name and its bearer is *not* a prototype; nor is the referential relation between a pronoun and its bearer prototypical, as Quine suggests.[149] There are *no* prototypes as far as the theoretical relation of reference is concerned: all semantically significant subsentential lexical expressions are on a par, and all are, along with their

---

[141] Cf. my [15], ch. 6, §2. On the centrality of the sentence to semantics, see also Wiggins [1], p. 16; Tugendhat [2], pp. 55, 141–2; Dummett [10], pp. 15–16.

[142] Plato, *Crat.* 435d5–6.   [143] [3], p. 72; cf. [2], p. 40.   [144] [1], p. 277. Cf. [2], p. 11.

[145] See here my [15], pp. 107–8.   [146] [2], p. 200.

[147] Cf. Hale [2], pp. 153–4; Tugendhat [1], p. 67: 'die Entscheidung darüber, ob ein Satz wahr ist, ist keine innersprachliche'. Tugendhat's 'right approach' in that article, commended by me at [15], p. 207 n. 19, consists in his handling of reference as a purely theoretical relation; his further analysis of it as 'truth-value potential' (in effect, supposition) of course conflicts with my treatment. Unfortunately, the theoreticity of the reference relation is not a position that Tugendhat maintains consistently. In his [2], there are many passages in which he clearly thinks of the reference relation as pre-theoretically given in the case of proper name and bearer: see e.g. pp. 37, 50, 131, 176, 198, 323, 337–8, 341–6, 355, 363, 374–5, 501–2; and cf. my remarks on Tugendhat in §§36 and 40 above.

[148] See e.g. [2], p. 198.   [149] [7], pp. 166–8.

senses and referents, theoretical posits; in any sense in which proper names can be said to 'pick out' objects, concept-expressions 'pick out' concepts or other functions (which are equally, by my lights, objects).[150] The context principle applies no less to the word–world relations exemplified by ordinary proper names and their referents than it does to the corresponding word–world relations of other expressions.[151] The nominalist claims to have some kind of pre-linguistic insight into the structure of the world that can then be used to test our language for adequacy; but the putative insight is illusory, and it is wrong to concede, as John Searle does, that 'insofar as the nominalist is claiming that the existence of particulars depends on facts in the world and the existence of universals merely on the meaning of words, he is quite correct'.[152] The existence of concrete individuals is just as much a matter of the meanings of words as is the existence of abstract universals; in any sense in which the existence of abstract objects is, in Dummett's phrase, 'internal to language', so too is the existence of all objects. Dummett himself well exposes the nominalist's error in several of his writings,[153] and it is surprising and disappointing that he undermines what would otherwise be a highly effective anti-nominalistic polemic by (in effect) excepting proper names of concrete objects from the scope of the context principle.

If concrete individuals are as much meanings of words, and are as dependent on the transcendental existence of language as abstract universals are, the reverse side of that coin is that meanings, of whatever sort, are objects. If even entities that are purportedly the most objective and objectual of things still are no more than meanings, other things too that are only meanings can be seen to be no less objective, and no less objectual, than the supposedly privileged entities. So, for example, the meanings of sentences are objects. It is common for philosophers to restrict the term 'object' to a proper part of the objective, that is, to a proper part of what grounds the meaningfulness of language.[154] But there is no justification for the restriction, or for the traditional claim that what a sentence names is not a *res* but a non-objectual *status rerum* or *rerum modus habendi se*, as Abelard puts it.[155] There is nothing more to being a *res* than being something that theory posits to ground understanding, and that role attaches to entities like *that Socrates is wise* as much as it does to the man Socrates. If Plato's Eleatic Stranger meant to imply, in the quotation from the *Sophist* given at

---

[150] Contra Dummett [2], p. 244; Bell [1], p. 48.

[151] See here Wright's excellent discussion in his [1], §x.

[152] [1], p. 105; cf. pp. 114–15.   [153] See e.g. [1], ch. 4; [2], ch. 14.

[154] See e.g. Künne [1], p. 128; Hale [2], pp. 165–6. Cf. MacBride [6], p. 425. In Hale's case, the restriction is consequential on his acceptance of the 'syntactic priority thesis', which I discuss (and reject) later in this chapter (§§57–61).

[155] See e.g. [2], p. 160.35–6. Cf. Haller, pp. 103–4.

the beginning of §1, that sentences do not name at all, he was mistaken: the difference between an ordinary proper name and a declarative sentence is not that the former refers to an object while the latter does not, but that they refer to different sorts of object—in particular, the object that the latter refers to is inherently true or false.

The Dummettian view that reference is not a purely theoretical relation is unfortunately widespread.[156] I suspect that it traces its origin to an old but incoherent philosophy of reference, according to which words 'stand for'—that is, stand *in* for, go *proxy* for—things. A traditional feature of this approach to reference, and one that nicely brings out its inherent absurdity, is the claim that, though it would ideally be preferable to speak and write the things themselves, the practical inconvenience of doing so obliges us to employ words instead as a technical expediency. Consider a school geography lesson: how much easier to speak words that go proxy for the Himalayas than to speak the Himalayas themselves! Undaunted by this consideration, the academicians of Lagado in Swift's pastiche of the Royal Society devised

a scheme for entirely abolishing all words whatsoever; . . . since words are only names for *things*, it would be more convenient for all men to carry about them such *things* as were necessary to express the particular business they are to discourse on.[157]

In the Parisian anti-Ockhamist statute of 1340 we are instructed as follows:

No one should say that there is no knowledge of things other than signs, that is, which are not terms or phrases, for in the sciences we use terms to stand for things, which we are not able to carry to our disputations.[158]

Of course the position, though it can boast the authority of Aristotle, Descartes, and the early Wittgenstein,[159] is hopeless: no serious philosophy of language

---

[156] See e.g. Bell [1], ch. 1; Searle [1], pp. 26–7, 81; Burge [2], pp. 87–8; Schnieder [1], p. 248; King [5], pp. 103–11. Evans starts his [1] by quoting (p. 2) Strawson's remark that 'the task of forestalling the . . . question ["What (who, which one) are you talking about?"] is the referring . . . task' ([2], p. 17). But (recall §45) if you say 'Socrates is wise' and are asked 'Who/what are you talking about?', you may, depending on context, reply with any or all of 'Socrates', 'wisdom', and 'predicative being/instantiation'. Now I have no objection if application of Strawson's test takes us to the view upheld in §40 above, namely that *all* words are referring expressions. But I do not think that that is quite what either Strawson or Evans intended. In his [2], Davidson, though maintaining his previous line that the reference relation is an essentially theoretical one (e.g. pp. 1, 35–6, 55 n. 8, 155), is in more than one place sympathetic to Dummett's suggestion that we need (and have) a pre-theoretical insight into the workings of the name–bearer relation (pp. 131, 142–3). I return to this point in §89.

[157] Swift, III, ch. 5, p. 230. Cf. Land, p. 35.

[158] Paqué, p. 10. Cf. Leppin, p. 275. Actually, Ockham himself would have agreed with the latter part of this assertion, since he defines *suppositio* as 'pro alio positio, ita quod quando terminus in propositione stat pro aliquo' ([1], I, §63). Cf. Panaccio [1], p. 271.

[159] Aristotle, *SE* 165a6–10; Descartes, *Principles*, I, §74 (viiiA, pp. 37–8); Wittgenstein [1], esp. §§3.1431, 3.22, 3.221, 4.0312. Cf. Schlick, p. 94.

can expect to make progress if it starts from the ludicrous view that words go proxy for things. As the later Wittgenstein realized,[160] language's being *about* worldly objects is a much more intimate property of it than can be accommodated by a model of reference according to which our using words to refer to things has merely instrumental value, that is, would in principle be dispensable in favour of using the things themselves.[161]

It is true that we often need to point to objects in order to be able to talk about them. This particularly applies to cases where we are trying to describe what something is like (as we say). If I want to convey to someone who has never heard a clarinet what the instrument sounds like, I can do no better than play a note on it and say '*That* is how a clarinet sounds.'[162] (I may try verbal explanations instead of, or as well as, an ostensive definition, such as 'A clarinet has a reedy sound', but these explanations will ultimately be parasitic on ostensive situations: to appreciate what a reedy sound is like, one has to hear it.) But the presence of the instrument itself is an enabling condition; it cannot replace the use of language. A note sounded on a clarinet followed by the words '. . . is how a clarinet sounds' is not as such a sentence: if in context it works as a way of conveying the necessary information, that is because the hearer tacitly completes the phrase with a suitable deictic word whose job is to refer to the sound, not to 'stand in for' it. The idea of 'standing in for' is at home in descriptions of how some items of language can represent other items—in particular, how pronouns (in general: proforms) may stand in for nouns (forms)—but it has no role to play in elucidating the referential relation between words and things. For the truth is that natural language is *already* a Leibnizian *characteristica universalis*; it is *already* a Fregean *Begriffsschrift*. The purpose for which Leibniz and Frege conceived these ideal languages, namely to 'express things immediately' (*unmittelbar die Sache ausdrücken*), as Frege put it,[163] is already attained—at least to the extent that makes sense—by natural language.

54 Alternative Hierarchies and the Context Principle

In the long passage quoted in the previous section, Dummett alludes to the Aristotelian thesis that a substance has no contrary. In fact, as I shall show below in this chapter, that thesis does not support the Fregean strategy

[160] [5], I, §120.   [161] Cf. Chomsky [6], p. 103.
[162] Cf. Künne [1], p. 207; McDowell [1], pp. 56–7.
[163] Frege [2], p. 54 ([25], p. 96). Note also [1], pp. vi–vii. Cf. Carl [2], p. 10.

over the anti-Fregean one: for when interpreted as a syntactic test, it fails to isolate just those expressions which Frege assigns to the zeroth level. Aristotle, of course, did not intend his thesis to be understood as a syntactic test of substancehood, nor indeed as any kind of test of substancehood, for he observes that failure to take a contrary is not peculiar to substances but holds of 'many other things as well': he tells us, for example, that a particular quantity, such as a length of two cubits, has no contrary.[164] But if we recur to Aristotle's own conception of substance (at least as that is promulgated in the *Categories*), we shall fail on two counts to provide anything that can shore up the Fregean hierarchy against a challenge from its rival. For, in the first place, there is nothing especially fundamental, metaphysically speaking, about Aristotle's category of substance. It is true that Aristotle himself evidently thought otherwise, as may be gathered from the privileged position he accords substance in the list of categories, and from a number of remarks he makes about the relations between substance and the other categories. Of these perhaps the most telling is his observation that if primary substances (individual human beings, individual horses, etc.) did not exist, the things in the other categories would not exist either.[165] But it is not clear that this observation is correct, and in any case the implied asymmetry fails to obtain. For it is equally (indeed more obviously) the case that, if the things in the other categories did not exist, primary substances would not exist either: individual substances must at the very least have qualities, dimensions, relations to other things; they must be in a particular position; and they must exist at particular times and in particular places. Hence no metaphysical asymmetry between the category of substance and the other categories—at least: no metaphysical asymmetry between substance and the categories of quality, quantity, relation, being-in-a-position, when, and where—is in prospect. (We might envisage, in parallel to the anti-Fregean strategy, an anti-Aristotelian list of the categories, granting prime location to the category of quality.) In the second place, and more importantly in the present context, Aristotle's (indeed anyone's) conception of substance is *metaphysical*, not *syntactic*. But our conception of what it is to be a proper name is syntactic: perfectly genuine proper names, such as the numerals, have referents that do not belong to the Aristotelian category of substance. Aristotelian category theory is therefore irrelevant to our purposes, and the Aristotelian doctrine of substance cannot be appealed to in support of the Fregean linguistic hierarchy.

Observe that, when assigned to the first level of the anti-Fregean hierarchy, proper names like 'Socrates' are true or false of objects like wisdom, and can take

---

[164] *Cat.* 3b24–32.   [165] *Cat.* 2a34–b6; cf. *Met.* 1028a10–b7.

significant conjunction, disjunction, and negation.[166] Hence the suggestion, frequently met in the literature,[167] that these properties serve to distinguish proper names from concept-expressions must be rejected. At the ontological level, on a suitable (anti-Fregean) construal of the ontological hierarchy, it will be true to say that monadic properties like being wise 'fall under' objects like Socrates, rather than vice versa. Hence if, like Davidson,[168] we wish to treat 'falling under' as designating a logical relation—in effect following Frege's and Russell's logicisms (recall §48), for whom (respectively) subsumption and set membership counted as logical relations—it will follow that, on the anti-Fregean approach, objects can enjoy logical relations, and that Davidson's absolutist assertion that 'material objects do not have logical relations, while properties do' is, as it stands, false—or at least misleadingly incomplete—as is its linguistic counterpart, the claim that 'predicates are logically related to other predicates; names have no logical relations'.[169]

Again, we may reject as spurious a disanalogy that Dummett seeks to establish between the reference relation as it applies to proper names and as it applies to concept-expressions.[170] The disanalogy is said to arise from different ways in which reference-failure purportedly affects proper names and concept-expressions: Dummett claims that there is no analogy, for the case of concept-expressions, to the fact that atomic sentences containing bearerless names are truth-valueless. But there is. Consider that a bearerless name is only a *name* by courtesy: it is really a nonsense word—which is itself only a *word* by courtesy. The analogy in the case of concept-expressions will then not be an empty concept-expression, not even a self-contradictory such expression,[171] for in neither of these cases is there any question of lack of either sense or reference—such concept-expressions lack not *referents* (and so not senses either) but *satisfiers*. Rather, the analogy in the case of concept-expressions will be a nonsense item lacking sense and reference, and so only by courtesy called a concept-expression. And such nonsense items will indeed infect sentences in which they figure with failure to take a truth-value.

In default of any other means of motivating the Fregean way of modelling the asymmetry between proper names and the expressions classified by Frege as first-level concept-expressions—his insistence that the former are basic to the linguistic hierarchy—we should conclude that there is no such

[166] Dummett [2], p. 66; Stirton [2], pp. 205–7; Hale [3], pp. 70–1.
[167] See e.g. Geach [1], pp. 474–5; [3], pp. 32–3, 59; [10], pp. 184–8; Strawson [2], p. 69; [6], pp. 4–9; Anscombe [1], p. 108; Dummett [2], pp. 63–4; Denyer [1], pp. 170–9. For a cogent critique of Geach's and Strawson's treatments of negation, see M. C. Bradley [2].
[168] [2], p. 89.   [169] Ibid., pp. 89, 112.   [170] [2], pp. 243–4.
[171] Cf. Dummett [2], p. 219.

asymmetry. Note this way of putting it: the conclusion is not that there is no asymmetry *simpliciter*, but that there is no *such* asymmetry. For there remain the absolute distinctions of grammatical congruence. That is to say, there *is* a linguistic hierarchy comprising distinct levels, at least for natural languages like English and German (though not for all conceivable languages, a point which will be important later in this study), and Geach and Dummett are quite wrong to suggest that pursuing what I am calling the anti-Fregean strategy would 'destroy our fundamental distinction' between proper names and concept-expressions (Geach),[172] or that Ramsey's criticism of the idea that some subsentential expressions are complete and others incomplete constitutes an attack on 'the whole conception of a hierarchy of expressions of different level' (Dummett), and that on such an approach we are not justified 'in taking the different *kinds* of incompleteness—the different valencies [i.e. congruence relations: RG]—as being different *levels*' (Dummett).[173] It is an interesting question whether Ramsey himself would have concurred with these claims.[174] But if he had been tempted to agree with them, he would have been mistaken. The conclusion to be drawn from the viability of the anti-Fregean strategy is not that the idea of a linguistic hierarchy of levels is redundant or incoherent, but that the fact that there is more than one level in that hierarchy—that there are subsentential expressions with distinct grammatical congruence relations—has, as such, no implications concerning the relative ordering, in such a hierarchy, of different sorts of subsentential expression (and of their corresponding references in an ontological hierarchy): more than one such ordering is possible. For we have seen that while there are absolute constraints on how we may dispose expressions within a linguistic hierarchy, these constraints fail to adjudicate between the Fregean disposition and that of its anti-Fregean rival.

The Fregean strategy treats proper names as saturated expressions, like sentences, and locates them at the zeroth level of its linguistic hierarchy; the anti-Fregean strategy treats primary monadic concept-expressions as saturated and locates them at the zeroth level of *its* linguistic hierarchy. Both strategies, then, identify saturated expressions with those housed at the zeroth level of a linguistic hierarchy. The availability of the anti-Fregean strategy shows that Frege was wrong to regard proper names as peculiarly saturated and (monadic) first-level concept-expressions as peculiarly unsaturated, if being saturated is

---

[172] [1], p. 474.   [173] [2], p. 62.
[174] MacBride seems to suggest that he would ([3], p. 71); Hale argues ([4], pp. 194–5, 199), convincingly I think, that he would not.

tantamount to belonging to the zeroth level of a linguistic hierarchy and being unsaturated tantamount to belonging to one of the higher levels. But I do not think that we should conclude from this that the category of saturated subsentential expressions is simply indeterminate as between Frege's way of calibrating the syntactic facts and the anti-Fregean way. It is true, as we have seen, that we must populate the zeroth level *either* in the Fregean way *or* in the anti-Fregean way. But we should divorce the label 'saturated' from its presumptive universal application to expressions of the zeroth level. For, as I suggested in Chapter 3, if sentences are to be classified as saturated in the sense that they are capable of saying something true or false, there is no warrant for extending the label 'saturated' to *any* subsentential components: subsentential components must all alike count as unsaturated. That, I suggested, is a consequence of the context principle. If we accept this revision to the way we apply Frege's chemical metaphor, we must also revise the statement of the constructional principle of the linguistic hierarchy offered at the beginning of this chapter. Sentences retain their *ex officio* position at the zeroth level of the hierarchy, of course, but the subsentential expressions with which they share the zeroth level (whether these be established in the Fregean or in the anti-Fregean way) are not to be classified as saturated in contrast to unsaturated expressions at all other levels.

We must thus clearly separate the application of the distinction between saturated and unsaturated expressions, on the one hand, from the project of constructing a linguistic hierarchy, on the other. In effect Frege thought of saturatedness as a property of, in the first instance, sentences, located *ex officio* at the zeroth level of a linguistic hierarchy, and then because he thought (in effect) that there was only one way to populate the zeroth level with subsentential expressions, he saw no difficulty in allowing (in effect) 'saturated' to function as a synonym for 'zeroth-level'. But reflection on the fact that there *is* more than one way to dispose subsentential expressions in a linguistic hierarchy suggests that it would be wiser to break the (in effect) definitional connection between 'saturated' and 'zeroth-level', confining the former term to sentences, and allowing the latter term to apply both to saturated sentences and to those subsentential expressions, whatever these are, which are also assigned to the lowest level of a linguistic hierarchy, and which, in virtue of being subsentential, count as unsaturated. That terminological policy embodies the crucial lesson I have drawn from the context principle, namely that zeroth-level subsentential expressions have, from the point of view of philosophical grammar, more in common with other subsentential expressions than they do with sentences.

55 The Linguistic Hierarchy and Categorial Nonsense

The phenomenon of congruence, keyed as it is to distinctions between levels of a linguistic hierarchy, makes available a certain kind of categorial nonsense, which arises when the principles of the hierarchy are breached. It is worth pausing to confirm this point, which has indeed been denied, before moving on. I start with a general distinction between ordinary and categorial nonsense.[175]

Ordinary nonsense, as we may here understand that notion, arises through failure of meaning: part or all of a purported stretch of discourse has no meaning in the language to which that stretch of discourse purportedly belongs. A case of ordinary nonsense would be an example which Moore is said to have used:[176]

(6) Scott kept a runcible at Abbotsford.

Here the word 'runcible', though it may easily enough be supplied with a meaning, does not yet have a meaning in our language. That (6) is indeed nonsense, rather than false, is confirmed by the fact that its negation is also nonsense, rather than true.[177]

We may contrast ordinary with *categorial* nonsense. The latter purportedly occurs when a sentence, which may or may not be grammatically correctly formed, contains words which already have a determinate meaning in the language, but which are combined in a way that is in some sense improper. One kind of categorial impropriety we might dub 'Aristotelian' nonsense. We are given a category theory which divides things into distinct sorts: individual substances, qualities, quantities, and so on. We might then be told that certain trans-categorial predications, such as

(7) The colour red weighs three pounds,

are nonsensical.[178] It is actually quite remarkable how often one meets claims of this sort. A few examples will suffice. Ryle asserts that 'Saturday is in bed' is not true or false, but 'absurd', 'unthinkable'.[179] Fred Sommers tells us that

If I say 'his anger was triangular and not triangular' I have not contradicted myself; I have said nothing and retracted nothing . . . . A horse which is a prime number neither

---

[175] Cf. Husserl's distinction between *Unsinn* and *Widersinn* at [2], iv, §12; Conant [1], pp. 18–21.
[176] Diamond, p. 95.
[177] See Frege [11], p. 453 ([21], p. 209); Kienzler, pp. 187–90; my [11], p. 201.
[178] Cf. Wittgenstein [3], p. 126.
[179] Ryle, ii, pp. 174, 179–80; cf. p. 7. Cf. Kneale and Kneale, p. 671.

exists nor does not exist. But in saying that I predicate nothing of horses . . . 'A horse which is a prime number' is not in the language, and neither is 'round anger'.[180]

And Chomsky states that, while there is no grammatical objection to 'the ant has a kidney', 'the kidney has an ant', by contrast, 'is not false or impossible but senseless'.[181] But as they stand these claims are easy to refute. Consider (7). There is a simple argument showing that this sentence is not meaningless, but false.[182] For its (external) negation is true. That its (external) negation is true is indicated by the fact that it can be derived as the conclusion of an argument whose premises are true (and indeed necessary), namely:

(8)   No colour has a weight;

    the colour red is a colour;

    anything that weighs three pounds has a weight.

    Hence it is not the case that the colour red weighs three pounds.

Similar arguments can be constructed to show that the relevant sentences in the examples propounded by Ryle, Sommers, and Chomsky are not nonsensical but false.

Elsewhere, Chomsky suggests that sentences like 'John amazed the injustice of the decision', 'The harvest was clever to agree', and 'John frightened sincerity' have a borderline character between syntactic and semantic deviance.[183] He concedes that, if embedded in certain contexts, as when prefixed by a phrase like 'It is absurd to say that . . .', the deviance of these sentences may be cancelled, but he supposes that such cancellation is best accommodated by ad hoc lexical rules (of words like 'absurd', 'nonsense', etc.). This approach is unattractive for two reasons: (i) the kinds of verbal context which cancel deviance are potentially unlimited in syntactic form, so that to adduce ad hoc rules is surely to miss a generalization; and (ii) the sentences in question may, given suitable discourse contexts, such as a children's story, even be true (true in the fiction).[184] The fact is that these sentences are not in any way syntactically deviant. Again, to engage with Sommers's second example, the phrase 'a horse which is a prime number' is certainly in the language, and I have no difficulty in understanding it. It is indeed not satisfied by anything, and necessarily so: for, necessarily, nothing which is an animal is a number, etc. But the mere possibility of constructing an argument to *show* that, necessarily, nothing is both a horse and a prime number *presupposes* that phrase's meaningfulness.

---

[180] Sommers, pp. 157, 161.   [181] [2], p. 161. Cf. Kimball, pp. 66–7.
[182] Cf. Pap; Prior [2]; [3], p. 104; M. C. Bradley [1]; Cartwright [1], p. 52.
[183] [2], pp. 75–9, 156–8.   [184] Z. Harris has a more nuanced account: pp. 51–3.

(If the phrase were not in the language, Sommers could not claim, as he wishes to, that a horse which is a prime number neither exists nor does not exist.[185]) In sum, if we admit necessary falsehoods of the Aristotelian variety as bona-fide cases of categorial nonsense, we must distinguish between nonsensicality and meaninglessness. (7) is nonsensical, in the defined sense, but it is not meaningless, because it has a truth-value.

Distinct from Aristotelian nonsense is a variety of categorial nonsense that we may label *breach of logical syntax*. This is the kind of nonsense that 'Socrates Plato' and 'is wise drinks hemlock' exemplify. It arises when the principles of the linguistic hierarchy of levels are breached. The examples just cited breach the canons of logical syntax by trying to put together expressions from the same level of the linguistic hierarchy, as do the examples of nonsense Plato introduces towards the end of the *Sophist*, which we have already mentioned (§5):

(9)   walks runs sleeps

and

(10)   lion stag horse.

Note that (9) and (10) are ungrammatical, as is the following attempt to put together the existential quantifier with a proper name, that is (to cast the operation in terms of the Fregean hierarchy), an expression of the second level with an expression of the zeroth level:

(11)   There are Julius Caesar.[186]

Categorial nonsense of this type need not be ungrammatical, however. Exactly the same sort of nonsense is conveyed by

(12)   Julius Caesar has an instance,

which is, though a logical absurdity, perfectly grammatical. Similarly, we are told that

(13)   Chairman Mao is rare

is logical nonsense, since it seeks to combine a zeroth-level proper name with a second-level concept-expression, but it is perfectly grammatical.[187]

Will an argument parallel to the one offered above, to the effect that (7) is false rather than nonsensical, work for breaches of logical syntax? In the case

---

[185] Sommers's discussion nicely demonstrates the perennial nemesis of type theories—that in setting them up one violates them: recall §28.

[186] Cf. Frege [7], p. 200 ([21], p. 174); [13], p. 373 ([21], p. 271).   [187] Dummett [2], p. 51.

of ungrammatical categorial nonsense like (9) and (10), there is no way of reconstructing nonsensicality as falsehood. One can indeed devise a parallel argument to (8), in respect of (9) and (10), by engaging in semantic ascent, but that would not be to reconstruct (9) and (10) *themselves* as falsehoods, but to retreat to a metalinguistic transform of the nonsensicalities in question. But in the case of grammatical categorial nonsense like (13) there is more to be said. Consider the argument:

(14)   Whatever is rare is a (first-level) property/concept;

  Chairman Mao is a (zeroth-level) object;

  no (zeroth-level) object is a (first-level) property/concept.

_____

  So it is not the case that Chairman Mao is rare.

The argument looks sound. There is of course a serious problem with (14) *for the historical Frege*: it is not expressible within the resources he officially provided, because to formalize it we should require a variable ranging over both zeroth-level objects and first-level concepts/properties, but it was, as we have seen, fundamental to Frege's conception of the hierarchy that there is no such variable. At the zeroth level there are objects, whereas what we find at other levels are incomplete items—not objects, but (to put it in the paradoxical terms which are officially banned in the position of the reformed Fregean) non-objectual concepts (in general: functions). To admit a variable ranging over both objects and concepts would be, in effect, to assimilate concepts to objects: but that would be to renege on the basic constructive principle of the hierarchy, as Frege conceived it, and ultimately to render void his entitlement to his own account of the unity of the proposition, which in the basic case depends on there being two fundamentally different types of contributor to propositional unity, namely a complete and an incomplete one.

But now the principle that no (zeroth-level) object is a (first-level) concept, while not expressible within the resources provided *by* the hierarchy of the historical Frege, is nevertheless true *of* it, and is indeed, as I have just said, a basic principle of its construction.[188] So there must be a good philosophical sense in which, for the historical Frege, the premises of (14) are true and the argument itself valid. But then (14)'s conclusion, 'It is not the case that Chairman Mao is rare', must be true. Hence (13) is false, and indeed necessarily false, since the premises of (14) are all necessarily true. If that is right, we should not jib at reconstructing grammatically well-formed logical nonsense as falsehood.

---

[188] Cf. Conant [2], p. 385, on the connection with Wittgenstein's ladder.

I have been careful here to restrict the comparison to the historical Frege, because the position for the reformed Frege is of course different. The historical Frege can be forced to accept (14), in some sense, simply because he paradoxically acknowledged that concepts are, in some sense, objects (or are proxied by objects), given that they (or their proxies) can be referred to by means of proper names. But the reformed Frege rejects this, thereby avoiding paradox. Accordingly, the reformed Frege will not admit the conclusion of (14): he avoids it by refusing to accept the truth of the first and third premisses. He is enabled to repudiate these premisses because he rejects the existence of concepts (and of objectual proxies for concepts). On his adverbial approach to the reference of concept-expressions, these expressions refer in a conceptual way, but there are no such things as concepts to which they refer. Hence for the reformed Frege an argument along the lines of (14) cannot even be formulated grammatically. For the reformed Frege, (14) as it stands is unacceptable, because two of its premisses are false; if it were reformulated to make them conform to his principles, we would end up with logical nonsense all right, but it would be nonsense along the lines of (9), (10), and (11), not (12) or (13): that is, it would be ungrammatical breach of logical syntax, from which no conclusions could be drawn. Since we have rejected the position of the reformed Frege, in favour of what I called the impartial strategy (§41), we are entitled to accept (14), but without the embarrassment consequent on this acceptance which must be felt by the historical Frege.

56 Logical Syntax and the Context Principle

The assimilation of breaches of logical syntax to ordinary nonsense is characteristic of Wittgenstein's thought at all periods of his activity. Perhaps his best-known exposition of the point comes in the *Tractatus*:

'Socrates is identical' means nothing, because there is no [sc. monadic] property called 'identical'. The sentence is nonsense because we have not made an arbitrary stipulation, and not because the symbol in and of itself would be impermissible.[189]

'Socrates is identical' says nothing, because we have given no meaning to the word 'identical' as expressive of a [sc. monadic] property. For when it occurs as the sign of identity it symbolizes in a quite different manner—the signifying relation is a different one—and so the symbol too is in each case quite different: it is only an accident that both symbols have the sign in common.[190]

---

[189] [1], §5.473.   [190] [1], §5.4733. Cf. [5], I, §500.

According to the view outlined by Wittgenstein in these Tractarian passages, the sentence 'Socrates is identical' is meaningless because we have not given the word 'identical' a meaning as a monadic concept-expression. The sentence is *not* meaningless because of the meaning we *have* given to the word 'identical': it is not that 'identical' in that sentence *is* a dyadic concept-expression, and so renders that sentence meaningless since it in effect occurs there with an unfilled argument-place. For according to Wittgenstein, the sign 'identical' in the sentence 'Socrates is identical' is not the same symbol as the sign 'identical' in 'Socrates is identical with Plato'.[191] (We might say: it is the same sign but not the same word.)

The implications of this position are explored, and the position itself defended, by Cora Diamond.[192] One important consequence which she stresses is that we cannot identify the logical category of an expression outside a particular sentential context; nor can we identify a gap in a sentence as keyed to a particular grammatical category in isolation from any given completion. Dummett's example,

(13)   Chairman Mao is rare,

will illustrate this point. Dummett simply assumes that the word 'rare' is certifiable in advance of any given completion as a second-level expression, so that, given that 'Chairman Mao' is a proper name of the zeroth level, (13) can be branded without further ado as a piece of categorial nonsense. But that is surely incorrect. For in the sentence

(15)   These steaks are rare

the word 'rare' evidently functions as a first-level expression, at least assuming that we are working within the terms of the Fregean linguistic hierarchy, and that 'these steaks' belongs to the zeroth level. The latter proviso here is crucial, because the Wittgenstein–Diamond position is actually more radical than I have so far suggested: it is not merely the case that any given expression or gap in a sentence cannot be identified as keyed to any particular grammatical category in advance of producing a complete sentence; even the production of a complete sentence will not settle that question unequivocally. I assumed that 'these steaks' in (15) is a zeroth-level expression, but nothing in the sheer string of signs making up (15) settles that. There is nothing to prevent us, by dint of a stipulation which is metaphysically arbitrary (if psychologically or

---

[191] Cf. [1], §3.323.

[192] Diamond, esp. chs. 2 and 3. Cf. Palmer, pp. 52–3; Conant [1] and [2].

pragmatically non-arbitrary), from giving that sentence the meaning we would normally convey by

(16)   Wrynecks are rare

in which (again, assuming that we are deploying the Fregean hierarchy) 'rare' once more appears to be a second-level concept-expression.

I said that (15) could be read as bearing the meaning of (16), if we so stipulated, and that depending on which way it is read, different logical analyses would be forthcoming. But what *is* the logical analysis of (16)? I tried to fix that by inserting the proviso that (16) is to be understood as bearing its *normal* meaning. But what is that meaning? There is nothing in the string of signs composing (16) to fix its own normal meaning, because, as we have seen, that depends on how we stipulate the meanings, and grammatical categories, of its constituent expressions. That was indeed the problem with (15). There is no saying, just from (16) itself, whether (for example) 'wrynecks' occurs in it as a first-level expression, and 'rare' as a second-level expression, or whether 'wrynecks' is a zeroth-level expression and 'rare' a first-level expression. The appeal to *normal* meaning was an attempt to single out determinately one of the available options, but on the Wittgenstein–Diamond approach it is simply not possible to identify the grammatical category of an expression either taken on its own or by producing it in a sentential context: on this approach there are no 'normal' meanings. Conversely, to the extent that 'normal' meanings are admitted, the possibility of 'logical nonsense' will be genuine.[193]

The view that Diamond attributes to Wittgenstein,[194] namely that 'there is no such thing as putting together words with a certain [sc. antecedent] role in the language, or with certain [sc. antecedent] logical powers, so that on account of these roles or these powers, the whole is nonsense',[195] is an unacceptably extreme version of the context principle. That principle tells us that sentences are metaphysically prior to words (words are *made for* sentences); but a semantic theory works by applying the principle of compositionality—specifying word-meanings and rules of combination by which someone who has (explicit or

---

[193] Hence I do not find Conant's attempt at [2], nn. 74, 83, 84, 88 (pp. 442, 445–6), to limit the radical implications of his and Diamond's position convincing. For, in conceding that the understanding of a sentence requires that at least *some* of its signs symbolize in a precedented way (n. 83), Conant cannot (nor would he wish to) rule out the possibility that, in a given sentence, they *all* do. But in that case we cannot rule out 'a sentence's having a fully determinate yet logically impossible sense' (p. 404), its being logical nonsense consisting in 'the logically determinate but logically mutually incompatible senses that its parts already have' (p. 405).

[194] She also attributes the view to Frege, though I think with less justification: see §66 below.

[195] Diamond, p. 91; cf. Conant [1], pp. 44–5, 51–3; [2], pp. 398, 404–5, 414–24.

tacit) knowledge of the theory can construct, and understand, sentences. These constraints certainly pull in opposite directions,[196] but there is no need to react to this tension by jettisoning either the context principle or the principle of compositionality. Instead we should relativize the different priorities to distinct projects or points of view. Dummett provides us with a handy characterization of the needed relativization, noting that 'in the order of *explanation* the sense of a sentence is primary, but in the order of *recognition* the sense of a word is primary'.[197] Sentences are, by definition, the smallest unit of language by means of which we can *say* anything, so that we must treat word-meaning as conceptually dependent on sentence-meaning: what it is for a word to have meaning is for it to be fitted to play a certain role in a sentence. That is what Dummett means by ascribing explanatory priority to sentences. But sentences are discerned by the application of semantic theory to be composed of words, and new sentences are (usually) composed of old words: if we are to understand the phenomenon of creative language use—the ability of speakers to understand new sentences on the basis of their understanding of old ones—then we must regard sentence-meaning as a function of the meanings of the words composing it, and speakers' ability to comprehend new sentences as functionally dependent on their understanding of the meanings of old words and their familiarity with grammatical modes of composition. That is what Dummett means by ascribing recognitional priority to words.[198]

Diamond tries to accommodate the sense in which sentence-meaning is a function of word-meaning by adverting to 'the general rules fixing the content of expressions of the language',[199] but if 'the identification of a word in a particular sentence as playing a certain role there, as meaning a certain kind of thing, cannot be read directly off the rules', it is unclear what these rules are supposed to tell us, or how they are supposed to help us. It is true that 'we cannot speak about the meaning of expressions unless we know how to tell when two expressions *have the same meaning*'. But it does not follow that 'they do not have the same meaning unless the sentence in which the first occurs expresses a thought . . . which has an element in common with the thought expressed by the sentence in which the other occurs', since that ignores the possibility that we might determine two expressions to have the same meaning

---

[196] Cf. von Kutschera [1], p. 67.

[197] [2], p. 4. Cf. Thiel, pp. 124–32; Wiggins [1], pp. 24–5; Milne [2], p. 458; Davidson [2], pp. 35–6; Sullivan [4], p. 86.

[198] Ironically enough, Wittgenstein himself stressed the phenomenon of creative language use: [1], §§4.02–4.03. For Frege's commitment to this principle, see an undated letter to Jourdain, [22], p. 127, together with [19], pp. 36–7 ([21], pp. 378–9), and [26], pp. 243, 262.

[199] Diamond, p. 109. The ensuing quotes are from pp. 104, 109, and 109 respectively.

regardless of the particular sentences they occur in: that is, we have *no particular* sentences in mind.[200] And we are indeed obliged to recognize an activity of determining the meanings of words independently of their occurrence in particular sentences; otherwise we would render the learning of language, and the phenomenon of creative language use, mysterious. That recognition then makes theoretical room for a peculiarly syntactic kind of nonsense distinct from ordinary nonsense.

57 Proper Names, Singular Terms, and the 'Identity' Test

In Chapter 3 we saw that the historical Frege's attempt to secure the unity of the proposition by distinguishing between complete, or saturated, proper names and incomplete, or unsaturated, concept-expressions failed because he landed in a paradox, the notorious paradox of the concept *horse*. What I called the reformed Fregean strategy, which dispensed with concepts as referents of concept-expressions in favour of a conceptual way in which such expressions refer, managed to avoid paradox, but succumbed to another objection, that of arbitrariness: there was no reason to adopt a nominal approach to proper names and an adverbial approach to what I am calling primary monadic concept-expressions (i.e. to those monadic concept-expressions that Frege assigns to the first level of his linguistic hierarchy) rather than vice versa. One of the lessons of Frege's context principle, I argued, was that, if we regard sentences as saturated, all semantically significant subsentential lexical components (words) must be regarded as alike unsaturated. Since we have no independent reason to abjure the categories of name and object, we may as well apply them across the board, that is, to all words discerned by some adequate theory of meaning for the language in question, and their referents: at least, we must either do that or reject the categories altogether. If we continue to maintain the categories, as we surely may, it will follow that objects are, like their linguistic counterparts (their names) unsaturated.

The context principle has, then, an ontological as well as a linguistic version. (Of course there is also a corresponding context principle for the level of sense.[201]) In the familiar linguistic version, it states that words only have meaning in the context of a sentence: words are *made for* sentences. The

---

[200] But if 'the sentence' is changed to 'a (any) sentence', the passage quoted from Diamond can stand.

[201] See here Kleemeier, ch. 1.

ontological version of this principle might run: objects are *made for* propositions. Recall that, in my view, propositions are located at the most fundamental level of our ontology, as fundamental as that housing the entities making them up (objects and properties): I do not recognize worldly entities, such as actual or possible states of affairs, obtaining at a distinct and lower ontological level (§§23–4). Objects are not made for propositions in just any way: at least, not if their names are of distinct grammatical categories. For, as we have just seen, if their names are of distinct grammatical categories, it will be possible to produce combinations of words which breach the principles of congruence, and which accordingly are, in a categorial sense, nonsense. Corresponding to such nonsense items at the ontological level will be impossible combinations of objects—combinations that do not yield propositions.

Dummett has taken one of Frege's most important philosophical contributions to be not merely the formulation of the context principle in its linguistic version, but also the promulgation of a thesis to the effect that the linguistic version has conceptual priority over the ontological version in the sense, as Wright puts it,

that the notion of an object is posterior in the order of explanation to that of a singular term; that no better general explanation of the notion of an object can be given than in terms of the notions of singular term and reference; and that the truth of appropriate sentential contexts containing what is, by syntactic criteria, a singular term is sufficient to take care, so to speak, of its reference.[202]

We may dub this claim, following Wright, the 'syntactic priority thesis'. (Actually, as we shall see, the criteria employed to test for singular termhood, under the aegis of this thesis, are not purely syntactic in nature.[203] But the label is convenient and I adopt it.) Two points need to be noted immediately in connection with this thesis and Wright's way of expressing it.

The first point is terminological: as the reader will have noticed, Wright talks about the conceptual priority, in respect of the notion of an object, of the notion of a *singular term* rather than that of a *proper name*. We may take singular terms to constitute an even wider class of expression than what I have so far called proper names 'in Frege's broad sense'. The latter include not just proper names strictly so called (proper names whose sense is *de re*), but also definite descriptions; singular terms may be taken to embrace both these classes, and also noun-phrases such as 'what we need to complete the

[202] [1], p. 24. See further ibid., chs. 1 and 2; Dummett [1], pp. 38–41; [2], pp. 55–8, 254–6, 494–8; [3], pp. 234–48, 382–4; Tugendhat [2], esp. chs. 3 and 20; Stevenson, pp. 218–19; Brandom [1], p. 279; Hale [2], pp. 1–14 and [3], pp. 31–71; Stevens [1], p. 230 n. 37; Potter [1], pp. 65–8.
[203] Rumfitt [3], pp. 197–8.

puzzle', indefinite descriptions such as 'a policeman' (at least on some occasions of use: §60 below), and indeed any nominal expression to which the notion of non-referential satisfaction by an object is applicable. By my lights (§15), only proper names strictly so called *refer to* their satisfying objects; descriptions and noun-phrases refer to complex conceptual entities, and are *satisfied by* the (concrete or abstract) objects (if any) which they are, in an intuitive but non-semantic sense, 'about', not by the complex conceptual entities to which they refer. For the moment, however, we can assume that satisfaction by objects is good enough for the purposes of the syntactic priority thesis, so that the theoretical priority asserted by that thesis attaches to singular terms in general, as I have defined them, not proper names in particular (either in Frege's broad or my narrow sense); the passage I have quoted from Wright can accordingly be read as though by 'reference' he meant 'reference or satisfaction'. But the importance of the distinction between reference and satisfaction will reassert itself in due course.

The second preliminary point to note is that the syntactic priority thesis is quite distinct from the doctrine of linguistic idealism. Both theses can be represented as taking their cue from the context principle: but whereas linguistic idealism interprets this principle as teaching us that we have, in general, no pre-linguistic access to reality and, ultimately, that reality is itself constituted by our linguistic access to it, the syntactic priority thesis is the much more precise claim to the effect that the syntactic category of *singular term* (as opposed to concept-expression) has priority over, and provides a theoretical route to, a corresponding ontological 'category' of *object* (as opposed to concept). Both linguistic idealism and the syntactic priority thesis may be thought of as interpretations of the context principle, but they are independent such interpretations: at least they are one-way independent, for although it is plausible that the syntactic priority thesis entails some version of linguistic idealism, there is no reverse entailment from linguistic idealism, as I have stated that, to the syntactic priority thesis. The syntactic priority thesis goes beyond a bare linguistic idealism to the extent that it seeks to ground an object–concept distinction in the linguistic distinction between singular term and concept-expression. So in rejecting the syntactic priority thesis, as I shall go on to do, I am not threatening the linguistic idealism which is the ground of this investigation.

It was allegedly on the basis of an (implicit) appeal to the syntactic priority thesis that Frege sought to show, in the *Grundlagen*, that numbers are objects: according to this interpretation, Frege did not try to argue that in establishing canonical means of referring to numbers we must resort to the use of singular terms *because numbers are objects* (as opposed to concepts); rather, the idea is that, contrariwise, *because we refer to or talk about numbers using singular terms*—that is, because we can make true statements in which mathematical properties are predicated of entities apparently introduced by singular-term number words—numbers must be objects. I am not now going to pursue the exegetical questions that this issue raises, though in the next chapter I shall enter a reservation about the extent of Frege's commitment to a syntactic priority thesis, at least in his mature writings.[204] Here I wish to examine the syntactic priority thesis from a systematic point of view.[205]

If the syntactic priority thesis is to have any force, it must be possible to isolate purely linguistic tests for singular termhood, and there has accordingly been some expenditure of effort in the literature to identify such tests. Frege himself started this trend in the *Grundlagen* by observing that statements of number—what he neutrally calls 'Zahlangaben', that is, statements of the form 'There are nFs'—can be parsed as identity statements of the form 'The number of Fs is n',[206] the nominal status of the numerical term here being indicated by its figuring (in the right way) in an identity statement: for (we may take Frege to be supposing) the sign of identity is constitutively flanked by singular terms.[207] But how can we be sure that the 'is', in 'The number of Fs is n' is genuinely a sign of identity, as Frege claims, rather than a sign of predication? In particular, how can we assure ourselves of this without presupposing an independent ability to identify the category of singular terms? For any such presupposition would clearly import a vicious circularity into the project of giving syntactic criteria for singular termhood. Frege himself seems to rely on just such a presupposition when he argues that the identitative status of the 'is' in 'The number of Jupiter's moons is four' is guaranteed by our being able to rewrite this sentence—here exploiting the fact that the construction of a numeral with the definite article is available in German—as 'The number of Jupiter's moons is [the] four' (*Die Zahl der Jupitersmonde ist die vier*), or 'The number of Jupiter's moons is the number 4', together with the fact that the definite article serves to ensure that the referent (or, as we should rather say: the satisfier) of descriptions such as 'the number four' is objectual.[208] But, clearly, if we already knew that the definite article had this property, we should not need to be engaged in seeking a warrant that the 'is' of the sentence 'The number of Jupiter's moons is the (number) four' is identitative: for we wanted

---

[204] For reservations about Frege's commitment to the syntactic priority thesis in the *Grundlagen*, see Milne [1].

[205] For an early version of the syntactic priority thesis, see Geulincx [2], i/i, pp. 211–15, esp. p. 212. Cf. Nuchelmans [5], p. 116.

[206] [3], §57.   [207] So too Tugendhat, [2], chs. 19–21. Cf. Künne [1], pp. 23–4, 105–6.

[208] [3], §§38, 51, 57, 66 n., 68 n.

the successful outcome of this search to yield an *argument* for the nominal status of terms flanking the identity sign. Moreover, the suggestion that we *can* identify expressions formed with the definite article as singular terms suffers from the drawback of parochialism, and so, ultimately, of circularity: for we have not been provided with any means of identifying an expression of an arbitrary language *as* the definite article, and it is hard to see how such means could be provided in a non-question-begging way.[209]

58 Proper Names, Leibniz's Law, and the Identity of Indiscernibles

A potentially more promising line would be to pursue another suggestion of Frege's, namely that what distinguishes the identity relation from predication, in general, is that identity obeys the following principle, obtained by combining Leibniz's Law (the indiscernibility of identicals) with the principle of the identity of indiscernibles:

(ID) $x = y \leftrightarrow \forall F(Fx \leftrightarrow Fy)$.

Frege explicitly calls (ID) a 'definition' of identity.[210] Does (ID) now enable us to isolate the singular terms of a language, as those terms that can meaningfully and truly flank the sign of identity so defined? It does not enable us to do so if we maintain our rag-bag category of singular terms. For, as is familiar, (ID) does not hold without exception in modal and epistemic contexts if the substitution class for expressions occupying the 'x' and 'y' positions include definite descriptions;[211] and a little thought shows that the same stricture applies to noun-phrases, and indeed to any linguistic expression to which the notion of non-referential satisfaction by an object is applicable. By contrast, it is now widely accepted that (ID) *does* hold, at least in modal contexts, where the substitution class for these variables is restricted to proper names strictly so called (names whose sense is *de re*). And it can be argued—though this point is admittedly more controversial—that the same goes for epistemic contexts.[212] If that is right, these contexts do not prevent obedience to (ID) from serving as a criterion for *strict* proper namehood.

But even if we accept that modal and epistemic contexts do not present a problem for the enterprise of using (ID) to yield a purely syntactic test

---

[209] See here Wright [1], p. 54.
[210] [3], §65. Cf. Church [6], p. 300 n. 502; Wright [1], pp. 3, 27; Dummett [5], pp. 112–13.
[211] Rumfitt [3], p. 206.   [212] See here my [4].

of (strict) proper namehood, there remains the following difficulty. Wright notes that the proposal fails to distinguish between statements of identity and what Russell called 'formal equivalences', that is, statements of the form '$\forall x(Fx \leftrightarrow Gx)$':

> Frege himself regarded such statements as expressing the *analogue* of identity for *concepts*; and the analogy is precisely in respect of the logical properties of identity statements. The difference is only and purely in respect of the type of expression needed to fill in the blanks—but that is just what, in the present context, we are not allowed to appeal to.[213]

Wright's point is that (ID) might be subject to a systematic permutation, so that the lower-case letters are taken to range over Fregean first-level concepts, and the upper-case letters to range over Fregean zeroth-level objects, without upsetting the truth of the law, so formulated, provided that we restrict ourselves to a first-order language without modal or epistemic vocabulary.

It is natural to object here that (ID) will be false if the customary interpretation of the lower- and upper-case variables is permuted in the manner indicated: for the mere co-extensiveness of two concept-expressions in the actual world—and that is all the right-hand side of (ID) gives us—while a necessary condition, is not a sufficient condition for the identity of the concept or property introduced by one concept-expression with that introduced by the other. In order to secure that identity, we need to be assured that the concept-expressions are co-extensive in all possible worlds, and are either semantically simple, or identically constructed from concept-expressions which are co-extensive in all possible worlds (or are themselves identically constructed from concept-expressions which are . . . co-extensive in all possible worlds). This feature of concept-expressions does not, however, drive a wedge between their behaviour and the behaviour of proper names when expressions of these types are plugged into the left-hand side of (ID), for it is true of Fregean objects too that mere possession of the same properties in the actual world, while necessary, is not sufficient for identity. We can only be assured of the identity, in this world, of one purported Fregean object with 'another' if it is guaranteed that 'they' share the same properties in all possible worlds. It appears, then, that (ID) is false *both* when the variables are given their customary interpretation, according to which the lower-case variables range over Fregean objects and the upper-case ones over Fregean first-level concepts, *and* under the permuting interpretation which reverses these assignments.

[213] [1], p. 55. Cf. Frege [9], p. 320 ([21], p. 184); [26], pp. 131–3, 197–8; Geach [7], p. 227; Bell [1], p. 30; [3], p. 185.

Of course, it follows from what has been said that we can generate a true version of (ID) if we suitably modalize its right-hand side, to obtain:

(IDM) $x = y \leftrightarrow \Box \forall F(Fx \leftrightarrow Fy)$.

But (IDM) is now true not merely under the customary interpretation of the variables, but also under the permutation. (I am continuing to assume that epistemic contexts do not present a problem for the truth of this formula: what is certain is that if they do present a problem, they present it even-handedly in respect of both proper names and concept-expressions.) Hence our formulation, whether in the original version (ID) or the revised version (IDM), does not permit us to isolate proper names, and the reason is that the relationship these formulations chart between proper names and (Fregean first-level) concept-expressions is isomorphic to an inverse relationship obtaining between (Fregean first-level) concept-expressions and proper names.

In the light of our reflections so far in this chapter, this upshot should come as no surprise. What we have already seen is that, if we try to construct an alternative linguistic hierarchy to Frege's, one that locates Frege's zeroth-level proper names at the first level, his monadic first-level concept-expressions at the zeroth level, and makes further consequent adjustments, we arrive at a hierarchy that is as adequate as Frege's for the purpose of imposing a categorial syntax on an object-language. That reflects the fact that the Fregean asymmetry between saturated proper name and unsaturated concept-expression cannot, absolutely speaking, be justified. Nor, of course, as we have observed, can the alternative, anti-Fregean asymmetry: as far as the saturated–unsaturated distinction goes, we should regard all semantically significant subsentential lexical components as unsaturated names, the distinct levels of the hierarchy then being taken to correspond not to any fundamental ontological differentiation, such as Frege envisaged to obtain between the references of proper names and those of concept-expressions, but merely to distinctions of grammatical category. If that is the right picture, it should come as no shock now to discover that the syntactic test we wish to associate with the identity relation for zeroth-level proper names, as captured in the above formulations (ID) and (IDM), can individuate that relation only up to isomorphism with the analogue of that relation obtaining in respect of Fregean first-level monadic concept-expressions, to which proper names have equal and opposite valency. For if, as I have argued, there is no absolute respect in which whatever items we locate at the zeroth level of a linguistic hierarchy belong there rather than at the first level, we should indeed not expect the (absolute) syntactic characteristics of the monadic items we choose to locate at the zeroth level to differ from those of the monadic items we choose to locate at the first level.

We have also noted that the fact that proper names and the monadic concept-expressions of a language do not bear a unique allegiance to any particular level of a linguistic hierarchy does not mean that the different levels of a linguistic hierarchy collapse. It remains the case that the zeroth and first levels, however they are populated, must be *differently* populated: they are keyed to the distinct categories of two fundamental types of expression—proper names and primary monadic concept-expressions—so that one of these types of expression must be assigned to the zeroth level and the other to the first level (though we cannot be more precise than that), and the failure of speakers to give tacit recognition to this point would lead to their producing nonsense. Application of (IDM) will now determine the identity relation for zeroth-level expressions, whatever these are; its analogue will determine the corresponding relation for monadic first-level expressions, whatever these are. But since (IDM) is not, within the resources of an object-language, syntactically distinguishable from its analogue, it will not be determinate at the level of the object-language, in any given case of application, whether we are applying (IDM) or its analogue. It will, of course, be determinate at the level of the metalanguage which of (IDM) and its analogue we are applying to any given fragment of object-language discourse, assuming that the metalanguage contains an internalized philosophical grammar assigning object-language expressions to levels of a linguistic hierarchy. But since there is no uniquely correct way of making these metalinguistic assignments, there is no uniquely correct way of settling which of the isomorphic applications of (IDM) a given fragment of object-language discourse embodies: there will be distinct equally good ways of arranging the matter. So there is a sense in which, for the speakers of an object-language who apply (IDM), it is indeterminate which level of a linguistic hierarchy they are applying it to: but that is no embarrassment, because it merely reflects the fact, which obtains anyway, that there is no fixing uniquely to which level of a metalinguistically specified linguistic hierarchy a given (primary) monadic expression belongs.

The upshot of these considerations is that we can expect no assistance from the direction of (IDM) towards the project of giving a purely syntactic characterization of proper names (and hence of singular terms in general). The appeal to the unique status of the identity relation as embodied in (IDM) will fix relative categories of relevant monadic expressions: it will partition expressions which pass the test into distinct congruence classes, comprising proper names strictly so called on the one hand, and primary monadic concept-expressions on the other: for, of these categories of linguistic expression, the identity sign may only be significantly and truly flanked by expressions drawn from the same category. But it will not fix uniquely which level of the linguistic hierarchy these expressions inhabit.

59 The Negation Asymmetry Test

A second test which has been proposed for the purpose of isolating singular terms is the so-called 'negation asymmetry test'.[214] According to this test, the principle

$$\forall A \exists B \forall C(A^*C \text{ is true iff it is not the case that } B^*C \text{ is true}),$$

where 'A', 'B', and 'C' range over expressions and the star indicates concatenation, is said to be true if we let 'A' and 'B' range over concept-expressions and 'C' over singular terms, whereas it is false if we let 'A' and 'B' range over singular terms and 'C' range over concept-expressions. The test is held to work because for any given singular term 'a' and concept-expression 'F', such that 'Fa' holds, we can always find a complementary concept-expression 'G' such that 'Ga' fails to hold. If necessary, 'G' can be specially introduced and simply defined to hold of all and only those objects of which 'F' fails to hold. But for any given object a there is not, in general, another object b such that b fails to possess all and only those properties possessed by a. Indeed we can put it more strongly: there is necessarily not such an object, for (here we may temporarily invoke Aristotelian category theory) among the properties of any given object there will be both generic and specific ones: an object might be, for example, both an animal and a man. Now another object which lacked all and only properties possessed by the given object would—if, counting negative properties as properties, we infer that the other object also possesses all and only those properties lacked by the given object—have *both* to enjoy a different specification under the same genus (and indeed more than one such specification, where available) *and* to fall under another genus (indeed to fall under all the other genera). But that is clearly an impossible demand: for then the 'contradictory' of Socrates would have to be (at the very least) both another sort of animal than a man, and not an animal at all. The negation asymmetry test is typically regarded as embodying Aristotle's claim that a substance has no contrary (though it is better to put the point by saying that a substance has no 'contradictory').[215]

As commentators have noted, however, the test fails to isolate just the items Frege wishes to locate at the zeroth level.[216] We cannot get at these expressions by defining them as the ones for which the principle *fails* to hold when they

[214] Geach [1], p. 463; [8], pp. 143–6; Strawson [2], ch. 5; [6], pp. 15–24; Dummett [2], pp. 63–4; Künne [1], pp. 24–7; Wright [1], pp. 11–12, 55–7; Denyer [1], pp. 176–9; Hale [3], pp. 39–47, 52–3, 67–71; [4], pp. 191–2; Stirton [2], pp. 197–205. I follow Wright's formulation of the test.
[215] *Cat.* 3b24–5.   [216] Wright [1], pp. 55–6; Hale [3], pp. 42–7, 52–3; [4], p. 197.

are selected for 'A', for the principle will also fail when Fregean first-level concept-expressions are selected for 'A' and second-level concept-expressions for 'C' (for example, it is not in general the case that something in the room is red if and only if it is not the case that something in the room has the same or another property, such as the property of being non-red). Nor can we isolate singular terms by defining them as those expressions for which the principle *holds* when they are selected for 'C', for the principle will hold, not merely when singular terms are selected for 'C' and Fregean first-level concept-expressions for 'A' and 'B', but also when Fregean first-level concept-expressions are selected for 'C' and suitable unary first-order quantifiers, which are Fregean second-level concept-expressions, are selected for 'A' and 'B' (for example, something in the room is red if and only if it is not the case that nothing in the room is red). Generalizing—that is, leaving it open that a language may contain (uses of) expressions assigned to arbitrarily high levels of a linguistic hierarchy—if we have groups of expressions 'A', 'B' and 'C' for which the principle *fails*, the best we can say is that, if the expressions 'A' and 'B' are of level n, the level of 'C' is $n + 1$, whereas if the principle *holds* of these expressions, the best we can say is that, if the expressions 'A' and 'B' are of level n, the level of 'C' is $n - 1$.

The importance of the generalization is this. If one ignored the general case, one might be tempted by the following strategy mooted by Bob Hale to employ the negation asymmetry test in order to isolate singular terms.[217] First we isolate quantifiers, taking these to be expressions which pass the test come what may, when selected for 'A' and 'B';[218] then, progressively, we isolate first-level concept-expressions, these being expressions which pass the test when selected for 'A' and 'B', so long as quantifiers (already identified) are not selected for 'C'; finally, we can isolate singular terms, since these are identifiable as expressions which fail the test when selected for 'A' and 'B', so long as first-level concept-expressions (already identified) are selected for 'C'. The reason why this strategy yields no general method of isolating singular terms is correctly identified by William Stirton, who notes that the strategy rests on the unwarrantable assumption that the language to which the tests are being applied contains no expressions (or uses of expressions) whose location in the linguistic hierarchy is above the second level.[219] Of course, it would be open to Hale to extend his method so as to meet the strict letter of Stirton's objection, that is, so as to deal with languages keyed to linguistic hierarchies comprising more than three levels. Evidently, we could construct a

---

[217] [3], pp. 42–7. Hale himself rejects the attempt, though not for the reason I go on to give.
[218] Cf. Rumfitt [3], p. 205.   [219] [2], pp. 202–5.

more general algorithm along the suggested lines that would be adequate to a language whose linguistic hierarchy comprised four, five, or indeed any finite number of levels. But what the method cannot do is yield an algorithm for the infinite case, the problem being, to put it briefly, that when faced with a linguistic hierarchy comprising infinitely many levels, there would be no point of entry at which we might start applying the method.

Applying Hale's strategy by starting at the highest level of the linguistic hierarchy does not in general work, then, because a linguistic hierarchy is not guaranteed to have a highest level. But it must have a lowest level. Perhaps, Wright conjectures,[220] we may still be able to distinguish singular terms from other kinds of expression by deploying the following thought. What distinguishes singular terms is not simply that the principle fails when they are selected for 'A', but that there is then no range of selection for 'C' for which the principle holds; on the other hand, when Fregean first-level concept-expressions or second-level concept-expressions are selected for 'A', there is in each case a restriction on the range of 'C' for which the principle will hold, namely the restriction to singular terms or to Fregean first-level concept-expressions respectively. (Clearly the strategy is generalizable to hierarchies with any number of levels, even infinitely many.) Wright rejects this attempt to isolate singular terms on the basis that there will normally be expressions in a language falling outside a linguistic hierarchy of levels: such expressions, he claims, will not only fail the test when selected for 'A', but will also fail to determine a range of selection for 'C' for which the principle holds. Wright offers the preposition 'of' as an example of a selection for 'A' for which there is no 'B' such that the principle holds for all 'C', and no restriction on 'C' enabling the principle to hold in the restricted cases. Wright's claim that there are expressions that share these features with singular terms is surely correct. But it is incorrect to imply that the claim depends on assuming that not all semantically significant subsentential lexical expressions are assigned a place in the linguistic hierarchy; and the assumption is anyway false. Let me explain.

My argument so far has been, briefly, that the context principle tells us that all semantically significant subsentential lexical expressions are unsaturated, if any are. But, I have suggested, that does not mean that we should jettison the concept of reference or the notion of an object. On the contrary, the way is now clear to regarding all such expressions as referring to objects. For each expression that object will be just what the speaker of the language has to think of in order to count as understanding the expression. A theory of meaning for the language will have as its task the specification of referents for each semantically significant subsentential lexical component of the language, together with appropriate compositional clauses. What *counts* for these purposes as semantically significant is fixed for us, theoretically, by the conception of a correct theory of meaning. That is, a semantically significant expression is determined as being just that sort of expression for which a correct, recursively based theory of meaning for the language in question has to give a meaning-specification; and a correct theory of meaning, for these purposes, is a theory explicit knowledge of which would suffice for understanding the language.

Now, given that all semantically significant subsentential lexical expressions are unsaturated, they will perforce combine in ways appropriate to their respective grammatical categories with other such expressions, and the linguistic hierarchy of levels simply has the function, as we have seen, of modelling these relationships—nothing more than that, but also nothing less. Consequently, it would introduce an intolerable tension into the proceedings to acknowledge a kind of expression, such as Wright supposes the preposition 'of' to be, which is a semantically significant subsentential lexical component (a word) but which occupies no position in the hierarchy. To be a semantically significant subsentential lexical component just *is* to enjoy some location in the linguistic hierarchy—not necessarily an absolute location, as I keep stressing, but at any rate a relative one. (Wright is in effect proposing to treat 'of' as syncategorematic;[221] but the reader will recall that I rejected the traditional distinction between the categorematic and the syncategorematic in §§38–40.) The specification of the meaning of 'of' may not be a very straightforward matter, because it may be the case that that sign is associated with a number of different, if related, meanings. But at any rate in what we can perhaps regard, for the sake of illustration, as the basic case, namely its occurrence in possessive phrases of the form *the F of N.N.* ('the death of Hector', 'the reign of Charlemagne' etc.), 'of' refers to a function from the referent of a definite description to a function from the referent of a proper name to the referent of a definite description, and hence, assuming that proper names are located at the zeroth level, and so definite descriptions at the second level, is an expression of the third level.[222] It remains the case, as Wright observes—this is correct,

---

[221] Cf. J. Harris, II. iii, p. 261: 'A PREPOSITION is a Part of Speech, devoid it self of Signification, but so formed as to unite two Words that are significant, and that refuse to co-alesce or unite of themselves'.

[222] Cf. Cresswell, p. 98. Note that the fact that some uses of 'of' are syntactically redundant ('all of the men') does not show that, in such uses, the word is syncategorematic, as Larson and Segal imply (pp. 89–91). Similarly, their suggestion that the fact that in some languages conjunction is expressed by appropriate juxtaposition does not show that 'and' is 'a purely formal mark of the conjunction structure, rather than . . . an autonomous lexical item that actually contributes the meaning of conjunction' (p. 91). Rather, what such examples show is that syntactic relations may themselves 'contribute the meaning

and independent of his mistaken claim that some expressions cannot be placed in the linguistic hierarchy—that where we have groups of expressions '*A*', '*B*', and '*C*' for which the principle fails, and where the expression we select for '*A*' introduces no restriction on the range of selection for '*C*' enabling the principle to hold in those cases, there is insufficient evidence to warrant the conclusion that the expression we have selected for '*A*' is a singular term.

But one might now raise the following query: even if singular terms are not the only expressions which fail the test, in general, when selected for '*A*', and which introduce no restriction on the range of selection for '*C*' enabling the principle to hold in those cases, can we not isolate singular terms as the only expressions which *both* (i) satisfy this condition *and* (ii) when they are selected for '*C*', determine a restriction on the range of selection for '*A*' (namely, to Fregean first-level concept-expressions) such that the principle then *holds*? Can we not, in other words, effect a pincer movement on singular terms by isolating them as those expressions for which our principle both fails, under certain specified circumstances, and holds, under other specified circumstances? The answer to this question, it seems to me, is that, insofar as this pincer movement is successful, what it isolates is not the class of singular terms, but that of singular terms and primary monadic concept-expressions. (Unary first-order quantifiers fail (i).) For consider again the anti-Fregean strategy, which locates a concept-expression like 'is wise' at its zeroth level. This strategy thinks of a sentence like 'Socrates is wise' rather as the Fregean would think of the equivalent sentence 'Wisdom Socratizes'. What will the anti-Fregean strategy say of the behaviour of the concept-expression 'is wise' when it is plugged into the negation asymmetry test? It will say exactly the same as what the Fregean strategy says of the behaviour of 'Socrates'. On the anti-Fregean account of the matter 'is wise' passes tests (i) and (ii): when 'is wise' is selected for '*A*', the principle fails, and there is no restriction on the range of selection for '*C*' enabling the principle to hold in these cases; and when it is selected for '*C*', there is a restriction on the range of selection for '*A*' such that the principle holds. The second of these claims is obvious: a restriction to the unary first-order quantifiers will fill the bill. But the first claim may well seem implausible, and appears to conflict with what I reported, when I introduced the negation asymmetry test, to be the received view of the cases in which the test's associated principle holds and fails to hold. Let us therefore consider this claim in more detail.

Clearly the principle will not hold, if 'is wise' is selected for '*A*', come what may, and equally clearly it is no good restricting the range of '*C*' to

---

of conjunction': it is not that 'and' is semantically redundant, but that syntax may be semantically significant. This idea will be important when we come to examine the logical copula.

the unary first-order quantifiers. But suppose we select a proper name like 'Socrates' for '*C*': will that restriction not enable the principle to hold, when we select 'is wise' for '*A*'? As I noted above, this is the received view of the way the test works out given these selections. But that view trades on a Fregean understanding of the selected terms; on an anti-Fregean understanding of them, things look different. In this case the principle fails because there is (to put the anti-Fregean's case in Fregean terms) nothing that does *not* Socratize if and only if wisdom *does* Socratize. It might be protested that there is indeed such a thing, namely what we might call non-wisdom, which is really the property of *not being wise*. But that manœuvre, if it worked, would also entitle us to introduce a purported contradictory object to Socrates—call it 'Non-socrates'—defined as instantiating all and only those properties Socrates does not instantiate. For the 'negation' of the zeroth-level object that the anti-Fregean identifies with the referent of 'is wise' (in Fregean terms this is the object wisdom) is not the Fregean first-level property of not being wise: rather, it is the saturated entity instantiating all and only those properties which count (on the anti-Fregean strategy) as referents of first-level concept-expressions, and which are not instantiated by the zeroth-level referent of 'is wise', just as, when Socrates is located at the zeroth level of the ontological hierarchy, the 'contradictory' of Socrates, Non-socrates, would, if such a curiosity existed, be just that object instantiating all and only those (Fregean) first-level properties (of all sorts, so including negative, disjunctive, etc. ones) that are not instantiated by Socrates. In this latter case, we agreed earlier that there is and indeed could be no such object; likewise, there is and can be no such object as the referent of 'is not wise' when this referent is conceived, as it is on the anti-Fregean strategy, as a zeroth-level object. For given that the anti-Fregean referent of 'is wise' does not instantiate Hesperus the cat and does not instantiate Xanthos the horse either, the entity we introduced as the 'contradictory' of the referent of 'is wise', taken as a zeroth-level object, would have the remarkable feature of instantiating both Hesperus the cat and Xanthos the horse, not to mention a huge assortment of other disparate properties. Anyone who thinks that the resulting combination of properties is not too outrageous to be ascribed to the anti-Fregean referent of 'is not wise' should re-examine his or her conscience on the viability of Non-socrates.

Consider the point in this way. For the Fregean, 'wisdom' is a proper name referring to a zeroth-level object, the property of being wise, and as such it passes the test for singular termhood based on the negation asymmetry test. That is, there is no object non-wisdom lacking all and only the properties wisdom has, and so (taking negative properties to be properties, as before) having all and only the properties it lacks. For, to make the move parallel to the one we made when originally considering the viability of Non-socrates, such an object would both have to fall under the same genus as wisdom, but under a different species—and so would have to fall under a virtue other than wisdom, say justice—and would also have to fall under a different genus altogether (indeed under all other genera), so that non-wisdom would have the contradictory status of being both a virtue and not a virtue. But now the anti-Fregean strategy classifies 'is wise' as a zeroth-level expression, referring to (in Fregean terms) the property of being wise. (Recall that we are obliged to employ these terms, given that English has an internalized Fregean grammar: it would be nonsense to say, what one would like here to say, that the zeroth-level expression 'is wise' refers to the zeroth-level object is wise.) So on the anti-Fregean strategy 'is wise', and not 'Socrates', satisfies the conditions established above ((i) and (ii)) for singular termhood. Hence, in summary, those conditions lay down criteria met by potential zeroth-level expressions in general, not singular terms in particular.

The test we examined in the previous section, based on (ID) and (IDM), did not, as we saw, isolate singular terms; what it did achieve was a partitioning of expressions satisfying it into distinct congruence classes comprising proper names (strictly so called) and primary monadic concept-expressions. The application of the negation asymmetry test in this section has had a similar though not identical upshot. As we have seen, the application of that test and its associated principle in (i) and (ii) above does not isolate only singular terms, but rather, when the anti-Fregean strategy is taken into account, both singular terms and primary monadic concept-expressions. The application of the negation asymmetry test, via tests (i) and (ii), suffices, then, to distinguish these two basic types of expression—singular terms and primary monadic concept-expressions—though it does not determine a unique assignment of them to the levels of a linguistic hierarchy.

60 Dummett's Tests for Singular Termhood

With these points in mind we can approach a final set of tests for singular termhood, originally proposed by Dummett, which we may reproduce as follows:[223] '*a*' is a singular term if and only if

(1) For any sentence '$F(a)$', the inference from '$F(a)$' to 'There is something such that '$F(it)$' is valid; and

---

[223] See Dummett [2], pp. 58–60; Wright [1], p. 57. Cf. Strawson [1], p. 157.

(2) For any sentences '$F(a)$' and '$G(a)$', the inference from '$F(a)$' and '$G(a)$' to 'There is something such that F(it) and G(it)' is valid; and

(3) For any sentences '$F(a)$' and '$G(a)$', the inference from 'It is true of a that F(it) or G(it)' to '$F(a)$ or $G(a)$' is valid.

The point of these tests is to exclude certain pretenders, grammatically congruent with singular terms, to the status of singular termhood. Thus (1) is designed to exclude 'nothing', along with cognate phrases of the form 'no Fs', (2) to exclude 'something', and cognate phrases of the form 'some Fs', and (3) to exclude 'everything', and cognate phrases of the form 'every F'. And the tests exclude other quantifiers, such as 'most', 'many', 'several', and cognates. (It has been objected that the tests do not exclude quantifier-phrases that are necessarily uniquely satisfied, such as 'some even prime'.[224] But this objection confuses logical and mathematical necessity.[225])

One apparent difficulty with the tests as they stand—this difficulty is raised by Dummett himself—is that although they exclude the quantifier-phrases they are designed to exclude, they do not appear to exclude indefinite descriptions such as 'a policeman', at least not when these occur as grammatical complements in sentences like 'John is a policeman', and where the generalizations introduced by the test count (in Fregean terms) as second-order. (This is obvious for tests (1) and (2); (3) is a more problematic.[226]) To deal with this kind of case—in effect, to discriminate between applications of tests (1) and (2) in which 'something' is a first-order quantifier and applications in which it is a second-order quantifier—Dummett introduces a fourth condition, which may be reproduced as follows:[227]

(4) The conclusion of an inference of the sort described in (1) or (2) is never such that requesting specification can lead to a point at which the demand for a further specification, although grammatically well-formulated, would be rejected as evincing a misunderstanding of the conclusion.

[224] Rumfitt [3], pp. 203–5.   [225] Cf. Etchemendy, p. 25.   [226] Wright [1], p. 58.
[227] Dummett [2], pp. 67–9. I follow Wright's version ([1], p. 62), which adapts Dummett's own expression of the test in the light of criticisms by Hale ([1], pp. 291–3), the details of which need not concern us here. See further Hale [2], pp. 15–21, and [3], pp. 37–9, 53–67: Hale modifies tests (1)–(4) in order to cater for the fact (which Dummett himself stresses at [2], p. 59) that the classification of linguistic expressions as singular terms or otherwise must be conceived to be arrived at not *simpliciter*, but relative to particular contexts of use. We can, however, abstract from these refinements, because Hale's modifications of Dummett's tests (and his putting them together with the negation asymmetry test in order to deliver a complete package capable of testing for singular termhood: cf. his [4], pp. 197–9) do not engage with the difficulty which interests me here, namely the question whether the tests can distinguish between singular terms and primary monadic concept-expressions when the anti-Fregean strategy is taken into account. A similar remark applies to Stirton's discussions ([1], and [2], pp. 194–6) of the problems posed for the tests by existential statements.

The point here is this: if the inferences in (1) and (2) are, on any occasion of use, applied to singular terms as substituends for '*a*' and Fregean first-level concept-expressions as substituends for '*F*' and '*G*', then the question 'Which *F*?' ought to have a determinate answer. For example, if the inference in question is from 'John has great respect for a Dundee policeman' to 'There is something such that John has great respect for it', and the question 'Which Dundee policeman?' is, on some occasion when this inference is performed, accepted as legitimate, and in principle capable of receiving an answer like 'That one over there', or 'The one mentioned in this newspaper report', etc., then the 'something' of the inference's conclusion was on that occasion functioning as a first-order quantifier (a Fregean second-level concept-expression), and the indefinite noun-phrase of the premiss was consequently functioning as a singular term. If, on the other hand, the question is on some occasion rejected as, though grammatically well formed, having no answer (perhaps accompanied by such words as 'No, I meant Dundee policemen in general'), then the 'something' of the inference's conclusion was on that occasion functioning as a second-order quantifier (a Fregean third-level concept-expression), and the indefinite noun-phrase of the premiss accordingly as a Fregean second-level expression.

Further, we need (4) to rule out words that can occur either as adjectives or as nouns, such as names of colours and numbers.[228] 'Vermilion', for example, passes (1)–(3), but is weeded out by (4). Likewise for definite descriptions such as 'the whale', when these function as Fregean first-level concept-expressions.[229] But what about words and phrases which can only occupy (grammatical) *predicate* position in a sentence? Hale has argued that these raise a serious problem for the tests.[230] The suggestion is that the tests do not after all succeed in isolating singular terms, for while they are competent to distinguish singular terms from quantifier-phrases and indefinite descriptions (when these function as second-level expressions), they do not distinguish them from pure adjectives and other non-substantival expressions when these occur as grammatical predicates. In other words, the claim is that these tests are incompetent to fix the levels of expressions which pass them, for they will be satisfied not only if '*a*' is a singular term, '*F*' and '*G*' primary monadic concept-expressions, and 'something' a first-order quantifier, but also if '*a*' is a non-substantival primary monadic concept-expression of adjectival or verbal form, such as 'good at squash' or 'runs', '*F*' and '*G*' singular terms, and 'something' a second-order quantifier. The extra test (4) does not help to rule

---

[228] Cf. Dummett [2], p. 72.   [229] On both these cases see Wright [1], p. 59.
[230] [3], pp. 38–9, 51–2, 53–4.

out this latter scenario, because the relevant request for specification which it introduces into this scenario will not be grammatically well formed, and so (4) will be satisfied by default: if, for example, the conclusion of an inference under (2) is 'There is something such that Henry is it and George is it', and in reply to an initial request for specification I answer 'namely, good at squash', it is not possible to formulate a grammatically acceptable request for further specification, for—in contradistinction to the case where the reply was, say, 'a policeman'—you cannot within the bounds of acceptable grammar ask 'Which good at squash?'. A parallel problem arises for verbal expressions like 'runs'.

To this objection the obvious response is that the cases Hale has in mind will have been ruled out anyway by the first three tests—so before we get to test (4)—on the basis of considerations of grammaticality. Take first adjectival phrases (what I earlier called verb radicals: §26). These will fail the third test, for it is not possible to infer from 'It is true of good at squash that Henry is it or George is it' to 'Henry is good at squash or George is good at squash', for the premiss is not well formed. The situation is even worse for verbal concept-expressions like 'runs', since they will fail the first two tests, as well as the third, on grounds of grammaticality: for example, from the sentence 'Henry runs' it is not possible to infer 'There is something such that Henry it'. Hale's objection also requires us to play fast and loose with the copula, first inserting it and then removing it in the statement forming the conclusion given above of an inference under (2) and its gloss under (4). But I have rejected Fregean laxity on the status of the copula (§30): strictly, the conclusion and its epexegesis offered above should have read either 'There is something such that Henry is it and George is it—namely, is good at squash' or 'There is something such that Henry it and George it—namely, good at squash'; but both of these are ungrammatical.

Hale's objection thus seems inconclusive, at least as stated; but there is a deeper problem with the tests that we need to consider, and one that indeed involves an application of Hale's objection in a modified form. We start from the observation that Dummett's tests are specified in English and are designed to isolate the singular terms of English. That observation, of course, immediately suggests a difficulty,[231] namely that the tests are, as promulgated by Dummett, excessively parochial. To overcome that parochialism, the tests must be generalized beyond the case of English: they must, ultimately, be stated in an entirely non-language-specific way. Now it is plausible that we could only formulate the needed generalized version of the tests in terms of a language-neutral notion of existential quantification, conceived as already

[231] Hale [1], pp. 289–90; [2], pp. 412; Wright [1], pp. 62–4.

understood. But how can existential quantification, in general, be understood save in tandem with a coeval notion of the category of singular terms? It is hard to see how the tests can be, as Wright puts it, *internationalized*, without presupposing a prior grasp of the very thing they are designed to explain. And it would clearly be just as objectionable, given that the tests are designed to subserve the syntactic priority thesis, to aim at a language-neutral notion of singular term by reference to 'the general conception of a singular term as one whose function is to identify an object',[232] for the whole purport of the syntactic priority thesis was that 'the notion of an object is posterior in the order of explanation to that of a singular term'.[233]

There is another dimension to the charge of parochialism. This concerns not the possibility of applying Dummett's tests to languages other than English—and so of arriving at a specification of them which is neutral with respect to all empirical *object-languages*—but rather the possibility of framing the tests in such a way as to preserve neutrality between Fregean and anti-Fregean *metalinguistic* analytical strategies, in respect of any (natural or artificial) object-language. For consider a theory of meaning for English stated in a metalanguage governed by a grammar along the lines of the anti-Fregean strategy, namely one that locates primary monadic concept-expressions at the zeroth level of a linguistic hierarchy, and disposes other expressions in the hierarchy in the ways we have explored. If the tests are stated in this metalanguage, the criticisms which Hale directed at them can be revived, at least in respect of primary monadic concept-expressions. That is, to repeat one of the examples I used earlier, the inference from 'Henry runs' to 'There is something such that Henry it' will now not only be grammatically well formed, but valid. And from 'Henry is good at squash' and 'George is good at squash' we will be able validly to infer, not indeed 'There is something such that Henry is it and George is it—namely good at squash'—in the envisaged metalanguage this sentence is nonsense—but 'There is something such that Henry it and George it—namely is good at squash'. For 'is good at squash' is a zeroth-level expression according to the grammar of this metalanguage, and correspondingly its referent is a basic object. (Of course we cannot state what its referent is—is good at squash—without descending into what we would regard as nonsense.)

It follows that the Dummettian tests, when conceived as utterly general, non-language-specific tests, formulated in a metalanguage whose categorial

<hr/>

[232] Hale [2], p. 44. In effect Hale appears here to concede to Dummett (see also ibid., pp. 165–6) that there is more to reference than semantic role, the view I rejected in §53 above.
[233] Wright [1], p. 24, quoted above, §57.

grammar may be either Fregean or anti-Fregean, do not succeed in isolating singular terms as such, but rather singular terms and primary monadic concept-expressions. The Dummettian tests take us precisely as far as, and not an inch further than, the tests (i) and (ii) which were constructed in the previous section using the negation asymmetry test. On the basis of the Dummettian tests we can, once again, partition expressions which pass them into distinct congruence classes. And of course it is open to us to label the resulting classes in different ways—as it might be, 'singular terms' and 'primary monadic concept-expressions'. But from a logical point of view these are mere labels: what we are really doing is distinguishing two different kinds of candidate zeroth-level expression. That is the real logical significance of these tests.

61 Discarding the Syntactic Priority Thesis

The upshot of the considerations we have rehearsed in §§57–60 is that the syntactic priority thesis is empty, and that is a conclusion we had in effect already reached by other means. My claim has been that all semantically significant subsentential lexical expressions are, as far as their ontological import is concerned, on a level: we should regard them all as unsaturated, referring to correspondingly unsaturated objects. Our examination in the foregoing sections of the various tests for singular termhood that have been discussed in the literature has confirmed this picture, at least with respect to what I have been calling primary monadic concept-expressions—the monadic concept-expressions that Frege assigns to his first level. For the tests are not able to distinguish singular terms from these expressions: in the case of the test based on (ID) and (IDM) (§58), we can distinguish within the broad category of singular terms between proper names strictly so called (which pass the test) and other singular terms (which do not), but we cannot then distinguish between proper names strictly so called and primary monadic concept-expressions; in the case of the other two tests (§§59–60) we can make neither the former nor the latter distinction. The tests do succeed in partitioning the expressions that are capable of occupying the zeroth level of a linguistic hierarchy into distinct congruence classes, based on considerations of grammatical congruence. The availability of such a division we of course knew about anyway: the tests perhaps help deepen our appreciation of the different allegiances of potential zeroth-level expressions belonging to different categories, but they take us no further than that.

Someone might say, to recur to a point that was left unresolved in §51, that proper names and concept-expressions can be distinguished at the level of ordinary language by dint of the fact that proper names are all multigrade, whereas concept-expressions, as a congruence class, include unigrade examples. But even if these differences are admitted, they do not justify a differential application of the saturated–unsaturated distinction to subsentential expressions: they do not warrant saying that the concept carries 'the form of the fact (proposition) into which it enters as a constituent',[234] whereas the name or names do not. After all, the monadic first-order quantifiers ('something', 'no one', etc.) are uniformly multigrade, just like proper names; yet they are supposed to be unsaturated, given that they are, for Frege, second-level concept-expressions. More importantly, the application of the point in question is, as I observed when I introduced it, limited to English and languages resembling English in the relevant respect, so that a suspicion of parochialism attaches to the claimed principle. In §51 this suspicion was confirmed by the fact that we do not know whether the alleged difference between proper names and concept-expressions obtains at the atomic level, assuming with Russell and Wittgenstein in their early period that there is, in an absolute sense, an atomic level. Here the point is rather that, as far as developing a non-language-specific test to distinguish between proper names and concept-expressions is concerned, and to obviate the charge of parochialism which, as we saw, has been rightly levelled at Dummett's tests, the assumed principle of distinction is useless. For it would direct us to classify a group of expressions whose members were uniformly multigrade as proper names, so ruling out a priori the possibility that a language might contain exclusively multigrade concept-expressions. We cannot employ the notion of the multigrade as a test for proper namehood if we wish, as we should, to leave open the possibility that a language's concept-expressions might be exclusively multigrade.

These considerations show, incidentally, that the project (sponsored by Strawson, for example) of justifying the subject–predicate distinction in terms of ontological categories is hopeless; and that, conversely, as Ramsey puts it, 'no fundamental classification of objects can be based upon [the subject–predicate] distinction'.[235] In traditional grammar, the sentence 'Socrates is wise' is analysed as having a subject 'Socrates' and a predicate 'is wise', and in the Fregean linguistic hierarchy this is expressed by locating 'Socrates' at the zeroth level and 'is wise' at the first level. But the anti-Fregean strategy reverses these allocations, with the consequence, as we have seen, that those syntactic tests that are designed to indicate which linguistic expressions are proper names (or singular terms)—and so to show which expressions are fitted to function as the subjects recognized by traditional grammar, and hence, by elimination, which

---

[234] Hochberg [2], p. 230. Cf. §69 below.   [235] [2], p. 116.

other expressions are fitted to function as predicates—yield opposite results, when applied to our sample sentence 'Socrates is wise', according as they are deployed by the Fregean or the anti-Fregean strategy. The fact that traditional grammar and the Fregean strategy line up in the way they do is neither surprising nor of especial philosophical interest: what is rather of interest is the point that when we substitute for the subject–predicate distinction of traditional grammar what I called (§45) the *analytical* subject–predicate distinction, the neat match between ontological and linguistic categories supported by traditional grammar disappears. Recall that the analytical predicate of a sentence (or subsentential clause) is the expression of highest level in that sentence (clause), according to some adequate allocation of that sentence's (clause's) semantically significant subsentential lexical expressions to the levels of a linguistic hierarchy. Hence, given the availability of an anti-Fregean as well as a Fregean syntactic treatment of our sample sentence, it follows that there is no unique way to divide the *analytical* subject–predicate labour between its key subsentential parts, namely 'Socrates' and 'is wise', and so no unique way to correlate the functional subject–predicate distinction with the ontological individual–universal distinction.

That does not mean that the ontological distinction is ungrounded or arbitrary, as Ramsey held.[236] But it does mean that we should not try to ground it in the subject–predicate distinction; nor should we try to ground the subject–predicate distinction in the individual–universal distinction, or in empirical facts purportedly differentiating individuals from universals, as Strawson wants.[237] In fact the subject–predicate distinction of traditional grammar and the individual–universal distinction of traditional ontology are orthogonal to one another. There is a distinction between individuals and universals, but it is constituted by their different metaphysical properties, not by the different grammatical functions of words that refer to them.

---

[236] [2], p. 117.   [237] [1], pp. 161, 167–247; [6], ch. 1 and p. 98. Recall §36 above.

5

Logical Predication, Logical Form, and Bradley's Regress

62 Names, Verbs, and the Replacement Test

I have argued so far that, if there is a distinction between saturated and unsaturated linguistic items in the offing, then, if the declarative sentence is to be regarded as paradigmatically saturated, in the sense that it is capable of saying something true or false, there can be no warrant for extending the label 'saturated' to any subsentential components, and hence no basis for refusing to extend the label 'unsaturated' to all subsentential components alike. And I have suggested that, unless we want to jettison the name–object duo, we have no genuinely compelling motive to do other than regard all semantically significant subsentential lexical components as names referring to objects, if any are to be so styled. But, having arrived at this position, it is borne in on us that the problem of unity arises in its starkest form for sentences as these are conceived by the approach to subsentential components which I am recommending. For since this approach regards all semantically significant subsentential lexical expressions as alike names, the question urgently presses: in what does the distinction between a *sentence*, composed as it is in the view I am recommending of nothing but names, and a mere *list* of names, consist? The question can be most pointedly addressed if we first consider not sentences like 'Socrates is wise', in respect of which the claim that sentences are composed of names is controversial, but a kind of sentence in respect of which even a Fregean would have to allow that it is composed of nothing but (proper) names.

Here I want to adduce a suggestive distinction between three artificial primitive languages devised by Nicholas Denyer, which he calls Agglomerative (**A**), Orthographic (**O**) and Sentential (**S**).[1] The three languages have in common that their basic 'sentences' all consist of linear strings of unambiguous names of primary elements, themselves arranged linearly. Thereafter they

---

[1] [1], pp. 117–27.

diverge in the following respects. In **A** and **O**, these basic 'sentences' are, according to Denyer, only by courtesy so called, for they are really complex names; but whereas in **A** the order in which the names are listed is insignificant, in **O** it is significant. Thus '*ab*', for example, would in **A** merely designate a complex object composed of the simple objects designated by '*a*' and '*b*', and is not semantically distinguishable from '*ba*'; in **O**, on the other hand, these two composite names additionally signify two different ways in which the complex consisting of *a* and *b* may be composed, for example, that *a* is to the left of *b*, and that *b* is to the left of *a*, respectively. In **S**, by contrast with both **A** and **O**, the basic 'sentences' are said to be genuine *sentences*: they are not merely lists of names, but are suitable for the making of assertions. In **S**, a symbol such as '*ab*' *says that* (for example) *a* is to the left of *b*. (Denyer notes the parallels between **S** and the fully analysed language of the *Tractatus*:[2] I recur to this below.)

Denyer's characterization of the three languages naturally prompts the following observations. First, although the basic sentences of **S** are not *mere* lists of names, they are *at least* lists of names. That does not, however, prevent them from being sentences as well; it does not deprive them of just that kind of sentential unity which mere lists of names lack. What does that unity consist in? Denyer does not seek to answer this question directly. But some of his incidental remarks seem to me to point to a response. He implies that if we try to supplement **S** with words specifying how the objects to which its component names refer are configured, we risk falling into a regress. If, for example, we try to say that *a* is to the left of *b* by writing '*a left b*', we now need to be told how to read *this* sign (what the significance of placing '*a*' to the left of '*left*' is, etc.). If we try to meet that requirement by writing in further signs, the same problem arises. The moral appears to be that at some point the way in which a composite sign is to be construed must rest on a convention which remains unspecified in the sign itself. As Denyer puts it: 'How [the] names [of **S**] are interwoven will of course . . . be significant. But a manner of interweaving is not itself one of the ingredients interwoven.'[3]

Secondly, although Denyer does not mention the possibility of generating such a regress in the cases of **A** and **O**, it is clear that it obtains there too. That is because the 'sentences' of these languages, and hence the referents of their component signs, are structured. Since the generation of **S**'s regress depended not on what distinguishes it from **A** and **O**—that it contains genuine sentences—but merely on the fact that the referents of its sentences' component signs are structured, and since the regress arises just when one tries to specify the relation between structuring and structured elements of the

---

[2] Ibid., p. 125 n. 3.　　[3] Ibid., p. 125; cf. p. 158. Cf. Armstrong [3], p. 192.

referents of its component signs, the fact that the 'sentences' of **A** and **O** have referents which are also structured (however barely) is enough to ensure the availability of the regress in their case too.

Now Denyer tells us that the 'sentences' of **A** and **O** merely *name* complex objects: they do not *say anything about* those objects, or their elementary components. In **S**, by contrast, the leap to declarative form has apparently been achieved: its sentences, though composed of names of elementary objects, are not to be conceived as mere names of complex objects; rather, they are capable of *saying something true or false* about the configurations of elementary objects. But this difference between **A** and **O** on the one hand, and **S** on the other, can only amount to this, that the complex names of **S** are *actually used* by its (hypothesized) speakers to advance declarations—that is, to make statements capable of being true or false, whether in an asserted or an unasserted context—whereas those of **A** and **O** are not.[4] For there is nothing on the side of their languages preventing speakers of **A** and **O** from using the complex names of their respective languages to advance declarations about the objects *a* and *b*: in **A**, '*ab*' could be used to say that *a* and *b* are related; in **O**, the same symbol could tell us not merely that *a* and *b* are related, but also how they are related.

It would appear, then, that the fact that a candidate sentence's component words are all *names* does not deprive it of the possibility of being used to advance a declaration, and hence of enjoying the semantic property of sentencehood. None of the sentences of **S** (or of **A** or **O**, supposing their complex names are used to advance declarations) contains any special, non-nominal component whose job it is to effect the unity of the sentence or expressed proposition. According to the account of the unity of the proposition which Denyer officially seems to offer, however, unity resides in the special nature of the verb: it is essential to that nature that verbs are not names, and do not refer to objects.[5] This position is, as we have seen, a traditional one, having been championed by Frege, Russell, and many of their predecessors and successors. Now I have rejected the view that there is anything special about the verb—generally, the concept-expression—in constituting the unity of the sentence: proper name and concept-expression stand on all fours in point of unsaturatedness, or unity-constituting properties. And reflection on Denyer's language **S** shows that it is not even the case, contrary to Plato's claim in the *Sophist*, that a sentence has to contain a verb or concept-expression: a unified sentence *can* be composed exclusively of proper names. That is, a sentence can be composed of linguistic items which are not merely names in the liberated sense of that word I have introduced, according to which any semantically

---

[4] On the notion of advancing a declaration, see §85 below.   [5] [1], pp. 179–82.

significant subsentential lexical component counts as a name, but which are proper names strictly so called. Making this point should go some way to disarming any residual resistance to taking 'is wise' in a sentence like 'Socrates is wise' to be a name (in the liberated sense) referring to an object: nothing is gained by insisting that 'is wise' is not a name on the basis that a sentence needs a verb or concept-expression to be constituted as a unity, for there are examples of unified sentences not containing a verb or concept-expression, so that the purported requirement is a spurious one.[6]

Recall that it is not *sufficient* for sentential unity that sentences be composed of words of different lexical types—however these types are specified (§5). For any sentence composed of the right kinds of word in the right order can be duplicated by a list of the same words in the same order, so that Mill was quite wrong to imply, in the passage quoted in §26, that the presence of the copula (or suitable inflection) in a sentence suffices to unify it. Again, Siderits is wrong to say that 'precisely because [Fregean] concepts are unsaturated, we no longer have to contend with those relations which mediate between universals and particulars'.[7] Rather, as MacBride notes, 'a mere grasp of [the] distinction [between complete and incomplete entities] does not enable us to distinguish a genuinely judgeable content from a mere collection of complete and incomplete items listed one after the other'.[8] Hence we are not absolved, by virtue of the claim that concepts are unsaturated and objects saturated, from asking after the principle of distinction between a mere aggregate comprising, say, a concept and an object, and a proposition (true or false) formed from that concept and that object. But my principal concern in the present context is with the converse point, namely that it is not *necessary* for sentential unity that sentences be composed of words of different syntactic types, either: sentences may be composed of expressions of just one type without detriment to the unity of those sentences.

In spite of the fact that he himself has succeeded in characterizing unified sentences which contain no verbs and are composed exclusively of items which anyone would be obliged to regard as proper names—an achievement which suggests that nothing deriving from considerations of sentential unity prevents us from construing *all* sentences as composed of names—Denyer argues that verbs cannot be taken to be names because they fail what he calls the replacement test.[9] Any genuine name 'a' can, according to this test, be replaced by the circumlocution 'the object designated by the word "a"'. Applying this test to

(1)   Socrates is wise

⁶ Cf. Hobbes [1], I. iii, §2.   ⁷ [3], pp. 58–9.   ⁸ [4], p. 605.
⁹ [1], pp. 164–73. Cf. Wright [1], pp. 19–20.

yields the result that 'Socrates' is a name, for

(2)   The object designated by the word 'Socrates' is wise

is a perfectly intelligible, if stilted, English sentence, with recognizably the same purport and truth-value as (1), whereas

(3)   Socrates the object designated by the words 'is wise'

is nonsense.

However, we are now in a position to see what is wrong with this argument. Of course (3) is nonsense *as a sentence of English*, but that is merely because English adopts the convention of employing a separate symbol for the copula (here figuring as a distinct word, in other contexts as the finite verb ending), rather than absorbing its function into the concatenation of the other subsentential components, as **S** does. But the fact that English symbolizes the copula separately is a contingent feature of the language: instead of producing sentences like (1), we might have had sentences like

(4)   Socrates wisdom,

determined to be true just in case the object designated by the first name instantiates the object designated by the second name.[10] Both lexical components of (4) pass the replacement test. What is more, we might, in applying a semantic theory to English, first regiment sentences like (1) along the lines of (4), as a preliminary to specifying objectual referents for its components, or indeed simply specify objectual referents for the components of (1) directly, in the manner of what I earlier called the 'impartial strategy' (§41)—

(5)   'Socrates' refers to Socrates
(6)   'is wise' refers to wisdom—

together with a suitable combinatorial axiom. That these manœuvres are available shows that it is a mistake to place any weight on the fact that English, or any other language, symbolizes the copula: we could achieve the same effect without doing so, and hence it is pointless to try to attach a special logical significance to the fact that a given language does symbolize it.

All the replacement test shows is that verbs and proper names are not intersubstitutable in English. Of course we knew that anyway: it emerged in our reflections on the linguistic hierarchy of levels as the point that proper

---

[10] Interestingly, Priestley suggested that languages went through a developmental phase in which just this happened—a phase in which speakers used sentences of the form 'a lion strength' to mean 'a lion has strength' (iv, p. 56). Cf. Nuchelmans [5], p. 167.

names on the one hand, and the concept-expressions that Frege assigns to the first level of his hierarchy on the other, must go to *different* levels of a linguistic hierarchy, whether we make our dispositions in the Fregean or in the anti-Fregean way. But the replacement test is not competent to show that an arbitrary language must *have* non-congruous and hence non-intersubstitutable expressions, or in other words that the grammar of any conceivable language must be governed by a linguistic hierarchy comprising *distinct* levels: Denyer's language **S** generates no such linguistic hierarchy—the hierarchy it generates is a hierarchy in a degenerate sense, comprising just one level. Nor does the test show that any particular kind of word—the verb, as it might be—is peculiarly responsible for unity. The verb or concept-expression cannot, as such, be what unifies the sentence or its expressed proposition: for we have examples of unified sentences that contain no verb or concept-expression, as those grammatical categories are ordinarily understood, and nothing would be lost if the grammatically distinctive features of the verb or concept-expression (such as inflection for tense, voice, aspect, and person) were 'regimented out' of languages which contain it and assigned to special operators (as is achieved in the case of tense by modern tense logic), or if those features were processed separately from the core semantic content of the verb (its nominal content, so to speak) in a theory of meaning for the language in question. In fact, the moral yielded by reflection on cases like the sentences of **S** is that *no* subsentential component of a sentence—in the sense of an antecedently available *ingredient*—can be the thing that unifies it or its corresponding proposition: rather, what unifies sentence and proposition must be a *structural* feature.

We already knew that no ingredient of the sentence can effect unity in the sense of being *sufficient* for unity: for, as we have said, no ingredient can enter into a sentence in such a way that the resulting sentence cannot be duplicated by a mere list comprising exactly the same components as that sentence, including the magic 'unifying' ingredient. What we now see in addition is that no special ingredient—at any rate, not the *verb* or concept-expression—is *necessary* for unity either. For we can construct bona-fide sentences lacking a verb or concept-expression. Of course, you might say that the *name* is necessary for unity, given that we need names to constitute a sentence in the first place: but that is simply a function of the fact that, as we have seen, all semantically significant subsentential lexical components can be regarded as names (§40). In that sense the name is indeed indispensable. But although this is by no means a trivial point, since it embodies the substantial lesson of the context principle, it nevertheless remains the case that the name whose presence in the unified sentence is indispensable is not making a contribution to unity *by virtue of any peculiar syntactic properties it may possess*: its contribution to the unity of sentences in which it figures is just its necessary presence, perhaps along with other names, in those sentences. They are, as it were, the sentence's matter. The verb or concept-expression does not constitute the moment of unity because it is dispensable in the sentence; the name, by contrast, is not dispensable in the sentence, but even so it does not *as such* constitute the moment of unity. That moment must, as we have said, be effected by some aspect of the structure of the sentence, and that unifying aspect must be something that *cannot* be duplicated by mere lists.

63 Analysis and Paradox

In this connection it is worth commenting on an argument of Geach's drawn from considerations having to do with Russell's paradox. The argument is directed against the suggestion that sentences might be composed of words of the same syntactic type—and, in particular, against the claim that sentences might be composed exclusively of proper names. Since the viability of such languages is an important presupposition of my investigation, and since Geach's objection, if left unaddressed, is one that might well occur to the reader as a possible stumbling-block, it is a good idea to tackle it here and now. Geach writes:

> Let us suppose that in sentences of the form 'A is B' or 'A is a B' the subject 'A' and the predicate 'B' are signs of the same sort. In that case 'A is (an) A' will be a possible form . . .; and so will 'A is not (an) A'. Consider now the matrix 'x is not (an) x'; this will express a certain property of the object indicated by the variable 'x'. Let us express this property by the predicate 'W', or the matrix 'x is (a) W'. Then we have:
>
>> For any x, x is (a) W if and only if x is not (an) x.
>
> But on our present hypothesis the predicate 'W' is itself a possible subject; 'W is a W' is an admissible sentence. We may therefore substitute 'W' for the variable 'x' in the above universally quantified matrix; and we shall then get Russell's Paradox:
>
>> W is (a) W if and only if W is not (a) W.
>
> To avoid this contradiction, we must hold that in 'A is (a) B' 'A' and 'B' are signs of completely different kinds; that a predicate cannot become a subject without a radical change of sense; that the form 'A is (an) A' never genuinely occurs.[11]

To which the obvious retort is: if 'the form "A is (an) A" never genuinely occurs', what does Geach suppose he is doing in reciting this version of

---

[11] [1], p. 476.

Russell's paradox? The form must occur, if the paradox is to be stateable, as it evidently is.

Geach has surely conflated two quite different projects: one is giving a logico-syntactic characterization of a natural or an artificial language; the other, distinct project is legislating, usually in the context of setting up a formal language which we intend to deploy in a particular area of mathematics, to avoid paradox. For certain mathematical purposes—for example, when we are seeking to establish set-theoretical foundations for mathematical analysis—we may have an interest in specifying our formal language in such a way as to block the derivation of Russell's paradox and its congeners. But these purposes have nothing to do with providing a perspicuous grammar of a natural language, or of an artificial language which has not been established with the purpose of providing a contradiction-free way of expressing results in some area, foundational or otherwise, of mathematics. And of course Russell's paradox *does* arise in natural language, as Geach's statement of it indeed demonstrates, and as Russell himself stressed (the paradox 'springs directly from common sense', as he put it),[12] so that a characterization of the grammar of a natural language which rendered the derivation of that paradox impossible would inevitably be a *misdescription* of that language's grammar.[13] The fact that the form '*A* is (a) *B*' (or '*AB*', in **S**-notation), where '*A*' and '*B*' are signs of the same syntactic type, permits the derivation of Russell's paradox, together with the fact that, in any natural language, or in an artificial language like **S** (suitably extended), Russell's paradox *is* (would be) derivable, shows that the possibility of those forms' occurring in those languages cannot be ruled out a priori on the basis that their occurrence would permit the derivation of Russell's paradox. To repeat: we precisely *want* our characterization of the grammar of natural languages—and we may want our characterization of certain artificial languages—to permit that derivation; a characterization which rendered the derivation impossible would be failing in its descriptive duty.

It is sometimes argued that at least some paradoxical sentences are underivable in the language because ungrammatical. Zellig Harris, for instance, tells us that 'This sentence is false' fails to be grammatical unless 'this sentence' refers to a distinct, already given sentence.[14] But this must be mistaken, for there are many contexts in which we experience no difficulty in understanding exactly the kind of self-reference that is here held to be grammatically problematic:

---

[12] [3], §105. Cf. Küng, p. 73. Contrast the paradox of the concept *horse*.

[13] Cf. Etchemendy, p. 166 n. 4; Priest [2], pp. 10–25, 132–6, 203–4, where it is argued that if the theory of meaning for a natural language is to be based on an axiomatizable theory of truth, as Davidson has argued it should be, then that theory cannot be a consistent one.

[14] Z. Harris, p. 146.

'This is an English sentence', 'In this book I intend to solve the problem of propositional unity', and so on. It is significant that Harris (tentatively) admits the grammaticality of 'All sentences are false':[15] to propound a grammatical version of Russell's Vicious Circle Principle, arguing along the above lines that the totality picked out by the phrase 'all sentences' as it figures in this sentence must be given as a completed entity before the formation of this sentence, on pain of ungrammaticality, would indeed be a desperate strategy.[16]

Attempts in the philosophical literature to deploy Russell's paradox in a way that is undermined by the current considerations are fairly commonly encountered. For example, Rumfitt uses the paradox, as did Lewis before him, to argue that apparently plural referring expressions cannot be reduced to singular referring expressions.[17] For, in the case of an expression such as 'The sets that are not members of themselves', the singular surrogate would have to be an expression picking out the Russell set. But 'Russell's paradox shows that there is no such set'.[18] Now, I agree that plural reference should not, in general, be construed as a kind of singular reference; but I do not think that the cited argument is the right way to establish that claim. Suppose that Russell's paradox does indeed indicate that there is no such thing as the Russell set—as opposed to showing merely that the Russell set (exists but) is a paradoxical object. Of course, given the distinction between reference and satisfaction on which I have insisted (§15), we ought to say that both of the descriptions in play here—both the plural 'The sets that are not members of themselves' and its singular congener 'The Russell set'—necessarily have *referents*; that is just truistic, given that these expressions are perfectly comprehensible. The most that Russell's paradox can show is that the singular definite description 'The Russell set' is not *satisfied* by anything.[19] But even if this is taken to be shown by the standard reasoning, we lack an argument to demonstrate that the relevant plural referring expression is not equally paradoxical in its implications. And there is surely a presumption that it is: Rumfitt's opponent will simply insist that the same paradoxicality accrues, albeit indirectly, to the plural description, on the basis that, though that description in the first instance picks out an uncollected bunch of entities, namely all the non-self-membered sets, we cannot prevent the aggregation of these sets into a single set containing them all: if they exist, so does it. Attempts to deny this automatic process of aggregation always overbalance into self-refutation: one first has to gather the

[15] Z. Harris, p. 212.   [16] Cf. Fraenkel *et al.*, pp. 11–12.

[17] Rumfitt [4], pp. 89–91, relying on Boolos (p. 66; cf. p. 70) and Oliver and Smiley ([1]); Lewis [5], pp. 62–72. See also Oliver [2]; Hossack, p. 420.

[18] Rumfitt [4], p. 89.   [19] Cf. Zalta [1], pp. 11, 26.

non-self-membered sets together, by for example quantifying over them, in order then to deny that the collection one has just formed exists.

At this point the set-theorist might wish, following von Neumann, to introduce a distinction between sets, on the one hand, which may be elements (that is, may themselves be set members) and proper classes, on the other, which may not (a proper class being equipollent to the universal class).[20] The point of this move is to allow the formation of (say) the collection of all non-self-membered sets, without incurring paradox: for in ruling that this collection is not a set, but rather a proper class, the usual set-theoretical paradoxes are avoided. But the distinction between sets and proper classes is no more than a notational stratagem designed with the intention of maintaining consistency while liberalizing the domain of quantification; it tells us nothing about the ontological facts of the matter. That is to say, the move does not tell us whether (say) the set of all non-self-membered sets *really is* a set or a proper class: in some contexts that may be a matter for stipulation, but not in all.[21] Even the suggestion that, as Zermelo came to think,[22] proper classes may themselves be arranged in a hierarchy, and that the status of a collection as a set or proper class depends upon the perspective from which it is viewed within the hierarchy does nothing to remove the aura of artificiality surrounding the distinction between sets and proper classes. From this angle there seems little to be gained by moving away from standard Zermelo–Fraenkel set theory, one of the alleged advantages of which, as its aficionados remind us, is that it permits quantification over all sets *without* admitting a superset (proper class) to contain them all.[23]

But now, waiving the purely technical concerns of (at least orthodox) set theory, which are not at all the same as those that move the philosopher of language, we ought to regard it as obvious that, if there are some (zero or more) things, there is a collection of them.[24] If this insistence leads to paradox, well, that is just how things are. Of course it does lead to paradox—at least under the usual assumptions, which include the datum that collections are

---

[20] See von Neumann, p. 229; letter to Zermelo of 15 Aug. 1923 (Meschkowski, pp. 271–3); Fraenkel *et al.*, pp. 119–53; cf. Lewis [5], pp. 18–19. The distinction between sets and proper classes was prefigured in Cantor's distinction between consistent and inconsistent multiplicities: see his letter to Dedekind of 3 Aug. 1899 ([1], pp. 443–4); Simons [2], p. 484; [8], p. 144; C. Parsons [2], pp. 281–2; Jané, p. 375. In a letter to Hilbert of 10 Oct. 1898, Cantor wrote: 'Unter einer fertigen Menge verstehe man jede Vielheit, bei welcher alle Elemente ohne Widerspruch als zusammenseiend und daher als ein Ding für sich gedacht werden können' (cited by Felgner [1], p. 179).

[21] Contrast the anti-realist tenor of Fraenkel *et al.*, pp. 331–45.

[22] [4], pp. 46–7; cf. Ebbinghaus, pp. 190–3.   [23] See Boolos, p. 42; cf. pp. 33–6.

[24] *Pace* Boolos, pp. 70–2 (cf. pp. 75–83), who not only takes this claim to be false, but even holds its denial to be obvious. Cf. also Lewis [5], p. 8; Hallett [2], p. 1212.

things and so may themselves be members of collections—because the stated principle is even stronger than the (universal closure of the) first-order naïve comprehension axiom-schema

$$\exists \gamma \forall x (x \in \gamma \leftrightarrow \phi x),$$

from which Russell's paradox is an easy consequence.[25] On a certain understanding of it, our principle is equivalent to the second-order comprehension axiom

$$\forall F \exists \gamma \forall x (x \in \gamma \leftrightarrow Fx),$$

where the second-order variable ranges over arbitrary collections in the sense of §1 (collections that need have no purely general collecting principle). If we say that there are some things, then we are implicitly quantifying over them, and that idea in turn imports the idea of a collection to which those things all belong.[26] And perhaps we should after all say that the description 'the Russell set' *is* satisfied by something—a paradoxical object that both is and is not a member of itself—in which case we will no doubt want to add that the relevant plural description is satisfied by sets that, taken collectively, are this very paradoxical object. Either way, Russell's paradox cannot be deployed in the way some have hoped as a simple conversation stopper.

Similar remarks apply to the so-called Russell–Myhill antinomy, which has on occasion been taken to tell against the existence of propositions. In *The Principles of Mathematics* Russell gives two versions of this paradox, which was independently rediscovered by Myhill in 1958.[27] The first version is stated in terms of propositional functions, the second in terms of sets.[28] The first version proceeds as follows. Plausibly, all propositional functions are objects, the category of *object* being Russell's most comprehensive ontological category in *Principles* (wider even than that of *term*). So there are at least as many objects as propositional functions. But it can be shown, by an application of Cantor's diagonal method, that there are more propositional functions than objects:

For suppose a correlation of all objects and some propositional functions to have been effected, and let ϕ_x be the correlate of x. Then 'not-$\phi_x(x)$', i.e. 'ϕ_x does not hold of x' is a propositional function not contained in the correlation; for it is true or false of x according as ϕ_x is false or true of x, and therefore it differs from ϕ_x for every value of x.[29]

---

[25] Boolos, pp. 15–16; Fraenkel *et al.*, pp. 31, 155–6.
[26] In essence this is Cantor's 'domain principle' (see §77 below). Cf. Potter [2], pp. 303–6.
[27] Myhill, pp. 81–2.
[28] [3], §§348, 500. Cf. L. Linsky [1], pp. 636–42; Potter [1], pp. 131–2; Stevens [3], pp. 66–70.
[29] [3], §348.

The version for sets is similar: on the one hand there are at least as many propositions as sets, for to each set there corresponds a proposition containing it; on the other hand there are more sets than propositions, for given any enumeration of sets in one-to-one correspondence with propositions, the Russell–Myhill set—the set containing all and only those propositions that are not members of the set with which they are correlated—will 'diagonalize out' of the list of sets.[30]

The fundamental mechanism of the Russell–Myhill antinomy is Cantor's diagonal method; as I observed earlier (§33), that procedure is also the crux of Russell's paradox. The doctrine of Russellian propositions (and the associated commitment to propositional functions) leads straight to the Russell–Myhill antinomy, in a way that parallels the generation of Russell's paradox for sets. Essentially the same impredicative circularity is generated by my claims that (i) propositions at the level of reference are composed of worldly things including, sometimes, propositions, and including, sometimes (as for instance in the proposition expressed by this very sentence) even the world itself (for 'the world' is a strict proper name), and (ii) the world is to be identified with the totality of propositions at the level of reference. Given (i) and (ii), there is a mutual dependence between the world and what it contains: it is impossible to close off either entity or totality before the other is established. The world quite literally contains itself. Here we may observe that, given the close association between functions and sets (§§16, 33), it follows that the existence of propositions about the world, on my conception of what the world is, will generate an ontology of non-well-founded sets.[31] But again, I take these consequences to be just the way things are, not a *reductio ad absurdum* of the doctrine of Russellian propositions in the context of a philosophically pregnant linguistic idealism. Of course, different strategies may be proposed for dealing with the Russell–Myhill antinomy, such as (Russell's favoured solution) some version of the theory of types;[32] but however we try, for particular purposes, to avoid or neutralize it, the fact remains that, assuming the soundness of the diagonal method (an assumption that is virtually universal among mathematicians, though not among philosophers),[33] this antinomy, just

---

[30] There is a formal reconstruction of the version of the antinomy given by Russell at [3], §500 in Church [9], at pp. 516–18. A variant involving concepts is given by Hale: [2], p. 246.

[31] Cf. Bealer [4], p. 53 n. 28.

[32] As Russell notes at the very end of [3] (§500, final paragraph), the simple theory of types presented in [3] itself does not solve the Russell–Myhill antinomy. To achieve that we need the ramified theory: cf. Church [9], pp. 519, 521; B. Linsky [2], pp. 65–6. That is because of the essentially intensional way the antinomy is generated (§43 above).

[33] See Hodges [1]; Stevens [3], p. 64; Potter [2], pp. 137–8, 158–9. The method is criticized from a finitist perspective by Kaufmann, ch. 5.

like Russell's paradox, arises in natural language in advance of the application of any theoretical apparatus (such as the stratification of propositions and propositional functions) we may devise for coping with it; and it is at that point—at the stage, as it were, of pre-Cantorian innocence—that the doctrine of propositions arises and the question of their unity must be addressed.

64 Simple, Complex, and Logical Predicates

In §45 I distinguished between a sentence's grammatical subject and predicate and what I called its analytical subject and predicate: the analytical predicate of a sentence was the highest-level expression in that sentence as discerned by some suitable syntactic analysis of it, and the notion of an analytical subject was correlative with that of an analytical predicate. I now need to introduce a third distinction between what we may call the *logical subject* and *logical predicate* of a sentence. We can best approach this further distinction by way of a discussion of a distinction that Dummett makes between what he calls simple and complex predicates.[34] As Dummett expounds it, the notion of a simple predicate is needed in specifying constraints on a correct theory of meaning for a language: the simple predicates of a language are those predicates which an empirically adequate theory of meaning would discern as its basic predicative units. The notion of a complex predicate, on the other hand, is required for the exhibiting of correct inference patterns involving quantified sentences: when they are first introduced by Dummett, complex predicates are said to be formed from a complete sentence by the omission of one or more occurrences of a proper name, the resulting gaps being annotated in some perspicuous way, for example by the insertion of lower-case Greek letters.[35] In Dummett's terminology, sentences are *analysed* into their semantically simple components, including simple predicates (concept-words), but *decomposed* into complex predicates plus remainder.[36]

Dummett's characterization of complex predicates raises several problems. First, the characterization is deficient, since it covers only the formation of 'first-level' complex predicates, and is restricted to the approach adopted by the Fregean version of the hierarchy of levels. To capture the general notion of a complex predicate in which we are interested, we need to say that a

---

[34] [2], pp. 27–33, 62–6; [3], chs. 15 and 16; [5], pp. 36–42. Cf. [4], pp. 192–8, 301–2. Dummettian complex predicates are what I called annotated predicates in §31.

[35] Cf. Bostock [1], p. 69.

[36] The distinction between analysis and decomposition is controversial as an interpretation of Frege: it is attacked by e.g. Hodes; Currie [2]; Levine [2].

complex predicate is formed from a sentence by the omission of one or more expressions and by the suitable annotation of the resulting gap(s): the level of the omitted expression—or, if there is more than one, the level of the highest-level omitted expression—counts, from the point of view of the remaining expression, taken to be of level n, as being of level $n - 1$. Note that I here place no restrictions on the type of expressions that may be omitted to form a complex predicate. This is as it should be: it is a consequence of the way I have interpreted the context principle that all semantically significant subsentential lexical expressions are names if any are, and accordingly enjoy equal rights in point of suitability to supply the substantial semantic content of a complex predicate or, to put it the other way round, are equally available to be omitted from a sentence in the process of forming a complex predicate out of the remainder. So we do not want to follow Dummett in his official restriction of the category of expressions that may be omitted in forming complex predicates to proper names; it is quite obscure to me why he says that the symbol '>' in the sentence 'If $5 > 3$, then $5 + 2 > 3 + 2$' cannot be omitted from that sentence to form a complex predicate.[37]

Secondly, we need to avert a risk of terminological confusion, and also clear up an inconsistency in Dummett's application of his distinction. The terminological point—which amounts to the charge that the phrase 'complex predicate' is, in this context, a misnomer—is this. As they are defined, complex predicates in Dummett's sense are 'complex' in a quite different sense from that in which complex names are 'complex': a complex name is complex in the untechnical sense that it is put together from several semantically simple components. But it ought to be possible for a complex predicate, in Dummett's sense, to be (in the untechnical sense) simple: what marks it out as complex, in Dummett's sense, is that it contains its argument-place(s) essentially. As Dummett himself puts it, the slots for singular terms (that is, for proper names, in Frege's broad sense) are *external* to simple predicates, whereas they are *internal* to complex predicates.[38] Of course, as I have just remarked, this characterization is insufficiently general. But that does not affect the present point, which is that the predicate 'ξ runs' should, according to Dummett's definition of complex predicates, count as complex, by contrast with the predicate 'runs', which would count as simple. Dummett notes that, strictly speaking, there is a distinction between the complex predicate 'ξ runs'

---

[37] [4], p. 198. But at [3], p. 275, Dummett allows that the expression removed in the formation of a complex predicate 'may be a predicate or a functor, indeed one of any level'.

[38] [2], p. 32. Cf. Simons [6], p. 83, who rightly remarks that the distinction between what Dummett calls simple and complex predicates is 'a difference in kind, not in complexity'. See also Currie [2], p. 287.

and the simple predicate 'runs', but suggests that in this kind of case the complex predicate is complex in a merely 'degenerate' sense, and that it is an allowable economy to dispense with it, and regard the sign of generality in, say, 'Everyone runs' as attached directly to the simple predicate.[39]

But this will not do at all. If complex predicates are arrived at by omission of a name from a complete sentence—generally, by the omission of one or more expressions of which the highest-level omitted expression counts as being of one level lower than that of the remaining expression—the resulting gap(s) being then suitably annotated, it follows that such predicates are being conceived to carry with them the essential structure, and hence the unity, of the whole sentence. For a complex predicate is in essence a *schematic* unified sentence, rather than a non-sentential element or ingredient out of which a sentence is constructed.[40] Hence there can be no question of economizing on predicates: 'ξ runs' has no worse a claim to be complex, in the relevant sense, than 'If ξ will have me king, why, ξ may crown me, without my stir', and there can be no question of dispensing with it in favour of the simple predicate 'runs'. There could only be a question of dispensing with one type of predicate in favour of the other if they discharged the same theoretical role: but that is not the case, as Dummett himself quite clearly states.[41] (That is also why we cannot dispense with the whole category of simple predicates, as Geach suggests: the particular theoretical role discharged by simple predicates cannot be assumed by complex predicates.[42]) Further, Dummett's assimilation of complex predicates constructed from atomic sentences (such as 'ξ runs') to simple predicates has the consequence that atomic sentences will consist of exclusively saturated components (with correspondingly saturated senses and referents), an upshot which conflicts with Frege's doctrine of the essentially unsaturated nature of concept-expressions, their senses, and referents (concepts).[43] Therewith Frege's account of the unity of the proposition would collapse. Dummett tries to circumvent this difficulty by suggesting that simple predicates have *incomplete* senses and referents, just like complex predicates.[44] But this is surely a mistake. Complex predicates contain argument-places internally and essentially, as we have said, whereas simple predicates do not. If this is to be a genuine (semantic) distinction between them, it must impinge on their senses: so they cannot possibly have the *same* kind of sense. A schematic unified sentence cannot possibly have the same sense and reference as a constituent concept-expression

---

[39] [2], pp. 30–1.
[40] Cf. Frege, Letter to Marty of 29 Aug. 1882, [22], p. 164; [26], pp. 18, 273.
[41] [2], p. 27.   [42] Geach [8], pp. 147–8; cf. Simons [3], pp. 92–5.
[43] Kleemeier, p. 46 n. 1.   [44] [3], pp. 318–19.

whose meaning is given and understood in advance of its entering as an ingredient into this (or another) sentence.

We must insist, then, that Dummettian complex predicates are complex in a quite different sense from that in which complex names are complex. Whereas for names the complex–simple division is both exclusive and exhaustive, for predicates the Dummettian complex–simple division, rightly understood, is exclusive but not exhaustive. Exhibiting the soundness of the inference from the premiss 'Devereux killed Wallenstein' to the conclusion 'Someone killed Wallenstein' requires us to abstract the complex predicate 'ξ killed Wallenstein' from the premiss; the predicate 'killed Wallenstein', on the other hand, conceived as built up from the simple predicate 'killed' (or rather the third-personal inflection of the simple predicate 'kill' and the past-tense operator) together with the proper name 'Wallenstein', is neither complex nor simple. It is not complex, in Dummett's technical sense, because it is not conceived as arrived at by omission of an expression from a complete sentence and does not contain a marker indicating its argument-place; it is not simple, because it would not (it is plausible to suppose) feature as a primitive predicate in a theory of meaning for English. But this way with the terminology is a recipe for confusion. It is plainly preferable to use the terms 'simple' and 'complex' in a uniform way in their application to both names and predicates, and to use them moreover in what I have called the untechnical sense. It will then be mandatory to introduce a new term to cover the case of a sentence frame which contains one or more annotated argument-places essentially.

I shall use the term 'logical predicate' for the notion arrived at by generalizing Dummett's notion of a complex predicate in the way indicated above: that is, by the logical predicate of a sentence we will understand a suitably annotated expression, of any degree of complexity (in the untechnical sense) and of any level, such that it counts, according to some suitable syntactic decomposition, in Dummett's sense, as the highest-level expression of the sentence. The omitted expression counts as the sentence's logical subject and, if the logical predicate is of level n, is of level $n - 1$. No restrictions are here placed on which types of expression may figure as logical subject: there is nothing to prevent us, if our interests so dictate, from counting the expression '$>$' in the sentence 'If $5 > 3$, then $5 + 2 > 3 + 2$' as its logical subject. Strictly, as they have been defined a sentence *contains* an analytical predicate as a component, whereas a logical predicate is *abstracted from* a sentence; however, it will often be convenient in what follows to work with a slightly more relaxed conception of the logical predicate, according to which it does count as a feature of the sentence. On this more liberal conception, we think of the logical predicate as being like the analytical predicate save that it carries implicit—unannotated—gaps, by contrast with the logical predicate strictly so called, in which the gaps are explicitly annotated. I shall continue to use the term 'grammatical predicate' to cover simple predicates like 'runs' and complex (in the untechnical sense) constructions from simple predicates and other lexical items, such as 'killed Wallenstein', or 'is an *F* unless everything *G*s'.

65 The Grammatical Copula and the Logical Copula

With these distinctions in place, consider the following gloss on the position we have reached so far. What has in effect been shown, someone might say, is just that *grammatical* predicates, being lexical components of the sentence, may, without detriment to the unity of the sentence and of its corresponding proposition, be regarded as names; *logical* predicates, on the other hand, are a different matter. That is because logical predicates are—like Dummett's complex predicates, of which they are a generalization—so defined that they carry with them (whether annotated or unannotated) the essential structure, and hence unity, of the complete sentence.[45] The constitutively unifying quality of logical predicates, it might now be said, unfits them to be names, at least in any obvious sense, since to nominalize the logical predicate is surely to conceive it as having a referent, which in turn is tantamount, one might suppose, to treating that referent as a mere ingredient of the relevant proposition. But we have agreed that no ingredient of the proposition can be what constitutes its unity, because the presence of any ingredient in the proposition can be duplicated in a mere aggregate; likewise, the presence of any name in a sentence can be duplicated in a mere list. Let us explore this line of thought in more detail.

Nominalizing the logical predicate generates a regress of a kind that has already surfaced in the present chapter. Take the sentence 'Socrates is wise'. In this sentence we can discern at least two distinct analytical predicates, from which we may form two logical predicates, namely 'ξ is wise' and '(Φ) Socrates'. The distinction between upper- and lower-case Greek letters represents the relevant distinction of grammatical category—the fact that the expressions for which these schematic letters are holding place must be assigned to different levels of a linguistic hierarchy (although as we have seen there is no unique way of carrying out such an assignment). What now distinguishes these logical predicates from *mere* lists comprising names and placeholders

---

[45] Cf. Carruthers, pp. 55–6.

for names? Well, it is natural to reply that since these predicates are *formed* from a complete sentence by the omission of one or more of its constituent expressions, whose places are then optionally annotated, they are to be so read that they *incorporate* the unity of the sentence and of its corresponding proposition; the logical predicate does not merely contain within itself names and placeholders for names, but also expresses the copulative structure of the unified sentence, which we may represent schematically as 'ξ is Φ' in the case of the first logical predicate mentioned above, and as 'Φ is ξ-instantiated' in the case of the second one.[46] These abstracted copulas, which we may call copulas in the logical sense, are to be distinguished from the copula in the merely grammatical sense. The grammatical copula typically arises when a language explicitly symbolizes the instantiation relations obtaining among the objects that constitute its basic reference class: it is the role of the grammatical copula to symbolize the directionality of the instantiation relation. But languages like **S** that lack a grammatical copula, and have indeed no obvious use for one, since the objects in their basic reference class are not (said to be) related to one another by asymmetrical relations like that of instantiation, nevertheless possess a logical copula: for they are structured in a way that can be schematically represented along the lines of the logical predicates I have exhibited. So if '$\Phi(a)$' and '$\Phi(b)$' are logical predicates abstracted from the sentence 'ab', we can represent their logical copula by a further abstraction: '$\Phi(\xi)$'. (In parallel with my liberal policy on the use of the phrase 'logical predicate', I shall often deploy a relaxed conception of the logical copula, according to which it is thought of as an unannotated feature of the sentence, by contrast with the logical copula strictly so called, which is conceived as abstracted from the sentence and appropriately annotated.)

But how should we parse the logical copula? If it is a name, what is its referent? Here the problem immediately strikes us that when we try to state a referent, our attempt seems to fall short of its target. Suppose we wish to specify copulative reference for the case of a language that contains a grammatical copula symbolizing an asymmetric relation of instantiation: we will perhaps start with 'the relation of instantiation' as our specification of that reference. We may indeed start with this characterization, and possibly it will serve as an adequate specification of the reference of the *grammatical* copula; but it cannot

---

[46] These representations are imbued with the Fregean perspective, which construes the instantiation relation as running from objects (i.e. the referents of proper names) to concepts (i.e. the references of concept-expressions) rather than vice versa. The anti-Fregean strategy reverses the direction of the instantiation relation (while retaining its asymmetry, of course). My adoption of the Fregean perspective is simply a function of the fact that I am writing in a language which has internalized that perspective, and is thus illustrative only.

serve as a complete specification of the reference of the *logical* copula. For then our sample sentence, 'Socrates is wise' will by implication degenerate into a mere list of names: its components will designate the object Socrates (the referent of 'Socrates'), the object wisdom (the referent of 'wise'), and the relation of instantiation (the referent of 'is'); but we shall have failed to capture the *connection* between these three elements in the proposition expressed by that sentence. So we must add to our characterization that the logical copula of the sentence 'Socrates is wise' refers not merely to a single relation of instantiation (the one that is satisfied by Socrates and wisdom, appropriately ordered and typed), but also to a further relation of instantiation (the one that is satisfied by Socrates, wisdom, and the initial relation of instantiation, appropriately ordered and typed). But here it might still seem as though we had failed adequately to specify the reference of the logical copula. For surely all we have done is introduce a fourth object—the further relation of instantiation—and the now four objects remain every bit as aloof from one another, to borrow Frege's poignant phrase,[47] as did the erstwhile three objects from each other before we adduced the further relation. To connect these now four objects, we surely require a fifth relation of instantiation. And so on, into a regress. At each stage of this regress we seem to arrive at a set of mere objects, and so apparently lose the essential unity of the proposition which the logical predicate somehow embodies.[48] At each stage of the regress we try, but fail, to specify the total referent of the logical copula.

The problem apparently confronting us here, of specifying a reference for the logical copula, wears different aspects depending on whether we view it from (the reformed) Frege's perspective, or from the perspective I have been recommending. In Fregean terms, at each stage of the regress we seem to arrive at a set of *saturated* items, and so lose the essential unity of the proposition which the unsaturated logical copula somehow embodies; so the apparent problem for the (reformed) Frege is how to recover the unity of the proposition, and derivatively that of the sentence expressing it, from a bunch of saturated items. Put in the terms I have recommended, in contradistinction, the apparent problem is that, whereas at each stage of the regress we do indeed arrive at a set of *unsaturated* items, that way round with the terminology does not, as I remarked at the end of §42, help us just as such. For the fact that, on my approach, names and their referents are in the relevant sense unsaturated merely amounts to the point that names are essentially semantically significant *subsentential* items and their referents essentially correspondent *subpropositional* entities—regardless of the way in

---

[47] [7], p. 205 ([21], p. 178).   [48] Cf. Dummett [2], pp. 251–2, 256; Davidson [2], p. 85.

which these subsentential items or subpropositional entities occur, whether as parts of sentences or propositions on the one hand, or as parts of lists or aggregates on the other. Hence the observation that, on my approach, the referents of subsentential expressions are unsaturated is (at least in this context) a merely terminological move, which does not assist in any substantial way with the problem of unity.

Still, in the light of the discussion so far in this chapter, we can place two substantial points on the table. The first is that the phenomenon of congruence cannot, as such, be what constitutes the unity of the sentence and its corresponding proposition. There is no purely grammatical solution to the unity problem. There are two reasons for this. One is that we have examples of sentences—the sentences of Denyer's artificial language **S** are such—which are certainly unities in the required sense, but whose component names all exhibit exactly the same congruence value. So the phenomenon of *differential* congruence, which is a significant determinant of the well-formedness of sentences in natural languages like English, plays no role here. The second reason why the phenomenon of congruence—even the *degenerate* congruence exhibited by the words of **S**—cannot be what is responsible for unity is that nothing prevents us from compiling lists of (type) words (referring to aggregates of objects) which are of the right grammatical category to constitute a sentence (proposition), but which do not, as it happens, do so—or are not conceived, in this context, as doing so; for recall (§5) that the distinction between a sentence and a mere list is a *conceptual* one. (Parallel points apply to word-order or inflection for case.)

The second point to emerge from our discussion so far in this chapter is that what unifies a sentence and its corresponding proposition is not an ingredient of the sentence or proposition, in the sense of a component that is antecedently available to be configured with other, similarly available ingredients, but a structural property. If we think of that structural property in functional terms, as a unifying function (§19), then I suggest that nothing prevents our conceiving the function in question as a part of the proposition which it goes to unify and which is its value for the objectual and conceptual components of the proposition taken as arguments, so long as we are careful to distinguish *parts* from *ingredients*: the unifying function counts as an *ex post facto* part, and is not an ingredient in the sense we have already exploited, namely, an antecedently available component that, when combined with other similarly available components according to a recipe, yields a proposition. In the case of the sentence, the unifying structural feature is what I have called the logical copula, whose structuring activity is somehow embodied in a regress that arises when we try to specify a reference for it—in other words, when we try to specify the corresponding structural property at the level of the *proposition*. In the bulk of the remainder of this study I shall be concerned to elucidate the nature of this involvement, and to say what our response to the regress should be.

66 Predication in Frege

As we have seen (Chapter 3), Frege's answer to the problem of unity was to say that unity is effected by the unsaturatedness of certain subsentential components. In the case of our sample sentence 'Socrates is wise', Frege would claim that its unity is effected by a peculiarly unsaturated concept-expression, namely the (grammatical) predicate 'is wise'. Against this, I have argued that the selection of this predicate to be *the* unsaturated component of our sample sentence cannot be justified. In attacking the Fregean position I have been assuming that 'concept-expression' and 'predicate' do not in general function as synonyms, in Frege's usage, for either 'analytical predicate' or 'logical predicate' in the senses of these phrases that I have introduced in this chapter. Our characterizations of the analytical and logical predicates do not have any implications concerning the way in which we should populate the linguistic hierarchy of levels. But, as I have remarked (§52), it is quite clear that Frege held substantive views on that question, and did not regard it as an arbitrary matter whether we assign 'Socrates' in the sentence 'Socrates is wise' to a level one higher or one lower than 'is wise'.

At least, this is quite clear in connection with Frege's discussions of *natural-language* predications, particularly in the article on which I have been focusing for most of my exposition of Frege's thinking on predication and unity, namely 'Über Begriff und Gegenstand'. A reading of this article will confirm that, for Frege, the predicate of a sentence is its *grammatical* predicate, rather than its *analytical* (or logical) predicate. This is stated explicitly in the first footnote and its associated text: there it is said that the predicative nature of the concept—by which Frege means its unsaturated nature, as the eleventh footnote[49] makes clear—is explained by its being the *Bedeutung* of a grammatical predicate. Further confirmation may be gleaned from Frege's remark that 'We can say in summary, understanding "predicate" and "subject" in the linguistic sense: a concept is the *Bedeutung* of a predicate; an object can never be the entire *Bedeutung* of a predicate, but can be the *Bedeutung* of a subject'.[50] And examples

---

[49] [7], p. 197 ([21], p. 171).   [50] [7], p. 198 ([21], p. 172).

of predicates given in this article include 'is green', '(is) nothing other than Venus', '(is a) planet', 'is red' and 'falls under', which are all straightforwardly grammatical predicates. This restrictive policy contrasts with a more generous approach that was at least intimated in the *Begriffsschrift* where, as we saw (§35), Frege seemed to allow—at least in principle if not in practice—any grammatically integral part of a sentence to serve as (the name of) a function or as (the name of) an argument, and so in effect as the analytical predicate or the analytical subject of the relevant sentence.[51]

As we have noted, Frege assimilates concepts to functions (mapping objects to truth-values), and in his more technical works he insists that when we write down expressions for functions we should always include explicit annotation of number and type of argument-places.[52] Correspondingly, in these writings Frege appears to operate with a relatively thin conception of objecthood—his examples of objects at *Grundgesetze*, I, §2 are numbers, truth-values, and *Wertverläufe*. It might, then, seem that in technical contexts Frege deploys a notion of logical, rather than grammatical, predication, and that, correspondingly, his conception of objecthood is syntax-based.[53] But the claim that Frege adopts a *purely* syntax-driven approach to objecthood in his technical writings would be an idealization of his position.[54] In some passages he evidently supposes that we operate with a prior conception of objecthood, and arrive at our conception of a proper name on its basis. This is already indicated by the Dummettian reading of Frege, which I have accepted (§14), according to which a pre-theoretically conceived name–bearer relation serves as a prototype for reference. For that idea assumes that we have a language-independent access to objects. The passage in the *Grundgesetze* from which I above drew Frege's examples of objects reads as follows:

I include among objects everything that is not a function: e.g. numbers, truth-values, and courses of values . . . The names of objects, proper names, therefore carry no argument-places; they are saturated like the objects themselves.[55]

This passage suggests ('therefore') that it is *because* proper names refer to *antecedently constituted* objects that they carry no argument-places and are

[51] Frege sometimes talks as though his aim were to get rid of the subject–predicate distinction: e.g. [1], p. vi, and §3; letter to Husserl of 30 Oct. 1906 ([2], p. 103). But he is not consistent in this, and in fact the subject–predicate distinction, as we see here, plays a significant role in Frege's mature thinking: Angelelli [1], p. 94. Angelelli plausibly suggests (pp. 151–2) that Frege's real target in §3 of [1] is the subject–*object* distinction.

[52] See e.g. [10], I, §§1, 19, 26; II, §147 n. 2; [14], p. 664 ([21], pp. 278–9); letters to Peano of 29 Sept. 1896 and to Russell of 13 Nov. 1904 ([22], pp. 184, 243); [26], p. 19.

[53] Cf. C. Parsons [2], p. 283.   [54] Cf. Kleemeier, pp. 204–26; Rumfitt [3], pp. 199–200.

[55] [10], I, §2.

saturated, rather than its being because objects are referred to by (antecedently identified) proper names with no argument-places that *they* (the objects) are saturated.

The same failure to grasp wholeheartedly the syntactic priority thesis, and therewith the thesis of linguistic idealism—which, as we have seen, is entailed by (though it does not entail) the syntactic priority thesis—is observable in Frege's lecture *Funktion und Begriff*, where at one point it is stated that when we analyse (in Dummett's terminology: decompose) the expression '$2 \times x^3 + x$' into the functor '$2 \times (\ )^3 + (\ )$' and the variable 'x', 'the two parts into which the computational expression is so analysed, the sign for the argument and the expression for the function, are unlike, for the argument is a number, a whole complete in itself, which the function is not'. And later he adds: 'We should admit not merely numbers [as arguments], but objects in general, and here of course I have to reckon persons among objects'.[56] It is surely implied here that we have an antecedently constituted grasp of what counts as an object—one that, for example, allows us to say without further ado that persons are objects—by dint of which we are entitled to introduce proper names as expressions defined to refer to objects, thus understood. So too in 'Über Begriff und Gegenstand' a footnote tells us that 'I call a proper name any sign for an object',[57] not, as the syntactic priority thesis would surely demand: 'I call an object anything referred to by a proper name'.[58] Hence even in contexts where Frege is clearly seeking to adumbrate a conception of the logical predicate, in the defined sense, his attempt is undermined by a tendency to sully the purity of the correlative conception of proper namehood by having improper recourse to ontological considerations, conceived as antecedent to linguistic ones.

But the important point for our purposes here is not Frege's tendency to jettison the syntactic priority thesis in favour of an ontological priority, but rather his tendency, when he turns from mathematical to natural-language predication, to abandon the technical notion of the logical predicate, putting that of the grammatical predicate in its theoretical place. A corollary of the fact that Frege's conception of natural-language predication is essentially a grammatical one is that a proper name cannot be regarded as a predicate. This

---

[56] [5], pp. 7, 17 ([21], pp. 128, 134).   [57] [7], p. 197 n. 10 ([21], p. 171).

[58] And recall the passage quoted above (from p. 198 of [7]), where instead of saying that an object is (sc. constitutively) the *Bedeutung* of a grammatical subject, Frege remarks that it *can* be the *Bedeutung* of a grammatical subject, thereby implying that it is constitutively something else: cf. [14], p. 665 ([21], pp. 279–80). Similarly, in [6] at p. 42 ([21], p. 155) we are told that places, instants, and stretches of time are objects and *hence* that their linguistic designations are proper names. See also [26], p. 67; Resnik [3], p. 45; Stevenson, pp. 220–1.

implication is explicitly embraced by Frege in 'Über Begriff und Gegenstand'.[59] One of his examples is the proper name 'Venus', of which he remarks that it can never be a predicate, although it can form part of a predicate, and hence that the *Bedeutung* of this word can never appear as concept, only as object.[60] Here we have a striking convergence with Russell's claim in *Principles* that 'Socrates is a thing, because Socrates can never occur otherwise than as term in a proposition: Socrates is not capable of that curious twofold use which is involved in *human* and *humanity*.'[61] That is, 'Socrates' has to be a zeroth-level expression: there is nowhere else in the linguistic hierarchy of levels to place it. In effect, the claim is that a sentence like 'Socrates is wise' cannot be given an analysis (decomposition) that discerns 'is wise' as the subject and 'Socrates' as the predicate; it cannot be given a metalinguistic analysis along the lines that a Fregean (and the Russell of 1903) would be obliged to accord to the sentence 'Wisdom Socratizes'. But the truth is that Russell, like Frege, has not thought of the possibility of constructing such sentences: had he done so, he would have realized that, in any sense in which 'human' and 'humanity' are capable of a 'curious twofold use', 'Socrates' is equally capable of it.

67 Two Exegetical Problems in Frege

There are two points in Frege's 'Über Begriff und Gegenstand' which might appear to conflict with his official adoption there of an essentially grammatical conception of predication. One is his observation, in apparent contradiction with the above claim about 'Venus', that 'language uses the same word sometimes as a proper name and sometimes as a concept-word'.[62] His example is 'Vienna', which, though normally a proper name, functions as a concept-word in the sentence 'Trieste is no Vienna'. That might seem to license treating 'proper name' and 'concept-word', in Frege's usage, as purely *logical* categories. It was presumably this kind of point which led Diamond to range Frege along with Wittgenstein as a defender of the extreme version of the context principle we examined in §56. But I think it exegetically sounder to say that Frege has slightly misexpressed himself in lodging the claim that

---

[59] [7], pp. 193, 194–5, 197, 200 ([21], pp. 167–9, 171–4).   [60] [7], pp. 194–5 ([21], p. 169).

[61] [3], §48. Confusingly, Russell defines 'term of/in a proposition' in such a way that not all terms (in the sense of [3], §47) occurring in propositions count as 'terms of/in a proposition', but only those occurring *as logical subject* (§48). A 'term in a proposition' is what the proposition is 'about' (§§48, 482), and may be intersubstituted with any other *thing* (as opposed to *concept*: §48) *salva propositionalitate* (§48). Cf. Cartwright [3], pp. 916–17.

[62] [7], p. 200 ([21], p. 174).

language uses the same *word* sometimes as a proper name and sometimes as a concept-word. What he should have said, in conformity with the tenor of the earlier remarks on 'Venus' and the rest of his article, is that while any given *word* is determinately a proper name or a concept-word, and cannot swap these roles, any given *sign* can correspond to different words discharging different grammatical roles. On that approach the right thing to say will be that the sign 'Vienna' functions as one word in 'Vienna is a beautiful city' and quite another in 'Trieste is no Vienna' (though of course the meaning of 'Vienna' the concept-word is systematically related to the meaning of the corresponding proper name). It is no part of Frege's purpose to argue that the logical category of 'Vienna' as it figures in, say, the sentence 'Trieste is no Vienna' is not yet fixed, so that alternative readings of that sentence are possible. For Frege there is only one possible reading of that sentence, which treats 'Vienna' as a concept-word. It is just that in *other* sentences the very same sign appears in a different (though systematically related) guise, as a proper name—and again determinately so.

Again, the attribution to Frege of a grammatical conception of predication might seem to be undermined by his remark that a Thought can be analysed (in Dummett's terminology, decomposed) in many different ways, and that depending on how it is analysed different components will appear as subject and predicate, and hence that 'the subject of this judgement' only signifies something determinate in connection with one particular such analysis.[63] But there is no conflict. For Frege, 'Thought' (*Gedanke*) and 'judgement' (*Urteil*) reside at the level of sense:[64] they are not components of symbolic language, but senses of such components. It is somewhat odd to talk of *sentences* analysing *Thoughts*—one would have expected analysis to operate at the same level of the semantic hierarchy, not across levels—but the use of the notion of analysis in this context is not a technical one, and the point is just that different linguistic expressions can correspond to the same Thought at the level of sense. The claim is not that any given *linguistic expression* can be given alternative analyses in respect of its subject–predicate composition.[65] Indeed that cannot be Frege's point, since if it were his argument would collapse. For his claim is that subject and predicate can only be fixed—but they *can* be fixed—*in relation to* given linguistic expressions of the relevant Thought, these expressions being accordingly viewed as possessing allegiance to determinately either the

---

[63] [7], pp. 199–200 ([21], pp. 172–4). Cf. Letter to Marty of 29 Aug. 1882 ([22], p. 164); [26], pp. 203, 209, 218.

[64] On *Gedanken*, recall §13; cf. [15], pp. 377, 387 ([21], pp. 295, 303–4); [26], p. 271. On Frege's conception of *Urteil* see Thiel, pp. 106–7; Kleemeier, pp. 76–7.

[65] Cf. Bell [4], p. 41 (Thesis 3); Dummett [4], pp. 195–7, 291–2.

subject category or the predicate category. And Frege suggests elsewhere that alternative analyses of one and the same Thought at the level of the language are only possible if the analysing sentences contain *more than one occurrence of a proper name*, the senses of these different occurrences then constituting alternative subjects of the analysed Thought.[66]

In connection with this point it is worth while examining the relevant passage from 'Über Begriff und Gegenstand' in its entirety:

In the sentence 'There is at least one square root of 4', we are saying something, not about (say) the definite number 2, nor about −2, but about a concept, *square root of 4*; viz. that it is not empty. But if I express the same Thought thus: 'The concept *square root of 4* is realized', then the first six words form the proper name of an object, and it is about this object that something is being said. But notice carefully that what is being said here is not the same thing as was being said about the concept. This will be surprising only to somebody who fails to see that a Thought can be split up in many ways, so that now one thing, now another, appears as subject or predicate. The Thought itself does not yet determine what is to be regarded as the subject. If we say 'the subject of this judgment', we do not designate anything definite unless at the same time we indicate a definite kind of analysis; as a rule, we do this in connection with a definite wording. But we must never forget that different sentences may express the same Thought. For example, the Thought we are considering could also be taken as saying something about the number 4: 'The number 4 has the property that there is something of which it is the square'. Language has the means of presenting now one, now another part of the Thought as the subject; one of the most familiar is the distinction between active and passive forms. . . . It need not then surprise us that the same sentence (*Satz*) may be conceived as a statement about a concept and also as a statement about an object; only we must observe that these statements are different.[67]

I have already, in effect, dealt with one confusion in this passage: the use of the word *Satz* (sentence) instead of *Gedanke* (Thought) in the final sentence. Frege has misexpressed himself here, for his meaning is that one and the same *Thought* can be 'analysed' into different sentences at the level of language, and that these sentences are different in the sense that they have different grammatical subjects and predicates. For this 'analysis' to be possible, the grammatical subject–predicate structure of the analysing *sentences* must be fully determinate, not open to further 'analysis'. It is interesting to note that in his draft of 'Über Begriff und Gegenstand' Frege had expressed himself correctly: instead of the word 'Satz', adopted in the published version of the article, he had used 'Inhalt' ('content').[68] Recall too the discussion of

[66] Frege [26], p. 209; cf. Dummett [4], pp. 295–6.
[67] [7], pp. 199–200 ([21], p. 173). I have adapted the tr. given at [20], p. 49.
[68] [26], p. 118.

Begriffsschrift, §9, in §35: there I reported Frege's view that in the conceptual content (*begrifflicher Inhalt*) expressed by a sentence like 'Hydrogen is lighter than carbon dioxide' we may regard 'hydrogen' as the argument and 'is lighter than carbon dioxide' as the function, or 'carbon dioxide' as the argument and 'is heavier than hydrogen' as the function. There is no suggestion here that one and the same *sentence* may be subjected to alternative analyses: that would not make sense, for we have to do with two different sentences here. Rather, it is its *conceptual content* that may be so subjected. Clearly the point is that (to put it in Frege's mature terminology) the *Thought* expressed by our sentence 'Hydrogen is lighter than carbon dioxide' can *also* be expressed by the sentence 'Carbon dioxide is heavier than hydrogen': these two sentences express the same Thought (and so may both be said to analyse that Thought), but at the level of symbolic language they have *distinct* subject–predicate structures.[69] However, that observation throws up a further difficulty with our passage.

If the sentences 'There is at least one square root of 4', 'The concept *square root of 4* is realized', and 'The number 4 has the property that there is something of which it is the square' are genuinely to express the same Thought, then what they express at the level of reference (in my terms: the corresponding Russellian proposition) must also be the same. But given that these sentences are composed of different linguistic items corresponding to different entities in the realm of reference (or so one would assume), the items at the level of sense mediating between the sentences at the level of symbolic language and whatever we regard as corresponding to them at the level of reference cannot, it is natural to suppose, be the same, on pain of abandoning either the principle of compositionality for sense or the principle that sense determines reference but not vice versa (that is, that senses are related many–one to referents):[70] so surely Frege should say that the sentences in question express different—if significantly related—Thoughts. The Thoughts are related in the sense that it is not possible, for a thinker who understands all three sentences, coherently to take different attitudes to them (to accept or reject one but not either of the others). But this test for sameness of sense yields only a *necessary*, not a *sufficient*, condition of sameness of sense.[71] In other words, it is really a test of

---

[69] Cf. Bell [4], p. 44 (the second interpretation).   [70] Cf. Künne [2], pp. 145–7.

[71] Unfortunately, as Dummett notes ([4], p. 298; [5], p. 171; cf. Rumfitt [1], pp. 608–9), Frege wrongly thought that the criterion does give a sufficient condition for sameness of sense: see [26], pp. 213–14. Actually, to be fair to Frege, he does show awareness of the point that to take the test for sameness of sense as a sufficiency test would be to rule, implausibly, that all logical truths have the same sense, for he expressly excludes them from the scope of the test (letter to Husserl of 9 Dec. 1906, [22], p. 105). But he does not take account of the point that *logically equivalent contingent* sentences may be differently structured or have semantically distinct components, and so may differ in sense. Cf. von Kutschera [1], p. 71.

difference of sense (and hence was appropriately called by Evans the intuitive criterion of *difference*):[72] two sentences express different Thoughts if (but not also: only if) it is possible for someone to understand both sentences at a given time while coherently taking different attitudes to them. What Frege appears to need in order to make the point he is driving at in the above passage is a conception of what we might (adapting Evans's terminology) call 'intuitively similar' Thoughts,[73] which we may define as Thoughts whose corresponding sentences satisfy the *necessary* condition for sameness of sense laid down by the test, but not necessarily a *sufficient* condition. The claim will then be, not indeed that a *Thought* can be 'analysed' at the level of language in many different ways, but that the members of a *class of intuitively similar Thoughts* may be so analysable.[74]

As Bell remarks, Frege appears to commit himself to two conflicting theses, namely the thesis that the sentence is a model of the Thought (the principle of compositionality for sense), and the thesis that two structurally different sentences can express the same Thought.[75] If what I have said is right, to resolve the tension Frege must abandon the latter thesis. (Here I am in agreement with Dummett,[76] but not with Bell, who wishes to maintain both theses and is in consequence forced to abandon the univocity of 'Thought'.[77]) It follows, too, that we must say, against Frege[78] and Ramsey,[79] that in definitions the definiens and definiendum will not in general coincide in sense—for they will not in general even coincide in reference—though they will express intuitively similar Thoughts.[80] Likewise, translation from one language to another will not in general preserve sense, as Frege held,[81] but at best intuitive similarity of Thoughts. (These materials suggest a solution to the so-called paradox of analysis; but I will not pause to pursue that topic.)

Frege claims in the quoted passage as well as elsewhere that active sentences express the same Thought as their passive transforms,[82] and Bell supports this on the basis that the sentences would receive the same formalization in a

---

[72] [1], pp. 18–19: cf. §14 above.

[73] Chomsky calls them 'cognitively synonymous' ([2], p. 22), Künne 'cognitively equivalent' ([1], p. 256; [2], p. 142).

[74] 'May be' rather than 'must be', because all sets of analytic truths (and all sets of analytic falsehoods) will satisfy the necessary condition for sameness of sense, but some of these sets (presumably) will *not* admit of different 'analyses': cf. Künne [2], p. 143.

[75] Bell [5], §1; cf. Kemmerling [1], pp. 10–11; Carl [2], pp. 108–14. See e.g. Frege [19], p. 36 ([21], p. 378) and [26], pp. 243, 275 for the former thesis; [7], p. 196 n. ([21], p. 170) and [26], pp. 222, 288 for the latter.

[76] [5], pp. 168–76; [4], pp. 289–301.   [77] [5], §VI.

[78] [9], p. 319 ([21], p. 183); [10], I, §27; [26], p. 225; cf. Bermúdez, p. 93.

[79] [2], pp. 118–19; cf. Bostock [2], p. 46.   [80] Here I differ from Künne [1], p. 259.

[81] [26], p. 222; cf. Church [6], p. 25 (cited in §14).   [82] See [1], §3; [17], p. 64 ([21], p. 348).

logically primitive notation.[83] But if this argument worked for active–passive transformations, it would also work for more controversial cases where Frege associates differently structured sentences with a single Thought,[84] such as the members of the following pairs:

a is parallel to $b \approx$ the direction of $a =$ the direction of b;

$\forall a(f(a) = g(a)) \approx$ the value-range of $f =$ the value-range of g;

There exist $Fs \approx$ the number of $Fs \neq 0$;

There are just as many Fs as $Gs \approx$ The number of $Fs =$ the number of Gs.[85]

Certainly, it will not *normally* be the case that differently structured sentences express exactly the same Thought; for differently structured sentences will not normally be co-referential, and if they are not co-referential they cannot express the same Thought either, co-referentiality being a necessary (though not a sufficient) condition for identity at the level of sense. In the normal case, we must go along with Dummett:

To say that the sense of a sentence is composed out of the senses of its constituent words is to say . . . that we can grasp that sense only as the sense of a complex which is composed out of parts in exactly that way; only a sentence which had exactly that structure, and whose primitive constituents corresponded in sense pointwise with those of the original sentence, could possibly express the very same sense.[86]

Or, as I would prefer to say, only a sentence which had exactly the same structure as that of the original sentence, and whose primitive constituents corresponded in reference pointwise with those of the original sentence, could possibly express the very same reference, and so a fortiori the same sense, too.

At least, that will be the normal case, but we should allow that sentences may under certain circumstances coincide in reference even if they do not satisfy the above condition: that will be the case if, for instance, they differ in purely formal respects. Perhaps active–passive transformations, even if they do not preserve sense as Frege thought, may at least be permitted to preserve reference, so long as we confine our attention to quantifier-free sentences.[87] It has been suggested that relations and their converses are identical, so that 'the proposition that a is before b is the proposition that b is after a';[88] but this strikes me as implausible, for the propositions in question differ not merely formally, but substantially, given the opposite meanings (which here fortuitously cancel out) of 'before' and 'after'. And certainly if the view is motivated by the kind

---

[83] [4], p. 44.   [84] Cf. Bermúdez, p. 88; van Heijenoort [2], p. 104; Potter [1], pp. 109–10.
[85] See here Dummett [4], p. 292; Künne [2], p. 142.   [86] [2], pp. 378–9 (cf. [4], p. 94).
[87] Chomsky [1], pp. 100–1; [4], pp. 104–5; Kimball, p. 118.   [88] Williamson, p. 257.

of transcendental realism I rejected in Chapter 2, namely the thought that the proposition that *a* is before *b* and the proposition that *b* is after *a* are both made true by the same chunk of brute, pre-propositional reality, and hence are the same proposition (so that the relation in question is the same as its converse, or alternatively does not have a converse),[89] then of course I reject it. On the other hand, in certain cases discussed by Bealer and involving artificially constructed relations that are interdefined, it seems to me plausible that relevant propositions will collapse to a single proposition.[90] So if we set

$Fx =_{df} x$ follows a

$Gy =_{df} b$ follows y,

then it would be quite attractive to say that the proposition *that Fb* is the same as the proposition *that Ga*: but of course that upshot is just an artefact of the definitions, which guarantee that, though the relevant *sentences* are distinct, their corresponding *propositions* match one another pointwise in content and so are identical. Further, I argued earlier (§21) that sentences and their nominalizations are co-referential despite their failure to intersubstitute *salva congruitate*—and so despite their failure to satisfy the above condition. But it would be implausible to claim that any of the members of the four Fregean pairs mentioned above is co-referential with its paired member. Equally, Frege's suggestion that '*A*' has the same sense as '*A* & *A*', and as '¬¬*A*', is surely mistaken, though the further claim that '*A* & *B*' and '*B* & *A*' express the same Thought is much more plausible (assuming that '&' is the familiar connective).[91] But nothing prevents our recognizing the phenomena to which Frege is responding by saying that the members of the pairs in question express intuitively similar Thoughts:[92] I have in effect made this suggestion already (§40) in connection with Ramsey's treatment of sentences and their double negations.[93]

---

[89] So Fine [2], pp. 3–5. Fine's argument is criticized by MacBride ([7]), but he does not question its assumed transcendental realism, apparently accepting (p. 54) that the cat's being on the mat and the mat's being under the cat involve the same relation *in re*.

[90] Bealer [2], pp. 5–10; cf. Menzel, p. 63.

[91] Frege [19], pp. 39, 44, 49 ([21], pp. 381, 386, 391–2). Cf. Künne [2], p. 141 with n. 48; Currie [2], pp. 296–7; Bermúdez, pp. 99–100; King [5], pp. 14–15.

[92] Bostock ([1], pp. 36–7) and Potter ([1], p. 117) would except Basic Law V on the ground that Russell's paradox shows it to be false and so not analytic.

[93] On the issue of this paragraph see King [2], who argues against admitting exceptions to what I have called the normal case. But that such exceptions arise seems to me guaranteed by the fact that the proposition *that Socrates is wise* (i) must indeed be a proposition, and (ii) must be named by the noun clause 'that Socrates is wise'; but (iii) the sentence 'Socrates is wise' is also a name of that proposition (as King would agree), from which it follows that syntactically non-congruous expressions may be co-referential. King would dispute (ii), but his grounds for doing so are essentially the Dummettian considerations I rejected in §53 (see his [5], pp. 106–7; note that on p. 137 that-clauses are said to 'designate' propositions).

68 Inference and the Logical Predicate

As far as the project of displaying correct inference patterns is concerned, the significant distinction is not that between grammatical subject and predicate, but between what I am calling logical subject and predicate. For that project may require us to take any semantically significant part of the sentence as our topic. And any semantically significant subsentential lexical component can be treated as its (unannotated) logical predicate, by omitting the remainder of the sentence and conceiving the expression so derived as carrying essential argument-places. The expressions that Frege called concept-words exhibit no *special* aptness for the role of logical predicate. As Ramsey put it: 'with a sufficiently elastic language any proposition can be so expressed that any of its terms is the subject'.[94] Ramsey himself, it may be noted, spoiled his insight by wrongly trying to restrict its scope. He argued that his principle does not apply to complex sentences like 'Either Socrates is wise or Plato is foolish', for if we construe 'Socrates' as the logical subject of this sentence, and 'ξ is wise unless Plato is foolish' as its (annotated) logical predicate, we will have to regard that logical predicate as standing for a complex universal, which Ramsey held to be incoherent. Why? Ramsey considered the schematic relational sentence 'aRb', and pointed out that if there are such things as complex universals, this sentence will generate three such universals, each correlated with a distinct proposition, namely the propositions *that R holds between a and b, that a has R to b*, and *that b is such that a has R to it*. He then remarked:

These must be three different propositions because they have different sets of constituents, and yet they are not three propositions, but one proposition, for they all say the same thing, namely that *a* has *R* to *b*. So the theory of complex universals is responsible for an incomprehensible trinity, as senseless as that of theology.[95]

But this argument is inconclusive.[96] Assuming that Ramsey intends 'proposition' to mean 'Russellian proposition',[97] that is, an entity at the level of reference with worldly things and properties as constituents, we may confront him with a dilemma. Either the three sentences 'R holds between a and b', 'a has R to b', and 'b is such that a has R to it' refer to distinct Russellian propositions, or they do not. If we say that they do, on the basis that they are composed of distinct words constructed in distinct ways, then it is open to us to say that the propositions they express, while not identical, are significantly related: the senses of those sentences form, in fact, a class of what I have called

---

[94] [2], p. 116.   [95] Ibid., p. 118.   [96] Cf. Hale [4], pp. 189–90.
[97] MacBride [5], p. 88.

intuitively similar Thoughts and, by a natural extension of the terminology, we may say that the corresponding Russellian propositions form a class of intuitively similar propositions. Alternatively, if we allowed this case to constitute an exception to the general rule (§67) that only sentences which have exactly the same structure, and whose primitive constituents correspond in reference pointwise, can be co-referential—and there would be some basis for this line, in the structural (a logicist would say: logical) nature of the vocabulary by which the sentences differ ('holds between', 'such that')[98]—then we might say, following Geach and Dummett, that one and the same proposition can admit of different analyses (that is, decompositions, in Dummett's sense), just as a single country can admit of different divisions into regions.[99] On this approach, when asked of the schematic sentence 'Raa' what the (unique) proposition it expresses says about a—which of

$$\lambda x(Rxx)(a),$$
$$\lambda x(\lambda y(Rxy)(a))(a), \text{ or}$$
$$\lambda y(\lambda x(Rxy)(a))(a) —$$

we should reply: all three.[100] (Note that the admission of alternative 'analyses' of particular propositions is not incompatible with the identification of the world with all the propositions.) Either way, then, however matters stand with the theological trinity there is nothing incomprehensible about Ramsey's linguistic trinity. The claim that any lexical part of a sentence may be regarded as its analytical predicate, and the sentence as a whole abstracted upon to form a corresponding logical predicate (that is, a logical predicate with the same substantial semantic content as an analytical predicate), can be taken to apply to all sentences, complex as well as simple ones.

69 Unity and the Logical Predicate

Frege's answer to the problem of unity—the claim that unity is effected by just one sort of subsentential expression, namely the grammatical predicate—cannot, so I have argued, be upheld. It is not, in general, either necessary or sufficient for the unity of a sentence that it contain a grammatical predicate. But suppose we try to deal with our problem by saying that unity is effected by the *logical* predicate, as I have defined this. In one way the

---

[98] Cf. Russell [11], p. 200.
[99] Geach [8], p. 146; Dummett [3], p. 264; cf. Rumfitt [1], pp. 607–8; Oliver [1], pp. 92–4.
[100] Cf. Humberstone, pp. 4–6.

answer cannot be faulted.[101] That is because the logical predicate is, as we have said (§65), so defined that it indeed incorporates the unity of the sentence and its corresponding proposition: for it is essentially a partially specified sentence, or we might call it a partially determined sentence-frame. Since the (unannotated) logical predicate is, like the analytical predicate (from which it differs by virtue of containing essential argument-places), the highest-level subsentential expression in the sentence (§64), and since, as we have seen (§46), the negation of the highest-level subsentential expression in a sentence cannot be distinguished from the negation of the sentence as a whole, we have here the grain of truth in the traditional view that it is the predicate of a sentence, rather than its subject, that is peculiarly responsible for the sentence's unity. But, while the tradition has tended to assume that the 'argument from negation' bestows the unity-constituting property on the *grammatical* predicate, we have seen that this is incorrect: the only predicate that can reasonably be thought to bear responsibility for the unity of a sentence and its corresponding proposition is the *logical* predicate. But it bears that responsibility in an entirely trivial sense.

Here it may be helpful to recall a point discussed earlier in this study. In his lectures 'The Philosophy of Logical Atomism', Russell argued that

to understand a name you must be acquainted with the particular of which it is a name... You do not... have any suggestion of the form of a proposition, whereas in understanding a predicate you do. To understand 'red', for instance, is to understand what is meant by saying that a thing is red. You have to bring in the form of a proposition.[102]

But Russell's attempt here to establish an asymmetry between a name and a predicate fails for a reason we explored in Chapter 3. There is indeed a sense in which we should want to say that a predicate like 'red' (or 'is red') 'brings in the form of a proposition': but the sense in which it does so is sponsored by the context principle, and in *that* sense, as we have seen, a name like 'Socrates' brings in the form of a proposition no less than '(is) red' does.[103] Contrariwise, in any sense in which 'Socrates' *fails* to 'bring in the form of a proposition', a predicate like 'red' (or 'is red') does not do so either; in *that* sense, as we are now in a position to add, only a *logical* predicate such as 'ξ is red'—to specify that logical predicate in its annotated form—can be said to 'bring in the form of a proposition'. But in that sense, too, the expression '(Φ) Socrates', being no less a logical predicate than 'ξ is red', has just as good a claim to 'bring in

---

[101] Cf. Davidson [2], p. 132.   [102] [13], p. 205. Cf. pp. 337–8.
[103] Cf. Grossmann [1], p. 78; Sellars [1], p. 234.

the form of a proposition': for a logical predicate may, as I have stressed, derive its substantial semantic content as well from the subject of traditional grammar as from the predicate. (Putting it the other way round, a grammatical predicate may figure as a logical subject just as well as a grammatical subject may do so.) But now, given that the only predicate that can be regarded as conferring unity on a sentence, by virtue of 'bringing in the form of a proposition', is the logical, not the grammatical, predicate, the interest and explanatory value of the thesis under consideration—namely that the logical predicate bears responsibility for unity—evaporates; for since the logical predicate is no more than a schematic sentence, whatever unity-conferring virtues it possesses it has inherited from the sentence from which it was formed, taken as theoretically prior.[104] Hence if one is asking after the principle of unity in the sentence and its corresponding proposition, to have one's attention directed to the evidently derivative unity of the logical predicate is to be taken, at least in the first instance, on a detour. Still, as we shall see presently, this does not mean that the logical predicate has *no* role to play in an account of unity: far from it. After all, detours are not always pointless.

Davidson once aptly remarked that Frege's doctrine of unsaturatedness seems to 'label a difficulty rather than solve it'.[105] The same point may be made in connection with a claim of Hylton's:

Only those who take objects (in the most general sense) as fundamental are faced with the problem of saying how they combine to form propositions or judgements. This cannot be a question for those who, with Kant and Frege, take the concept of an object to be derivative upon the fundamental notion of a complete proposition or judgement.[106]

As for Frege, Hylton has the context principle in mind;[107] I have sufficiently indicated why I think that the context principle in fact tells against Frege's solution to the unity problem rather than in its favour. Kant is allowed to sidestep the problem because of his anti-empiricism: if the objects given originally in experience are not bare, but already conceptualized, it follows that, at that original stage, complete propositions or judgements—judgements to the effect that such-and-such objects *are* thus and so—are already in the picture, and do not need to be subsequently constructed from more basic materials.[108] That is true,[109] but the question still arises: what distinguishes a proposition—an

[104] Cf. Dummett [3], pp. 482–6.
[105] [1], p. 17. Cf. Bell [1], pp. 9–10, 16; Hanks [1], p. 159; King [5], p. 18.
[106] [1], p. 173 n. 7. Cf. Bell [1], pp. 4–5; Tugendhat [2], pp. 140–1.
[107] Hylton [1], p. 223. Cf. Goldfarb [2], pp. 190, 194. Hylton rightly notes that Frege's doctrine of the unsaturatedness of concepts is unfit to solve the problem: [2], p. 15 n. 6.
[108] Hylton [1], pp. 177–8; cf. [2], pp. 11–13.
[109] See my [15], esp. chs. 5 and 6. Cf. Tugendhat [2], pp. 202–3.

entity composed in the right way of conceptualized objects—from a mere aggregate of such objects? The sheer fact that all objects are unsaturated, and that they are, in appropriate combinations, of the right shapes to form propositions is not of itself enough to *effect* their being fitted together into propositions. This is the ontological image of a point I have already insisted on at the level of language (§§5, 62, 65). The moment of propositional unity must be something over and above the mere suitability and availability of objects to be combined in the right way to form a proposition.

70 Bradley's Regress and the Tradition

The instantiation regress to which I alluded in §65, and which has surfaced elsewhere in this study, was well known to the major medieval thinkers, and it appears in various guises in the writings of Abelard,[110] Avicenna,[111] Scotus,[112] Ockham,[113] Buridan,[114] Gregory of Rimini,[115] and Suarez,[116] as well as in the writings of later thinkers such as Leibniz who were influenced by scholasticism.[117] The instantiation regress also bears some recognizable kinship to the regress arguments developed in the first half of Plato's *Parmenides*,[118] and the common view that it is cognate with the Third Man regress has some plausibility:[119] for, as we shall explore in more detail in the next chapter, the instantiation regress echoes the two key features of the Third Man regress, namely the self-predication and non-identity assumptions (the point that Forms can be predicated of Forms, and that instantiating Forms are not identical with the Forms they instantiate).[120] The familiarity of the regress to modern readers, however, derives not from its ancient, medieval, or early modern incarnations, but from its prominence in the philosophy of F. H. Bradley, and it is standard practice, which I shall follow, to call it Bradley's regress. Here is Bradley's description of the way in which the regress arises:

[A] relation . . . without qualities is nothing. But how the relation can stand to the qualities is . . . unintelligible. If it is nothing to the qualities, then they are not related at

---

[110] Abelard [2], II. i, pp. 158.34–159.5; cf. Kneale and Kneale, p. 208.

[111] Avicenna, 3. 10, pp. 178–83; cf. Weinberg, p. 93.

[112] Scotus, *Ordinatio*, II, d. 1, qq. 4–5 (vii, pp. 132–4); cf. Beckmann, p. 78.

[113] Ockham [1], I, 51, pp. 169–70; [4], I, d. 30, p. 317.

[114] Buridan [1], V, q. 8, fo. 31^{rb-va} (see Normore, pp. 198, 202).

[115] Gregory [2], dd. 28–32, esp. pp. 86–7, 123–7, 132–3, 139.

[116] Suarez, VII. i, §18, p. 256.   [117] See Mugnai, pp. 18, 32.

[118] See here Ryle, i, pp. 9–11.

[119] See e.g. Priest [1], p. 188; cf. Ricketts [3], p. 193 n. 12.   [120] Owen, pp. 207–8.

all; and, if so, . . . they have ceased to be qualities, and their relation is a nonentity. But if it is to be something to them, then clearly we now shall require a *new* connecting relation. For the relation hardly can be the mere adjective of one or both of its terms; or, at least, as such it seems indefensible. And, being something itself, if it does not itself bear a relation to the terms, in what intelligible way will it succeed in being anything to them? But here again we are hurried off into the eddy of a hopeless process, since we are forced to go on finding new relations without end. The links are united by a link, and this bond of union is a link which also has two ends; and these require each a fresh link to connect them with the old. The problem is to find how the relation can stand to its qualities; and this problem is insoluble.[121]

The basic idea of the regress is the following: if we analyse the connection between object and property as the obtaining of a real relation of instantiation of the property by the object, we are launched on an infinite regress, because we shall have to analyse the introduced relation of instantiation as the obtaining of a yet further relation of instantiation, connecting object, property, and instantiation. And so on.

  Notice that Bradley states the problem in terms of actually obtaining relations of instantiation—the problem as it arises in connection with facts or states of affairs—and in this respect most of his medieval forebears adopted the same approach. But it is possible—and this will be crucial in the sequel—to cast the problem not specifically in terms of true propositions (remember that I simply identify facts or states of affairs with true propositions at the level of reference), but in terms of propositions in general, whether true or false. Here is a modern statement of the genesis of the regress, given by Francesco Orilia, which adopts this broader perspective:

[I]f a proposition is an entity constituting a complex unity of a certain sort and it is such that its constituents are, say, $R^n, a_1, \ldots, a_n$, then there must be a relationship holding together $a_1, \ldots, a_n$ and R^n to the effect that the proposition has a certain form, e.g., $R^n a_1, \ldots, a_n$. If this relation is I^{n+1}, then the constituents of the proposition are really $I^{n+1}, R^n, a_1, \ldots, a_n$, and the proposition must have a form such as $I^{n+1} R^n a_1, \ldots, a_n$ (where 'I^{n+1}' is meant to represent the $(n+1)$-adic exemplification (instantiation) relation or copula).[122]

But, he adds, this line of argument can clearly be iterated ad infinitum, generating a 'Bradley series':

(BS) $R^n a_1, \ldots, a_n; I^{n+1} R^n a_1, \ldots, a_n; I^{n+2} I^{n+1} R^n a_1, \ldots, a_n;$ etc.

The medieval tradition regarded the regress as vicious, as did Bradley himself. For it was widely accepted among medieval thinkers, and Leibniz agreed,[123]

[121] [2], pp. 27–8. Cf. [2], pp. 16–18; [1], pp. 240, 264 n.; [3], pp. 641, 643.
[122] Orilia [1], p. 104; cf. Hochberg [6], pp. 75–6.   [123] Mugnai, pp. 42–3.

that relations must have a non-relational *fundamentum in re*, that is, that while relations of relations are possible, and perhaps relations of. . . relations of relations, to any finite degree, there can be no infinite regress of such relationally based relations: ultimately any such chain must bottom out in absolute, non-relational properties. In Bradley's case, his rejection of the innocence of the regress is connected with his idealism. The argument seems to be: if relations were real the regress would arise; since the regress is a vicious one, we must conclude that relations are ideal.[124] If that is the position, it is obviously a weak one: for if the regress is vicious, why should regarding relations as mere abstractions (or as 'relatively true', or as 'belonging to appearance' as opposed to 'ultimate reality') draw its sting?[125] Somewhat similarly, Leibniz held that while real bodies are actually divided to infinity (by contrast mathematical entities, such as lines, are merely potentially infinitely divisible),[126] the infinite division of body entails that bodies as such have no genuine unity and are mere phenomena, such unity as is found in body being supplied by the involvement of mind in matter.[127]

The traditional branding of Bradley's regress as vicious seems to have met with almost unanimous concurrence among philosophers and commentators in the analytic tradition including, as we have seen, Frege,[128] as well as such influential contemporary or near-contemporary figures as Ryle, Sellars, Strawson, Dummett, Simons, Armstrong (at least sometimes), Davidson, Lewis, and Priest.[129] Even Aristotle can plausibly be enlisted among the regress's opponents.[130] But the critics have not had things all their own way: a few voices—initially isolated, but the chorus is gradually growing stronger—have suggested that the regress might be innocent after all. These heterodox voices have so far included McTaggart, Orilia, Armstrong (again), Klein, and myself.[131]

[124] See here Bradley [2], pp. 16–29; [3], pp. 630–50; Hylton [1], pp. 48–9. Cf. Vallicella [3]; [4], p. 163; Imaguire, p. 102; Davidson [2], pp. 106, 144.

[125] Cf. Horstmann, pp. 127–8 n. 45.   [126] See here Phemister, pp. 106–9.

[127] See the passages cited by Arthur in Leibniz [6], pp. lxix, lxxiii, 259, 271–2. Cf. the Fifth Letter to Clarke, §42 ([1], vii, p. 401); the letter to de Volder of 30 June 1704 ([1], ii, p. 268).

[128] Recall the long passage from [7] cited in §27 above.

[129] Ryle, i, p. 10; Sellars [2]; Strawson [1], pp. 167–76; [6], pp. 18, 21; Dummett [2], pp. 251–2; Simons [3], p. 80; Armstrong [2], p. 108; [4], pp. 108–11; [6], p. 242; Davidson [1], p. 17; [2], pp. 79, 85, 87, 93–4, 114–15, 143–5; Lewis [8], pp. 6–7; Priest [1], pp. 188–9. To this list may be added: Fisk [2], pp. 141–2; Grossmann [1], pp. 78–83, 209; Dodd [2], p. 150; Maurin and Sahlin, pp. 23–7. On Vallicella, see §81 below.

[130] At *Met.* Z. 17 (1041b11–33), Aristotle does not mention a relations regress, but rather a regress of elements. Still, we can deduce from this passage what his attitude to Bradley's regress would be, given his opposition to the reality of relations (cf. §47 above): in rejecting the coherence of an elements regress, he a fortiori rejects that of a relations regress.

[131] McTaggart, I, §§88–91 (cf. Vallicella [2], pp. 209–11); Orilia [1], pp. 107–8; [2], §7; Armstrong [5], pp. 118–19; my [1]; [10]. I shall discuss Klein's relevant publications in due course. Cf. also

The list of the supporters of Bradley's regress, if I can put it that way, is not perhaps quite as authoritative as the list of its detractors, but then the argument from authority nowadays enjoys about as much credibility as Uncle Toby's *Argumentum Fistulatorium*.[132] The widespread desire among philosophers who have confronted the issue to be seen to excoriate Bradley's regress well illustrates Davidson's remark that 'the difficulty of avoiding one infinite regress or another might almost be said to be *the* problem of predication'.[133] By my lights, however, Davidson's remark is importantly inaccurate: for it would be better to say, not that the difficulty of avoiding Bradley's regress *is* the 'problem of predication', but that that is the way in which that problem *has been viewed* by the majority of thinkers who have considered it at all (including Davidson himself). I regard this way of putting things as more accurate than Davidson's own formulation because, as I shall suggest in due course, the solution to the 'problem of predication' lies not in avoiding Bradley's regress, but in embracing it (with the right attitude). The regress seems to prompt a kind of phobic reaction in many philosophers when they sense its presence just around the semantic or ontological corner; but the phobia should be dispelled, not indulged.

Russell's position on the regress, at least in *Principles*, is somewhat equivocal: the fact that each stage of the regress entails the next stage he regards as harmless, but if the regress arises in the analysis of meaning then it is, in his view, vicious.[134] He applies this point to, for example, the attempt to analyse '*A* differs from *B*' into '*A*, referent, difference, relatum, *B*', which occurs in a passage I have already quoted (§29).[135] Russell notes the regressive tendencies of this analysis, remarking that the regress thereby generated is not *in se* vicious, but is so only if it arises in the analysis of meaning.[136] This problem led Russell to the two-aspect doctrine of concepts (the relation in itself/the relation actually relating) that I have already examined.[137] But it is clear that, in the present context, the regress, if it arises at all, will arise precisely in the analysis of meaning. For we are aiming to give a general account of the unity of the proposition, that is, an account of how it is that a declarative sentence can have the distinctive kind of meaning it has. Hence Russell, for my purposes, counts

---

K. Campbell, pp. 34–6; Trettin, p. 212; Schnieder [1], p. 227; Hochberg [6], pp. 75–9. But note that although Hochberg has some preliminary remarks on the innocence of Bradley's regress (pp. 76–7), he really counts as an 'opponent' of it, because he ends up legislating to avoid it (p. 78), claiming that exemplification is not 'a relation among relations', a move which, as I shall argue in due course (§84), is unacceptably ad hoc.

[132] Sterne, i, ch. 21, p. 93.   [133] [2], p. 79. Cf. Siderits, [3], pp. 58, 64.
[134] [3], §§55, 99, 329. A similar approach is found in Currie [1].   [135] [3], §54.
[136] [3], §55.   [137] Cf. N. Griffin [4], p. 166.

as an 'opponent' of the regress. In the remainder of this chapter I shall show that the early Wittgenstein must also be ranged among its 'opponents'. For although Wittgenstein does not explicitly mention the regress in the *Tractatus*, he can nonetheless be read as trying to prevent its arising by relegating logical form to the status of the ineffable.

71 Russell and the General Form of the Proposition

Wittgenstein's treatment of logical form in the *Tractatus* may usefully be read as a direct response to the difficulties Russell encountered when he dealt with the issue in his manuscript *Theory of Knowledge*, composed in 1913. We know that Russell discussed the contents of this work with Wittgenstein, and that he abandoned it under the onslaught of Wittgenstein's criticisms.[138] One important aspect of the theory developed by Russell in that manuscript was his inclusion in the act of judgement of the general form of the proposition: this we have already noted (§11). In the case of dyadic relations, Russell expressed this general form by means of the locutions 'something has some relation to something', and 'something and something have a certain relation'.[139] It is clear that, at this point, Russell has abandoned his 1903 account of unity in terms of the 'relation actually relating', and has moved to regarding the form of a proposition as its unifier.[140] But how does this form enter into the act of judgement? Here Russell falls into antinomy.

On the one hand, he tells us that when we replace the constant constituents of a proposition (by which Russell now means 'declarative sentence')[141] by variables, what we arrive at is 'the pure *form* of the proposition, and the form is not a "thing", not another constituent along with the objects that were previously related in that form'. In the proposition 'Socrates is human', we are told,

'is' represents merely the way in which the constituents are put together. This cannot be a new constituent, for if it were, there would have to be a new way in which it and the other two constituents are put together, and if we take this way as again a constituent, we find ourselves embarked on an endless regress.[142]

On the other hand, we are subsequently assured that propositional forms are indeed objects, but utterly simple ones: the form of dual complexes 'seems

---

[138] See here Monk, ch. 10.   [139] [9], pp. 114, 116.   [140] Cf. Johnston, pp. 234–5.
[141] See Russell [9], p. 105.
[142] Ibid., p. 98; cf. [11], p. 198. See N. Griffin [4], p. 168; Stevens [3], p. 94.

to have a structure, and therefore to be not simple; but it is more correct to say that it *is* a structure. Language is not well adapted for speaking of such objects.'[143] And the antinomy is replicated at the epistemological level, where Russell wants to say both that logical objects such as propositional forms 'cannot be regarded as "entities", and that, therefore, what we call "acquaintance" with them cannot really be a dual relation', and also that 'there certainly is such a thing as "logical experience", by which I mean a kind of immediate knowledge, other than judgment, . . . something which seems fitly described as "acquaintance with logical objects" '.[144] Here Russell manages perhaps verbally, but hardly materially, to avoid falling into contradiction.[145]

If forms are objects, what distinguishes them from more ordinary objects figuring in acts of judgement? This problem cries out for an answer, particularly when Russell attempts, in his chapter on how propositions can be objects of understanding—a mental act which Russell now regards as basic to acts of judgement and belief[146]—to symbolize acts of understanding, for instance the act of understanding that *A* and *B* are similar, which he represents as

$U\{S, A, B, \text{similarity}, R(x, y)\}$.

Here *U* is the act of understanding, *S* the subject (i.e. the understander), and $R(x, y)$ represents the form 'something and something have some relation'.[147] But surely now the very regress which Russell had so accurately diagnosed in the earlier passage from 'Logical Data' threatens. Do we not need another form to unite the disparate components of the act of understanding? Russell makes a half-hearted attempt to circumvent this problem by observing that

it is obvious . . . that $R(x, y)$ enters in a different way from the other three objects [i.e. *A*, *B*, and similarity], and that 'similarity' has a different relation to $R(x, y)$ from that which *A* and *B* have, while *A* and *B* have the same relation to $R(x, y)$.[148]

But the 'different way' in which $R(x, y)$ is said to enter into the understood complex receives no symbolic expression in Russell's formalization of the complex itself: as far as that formalization goes, all components seem to be on a level. There is nothing to tell us that $R(x, y)$ is supposed to represent the structure of the other components; there is nothing to tell us that $R(x, y)$ is supposed to be absolutely simple in the sense that, rather than *having* structure, it *is* the structure of the complex. On the contrary, by giving this structure an explicit representation and placing that representation alongside

[143] [9], p. 114; cf. p. 130.   [144] Ibid., p. 97.   [145] See Monk, p. 296; Candlish [2], p. 72.
[146] See [9], p. 115; cf. Sommerville, p. 183.   [147] [9], p. 117.   [148] Ibid.

other components of the understood complex in his representation of the act of understanding, Russell implies that $R(x, y)$ is a component just like these others, itself standing in need, just like them, of *being constructed with* the remaining components of the complex.[149] Hence there immediately arises the need for a representation of *another* structure, namely one that unites the first structure, $R(x, y)$, with the components A, B, and similarity: which evidently launches us on the regress. Russell seems to have forgotten his own earlier claim that the structure—the form—of a proposition cannot itself be a constituent of the proposition.

72 Wittgenstein's Criticism of Russell

The objection which Wittgenstein raised against Russell's theory of judgement, and which brought the project to a standstill,[150] was that, as he said to Russell in June 1913,

> from the prop[osition] 'A judges that (say) a is in the Rel[ation] R to b', if correctly analysed, the prop[osition] 'aRb. ∨ . ¬aRb' must follow directly *without the use of any other premiss*. This condition is not fulfilled by your theory.[151]

What this objection amounts to is expressed by Nicholas Griffin as follows: 'the requirement that aRb. ∨ . ¬aRb follow directly from the judgement that aRb imposes a significance constraint on judgements. For aRb. ∨ . ¬aRb is a tautology and thus follows classically from any proposition, *provided* that aRb is significant.'[152] The objection thus coincides with the one Wittgenstein went on to make against Russell's theory of judgement in the *Tractatus*, where he wrote that 'the correct explanation of the form of the sentence "A judges that p" must show that it is impossible to judge nonsense. (Russell's theory does not satisfy this condition).'[153] The point had already been made by Wittgenstein to Russell in a letter of January 1913, when he wrote that

> every theory of types must be rendered superfluous by a proper theory of the symbolism: For instance if I analyse the prop[osition] Socrates is mortal into Socrates, Mortality and $(\exists x, y)\varepsilon_1(x, y)$ I want a theory of types to tell me that 'Mortality is Socrates' is nonsensical, because if I treat 'Mortality' as a proper name (as I did) there is nothing to prevent me to make the substitution the wrong way round. *But* if I analyse [it] (as I do now) into Socrates and $(\exists x)x$ is mortal or generally into x and $(\exists x)\phi(x)$* it becomes

---

[149] Cf. Hochberg [8], pp. 15–16; Stevens [3], p. 94.
[150] See here again Monk, ch. 10; N. Griffin [2], pp. 142–3; Hylton [1], pp. 357–9.
[151] [9], p. 237.   [152] [2], pp. 143–4.   [153] [1], §5.5422.

impossible to substitute the wrong way round, because the two symbols are now of a different *kind* themselves.[154]

The last sentence contains a flag for a footnote which reads:

*Prop[osition]s which I formerly wrote $\varepsilon_2(a, R, b)$ I now write $R(a, b)$ and analyse them into a, b, and $(\exists x, y)R(x, y)$.[155]

To this Wittgenstein adds the remark that the expression '$(\exists x, y)R(x, y)$' is 'not complex'. Is Wittgenstein's criticism fair? Yes and no: the criticism hits its target all right; but it does not quite lie in Wittgenstein's mouth to make it.

Russell, as we have seen, agrees that, in the act of understanding (and judging) that A is similar to B, the form of the understood entity, namely $R(x, y)$, 'enters in a different way from the other three objects' (i.e. A, B, and similarity), and further that ' "similarity" has a different relation to $R(x, y)$ from that which A and B have, while A and B have the same relation to $R(x, y)$'.[156] The trouble with Russell's theory, according to Wittgenstein, is that the content of this observation is not built into the symbolism itself, so that the bare symbolism requires an 'extra premiss', if nonsensical combinations are to be ruled out. Here Russell will insist that the formula '$R(x, y)$' shows, by exploiting the distinction between upper- and lower-case letters, that whatever we can substitute for 'R' is of a different logical type from whatever we can substitute for 'x' and 'y'.[157] Unfortunately that does not help. For one thing, the use of distinct types of letter (upper- and lower-case, as it might be) requires an explicit verbal gloss if it is to achieve its aim of discouraging us from making inappropriate substitutions. But even if we waive that point, it remains the case that there is nothing in the sheer formula

$$U\{S, A, B, \text{similarity}, R(x, y)\}$$

to tell us that similarity is the relation, and A and B the relata, rather than (for example) A the relation, and similarity and B the relata: incorporating a representation of the general form of similarity judgements into the formula does not settle this matter. Wittgenstein is right, then, that an extra premiss

---

[154] [9], p. 236. Cf. the remark in 'Notes on Logic' that 'Every right theory of judgement must make it impossible for me to judge that this table penholders the book. Russell's theory does not satisfy this requirement' ([6], p. 103); [1], §§3.331–3. See further J. Griffin, pp. 113–14; Stevens [2], pp. 40–2; [3], pp. 95–6.

[155] Wittgenstein had hitherto in his letters to Russell symbolized the copula using a subscripted epsilon, the subscript indicating order (i.e. level): [9], pp. 232–3; cf. N. Griffin [4], p. 176.

[156] [9], p. 117.

[157] So ibid., p. 98: 'we may naturally symbolize the form [of a dual complex] by "xRy", where we use a different sort of letter for the relation, because the difference between a relation and its terms is a *logical* difference'. Cf. p. 90; N. Griffin [2], p. 140.

is required by Russell's theory, and the observation of Russell's quoted at the beginning of this paragraph can serve as a programmatic move in the direction of supplying the needed supplementation.[158]

But how is the supplementation to be rendered superfluous, as Wittgenstein claims it must be? Surely *any* symbolic representation of the form of an act of understanding or judgement, or generally of a proposition, will need to be eked out by a natural-language key to its interpretation. And what Wittgenstein tells us, in the part of the January 1913 letter quoted above, clearly does nothing to obviate the need for supplementation. To say, as in effect Wittgenstein does (I extrude the supernumerary existential quantifiers from his formulations), that 'Socrates is mortal' has the general form $\phi(x)$—where 'ϕ . . .', not 'x', is supposed to 'bring in the form of a proposition', as Russell (under Wittgenstein's influence) would later put it[159]—while perhaps going some distance towards building a theory of types into the symbolism itself, obviously goes no distance at all towards rendering any such theory superfluous, because in order to interpret the symbol '$\phi(x)$' correctly we need to be told, in an 'extra premiss' (really a key), that small Greek letters hold place for expressions like 'mortality', and small Roman letters for expressions like 'Socrates', that is, that these letters hold place for primary monadic concept-expressions and for proper names respectively. The expression '$\phi(x)$' does not itself give us this information: that bare symbol tells us *nothing at all* about how it should, or even might, be interpreted. So if Wittgenstein really does wish to do away with the need for a theory of types, it would appear that he has not managed to say quite what he intended.

A hint of what he perhaps meant is provided by the footnote, in the comment to the effect that '$(\exists x, y)R(x, y)$' is 'not complex'. The remark, which recalls (and may have inspired) Russell's repeated insistence in *Theory of Knowledge* that the general form of a proposition is simple,[160] is immediately suspicious, for the expression certainly *looks* complex: Russell's assertion that such expressions of pure form are, despite appearances, really logically simple constitutes one of the more evident difficulties of the 1913 theory.[161] If we

---

[158] I do not see that, as Hanks suggests ([2], pp. 129–30), Russell had 'an obvious reply' to Wittgenstein along the lines of pointing to the fact that his symbols had 'ranges of significance': specifying those ranges is precisely what requires an extra premiss.

[159] [13], p. 205, quoted above, §69; cf. Johnston, pp. 236–7.

[160] See N. Griffin [4], p. 177. Wittgenstein subsequently abandoned this position in his 'Notes on Logic' of Oct. 1913 ([6], p. 97): Griffin [4], p. 178.

[161] Russell's embarrassment surfaces on p. 130 of [9]: 'although "something has some relation to something" is a proposition, and is true, it is nevertheless simple. . . . How can an object be at once simple and a "fact"?' But this 'logical' difficulty is put aside, because there are more pressing 'epistemological' questions.

examine the beginning of Wittgenstein's January 1913 letter, we find there too the claim that the non-nominal part of the new propositional analysis is not complex:

I have changed my views on 'atomic' complexes: I now think that Qualities, Relations (like Love), etc. are all copulae! That means I for instance analyse a subject–predicate prop[osition], say, 'Socrates is human' into 'Socrates' and 'Something is human' (which I think is not complex).[162]

And Wittgenstein goes on to explain that 'the reason for this is a very fundamental one: I think that there cannot be different Types of things!'[163] The emphasis in this sentence falls on the word 'things': what Wittgenstein in effect means is that there cannot be different types of *Fregean object*. This becomes clear in the sequel, for Wittgenstein glosses the above claim as: 'In other words whatever can be symbolized by a simple proper name must belong to one type',[164] and adds, as a further point, the passage I quoted at length above. Immediately after that passage he writes:

What I am *most* certain of is not however the correctness of my present way of analysis, but of the fact that all theory of types must be done away with by a theory of symbolism showing that what seem to be *different kinds of things* are symbolized by different kinds of symbols which *cannot* possibly be substituted in one another's places.[165]

In other words, type distinctions should emerge in a correct philosophical grammar at the level of *symbolic language* and not at the level of *reference*. (Compare the remark in the *Tractatus* that 'Russell's error is shown in the fact that in setting up his rules for signs he was forced to speak of the meaning of the signs'.[166]) But then, as I have pointed out, we shall certainly need an 'extra premiss' telling us how to *understand* the symbolism and preventing us from making substitutions the wrong way round. After all, wrong substitutions are not in any sense physically impossible; they will only count as logically impossible (that is, incorrect) if an 'extra premiss' expressly prohibits them. Hence his attack on Russell lays Wittgenstein himself wide open to a *tu quoque*.

A natural thought at this point would be this. What Wittgenstein surely should have done, if he really wanted to achieve the result that the *symbolism itself* rules out nonsensical combinations, without being beholden to an 'extra premiss', was to take his initial insight that 'Qualities, Relations (like Love), etc. are all copulae' more seriously. Plausibly, it is an implication of this claim that, in an adequate symbolism, concepts (including relations) *will not be explicitly symbolized at all*, not that they will be expressed in a special

---

[162] [9], p. 235.   [163] Ibid.   [164] Ibid., pp. 235–6.
[165] Ibid., p. 236.   [166] [1], §3.331. Cf. Potter [1], p. 169.

symbolism, for this latter strategy imports the requirement of an extra premiss indicating what that special symbolism is, and providing a key to it. Rather, the real insight (if that is what it is) which Wittgenstein is struggling towards in this letter but has not yet managed to formulate is that an adequate symbolism, rendering any theory of types superfluous, must admit just *one* type of expression into its symbolism—for want of a better label we can call expressions of this unique type 'names'—thereby doing away with all other kinds of symbol and absorbing their functions into syntax. This is the position which is inchoately expressed in the exclamation 'I think that there cannot be different Types of things!'; but it is submerged, in the letter, in an inappropriate symbolism—inappropriate because while different types of *things* (objects in the Fregean sense) are abolished, we still need different types of *symbol*, which is what brings down the charge that Wittgenstein is caught by his own criticism of Russell. Even at the stage of writing the *Notebooks* Wittgenstein still thinks that 'Relations and properties, etc. are *objects* too',[167] so that presumably, if nonsense sentences along the lines of 'this table penholders the book' are to be avoided,[168] relations and properties must be different *types* of object from objects like Socrates. (At one point in the *Notebooks*, 'the thing Socrates' and 'the property of mortality' are said to 'function as simple objects',[169] but observe how Wittgenstein specifies these objects: they are the *thing* Socrates and the *property* of mortality. Clearly, these entities are conceived to be objects of different *types*.)

Why does Wittgenstein think that a correct symbolism must render any theory of types superfluous? My suggestion[170] is that Wittgenstein is moving towards his Tractarian position that all necessity is logical necessity,[171] and that logical necessity is, in turn, a matter of truth-functional tautology.[172] For if there were different types of things, there would be a kind of ontological necessity (impossibility) inherent in permissible and especially impermissible combinations of variously typed individual *objects*, rather than exclusively the kind of necessity evinced by truth-functional tautologies, which obtain at the level of the *sentences* formed from names of those objects. There would thus be an 'order of things a priori', contradicting Wittgenstein's express statement in the *Tractatus* that there is no such order.[173] The existence of any a priori constraints on permissible combinations of objects would represent a retreat from pure atomism.[174]

---

[167] [6], p. 61.   [168] Ibid., p. 103.   [169] Ibid., p. 69.
[170] See Sommerville, pp. 186–7, and N. Griffin [2], p. 144, for an alternative explanation, based on Whitehead and Russell, i, pp. 44–6. Their attempt is criticized in Hanks [2].
[171] [1], §§6.37, 6.375.   [172] [1], §§5–5.133, 6.1, 6.1221.   [173] [1], §5.634.
[174] Cf. Fogelin, pp. 12–13.

It is, I think, not until the *Tractatus* that Wittgenstein finally produces a theory that captures the core insight of the January 1913 letter. According to this theory there is, at the final stage of analysis, just one type of symbol: there are only names. The functions of concept-expressions (including relational expressions) are taken over, at this ultimate point, by the syntactical properties of sentences, and sentences are just configurations of names. Those syntactical properties of sentences are not *expressed by* the sentences, but rather *inexpressibly shown*: properties and relations no longer feature as objects, but have their functional specificities absorbed into configurations of objects, and these configurations now discharge the semantical obligations of all concept-expressions.[175] This, I suggest, is the line of thought that Wittgenstein in effect followed through in the *Tractatus*, so playing out the implications of his 1913 remark that 'Qualities, Relations (like Love), etc. are all copulae'. We thereby arrive at a pure form of logical atomism, shared by Russell,[176] in which basic objects occur as, in themselves, undetermined, featureless *Dinge an sich*—no more than bare possibilities of combination. These possibilities of combination must, in order to ensure an absence of a priori constraints at the atomic level, be conceived along maximally permissive lines, so that any combinations of any objects are allowed.[177]

But, though one can appreciate why Wittgenstein might have thought that it worked, the strategy is nevertheless, by his own lights, a failure. Reducing the expressive resources of language to just one type of symbol, together with its permitted configurations, does not eliminate the need for an 'extra premiss' or key: obviously we now need to be told which combinations of names are permitted. And it will not help to reply here—as, so we have just conjectured, the Wittgenstein of the *Tractatus* would have wished to reply—that at the ultimate level of analysis *all* combinations are permitted, or more precisely that all combinations are *in principle* permitted, and that which combinations are *in practice* permitted will be shown by which combinations we are actually prepared to regard as having sense, and which not.[178] For to say that much just *is* to give an essential 'extra premiss': the admissibility of all combinations

[175] The claim is controversial—it has been denied by e.g. Hintikka and Hintikka (ch. 2)—but it seems to me the most natural interpretation of §§3.1431–3.1432, and the only reasonable interpretation of §§2.0231–2.02331. See Wittgenstein [6], pp. 98–9, 109–112; Urmson, p. 79; Keyt, pp. 383–4; Copi; Anscombe [1], ch. 7; J. Griffin, ch. 6; Küng, ch. 6; Carruthers, pp. 78–81.

[176] Horstmann, pp. 228–31; see esp. Russell [3], §443.

[177] So, rightly, Küng, p. 84: 'The ultimate logical atoms, which must be points with no further internal structure, must all have the same logical form; the only distinction possible is that they are numerically different and that they have different external properties, i.e. that they enter de facto into different configurations'. See too the helpful study by Goddard and Judge.

[178] [1], §§5.473–5.4733. Cf. §56 above.

of names is still something that has to be *said*; it cannot be merely *shown*. For how could it be shown? No amount of liberal practice with the combinations that have been encountered so far can rule out the possibility that in the future some other, so far unencountered combinations will be judged illicit on a priori grounds or, even more radically, that some combinations will turn out to be literally unthinkable. So the need for an 'extra premiss' is not obviated by declaring that anything goes—that declaration just becomes the extra premiss. Likewise, a theory stating that there is just one type of symbol is still a type theory, and one whose content cannot simply be taken as understood, but must be explicitly conveyed.[179]

The important point for our purposes is that although Wittgenstein's criticism of Russell's theory of judgement is superficially distinct from mine, in its ultimate effect it is rather similar. My criticism (§71) was that, while officially regarding a certain regress as vicious, Russell could not prevent its arising in his theory of judgement, because he introduced the representation of the form of an act of understanding into the representation of the act of understanding itself, alongside the representation of the other components, thereby reifying that form and treating it as an entity to be *configured with* the other components of the act of understanding, and hence requiring, regressively, a further representation of the form of that act. Wittgenstein does not allude to this point, but the thrust of his criticism, when it is taken as anticipating the theory of symbolism offered in the *Tractatus*, in which both monadic and polyadic concept-expressions are absorbed at the final stage of analysis into syntactic relations among names, is exactly to stop the regress in its tracks. Beside the official motive of seeking to provide a theory of judgement that makes it impossible to judge nonsense, Wittgenstein can be regarded as additionally aiming to provide a theory that is not liable to the regress which, if it be regarded as vicious, devastates Russell's theory. That Wittgenstein was indeed motivated by this consideration can be shown by a brief recapitulation of some of the salient features of Tractarian metaphysics.

73 Logical Form in the *Tractatus*

Early on in the *Tractatus*, Wittgenstein puts forward the so-called Picture Theory of meaning. At the limit of analysis we arrive at elementary sentences

---

[179] And of course in practice Wittgenstein himself does not shrink from laying down rules on permissible combinations of symbols, as e.g. in the section dealing with Russellian type theory: [1], §3.333. Cf. Hochberg [6], p. 79.

(*Elementarsätze*), which consist of simple signs in immediate combination.[180] Each simple sign stands for a (simple) object,[181] and the way in which the signs are put together in the sentence represents the way the corresponding objects are configured in the world.[182] Pictures can represent facts (configurations of objects) because they are themselves facts (configurations of names).[183] Any picture must share its form of representation with the pictured reality;[184] in the case of the sentence, that form is the logical form of reality itself.[185] That form is not *represented* (*dargestellt*) by the sentence; it is *shown* (*gezeigt*). For a sentence cannot state its own conditions of application to the world.[186]

It is natural to read these claims in the light of what is said in a later part of the work, where Wittgenstein talks about the general form of the sentence, and of the capacity of sentences, by virtue of their general form, which he calls their essence, to express the essence of the world.[187] Now it is surely plausible to identify the logical form of reality with the essence of the world.[188] But in that case the form of sentential representation would be just the general form of the sentence, which Wittgenstein identifies with the one logical constant that all sentences, by their nature, have in common with each other, and which he conveys in the words 'This is how things are' ('Es verhält sich so und so').[189] But has not something gone wrong? For we have arrived at a sentence—'This is how things are'—which purportedly represents the logical form of reality, contrary to Wittgenstein's claim that the logical form of reality can be shown, but not represented. Nothing has gone wrong, however: we have arrived, rather, at a piece of Tractarian 'nonsense',[190] something that tries to state what can, officially, only be shown.

Logical form—the essence of both sentence and world—is Wittgenstein's solution to Frege's paradox of the concept *horse*—in general, it is Wittgenstein's response to the fact (§28) that there are truths *about* Frege's system that cannot be stated *in* the system—and at the same time it is his solution to the problem of the unity of the proposition. Wittgenstein thus replaces Frege's notion of the unsaturated concept, which both leads to the paradox and is the underpinning of Frege's account of the unity of the proposition, with his own notion of logical form.[191] By the same token, logical form must be that in virtue of which a sentence manages to say something—is prevented from degenerating into

---

[180] [1], §4.221.   [181] [1], §§3.22, 3.26.
[182] [1], §§2.15, 3.1432, 3.21, 4.011–4.012, 4.0311.   [183] [1], §§2.14–2.15; cf. 3.14.
[184] [1], §2.17.   [185] [1], §§2.18–2.2.   [186] [1], §§4.12–4.1212; cf. 2.172.
[187] [1], §§5.47–5.472.   [188] [1], §§2.18, 5.4711.   [189] [1], §4.5.   [190] [1], §6.54.
[191] See Anscombe [1], pp. 108–9; van Heijenoort [1], p. 445 n. 5; Resnik [4], pp. 96–7; Priest [1], p. 192. Hochberg ([2], p. 230) makes a similar point about Sellars's Jumblese ([1], ch. 7), a sign system closely related to Wittgenstein's conception of what language would look like after analysis, in that it represents relations by the syntactical arrangement of names.

a list of names.[192] Wittgenstein must now insist on the ineffability of logical form, if he is to avoid the regress that threatened Russell's 1913 theory of judgement.[193] For the form of a sentence consists in the fact that its names are configured in a certain way, which shows that the objects of the represented reality are configured in the same way. If the configuration of the names in the sentence—its particular syntax—were itself a picturing component of the sentence, we would need a further component in the sentence to configure the picturing component with the other components. We would be launched on the familiar regress. That Wittgenstein regarded the regress as vicious may be gathered from the fact that his (official) doctrine of the ineffability of form is precisely tailored to inhibit the regress before it can get off the ground. Objects in the world are configured, and names in elementary sentences are configured: but those configurations are not themselves further objects, or further names.[194] As he put it in his remarks on Ogden's translation of §2.03: 'The meaning is *that there isn't anything third* that connects the links but that the links *themselves* make connexion with one another'.[195]

I noted above that Wittgenstein was led to state the general form of the sentence ('This is how things are'), which on his official view cannot be stated. This is not an isolated breach. Consider this passage:

> The name occurs in the sentence only in the context of the elementary sentences. Names are the simple symbols; I indicate them by single letters (x, y, z). I write the elementary sentence as a function of its names in the form 'fx', '$\phi(x, y)$', etc.[196]

What is the status of the functional expressions? They cannot be names, for Wittgenstein expressly tells us that he indicates names by the letters 'x', 'y' etc.[197] Furthermore, there is a good reason why it would be disastrous for Wittgenstein to classify the functional expressions as names: it would bring down the very regress which, as I have argued, he seeks to avoid, for we should need a further functional expression to represent the configuration of the referent of the original functional expression with the referents of the non-functional names, and so on. But if the functional expressions are not names, they can only be intended to fulfil a role that on Wittgenstein's official view does not exist: to represent (what can strictly only be shown) logical form.[198]

It might now be thought that the aporia we have reached is not insuperable: could we not mend matters if we simply dropped Wittgenstein's unhappy

[192] [1], §§3.142, 4.022.   [193] See here again Priest [1], pp. 188–9.
[194] Cf. McGuinness, p. 145 n. 2; Keyt, p. 381.   [195] [4], p. 23.
[196] [1], §§4.23–4.
[197] Cf. [1], §4.1272 with 5.5261; J. Griffin, pp. 57–9; Carruthers, p. 82, point G.
[198] Cf. Sellars [1], p. 237.

attempt to represent form by writing functional symbols into the expression of the forms of elementary sentences? This proposal is certainly true to one strand in Wittgenstein's thinking, namely to the doctrine that elementary sentences are concatenations of simple names and that their logical form, and correlatively the form of the world, is *shown* by the way their constituent names are configured, not *represented* by these or other names. The proposal thus tends to be favoured by commentators who wish to stress the point that, as we have noted, Wittgenstein's doctrine of logical form is intended to supplant Frege's notion of the unsaturated concept as a solution to the problem of the unity of the proposition.[199] But there are difficulties. Wittgenstein insists, not only in the previously cited passage, but also in a subsequent one, that elementary sentences contain 'argument and function':

All logical operations are already contained in the elementary sentence. For 'fa' says the same as '$(\exists x). fx. x = a$'. Where there is composition, there is argument and function, and where these are present, all logical constants are already present.[200]

It is essential to Wittgenstein's enterprise that all logical constants be already implicitly present in the sentence, in virtue of its form, for 'My fundamental thought is that the "logical constants" do not represent, that the *logic* of the facts cannot be represented'.[201] If apparent logical constants did not 'disappear' on analysis,[202] being absorbed into the form of the elementary sentence, they would be genuine names, in which case the logic of the facts certainly could (and would) be represented. But, Wittgenstein supposes, only if elementary sentences have the form '$R^n(x_1 \ldots x_n)$' will it be clear a priori that they already implicitly contain all logical constants. It seems, then, that if Wittgenstein's 'fundamental thought' is to be given a priori, it must be guaranteed a priori that an elementary sentence will have the form: '$R^n(x_1 \ldots x_n)$'. But this schema tries to say what can only be shown.

On the one hand, then, Wittgenstein would like to avoid the regress generated when one explicitly symbolizes logical form—when one regards the schematic functional expression in '$R^n(x_1 \ldots x_n)$', where the individual variables range over simple objects, as a name of that form—and he seeks to do so by banishing all but names of objects from the elementary level and confining logical form to the status of what is shown rather than represented. But pressures from elsewhere in his metaphysical economy force him, or so he imagines, to admit functors to the elementary level, where their role can only be to symbolize form. Just as, in criticizing Russell's theory of

---

[199] See e.g. Bell [1], pp. 130–3.   [200] [1], §5.47.   [201] [1], §4.0312: tr. Ogden.
[202] Cf. [1], §5.441.

judgement, Wittgenstein himself failed to avoid the aim of his own shaft, so too, we may say, while (in effect) seeking to rid his own theory of the defect which had vitiated Russell's theory of judgement—namely, that it could distinguish a sentence from a mere list only at the cost of precipitating a regress—Wittgenstein unwittingly produced a theory which was liable to exactly the same failing, if failing it is: for the drive to represent all elementary sentences as having the general form '$R^n(x_1 \ldots x_n)$', within the context of the claim that the elementary sentence is a concatenation exclusively of names of objects (which do not include properties and relations), can only—if it is not to be a sheer contradiction—precipitate the familiar regress. Perhaps, in view of the concluding remarks of the *Tractatus*, as well as the general thrust of Wittgenstein's treatment of logical form, as I have characterized that, we will think that he would have preferred to embrace the contradictory implication that the functional symbol in the above formula both is and is not a name to saying outright that it is a name and accepting the ensuing regress. But, when we advance from the purely exegetical business of elucidating Wittgenstein's Tractarian position to the systematic question how we ourselves should react to the above dilemma, it will surely strike us that there is a case for entertaining the option of accepting the nominal status of functional symbols and allowing the associated regress to unfold: after all, that would seem to suit the kind of posture in the philosophy of language that I have taken up, according to which all words, including functional symbols, are names.

6

Bradley's Regress and the Unity of the Proposition

74 The Logical Copula and Theories of Meaning

We have seen that Frege, Russell, and Wittgenstein all, in their different ways, sought to avoid the regress that I discussed in the previous chapter. None of their expedients is satisfactory. What should our response to the regress, which in deference to its most familiar modern formulation I am calling Bradley's regress, be? In answering this question we will perforce have to tackle the problem broached in §65, namely the question whether the logical copula is a name. For if it is a name and has a referent, presumably that referent can be nothing other than the totality of instantiation relations generated by Bradley's regress. (For the time being I shall focus on the unity of simple categorical propositions of the form *that a is F*.)

One strategy, recommended by David Wiggins (in effect following Russell), is to deny that the copula has reference on the ground that, if it did, its referent would have to be the infinitistic object generated by the regress; but the regress, if it so figured in the analysis of the meaning of the copula, would be vicious.[1] Wiggins accepts, against Frege, that we should take the contribution of the copula to sentential unity seriously, for he argues, again against Frege, that we need to isolate a saturated component from the concept-expression, if we are to make sense of second-order quantification. I rejected this argument in §34, but we have nevertheless arrived, in effect, at the same conclusion—that the Fregean concept-expression is just as saturated as the Fregean proper name or, as I prefer to put it, that the Fregean proper name is just as unsaturated as the Fregean concept-expression, and hence that namehood, and with it all the apparatus of objectual reference and quantification, attaches just as much to the one type of expression as to the other, and so to both types, given that we do not wish to jettison the category of names. But I argued for this view on

---

[1] [3], pp. 133–4, 142–3; cf. his [4], p. 8; Strawson [1], p. 167.

the basis of the context principle, not on the basis of considerations relating to quantification.

In connection with my notion of the logical predicate of a sentence, which was an extension of Dummett's notion of the complex predicate, and according to which the logical predicate is so defined that it embodies the copulative structure—and hence the unity—of the whole sentence, I noted (§64) that the upshot of my argument, on the basis of the context principle, for an even-handed approach to all semantically significant subsentential lexical components was that any such component could be regarded as providing the substantial semantic content of the logical predicate of a sentence: the concept-expression does not, as Frege and others have supposed, enjoy any kind of privilege in this regard. Now the logical copula is that part of the logical predicate in virtue of which this predicate counts as a schematic sentence; hence the (unannotated) logical copula is that feature of the sentence which is responsible for the unity of the proposition. But the logical copula no more attaches to or characterizes, as a matter of its nature, one part of the sentence than another: a given sentence may contain arbitrarily many ways of isolating a logical predicate, and so arbitrarily many distinct structures capable of serving (though not simultaneously) as that sentence's (unannotated) logical copula.[2]

As I have stressed (§69), attributing responsibility for unity to the logical predicate, and so ultimately to the logical copula, is not *eo ipso* to provide an account of the unity of the sentence: for just so far, given that the logical predicate is no more than a schematic sentence—a partially determined sentence frame—these moves are merely programmatic. Our question is not answered by saying that the unity of the proposition is constituted by the presence in the corresponding sentence of a logical copula: that is true, but simply postpones the real issue, which is what the logical copula *is*. By the same token, the logical copula is not an *ingredient* of the sentence whose presence in the sentence could be duplicated by a mere list: the logical copula is, one might say, too trivially *coincident* with the unity of a sentence and its corresponding proposition to admit of duplication by something lacking the requisite kind of unity; put differently, we might say that the logical copula just *is* what makes a bunch of words into a sentence, but it is 'what makes' them a sentence in the sense of being merely *the fact of their sentencehood*, not *that in virtue of which*, in any explanatorily helpful sense, those words constitute a sentence. Or again, we might say that the logical copula is *by definition* present to a sentence and absent from a mere list, but that means that it is the explanandum—the same

---

[2] Recall (§5) that I set no upper bound, finite or transfinite, on sentence length. On the distinction between annotated and unannotated logical copulas, see §§64–5.

explanandum as the unity of the sentence itself—not the explanans. (As I have made clear—and I shall return to the point—I take it to be essential to the 'ingredient' solution that the alleged unifying component is held to be available *in advance* of the construction of the sentence, as one item in a construction kit that includes all the other constituents of the sentence.)

If we simply treat the concept-expression as a species of name in as good a sense as the items Frege called proper names, so as something with a proprietary semantic content, specifiable independently and in advance of its occurring in any particular sentence, we are in effect forced to find something else in the sentence, other than the concept-expression, to support the sentential status of the combination of names and prevent it from disintegrating into a mere list of words. The 'double function' or 'twofold role' of the concept-expression or verb favoured by Frege, Russell, Strawson, and others—the supposed fact that the concept-expression or verb *both* has a proprietary semantic content *and* discharges the unifying role in the sentence—is not an option. It is not an option for Frege and Russell because, as we have seen, they invite paradox (the paradox of the concept *horse*). Strawson need not incur problems of this nature, because he need not be saddled with the special non-nominal status of the unifying concept-expression or verb, and the corresponding non-objectual status of the concept, as Frege and Russell wanted. But he is liable to the standard difficulty confronting the ingredient solution, namely that the proposed method of unifying the proposition cannot distinguish it from a replica aggregate, and the corresponding sentence from an equiform list. For to treat the concept-expression or verb as having its own proprietary semantic content, in addition to performing the unifying task, just *is* to turn the sentence into something that can be duplicated by a mere list. That is because the specific type of semantic content which we will want to ascribe to concept-expressions and verbs is, like that ascribed to a proper name, given independently and in advance of the relevant expressions' occurring in any particular sentences. In effect, we associate a universal content with the concept-expression or verb in question, quite irrespective of its figuring in any particular sentence; and that association has, as such, nothing to do with the unifying of any given sentence in which that expression may occur. Strawson has no answer to the question what distinguishes a mere list containing a concept-expression with its proprietary semantic content, on the one hand, from the same linguistic items with the same semantic contents, on the other, but in which that concept-expression now additionally discharges the role of unifying the elements into a sentence.

At this point we are obliged to go beyond Frege, Russell, Strawson, and all previous attempts to solve the unity problem: for we are in effect forced to find a logical *tertium adiacens*—what I am calling the logical copula—in the sentence, as the actively unifying feature of the logical predicate, that predicate being, as we have seen, (trivially) present to any unified sentence, but not constitutively associated with the concept-expression or indeed with any other specific type of linguistic expression. That brings us back to the question of the logical copula's status: is it a name and, if so, what kind of reference does it have? We must now choose one of three options. The first option is the radical one of denying that the logical copula has *reference* at all. Given the theoretical role played by the notion of the reference, that option in turn amounts to a denial that the logical copula is a semantically significant feature or component of the sentence: our theory of meaning must accordingly contain no clause for the logical copula. Alternatively, drawing on the distinction made in §32 between having reference and having a referent, we might say, less radically, that the logical copula does indeed have *reference*, but does not have a *referent*. On this line, we transfer the moves which I contemplated a reformed Frege making in response to the paradox of the concept *horse* from the concept-expression to the logical copula. Finally, we have the option of saying that the logical copula has not only reference, but also a referent.

The motivation for choosing the first option is just the desire to escape from Bradley's regress. But what is the point of this tactic? Why avoid Bradley's regress? I have already mentioned Russell's 1903 response to this question: regresses which arise as a matter of sheer entailment are harmless, but regresses which arise in the analysis of meaning are vicious. It might now be said that Bradley's regress is vicious because if a theory of meaning contained an explicit primitive clause for the logical copula it would have to contain an infinity of (primitive) clauses, given that each stage in Bradley's regress is distinct from every other stage: for each instantiation relation drawn on as we proceed into the regress is distinct from every other such relation, because each relation contains a distinct number of argument-places. (Recall Orilia's formalization of the 'Bradley series' (BS) in §70:

$$R^n a_1, \ldots, a_n; I^{n+1} R^n a_1, \ldots, a_n; I^{n+2} I^{n+1} R^n a_1, \ldots, a_n;$$

and so on.) Hence a theory of meaning that attempted to specify a relation purportedly designated by the logical copula would contain an infinite number of primitive axioms. But it is a clear constraint on any theory of meaning for a *learnable* language that its primitive structure be finite. If this reasoning is correct, it follows that there can be no axiom, in a finitistic theory of meaning, for the logical copula.

But would a theory of meaning with a clause for the logical copula be committed to an infinite primitive structure? Let us assume, for the moment, that a clause for the logical copula is a combinatorial axiom telling us how to concatenate significantly to produce a declarative sentence. In the case of Denyer's primitive language **S**, for instance, such a clause might look like this:

$\forall\alpha\forall\beta(\alpha^*\beta$ means that $Ref(\alpha)$ is to the left of $Ref(\beta))$,

where small Greek letters range over the simple names of the language, an expression of the form '$Ref(\gamma)$' designates the referent of γ and, as usual, the star represents concatenation. (For simplicity's sake I restrict the discussion to two-name strings: longer strings can be handled recursively, but the complications required to deal with them can be left aside here.) Now, recall that the 'impartial strategy' semantics outlined in §41 offered a way of specifying the semantics of a natural language containing a grammatical copula by means of regimenting sentences of the object-language into a form in which they had been stripped of that grammatical copula and left (in effect, and to put it in my current terminology) with a merely logical copula. Hence, in asking quite generally after the meaning of the copula, we can, with no loss of generality, consider how to specify the meaning of the logical copula in the style of the impartial strategy for such a regimented language. The sentences of such a language were more developed than those of **S**, because they contained different types (categories) of name, but otherwise they shared with **S** the feature that the grammatical copula was in effect absorbed into a logical copula, the meaning of which we might assume in their case to be expressed by:

(1) $\forall\alpha\forall\Pi(\alpha^*\Pi$ means that $Ref(\alpha)$ instantiates $Ref(\Pi))$,

where small Greek letters range over actual and possible proper names and capital Greek letters over actual and possible concept-words. If it is fair to regard (1) as providing the meaning of the logical copula, as this characterizes sentences of the regimented language (and hence sentences of any language which can be so regimented), then the answer to our question—whether a theory of meaning with a clause for the logical copula is committed to an infinite primitive structure—is plainly negative. For we appear to have specified that meaning in a single axiom.

But we cannot yet regard (1) as, on its own, specifying the meaning of the logical copula. We assumed *pro tempore* that a clause for the logical copula would be a combinatorial axiom telling us how to concatenate significantly to produce a declarative sentence: but, as we have seen (§5), the operation of concatenation is not on its own enough to turn a bunch of words into a sentence as opposed to a list, seeing that lists may themselves be significantly concatenated, and for any given sentence there is an equiform list which looks (sounds) just like that sentence. In terms of (1), the problem can be put like this.

In specifying, in general terms, the meanings of object-language sentences, this axiom invokes something not explicitly mentioned in such sentences, namely a metalinguistic relation of instantiation; but so far this relation is, for anything that has been said to the contrary, just an object—saturated or unsaturated, depending on how we wish to regard objects—like the other (saturated or unsaturated) referents of the component words of the base sentence. So far we have done nothing to distinguish the regimented sentence theoretically from a list, whose components refer to the referent of the relevant proper name, the referent of the relevant grammatical predicate, and the relation of instantiation. How can we be sure that these three entities do not simply 'stand aloof' from one another?[3]

In order to secure the *propositional* unity of this collection and, derivatively, the unity of the corresponding sentence, we need to discern within the collected entities the operation of a principle of significant combination of the right (propositional) sort and, derivatively, we need to discern in the case of the sentence the operation of a principle of significant concatenation of the right (sentential) sort. That is, we need to regard the sentences of the metalanguage in terms of which we specify the meanings of object-language sentences as *themselves* capable of being subjected to regimentation in the style of the impartial strategy, and to regard the regimented items so produced as provided with some suitable combinatorial axiom. The regimentation, here as in the case of its application to object-language sentences, destroys the grammatical copula employed in the base (here metalanguage) sentences but restores unity to the fragments by providing them with a logical copula, that is, with a principle of significant concatenation of the right, sentence-yielding sort. The possibility of making this further move—that is, the possibility of discerning within metalinguistic meaning-specifications of object-language sentences an application of logical combinatorial principles to suitable regimentations of those specifications—is fundamental to our ability to give ourselves, as theoreticians, an assurance of the unity of the metalinguistic sentences in question. It is not that in practice we doubt their unity; it is just that the mentioned possibility is required to give us an analysis, and hence a theoretical assurance, of that unity.

We need, then, to regiment metalanguage sentences of the form '$Ref(\alpha)$ instantiates $Ref(\Pi)$' along the lines of

(2)   Instantiation $(Ref(\alpha), Ref(\Pi))$.[4]

---

[3] Frege [7], p. 205 ([21], p. 178).
[4] Strictly, the items inside the outer brackets of (2) should be ordered and typed, but we can ignore that point here. In (3) and (4) below punctuation marks figure autonymously.

We must then provide a clause like

(3) $\forall\alpha\forall\Pi$('Instantiation'*(*'Ref'*(*'α'*)*,*'Ref'*(*Π*)*) means that $Ref(\alpha)$ and $Ref(\Pi)$ instantiate Instantiation).

Taking into account the fact that the new relation of instantiation invoked on the right-hand side of (3) as the 'relating relation' has one more argument-place than the relation of instantiation which is invoked on the left-hand side as the 'relating relation' and which again figures on the right-hand side but this time as a 'related relation', the general content of this clause can be expressed as

(4) $\forall\alpha_1 \ldots \alpha_n\forall\Phi^n(\Phi^{n}*(*'\alpha_1*,* \ldots *,*\alpha_n*)$ means that $Ref(\alpha_1)$ and . . . and $Ref(\alpha_n)$ instantiate^{n+1} $Ref(\Phi^n))$,

where '$\alpha_1 \ldots \alpha_n$' range over metalinguistic names and 'Φ^n' over metalinguistic n-adic concept-expressions. Accordingly, (4) belongs to the metametalanguage. Like (2), it specifies the meaning of the logical copula in terms of the relation of instantiation. But now since instantiation is just another relation, (4) can obviously be run on instantiation itself as the referent of the concept-expression 'Φ^n' (the erstwhile Φ^n being, so to speak, demoted to the status of an α_i). The possibility of repeating this process is just the possibility of generating Bradley's regress.[5]

Let us now repose our worry: would a theory of meaning with a clause for the logical copula in its metametalanguage, along the lines of (4), be committed to an infinite primitive structure? Does such a clause generate *distinct* instantiation relations as the objection envisaged? That depends on whether we treat the superscripts in (4) as indices or as variables.[6] If they are regarded as indices, then the answer to our question is affirmative. (4) then constitutes an axiom scheme rather than an axiom. But its infinitism does not present a problem for a finitistic theory of meaning, any more than ascription to a speaker of knowledge of (say) the axiom scheme of separation in first-order set theory does:[7] in each case, the speaker is credited with knowledge of a possibly infinite number of axioms, but the fact that these axioms can be given a systematic representation renders the ascription unproblematic. (In the case we are interested in 'the speaker' is the theorist.) An alternative reading of (4) treats the superscripts not as indices but as variables. In that case the relation of instantiation figuring in (4) would be of no particular adicity. Mastery of (4) would again be finitely based, but there would now be an infinite number of possible *applications* of its universal closure. On either approach, we can

---

[5] Cf. Currie [1], p. 150; MacBride [6], pp. 430–1.
[6] On the distinction, cf. Boolos, p. 68. [7] See e.g. Potter [2], pp. 291–2.

rebut the objector's charge that the infinitism (4) imports renders its content unlearnable.

75 Reference and the Logical Copula

We have seen that including a clause for the logical copula in the metametalanguage in the style of (4) permits the generation of Bradley's regress. (4) shows how the regress arises naturally in the course of seeking to specify what the logical copula refers to. That now at least gives us an answer to the question whether the logical copula has *reference*. The answer is affirmative: the reference of the logical copula is exactly what (4) specifies. Not only *can* we specify the reference of the logical copula; we *must* do so. For when we are engaged in the project of giving, in a metalanguage, the semantics of some particular object-language, we must provide a general combinatorial axiom, and this axiom conveys a partial specification of the reference of the logical copula. The specification is merely partial, because it does not yet tell us in what way the object-language sentences, whose meanings it is the job of the combinatorial axiom to specify in general schematic terms, differ from mere lists of words; it does not give us this information, in turn, because it does not yet provide a theoretical guarantee that our metalinguistic meaning-specifications are themselves unities in the required sense. Only if we go beyond the inchoate specification of the logical copula's reference yielded by the metalinguistic combinatorial axiom—only if we dispose, in the metametalanguage, of a quite general specification, along the lines of (4), of the significance of the logical copula—will we capture in our linguistic net the reference of the logical copula itself.

It follows that the strategy concerning the semantics of the logical copula which denies that the logical copula has meaning, in the sense that we cannot specify a reference for it in a systematic theory of meaning, is mistaken. That leaves the further, and more interesting, question what we should say about the less radical second strategy, which allows that the logical copula has *reference*, but denies that it has a *referent*. An adherent of this strategy is quite happy to concede that we can specify, in a clause along the lines of (4), the reference of the logical copula, much as the reformed Frege was happy to agree that a clause like

$$\forall x(x \text{ satisfies 'is wise' iff } x \text{ is wise})$$

specifies the reference of the concept-expression 'is wise', while denying that that concept-expression has a referent. Hence the second strategy does not, in one sense, regard Bradley's regress as vicious. For (4), in specifying the reference of the logical copula, *eo ipso* permits the generation of Bradley's regress: so this strategy, which is comfortable with the idea that the reference of the logical copula *can* be specified, must be prepared to allow that the generation of the regress is, just so far, a harmless by-product of our semantics. But, just as the reformed Frege will insist that the above statement of the meaning of the concept-expression 'is wise', while it indeed specifies the reference of that expression, does not specify a referent for it, so too a supporter of the second strategy concerning the semantics of the logical copula will want to insist that (4), while it may indeed be taken to specify a *reference* for the logical copula, does not specify a *referent* for it.[8]

The idea behind the second strategy's resistance to accepting a referent for the copula would presumably be this. To specify the referent of the logical copula we would have to give an infinite list, comprising an initial relation of instantiation (instantiation$_1$), a further such relation (instantiation$_2$), being the instantiation of instantiation$_1$, a yet further such relation (instantiation$_3$), being the instantiation of instantiation$_2$, and so on into a regress.[9] Surely, one might think, what that shows is that the logical copula does not have a referent *simpliciter*, given that we cannot complete the specification of what that referent is. But why is it so damaging to the logical copula's prospects for being a genuine referring device that we cannot complete the specification of its referent? Well, one line of thought here would be the following. As Quine has urged, there is a constitutive connection between reference and objectual quantification: to be a referent is to be the value of a variable.[10] This slogan does not, as such, entail any version of nominalism: there is nothing in it to warrant (for example) Quine's own hostility to second-order quantification,[11] and nothing in it to support a programme of ontological parsimony.[12] I have argued that all semantically significant subsentential lexical components must be treated as having equal referential rights: all such expressions have a reference—and indeed a referent—if any does. Hence, if we wish to admit objectual quantification over the referents of one sort of semantically significant subsentential lexical expression, we have no basis on which to refuse to acknowledge the existence of a range of referents,

[8] Cf. Potter [1], p. 116.

[9] In the general case, taking into account languages such as Denyer's **S**, we will also have to specify an initial relation of sheer combination: but I ignore this complication in this section. I am also simplifying the proceedings by focusing on the regress of instantiation relations, as formalized in Orilia's (BS). The account will be generalized in §88.

[10] See e.g. Quine [1], p. 708; [2], pp. 13, 103; [3], p. 242; [5], p. 100.

[11] See e.g. [10], pp. 66–8.   [12] Cf. Searle [1], pp. 106–13.

equally available to be objectually quantified over, in respect of all such expressions.[13]

One might complain here that this liberal attitude to objectual quantification is liable to generate objects artificially, and that the lack of genuineness of the 'objects' so generated emerges in the fact that attempts to quantify into just any subsentential position precipitate ill-formedness.[14] So, for example, one might protest that the semi-formalized inference from 'John played the Ace of Hearts' to '∃x(John played the Ace x Hearts)' cannot be valid because it is not well formed. Of course, if the quantifier is read substitutionally the inference can, given an appropriate determination of the substitution class, be both well formed and valid, and the point to be made in response to the cavil is that it is always possible to read such quantifications substitutionally, if we need to do so in the interests of grammaticality. But our being sometimes obliged, in the interests of grammaticality, to resort to a substitutional reading does *not* go to show that the relevant quantification is *not* objectual. After all, the claim that all words are names (§40) is obviously not to be read as implying that all words function syntactically as (what we call) *proper* names, or even as nouns. It is rather to be understood as conveying the lesson of the context principle: that the philosophically pregnant notion of objecthood is not to be limited to the sorts of entity that can be referred to by a proper name; that there is no philosophically sound sense in which the objects that have been tagged as such by the tradition, and in particular by Frege, are more 'complete' or 'saturated' or 'objectual' than the referents of any linguistic expression. So the fact that the above inference has to be read substitutionally if it is to make grammatical sense is without philosophical significance: one might say that, philosophically speaking, to read that inference substitutionally *is* to read it objectually.

Plausibly, the liberal policy of recognizing objects as referents of any linguistic items we are prepared to classify as words should be extended to non-lexical but semantically significant features of the sentence, such as is the (unannotated) logical copula, which is not as such a lexical or morphological component of the sentence, but rather a principle of significant, sentence-yielding concatenation:[15] if such non-lexical and non-morphological features of the sentence are granted referents, those referents should stand on all fours

---

[13] Boolos (pp. 38–9) and Simons ([11], p. 265) allow objectual quantification into predicate positions without regarding predicates as names: cf. C. Parsons [2], p. 284. But since we are forced by the context principle to regard all words as names (§40), their position is, by my lights, doubly mistaken.

[14] Schiffer, p. 30; King [5], pp. 103–5.

[15] Recall my remarks on the reference of punctuation marks in §40. Note that the approach I am here recommending to the reference of the logical copula is one that—notwithstanding its derogatory remarks on punctuation—we can find prefigured in the *Tractatus*, which allows that features of words, as well as words themselves, may be symbolic: see esp. §§3.1432, 3.31, 3.344.

in point of availability to objectual quantification with the referents of lexical subsentential expressions. It follows that if the logical copula has a referent, it must be possible to quantify over that referent. But here it might be attractive to suppose that, if we are to find a role for quantification over the referent of the logical copula, we need first to articulate it into what one might call a strictly copulative component and a strictly nominal component. The thought here would be not the failed argument of the previous paragraph—that (in effect) objectual quantification only makes philosophical sense if the entities thereby quantified over would have been recognized as objects by Frege—but rather that quantification necessarily takes place over entities that are *surveyable*. But the 'entity' purportedly designated by the logical copula is infinitistic, in the way explained, so that if we admitted variables ranging over entities that included the 'referent' of the logical copula, just as such, we would surely forfeit the surveyability of the domain of quantification, in the sense that there would be no determinate answer to the question *what* was being quantified over. The idea would be that each stage of the 'instantiation' regress delivers referents of exclusively nominal items figuring as the partially specified referent of the logical copula. At each stage of the regress, on this line of thought, the referents generated by the regress will indeed sustain objectual quantification; but the *final* designatum of the logical copula—that retiring object which lurks, unattainably, at the end of the regress—will not.

This I take to be the basis of the resistance to the idea that the logical copula has not merely reference but also a referent. But when we spell out the qualm in the above terms, it is natural to respond to it as follows. Can we not collect together all the entities generated by the regress and speak of them collectively as *the* referent of the logical copula? Why not regard the logical copula as having a determinate, albeit infinitistic, *referent*, rather than as merely having *reference*, in the sense of this distinction exploited by the reformed Frege? After all, such an approach would not be obliged to break the constitutive connection between reference and quantification: what we quantify over, in quantifying over the referent of the logical copula, would be the totality of instantiation relations generated by Bradley's regress. Nor need a defender of this robust approach be impressed by an objection to the effect that in regarding the logical copula as having a referent, we face the disintegration of the proposition into a mere aggregate of objects and of its corresponding sentence into a mere list of words. That objection, it may be retorted, simply fails to take seriously the special, infinitistic nature of the referent of the logical copula invoked by the robust approach. For why should we not say that the unity of the proposition consists in the presence in it of a special sort of infinitistic object—not, as I have stressed, present as an ingredient, but as a structural feature constitutive of the proposition's being just the kind of unity it is—and that the derivative unity of the declarative sentence consists in the fact that, while *all* of its semantically significant features and components, including the logical copula, have a referent, one particular feature—the logical copula—has, in the explained way, a quite different sort of referent from all the others? So, while the mere presence of the (unannotated) logical copula in a sentence, and the presence of its referent in the corresponding proposition, is too close to being a merely definitional feature of sentence and correlative proposition to provide any kind of explanation of their respective unities, the special nature of the logical copula's reference—the infinitistic nature of its referent—can perhaps lay claim to having some explanatory value.

The difference between the robust view that the logical copula has a determinate, but infinitistic, referent (the third of the options mentioned above), and the more cautious view that it has reference, but no referent (the second option), is that on the former view, but not on the latter, it is possible to talk about the totality of instantiation relations generated by Bradley's regress. Priest argues that we can indeed talk about the referent of the copula,[16] and certainly the claim that we cannot talk about some totality or other that we appear to talk about in the very act of saying that we cannot do so is apt to seem paradoxical. Priest asks us to consider self-referential sentences like 'I am thinking about the referent of the copula of this very sentence'.[17] The truth of any such sentence depends upon its copula's having a referent. But, Priest in effect claims, that sentence can surely be true, given that it is meaningful. We must be careful here, however. Let us grant that the above sentence is meaningful, and given suitable compositionality principles for sense and reference, it will follow that the definite description 'the referent of the copula of this very sentence'—assume that it occurs in a sentential context fixing the reference of 'this very sentence'—has sense and reference. But recall that the referent of a definite description is not to be identified with its satisfying object(s), if any: so it does not follow that the description in question is satisfied by anything. It would be open to someone to hold that the above sentence is indeed meaningful (has sense and reference), but false, which it will be if, as the more cautious approach to copulative reference supposes, there simply is no such thing as the referent of the copula of the sentence in question—because there is no such thing as the referent of the logical copula of *any* sentence.

This unsuccessful argument aside, the question remains whether we should regard the logical copula as having a determinate, but infinitistic, referent, in line with what I have called the robust approach to the semantics of

---

[16] [1], pp. 192–4.   [17] Ibid., p. 193 with n. 22. I have altered his example slightly.

the logical copula, or whether, following the more cautious approach, we should regard it as having merely reference, but not a referent. That question transports us to a much wider field of conflict, the scene of a veritable battle of the gods and giants, between those who believe in the existence of actual, completed infinities, and those who hold that there are no actual, completed infinities, but at best potential infinities. The gods include Cantor,[18] the founding father of modern set theory, Gregory of Rimini,[19] Leibniz (at least in respect of body, though not, as I noted in §70, in respect of ideal entities such as mathematical lines),[20] Bolzano,[21] Dedekind,[22] Frege,[23] and Russell;[24] the giants include Aristotle,[25] Aquinas and the majority of medieval thinkers,[26] the British empiricists,[27] d'Alembert,[28] Kant,[29] Gauss,[30] Cantor's arch-antagonist Kronecker,[31] Poincaré,[32] Wittgenstein,[33] and the mathematical constructivists and intuitionists.[34] The robust approach is also reminiscent of Leibniz's treatment of contingent truths as necessary truths whose analysis is infinitistic:[35] for on the robust approach the copula is treated as a name, the specification of whose referent is infinitistic.

[18] See [1], pp. 165–83, 370–6, 390–417. Cantor cites Plato, Augustine, Nicolas of Cusa, and Giordano Bruno as inspirations: pp. 204–5, 401–2. See Dauben, esp. pp. 96–9, 120–48, 229–30; Hallett [1], esp. ch. 1; A. Moore [2], pp. 110–30; Priest [1], pp. 123–6. Cantor came to believe that 'absolute' infinity (inconsistent multiplicity), by contrast with the merely transfinite, has potential existence only: Jané; Felgner [1], pp. 178–9.
[19] See Maier, i, pp. 82–4; Murdoch [1], p. 174.
[20] Famously, Leibniz stated in a letter to Foucher written some time after 1692 that 'Je suis tellement pour l'infini actuel, qu'au lieu d'admettre que la nature l'abhorre, comme l'on dit vulgairement, je tiens qu'elle l'affecte partout, pour mieux marquer les perfections de son auteur. Ainsi je crois qu'il n'y a aucune partie de la matière qui ne soit, je ne dis pas divisible, mais actuellement divisée; et par conséquent la moindre particelle doit estre considerée comme un monde plein d'une infinité de créatures différentes' ([1], i, p. 416; cf. iv, p. 492). This passage was cited in part by Bolzano at the beginning of his [1], and in full by Cantor in his *Grundlagen*, §7 ([1], p. 179). On the fortunes in Leibniz's thinking of his thesis that there are 'worlds within worlds to infinity', see [6], pp. xxxii–iv, xliv–xlv, li–lxii.
[21] See [1], §13; A. Moore [2], p. 112.   [22] See Maddy, p. 114.
[23] [8], p. 269 ([21], p. 163); [10], II, §123; [26], p. 77.   [24] [3], §§140, 179–86, 322.
[25] See A. Moore [2], pp. 34–44, 206–8; Priest [1], pp. 25–34.
[26] Aquinas [1], Ia, q. 7, a. 4; cf. Cantor [1], pp. 399, 403–4; Hallett [1], p. 22.
[27] Locke, II. xvii and xxix, §16; Berkeley, esp. §50; Hume, I, ii, §iv.
[28] Diderot, viii, pp. 702–3 (Ewald, pp. 128–30).
[29] See A. Moore [2], pp. 84–95; Priest [1], pp. 85–101.
[30] Gauss, p. 216; Kneale and Kneale, p. 673.
[31] See Dauben, pp. 66–70, 127, 134–7, 253–9; A. Moore [2], p. 121.
[32] Poincaré, §xv (Ewald, p. 1070); Dauben, pp. 266–7; A. Moore [2], p. 121.
[33] See e.g. [10], p. 119; A. Moore [2], pp. 137–40.
[34] See Kleene, pp. 46–53; Hallett [1], pp. 27–8; A. Moore [2], pp. 131–7; Priest [1], pp. 159–61; Giaquinto, pp. 136–9. The intuitionist need not baulk at Bradley's regress construed as comprising a potential infinity of instantiation relations, because as we have seen (§74) it has an effective principle of generation: cf. Fraenkel *et al.*, p. 231; Dummett [8], pp. 40–7.
[35] [1], vii, p. 309.

Though the Cantorian position can no doubt claim the status of orthodoxy, and is what I am committed to by virtue of the realism I espoused in §1, we do not strictly need here to decide the issue between the robust and cautious approaches to the semantics of the logical copula. For what these rival approaches have in common—a rejection of the claim that the copula lacks reference *simpliciter*—is surely something we can accept without investigating the relative merits of these approaches. Indeed it is rather unclear that such a further inquiry would yield dividends.[36] Of course there is a general issue of coherence between the rival approaches to infinite totalities, to be settled by consideration of the metaphysics of the infinite. But it is not clear that examination of the semantics of the copula would have anything to contribute to this general issue. Rather, it seems obvious that our choice between these rival approaches to the semantics of the logical copula must be determined by the outcome of that wider inquiry. Pending that outcome (that is, supposing we do not think the issue is already settled), we can refuse to adjudicate between the two approaches. In fact it is a clear possibility that the two approaches will turn out to be, for our purposes, mere notational variants of one another. For whatever we end up saying about the precise way in which the logical copula has reference, it will remain the case that the logical copula relates to whatever sort of reference it has in a quite unique way, and that suffices for our purposes to distinguish it from all other semantically significant features of the sentence. It also vindicates at least one version of the *tertium adiacens* approach to the copula (§42): for there is a sense in which the logical copula provides the *form* of the declarative sentence, by contrast with the *matter* which is provided by all other semantically significant parts (expressions or features) of the sentence.[37]

76 Bradley's Regress and the Analysis of Meaning

Allowing the (unannotated) logical copula to be a part of the sentence, we may now say that it is the only part of the sentence whose reference or referent is infinitistic in the defined way. Previously I have put this by saying

---

[36] Though one possible line of investigation would exploit the traditional assimilation (found in medieval authors, and again in Leibniz) of the distinction between categorematic and syncategorematic terms to the distinction between the actual and the potential infinite: see Murdoch [2], pp. 567–8. Cantor approves of this assimilation, because the potential infinite has 'nur eine geborgte Realität' ([1], pp. 391, 404; Jané, pp. 378–9). I am inclined to agree with Maier's remark that the assimilation is 'nichts weiter als eine terminologische Festsetzung' (i, p. 44 n. 7; cf. Geach [5]): but the matter is, I should say, open.

[37] Cf. Simons [3], p. 90.

that the copula is *the* carrier of unsaturatedness in the sentence.[38] Since I am now, on the basis of the context principle, taking *all* semantically significant parts of the sentence to be unsaturated, this manner of speaking is no longer available to me. But the basic point—that the logical copula is that sentential feature which, by virtue of its having reference in a quite special way, captured by the regress, unifies the proposition—remains intact. It follows now that far from being vicious, it is exactly the generation of Bradley's regress that guarantees our ability to *say* anything at all. Bradley's regress emerges not as an embarrassment, something to be circumvented by careful legislation, but as the metaphysical ground of the unity of the proposition. Reverting to the original terms of the unity problem, we might say, perhaps riskily, that what stops a proposition from being a *mere* aggregate of entities, and the corresponding sentence from being a *mere* list, is that the proposition unfolds into an *infinite* aggregate, and the sentence into an *infinite* list.

But we must be careful how we specify the mode of generation of the relevant infinities. Davidson remarks that 'Viewing concatenation as a significant piece of syntax, we may assign to it the relation of participating in or instantiating; however, it is obvious that we have here the start of an infinite regress'.[39] And Simons writes:

[A] sentence . . . will need to be discernible from its surroundings, and its parts will have to stand in relations to one another, in which they do not stand to parts of other sentences. In natural languages, spatial or temporal contiguity obviously play a crucial role in holding perceptible sentences together, and apart from others. In general, especially in connected speech or prose, the unifying relations will be far more complicated—one need only think of such varied devices as full stops (periods) in punctuation, or pauses and intonation-pattern in diction. Nevertheless, the single function these many devices fulfil is that of satisfaction relations.[40]

But the first clause of Davidson's claim, and the last sentence of Simons's, are surely incorrect. The relations of concatenation or ordering do not have anything, as such, to do with the relations of participation, instantiation, or satisfaction. Indeed the relations of concatenation or ordering at the level of symbolic language (token or type) do not even have anything, as such, to do with a basic relation of configuration at the level of reference. For a list may comprise concatenated or ordered symbolic items, and there is nothing in a list as such (token or type), even when its component words are concatenated or ordered, to ensure that the corresponding entities at the level of reference are configured or combined in any way at all, let alone organized by such substantial relations as instantiation or satisfaction. The items in a list

---

[38] [1], §VII. [39] [1], p. 17. Cf. Orilia [1], p. 109 n. 8. [40] [3], pp. 89–90.

may—perhaps must—*be* ordered, but if they are, it does not follow that their referents are (being said to be) ordered, or configured in any other way. Indeed we shall see in more detail below (§79) that, to the extent that a list really falls short of having sentential unity, it follows that its referents are (being said to be) *not ordered*.

This fits with the fact that, as we have noted (§5), significant concatenation is not the special prerogative of sentences as opposed to lists: items figuring in mere lists are or can be significantly concatenated or ordered in a way that duplicates any concatenative or ordering devices employed in the formation of sentences. At least, that is clearly so of spoken language: Simons is wrong to suppose (in effect) that concatenative devices such as intonation patterns cannot be duplicated by mere (spoken) lists. Insofar as written language deploys punctuation marks it may be in a different case: for punctuation enables us to differentiate sentences visually from lists. But punctuation (i) is an accidental, not an essential, feature of written language, as shown by the fact that some empirical languages do not employ it (or do so only to a minimal degree),[41] and (ii) it is, like written language in general, a secondary phenomenon, dependent on a prior constitution of grammatical categories in respect of spoken language. It is not because the written string 'Socrates, is, wise' is punctuated in that particular way that the identity of the type expression of which this is a token is constituted as a list rather than as a declarative sentence; rather, that is one agreed way to punctuate an expression whose identity as a list precedes and is presupposed to the possibility of its being so inscribed.

The general bearing of Bradley's regress on our problem is relevantly similar to this. Imagine a regimented language in which declarative sentences are arrived at by suffixing the predicate 'trues' to nominalizations of sentences. 'Socrates is wise' becomes 'The wisdom of Socrates trues', etc. Bradley's regress then takes the form: the truth of the wisdom of Socrates trues, the truth of the truth of the wisdom of Socrates trues, etc.[42] Such a regress—a version of the regress

p,
it is true that p,
it is true that it is true that p, etc.[43]—

[41] Oliver and Smiley [2], p. 657 n. 39.　　[42] Cf. Bolzano [1], §13; [2], §32; Frege [1], §3.

[43] Or: p, 'p' is true, '"p"' is true' is true, etc. Hochberg states that the truth regress is innocent because it is a linguistic regress *rather than* an ontological one ([9], pp. 37–8), but, so far as I can see, it is both: the version I give in the text applies at the level of the proposition, and so, by my lights, is ontological; the version given in this note is linguistic. I do not see how one version could be more or less innocent than the other.

is surely not only harmless but fundamental to the ability of speakers of this language to say anything true (and so to say anything at all),[44] for the truth of the $n + 1$th stage is a necessary (and sufficient) condition of the truth of the nth stage.[45] (This was in effect the construction used by Dedekind when he sought to prove the existence of an infinite set, with 'it is thought that' in place of 'it is true that'.[46]) Russell then turns out to have been both right and wrong (§70). Each stage in the regress entails (and is entailed by) the next stage, so the regress is (on one of his intuitions, which I accept) harmless. But the fact that it arises in the analysis of meaning does not, as he supposed, destroy its innocence. A regress which arises in the analysis of meaning is not *eo ipso* vicious.

Here we may recall the passage from Russell's 1899 paper 'The Classification of Relations' with which I prefaced this investigation, and compare it with a remark from *The Principles of Mathematics* that all but anticipates my proposed solution to the unity problem. Russell writes:

> It may be urged that it is part of the very meaning of a relational proposition that the relation involved should have to the terms the relation expressed in saying that it relates them, and that this is what makes the distinction, which we formerly (§54) left unexplained, between a relating relation and a relation in itself. It may be urged, however, against this view, that the assertion of a relation between the relation and the terms, though implied, is no part of the original proposition, and that a relating relation is distinguished from a relation in itself by the indefinable element of assertion which distinguishes a proposition from a concept.[47]

I have already sufficiently censured Russell's own positive proposal, given at the end of this passage, for what distinguishes a 'relation actually relating' from a 'relation in itself'. Here I am interested in the initial suggestion that Russell rejects ('it is part of the very meaning . . .'). As we saw in my opening quotation from 'The Classification of Relations', Russell was aware of the regressive tendencies of this suggestion, and he repeats the point in *Principles*, adding that

> when a relation holds between two terms, the relations of the relation to the terms, and of these relations to the relation and the terms, and so on ad infinitum, though all implied by the proposition affirming the original relation, form no part of the *meaning* of this proposition.[48]

Russell is considering relational sentences in these passages, whereas I have largely concentrated on non-relational sentences and their corresponding

[44] See §83 below.   [45] Cf. Hochberg [6], p. 78; Armstrong [5], pp. 118–19.
[46] Dedekind, §66. See Hilbert, pp. 32–3; Russell [11], pp. 138–40; Boolos, ch. 13.   [47] [3], §99.
[48] [3], §55. Cf. §214: the relevant part is quoted in §82 below; [7], pp. 375, 377.

propositions in my exposition of the unity problem and its solution. But that difference is slight, given that Bradley's regress very quickly generates relational out of non-relational propositions, and given that, as the 1899 paper makes clear, and as we noted in §29, it is in any case Russell's view that subject–predicate propositions are reducible to relational ones.[49]

Waiving, then, that insignificant difference, it can be seen that, with one crucial change, these Russellian passages anticipate my solution to the unity problem. If Russell is right that subject–predicate sentences are deeply relational in form, the problem of unity might be said to be reducible to the question how relations in propositions relate their relata—by which I mean, not how relations *actually* relate their relata (in *true* propositions), but how they *are said to* relate them (in *true or false* propositions). But instead of maintaining, as Russell does in rejecting the suggestion that (in effect) a relation must itself be (said to be) related to its relata if it is to (be said to) relate them (truly or falsely), that the relation (or, in my terms, instantiation) regress, though implied by the original sentence, is *not* part of its meaning, we should accept that it is not only implied by the original sentence but *is* part of its meaning.[50] So we should accept the first of the two options Russell offers us at the beginning of the passage I quoted from 'The Classification of Relations' at the outset of this study and between which Russell himself declines to choose: that is, we should accept that, when two terms are (said to be) related, the relation is indeed (said to be) related to each term, regress and all.

77 Vicious Practical Regresses

Perhaps it may be helpful in giving a sense of what is at stake here if we consider, by way of contrast, some other regresses which arise in the analysis of meaning but which, unlike Bradley's regress, are plausibly regarded as vicious. Consider, first, a regress that occurs in the reflections of the later Wittgenstein on the notion of following a rule, namely the regress that arises if understanding is construed as a matter of having an interpretation, which is defined for these purposes as the substitution of one expression of the rule for another.[51] This regress presents us with a practical impossibility: if understanding a given sign always consisted in understanding a prior sign, the business of linguistic understanding could never get off the ground. A similar vicious regress is

---

[49] See e.g. [2], p. 15; [13], p. 123. Cf. Horstmann, p. 203.
[50] Here I differ from N. Griffin [3], pp. 345–6, and Sainsbury [3], p. 150.
[51] [5], I, §§198–201. See Bell [4], pp. 47–8; McDowell [4], pp. 264–6; and my [15], p. 188.

hiding under the surface of Wittgenstein's charge that Augustine's picture of language represents the language-learning child as already in command of a language, only not the one being taught.[52] Regresses of this general shape are quite common in the tradition: for instance, the eighteenth-century writer Johann Peter Süssmilch, relying on Christian Wolff, argued that language is so sophisticated and complete a system that it could only have been devised by a being endowed with reason—and language.[53] Süssmilch essays a theological escape route, but the regress, if we got into it, certainly would be vicious.

A second example of a vicious practical regress is the epistemological regress that arises when the criteria of the justification of a belief themselves have to be subjected to a *process* of justification if the original criteria are to serve as such: if the process never terminates, justification for the original belief cannot be established.[54] Note the emphasis: I see no objection to a justification or explanation regress in which each stage is *in fact* justified by the next stage. In other words, there is no reason why infinite chains of justification or explanation *as such* should be branded as vicious, so long as they do not require us to go through an infinity of *procedures*. Here I agree with Peter Klein, who has argued forcefully that there is no good a priori reason why we should insist that all justificatory chains must terminate.[55] In practice, it seems to me (and against Klein), most ordinary justificatory chains *do* terminate: for example, in the case of perceptually based beliefs, it is plausible that, as Wittgenstein suggested in some of his later writings (especially in the remarks collected in *Über Gewissheit/On Certainty*), in tracing justifications, rather than falling into a regress we quickly reach a bedrock constituted not by beliefs that are self-justifying, but rather by beliefs that do not need to be justified because they are, in some sense, *too deep* for justification.[56] But I see no reason why we should insist as a matter of a priori principle that all explanatory chains must terminate, and I shall suggest shortly that Bradley's regress can be regarded as an explanatory chain which does not do so.

Thirdly, we might cite Cantor's 'domain' principle. The core of Cantor's argument for the existence of an actual, not merely potential, infinite was that if statements incorporating a variable are to be determinate in sense the domain of variability must be determinate, and in the case of statements involving a potential infinity, the domain of variability will be an actual infinity. If the domain of variability were itself variable, and the domain of *that* variability's variability in turn variable, and so on ad infinitum, the original statements

---

[52] [5], I, §32.   [53] Süssmilch, esp. §22.   [54] See Priest [1], pp. 43–4; Norman.
[55] See the papers of his mentioned in the bibliography.
[56] Cf. Ginet's contribution to Klein and Ginet, esp. pp. 141–3.

would lack determinate sense.[57] Here again the point is that in order to *understand* a statement involving a variable, one must know what its domain of variability is: if that domain were itself variable, and so on ad infinitum, the would-be understander would be 'hurried off into the eddy of a hopeless process'. The original statement would lack determinate sense, so that there would be nothing for the understander to understand.

Consider, finally, a standard rebuttal of the suggestion that objectual quantification can be 'analysed out' in favour of substitutional quantification. The rebuttal proceeds by pointing out that substitutional quantification is itself conceptually dependent on objectual quantification: since substitutional accounts presuppose that for every object there is (or can be created) a sign that denotes that object, it plainly involves quantification (i) over the domain of objects (the ones to be correlated with signs),[58] and (ii) over signs themselves taken as objects.[59] If one tried to construe these apparently objectual quantifications substitutionally, as some have suggested we might do,[60] one would both—in case (i)—be involved in a vicious circularity, and—in case (ii)—be launched on a regress.[61] The regress is vicious because, if one enters it, then in order to understand the original substitutional analysans ('there are signs...') one needs already to have performed infinitely many discrete acts of identifying potentially distinct sets of actual and possible signs. For here, as also in the case of the domain regress, but in contrast with Bradley's regress, the infinitely many stages in the regress are not mechanically generated from a finite base—there is and can be no algorithm for generating all actual and possible names of objects, names of names, names of names of names, etc.—and so are not capable of being grasped in a single act, or finite series of acts, of understanding, but must be individually computed ad infinitum, a task which it is evidently beyond our capacities to compass.

78 Bradley's Regress and the Solution to the Unity Problem

I claim that a regress that arises in the analysis of meaning will be vicious just if it is a 'practical' regress, in the sense that it presents an infinite series of

---

[57] See Cantor [1], pp. 393 n., 404, 410–11; Jourdain at Cantor [2], p. 79; Hallett [1], pp. 7, 24–32, 195–6; Tiles, pp. 29–30; Jané, pp. 385–6; Priest [1], pp. 125–6.
[58] See Hochberg [7], p. 177.   [59] Cf. Quine [4], pp. 106–7.
[60] Cf. Dunn and Belnap, p. 184 (point 4); Bonevac, pp. 230–1; Priest [2], pp. 154–5.
[61] Cf. Quine [5], p. 119.

discrete epistemic tasks to be completed by the would-be understander. By contrast, a regress that arises in the analysis of meaning will be innocent just if it is a 'metaphysical' regress, in the sense that it places an infinitistic structural condition on what it is to understand; its stages are not epistemically discrete moments, requiring to be processed seriatim by the understander, but are rather acquired all at once and in their entirety as an epistemological package. Of course a metaphysical regress *as such* need not have anything to do with understanding: in general, such regresses place structural conditions on reality. That suggests an analogy.

At the beginning of §70 I gave a list of philosophers who have held Bradley's regress to be vicious, and I mentioned the cases known to me of those who have repudiated this orthodoxy. Two major thinkers who perhaps have some claim to be included under the latter rubric, on the basis that they at least came close to regarding the regress (or something like it) as innocent, are Bolzano and Meinong. Implicit in Bolzano's *Paradoxien des Unendlichen*, and explicit in Meinong's *Über Gegenstände höherer Ordnung*,[62] is an analogy between the instantiation regress and the continuity of the real number line. (We also find in Geulincx an analogy between the truth regress and the infinite divisibility of body.[63]) The profundity and aptness of the analogy surely reside in (i) the fact that the continuity of the real number line is not mysterious, but is generated in a well-understood way by a particular analytical condition, which is infinitistic in its implications but is finitely expressible, and (ii) the additional fact that the condition in question is not viciously infinitistic, but on the contrary innocently constitutes a number line (a dimension of space, a material extension, and so on) as having that particular order-type—the order-type of the continuum.[64] It should be remarked that the analogy is not perfect: for one thing, the instantiation regress is an ω-sequence; that is, it has the order-type of the natural numbers, not the rationals (which Bolzano, following Aristotle, understood to compose the continuum), nor the reals (which are now held to compose it).

Bradley's regress, like the structure of the rational or real line, is infinitistic in a metaphysical, not a practical, sense, and for that reason is not vicious: it imposes a specific infinitistic condition on the structure of propositions—and so ultimately (recall the argument of Chapter 2) on the structure of the world itself—and not an infinitistic, and so unperformable, task for the understander. The condition imposed by Bradley's regress on the proposition, and on the world, can be captured in a finitely based theory of meaning, and so is within

---

[62] Of the latter see esp. §5 ([1], p. 390).   [63] [1], II. i, §3, p. 238. Cf. Olson, p. 49.

[64] Bolzano [1], §§38–41. Cf. Russell [3], §330; Cantor [1], pp. 190–1; Dauben, pp. 107–11.

the grasp of the understander. Accordingly, though acquaintance with the unified proposition involves acquaintance with an infinity of entities, the process of becoming acquainted with it and them does not involve performing the impossible feat of, in Aristotle's phrase, 'going through infinitely many things'.[65] The regress unpacks the original proposition into an infinity of further propositions, and it structures, infinitistically, our understanding of that original proposition, but it does not present us with a series of discrete epistemic tasks: we do not have to perform an infinity of such tasks corresponding to the stages of the regress before we can assure ourselves of the unity of a given proposition. Even so, its unity depends on the presence, in the unspoken and unwritten background, of the members of the regress: were that background not fully in place—if the regress did not get going, or if it faltered at some point—the proposition in question would not be unified, but would fall apart into a mere aggregate.

In the first instance, what distinguishes a declarative sentence from a mere list of words is that a sentence has the capacity to say something *true or false*, whereas a list does not. What constitutes this distinction? The *initial* answer we can give to this question is that a sentence is distinguished from a mere list by the presence in it of a logical predicate or, more precisely, of a logical copula. But, as I noted in the last chapter (§69) concerning the logical predicate, and earlier in this chapter (§74) concerning the logical copula, that move cannot possibly represent the final answer to our question: it is, rather, best thought of as a framework for an answer. Bradley's regress arose in an attempt to specify the reference of the crucial copulative feature of the sentence unifying it and the proposition it refers to. But the regress can also be regarded as, at each stage, comprising *necessary and sufficient conditions* for the presence of that crucial feature at any preceding, and each succeeding, stage: in particular—to take the case where the language contains asymmetric relations of instantiation[66]—it is a necessary and sufficient condition of *a*'s being (said to be) *F* that *a* (be said to) instantiate *F*-ness, and it is in turn a necessary and sufficient condition of *a*'s instantiating (being said to instantiate) *F*-ness that *a* (be said to) instantiate the relation of instantiation with respect to *F*-ness, and so on. Since the initial stage of the regress comprises a complete, unified proposition, constituted in the first instance by its capacity to be true or false, a capacity it enjoys in virtue of its possession of a logically copulative feature corresponding to the logical

---

[65] *An. Po.* 72b10–11. Cf. Bell [4], pp. 39–40, 46–7.

[66] The case of languages like Denyer's **S** which do not contain explicit symbols for universals will not introduce any new distinction of principle, but merely complicate the regress by adding an extra stage at the beginning of the specification of the copula's referent ('the relation of configuration') before we get into the regress of instantiation relations. I shall return to this point in §86.

copula of its governing sentence, it follows that the regressive unfolding of the necessary and sufficient conditions for possession of that feature is constitutive of the base proposition's unity. In that sense, the regress *itself* is ultimately constitutive of that unity.

Note that, as we have said (§74), the various stages of Bradley's regress are genuinely distinct from one another, and that this is so quite regardless of whether the superscripts in the formula (4) above (§74) are treated as indices or variables: for there is no question of a relation of synonymy's obtaining, at the level of language, between any two stages, and so correspondingly no question of a relation of identity's obtaining between any two stages at the level of the expressed proposition.[67] (Bolzano stressed—surely correctly—the distinctness of each stage of the truth regress from all other stages.[68]) By contrast, what might be called the 'Russellian liar'[69]—the Russellian proposition to the effect that this very proposition is false—generates a collapsing regress. If we call the Russellian liar 'f', we have

$$f = [(\text{false})f],$$

where the square brackets are a device to name a Russellian proposition (or its set-theoretic representative).[70] By substitution, we may then generate the regress

$$f = [(\text{false}) \, [(\text{false})f]],$$
$$f = [(\text{false}) \, [(\text{false}) \, [(\text{false})f]]],$$

and so on. But it is clear that at the level of the proposition the stages of the regress collapse to f.[71] Bradley's regress contains nothing like the self-referentiality feature that engenders collapse of the stages of the Russellian liar regress. Rather, at each stage of Bradley's regress we find either *distinct* instantiation relations of *distinct* adicities (if the superscripts in (4) are understood to be indices), or *distinct applications* of an initial, multigrade instantiation relation (if the superscripts in (4) are understood to be variables). Hence the claim that each stage of the regress at the level of language supplies necessary and sufficient conditions for the presence of the logical copula at each preceding and succeeding stage is not a trivial one. But, although we do not want to say that each stage of the regress at the level of language is synonymous with the others, so collapsing the stages at the level of reference into a single proposition, it is plausible that those stages do satisfy, pairwise, the intuitive criterion of

---

[67] So the regress is not an *internalist* regress in Orilia's sense: [2], §6.
[68] [2], §32 n.; cf. Textor [2], pp. 190–1.   [69] So Barwise and Etchemendy, p. 65.
[70] Ibid., p. 64.   [71] Ibid., p. 67.

difference, so that at the level of sense the stages of the regress do express intuitively similar Thoughts (§67).[72]

Further, the explanatory value of the regress attaches both to the regress as a whole and to each stage of it: indeed, one must surely say that that explanatory value attaches to each of these *in virtue of* its applying to the other. To draw on a useful distinction made by Klein,[73] the infinitism I embrace is of both a *holistic* and a *dependent-property* variety, and it is each of these *because* it is the other: for the two varieties point at one another. The holistic variety of Bradley's-regress infinitism takes the unity of a given proposition to consist in its generating an infinite set of propositions—those constituting the regress that arises in respect of that proposition. The dependent-property variety of Bradley's-regress infinitism holds that unity is conferred piecemeal on proposition by proposition as we move through the regress. (This conferral of unity operates in both directions: see below in this section on this point.) Klein himself supports a holistic infinitism for the regress of justifications (§77), but argues that the dependent-property variety is not vicious. He does not consider the possibility that the two varieties of infinitism might actually be mutually supporting. At least as far as the present context is concerned, and the role of Bradley's regress in unifying the proposition, that seems to me the right thing to say.

What we should affirm is that the regress as a whole is explanatory because each stage is; and, by contrast with the kind of terminating explanatory chain that we considered above (§77), each stage in Bradley's regress owes its explanatory status to the fact that it is indeed a stage in an *infinite* regress. Were this latter not the case, one would have to allow that it is not explanatory of an instantiation relation's occurring at a given stage n that an instantiation relation of higher adicity occurs suitably at stage $n + 1$ (or that the same multigrade instantiation relation is applied to one more object at stage $n + 1$). But the fact that any given stage of Bradley's regress is indeed, and essentially, a *stage of that infinite regress* entitles us to overcome this objection. And it would evidently be an egregious fallacy—the familiar fallacy of composition—to move from the admitted fact that any given stage of the regress, taken in abstraction from its position in the regress as a whole, lacks explanatory value to the conclusion that

---

[72] I distinguish here between the regress as it arises at the levels of symbolic language, sense, and reference. When it was introduced, Bradley's regress was taken to operate at the level of reference, where it indeed arises in its fundamental form. But it is convenient to be able to talk about its images at derivative levels of sense and symbolic language: these images of the basic ontological regress are presentations of that ontological regress. I shall continue to regard the level of reference as being the default location of the regress, inserting appropriate qualifications when its images at the levels of sense or symbolic language are in question.

[73] [3], pp. 726–9; Klein and Ginet, p. 152.

the regress as a whole lacks explanatory value; equally, it would be fallacious to suppose that, because any given stage of the regress, taken in abstraction from its position in the regress as a whole, lacks explanatory value, that stage *continues* to lack explanatory value when we consider it *without* abstracting it from its place in the regress as a whole, that is, when we consider it *as* being a stage in Bradley's regress.[74]

So when William Vallicella puts Bradley's point by saying that 'the unity of *a*'s being F cannot be explained by saying that the connector EX (exemplification) connects *a* and F-ness, for the unity of *a*, F-ness and EX is just as much in need of explanation as the unity of *a* and F-ness',[75] we may reply by agreeing with the content of the 'for' clause but disagreeing with the 'for': it does not follow from the agreed fact that the unity of *a*, F-ness, and EX is just as much in need of explanation as the unity of *a* and F-ness that the unity of *a*'s being F cannot be explained by saying that exemplification connects *a* and F-ness. An explanation that itself stands in need of explanation may, for all that, *be* an explanation. Lewis tells us that Bradley's regress is harmless so long as its stages are taken to be mere equivalences, not explanations, and he adds that 'Bradley's regress shows that if we insist on trying to explain having [i.e. instantiation] *simpliciter* in terms of relational having, the explanation we seek will never be finished'.[76] But the fact that a given explanation will never be finished does not mean that it cannot get started or that it cannot, so far as we take it, be a good explanation. Wittgenstein once remarked that explanations have to come to an end somewhere,[77] by which he meant that, when we *in practice* provide explanations we perforce come to rest on a basis that we do not explain. But I do not think he should be taken to imply—and it would not be correct to say—that the fact that explanations must in practice come to an end means that there can be no infinitely long explanatory chains—chains which we cannot go through stage by stage, but which for all that exist, and are such that each stage (and the chain as a whole) is indeed genuinely explanatory.[78] This is denied by Alan Weir, who claims that an infinite regress which is such that 'there is *no* explanatory power at all at level α unless the explanation at level α + 1 works is indeed vicious, for the usual reason: explanation must come to an end'.[79] But I see no basis for this asseveration, no reason in general metaphysics why an explanatory chain may not exist in which, for each stage α, α's having

[74] See here Orilia [2], §7; Hochberg, [6], p. 77.

[75] [1], p. 239. Note that Vallicella is talking about the unity of states of affairs, whereas I am interested in the unity of propositions, whether true or false; but his point can be transferred to the present context. (The same applies to Orilia's relevant publications.)

[76] [8], p. 6.   [77] [5], I, §1.

[78] Cf. Priest [2], p. 32 (on regressive arguments).   [79] Weir, p. 780.

explanatory efficacy depends partly or even entirely on the explanatory efficacy of stage $\alpha + 1$.

Given the symmetry imported by the claim that each stage in the regress at the level of language supplies both a necessary and a sufficient condition for the presence of the logical copula at any immediately preceding and succeeding stages, it seems to me that we are obliged to say that at each non-initial stage of the regress at the level of reference the direction of explanation is both downwards and upwards—down towards the original unified proposition, up through the increasingly complex stages of the regress. (At the initial stage, of course, the direction of explanation is just upwards.) Here I am in disagreement with Gregory Currie, who suggests that, though the regress, as such, is innocent, 'the direction of the *in virtue of* relation is . . . downwards to the base level of the hierarchy, rather than upwards'.[80] Orilia, by contrast, thinks that the 'in virtue of' relation runs upwards, not downwards: that is, at any given stage of the regress, where an instantiation relation unites n appropriate arguments, it does so in virtue of an instantiation relation's uniting $n + 1$ appropriate arguments at the next stage up.[81] (The instantiation relations in question will be the same or different depending on how we interpret the superscripts in formula (4).) My position, against both Currie and Orilia, is that the explanatory 'in virtue of' relation operates in both directions, rather as—to borrow a point of Wiggins's from a different area[82]—the presupposition relation which Locke thought linked personal identity and memory in one direction, and which Butler thought linked them in the opposite direction, indeed connects them in both directions.

The solution I propose parallels in certain respects—to compare small things with great—Cantor's founding move in the theory of cardinality. The fact that of two denumerable infinities one might be a proper subset of the other—that (for instance) the positive integers can be put into one-to-one correspondence with the positive even integers—had long been familiar.[83] Leibniz held that this fact showed the idea of infinite number to be contradictory.[84] In his *Paradoxien des Unendlichen*, Bolzano rejected Leibniz's position, and went so far as to entertain the possibility of defining cardinality, quite generally, in terms of equinumerosity; but he did not actually cross the Rubicon and adopt

[80] [1], p. 151. Cf. Maurin, p. 101; Cameron.   [81] [2], §7.   [82] [2], p. 159 n. 13.
[83] See Murdoch [1]; [2], pp. 569–70; A. Moore [2], pp. 53–4, 111; Priest [1], pp. 32–3.
[84] Letter to Malebranche of 22 June 1679 ([1], i, p. 338); [3], II. xvii ([1], v, p. 144). Cf. Russell [3], §285; A. Moore [2], p. 79; Arthur's introduction to [6], pp. liv–lv, lxi–lxiii. Leibniz also recapitulates the fact, already noted by Galileo (Kneale and Kneale, p. 440 n. 5), that the integers can be put into one-to-one correspondence with their squares, which ought to establish equinumerosity, whereas one might suppose that there are fewer squares than integers, given that many integers are not squares: [6], pp. 176–7 (cf. pp. lxxvii, 356).

that definition.[85] It seems that towards the end of his life he may have gone further,[86] but Cantor was the first publicly to promote equinumerosity to definitional status in the transfinite as well as the finite domain:[87] henceforth the availability of bijective relations between sets was to be regarded as delivering a *criterion* of a set's cardinality. (Making this move then enabled Cantor to argue, by the method of diagonalization, that there are infinite collections of different sizes,[88] a possibility that had always struck philosophers as highly counterintuitive—Locke described it as an absurdity 'too gross to be confuted'[89]—and it enabled Dedekind and Cantor, again anticipated by Bolzano, to define an infinite set as one equinumerous to a proper part of itself.[90]) Somewhat in the same spirit as the radical shift in perspective on the metaphysics of the infinite inaugurated by Cantor, my proposed solution to the problem of the unity of the proposition invites us to see the instantiation regress, which has generally been regarded as vicious, and so to be avoided in philosophical accounts of the nature of predication, as not only innocent but constitutive of the very thing—the possibility of predication—that it was previously thought to endanger or undermine if permitted to unfold unchecked.

79 Propositions, Sets, Sums, and the Objects Themselves

There is another respect in which Cantor is important to my project, one that takes us back to my opening remarks (§1) on the difference between propositions and mere aggregates, and correspondingly between sentences and mere lists. The point I made there was that mere lists, though they may have some kind of unity, and in particular cases may even have an implied sentential unity, do not, in general and as such, have the kind of unity that is distinctive of sentences, so that their corresponding aggregates do not, as such, have the kind of unity that is distinctive of propositions—perhaps do not even have any kind of unity at all. The conception of a mere aggregate and of its linguistic counterpart, a mere list, which I am relying on here was not always regarded as a matter of course: winning through to it was an intellectual achievement, and

[85] [1], §§19–24; cf. A. Moore [2], p. 113; Potter [2], p. 155.
[86] See Berg, p. 170.   [87] [1], pp. 119, 167, 379, 380, 387, 412–20.
[88] [1], pp. 115–18, 278–80. See Dauben, pp. 165–8.   [89] Locke, II. xvii, §20.
[90] Bolzano [1], §21; Dedekind, §64; Cantor [1], pp. 414–17. See Russell [11], pp. 78–81; Maier, i, p. 46; Berg, pp. 169–70; Enderton [1], p. 157; A. Moore [2], p. 113; Potter [2], p. 68.

the outstanding figure in this story was Cantor. It was above all the influence of Cantor's work that led to the replacing of the 'logical' conception of a set or aggregate, which had been and continued to be dominant in mathematical thinking (influencing, for example, Bolzano,[91] Russell,[92] Frege,[93] and even Zermelo),[94] with a 'mathematical' conception.[95] The 'logical' conception of sets defines them as collections of objects evincing some antecedently available property, in the sense of §1, that is, as satisfying some purely general and antecedently formulable concept-expression collecting the objects in a lawlike way. This conception works by dichotomizing the totality of all things into two groups—those that satisfy the relevant property and the rest.[96] The 'mathematical' approach, by contrast, treats sets as collections of objects that need have no such property in common.[97] As Ramsey, a prime exponent of the 'mathematical' approach, put it, a class in this sense need involve no principle of classification, and need not 'be definable either by enumeration or as the extension of a predicate'.[98] Frege's intensional conception of classes survives in some modern writers;[99] indeed Gödel continued to associate classes with concepts, conjecturing that every set is the extension of some concept.[100] By contrast, in §1 I in effect supported the 'mathematical' approach to collections, agreeing that there may be (and so are) collections, whether finite or infinite, disposing of no antecedently available collecting concept in the defined sense. (Of course anti-realists are uneasy about the idea of an entirely arbitrary set;[101] but in the same place I set that anti-realism aside.)

---

[91] See e.g. [1], §14; on Bolzano's extensionalism, see Felgner [1], pp. 176–7.

[92] See e.g. [3], §23; on Russell before *Principles*, see Imaguire, pp. 130–5, 163–5; on Russell at the time of *Principia*, see Ramsey [2], p. 22; Hintikka, pp. 33–6. After Russell adopted the 'no class' theory of classes, his conception of them was perforce intensional, since they were reduced to propositional functions, which were *ex officio* intensional entities: recall §§19, 33.

[93] See §33 above.

[94] Zermelo appealed in 1908 and again in 1929 to a comprehension principle in justification of his *Aussonderungsaxiom* ([1] pp. 263–4; [3]): Hallett [1], pp. 240–4, 266–9; Ebbinghaus, pp. 86–8, 179–86. But in 1930 this restriction was withdrawn and arbitrary functions were permitted to constitute subsets of a given set: [4], p. 30 n. 1, with Ebbinghaus, p. 189.

[95] See Hallett [1], pp. 299–300. On the terminology of 'logical' vs. 'mathematical' conceptions of a set, see Cocchiarella [1], p. 152; Maddy, pp. 118–19.

[96] Cf. Wang [1], p. 187; Boolos, p. 14. Cantor sometimes expresses his set concept intensionally: see e.g. [1], p. 204 n. 1. But it seems clear that his 'best' position is extensionalist: Hallett [1], p. 34; Hintikka, pp. 29–31.

[97] See Cantor [1], p. 379; Hallett [1], pp. 135–6; Wang [1], p. 196; C. Parsons [2], pp. 217–18. Cf. also Dedekind, §2.

[98] [2], p. 15.

[99] See e.g. Marcus, ch. 6; Tugendhat [2], pp. 294, 328; von Kutschera [2], p. 324. On earlier manifestations of the conceptions, see Land, p. 158; Prior [3], p. 72.

[100] See here Wang [3], pp. 274–6.

[101] For expressions of this unease, see Hale [2], pp. 242–3; Wright [4], pp. 400–2.

But, though the 'mathematical' approach to sets or classes is an important precursor to my project, it does not go far enough for my purposes. For, even assuming that approach to sets, we can and indeed must recognize a property that the members of any given set, no matter how arbitrarily assembled, may be said to share: objects share this property just in case they are members of the set.[102] And we can, in turn, provide a specification of these specially constructed properties in terms of sets' characteristic functions, that is, in terms of mappings from objects to truth-values. On the 'mathematical' as on the 'logical' approach, then, the members of a set must be held to share a common property; but on the 'mathematical' approach, by contrast with the 'logical' approach, that property is not necessarily antecedently available, in the specified sense, and the corresponding characteristic function may accordingly be wholly arbitrary.[103] We might capture the difference between the rival approaches' understanding of the property shared by members of a set by saying that, whereas on the 'logical' approach that property is *conceptually anterior* to the set (the set exists in virtue of the property's existence), on the 'mathematical' approach it is the other way round. And it is obvious that the two operations in question here—forming sets and taking characteristic functions—can be iterated alternately into the transfinite. Or one can think of the availability of these operations as generating a regress: a given set generates its characteristic function, which in turn can be represented as a new set of ordered pairs, which in turn generates its own distinctive characteristic function, and so on. This regress is not vicious, but an innocent regress constitutive of the membership relation; to that extent it is relevantly similar to Bradley's regress and other innocent regresses that I will discuss below in §82.

If, now, we ask what the bearing of these constructions, whether iterated alternately into the transfinite or not, is on the unities of the set and of the proposition, it seems plausible to reply that a given set, regardless whether it is conceptually anterior or posterior to the property shared by its members, is logically and ontologically *coeval* with that shared property, and correspondingly coeval with the correlative characteristic function, and accordingly that the existence and unity of a set are logically and ontologically *coincident* with the existence and unity of the proposition specifying that set's membership. And, plausibly, it is a consequence of my realism about arbitrarily constituted sets (§1) that the proposition with which a set is constitutively associated—the proposition stating the membership condition of that set—does not have to

---

[102] Cf. Potter [2], p. 314.
[103] On the historical origins of the idea of a wholly arbitrary function, see Felgner [2], p. 624; Marion, p. 344; Kanamori, pp. 276–7, 290–1.

be known, knowable, or even finitely stateable. For example, its complexity might be constituted by an infinity of randomly selected elements going well beyond anything that could be encompassed by a human cognitive capacity. Russell held that while all propositions known to us are finitely complex, infinite complexity of propositions is in principle possible,[104] though his unease with the axiom of choice suggests that he would have found the idea of an infinitely complex and randomly constituted proposition problematic.[105] I have accepted (§5) that infinitely complex propositions are not merely possible but actual (as abstract objects their actuality coincides with their possibility). And, in line with the liberal view I have taken (§5) on the question of sentence size, I see no reason to impose any limits, finite or transfinite, on the possible complexity of propositions.[106]

My claim is this: not only is a given set logically and ontologically coeval with an associated proposition specifying its membership; it is further the case that the unity of a set *is* the unity of that associated proposition. Here we must guard against building too much into our notion of set-membership. We are accustomed to call the relevant relation between its elements and a set 'membership', but what is important about the relation in question is not this particular label with its ordinary, extra-mathematical connotations, but rather the fact that, given a bunch of elements and the relation in question, the relatum—the set that we want these elements to make up—is uniquely determined.[107] There is nothing more to set-membership than this, and a consequence of that fact, it seems to me, is that the unity of a set *just is* the unity of the relevant proposition specifying its membership. (Recall that von Neumann axiomatized set theory on the basis of sets' characteristic functions rather than a primitive membership relation.[108]) The bearing on our inquiry of the 'mathematical' revolution in set theory is, then, that although a 'mathematical' understanding of sets takes us in the right direction, away from a conception of sets as exclusively constructed on the basis of antecedently available properties, in the defined sense, it does not go far enough for our purposes. That is because, like Frege's 'logical' approach, the 'mathematical'

---

[104] [3], §§72, 141; [13], pp. 202, 337; cf. B. Linsky [3], p. 383; Grattan-Guinness, p. 341. In the *Notebooks* Wittgenstein had wavered on the question whether infinite complexity is possible: Simons [7], p. 213. By the time of the *Tractatus*, he is prepared to envisage (§4.2211) the possibility of 'horizontal' infinite complexity (i.e. the possibility that there are infinitely many facts, and that some of these facts contain infinitely many simple objects); §§2.021–2.0212 only rule out the possibility of 'vertical' complexity (i.e. a complexity all the way down, entailing that we can never arrive at simple objects): cf. Oliver [1], pp. 94–6.

[105] Cf. Hintikka, pp. 37–42.   [106] Here I am in disagreement with Wright [4], p. 401.

[107] Stenius [2], pp. 181–5; cf. Potter [2], p. 231.

[108] Von Neumann, pp. 221–2; Fraenkel et al., p. 135.

approach to sets still provides us with objects that, insofar as they are unified, are *propositionally* unified, and so are unfit to serve as a point of contrast with propositions and their distinctive kind of unity.

The contrast we have been working with is between a sentence and a mere list on the one hand, and between a proposition and a mere aggregate on the other, and about lists and aggregates little has been said hitherto by way of characterization except that, in themselves, they constitutively lack the kind of unity that is distinctive of sentences and propositions respectively. But now we are in a position to say more. First, we need some distinctions: I start by distinguishing among what I shall call 'Cantorian sets', 'sums or classes', and 'the objects themselves'.[109] Cantorian sets are marked out by (at least) the following features: (i) they are abstract objects over and above their so-called members—that is, the set is abstract regardless of the status (abstract or concrete) of its members; (ii) the membership relation is not transitive; (iii) Cantorian sets may be referred to by means of genuinely singular referring expressions, and such expressions are not a mere *façon de parler*; (iv) there is a (unique) null set, and a singleton is ontologically distinct from its member;[110] (v) the cardinality of the power set of a Cantorian set containing n members is 2^n. Less ontologically special than Cantorian sets are sums or classes conceived as follows:[111] (i) they are nothing over and above their members—that is, if the members of a sum or class, in this sense, are concrete individuals, then the sum or class is also concrete;[112] (ii) the membership relation is transitive; (iii) we can refer to sums and classes (in this sense) using singular referring expressions, but the collections of entities thereby generated are no more than useful fictions, and the singular referring expressions we employ no more than convenient shorthand for plural referring expressions (a style of reference that Max Black calls 'ostensibly singular reference');[113] (iv) there is, on this understanding of sums or classes, no null sum or class, and no distinction to be made between an individual and the sum or class comprising just that individual; (v) the cardinality of all the sums or classes (in this sense) of n individuals is 2^n-1.[114] Finally, at the lowest level of ontological commitment, there are just the objects themselves, any or all of them: they do not, at this level, constitute a unity of any kind.[115] At this level, only plural referring devices are competent to designate the unassembled bits of reality we wish to talk about. In *Principles*, as

---

[109] Cf. Simons [10], pp. 87–92.

[110] Cf. Potter [2], p. 22 (cf. pp. 58–60). Contrast Black [3], p. 633; Muller, p. 446.

[111] On sums, see Bolzano [2], §84; Frege [26], p. 199. On Leśniewski's related distinction between distributive and collective classes, see Küng, ch. 8; Simons [8], esp. pp. 144–71.

[112] Cf. Frege's letter to Russell of 28 July 1902 ([22], p. 223).   [113] [3], pp. 631–3.

[114] Cf. Küng, pp. 136–7.   [115] Cf. Boolos, pp. 70–2; Oliver and Smiley [2], pp. 649–50.

we have seen (§33), Russell characterized a 'collection' of this kind (the word is scare-quoted because the point is that at this level of ontological commitment the objects are *not* collected) as a 'class as many' (as opposed to a 'class as one'). At this level, there is obviously no room for the notion of a null 'collection', or for a distinction between an individual and the 'collection' containing just that individual (for there is no place for a distinction between *any* number of individuals and the 'collection' containing them).

We should recognize that these three grades of ontological abstraction always and necessarily come together as an ontological package: that is, in any application, each one of the three categories—(some or all of) the objects themselves, sums or classes (in the above sense) of those objects, and Cantorian sets of them—exists if and only if the other two do. Russell and Whitehead exist if and only if the sum or (concrete) class of Russell and Whitehead exists, which in turn exists if and only if the (abstract) set containing Russell and Whitehead exists. The same applies to the non-self-membered sets, as I argued in §63: you cannot posit the existence of these sets without at the same time committing yourself to the existence of a set containing them all. No doubt you can *refer to* all those collections without referring to the supercollection containing them all:[116] but you cannot prevent your thereby being *committed to* the existence of that supercollection. There is no call to respond to this ontological parity by downgrading the reality of any of the three categories to the status of mere *entia rationis*, on the basis that we cannot permit entities whose existence is necessarily interdependent to exist as bona-fide distinct bits of the world: on the contrary, there is no difficulty in acknowledging that real objects, or collections thereof, whose existence is necessarily tied to the existence of other real objects or collections thereof, may exist as distinct objects or collections with their own ontological integrity. Here we set our face against considerations that have often appealed to philosophers. The scholastic tradition, in particular, has always taken the possibility of *A*'s independent existence from *B*, and vice versa—the possibility that *A* may exist though *B* does not, often more concretely expressed in terms of God's having the power to create *A* without *B*, or destroy *B* while preserving *A*—to be necessary and sufficient for the real diversity of *A* and *B*.[117] But, while the *sufficiency* component of the condition is no doubt unimpeachable, it is not hard to think of counterexamples to the claim that any such independence is *necessary* for real diversity. (The natural numbers would be a counterexample.) It is true that, given a collection (or 'collection') of objects, we can think of and refer to them in any of the three ways mentioned—as just those objects (plural reference), as the sum or class of those objects (mere ostensibly singular reference), or as the set of those objects (genuine singular reference); but that fact does not show that to these three ways of representing the same objects nothing corresponds *a parte rei*.

Now all three grades of ontological commitment fall short of the kind of ontological commitment carried by propositions. For all three grades of collection (or 'collection') of objects conform to the axiom of extensionality—same objects, same collection (or 'collection'). By contrast, propositions on my understanding of them (Chapter 2), as on Russell's in his early period, are intensional entities (though intensional entities which may contain one or more extensional positions). It follows that propositions constitute a higher grade of ontological commitment than any of the three types of commitment so far mentioned: in terms of a familiar division, they are *wholes* as opposed to *sets* or *sums*.[118] In this higher grade of ontological commitment, extensionality fails to apply; the reasons for this failure may vary, depending on the type of whole in question. In some cases, extensionality fails because the *organization* of the parts making up the whole plays a role in constituting the whole as such:[119] this applies to many concrete wholes we encounter or construct, such as organisms and artefacts, for which the organizational factor is normally so important that such wholes may even gain or lose parts without forfeiting their identity, so long as their organizational integrity is preserved. In the case of interest here, namely Russellian propositions, extensionality fails because these propositions contain intensional components: for, on my construal of them, they contain Carnapian intensions, and so are themselves intensional entities (§§18–19).

But, though all three grades of ontological commitment examined above—Cantorian sets, sums or classes, and 'the objects themselves'—fall short of the level of ontological commitment accruing to propositions, as far as concerns the unity issue the matter is more complicated. For we have seen that Cantorian sets are *propositionally* unified. At the other end of the spectrum, the 'objects themselves' (Russell's 'class as many') have, as such, no sort of unity: it is these, then, that we should mean when we talk of a 'mere aggregate', and raise up for comparison entities enjoying propositional unity, on the one hand, and entities falling short of having propositional unity, on the other. As for sums or classes, in the defined sense, they seem to occupy a grey area between the clear extremes: insofar as they have an integrity of their own,

---

[118] Simons calls these entities 'groups': [2], p. 484; [8], pp. 168–9.
[119] Cf. Husserl's 'foundation relations': [2], iii, §14.

364 THE UNITY OF THE PROPOSITION

they fall like sets on the propositionally unified side of the divide; insofar as they are fictions, they fall on the 'mere aggregate' side of the divide, where we house 'collections' of entities with no sort of unity. Strictly speaking, then, there is no conceptual resting place between sheer disunity on the one hand and full propositional unity on the other. It has turned out that, in seeking pluralities that lack propositional unity, in order to isolate just what constitutes the moment of propositional unity, we have to adduce 'collections' of objects evincing no kind of unity at all: aggregates of objects are either not unified, or they are propositionally unified.

That does not now mean that the original terms of the comparison—between declarative sentences and 'mere lists'—collapses, and that all lists turn out to be sententially unified. For, as we have noted (§76), there is crucial mismatch between order or concatenation of words at the level of symbolic language, and basic relations of configuration on the ground: lists may—perhaps must—be ordered, but there is no implication that the corresponding objects referred to by the items composing the list are (being said to be) configured by any relations at all—such objects may be just 'the objects themselves' (the 'class as many') in the sense of this section, that is, a bunch of objects enjoying absolutely no unifying or organizing principle at all. Hence, insofar as we really do have to do with a 'mere list' in the relevant, contrasting sense, not only does it not follow that the corresponding objects are (being said to be) configured; it follows that they are (being said to be) not configured—they are (being said to be) just 'the objects themselves'. For example, lists of the form '*abc*' and '*bca*' differ as syntactic objects but, insofar as they really are mere lists in the contrasting sense, and not disguised sentences, they refer to the same aggregate.[120]

Of course, ordered lists are indeed *associated* with unified propositions—namely propositions specifying their linguistic constituents and principle of ordering. But that does not make the lists themselves sententially unified or their referents propositionally unified. One indication of this is that the associated proposition does not characterize a list *as opposed to* a sentence: exactly the same proposition specifying the linguistic constituents and principle of ordering of the mere list comprising the words 'Socrates', 'is', and 'wise', in that order, is associated with the sentence 'Socrates is wise'. For, taken as linguistic states of affairs, lists and sentences are (or can be) equiform, as we have observed. And, obviously enough, the relevant associated proposition, detailing the above list's constituents and principle of ordering, is *not* the proposition *that Socrates is wise*: but that is the proposition which, if our list

---

[120] Cf. Bostock [1], p. 35.

were sententially unified, it would express. Notice the crucial difference here between mere aggregates and sets: we have said that the unity of a set *is* the unity of the proposition specifying that set's membership; by contrast, the unity of a list's associated proposition (as I have termed it) does *not* confer unity on the aggregate correlated with that list, but only on the list itself, and the kind of unity it confers on the list does not distinguish that list from a sentence. Hence we may continue to contrast sentences and propositions with 'mere lists' and 'mere aggregates' respectively, in spite of the fact that lists may—or even must—have an ordering component and so may (must) involve an implied sentential unity: the implied sentential unity which a list involves is not the unity of the sentence it would be if it were a sentence, and the implied propositional unity of the aggregate corresponding to the implied unified sentence is not the unity of the proposition which the aggregate referred to by our list would be if it were a proposition. I shall return to this important point at the end of §84.

80 Bradley's Regress and the Infinite

It is important to see that discerning an infinity of instantiation relations (or different applications of a single such relation) as the reference or referent of the logical copula does not pose the problem of unity at a higher level. (Since nothing turns for present purposes on how we interpret formula (4) of §74, I shall henceforth assume that the superscripts therein are indices, and accordingly that Bradley's regress comprises distinct instantiation relations in its various stages.) One might be tempted to raise the question what unifies the infinity of instantiation relations figuring as the reference or referent of the logical copula with the referents of the lexical constituents of the base sentence. Does our unified proposition, analysed as I have proposed it should be analysed, fall apart into a mere aggregate of discrete objects—the referents of the corresponding sentence's constituents, and an infinity of instantiation relations of ever increasing adicity? Do we not need a further relation of instantiation—a transfinite one—to unify those referents and the infinity of instantiation relations we have so far, and does not the problem then continue to repose itself on an ever grander and more daunting scale as we proceed into higher and remoter regions of the transfinite? That is, if our original proposition is the schematic proposition *that a is F*, surely, it is tempting to suppose, we can simply collect up all the instantiation relations, of which there are countably many, adduced by the analysis, and summarize my proposed solution to the unity problem as discerning a transfinite relation of instantiation connecting a and F in the original proposition, thus:

(5) a instantiates$_\omega$ F.

What (5) means is that a instantiates F, a instantiates the instantiation of F, and so on. But if the original proposition disintegrates into a mere aggregate of discrete entities, and if the same fate befalls each finitely indexed stage of the regress, then an identical upshot surely awaits the first transfinite stage of the regress, represented in (5), and all subsequent such stages, as we advance from (5) to

a instantiates$_{\omega+1}$ F,
a instantiates$_{\omega+2}$ F,

and so on up into the dizzying heights of the transfinite ordinals,[121] with—so the Burali-Forti paradox, as it is familiarly known, assures us—no prospect of an end (indeed with the prospect of no end).[122] But if one relation of instantiation cannot unify the proposition, how, one might ask, can an infinity—no matter how large—of such relations fare any better? As Priest puts it: 'If one elephant will not support the world, then neither will an infinite regress of elephants.'[123]

If something like that were right, we should no doubt have to abandon the project of giving a philosophical account of the unity of the proposition; instead we should have to follow Russell, Wittgenstein, and (in effect) Frege in assigning to that unity the status of the ineffable. For in that case there would be, so to speak, no point in embarking on the regress at all: nothing would be achieved at any stage of it which was not already achieved—or not achieved—at the very first stage, where appeal is made to an initial relation of instantiation. If the relation of instantiation which we initially appeal to in trying to account for the unity of the schematic proposition *that a is F* does not succeed in unifying it, no appeal to more complex such relations, ultimately burgeoning into a transfinite stratosphere, is going to do the trick. Recall Russell's remark that 'a proposition . . . is essentially a unity, and when

---

[121] Cf. Cantor [1], pp. 195–7; Potter [2], p. 204.

[122] See Russell [3], §301; Enderton [1], p. 194; G. H. Moore, pp. 104–5; Hallett [1], pp. 165–75; A. Moore [1], p. 15; Potter [2], p. 181.

[123] [1], pp. 193–4. Cf. N. Griffin [4], p. 166; Vallicella [2], p. 210. Priest here adapts a well-known piece of philosophical folklore. Shaftesbury has (ii, p. 115): 'We ought not to laugh so readily at the *Indian* Philosophers, who to satisfy their People how this huge Frame of the World is supported, tell 'em 'tis by an Elephant.—And the Elephant how?—A shrewd Question! but which by no means shou'd be answer'd. 'Tis here only that our *Indian* Philosophers are to blame. They shou'd be contented with *the Elephant*, and go no further. But they have a *Tortoise* in reverse; whose Back, they think, is broad enough. So the Tortoise must bear the new Load: And thus the matter stands worse than before.' Cf. Locke, II. xxiii, §2.

analysis has destroyed the unity, no enumeration of constituents will restore the proposition',[124] and he adds that analysis destroys the unity of a proposition even if that unity is mentioned as an element of the proposition.[125]

But the starting point of this tempting line of thought is mistaken. At each stage of Bradley's regress we have a unity: the initial analysandum—the schematic proposition *that a is F*, as it might be—is a unity, the first stage of analysis—the proposition *that a instantiates F*—is a unity, the next stage is a unity, and so on. The point about the regress, which does indeed burgeon into the upper reaches of the transfinite, is not that each stage of it seeks to restore a unity which has broken down at the previous stage—that would indeed be a hopeless task—but that each stage provides an *analysis* of the unity which was securely present at the previous stage. Each stage *guarantees* the unity of the previous stage, and tells us what that unity *consists in*. Embarking on Bradley's regress, in the present context, does not either destroy the unity of the original proposition or fail to unify an originally fragmented object; rather it analyses a proposition's original unity. It does so by producing, at each stage of the regress, another propositional unity. That further propositional unity *itself* stands in need of analysis, and so on, with the result that the *final* analysis is, in a sense, indefinitely deferred, but at no stage do we arrive at a mere aggregate of constituents from which the original unity has to be pieced together. The analysis does not *mention* the unity of the original proposition as a constituent, as Russell has it, so (in effect) destroying that unity, but preserves it by *producing another* unity, and so on indefinitely.

We might here recall a couple of analogies that I offered earlier in this chapter to the way Bradley's regress arises in the present context: the truth regress (§76), and the composition of the continuum (§78). As for the first of these:[126] the point is that *if* a proposition is true, then it is true that it is true, etc.; the truth regress does not constitute a proposition as true in the sense of turning a proposition which is false or lacks a truth-value into a true proposition, but analyses the truth of a proposition which is (already and anyway, so to speak) true. Just so, Bradley's regress analyses the given unity of a proposition; it does not construct that unity out of an assemblage of otherwise incoherent bits. Again, the division of the continuum is constitutive of the whole in the sense that the division analyses the composition of the whole, not in the sense that the whole is conceived to have been literally and antecedently constructed out of an assemblage of discrete points.[127]

---

[124] [3], §54; cf. [7], p. 373.   [125] [3], §55. Cf. §§81, 138.
[126] Cf. Armstrong [5], pp. 118–19; the aptness of the analogy is contested by Dodd [2], pp. 150–1.
[127] Cf. Leibniz [6], pp. 184–7.

Perhaps one elephant can indeed support the world, but only if it is in turn supported by a second elephant, and that one supported by a third elephant, and so on. If you object that that is as much as to say that a single elephant *cannot* support the world, I reply that the original thought ('If one elephant will not support the world, then neither will an infinite regress of elephants') contains a fallacy. It does not follow, if one elephant cannot support the world (on its own)—or indeed if any finite number of elephants cannot support it—that an infinitude of elephants cannot do so either. For suppose the world is too heavy for one elephant to support, too heavy for two elephants to support, . . .; if the world is infinitely heavy, an 'infinite regress' of elephants may be just what is needed to support it. For the point is that it could be a condition on one elephant's supporting the world that it be supported by a second elephant, and a condition on the second elephant's supporting the first elephant that it in turn be supported by a third elephant, and so on. Just so in the case which interests us here: it is a condition on one instantiation relation's unifying a proposition that a second instantiation relation unify the first instantiation relation with its relata, and so on. It's elephants all the way down.[128]

Reverting to the terms in which, at the beginning of this section, I raised the difficulty to which I have been responding, we can say that discerning an infinity of instantiation relations as the reference or referent of the logical copula does not pose a higher-level problem of unity, because the regress generated at the level of reference by the semantics of the logical copula comprises unified propositions at each of its stages. Viewing the structure vertically, with the unified proposition *that a is F*, as it might be, at the base of the hierarchy, and the regress unfolding above it, we might regard the reference or referent of the corresponding sentence's logical copula as a procedure running systematically through the consecutive stages of the regress, at each stage picking up the new instantiation relations housed at that stage. Lest that picture look as though it would throw up a higher-level (transfinite) problem of unity, we insist that *each stage* of the regress comprises not a bunch of unconnected elements, but a unified proposition. The fact that the components of the infinitistic reference or referent of the logical copula are, taken collectively, not propositionally unified no more constitutes a difficulty than does the fact that the stages of the regress itself are, taken collectively, not propositionally unified.

We need to be clear about what my solution to the problem of unity does, and what it does not, purport to do. The regress, I claim, analyses the

---

[128] For the allusion, see Partee *et al.*, p. 72. For discussion, see Nolan, who argues that 'the ontological extravagance of infinite regresses can be in itself a cost' (p. 536). Against this, I hold the ideal of ontological parsimony to be a false god: cf. Lewis [4], p. 87.

unity of the original proposition, in the sense that each stage of the regress yields necessary and sufficient conditions for unity at each preceding and succeeding stage. The regress works by generating relations of instantiation of ever-increasing adicity; it does not give us—and does not purport to give us—a *reductive* analysis of the basic relation of instantiation. But it does not follow that the regress tells us nothing interesting about instantiation: on the contrary, the specification of necessary and sufficient conditions for the relation of instantiation to (be said to) obtain, generating as it does the instantiation regress, tells us something substantial about the nature of that relation. It does throw light on the nature of instantiation to be told that a instantiates F just if it instantiates instantiation with respect to F, and so on.[129] That is, it casts *theoretical* light on the nature of the instantiation relation to be told this. The regress does *not* give us the wherewithal to specify the meaning of the sentence whose unity generates it in terms that could be apprehended by someone who did not yet understand that sentence, or who had no grasp of the relation of instantiation: but I take it to be an uncontroversial datum of philosophical method that an analysis can be illuminating without being reductive.

It has emerged from the foregoing that there is a sense in which you cannot go about constructing a sentence from bits; you can only find that you have constructed one. Of course in any ordinary sense of the phrase you can construct a sentence: what my paradoxical-sounding expression is meant to highlight is the point that there is no *procedure* which, if followed, allows you to start with some bits and end up, uniquely, with a sentence; that is to say, there is no method of constructing a sentence *as opposed to* a mere list. Whether what you end up with when you have, so to speak, followed the instructions in your assembly kit is a sentence or mere list depends on its *ex post facto* analysis, not on what you do with any components, internal or external, to arrive at the finished product (so long, that is, as they are put together in the right way, if there is a right way). If the finished product is analysable as generating Bradley's regress at the level of reference, in the manner I have indicated, then it refers to a proposition and so is itself a declarative sentence; if not, then it is a mere list and its referent a mere aggregate. Taken in itself, the item of language might be either sentence or list. If, as one critic has suggested, 'Bradley's point was that the unity of a judgement cannot be thought of as arising from the union of things that can be itemized',[130] because their relational and structural

---

[129] Compare the truth-table definition of logical constants like 'and': 'P and Q' is true just if 'P' is true *and* 'Q' is true. The definition uses the word 'and', but is for all that of explanatory value: cf. Tugendhat [2], pp. 301–3.

[130] Palmer, p. 5. Cf. the passage of Carruthers cited in §5.

components must be itemized too, so generating Bradley's regress, then my point has been that the unity of a proposition can (and must) be thought of as arising from the union of things that can be itemized *because*, or rather *insofar as*, the itemizing generates Bradley's regress.

81 Vallicella's Onto-theology

This puts me in opposition to Vallicella, who writes:

> Bradley's problem concerns the very constitution of a state of affairs in the first place, not what happens once there is a state of affairs. *Given* a state of affairs, the ensuing regress is of course benign. Bradley's regress, however, is *internal* to would-be states of affairs. There must be something that binds together the constituents of a would-be state of affairs; but if this is a further constituent, a vicious infinite regress breaks out that prevents the formation of a state of affairs.[131]

What is 'Bradley's problem'? That question is answered for us by the following passage:

> The problem is that the mere existence of a and—F does not entail the existence of a's being F. What then accounts for the difference between the sum $a+$—F and the corresponding fact? It is no answer to say that in the former case a does not saturate—F while in the latter case it does. For that merely redescribes the problem. The problem is to specify ontologically what the saturation consists in.[132]

Vallicella's example is of a monadic predication, but clearly the problem concerns predication in general whether monadic or polyadic.[133] Vallicella rightly notes that the problem is not solved by adopting an Aristotelian realism about universals—the view that only instantiated universals exist—for the mere fact that a universal (the relation R^2, say) is instantiated does not guarantee its being unified with any given entities, a and b, say, and does not tell us, in any case, *what it is* for R^2 to be instantiated by a and b.[134] But he wrongly restricts the problem of unity to the unification of objects and *contingent universals*, suggesting that no corresponding problem arises for *necessary* universal properties or *individualized* properties (tropes).[135] This is connected with the fact that (in the quoted passages and elsewhere) Vallicella states the problem in terms of the question what constitutes the unity of *facts* or *states of affairs*, and with his acceptance of the view that certain kinds of truth—precisely

---

[131] [2], p. 208. Cf. p. 238.   [132] [3], p. 33. Cf. [1], pp. 242–3; [2], p. 205.
[133] Cf. [2], pp. 201–3, 206–7.   [134] [3], pp. 13–15, [4], pp. 160, 164.
[135] [1], pp. 241, 243, 245, 257 n. 7, 258 n. 45; [2], pp. 206, 225–6.

the instantiation by objects of contingent universal properties—stand in need
of a general metaphysical explanation. But by my lights, since facts are just
true propositions, Vallicella's way of stating the problem in terms of facts is
relatively superficial: the real question is what unifies propositions whether
they are true or false. And I have rejected (§24) the idea that the truth of
true propositions, whatever their modality, requires a general metaphysical
underpinning. Even if we restrict our attention to the case of true propositions,
it seems to me that Vallicella is wrong to suppose that the problem of unifying
properties with objects only arises for contingent universals: the fact that, say,
the number three necessarily instantiates oddness does not absolve us from
asking *how* this instantiation is possible and what it involves; similarly, the
fact that tropes are individuated by the objects instantiating them does not
absolve us from asking how that instantiation is possible—how it is possible
for properties and objects so to combine that properties can be thereby
individualized. Tropes are, after all, secondary phenomena whose existence
depends on a conceptually prior instantiation by objects of universals, and
it is that prior instantiation which—assuming Vallicella's restriction of the
question—is problematic.

Vallicella's view is that a state of affairs is unified by an external unifier, not
by an internal constituent.[136] Now I have already (in effect) rejected the idea
of an external unifier for states of affairs (facts)—for an external unifier for a
state of affairs would be a truth-maker—and I see no reason to revive a solution
of that form for propositions taken generally, whether true or false. To add an
external unifier would, like adding unity as a purported internal constituent
of the complex, simply be to add another component to the components
we already have: the objection to that move is not that it is regressive but
that it is an ingredient solution, and accordingly does not supply us with a
principle of distinction between a unified proposition and a mere aggregate.
For any assemblage of bits—whether supplemented by 'external' components
or no—can be duplicated by a mere aggregate. Vallicella concedes that 'the
fundamental problem is to secure unity, not to avoid a regress',[137] but he
certainly regards Bradley's regress, if it arises in a purported attempt to secure
unity, as vicious. My position is that one secures unity *by* producing and *insofar
as* one produces a structure that generates Bradley's regress. As the opening
quotation in this section shows, Vallicella seems to suppose that if Bradley's
regress arises as a matter of the constitution of a unity it must be a practical,
and so a vicious, regress. But that is surely mistaken: we have seen how the
generation of Bradley's regress can be a necessary and sufficient condition for

---

[136] [1], p. 247; [2], pp. 199, 239; [4], p. 180.   [137] [2], p. 207.

propositional unity, and so can be involved in the very constitution of that unity, without being a vicious practical regress.

Elsewhere, indeed, Vallicella rightly remarks that it is unintelligible to suppose that two distinct complexes—as it might be, a unified proposition and its duplicating aggregate—could just differ as a matter of brute fact:

[T]here is a need for a ground of their difference. There must be a ground of unity, because, without a ground, there is no explanation of the difference between the sum, $a + F$-ness, and the fact, a's being F. This is a genuine difference given that both a and F-ness can exist apart from the fact in question.[138]

The point is well made, and it holds even though, when we widen our purview to encompass propositions in general, an important metaphysical symmetry sets in which failed to obtain when we focused exclusively on facts (true propositions): for facts in general are not, but propositions are, ontologically coeval with their components. That is, while the existence of (say) a and of F-ness does *not* in general entail the existence of the *fact that a is F*, the sheer existence of these two entities *does* suffice for the existence of the *proposition that a is F*. So a guiding principle of Vallicella's discussion,[139] namely that the existence of a fact is asymmetrically dependent on the existence of its constituents, does not hold when we consider propositions in general, rather than just the true ones. For us (recall my remarks in §79 on the scholastic criterion for real independence), the distinction between the component bits of a proposition and the proposition itself is a purely theoretical or conceptual one—in practice, so to speak, you cannot have the bits without the proposition or the proposition without the bits—but real for all that. So Vallicella is right to imply that there is a need for something to *ground* the difference between (in my terms) a proposition and the mere aggregate of its bits.

But that ground can lie in the *semantics* of the linguistic correlate of the complex in question; it need not—indeed cannot—lie in any (internal or external) *ingredient*. Vallicella considers the difficulty that any external unifier needs *itself* to be unified with the bits it is supposed to unify, and his response is that the external unifier may manage not only to unify the other bits, but to unify itself with those bits. Such an external unifier would be unique among relations in having the power, not only to unify its relata, but also to unify itself with its relata.[140] Clearly only a very special entity would be capable of fulfilling this task, and indeed Vallicella tells us that nothing empirical is good enough: only a 'metaphysical agent or perhaps some sort of ontological

---

[138] [1], p. 248; [2], p. 229; cf. [4], p. 165.   [139] [2], p. 233.   [140] [1], pp. 254–6; [2], p. 252.

operator'[141] has the necessary wherewithal to unify the complex; at this point God is called upon to perform the feat that no empirical agent is capable of achieving. In effect Vallicella offers us a theological version of Russell's multiple relation theory of judgement: the proposition (or state of affairs) is in itself just a collection of pieces, which nothing short of a transcendent mind can knit together in the right way.[142] But this is just mystery-mongering. I shall reject in due course the pragmatist suggestion that *human* mental activity might provide the key to the unity of the proposition (see below, §85); and if that is right, or even if it is not, it is in any case impossible to see how ascent to the *theological* level might fill the gap. Vallicella suggests that 'the theist already has an entity in his ontology that can play the role of external unifier';[143] but in truth the appeal to a supernatural agency in this context (as in others) merely creates a host of extra problems, while leaving the original difficulty in place.[144] Vallicella rejects the idea that a state of affairs (or, in my terms, a proposition) might simply unify itself: that is in effect the 'no ground' position which, as we saw above, he rightly dismisses.[145] How, then, can anything else not only unify the constituents of a proposition or state of affairs, but also unify *itself* with those constituents? How is the bootstrapping to be done?

Vallicella's resort to legerdemain is puzzling in view of his clear-sighted criticism of D. W. Mertz's account of unity, which proceeds in terms of the alleged unifying power of relations. According to Mertz, a relation instance R that is truly predicable of its relata $<a, b, \ldots>$ *causes* the fact that $R(<a, b, \ldots>)$, and this fact has R and $a, b, \ldots$ as its *constituents*; the relation instance R is said to be *nothing other* than the proposition—in Mertz's story, fact—that $R(<a, b, \ldots>)$, for we are told that 'R' abbreviates '$R(<a, b, \ldots>)$', and further that 'predicate instances do not exist independently of their relata'.[146] So we are invited to suppose that R is both cause and proper constituent of itself, which is absurd.[147] Vallicella argues that the basic mistake Mertz makes is to overlook the point that relational constituents of facts, and of propositions in general (whether true or false), are, in the first instance, universals: they therefore need to be unified with their relata in the proposition and cannot perform this feat on their own, given that they are essentially independent of

---

[141] [1], p. 250; cf. [2], pp. 249–56, 267–9.

[142] Cf. [2], p. 243. Recall (§77) Süssmilch's argument that the sophistication and perfection of language require a divine origin: see esp. his §3. It is strange to see these pre-Enlightenment arguments once more emerging from their dark cupboards.

[143] [1], p. 252.

[144] Cf. Potter's remarks on the ineptness of appealing to an infinite being in our efforts to understand infinity: [2], pp. 38–9.

[145] Cf. [2], pp. 227–38.   [146] Mertz, pp. 131, 136.

[147] Cf. Vallicella [2], pp. 211–13; [4], pp. 173–4.

any given proposition:[148] a relation does indeed relate its relata but it cannot relate *itself* to those relata.[149] There must, then, be something grounding the unity of a proposition (and, if appropriate, fact), and that ground cannot be the proposition (fact) itself, since a proposition's (fact's) unity cannot be *causa sui* (any more than anything else can be, I would add).[150] These criticisms of Vallicella's are all very much to the point, though I should prefer to say (recall the elephants of §80), not that a relation *cannot* relate itself to its relata, but that it is a *condition* of its so doing that it is related to its relata by a further relation, and so on into the regress. For it would be absurd to say that relations can connect entities without having themselves to be connected to the entities they connect.[151] How could relations connect their relata if they were not them- selves connected to their relata? Then they would be disconnected from their relata, in which case the relata would not, after all, be related to one another by that relation: what we took to be a relational structure would dissolve into an atomistic armed neutrality. But if relations are connected to their relata, then we have Bradley's regress. Vallicella claims that 'a ground must be something whose existence is independent of the existence of what it grounds'.[152] But if this is meant to invoke the scholastic criterion of independent existence, we must demur: for Bradley's regress is not thus independent of the existence of the proposition that generates it, but even so grounds that proposition's unity by giving necessary and sufficient conditions for it.

82 A Comparison with Other Innocent Regresses

There is a general point to be made in connection with the constitutive status of Bradley's regress. The student of metaphysics encounters numerous regresses, and of these many are not only innocent but also explanatory of the phenomena to which they are keyed. In this section we will look at some examples. I start with a well-known regress in the philosophy of time.[153] McTaggart argued that the concept of time involves that of change, which in turn requires the concept of A-series time (the series of past, present, and future positions in the time series), but that the concept of the A-series is incoherent, and hence also that the concept of time in general is incoherent, rendering time itself (so McTaggart concluded) unreal. The incoherence allegedly arises

[148] Cf. Vallicella [2], pp. 201–2, 216–17; Clark, p. 263.
[149] [1], pp. 254–6; [4], p. 165. A fortiori, relations are independent of facts in which they figure as the 'relation actually relating'. Contra Read: see esp. pp. 319, 331.
[150] [2], p. 235.   [151] Contra Grossmann [1], p. 209.
[152] [2], p. 235.   [153] McTaggart, §§303–33.

because the A-series generates incompatible properties, since any given event will attract all three temporal attributes, being variously past, present, and future. The attempt to relativize these ascriptions, as I just implicitly did (in the qualification 'variously')—by saying of a given event (occurring now, say) that it is present in the present, past in the future, future in the past—simply generates a fresh set of complex temporal properties (nine, in fact) of which some are mutually incompatible (for instance: past in the present, present in the present, future in the present). If we seek to obviate these incompatibilities by relativizing again, we will merely generate still more complex temporal properties (twenty-seven this time), again in part mutually incompatible. Clearly we are launched on a regress, and it has generally been held that the regress is vicious, in the sense that, if at the initial stage the ascription of A-series attributes is incoherent, ascent into the regress will do nothing to remove the incoherence, which will simply be replicated at each stage of the regress.[154] But it is a mistake to suppose that the initial position involves the ascription of incompatible attributes to a given event: in the only sense in which an event can sensibly be said to *be* past, present, and future—namely, in an *atemporal* (timeless) sense of 'be'[155]—the attributes are *not* incompatible (still less are they contradictory, as McTaggart says),[156] for it is atemporally *true* that a given event is present, past, and future: it is present at one time, past at another time, and future at yet another time. Once this point is firmly in place we are free to regard the A-series regress as an innocent, constitutive regress, analysing what it is for an event to have A-series attributes.[157]

Lewis Carroll famously pointed out that a regress arises when we try to formalize the rule of *modus ponens* as an axiom. The threat of the Lewis Carroll regress is particularly real for the Russell of *Principles*, because he here (and in *Principia*)[158] treats rules of inference as theoretic, as opposed to metatheoretic, statements: this is part and parcel of the doctrine (which he shares with Frege) of the universality of logic, according to which there is no distinction between theory and metatheory.[159] But shifting rules of inference from theory to metatheory, as is standard practice today, does not get rid of the regress:[160] it merely displaces it.[161] However, the *modus ponens* regress is, I claim, not

---

[154] See e.g. Dummett [1], pp. 351–2; Dainton, pp. 15–17.
[155] This is the 'true verb' of the Port-Royal (§26), which has no tense but is, as McTaggart puts it (§331), 'simply for predication'.
[156] McTaggart, §332.   [157] On this topic see further Q. Smith, esp. pp. 388–90, 394–5.
[158] See e.g. Whitehead and Russell, i, p. 106.
[159] On the significance of the regress for Frege and Wittgenstein, see Ricketts [1], pp. 11–12.
[160] As is perhaps implied by Ricketts [2], p. 83, and Grattan-Guinness, p. 319.
[161] See Hylton [2], pp. 84–6; Goldfarb [1], §II; Potter [1], pp. 144–5.

vicious, but constitutive of that rule of inference.[162] In moves parallel to what I have said about Bradley's regress, I say that it is the underlying presence of this regress which entitles us to think of ourselves as deploying a rule of *modus ponens* at all. So there is no question here of my pleading for a revised formalization of logic or mathematics; what is rather at issue is a philosophical point about how we should understand the formalizations we already have.

The rule of *modus ponens* pervades logic and mathematics, so that the regress constituting the acceptability of that rule is of correspondingly broad significance. The same may be said of the definite-description regress that was briefly mentioned at the end of §15. Russell observed, as we there noted, that ordinary mathematical functional expressions are of definite-description form. Now Russell's own 1905 analysis of statements containing definite descriptions does not precipitate a regress, because the descriptions are 'analysed out' in favour of existential quantifiers. But, as I remarked in the earlier discussion, if we follow Evans in rejecting Russell's cavalier approach to the analysis of descriptive statements, and instead treat the description operator as primitive, our analysis of statements involving definite descriptions will perforce be regressive, given that the truth-conditions of such statements must be specified in terms of the satisfiers of relevant descriptions, not their referents. So, for example, the truth-conditions of the statement 'sin $\pi = 0$' are specified by saying that it is true just if the object satisfying the description 'sin π' equals zero. That statement is in turn true just if the object satisfying the description 'the object satisfying the description "sin π"' equals zero. And so on. The regress is perfectly innocent; and again I hope it is obvious that I am not putting in a plea for a revision of our mathematical notation.

I mentioned another innocent metaphysical regress—again fundamental to logic and mathematics—in the context of discussing the role played by inference in securing the essential compositionality of the sentence (§6). Consider the inference:

Hesperus is F
Hesperus is G

_____

Hence, Hesperus is both F and G.

We say that arguments of this shape are formally valid, but of course their formal validity depends on the assumption that the name 'Hesperus' in the first premiss is the same name as the name 'Hesperus' in the second premiss. However, the sheer fact that orthographically identical signs are used in the

---

[162] Here I am in disagreement with Priest: [1], p. 45; [2], pp. 259–60.

two premisses does not *of itself* guarantee that identity: if the 'Hesperus' of the first premiss were, as usual in discussions of sense and reference, a name of the planet Venus, and the 'Hesperus' of the second premiss a name of my cat, the argument would no longer be formally valid. We might now try to secure formal validity by writing in an extra premiss, so as to guarantee the identity of the Hesperus mentioned in the first premiss with the Hesperus mentioned in the second. If $Hesperus_n$ is the Hesperus referred to by the use of 'Hesperus' in the nth premiss, then we might put:

Hesperus is F
Hesperus is G
$Hesperus_1 = Hesperus_2$

_____

Hence, $Hesperus_1$ (or $Hesperus_2$) is both F and G.

Does the move achieve its objective? Yes, but only on condition that we add—or rather discern the tacit presence of—two further premisses aimed at securing the identities of the objects mentioned in the first two premisses with the relevant objects mentioned in the third, thus:

$Hesperus_1 = Hesperus_{3/1}$
$Hesperus_2 = Hesperus_{3/2}$

where '$Hesperus_{m/n}$' takes us to the nth occurrence of the name 'Hesperus' in the mth premiss. And so on, into a regress.

    John Campbell, from whom I have drawn the above example,[163] takes these points to show that the original argument is valid as it stands without being enthymematic: it simply *trades on* the identity of the Hesperus mentioned in the first premiss with the Hesperus mentioned in the second premiss; that identity does not figure in the form of an extra, suppressed premiss. But if the argument trades on that identity, does that not mean that the identity is indeed present in the background of the deduction? Surely it is clearer-headed to admit that the formal validity of the argument *does* depend on a suppressed premiss, explicit mention of which takes us into a regress of further suppressed premisses, but to insist that the regress is of a harmless, constitutive sort, not a vicious practical one. For, to adapt what I said (§78) about the case of the proposition, we do not have to *write down* (or even consciously think of) any—let alone all (an infinite totality)—of the suppressed premisses before we can assure ourselves of the formal validity of our argument; nevertheless, its validity indeed depends on the presence, in the unspoken and unwritten background, of an infinity of

[163] J. Campbell, pp. 74–5.

satisfied conditions on the identities of objects mentioned in the (explicit and suppressed) premisses. If that background were not fully in place, the argument would be invalid. For example, suppose that we (rather rashly) undertook to render explicit all the suppressed premisses composing the regress, and suppose that (to our relief) at a certain point we produced a premiss that was false: so long as the premiss had been generated correctly, that would show that the original argument was invalid, for a condition on its validity would have been shown to fail.

Finally in this connection, we might usefully compare a regress which Russell mentions in *Principles* as arising when we try to analyse the relation 'is greater than' in purely monadic terms. Russell draws our attention to the fact that if we try to dissolve the relation into monadic properties—magnitudes—we find that we

> have to admit a relation between the magnitudes, which will be as asymmetrical as the relation which the magnitudes were to explain. Hence the magnitudes will need new adjectives, and so on ad infinitum; and the infinite process will have to be completed before any *meaning* can be assigned to our original proposition. This kind of infinite process is undoubtedly objectionable, since its sole object is to explain the meaning of a certain proposition, and yet none of its steps bring it any nearer to that meaning.[164]

Here we see clearly how Russell's approach to Bradley's regress and its congeners differs from mine. These regresses do indeed arise in the analysis of meaning: Russell is right about that. But I claim that they are not therefore vicious. In the case mentioned by Russell in the quoted passage, the regress that arises is specific to the phenomenon to which it is keyed—the dyadic relation consisting in something's being greater than something else—and to that extent the regress tells us an interesting fact about just what that dyadic relation involves. It would be fallacious to reason, as Russell implicitly does in this passage, that because no single step in the regress, taken in abstraction from its status as such, succeeds in analysing the meaning of the original, the regress as a whole does not do so either. For wholes may—indeed necessarily do—have properties lacked by their parts taken individually.[165]

Though Russell accepts, like Meinong, that a regress which arises in the analysis of infinite wholes is or at any rate can be innocent,[166] his restriction of the concession so as to exclude regresses which arise in the analysis of meaning necessarily rules out the kind of case we are interested in: for in our case the instantiation regress arises precisely in the analysis of the meaning of a unified proposition, taken just as such. Somewhat similar to Russell's position

---

[164] [3], §214; cf. Davidson [2], pp. 82–4, on a similar regress in Plato's *Sophist*.
[165] Cf. Bolzano [1], §38.   [166] [3], §143.

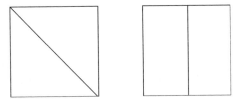

Figure 6.1

is Olson's: Olson suggests that 'explication' regresses are vicious, whereas regresses that are simply 'in the world' are not.[167] My position is that Bradley's regress is *both* in the world *and* explanatory of the unity of the proposition. In a further passage, Russell provides an illustration of the restriction:

> Take for example the following [definition]: 'Two people are said to have the *same* idea when they have ideas which are similar; and ideas are similar when they contain an identical part'. If an idea may have a part which is not an idea, such a definition is not logically objectionable; but if part of an idea is an idea, then, in the second place where identity of ideas occurs, the definition must be substituted; and so on. Thus whenever the *meaning* of a proposition is in question, an infinite regress is objectionable, since we never reach a proposition which has a definite meaning.[168]

Russell here seems to commit the fallacy I have already censured. Even if parts of ideas are themselves ideas, it does not follow that the identity of whole ideas entails a corresponding identity of parts, as we may illustrate by means of a simple analogy borrowed from Leibniz.[169] The squares in Figure 6.1 are geometrical shapes and are made up of parts that are themselves geometrical shapes, but though the wholes are identical the parts are not. It follows that it would by no means be trivial to affirm that identical whole ideas were composed of identical parts, and the regress that arose thereby would analyse what that identity consisted in.

83 Truth, Falsity, and Unity Revisited

At this point it would be well to check that my account of unity is not in breach of the important constraint which I insisted on in Chapter 1, and which, as we saw in that chapter, caused Russell problems, namely that our treatment must provide for the unity of false as well as true propositions, or equivalently that it must not be an implication of our treatment that only

---

[167] Olson, pp. 45–64.   [168] [3], §329.   [169] See [4], pp. 50–3; [6], p. lxix.

true propositions are unified.[170] The check is readily carried out. Recall first that propositions inhabit the level of reference, which is the level of what is *understood* when a declarative sentence is understood. They are also the content of what, as I shall put it, is *advanced* when a declarative sentence is advanced: a declarative sentence is advanced when it is uttered or inscribed or entertained as such, that is, with the intention of uttering, inscribing or entertaining the content of that very sentence.[171] But now the content of what is understood, or advanced, when the proposition *that p* is understood or advanced is equivalent to the content *that it is true that p*.[172] Here it is crucial to be clear that, where a declarative sentence is advanced, the claim that what is advanced is the truth of the relevant proposition holds quite independently of the speaker's pragmatic purpose in advancing the sentence: in particular, one must avoid the error of taking 'advance' to mean 'assert'. A speaker may, for example, advance a sentence hypothetically (by putting it forward as the antecedent of a conditional), or even by asserting the very opposite of the sentence (by embedding it within a negation and asserting the result).[173] Although it is not, in general, the case that a speaker asserts an advanced sentence or its corresponding proposition, nevertheless the proposition which is the content of the sentence so advanced remains equivalent to another proposition stating its truth.

In spite of the obviousness of this point when it is spelt out, writers in this area never cease to embroil themselves in hopeless muddles over the pragmatic–semantic distinction. Tugendhat, for instance, having noted the equivalence of '*p*' and 'it is true that *p*', adds that 'it seems to follow from that that the predicate "is true" expresses the assertoric moment'.[174] He is overlooking the point, of which he elsewhere shows awareness,[175] that 'it is true that *p*' can, like the bare '*p*', be employed on its own or embedded in hypothetical and other contexts in such a way that the stand-alone or embedded sentence cannot be conceived to carry any assertoric force, regardless of the pragmatic purpose of the context, if any, in which it is embedded.[176] He makes the same mistake about the bare '*p*', suggesting that 'anyone who says "*p*" does not merely designate a state of affairs, but also simultaneously asserts that it is true or "obtains" '.[177] Tugendhat is forgetting

---

[170] Cf. B. Linsky [2], p. 54 n. 12; MacBride [4], pp. 604–5; Olson, pp. 46–7.
[171] Cf. Strawson [2], p. 101.
[172] Cf. Geulincx [1], II. i, §1 and 3, pp. 233–4, 237–8 (see Nuchelmans [5], p. 110; cf. [3], pp. 45–6); Frege [10], I, §5 (see Carl [2], p. 155); Tugendhat [2], p. 241.
[173] Cf. de Soto, fo. 26ʳᵇ; Nuchelmans [5], pp. 52–3; Ryle, ii, pp. 28–9.
[174] [2], pp. 64–5.   [175] Ibid., p. 67.   [176] See here Frege [26], p. 271.
[177] [2], p. 157. Cf. [2], pp. 268, 281–2, 316, 509. So too Searle [1], p. 23.

that, given the question 'What is the commonest declarative sentence used by English-speaking philosophers to illustrate a contingent fact?', for example, one may reply with 'The cat sat on the mat' without *asserting* that the cat sat on the mat.[178] Hence neither the bare statement that p, nor the prefixing of 'it is true that . . .' to a sentence, has, as such, anything whatever to do with the pragmatic act of assertion (or with any other pragmatic act). Indeed the same goes for 'I assert that . . .', or any other form of words: for *any* form of words, legitimately prefixed to a sentence, can produce a whole that is advanced by a speaker (either on its own, or embedded in a larger linguistic context) in such a way that the whole is devoid of assertoric force. (Suppose I reply to the above question: 'I assert that the cat sat on the mat'. In so replying, I make no assertion.) A statement of the form 'p' or 'it is true that p' (or 'I assert that p', etc.) *may* be advanced on its own (or in context) in such a way as to effect an assertion: but that requires a suitable stage-setting going beyond the mere fact of its advancement.[179] It is accordingly a mistake for semantics to entertain imperialist ambitions in respect of pragmatics. (Equally, as I shall argue in §85, it would be a mistake for pragmatics to arrogate to itself the task of answering the distinctively semantic question what unifies the proposition.)

The question we are addressing in this section is whether our account of unity respects the constraint that requires the account to apply to false as well as to true propositions. With irrelevant pragmatic issues out of the way, we can see that the answer to our question is affirmative. False propositions exist at the level of reference as much as do true ones: false as well as true propositions form the content of what is understood or advanced when their corresponding declarative sentences are understood or advanced. Hence, as we in effect saw in §10, the equivalence between the proposition that is the referent of a declarative sentence and another proposition stating the truth of the first proposition holds as much for false declarative sentences and their propositional referents as for true ones. This point applies to what is *understood or advanced*: whether the sentence in question and its corresponding proposition are *in fact* true or false is a further question, not in general settled by the sheer acts of understanding or advancing the sentence. One might encapsulate the point I am making by saying that an account of the unity of the proposition applies, in view of what propositions are, to the level of reference, which is the

---

[178] Cf. Dummett [10], p. 4.

[179] Cf. Frege [17], p. 63 ([21], p. 347). Hanks argues ([1], pp. 153–6) that declarative sentences come packaged with a default assertoric force, which may be cancelled by extraneous factors. But the ascription of pragmatic force (by contrast with semantic mood: recall §2) to type sentences makes no sense: sentences do not assert themselves. Rather, tokens of sentences are invested with pragmatic force by speakers (in general: advancers) on occasions of use.

level of *what is understood or advanced to be the case*, and that that notion is quite distinct from the notion of *what actually is the case*.[180] It follows that, contrary to what some writers suggest,[181] we do not have to locate propositions exclusively at the level of sense if our account of propositional unity is to accommodate unified false propositions.

84 Bradley's Regress, Realism, and States of Affairs

It follows also that we should distinguish clearly between the instantiation regress as it arises in the present context, where what is in question is the unity of the proposition (whether true or false), and the same regress as it arises in the context of the debate between realists and nominalists, where what is in question is whether the correct analysis of true propositions and states of affairs—as it might be, the (schematic) true proposition or state of affairs *that a is F*—requires us to recognize the existence of an instantiation relation connecting entities at least one of which is a universal. Bradley's regress arises naturally in this latter context, because if we adopt the realist line of accepting the existence of universals, connected by relations of instantiation to other objects (individuals and universals), those instantiation relations will presumably themselves count as bona-fide universals standing in need of further relations of instantiation to connect them to the original relata, and so on.

Some philosophers think that realism about universals can only be viable if it is restricted so as to exclude the relation of instantiation or exemplification from our inventory of universals, and their grounds for adopting this restriction include the desire to avoid Bradley's regress.[182] A further motive is the desire to avoid Russell's paradox,[183] a version of which arises if we allow not only a universal of instantiation but also, naturally enough, one of self-instantiation, and hence one of non-self-instantiation (an entity which will then turn out both to instantiate and not to instantiate itself).[184] A realist simply concerned to avoid Russell's paradox might try the minimal strategy of banning a universal of non-self-instantiation.[185] Slightly less minimally, one might consider banning a universal of instantiation.[186] More radically, Geach is even prepared to

---

[180] This deals with a problem raised by Currie at [1], pp. 153–4.
[181] See e.g. Weiss, pp. 264–5; Read, pp. 325–6; Candlish [2], pp. 75–6, 88–9.
[182] See e.g. Strawson [1], pp. 167–76; Seargent, pp. 113–14.
[183] Strawson [1], p. 229; Künne [1], p. 100 n. 11; Lewis [8], p. 10.
[184] See e.g. Grossmann [2], p. 20; Loux, pp. 35–41; cf. Gödel *apud* Wang [3], p. 279.
[185] See e.g. MacBride [6], pp. 471–2; King [5], p. 56.
[186] See e.g. Menzel, pp. 74–8 with n. 29.

repudiate properties as referents of expressions like 'redness' or 'the property of being red', on the basis that

properties so regarded would involve all the difficulties that arise over classes; for instance, the property of being a property that does not belong to itself would involve a difficulty parallel to that about Russell's class of all classes that are not members of themselves.[187]

Geach's response to Russell's paradox is plainly an overreaction; but so are the less radical responses mentioned above. I have already rejected the line of thinking that would have us trying to prevent Russell's paradox from arising in our theoretical descriptions of ordinary discourse (§63), and I see no good reason to ban from our ontology 'structural' universals like instantiation, let alone 'substantial' ones like redness. But, having admitted a universal of instantiation to our ontology, we cannot reasonably exclude universals of self- and non-self-instantiation. These latter universals are formed from the base universal of instantiation by means of entirely unexceptionable operations *in re*. The fact that the universal of non-self-instantiation generates Russell's paradox is quite without significance in the present context, and certainly constitutes no compelling reason to detrude it from our ontology. As we noted in §23, ontology follows semantics, not vice versa: given that we talk meaningfully about these universals—it is not necessary to add 'in true sentences': meaningfulness is enough—they must exist at the level of reference, and so must exist in the world. There is no further question concerning their *existence*, though whether they are *instantiated* is another matter: the class of universals *in re* includes ones that are contingently, and ones that are necessarily, not instantiated by anything.[188]

So much for Russell's paradox. As far as Bradley's regress is concerned, it will come as no surprise to the reader to learn that I do not regard this regress, as it arises in the context of a realistic approach to the metaphysics of universals, as being any more vicious than it is when it arises in the context of my account of the unity of the proposition. The suggested restriction on realism has in any case a suspiciously ad hoc feel about it, aggravated in some accounts of the matter by the cosmetic shift of speaking of instantiation as a *nexus* or *tie*[189]— as opposed to a *relation*—as though this merely terminological move could somehow bring it about that the entity in question escaped the commitments

[187] [7], p. 223; cf. Cartwright [3], p. 918.
[188] Cf. Baylis on the harmlessness of such universals as round-squareness: pp. 56–7; Gödel *apud* Wang [3], pp. 272–3 ('The argument that concepts are unreal because of the logical-intensional paradoxes is like the argument that the outer world does not exist because there are sense deceptions').
[189] Strawson [1], pp. 167–73; Bergmann [2], pp. 94, 198.

accruing to a genuine relation. Lewis allows that 'it is all too obvious that "ties" are relations in all but name', but his response to this concession is not to admit that instantiation ('having') is a relation, but to suggest that it is neither a relation nor a tie:

it is one thing to have a property; it is something else to bear some relation to it. If a relation stands between you and your properties, you are alienated from them. . . . Having *simpliciter* is not a relation, whatever grammar may suggest. What is it then? I don't know what more can be said. . . . I conclude that reifying non-relational ties and giving an account of them is a thoroughly misguided thing to do.[190]

As I have noted (§78), Lewis's reason for rejecting the relational status of instantiation is the consequent generation of Bradley's regress; conversely, as soon as we have decided that the regress is innocent, the denial of relationality to instantiation is shown up for the grammatical and philosophical monstrosity it is. By the same token, so far from *alienating* something from its properties, it is precisely the instantiation relation that (what else?) *relates* a thing to its properties. Russell, as we have noted (§76), thought that subject–predicate propositions are reducible to relational ones; even Frege, though he rejects the *tertium adiacens* approach to the copula (§27), is quite happy to speak of the *relation* (*Beziehung*) of an object's *falling under* a concept.[191] At any rate, instantiation is plainly a relation if it is anything: to deny that obvious truth on the basis of a prejudice against Bradley's regress, while having confessedly no account to offer in place of the one that 'grammar suggests', seems to me rather an abdication of philosophical responsibility.

On the view I am rejecting, we are to suppose of the instantiation tie that, in Herbert Hochberg's words, 'what makes it special is that ties do not require further ties, while relations require ties'.[192] That formulation nicely brings out the inherent absurdity of the position. Actually, Hochberg's own account of the matter is not quite consistent: in one place,[193] he seems to agree that the 'tie' solution is ad hoc, but then shortly afterwards rejects the relational status of exemplification,[194] a move which is ad hoc for just the same reason. In another discussion, he seems to waver between the view that 'exemplification is a tie and is not a relation among relations', on the one hand, and accepting exemplification as a genuine relation which generates an innocent regress, on the other.[195] But that he eventually plumps for the former option is indicated by the fact that he contrasts realism favourably with nominalism on the basis

---

[190] [8], pp. 5–7. Cf. Tugendhat [2], pp. 171–4.
[191] See e.g. [9], p. 317 ([21], pp. 181–2); [11], pp. 455–6 ([21], p. 210). Frege calls this relation 'die logische Grundbeziehung' ([26], p. 128); cf. Tugendhat [2], p. 194.
[192] [9], p. 43.   [193] [6], p. 76.   [194] Ibid., p. 78.   [195] [2], pp. 228–9.

that the realist, exploiting the supposed non-relational status of exemplification, can avoid Bradley's regress, whereas the nominalist incurs a version of that regress in respect of the satisfaction relation.[196]

Hochberg's argument here is interesting from our point of view and worth recounting. His idea is that the nominalist, in analysing the meaning of concept-expressions in terms of the satisfaction relation (we have seen that this approach is common to Quine and Davidson: §7), is launched on a regress, for (to take the dyadic case as an illustration)

'xRy' is satisfied by $<a, b>$

can be true only if

'. . . is by satisfied by——' is satisfied by $<'xRy', <a, b>>$

is true (and vice versa); and so on. Now in the present context we naturally want to know whether the regress is a vicious one. Hochberg suggests that it is vicious because 'the nominalist solution . . . invites the kind of question it purports to answer'.[197] On the contrary, one might reply, the regress is surely an innocent, constituting regress of the sort we examined in §82: it constitutes the satisfaction relation, as that obtains between entities in the world and items of language, as being the very relation it is.[198] No doubt serious nominalists will be rather disconcerted to discover that their account of the relation between concept-expressions and worldly entities, while deftly avoiding the positing of universals (or so they claim), precipitates a regress.[199] But I at least would neither wish nor be entitled to turn the regress into a stick for the nominalist's back; in my view nominalism's problems arise elsewhere.[200] Now I am not concerned here to defend realism about universals. But the role of Bradley's regress in constituting the unity of the proposition by no means follows from its innocence in the context of an assumed realism about universals, and it is that constitutive role that I am here concerned to establish.

Given that, on my approach, facts and states of affairs are just true propositions at the level of reference, it follows that, while an account of the unity of facts or states of affairs will not on its own yield an account of the unity of the proposition—for we will still require an account of what unifies false propositions—an account of the unity of the proposition will yield

---

[196] Ibid., p. 232. Cf. his [5], p. 193.   [197] [2], p. 232.

[198] A similar response applies to Hochberg's argument elsewhere that the nominalist's attempt to capture *order* in relations is regressive: [5], pp. 203–7.

[199] Cf. Küng, pp. 167–8.

[200] See my [15], pp. 150, 186 n. 50. Similar remarks apply to the 'resemblance' regress, which Russell thought overturned nominalism: [8], p. 55; cf. Küng, pp. 68–9.

an account of the unity of facts or states of affairs. Orilia suggests that the entailment relationship is the other way round: given the property F and the object a, the proposition *that a is F* comes ontologically free, but the state of affairs *that a is F* does not—for the proposition *that a is F* may be false—and so stands in need of a general metaphysical explanation.[201] Orilia is right, as we have noted (§81), that, given the existence of the property F and of the object a, the proposition *that a is F* comes ontologically free: but, as I have stressed, though it comes *ontologically* free, it does not come *conceptually* free. We can compare the proposition *that a is F* with the mere aggregate of the entities F and a, and ask what their difference consists in. Even if such mere aggregates are never found *in pre-propositional reality*—since there is no such thing as pre-propositional reality for them to be found in: reality *is* propositional, so that at any ontological stage where the relevant objects are in the picture, the propositions formed from them are in the picture too—still they are *conceptually* available as such, in abstraction from any proposition their bits go to compose. Hence we can raise the distinctively theoretical question what differentiates a proposition from a mere aggregate—what constitutes the moment of propositional unity when we move in thought from a mere aggregate to a proposition. That propositional unity is not, from a conceptual point of view, simply given.

We can of course raise the further question why a given unified, true proposition *is* true, or a fact—why not merely the propositional unity but also the state of affairs *that a is F* exists, if it does exist. But, as I have indicated (§24), it would be wrong to look for a metaphysical explanation of the truth of true propositions. By contrast, the unity of the proposition is not, metaphysically speaking, a brute fact, but requires explanation; and since the distinction between a proposition and a mere aggregate is an essentially metaphysical one, the explanation sought will be of a correspondingly metaphysical nature. The truth of a true proposition is not a brute fact either, and so likewise requires explanation; but the distinction between a proposition, taken just as such, and a true proposition is not metaphysically grounded, so that the explanation sought will not be of a metaphysical nature. The truth of a true proposition will be grounded, insofar as it is grounded, in the truth of other true propositions of the same metaphysical status or level as the one to be explained—in ordinary facts about the history and make-up of the world, in causal and rational aetiologies.

In connection with my assertion that the instantiation regress as it arises in the context of facts or states of affairs is no more problematic than it is when it arises in the context of the unified proposition in general, it might

---

[201] [2], esp. §§2–4.

be wondered how any kind of actual relational linkage is possible at all. This
is in effect Russell's objection to Bradley. In *An Outline of Philosophy* (1927),
Russell discusses the passage from *Appearance and Reality* which I quoted at
the beginning of §70, and he tells us that he is going to point out Bradley's
'essential error':

> Bradley conceives a relation as something just as substantial as its terms, and not radically
> different in kind. The analogy of the chain with links should make us suspicious, since
> it clearly proves, if it is valid, that chains are impossible, and yet, as a fact they exist.
> There is not a word in his argument which would not apply to physical chains. The
> successive links are united not by another link, but by a spatial relation.[202]

And I take it that C. D. Broad's well-known criticism of Bradley aims in
substantially the same direction. Having remarked that the regress argument
'would disgrace a child or a savage', Broad goes on to say that 'Bradley's
argument depends on insisting that [relations] shall behave as if they were
particulars like the terms which they relate'.[203] In a similar vein, Meinong states
that the relation that unifies a complex is a something, but not the same sort
of thing as any of the components it unifies.[204] (Recall too the passage from
Destutt de Tracy quoted in §40.)

We have seen that Russell's solution to the unity problem, which involves,
like the solutions of Frege, Strawson, and others, treating the verbal element
of the sentence as 'radically different in kind' from nominal elements, will not
stand up: the context principle assures us that, as far as their (un)saturatedness
is concerned, all semantically significant components of the sentence are on
a par. We can, as we have seen, regard the logical copula as being 'radically
different in kind' from the other semantically significant components or
features of the sentence, but I have made clear that this move is, as such,
not yet the solution to the problem of unity but a mere placeholder for a
solution. Further, since the logical copula is, as such, not to be identified
with a lexical or morphological component of the sentence, but is properly
a *function* that may be taken over by such components—and indeed by any
such components—in the sentence, and since nothing about a given bunch
of words, taken just as such, indicates whether that function is present, or
whether they constitute a mere list, it follows that no purely grammatical
solution to the unity problem, such as was sponsored by Frege, Russell, and
Strawson, is in the offing. Now we have agreed that the logical copula will,
like any other semantically significant subsentential component or feature,
have *reference*, and if we are ready to accept Cantor's assertion of the existence

---

[202] [12], p. 202.   [203] Broad, p. 85.   [204] [1], p. 432.

of the actual infinite, we will also want to say that it has a *referent*. Hence Russell's insinuation in the quoted passage that Bradley was wrong to regard the 'relation actually relating', taken as unifier, as (in effect) a substantial part of the proposition is, whatever its merits as a criticism of Bradley,[205] from a systematic point of view thoroughly misguided: for the 'relation actually relating' taken as unifier—in general the reference or referent of the logical copula—*is* as substantial (albeit infinitistically so) as the referents of the other semantically significant components of the sentence.

So Russell's criticism of Bradley misfires. How, then, should we answer his point about physical chains—chains made of metal links, say? Why do we not need, as Russell implies we should need on Bradley's approach, an infinite supply of such links in order to make an ordinary chain? Why, in order to connect one metal link to another, do we not always need a third, thus precipitating a physical version of Bradley's regress? Or why does glue work? Why do we not need a second-order glue—that is, a glue for gluing the original glue to the materials to be glued—and then a third-order glue, and so on? Well, Russell is clearly right to say that, in the physical case, the connection is established by a spatial relation, not (in general) by a further metal link, or film of glue. But, in the physical case as in the metaphysical one, having a bunch of metal links, say, together with a sheaf of suitable (universal) relations, does not *as such* give us more than a mere aggregate of links and relations: to produce a chain, we must bring it about that, as Russell would say, the relations *actually relate* the other materials. And how can they do that without precipitating Bradley's regress? They cannot: as soon as one thing of any kind at all is related, in any way at all, to another thing of any kind at all, we have a relations regress on our hands. So Bradley's regress does indeed arise for metal chains and glued pieces of cardboard, but the regress involves *relations* (of course), not physical entities such as pieces of metal or films of glue. To join one metal link to another such link what you need is not (or not generally) a third such link, but a relation of the right sort between the two links you already have; to glue one piece of cardboard to another what you need is not (or not generally) a second-order glue, but a relation of the right sort between the pieces of cardboard and the glue you already have. It is true that, to take the case of physical chains, in order to put a couple of metal links into the desired relation you do indeed need *further* relations, and to put the links and the desired relation into these further relations you need yet further relations, and so on into the familiar regress. But the regress, notwithstanding the slightly imprecise way in which I have just described the situation, is not a

---

[205] The passage is attacked as unfair by Olson (pp. 60–4) and Candlish ([2], pp. 167–71).

practical one: in securing the first relation—or indeed any of the relations—in the regress, you *eo ipso* secure the others; the relations in the regress come not single spies, but in battalions.

In connection with the case that interests us here, that of sentences and propositions, Alex Oliver and Timothy Smiley remark that 'in general a grammatical unit needs no additional expression to link together its parts: think of "Jack smokes". At some stage mere juxtaposition of parts must be enough to create a larger unit, on pain of an obvious regress.'[206] Oliver and Smiley are right that mere juxtaposition of words suffices to create a larger syntactic unit, such as a sentence and list. To put some words together to form a sentence or list, you do not (in general) need more words, but a relation of (spatial, temporal, or merely conceptual) juxtaposition. So we do not get into a *word* regress at the level of the sentence or list, and it would be disastrous if we did. But we do get into a *relations* regress at that level, just as we did for metal chains, and, so far from its being vicious, the generation of such a regress is a condition on the possibility of our constructing a sentence or list in the first place. Sentences and lists are, after all, just linguistic states of affairs and so, like all states of affairs, involve relations (in this case, between words) in an essential way. And anything that involves relations generates Bradley's regress.

This consideration raises another, one that was broached at the end of §79. We have been concentrating throughout this study on the unity of the proposition and correlatively of the sentence; but the reader may be wondering what we should say about the unities of smaller and larger items of discourse—of words, on the one hand, and of arguments, say, on the other. Words are lists of letters; arguments are lists of sentences. Still larger expanses of discourse—histories, novels, and so on—are also lists of sentences. So the account I have just given applies to them: the unity of a word is constituted by the relations among its constituent letters together with the regress that its being unified generates, and similarly, *mutatis mutandis*, for the other examples. The same applies to the unity of a sentence-or-list, that is, to the unity of a string of words whose identity is just so far indeterminate as between sentence and list; as we have said, a group of words that may compose either a sentence or list has, just as such, that indeterminate status. But the unity of a sentence *as opposed to* a list is given not by the relations regress generated by the relevant component words—for that is common to both sentence and equiform list—but by the unity of the sentence's corresponding proposition.

85   Unity and Use

The solution to the problem of unity that I am offering is a semantic, not a pragmatic one. The level of reference is the level of what is understood and advanced, not in the sense that it is the level of what is *actually* (at some time, in some token utterance or inscription) *understood or advanced*, but in the sense that it is the level of contents that are *available to be understood and advanced*. That any purported solution to the problem of unity should be semantic rather than pragmatic is indeed what one would demand of it. It might be tempting to suppose otherwise: given, as I have insisted at several points, that a unified sentence may be duplicated by a mere list—that arranging a bunch of linguistic items, even arranging suitable items for constituting a sentence and in the right order to do so, does not of itself guarantee that a sentence, as opposed to a mere list, is thereby actually constituted—it might be tempting to suppose that what is required to turn a bunch of words into a sentence is the right kind of linguistic intention, that, for example, the words 'Socrates is wise' will constitute a sentence on any particular occasion of use, as opposed to a mere list, if they are uttered or inscribed with the right intention.[207] But when we spell out this idea as I have just done, it is plain that it gets matters back to front.

For the strategy of appealing to use, or the speaker's intention, or some such pragmatic notion, as the key factor distinguishing a sentence from a mere list of words inverts the correct order of dependency between speaker's meaning and semantic meaning: speakers use linguistic items, from occasion to occasion, with the imputed overriding intention of communicating the meaning which those items objectively have in the language, that is, have independently of their deployment on any particular occasion of use. Intentions are relevant when it comes to determining which linguistic counter a language-user means to put forward, so to speak; but what the semantic consequences of advancing exactly that counter are—in other words, what the linguistic item in question actually *means*—is a matter of its role in the public language.[208] Use in the pragmatic sense (use on any particular occasion) will not convert a bunch of words which is not already a (type) sentence into a (token) sentence; rather, a bunch of words which is already and anyway a (type) sentence can be used (tokened) as such from occasion to occasion. Of course, if by 'use' we mean not use on any particular occasion but something tantamount to semantic meaning ('how the word is used in the language'), then it would be correct,

---

[207] So e.g. Gibson; Hanks [1], pp. 159–60.   [208] See here Evans [1], pp. 67–9.

but unhelpful, to say that use is what unifies a sentence: the question will then be what that unifying use consists in. And to that question only a reply that specifies the *semantics* of sentences in a way that casts light on their unity will be satisfactory. What makes a bunch of words a sentence rather than a mere list—at least in the simple forms of sentence I have concentrated on for most of this study (I will generalize the account in §88)—is that its semantic analysis generates the instantiation regress.

The correct order of dependency between speaker's meaning and semantic meaning is a point of some importance, and worth pausing over before we move on. It may be as well to allow my opponents to state their position. This is how Davidson elegantly puts the pragmatic alternative:

> An utterance has certain truth-conditions only if the speaker intends it to be interpreted as having those truth-conditions. . . . A malapropism, or slip of the tongue, if it means anything, means what its promulgator intends it to mean. There are those who are pleased to hold that the meanings of words are magically independent of the speaker's intentions. . . . This doctrine entails that a speaker may be perfectly intelligible to his hearers, may be interpreted exactly as he intends to be interpreted, and yet may not know what he means by what he says.[209]

To which we may reply: what is so difficult about that entailment? The captured Second World War American soldier—to borrow John Searle's well-known example[210]—who tries to persuade his monolingual Italian captors that he is a German officer by uttering the one line of German that he recalls from his school days ('Kennst du das Land, wo die Zitronen blühen?') may indeed *intend* his hearers to think that he is saying, in German, that he is a Wehrmacht officer, and may further (let us suppose) succeed in getting his hearers to interpret him as saying exactly that, and thereupon to release him, but that is not what the line of poetry he remembers and utters *means in the language*.[211] There is nothing problematic about adding to the scenario as described by Searle the assumption that the soldier does not know what his words mean—he has, as we say, forgotten their meaning and, if so, he would be the first to admit his ignorance on this score—despite the pragmatic success (as we are supposing) of his act of communication; and there is nothing mysterious about the fact that words mean what they mean in the language independently of individual speakers' intentions in using those words on particular occasions. Incidentally, it is not essential to the description of this scenario that the

---

[209] [2], pp. 50–1. Cf. [2], p. 123. Curiously, Davidson's own solution to the unity problem (which I discuss in §89 below) is not a pragmatic one, though he is willing to concede that pragmatic solutions may contain a 'deep truth' (ibid., p. 147).

[210] See Searle [1], pp. 44–5; [2], pp. 45–6.   [211] Cf. Wittgenstein [5], I, §498.

quotation our soldier remembers does not objectively mean what he intends to convey by it in this one-off situation. For suppose that, instead of that line of Goethe's, the one German sentence which our American soldier remembers, without remembering its meaning, just happens to be 'Ich bin Offizier in der Wehrmacht', and suppose that as he uses it he says to himself 'I can't remember what this sentence means, but I'll come out with it in order to get my captors to think I'm saying that I am a Wehrmacht officer', and that his captors fall for his strategy. Even though, in this situation, there is a lucky coincidence between what he actually said and what he intended to convey, nevertheless the soldier quite literally did not know what he was saying.

The entire phenomenon of irony depends on there being a gap between occasion intentions and linguistic meaning. As the ballad singer tells us concerning the notorious Mack the Knife: 'Jenny Towler ward gefunden/Mit 'nem Messer in der Brust./Und am Kai geht Mackie Messer,/Der von allem nichts gewusst./Und das große Feuer in Soho—/Sieben Kinder und ein Greis—/In der Menge Mackie Messer, den/Man nichts fragt und der nichts weiß.'[212] What the singer says is one thing; what he actually intends us to extract from his words quite another. Such a dislocation between Mack the Knife's proclaimed ignorance and innocence, on the one hand, and the unmistakable subtextual message of his knowledge and guilt, on the other, would not be possible if Davidson's pragmatic account of linguistic meaning were correct. In fact, as far as the charge of magic goes, the boot is on the other foot: the thesis that speakers invest their words with particular meanings, from occasion to occasion, by forming special, meaning-conferring intentions whenever they utter or inscribe particular words is not only a travesty of the actual phenomenology of speaking and writing, but is also philosophically incoherent. For how could such intentions possibly *confer* meaning, and how could the meanings thereby (supposedly) conferred be *deciphered* by hearers and readers? The suggestion reduces the act of communication to a hocus-pocus performed by the communicator's soul, accompanied by a miraculous feat of divination on the part of the addressee. In the case of irony, the intended meaning is *systematically* related to (usually, it is just the negation of) the literal meaning of the words uttered or inscribed, so that, provided it is sufficiently clearly signalled that the words are intended ironically, there is nothing mysterious in the process by which the addressee arrives at the intended meaning.

---

[212] Brecht/Weill, *Die Dreigroschenoper*, Act 1, 'Moritat von Mackie Messer': 'Jenny Towler was found with a knife in her chest; meanwhile Mack the Knife, who knows nothing of all that, strolls the Embankment. And the great fire in Soho—seven children and an old man—in the crowd stands Mack the Knife, but he is not asked and he knows nothing.'

The pragmatic account obviously fails to capture what goes on when we communicate. The truth is rather that when we learn to speak a language, we join an institution that has a being and a life quite independently of our individual contributions to its existence.[213] I am exploiting that fact as I write these words, and when you read and understand them you rely on my having written words the meanings of which are fixed in the language. When we utter or write words, we participate in the language institution, and what that entails is that we have an imputed overriding intention, as I put it above, to use words with the meanings they objectively have in the language. Davidson's insinuation to the contrary notwithstanding, acts of communication may indeed—and often do—involve a speaker's using words correctly and being understood by the addressee, without that speaker's understanding what those words mean in the language: the speaker meant what the words meant, because he or she spoke with the imputed overriding intention to use words with the meanings they objectively have in the language. That overriding intention may indeed be cancelled by special factors, as in the scenarios I considered above involving the captured soldier, but even in these unusual situations the words go on meaning what they objectively mean in the language, and the speaker says what they mean.

The point that occasion intentions alone cannot constitute linguistic meaning applies to the case we are interested in, that of the unity of the proposition and of the sentence expressing it, in this way: how, we might ask, could a sheer intention convert a bunch of words from a list into a sentence, and how could such an intention be deciphered? If, on any particular occasion, you utter the token words 'Socrates', 'is', and 'wise' in that order, your intentions will be relevant to determining whether you uttered the type *sentence* 'Socrates is wise', or the type *list* comprising the type words 'Socrates', 'is', and 'wise', for indeed if there is any doubt on that score you can inform us what you intended ('I meant the sentence, not the list'), just as, if we are puzzled by the obvious ambiguity in your utterance of 'He sat near the bank' you can clear it up for us ('I meant the river bank'). But no intention of yours can be *what constitutes* the type sentence 'Socrates is wise' *as a sentence* or the type list comprising 'Socrates', 'is', and 'wise' *as a list*, just as no intention of yours can be what constitutes the semantic difference between 'bank' as a word for a

[213] The later Davidson's idiolectic conception of linguistic meaning, exemplified by the above quotation, sits uneasily beside his former insistence—still maintained only a few pages away from the quoted passage—that language is essentially a social phenomenon and that 'meaning is entirely determined by observable behaviour, even readily observable behaviour' ([2], p. 56). I do not know how Davidson thought these two tendencies in his later philosophy could be reconciled. See further my [15], ch. 3, §4; McDowell [5].

river bank, and 'bank' as a word for a financial institution. Settling the purely *pragmatic* question whether you intended to utter a sentence or a list does not answer the *semantic* question what the difference between sentence and list consists in: to answer this latter question we need an account that spells out what is involved in doing one thing rather than the other, advancing one type of linguistic counter rather than the other.

86 The Unity of Sentences and the Unity of Complex Names (I)

It may be objected that the generation of Bradley's regress cannot be *fully* constitutive of the unity of the proposition, because although it yields a specification of *necessary* conditions of possession of that unity, it does not yield *sufficient* conditions. That is shown, according to this objection, by the fact that the attempt to specify the unity of what a *complex name*[214] refers to generates a parallel regress. This regress arises when one tries to give a complete specification of the relation between structuring and structured elements of a complex object. But, so the objection continues, the referents of complex names, though unities in some sense, are surely not unities in the sense in which propositions are unities, since they are not true or false. Now it is certainly correct that this 'configuration' regress for the referents of complex names is in all relevant respects the same as the 'instantiation' regress we have just been considering in the case of propositions. In fact it is exactly the same as the regress that arises in respect of the referents of sentences of Denyer's language **S**, which is unsurprising, given that the sentences of **S** are syntactically indistinguishable from complex names. As the case of **S** already intimates, however, the objector is wrong to suppose that complex names are not unified in the relevant sense.

Here it is interesting to note that in his 1904 discussions of Meinong Russell regarded complex objects as indeed unified in the same sense as propositions, and identified the regress we have been concerned with—which however he failed to recognize as containing the solution to the problem of that unity—as arising in both cases.[215] Of course we have already seen this assimilation in *Principles*, §52, which I quoted in §10,[216] and in general the thesis that complexes are facts (and vice versa) may be said to be basic to Russell's logical atomism.[217]

---

[214] On the terminology recall §64.   [215] See [15], ch. 1, esp. pp. 28, 50–7, 62.

[216] Cf. [3], §135, with N. Griffin [4], pp. 165, 169–70.

[217] See Russell [7], p. 374; [13], p. 285; Meinong [2], §10, pp. 53–9. Cf. Hochberg [7], p. 174.

The question whether (obtaining or non-obtaining) complexes are (true or false) propositions was also the subject of debate in the late medieval period, when it was discussed in connection with (restrictive and non-restrictive) relative clauses.[218] The position of the logical atomists was in some degree anticipated in the Port-Royal *Logic*, where we are told, for example, that in the sentence 'minds that are square are sounder than those that are round' ('les esprits qui sont carrés sont plus solides que ceux qui sont ronds') the relative clauses (which Arnauld and Nicole call 'incidental propositions') are false.[219]

Russell's identification of complexes and true propositions was of relatively brief duration. Earlier, in a letter to Moore, he had objected to Moore's thesis that propositions are merely complex concepts, saying:

I believe that propositions are distinguished from mere concepts, not by their complexity only, but by always containing one specific concept, i.e., the copula 'is'. That is, there must be, between the concepts of a proposition, one special type of relation, not merely some relation.[220]

In the same place Russell reminds us of Leibniz's assertion (which was quoted in §5 above) that 'The wise man' is not a proposition. The 1905 theory of descriptions might be said to have maintained the 1904 doctrine that complexes are (deeply) propositional in form.[221] But when Russell came to adopt the multiple relation theory of judgement, propositions disappeared (at least officially) from his ontology as genuine individuals, though there were still complexes in the world. Thus we are told in the introduction to the first edition of *Principia Mathematica* that

when we judge (say) 'this is red', what occurs is a relation of three terms, the mind, and 'this', and red. On the other hand, when we *perceive* 'the redness of this', there is a relation of two terms, namely the mind and the complex object 'the redness of this'.[222]

Later still Russell abandoned the idea that complexes can be named, so adopting Wittgenstein's Tractarian position.[223]

Given that the Russell of 1903–5 regarded all 'complexes' as propositionally unified, he faced the problem, which was aired in §52 of the *Principles*, how it is that the proposition *that Caesar died* has a truth-value, whereas the complex object *the death of Caesar* does not. Of course, complex objects like the death of Caesar—and in particular those complex objects which it is natural to call states

---

[218] See here Nuchelmans [5], pp. 77–81.   [219] [1], II, ch. 7, p. 119. Cf. Chomsky [8], pp. 14–15.
[220] Letter of 1 Dec. 1898, [17], p. 186. Cf. Moore [2], p. 5, quoted in §6 above.
[221] Cf. Imaguire, pp. 189–91.
[222] Whitehead and Russell, i, pp. 43–4. See Cocchiarella [1], pp. 48–50.
[223] Russell [13], pp. 188, 267, 270; Wittgenstein [1], §§3.12, 3.14, 3.144, 3.221; Cocchiarella [1], p. 207.

of affairs—have something very like a truth-value, namely what one might call an 'obtaining-value': they either *obtain* or not, and their obtaining-values are clearly closely related to—indeed necessarily march in step with—the truth-values of their corresponding propositions. (I follow Wittgenstein here in supposing that states of affairs may obtain or fail to obtain.[224]) Plausibly, the terminological difference—the fact that we say that propositions are true whereas complex objects like the death of Caesar or the cat's being on the mat obtain—has no more depth than the syntactic differences between declarative sentences and complex names. Both propositions and complex objects have what we might call 'correctness' values, and the fact that there are two species of the genus—truth-values and obtaining-values—is without philosophical significance.

I shall return to this point. Certainly it is no part of my brief to deny that declarative sentences are syntactically distinct from complex names, and that this difference is reflected in distinct ways in which we talk about their corresponding referents. But the question is what the significance of this fact is; here I am interested in showing that what *unifies* a proposition is fundamentally the same as what *unifies* a complex object. It should be stressed again that, just as we are interested in the unity of a proposition whether true or false, so also we are interested in the unity of a complex object, whether it obtains or not. For the *existence* of a complex object as the referent of a complex name does not depend on its *obtaining*, in the sense of its being satisfied by something: the complex object that is the referent of the phrase 'Wallenstein's death in old age of natural causes' exists, just in virtue of the meaningfulness of that phrase, but, as a matter of (contingent) fact, that complex object does (did) not obtain, in the sense of being satisfied by an actual event. Again, the complex object referred to by the phrase 'the round square' exists, simply in virtue of the meaningfulness of that phrase, but as a matter of (necessary) fact does not obtain, in the sense of being satisfied by an object. (Note here that the locution 'in the sense of being satisfied . . .', which I have appended to occurrences of 'obtain', are not intended to be explanatory of that notion in any reductive sense: rather, the distinction between obtaining and not obtaining is metaphysically primitive, just as the general distinction between truth and falsity of propositions is, as we have said, metaphysically primitive.) Drawing on a useful distinction made by Edward Zalta, we might say that this complex object *encodes* just the joint characteristics of being round and being square, though nothing *exemplifies* both those characteristics jointly.[225]

---

[224] [1], §§2.04–2.063; Clark, p. 260.   [225] [1], pp. 15–37, 105–14, 120–3.

In the general case of a complex name there can be no doubt that the availability of the 'configuration' regress is what constitutes the unity of the corresponding complex object, in the sense of providing necessary *and* sufficient conditions for unity. For the presence of a certain structure at the ontological level of the complex object is exactly what its unity consists in, and that structure is just what the regress analyses: if there were no 'configuration' regress, or if it terminated at some point, the elements of the purported complex object would fall apart; contrariwise, if analysis uncovers a 'configuration' regress in respect of any given elements, that shows that those elements are unified by the structural relation(s) generating the regress. What now has to be shown is that the unified proposition simply inherits this feature of complex objects. But we have in effect already shown that, in observing (§62) that any complex name is *capable* of being used to advance a declaration. Aristotle's example of a complex name lacking declarative status is 'goat-stag':[226] but the phrase 'goat-stag' *could* be used to mean (for example) 'a goat is a stag'. No further linguistic element needs to be superadded to it to achieve this transformation: its referent already possesses enough structure to be capable of saying something true or false. Similarly, the 'sentences' of Denyer's primitive languages, though consisting of nothing more than strings of names, could, as we observed, be used to advance declarations, and in the case of **S** we are officially told that they are so used. And on the interpretation of the *Tractatus* that I favour, a fully analysed Tractarian sentence also consists of strings of type-identical names (primitive signs correlated with simple objects)—it is, in effect, a complex name—but for all that *says* that things stand as they are shown by the sentence to stand.[227] But if the mere act of stringing names together so as to form a complex name suffices, in these artificial cases, to yield linguistic items bearing a truth-value, it follows that, at least in these cases, the conditions that are necessary and sufficient for the unity of the relevant complex object are also necessary and sufficient for the unity of the relevant proposition. Those conditions are, I have argued, given by the availability of the 'configuration' regress.

What constitutes the unity of a proposition referred to by a declarative sentence is just the fact that its components are structured, that structure being in turn embodied in a regress which arises when we reify the structuring component and try to specify completely how that structuring component is itself structured with the other components. In the case of Denyer's language **S**, or the fully analysed Tractarian language, the regress initially takes the form of what I have called a *configuration* regress, since in these cases there are no intrinsic distinctions among the objects which compose the propositions of the

226 *Int.* 16a16–18.   227 Wittgenstein [1], §§4.22, 4.022.

398 THE UNITY OF THE PROPOSITION

languages in question, so that at the first stage the 'relating' relation is that of configuration; at the second and subsequent stages, however, given that the relation of configuration is indeed a relation, the regress will be an *instantiation* regress. In the case of natural languages containing a grammatical copula, which in consequence automatically exhibit a grammatical subject–predicate asymmetry, the regress, as it arises for predications of the basic form $R^n(a_1, \ldots, a_n)$, takes the form of an instantiation regress from the beginning. For, as Russell said (§76), predication essentially involves the relation of instantiation. In each case the mechanism by which the relevant regress—in the former case the regress takes the form of a configuration/instantiation regress, in the latter case it is just an instantiation regress—constitutes propositional unity is the same. The regress constitutes the unity of what is advanced or understood—*that this object is configured with that*, as it might be, or *that this object instantiates that (universal) object.*

Of course, in the case of languages which employ a grammatical copula, there remains a syntactic distinction, as we have agreed, between declarative sentences on the one hand and complex names, such as definite descriptions, on the other. But the distinction, though grammatically significant, is logically superficial. There are two reasons for this. One is that, as we have seen, the incorporation of the *grammatical* copula in a sentence does not effect a unity missing from the sentences of languages lacking such a device: unity is effected by the *logical* copula, which does not depend for its presence in a sentence on that sentence's having a grammatical copula—as we have said (§84), the logical copula is a function available to be taken over by any semantically significant component of a sentence—and so can be as much present to sentences of languages lacking a grammatical copula as it can to sentences of languages possessing one. Secondly, even in the case of languages that have a grammatical copula, the surface difference between complex names and declarative sentences, in virtue of which we say that mere complex names, unlike sentences, are not true or false, has, as I hinted at the beginning of this section, no logical depth. Definite descriptions entail, in context, an analysis which brings out a distinctively sentential content embedded in the nominal form of the description. (Russell had held this as part of his 1903 theory of denoting, but it is brought out more fully—perhaps carried too far—in the 1905 theory of definite descriptions.) Definite descriptions are nominal in form, but, in context, they are not merely nominal. The point is general to complex names.[228] Perhaps we do not want to agree with the early Wittgenstein and the Russell of 'On Denoting' that a sentence containing a complex name *says* that the components of the complex

---

[228] Cf. Simons [6], pp. 78–9.

name's referent are structured in such and such a way:[229] but at the very least it *presupposes* that they are so structured, and that is enough to give the complex name a logically sentential status.[230] That explains why the complex names of all three of Denyer's primitive languages are capable of being used to make statements: they are deeply sentential anyway, in the explained sense. We now have an explanation, too, of what ought otherwise to seem a highly surprising fact—namely, that something superficially nominal in form can be deeply sentential, that by saying 'The redness of the rose is F' I can mean, or presuppose, that the rose *is* red.[231] After all, one might think, in using the phrase 'the redness of the rose' I have simply *referred to* that particular object—the rose's redness: how can I thereby have said something that already carries a *propositional* commitment, namely that the rose *is* red? But the point is that what unifies a complex object is exactly what unifies a proposition: given this, the fact that a complex name has, in context, sentential implications should no longer be surprising.

87   The Unity of Sentences and the Unity of Complex Names (II)

It might look here as though there were a structural mismatch between explanandum and explanans. I have said that what unifies a complex object is exactly what unifies a proposition, which is a symmetrical fact, but I have adduced it to explain what is apparently an asymmetrical fact, namely that complex objects are deeply propositional and, correspondingly, that complex names are deeply sentential. Or is it possible to say, not only that complex objects are deeply propositional, but also that propositions are deeply objectual and, correspondingly, that sentences are deeply nominal? Of course, I have already argued on the basis of considerations deriving from linguistic idealism (§53) that sentences are names of propositions, which are objects in as good a sense as anything at all is an object. But the question here is the more precise one whether propositions are the *right sort* of object, that is, whether their kind of objecthood restores symmetry to the above-mentioned explanandum, and hence removes the apparent structural mismatch between explanandum and explanans. Well, surely the fact, already noted, that what I called the 'obtaining-value' of a complex object necessarily reflects and is reflected by the

---

[229] Wittgenstein [1], §§3.24, 4.022.   [230] Cf. Grossmann [1], pp. 170–8.
[231] On the connection between sentences and complex names, see Poole, pp. 116–17.

truth-value of its corresponding proposition gives us the resources we need to recognize a relevant symmetry in the relation between complex objects and propositions.

I have observed that the Russell of 1903–5 held that complex objects and propositions are indeed related in the relevant symmetrical way. Even after he had abandoned propositions as integral individual entities, Russell held that complexes 'on the ground' were propositionally structured, and in a passage in *Principia* which comes slightly earlier than the one quoted in §86, he suggested a significant relation between complex judgements and (as I would want to say) propositions asserting the existence of complexes:

> The universe consists of objects having various qualities and standing in various relations. Some of the objects which occur in the universe are complex. When an object is complex, it consists of interrelated parts. Let us consider a complex object composed of two parts *a* and *b* standing to each other in the relation *R*. The complex object '*a*-in-the-relation-*R*-to-*b*' may be capable of being *perceived*; when perceived, it is perceived as one object. Attention may show that it is complex; we then *judge* that *a* and *b* stand in the relation *R*. Such a judgment, being derived from perception by mere attention, may be called a 'judgment of perception'. . . . [I]f our judgment has been so derived, it must be true. In fact, we may define *truth*, where such judgments are concerned, as consisting in the fact that there is a complex *corresponding* to the discursive thought which is the judgment. That is, when we judge '*a* has the relation *R* to *b*', our judgment is said to be *true* when there is [=obtains: RG] a complex '*a*-in-the-relation-*R*-to-*b*', and is said to be *false* when this is not the case.[232]

Simons formulates the principle of symmetry that is (at least partially) expressed in this passage, as:

$aRb \leftrightarrow [aRb]$ exists.[233]

We might compare two of Wittgenstein's wartime diary entries, in which he says that

$\phi a. \phi b. aRb = \text{Def } \phi[aRb]$[234]

and also that

$aRb. aRc. bSc = aR[bSc] \text{ Def.}$[235]

(Wittgenstein here follows Frege's practice of placing the definiendum on the right and the definiens on the left.) To take the first of these: the point is that '$\phi[aRb]$' means, or presupposes, that, among other things, aRb.[236] (Those

---

[232] Whitehead and Russell, i, p. 43.   [233] [7], p. 207.   [234] [6], entry for 5 Sept. 1914 (p. 4).
[235] [11], entry for 6 Aug. 1914 (p. 18).   [236] Cf. Simons [7], p. 211.

other things do not, however, necessarily include ϕa and ϕb, as the definition Wittgenstein here considers states: for the redness of the rose can be F without its being the case that the rose, as such, or the redness, as such, is F.[237])

Simons traces the idea to Meinong, but I think it goes back further: we have already noted, in connection with our discussion of Frege's attitude to the copula and alternatives thereto (§27), that, at least on one occasion, Leibniz analyses sentences of the form 'a is F' as '$[aF]$ exists' (that is, 'The F-ness of a exists'), and in another passage, conveniently for our purposes, he actually asserts both directions of the above biconditional.[238] Simons thinks that the biconditional is in fact only true in one direction (right to left), for 'not every case of relatedness gives rise to a complex',[239] and the thought is presumably that a genuine complex object has some kind of natural integrity. But I have rejected that restriction: I did so when I remarked (§1) that any complex entity—no matter how artificially assembled—has a unity, and so a being, just as such. These reflections now suggest the following line of thought.

Just as a complex name can be 'augmented', in context, to yield a sentence, so a sentence can be 'reduced' to yield a complex name plus some additional context. The difference between these processes is that in the former case the context has to be supplied to complete the augmentation, whereas in the latter case the extra context is a by-product of the reduction. We find a similar procedure in Frege's *Begriffsschrift*. There we are told how a declarative sentence A can be nominalized by prefixing a horizontal content stroke to yield the symbol '——A', which can be read 'the circumstance/proposition that A' (or simply 'that A'); to this symbol in turn a vertical judgement stroke can be prefixed, yielding '⊢——A', which can be read 'the circumstance/proposition that A is a fact' (or simply 'it is a fact that A').[240] We are told that the symbol '⊢——' is the 'common predicate of all judgements'.[241] The general idea is

---

[237] Ibid., p. 211 n. 8.

[238] The passage occurs in marginal notes which Leibniz made on a letter from des Bosses of 12 Dec. 1712 ([1], ii, p. 472): 'Cum abstracta non sunt entia, reducuntur ad veritates, verb. g. rationalitas hominis nihil aliud est quam veritas huius enuntiationis: homo est rationalis. Unde patet incomplexa saepe fundari in ipsis complexis, quae tamen per se natura posteriora sunt ipsis incomplexis, quorum scilicet faciunt nexum. Et revera omnis propositio seu omne complexum potest vicissim reduci ad incomplexum per *est* primi adiecti, ut vocant. Ut si loco propositionis: homo est rationalis, dicam τὸ Hominem esse rationalem, est. Rosam esse odoratam, est. Nempe est verum, etsi forte non existat rosa, ut in hyeme.' (Note: here *complexa* are sentences, *incomplexa* subsentential expressions.) Cf. Nuchelmans [5], p. 219.

[239] [7], p. 209 n. 5.

[240] [1], §§2–3. Cf. Bell [1], pp. 21–4, 85–7; von Kutschera [1], p. 25 n. 7.

[241] [1], §3. Elsewhere, the judgement stroke has the role of asserting the propositional content that follows it: Wittgenstein [1], §4.442; Dummett [3], pp. 491–5; Carl [2], pp. 58–9. N. Smith interprets the *Begriffsschrift* passage in the same way: pp. 167–8.

that, by adding or removing suitable context, complex names and sentences are interconvertible (as one might put it: *propositiones et nomina complexa convertuntur*). That gives us sufficient symmetry in the explanandum—the unities of proposition and complex object—to provide for a structural match with the explanans, the 'configuration' regress that arises in each case. In fact the strategy mooted by Russell and Leibniz is just a notational variant of the first stage of Bradley's regress, which I have suggested (following Russell) the very nature of predication as a relational status forces us to take: for the analysis of '*a* is *F*' ('*a* has *R* to *b*') as '[*aF*] exists' ('[*aRb*] exists') is just a variant of its analysis as '[*aF*] is instantiated' ('[*aRb*] is instantiated'), which, when it is subjected to the same analysis, launches us on the familiar regress. That suggests a more direct way of restoring symmetry to the explanandum.

For there is a good sense in which we can regard the sentence as a kind of complex name, and its corresponding proposition as a complex object, without prejudice to their ability to *say* something. On a treatment of the logical copula that accords it a determinate, infinitistic referent (what I called the robust approach to the reference of the copula) the sentence is quite straightforwardly composed of items all of which have referents. What stops the sentence, on this approach, from degenerating into a mere list, and what prevents the corresponding proposition from degenerating into a mere aggregate is the quite special nature of one feature of the sentence, namely the logical copula, and the correspondingly special nature of its referent. For the presence of the logical copula is distinctive of sentential unity, and its special nature is analysed by the regress that arises when we try to describe its infinitistic referent. But I think that on the alternative approach that denies that the logical copula has a *referent*, insisting that it merely has *reference* (what I called the more cautious approach to the referential status of the logical copula) there is still a sense in which we can regard the sentence as a complex name. This works as follows.

A given expression, as it figures in a sentence, may be regarded as supplying the substantial content of the logical predicate (annotated and unannotated) of that sentence, or as a name with a referent which is available to be replaced by a variable bound by a quantifier. Both of these approaches are indeed available, according to the approach under consideration, but not from the same standpoint. Of course, as I have stressed, given any unanalysed sentence it may be quite arbitrary which of its expressions we assign to higher levels of a linguistic hierarchy, and which to lower levels, provided we observe the principles of congruence. But, once we have made a choice, the points of view from which any given expression is considered as supplying the substantial content of the logical predicate, on the one hand, and as a name with a referent, on the other, are distinct. This relativization is underpinned by the fact that, as we have said, the logical copula—that feature of the logical predicate which makes it the bearer of sentential unity—is, unlike the grammatical copula, not essentially a lexical or morphological component of the sentence, but a *function* which is available to be *taken over* by such components, and is so taken over when one or more of those components are regarded as themselves supporting the frame of the sentence. That function is just to provide a sentence with what it needs to be enabled to say something, rather than merely itemize its referents. Hence there can be no question of the *logical copula's* being seen to have a referent from one point of view and not to have a referent from another: according to the approach to copulative reference currently under consideration, the logical copula is essentially (from all points of view) such that it has a reference but no referent. Only *words* (or, in general, morphemes) can be subject to the relativization in question here: from one point of view a word may be seen to discharge the copulative function; from another point of view not. Words themselves, in advance of entering a particular sentence, have, in the relevant sense, no function. But on entering a sentence, they can assume either of these roles, depending on how they are viewed. There is nothing problematic about this relativization, so long as we do not mistake the kind of thing that is subject to it.

This position is structurally rather similar to one that Russell developed after writing *Principles*, and is preserved in a manuscript entitled 'On Functions'.[242] In this text Russell starts by noting that 'A *complex* is a unity formed by certain constituents combined in a certain manner', and 'A complex is determined by its constituents together with their mode of combination'. He remarks that 'The mode of combination of the constituents of a complex is not itself one of the constituents of the complex.'[243] As he notes elsewhere, any such supposition would generate Bradley's regress.[244] Russell then tells us that

A mode of combination, like everything else, is an entity; but it is not one of the entities occurring in a complex composed of entities combined in the mode in question. . . . Although a mode of combination is not a constituent of a complex in which constituents are combined according to the mode in question, yet there are complexes in which modes of combination are constituents. If this were not the case, there would be no propositions about modes of combination, which, being itself a proposition about modes of combination, is a self-contradictory hypothesis.[245]

The mode of combination of a complex is not an entity *in that very complex*,[246] but it can be an entity in another complex, one that has its own, different

---

242 Cf. N. Griffin [4], pp. 167–8.   243 [18], p. 98.
244 Cf. [9], p. 98 (cited in §71 above); [11], p. 198.   245 [18], pp. 98–9. Cf. [13], p. 239.
246 Cf. Vallicella [4], pp. 177–8.

mode of combination. This move rather resembles the strategy of the cautious approach to the reference of the logical copula, according to which any part of a sentence can be regarded either as nominal, in which case it has a referent capable of being subject to objectual quantification, or as the basis for abstracting out the sentence's (annotated or unannotated) logical predicate, in which case it contains the logical copula responsible for that sentence's unity, and is to that extent not nominal (having reference but not a referent).

Since, as we have seen (§75), Russell was on the side of the gods in the battle between Cantorians and Aristotelians on the metaphysics of the infinite, there might seem to be something peculiar about the similarity between his position on modes of combination and what I have called the cautious approach to the semantics of the logical copula, which was after all motivated by the desire to avoid an actual infinity—the infinitistic referent of the logical copula happily acknowledged by the robust approach. The cautious approach tries to make a rigorous separation between the nominal and the unifying—between parts of the sentence construed, on the one hand, as names with referents and, on the other, as discharging the function of the logical predicate: the same component or feature of the sentence may be regarded as playing either of these roles, only not from the same perspective. Likewise, Russell's 'mode of combination' serves as non-unifying entity in one context and as unifying non-entity in another. If, now, we ask what the difficulty about performing both naming and unifying tasks when viewed from the same perspective is supposed to be, exactly—why a linguistic item which is nominal in form cannot also *pro tanto* unify, or why something at the level of reference cannot both unify and be an entity in the same context—and if the only answer to this question is that we do not want the logical copula to refer to an actual infinitistic entity, namely the regress of instantiation relations, as opposed to a merely potential infinity of such relations, then it might seem as though Russell ought to have allowed a mode of combination to be an entity in the very proposition whose constituents are combined by that mode to form a unity. But this move is only open to someone who accepts that the regress thereby generated is innocent, and Russell, as we have seen, though he does not object to regresses as such, thinks that because the regress in question arises in the analysis of meaning, it is vicious. I have rejected that view, on the basis that the regress, though it indeed arises in the analysis of meaning, is 'metaphysical' rather than 'practical'. So Russell's position is consistent, but mistaken: given his Cantorian sympathies, he ought to have allowed a unifying mode of combination to be an entity, though not an ingredient, in the very proposition it unifies (the position paralleling the robust approach to the semantics of the logical copula). That is, the unifying mode of combination, while not an *ingredient* of the proposition in the sense of a component available alongside the other components in advance of the formation of the proposition, is nevertheless an *ex post facto part* of the proposition it unifies, available to be referred to by a word or structural feature of the corresponding sentence, and to be quantified over *in its capacity as unifier.*

In the light of the argument of this section and the previous one, we can say that there is nothing, deeply, distinguishing a sentence from a complex name. What distinguishes a complex name or sentence on the one hand from a mere list of names on the other is that in supplying semantics for the former categories of expression we will be obliged to provide suitable combinatorial principles that, when explicitly formulated, generate Bradley's regress. In the case of a mere list of names, on the other hand, this will not be so. Hence it turns out that a list in the relevant sense does not have the unity even of a complex name. That harmonizes nicely with one of the main conclusions of §79, which was that there is no conceptual resting place between sheer disunity on the one hand and full propositional unity on the other.

As we have seen, that a stretch of discourse is composed exclusively of items which we classify as names does not, as such, prevent its being treated by us as a sentence. Provided the concatenated names have congruence values that can be regarded as interlocking with one another appropriately—a condition that is trivially met by the sentences of Denyer's artificial language **S** and by the fully analysed sentences of the *Tractatus*, for in these cases all combinations of names are permitted—nothing stands in the way of our regarding those concatenated names as constituting a sentence *saying that* the corresponding referents engage with one another in the appropriate way. If we make this choice—if we promote a list to sentential status—its semantic analysis will change: its analysis will now generate Bradley's regress. That is *what it means* to classify a group of words as a sentence rather than as a list. That is what constitutes the moment of sentential unity.

88 Congruence, Functionality, and Propositional Unity

Congruence of subsentential expressions emerges in my account as supplying at best a necessary but not a sufficient condition for sentential unity. This is a point which I have insisted on throughout this study,[247] and which I have encapsulated in the claims that (i) the criterion for the unity of a sentence

---

[247] See esp. §§5, 62, 65, 74, 80.

cannot be merely *syntactic*—that there is a distinction between a list of words that are of the right syntactic form to constitute a sentence, and a sentence actually composed of those words—and, equivalently, that (ii) what unifies a proposition cannot be an *ingredient* of it, something that could be duplicated by a mere aggregate. Russell in effect makes this point in *Principles*, but he goes on to spoil the insight: 'A subject and an assertion, if simply juxtaposed, do not, it is true, constitute a proposition; but as soon as the assertion is actually asserted of the subject, the proposition reappears.'[248] But what does Russell here suppose effects the necessary asserting? If the account is intended to be a psychological or pragmatic one, we have seen that this gets matters back to front (§85); but if (as indeed the broader context suggests) the notion of assertion, as it figures in this passage, is really a disguised semantic notion, then the account is vacuous, for it then merely says that the unity of a proposition is constituted by whatever it is that connects the grammatical predicate of the corresponding sentence to its subject, which still leaves us in the dark about what actually does the connecting.

The same vacuity attaches to Wittgenstein's Tractarian account of declarative sentences as facts. As we have seen, Wittgenstein's view is that relation words have their semantic functions absorbed, on analysis, into the syntax of elementary sentences, the expressed relations being correspondingly taken up into the relations between the objects named by the sentences' component words, which, at the limit of analysis, are type-identical names of simple objects. But does this provide us with an illuminating account of the distinction between sentences and mere lists? Peter Carruthers is optimistic. In connection with *Tractatus*, §3.1432, he writes:

> If a sentence is a fact, with relations being expressed by relations between signs, then it is obvious why a mere string of names cannot constitute a sentence: if it *is* a *mere* string, then it does not contain any significant relations between signs, and so does not constitute—in the relevant sense—a fact.[249]

But this takes us back to the failed proposal of §5, according to which their divergent *syntactic analyses*, on the kind of conception of what that involves favoured by modern linguistic theory, might distinguish sentences from lists. The suggestion gets us precisely nowhere, for the question we are asking is: what *is* it for the relevant syntactic ('significant') relations to obtain between signs, constituting them as a sentence, say, rather than as a list. What is the 'relevant' sense in which a mere string of signs does not constitute a fact? Wittgenstein does not answer this question and Carruthers does not answer it

---

[248] [3], §81.   [249] Carruthers, p. 58.

on his behalf. Surely the point is simply that a list is not—or not necessarily, not just in virtue of being a list—structured *sententially*, and its referents *propositionally*. But that brings us round in a circle: what *is* it for a bunch of items to be structured sententially and their referents propositionally?

The distinction between a sentence and a mere list is, we can now say, supplied by the logical copula, that is, by a structural feature of the sentence. So far this assertion is, as I have emphasized, merely programmatic: what renders it a substantial, non-question-begging solution to our problem is that we can specify the logical copula as being that feature of a sentence which has, in the explained sense, an infinitistic reference—and Cantorians can add that it has an actually infinite referent. It is only if that logically copulative feature, with that kind of reference, is present at the sentential level that the corresponding entity at the level of reference is a proposition. Is the collection of (transliterated) Greek words *politikon ho anthrôpos*,[250] concatenated in that order, a declarative sentence, referring to a unified proposition—one which says that man is a political being—or is it just a list of words, referring severally to the properties of being political and manhood? Or rather—since that bunch of words, taken just as such, may be either a sentence or a list—what *is* it for it to be one of these rather than the other? Which it is depends on its semantic analysis: if, and only if, we discern the presence within these words of a logical copula, whose semantic analysis generates Bradley's regress, do the words stick together in the right way to say that man is a political being. Discerning the presence of that feature *is* to treat these symbols as forming a complex linguistic item which refers to a proposition, and vice versa. Whether, in any actual case, we want to discern the presence of that feature will, as we have noted (§85), be dependent on contextual factors and in particular on the intention with which the words in question are advanced; but what discerning that feature *involves* is a semantic, not a pragmatic, matter. And, as we have also seen and as this example well illustrates, the semantic property of collections of linguistic items in virtue of which they constitute sentences—the presence of the logical copula—need not find any explicit symbolic representation in the sentence itself: indeed, sentences may, unlike our example but like the sentences of **S** and fully analysed Tractarian sentences, even be composed entirely of symbols of exactly the same syntactic type.[251]

I have said that there need be no syntactic difference between a sentence and a list, in the sense that sentence and list may share a superficial linguistic form, and that what makes the difference is how we differentiate between their respective semantical properties. In characterizing the semantics of a

[250] Aristotle, *EN* 1097b11.   [251] Cf. Bell [1], pp. 130–1.

sentence, we discern the presence of a crucial structural feature, namely the logical copula with its infinitistic reference or referent. The logical copula, as I have stressed, is not a lexical or morphological component of the sentence; correspondingly, its infinitistic reference or referent is not an *ingredient* of the proposition in the sense identified earlier (§65): that is, it is not an antecedently available component which, when combined with other antecedently available components according to a recipe, automatically yields a proposition. At best that reference or referent may be discerned as an *ex post facto* part of the proposition in the contrasting sense: that is, it is a feature essentially isolated in thought from the unified proposition. With this in mind, it seems reasonable to identify the reference or referent of the logical copula, in the first instance,[252] with the unifying function that I introduced in §19 as taking (in the simple case) an object and a concept as arguments, and delivering a Russellian proposition as value. It was suggested there that nothing prevents us from regarding Russellian propositions both as values of appropriate unifying functions and as wholes with objects and concepts as parts. I implied that the unifying function might itself be treated as a part of the Russellian proposition which is its value for given arguments, and then in §65 I suggested that, provided we distinguish between *ex post facto* parts abstracted from wholes, on the one hand, and antecedently available ingredients, on the other, it is attractive and plausible to construe the unifying function as an *ex post facto* part abstracted from the proposition it unifies, though not as an ingredient of it.

One advantage of adopting the functional approach is that it helps us deal with the general case of propositional unity. In the general case, it will be recalled, we said (§18) that Russellian propositions are to be identified with the objects, simple concepts or properties, and structures of composition given (referred to) by the phrase markers which specify how the governing sentence is built up—that is, they are to be identified with what I called phrase markers *in re*. These phrase markers *in re* may be thought of in functional terms: we may conceive dominating (non-terminal) nodes, labelled in accordance with so-called projection rules,[253] as representing the value of a unifying function (§19) applied to the objects (including, of course, properties, relations, and the functions introduced by connectives) located at their daughter nodes, taken as arguments.[254] Insofar as we have to do with a simple monadic predication like 'Socrates is wise', we may think of the procedure as being just so far indeterminate between Fregean and anti-Fregean ways of selecting one of the daughter nodes to discharge the unifying function and its sister node that of the

---

[252] I shall explain this proviso shortly.   [253] Cf. Kimball, pp. 82, 119–20.
[254] See here Carpenter, p. 43; van Heijenoort [2], pp. 99–100; King [5], pp. 34, 47–8.

argument to that function. (In the 'principles and parameters' tradition only binary branching is permitted.[255]) Actually, there is more than one way to construct the details of the functionality of Russellian propositions in the general case: viewing phrase markers as trees, we may interpret their referents as functions from finite sequences of natural numbers to the objects designated by expressions located at the nodes.[256] So long as the construction proceeds in function–argument terms, the precise details do not matter.

I have affirmed more than once in this study (§§16, 33, 79) that, while Russellian propositions may be identified with the functional structures of appropriate phrase markers *in re*, the sets of ordered *n*-tuples with which, for technical purposes, functions are often identified, are not to be regarded as better than proxies, useful for certain purposes, of Russellian propositions. It is important to be clear that this latter identification *is* a matter of technical convenience, not of metaphysical truth:[257] the reality of the situation is that the *original* unity of a function with its argument is not a set-theoretical unity, and so is not identical with, but merely proxied by, the unity of the set constituting the graph of the function. Now we noted earlier in this chapter (§79) that sets have an essentially functional or propositional unity: they are conceptually posterior to functions and propositions. If not—if either the unity of a function with its argument(s) or the unity of a proposition were of an essentially set-theoretical nature—we would be led into a tight circle connecting the unities of propositions, functions with their arguments, and sets. The circle seems to me to be broken, however, at the point of the alleged dependence of propositional or function–argument unity on set-theoretical unity: there is no such dependence. Rather, set-theoretical unity depends *asymmetrically* on functional and propositional unity. These two latter forms of unity, however, *are* connected by a tight circle. For unlike Frege and the Russell of *Principles* (recall §33 above), both of whom held (though in opposite senses) that an asymmetric relation of dependence connects function–argument unity and propositional unity, I take these unities to be logically and ontologically coeval and interdependent.[258] There is, then, no bar from the direction of the metaphysics of unity to construing Russellian propositions both as values of appropriate unifying functions applied to one or more objects (including objects that are themselves functions), and as wholes made up of those functions and arguments as *ex post facto* parts abstracted from the proposition, so long as we do not conceive of this identification in a reductive spirit.

[255] Cook and Newson, p. 113.   [256] See here again van Heijenoort [2], p. 100.
[257] Cf. Stenius [2], p. 185; Vallicella [2], p. 253; B. Linsky [2], pp. 50–1, 136–7.
[258] Cf. Sainsbury [3], pp. 145–6.

I have been assuming so far in this discussion, as I assumed in §18, that the phrase marker *in re* with which we identify a given proposition is unique. But there is no difficulty in relaxing this assumption to allow for several distinct phrase markers, perhaps keyed to different levels of syntactic analysis in respect of the relevant sentence, to correspond to a single proposition. One could, for instance, identify a proposition with what we might call a transformational series *in re*, that is, with a series of phrase markers *in re* linked by appropriate transformations. Transformational series *in re* could then themselves be reconstructed in functional terms, namely as functions from phrase markers *in re* to (functions from phrase markers *in re* to (. . . to phrase markers *in re*)).[259] Alternatively, if one believes in the existence of distinct levels of syntactic analysis, one might identify propositions with phrase markers *in re* drawn exclusively from a privileged stage of syntactic analysis, say D-Structure or LF. Now it may be that, depending on how rigorously intensional we wish our individuation of propositions to be, we shall want to identify different phrase markers *in re* with one and the same proposition. In this connection, recall that I have both suggested that propositions should be individuated hyperintensionally (§16) and speculated that, although differently structured sentences cannot normally be allowed to express the same Thought, they may exceptionally be permitted to do so, and in these atypical cases they will (a fortiori) refer to the same Russellian proposition (§67). Do these conditions clash?

I see no strict clash between them, regardless which of the two approaches outlined in the previous paragraph we select. On the first approach, differently structured sentences may be associated with the same transformational series *in re*, while on the second approach they may be associated with the same phrase marker *in re* at a given level of syntactic analysis. Of course, since phrase markers *in re* (and hence transformational series *in re*) can be nothing but ontological precipitates of linguistic phrase markers (linguistic transformational series)—that is, items of symbolic language—it would not be plausible to suggest that the two might come apart structurally in respect of any given sentence and the proposition it refers to. There can be no question of anything other than an isomorphism between linguistic phrase markers and phrase markers *in re*. In that case, given that we wish to make room for many–one relations between sentences and propositions, we should admit the possibility that more than one phrase marker *in re* (transformational series *in re*) can be identified with a given proposition, and an obvious way to amend the identity-conditions of propositions as so far expounded would be to identify a proposition with an equivalence class of phrase markers *in re* (transformational series *in re*) collected by an appropriate

[259] Cf. Chomsky [2], pp. 12, 63–6; [3], pp. 80–1; Partee *et al.*, p. 556.

relation of synonymy at the level of the sentence. If we make this identification, there is no need to resile from our insistence that propositional unity is not, as such, a matter of set-theoretical unity. The unity of a proposition, we might say, is the unity of an *arbitrary member* of its associated equivalence class, and that member is unified by virtue of the unity of its function–argument structure. Of course, as we have said (§79), the unity of a set *is* the unity of a proposition; but the relevant proposition is the one specifying that set's membership, a proposition that will not, in general, be identical with any member of the set in question. The unity of a set is the unity of a proposition; but it does not follow, and it is not in general true, that the unity of a proposition is the unity of a set.

Stepping back now from these details, and presuming the correctness of the strategy of construing Russellian propositions in functional terms, we should expect our general account of functional unity to replicate in its essentials what we have said so far by way of accounting for propositional unity in the special case of sentences of the basic form $R^n(a_1, \ldots, a_n)$. And it seems to me that this is in fact the case. In moves parallel to ones made when we were considering simple monadic and polyadic predications, we can ask and answer the question: what *unites* the functions in question with their arguments? For analysing a sentence as referring to a Russellian proposition that is in turn construed as the value of an appropriate unifying function applied to appropriate arguments does not give us an account of the unity of the proposition unless we have a semantical guarantee that the function *really is applied* to the arguments[260]—not unless, in other words, we have a semantical guarantee that we do not merely encounter, at the referential level, an aggregate consisting of the function and its arguments as discrete entities, but are indeed presented with a function *of* the arguments. What makes it the case that we do not have to do with a mere aggregate of unconnected objects at the referential level—that we really do have a function ϕ^n, say, being applied to arguments $a_1 \ldots a_n$—is that we can discern the tacit presence of another function χ^{n+1}, whose job is precisely to apply ϕ^n to $a_1 \ldots a_n$. It is important to be clear that χ does not *compose* with ϕ^n in the standard set-theoretical sense; it takes ϕ^n and $a_1 \ldots a_n$ as its arguments, and *applies* the one to the other. That is, we have to do not with

$$\chi^1(\phi^n(a_1 \ldots a_n)),$$

but rather with

$$\chi^{n+1}(<\phi^n, a_1 \ldots a_n>),$$

where ϕ^n here represents the function ϕ^n *in extenso* (the graph of the function).

---

[260] Cf. MacBride [4], p. 607.

The function $\chi^{n+1}(<\phi^n, a_1 \ldots a_n>)$ is stipulated to have the same value as $\phi^n(a_1 \ldots a_n)$.[261] But we can ask the same question concerning its unity as was raised in connection with the simple function $\phi^n(a_1 \ldots a_n)$. Priest remarks that 'a mathematician might say that o is the *application* of the function sin to π: $Ap(\sin, \pi)$. But this does not solve the problem [of unity]: it just transfers it to this new functional expression'.[262] Similarly, a linguist in the Montague tradition might say that a truth-value is (the result of) the *application* of the function $\lambda x(x$ is wise) to the entity Socrates taken as argument.[263] And here, too, it will be said that appeal to an application function does not solve the problem of the unity of the function given by the lambda abstract with its argument, but raises that problem afresh for the specified application and *its* arguments. For, we might ask in the spirit of Priest's remark, what makes it the case that

$$\chi^{n+1}(<\phi^n, a_1 \ldots a_n>)$$

is a unity and not a mere aggregate of separate entities? But the answer now comes pat: we can construct another function ψ^{n+2} whose job is to apply χ^{n+1} to its arguments, ϕ^n and $a_1 \ldots a_n$. And so on, into a version of the familiar regress. Once again, I hope it is obvious that I am not making a plea for a revised notational practice, in which we attempt to give symbolic representation to all these application functions: the point is rather that these application functions must be considered to be already tacitly operative in our semantics for an expression like '$\phi^n(a_1 \ldots a_n)$'. That is just what entitles us to treat—more essentially, that is what it *is* for us to treat—the function designated by the expression '$\phi^n(a_1 \ldots a_n)$'—and derivatively that symbol itself—as a unity. If the reference or referent of the logical copula is, in the first instance, the unifying function of a phrase marker *in re* (or a transformational series *in re*), its ultimate reference or referent comprises the stages of the function-application regress, so that it is its generation of the function-application regress which is what the unity of the proposition, in the general case, consists in.

Earlier in this section I argued that, while there is a tight circle connecting propositional unity and the unity of a function with its arguments—neither of these unities being logically or ontologically prior to the other—the unity of a set, by contrast, is asymmetrically dependent on propositional or function–argument unity. The reader will recall that the basis of the asymmetry was the claim that, while functions may be proxied by sets, they are not literally identical with sets. It would be a good idea to allow for the possibility that this

---

[261] Cf. Frege [10], I, §34; von Kutschera [1], p. 104; Thomason, intro. to Montague, pp. 7, 24–5; Weiner [2], p. 338.
[262] [1], p. 181 n. 4.   [263] Cf. Simons [9], pp. 151–2.

claim is mistaken, because I do not think that this possibility carries any serious threat to the core of my account of unity. An objector to the claim might focus on the fact that I have been operating with the notion of a wholly arbitrary function (§79). Perhaps it will be said that such functions *must* be identical with—not merely proxied by—sets: for to say that functions may be wholly arbitrary is surely to say that they cannot, in general, be given intensionally (that is, by some formula); but then how can we conceive their identity to be constituted, if not extensionally by sets of ordered pairs? I agree, of course, that functions cannot, in general, be specified by a formula, if by that we mean an antecedently given formula in the sense of §1, that is, a finitely long formula involving reference only to purely general, lawlike concepts. An arbitrary function can be specified by a formula if we allow the formula in question to be infinitely long and do not require it to be antecedently given in the defined sense. But to specify a function in that way would not be to specify it intensionally within the meaning of the objection; and the objector would simply contend that such a specification was itself tantamount to a set-theoretical one.

I am not going to attempt to adjudicate this point here, but shall just note that, if the objector is right that function–argument and propositional unity are, at bottom, set-theoretical in nature, my account of propositional unity would have to be altered in its details but would not thereby be either impaired or compromised in its spirit. We would be led into the tight circle connecting the three types of unity—set-theoretical, propositional, and function–argument—that I earlier tried to avoid; but I tried to avoid that circularity simply because I do not believe it to obtain, not because I regard it as being any more vicious, if it genuinely arose, than the acknowledged circularity connecting propositional and function–argument unity. If it did obtain, then in effect the regress I mentioned in §79, in which sets and their characteristic functions iterate alternately into the transfinite, would turn out to be a regress comprising sets at each stage. If we started, to take a simple example, with the set

$$\{a, b, c\},$$

its characteristic function would be identified with (not merely proxied by) the set

$$\{<a, 1>, <b, 1>, <c, 1>, <d, 0>, <e, 0>, \ldots\},$$

which itself would generate, as its characteristic function, the set

$$\{<<a, 1>, 1>, \ldots, <<d, 0>, 1>, \ldots, <<a, 0>, 0>, \ldots, \\ <<d, 1>, 0>, \ldots\},$$

which in turn would generate, as *its* characteristic function, the set

$$\{<<<a, 1>, 1>, 1>, \ldots, <<<a, 0>, 0>, 1>, \ldots, <<<d, 1>, 1>, 0>, \ldots\},$$

and so on. This regress is closely related to Bradley's regress, and invites the same defence of its innocence and constitutive status as I have made in connection with Bradley's instantiation regress or the functional-application regress: that is, the unity of the initial set, $\{a, b, c\}$, would be constituted by its generating just that regress. Indeed, if the function−argument unity with which I am identifying propositional unity, in the general case, just *is* a set-theoretical unity, then this simple regress gives us an inkling of the form that, ultimately, Bradley's regress will take in the propositional case.

We are nearly at the end of the story, and this is a good place to summarize my systematic account of unity. A declarative sentence, which is constitutively capable of being true or false, is unified just if it refers to a unified proposition. It refers to a unified proposition just if it contains a logical copula as a structural feature. Here I note in passing that containing a logical copula is compatible with a sentence's exhibiting no name−verb or grammatical subject−predicate asymmetry: for it is possible to construct sentences which are composed exclusively of names, and indeed of type-identical names. In the case of simple predications of the form $R^n(a_1, \ldots, a_n)$, specification of the reference or (as I prefer) referent of the logical copula generates Bradley's regress, so that the analysis of propositional unity is inherently, but innocently, regressive. The stages of the regress constitute necessary and sufficient conditions of proposi-tional unity, and so constitute the unity of the original proposition; the regress does not, as has been traditionally supposed, undermine or unpick that unity. In the general case we may think of the reference or referent of the logical copula as, in the first instance, a unifying *function* that is applied to the proposition's other components as its *arguments*. The analysis of that operation of functional application draws down a regress that is in all relevant respects the same as Bradley's regress, and that serves as the ultimate reference or referent of the logical copula. It is its generation of the functional-application regress which is what the unity of a proposition, in the general case, consists in.

What, then, to recur to our governing question, is the distinction between a sentence and a 'mere list' of words, and between a proposition and a 'mere aggregate' of word-meanings? A mere list may—perhaps must—be inherently ordered, but even so it generates as a rule no such regress at the level of reference as the sentence generates: at the level of reference there may simply be nothing organizing the referents of the words in a list—no relation of instantiation, no relation of configuration, in general no relation of functional application. The elements of a genuine 'mere aggregate' are radically unrelated to one another. Conversely, if the elements of an aggregate at the level of reference are configured with (related to) one another in any way at all—that is, if they compose any kind of whole (no matter how unnaturally or arbitrarily assembled) constituting the value of a function applied to its parts as arguments, it being understood that the function may itself be one of those parts—then the elements of such an aggregate are indeed propositionally unified. Correlatively, linguistic structures which fall grammatically short of full sentential status but which, on analysis, generate the relevant regress turn out, upon examination, to be deeply sentential in form and their referents to be deeply propositional. Sentences may be mimicked by equiform lists: what it is for a group of words to compose (or be regarded as composing) a sentence as opposed to a list is for it to generate (or be regarded as generating) the relevant structural regress at the level of the expressed proposition.

89 Davidson on Predication

Before concluding, I should like to say something about the account of the unity of the proposition offered by Davidson in his posthumously published book *Truth and Predication*. Davidson thinks that Tarski's method for defining truth predicates solves what he calls 'the problem of predication': according to this method an account is given 'of how each predicate in a language contributes to the truth-conditions of the sentences in which it occurs'.[264] Davidson concedes that the account does not supply a 'general explanation of predication', but he adds:

What does emerge is a *method* for specifying the role of each and every predicate in a specific language; this role is given by a non-recursive axiom which says under what conditions it is true of any number of entities taken in the order in which its blanks occur. What more can we demand? I think the history of the subject has demonstrated that more would be less.[265]

And in this last sentence Davidson principally has in mind the failure of previous accounts to avoid Bradley's regress. Davidson's proposal, though in one way an unsurprising turn given the amount of philosophical capital he has invested over the years in the project of applying Tarski's formal work to natural languages, is, considered objectively, hard to make sense of as a solution to the problem of unity. Surely it is obvious that, as Wiggins remarks, 'from

---

[264] [2], p. 161. Sainsbury concurs: [3], pp. 147–8; [5], p. 61.   [265] [2], p. 161.

a standing start, we cannot . . . explain in [Tarskian] terms what distinguishes a sentence from a mere list'.[266] In his seminal paper 'The Concept of Truth in Formalized Languages' Tarski exploits the idea that, given a universe of discourse, predicates are true of, or satisfied by, objects in that universe, supplementing this for formal purposes by the technical trick of defining the satisfaction relation in question to obtain between predicates and infinite sequences of objects—infinite because a language may, in principle, contain predicates of arbitrary adicity. But, although Tarski himself does not put the matter in this way, it does not falsify his method to say that he identifies the *referent* of a predicate with a *function* from infinite sequences of objects to truth-values. Now that is, to all intents and purposes, Frege's story: the difference is simply that Tarski specifies more complicated (and technically more useful) entities to serve as *arguments* to the functions in question. But that merely technical difference makes no odds as far as the problem of unity is concerned; and we have seen that merely assimilating the referents of predicates to functions does *not* solve the problem of unity, for it does not tell us what *unites* function and argument, which is one way of stating what the problem of the unity of the proposition *is*.

Davidson expressly rejects Frege's functional account of unity,[267] which makes his adoption of Tarski's equally functional account (as it in effect is) puzzling. The solution to this exegetical problem seems to lie in the fact that Davidson takes Tarski's method—by contrast with Frege's—to be *nominalistic* in spirit:[268] it is Frege's casting of suitable functions as the *referents* of predicates that spoils the prospects for his delivering a satisfactory explanation of unity:

To say that predicates are functional expressions, and are therefore incomplete or unsaturated, and that what they refer to is similarly full of holes or spaces waiting to be filled in, does not help: entities are entities, whatever we call them.[269]

I have agreed with that. But now, in any sense in which Frege's concepts—functions from objects to truth-values—are entities, and so unfit (in Davidson's view) to help solve the problem of unity, in just the same sense Tarski's functions from infinite sequences of objects to truth-values are entities, and so ought to be equally unserviceable in an account of propositional unity. A nominalistic reading of Tarski's strategy is no more accurate than such a reading of Frege's would be, and Tarski's strategy does not differ from Frege's on what is for us the essential point: namely, insofar as it can be construed

[266] [4], p. 13.   [267] [2], p. 139.   [268] Cf. Siderits [3], p. 59; Sainsbury [3], pp. 147–8.
[269] [2], p. 156. Cf. [2], p. 145; C. Parsons's gloss, ibid., p. 152 n. 14.

as offering a solution to the unity problem, what Tarski's account offers, like Frege's, is an 'ingredient' solution—an attempt to unify the proposition by adding an antecedently available emulsifying ingredient. But any such account must fail, as we have said, because it will always be possible to produce a mere list that duplicates the recipe.

In an earlier part of his book, Davidson ascribes Tarski's purportedly revolutionary move—the supposed nominalistic adaptation of Frege—to Quine, and he writes, in the context of a discussion of Bradley's regress, that

Quine, alone among those I have discussed, escapes the usual regress by simply denying that predicates indicate, refer to, or are to be explained by their association with some simple entity, such as a property, quality, universal, or attribute. Quine relates predicates to the things of which they can be predicated—hence his phrase 'true of': predicates are *true of* each and every thing (or pair or triple, etc., of things) of which the predicate can be truly predicated. This cannot be called a full account of the role of predicates. Its merit is negative: it does not invite a regress.[270]

But if Quine's account cannot be called 'a full account of the role of predicates', how is it that Tarski's account, which is in all relevant respects the same, the differences being of a merely technical nature, does count as one? The fatal mistake which has to be avoided is, so Davidson thinks, the association of predicates with an entity: why does Tarski's account not effect just that association? Or indeed Quine's: for Quine sets up a semantic association, namely the relation *being true of*, between predicates and the objects in their extensions; but extensions are themselves objects. However he styles the matter, Quine is, as we observed in §7, in effect an adherent of the *suppositio* school of thinking about reference, according to which the extension of a predicate *is* its referent. Predicates are true of objects: you do not avoid ascribing reference to predicates by refusing to say anything more than that about their semantics. On the contrary, what you have said, in saying that predicates are true of objects, *becomes* your account of predicate reference.

A further difficulty with Davidson's account is revealed by the observation that his nominalistic reading of Tarski conflicts with his erstwhile insistence on the theoretical status of the reference relation.[271] That policy is still adhered to in *Truth and Predication*, but only patchily, for Davidson there evinces a contrary tendency to think that we have a pre-theoretical grasp of the reference relation in the case of the relation between name and bearer. What else can

[270] [2], p. 114. Cf. Quine [2], p. 21; [3], §§19–22; [5], p. 84; [9], §46; MacBride [6], pp. 428–9.
[271] See above Ch. 4 n. 156; and my [15], ch. 6, §2.

explain his failure to see that, so far from *avoiding* referents for predicates, Tarski and Quine simply give us *alternative candidates* for that referential status? But for an adherent of the theoretical status of the referential relation, the business of specifying which objects a given predicate is true of—in fact, of course, as we saw in Chapter 2, we need a more sophisticated account than Davidson, following Tarski and Quine, suggests, one which associates not sheer objects (or sequences of objects) with predicates (or concept-expressions) as their referents, but Carnapian intensions—is not essentially different from what Davidson, regrettably following Dummett in this matter, seems to regard as a prototypical case of specifying a referent, namely the associating of a proper name with its bearer. As we have already said (§53), the name–bearer relation is just one referential relation among others: it is not a prototype. I agree with Davidson that there is a limit to what we can demand from a theory of predication: in particular, I have conceded that my account of the unity of the proposition appeals to, but does not give a reductive analysis of, the relation of instantiation—and the same would apply to my deployment in the general case of the notion of functional application. I am unembarrassed by that feature of my account, because I strongly suspect that, were we to attempt an analysis of the instantiation relation or of the notion of functional application going beyond what I have attempted here, and certainly if we were to attempt a *reductive* analysis, we would indeed find that more was less. But I think that there is more to be had than Davidson allows, and that the regress which he, following Russell and a long line of thinkers, is so anxious to avoid does give us insight into what unifies the proposition.

90 Epilogue: The Limits of Language

In the *Tractatus* Wittgenstein states that it is essential to sentences that they can communicate a new sense with old words.[272] It is this thought which is fundamental to the project of constructing compositional theories of meaning for natural languages, for that project holds out the hope of explaining the evident compossibility of the creativity of a language (its power to generate an infinity of theorems) with its learnability (which requires a finite base). I argued in §73 that in employing a schema like '$R^n(x_1 \ldots x_n)$' to convey the logical form of the elementary sentence Wittgenstein faces a dilemma

---

[272] [1], §§4.027–4.03.

between construing the functional expression as a name—in which case we are launched on Bradley's regress—or treating it as a symbol expressing the logical form of the sentence—in which case we are trying to say what, strictly speaking, can only be shown. The point concerned the elementary sentences of the *Tractatus*, but it may be generalized in a way that casts further light on the conclusions we have reached about the logical copula. For the (unannotated) logical copula, as the *ex officio* unifier of the sentence, is thereby also the bearer of the sentence's logical form: it is that in virtue of which the string of words of which it is a semantically significant feature constitutes a sentence at all. Wittgenstein further connects the capacity of old words to express a new sense with the fact that the proposition is the logical picture of what it represents, that is to say, that it has logical form.[273] That suggests the following reflection, which I offer in closing this study.

The reason why the schema '$R^n(x_1 \ldots x_n)$' is (on the second horn of the dilemma) trying to say what can only be shown is precisely that (on the first horn of the dilemma) it is trying to say what cannot *finitely* be said. The attempt to express logical form—that in virtue of which old words can express a new sense—precipitates Bradley's regress. In other words, Bradley's regress, which tries to say in infinite compass what cannot finitely be said—*because* it is trying to convey logical form—underwrites not merely the unity of the proposition, but also the power of old words to express a new sense. We may fairly say, then, that the availability of the regress, so far from being vicious, is a necessary condition of the constitution of language.

The inability of language to get at the conditions of its own application without falling into regress is illuminated by a remark which Wittgenstein made in 1931, and which clearly harks back to the metaphysical outlook of the *Tractatus*:

The limit of language is shown in the impossibility of describing the fact that corresponds to a sentence (is its translation), without simply repeating the sentence. (We have here to do with the Kantian solution of the problem of philosophy.)[274]

Of course, in one sense the remark does not fit what I have said: for corresponding to a declarative sentence we have not merely one proposition, but an infinity of propositions—just the ones generated by Bradley's regress. (And these propositions do not have to be true, as Wittgenstein implies, but may be false—as they will be if the governing sentence is false.) Even so, the spirit of the remark is congenial to me. For there is obviously a good sense in which generating the propositions of Bradley's regress gets us no

---

[273] [1], §4.03.   [274] [8], p. 10.

further—gets us no nearer the 'world', in the philosophically contentious use of that word from which Wittgenstein, by appeal to Kant, in effect wishes to draw us away: the world thought of as brutely anterior to language—than does the original proposition. What for Wittgenstein in effect constitutes a limit of language—our inability to reach the 'world', in that philosophically contentious sense, no matter how far into the regress we proceed—I have suggested is a necessary condition of language's possibility. And if the generation of Bradley's regress is thus implicated in the metaphysical origin of language, linguistic idealism will tell us that it also sustains the very existence of the world in the philosophically hygienic sense of that word—the totality of (true and false) propositions at the level of reference. Bradley's regress cannot give us the 'world'; but it can and does give us the world.

References

Classical and late-antique authors are cited in the standard way and are for the most part not included in this list.

Aarsleff, H., [1] *The Study of Language in England 1780–1860* (London: Athlone, 1983).

―― [2] 'Philosophy of Language', in K. Haakonssen (ed.), *The Cambridge History of Eighteenth-Century Philosophy* (Cambridge: CUP, 2006), 451–95.

Abelard, P., [1] *Logica 'Ingredientibus'*, in B. Geyer (ed.), *Peter Abaelards Philosophische Schriften* (Münster: Aschendorff, 1919).

―― [2] *Dialectica*, ed. L. M. de Rijk, 2nd edn. (Assen: Van Gorcum, 1970).

Adams, M. M., *William Ockham* (Notre Dame, Ind.: University of Notre Dame, 1987).

Almog, J., 'Logic and the World', in J. Almog, J. Perry, and H. Wettstein (eds.), *Themes from Kaplan* (Oxford: OUP, 1989), 43–65.

Anderson, J., *Studies in Empirical Philosophy* (Sydney: Angus & Robertson, 1963).

André de Neufchâteau, *In Primum Librum Sententiarum* (Paris: Jean Granjon, 1514).

Angelelli, I., [1] *Gottlob Frege and Traditional Philosophy* (Dordrecht: Reidel, 1967).

―― [2] 'Friends and Opponents of the Substitutivity of Identicals in the History of Logic', in M. Schirn (ed.), *Studien zu Frege*, ii (Stuttgart: Frommann-Holzboog, 1976), 141–66.

―― [3] 'Predication Theory: Classical vs. Modern', in H. Hochberg and K. Mulligan (eds.), *Relations and Predicates* (Frankfurt and Lancaster: Ontos, 2004), 55–80.

Anscombe, G. E. M., [1] *An Introduction to Wittgenstein's Tractatus* (London: Hutchinson, 1959).

―― [2] 'Mr Copi on Objects, Properties, and Relations in the *Tractatus*', in I. Copi and R. Beard (eds.), *Essays on Wittgenstein's Tractatus* (London: Routledge, 1966), 187.

Aquinas, T., [1] *Summa Theologica*, i (Rome: Forzani, 1894).

―― [2] *De Veritate*, in *Quaestiones Disputatae et Quaestiones Duodecim Quodlibetales* (Rome and Turin: Marietti, 1942).

Armstrong, D., [1] *A Theory of Universals*, 2 vols. (Cambridge: CUP, 1978).

―― [2] *Universals: An Opinionated Introduction* (Boulder, Colo.: Westview, 1989).

―― [3] 'Classes are States of Affairs', *Mind* 100 (1991), 189–200.

―― [4] 'Against "Ostrich" Nominalism: A Reply to Michael Devitt', in D. H. Mellor and A. Oliver (eds.), *Properties* (Oxford: OUP, 1997), 101–11.

―― [5] *A World of States of Affairs* (Cambridge: CUP, 1997).

―― [6] 'Particulars Have their Properties of Necessity', in P. Strawson and A. Chakrabarti (eds.), *Universals, Concepts, and Qualities: New Essays on the Meaning of Predicates* (Aldershot: Ashgate, 2006), 239–47.

Arnauld, A., and Lancelot, C., *Grammaire générale et raisonnée* (Paris: Allia, 1997).

Arnauld A., and Nicole, P., [1] *La Logique ou l'art de penser* (Paris: Éditions Gallimard, 1992).

——[2] *Logic or the Art of Thinking*, ed. J. V. Buroker (Cambridge: CUP, 1996).

Arnold, E., 'Zur Geschichte der Suppositionstheorie', *Symposion Jahrbuch für Philosophie* 3 (1952), 1–134.

Ashworth, E. J., [1] *Language and Logic in the Post-Medieval Period* (Dordrecht: Reidel, 1974).

——[2] *Studies in Post-Medieval Semantics* (London: Variorum, 1985).

Austin, J. L., [1] *How to Do Things with Words* (Oxford: OUP, 1975).

——[2] *Philosophical Papers*, 3rd edn. (Oxford: Clarendon, 1979).

Avicenna (Ibn Sina), *Avicenna Latinus: Liber de Philosophia Prima sive Scientia Divina*, i–iv, ed. S. van Riet (Leiden and Louvain: Brill and Peeters, 1977).

Bäck, A., *Aristotle's Theory of Predication* (Leiden: Brill, 2000).

Baldwin, T., [1] 'Interpretation of Quantifiers', *Mind* 88 (1979), 215–40.

——[2] 'The Identity Theory of Truth', *Mind* 100 (1991), 35–52.

Barwise, J., and Etchemendy, J., *The Liar: An Essay on Truth and Circularity* (Oxford: OUP, 1987).

Baylis, C., 'Universals, Communicable Knowledge, and Metaphysics', in M. Loux (ed.), *Universals and Particulars* (New York: Doubleday, 1970), 50–61.

Bealer, G., [1] *Quality and Concept* (Oxford: Clarendon, 1982).

——[2] 'On the Identification of Properties and Propositional Functions', *Linguistics and Philosophy* 12 (1989), 1–14.

——[3] 'Universals', *Journal of Philosophy* 90 (1993), 5–32.

——[4] 'A Solution to Frege's Puzzle', *Philosophical Perspectives* 7 (1993), 17–60.

——[5] 'Propositions', *Mind* 107 (1998), 1–32.

Beaney, M., 'Russell and Frege', in N. Griffin (ed.), *The Cambridge Companion to Bertrand Russell* (Cambridge: CUP, 2003), 128–70.

Beckmann, J. P., *Die Relationen der Identität und Gleichheit nach Johannes Duns Scotus* (Bonn: Bouvier, 1967).

Bell, D., [1] *Frege's Theory of Judgement* (Oxford: Clarendon, 1979).

——[2] 'On the Translation of Frege's *Bedeutung*', *Analysis* 40 (1980), 191–5.

——[3] 'Reference and Sense: an Epitome', in C. Wright (ed.), *Frege: Tradition and Influence* (Oxford: Blackwell, 1984), 184–8.

——[4] 'Thoughts', *Notre Dame Journal of Formal Logic* 28 (1987), 36–50.

——[5] 'The Formation of Concepts and the Structure of Thoughts', *Philosophy and Phenomenological Research* 56 (1996), 583–96.

Benacerraf, P., 'What Numbers Could Not Be', *Philosophical Review* 74 (1965), 47–73.

Bentham, J., *Essay on Language*, in *The Works of Jeremy Bentham*, ed. J. Bowring, viii (Edinburgh: W. Tait, 1843), 294–338.

Berg, J., 'Bolzano's Contribution to Logic and Philosophy of Mathematics', in R. Gandy and M. Hyland (eds.), *Logic Colloquium 76* (Amsterdam: North Holland, 1977), 147–71.

Bergmann, G., [1] 'Propositional Functions', *Analysis* 17 (1956), 43–8.

_____ [2] *Logic and Reality* (Madison: University of Wisconsin, 1964).

Berkeley, B., *The Analyst*, in *The Works of George Berkeley*, iii, ed. G. Sampson (London: Bell, 1898).

Bermúdez, J. L., 'Frege on Thoughts and their Structure', *Philosophiegeschichte und logische Analyse* 4 (2001), 87–105.

Bernays, P., and Schönfinkel, M., 'Zum Entscheidungsproblem der mathematischen Logik', *Mathematische Annalen* 99 (1928), 342–72.

Black, M., [1] 'Russell's Philosophy of Language', in his *Language and Philosophy* (Ithaca, NY: Cornell University Press, 1949), 109–38.

_____ [2] 'Frege on Functions', in E. D. Klemke (ed.), *Essays on Frege* (Chicago: University of Illinois, 1968), 223–48.

_____ [3] 'The Elusiveness of Sets', *Review of Metaphysics* 24 (1971), 614–36.

Boethius, A. M. S., [1] *In Librum Aristotelis Peri Hermeneias*, editio secunda, ed. C. Meiser (Leipzig: Teubner, 1880).

_____ [2] *De Differentiis Topicis*, in *Patrologia Latina*, 64, ed. J. P. Migne (Paris: Garnier, 1891), 1174–1218.

Bolzano, B., [1] *Paradoxien des Unendlichen* (Leipzig: Reclam, 1851; repr. Darmstadt: Wissenschaftliche Buchgesellschaft, 1964).

_____ [2] *Wissenschaftslehre*, 4 vols., ed. W. Schultz (Leipzig: Felix Meiner, 1929–31; repr. Aalen: Scientia, 1981).

Bonevac, D., 'Quantity and Quantification', *Noûs* 19 (1985), 229–47.

Boole, G., *An Investigation of the Laws of Thought*, ed. J. Corcoran (Amherst, Mass.: Prometheus, 2003).

Boolos, G., *Logic, Logic, and Logic*, ed. R. Jeffrey (Cambridge, Mass.: Harvard University Press, 1998).

_____ and Jeffrey, R., *Computability and Logic*, 3rd edn. (Cambridge: CUP, 1989).

Bostock, D., [1] *Logic and Arithmetic: Natural Numbers* (Oxford: Clarendon, 1974).

_____ [2] *Intermediate Logic* (Oxford: Clarendon, 1997).

Bradley, F. H., [1] *Essays on Truth and Reality* (Oxford: Clarendon, 1914).

_____ [2] *Appearance and Reality*, 2nd edn. (Oxford: Clarendon, 1930).

_____ [3] 'Relations', in *Collected Essays*, ii (Oxford: Clarendon, 1935), 628–76.

Bradley, M. C., [1] 'On the Alleged Need for Nonsense', *Australasian Journal of Philosophy* 56 (1978), 203–18.

_____ [2] 'Geach and Strawson on Negating Names', *Philosophical Quarterly* 36 (1986), 16–28.

Brandom, R., [1] 'Frege's Technical Concepts: Some Recent Developments', in L. Haaparanta and J. Hintikka (eds.), *Frege Synthesized: Essays on the Philosophical and Foundational Work of Gottlob Frege* (Dordrecht: Reidel, 1986), 253–95.

_____ [2] *Making it Explicit* (Cambridge, Mass.: Harvard University Press, 1994).

Bridge, J., *Beginning Model Theory: The Completeness Theorem and Some Consequences* (Oxford: Clarendon, 1977).

Broad, C. D., *An Examination of McTaggart's Philosophy* (Cambridge: CUP, 1933).

Burge, T., [1] 'A Theory of Aggregates', *Noûs* 11 (1977), 97–117.

Burge, T., [2] *Truth, Thought, Reason: Essays on Frege* (Oxford: Clarendon, 2005).

Buridan, J., [1] *Quaestiones in Metaphysicam Aristotelis* (Paris, 1518; repr. Frankfurt: Minerva, 1964).

——— [2] *Sophismata*, ed. T. Scott (Stuttgart: Frommann-Holzboog, 1977).

——— [3] *Questiones Longe super Librum Perihermeneias*, ed. R. van der Lecq (Nijmegen: Ingenium, 1983).

Burleigh, W., [1] *Super Artem Veterem* (Venice, 1497; repr. Frankfurt: Minerva, 1967).

——— [2] *De Puritate Artis Logicae*, ed. P. Boehner (St Bonaventura, NY: Franciscan Institute, 1955).

Cameron, R., 'Turtles All the Way Down: Regress, Priority, and Fundamentality', *Philosophical Quarterly* 58 (2008), 1–14.

Campbell, J., *Past, Space, and Self* (Cambridge, Mass.: MIT, 1994).

Campbell, K., *Abstract Particulars* (Oxford: Blackwell, 1990).

Candlish, S., [1] 'The Unity of the Proposition and Russell's Theories of Judgement', in R. Monk and A. Palmer (eds.), *Bertrand Russell and the Origins of Analytical Philosophy* (Bristol: Thoemmes, 1996), 103–33.

——— [2] *The Russell/Bradley Dispute and its Significance for Twentieth-Century Philosophy* (Basingstoke: Palgrave, 2007).

Cann, R., *Formal Semantics* (Cambridge: CUP, 1993).

Cantor, G., [1] *Georg Cantor: Gesammelte Abhandlungen mathematischen und philosophischen Inhalts*, ed. E. Zermelo (Berlin: Springer, 1932).

——— [2] *Contributions to the Founding of the Theory of Numbers*, ed. and tr. P. E. Jourdain (New York: Dover, 1955).

Carl, W., [1] 'Freges Unterscheidung von Gegenstand und Begriff', in M. Schirn (ed.), *Studien zu Frege*, ii (Stuttgart: Frommann-Holzboog, 1976), 33–49.

——— [2] *Frege's Theory of Sense and Reference: Its Origins and Scope* (Cambridge: CUP, 1994).

Carnap, R., [1] *Der logische Aufbau der Welt* (Hamburg: Felix Meiner, 1998).

——— [2] *The Logical Syntax of Language* (London: Kegan Paul, 1937).

——— [3] *Meaning and Necessity* (Chicago: University of Chicago, 1947).

Carnie, A., *Syntax: A Generative Introduction*, 2nd edn. (Oxford: Blackwell, 2007).

Carpenter, B., *Type-Logical Semantics* (Cambridge, Mass.: MIT, 1997).

Carroll, L., 'What the Tortoise Said to Achilles', *Mind* 4 (1895), 278–80.

Carruthers, P., 'On Concept and Object', *Theoria* 49 (1983), 49–86.

Cartwright, R., [1] *Philosophical Essays* (Cambridge, Mass.: MIT, 1987).

——— [2] 'Russell and Moore, 1898–1905', in N. Griffin (ed.), *The Cambridge Companion to Bertrand Russell* (Cambridge: CUP, 2003), 108–27.

——— [3] 'Remarks on Propositional Functions', *Mind* 114 (2005), 915–27.

Chihara, C., 'Ramsey's Theory of Types: Suggestions for a Return to Fregean Sources', in D. H. Mellor (ed.), *Prospects for Pragmatism* (Cambridge: CUP, 1980), 21–47.

Chomsky, N., [1] *Syntactic Structures*, 2nd edn. (Berlin: Walter de Gruyter, 2002).

——— [2] *Aspects of the Theory of Syntax* (Cambridge, Mass.: MIT, 1965).

——— [3] *Cartesian Linguistics: A Chapter in the History of Rationalist Thought* (New York: University of America, 1966).

_____[4] *Studies on Semantics in Generative Grammar* (The Hague: Mouton, 1972).

_____[5] *Reflections on Language* (Glasgow: Collins, 1976).

_____[6] *Rules and Representations* (Oxford: Blackwell, 1980).

_____[7] *The Minimalist Program* (Cambridge, Mass.: MIT, 1995).

_____[8] *Language and Mind*, 3rd edn. (Cambridge: CUP, 2006).

Church, A., [1], 'A Note on the Entscheidungsproblem', *Journal of Symbolic Logic* 1 (1936), 40–1.

_____[2] 'On Carnap's Analysis of Statements of Assertion and Belief', *Analysis* 10 (1950), 97–9.

_____[3] 'A Formulation of the Logic of Sense and Denotation', in P. Henle, H. Kallen, and S. Langer (eds.), *Structure, Method and Meaning* (New York: Liberal Arts, 1951), 3–24.

_____[4] 'The Need for Abstract Entities in Semantic Analysis', *Proceedings of the American Academy of Arts and Sciences* 80 (1951), 100–12.

_____[5] 'Intensional Isomorphism and the Identity of Belief', *Philosophical Studies* 5 (1954), 65–73.

_____[6] *Introduction to Mathematical Logic* (Princeton: Princeton University Press, 1956).

_____[7] 'Propositions and Sentences', in I. Bocheński, A. Church, and N. Goodman (eds.), *The Problem of Universals: A Symposium* (Notre Dame, Ind.: University of Notre Dame, 1956), 3–11.

_____[8] 'Schröder's Anticipation of the Simple Theory of Types', *Erkenntnis* 10 (1976), 407–11.

_____[9] 'Russell's Theory of Identity of Propositions', *Philosophia Naturalis* 21 (1984), 513–22.

_____[10] 'Intensionality and the Paradox of the Name Relation', in J. Almog, J. Perry, and H. Wettstein (eds.), *Themes from Kaplan* (Oxford: OUP, 1989), 151–65.

Clark, R., 'What Facts Are', *Southern Journal of Philosophy* 14 (1976), 257–68.

Cocchiarella, N., [1] *Logical Studies in Early Analytic Philosophy* (Columbus, Ohio: Ohio State University Press, 1987).

_____[2] 'Predication versus Membership in the Distinction between Logic as Language and Logic as Calculus', *Synthese* 77 (1988), 37–72.

Conant, J., [1] 'Two Conceptions of *Die Überwindung der Metaphysik*: Carnap and Early Wittgenstein', in T. McCarthy and S. Stidd (eds.), *Wittgenstein in America* (Oxford: Clarendon, 2001), 13–61.

_____[2] 'The Method of the *Tractatus*', in E. Reck (ed.), *From Frege to Wittgenstein: Perspectives on Early Analytic Philosophy* (Oxford: OUP, 2002), 374–462.

Condillac, E. B. de, *Œuvres Philosophiques*, ed. G. Le Roy, i (Paris: Presses Universitaires de France, 1947).

Cook, V., and Newson, M., *Chomsky's Universal Grammar*, 3rd edn. (Oxford: Blackwell, 2007).

Copi, I., 'Objects, Properties and Relations in the *Tractatus*', in I. Copi and R. Beard (eds.), *Essays on Wittgenstein's Tractatus* (London: Routledge, 1966), 167–86.

Coronel, A., *Prima Pars Rosarii* (Paris, [*c.*1500]).

Cresswell, M., *Structured Meanings: The Semantics of Propositional Attitudes* (Cambridge, Mass.: MIT, 1985).

Crocco, G., [1] 'Gödel, Carnap and the Fregean Heritage', *Synthese* 137 (2003), 21–41.

——— [2] 'Gödel on Concepts', *History and Philosophy of Logic* 27 (2006), 171–91.

Currie, G., [1] 'Frege's Metaphysical Argument', in C. Wright (ed.), *Frege: Tradition and Influence* (Oxford: Blackwell, 1984), 144–57.

——— [2] 'The Analysis of Thoughts', *Australasian Journal of Philosophy* 63 (1985), 283–98.

——— [3] *The Nature of Fiction* (Cambridge: CUP, 1990).

Dainton, B., *Time and Space* (Chesham: Acumen, 2001).

Dauben, J., *Georg Cantor: His Mathematics and Philosophy of the Infinite* (Princeton: Princeton University Press, 1979).

Davidson, D., [1] *Inquiries into Truth and Interpretation* (Oxford: Clarendon, 1984).

——— [2] *Truth and Predication* (Cambridge, Mass.: Belknap, 2005).

Davies, M., *Meaning, Quantification, Necessity* (London: Routledge, 1981).

Dedekind, R., *Was sind und was sollen die Zahlen?* (Brunswick: Vieweg, 1888).

De Morgan, A., *Formal Logic, or the Calculus of Inference, Necessary and Probable* (London: Taylor & Walton, 1847).

Denyer, N., [1] *Language, Thought and Falsehood in Ancient Greek Philosophy* (London: Routledge, 1991).

——— [2] 'Names, Verbs, and Quantification', *Philosophy* 73 (1998), 619–23.

Descartes, R., *Œuvres de Descartes*, ed. C. Adam and A. Tannery (Paris: Vrin, 1964–76).

Destutt de Tracy, A. L. C., [1] *Grammaire*, in *Éléments d'Idéologie*, ii (Paris: Courcier, 1803).

——— [2] *Logique*, in *Éléments d'Idéologie*, iii (Paris: Courcier, 1805).

Deutscher, G., *The Unfolding of Language: The Evolution of Mankind's Greatest Invention* (London: Arrow Books, 2005).

Dever, J., 'Compositionality', in E. Lepore and B. Smith (eds.), *The Oxford Handbook of Philosophy of Language* (Oxford: Clarendon, 2006), 633–66.

Diamond, C., *The Realistic Spirit* (Cambridge, Mass.: MIT, 1995).

Diderot, D., *Encyclopédie, ou Dictionnaire raisonné des sciences, des arts et des metiers, par une société de gens de letters*, 28 vols. (Neuchâtel: Faulche, 1751–72).

Dodd, J., [1] 'McDowell and Identity Theories of Truth', *Analysis* 55 (1995), 160–5.

——— [2] 'Farewell to States of Affairs', *Australasian Journal of Philosophy* 77 (1999), 146–60.

——— [3] 'Is Truth Supervenient on Being?', *Proceedings of the Aristotelian Society* 102 (2002), 69–85.

——— and Hornsby, J., 'The Identity Theory of Truth: Reply to Baldwin', *Mind* 101 (1992), 319–22.

Donaho, S., 'Are Declarative Sentences Representational?', *Mind* 107 (1998), 33–58.

Dowty, D., Wall, R., and Peters, S., *Introduction to Montague Semantics* (Dordrecht: Kluwer, 1981).

Dudman, V., '*Bedeutung* for Predicates', in M. Schirn (ed.), *Studien zu Frege*, iii. (Stuttgart: Frommann-Holzboog, 1976), 71–84.

Dufour, C., *Die Lehre der Proprietates Terminorum: Sinn und Referenz in mittelalterlicher Logik* (Munich: Philosophia, 1989).

Dummett, M., [1] *Truth and Other Enigmas* (London: Duckworth, 1978).

_____ [2] *Frege: Philosophy of Language*, 2nd edn. (London: Duckworth, 1981).

_____ [3] *The Interpretation of Frege's Philosophy* (London: Duckworth, 1981).

_____ [4] *Frege and Other Philosophers* (Oxford: Clarendon, 1991).

_____ [5] *Frege: Philosophy of Mathematics* (London: Duckworth, 1991).

_____ [6] *Grammar and Style* (London: Duckworth, 1993).

_____ [7] 'Of What Kind of Thing is Truth a Property?', in S. Blackburn and K. Simmons (eds.), *Truth* (Oxford: OUP, 1999), 264–81.

_____ [8] *Elements of Intuitionism*, 2nd edn. (Oxford: Clarendon, 2000).

_____ [9] 'Comments on Wolfgang Künne's Paper', in M. Beaney and E. Reck (eds.), *Gottlob Frege: Critical Assessments of Leading Philosophers*, i (London: Routledge, 2005), 154–60.

_____ [10] *Thought and Reality* (Oxford: Clarendon, 2006).

Dunn, J. M., and Belnap, N., 'The Substitution Interpretation of the Quantifiers', *Noûs* 2 (1968), 177–85.

Ebbinghaus, H.-D., *Ernst Zermelo: an Approach to his Life and Work* (Berlin: Springer, 2007).

Eckermann, W., *Wort und Wirklichkeit: Das Sprachverständnis in der Theologie Gregors von Rimini und sein Weiterwirken in der Augustinerschule* (Würzburg: Augustinus, 1978).

Enderton, H., [1] *Elements of Set Theory* (San Diego, Calif.: Academic, 1977).

_____ [2] *A Mathematical Introduction to Logic*, 2nd edn. (San Diego, Calif.: Academic, 2001).

Etchemendy, J., *The Concept of Logical Consequence* (Stanford, Calif.: CSLI, 1999).

Evans, G., [1] *The Varieties of Reference*, ed. J. McDowell (Oxford: Clarendon, 1982).

_____ [2] *Collected Papers* (Oxford: Clarendon, 1985).

_____ and J. McDowell (eds.), *Truth and Meaning: Essays in Semantics* (Oxford: Clarendon, 1976).

Ewald, W., *From Kant to Hilbert: A Sourcebook in the Foundations of Mathematics*, 2 vols. (Oxford: Clarendon, 1996).

Felgner, U., [1] 'Zur Geschichte des Mengenbegriffs', in B. Buldt *et al.* (eds.), *Kurt Gödel: Wahrheit und Beweisbarkeit*, ii (Vienna: öbv & hpt, 2006), 169–85.

_____ [2] 'Der Begriff der Funktion', in F. Hausdorff, *Gesammelte Werke*, ii. *Grundzüge der Mengenlehre*, ed. E. Brieskorn *et al.* (Berlin: Springer, 2002), 621–33.

Ferrer, V., *Tractatus de Suppositionibus*, ed. J. Trentman (Stuttgart: Frommann-Holzboog, 1977).

Fine, K., [1] 'First-Order Modal Theories: Facts', *Synthese* 53 (1982), 43–122.

_____ [2] 'Neutral Relations', *Philosophical Review* 109 (2000), 1–33.

Fisk, M., [1] 'A Paradox in Frege's Semantics', *Philosophical Studies* 14 (1963), 56–62.

_____ [2] 'Relatedness without Relations', *Noûs* 6 (1972), 139–51.

Fitch, F., 'Propositions as the Only Realities', *American Philosophical Quarterly* 8 (1971), 99–103.

Fogelin, R., *Wittgenstein*, 2nd edn. (London: Routledge & Kegan Paul, 1987).

Fonseca, P., *Institutiones Dialecticae* (Liège: Hovius, 1608).

Forbes, G., *Languages of Possibility* (Oxford: Blackwell, 1989).

Fraenkel, A., Bar-Hillel, Y., and Levy, A., *Foundations of Set Theory*, 2nd rev. edn. (Amsterdam: North Holland, 1973).

Frege, G., [1] *Begriffsschrift* (Halle: Nebert, 1879; repr. Darmstadt: Wissenschaftliche Buchgesellschaft, 1964).

——[2] 'Über die wissenschaftliche Berechtigung einer Begriffsschrift', *Zeitschrift für Philosophie und philosophische Kritik* 81 (1882), 48–56 (= [25], 91–7).

——[3] *Grundlagen der Arithmetik* (Breslau: Koebner, 1884; repr. ed. C. Thiel, Hamburg: Felix Meiner, 1988).

——[4] 'Über formale Theorien der Arithmetik', *Sitzungsberichte der Jenaischen Gesellschaft für Medezin und Naturwissenschaft* (Jena: Fischer, 1885; = [21], 103–11).

——[5] *Funktion und Begriff* (Jena: Jenaische Gesellschaft für Medizin und Naturwissenschaft, 1891; = [21], 125–42).

——[6] 'Über Sinn und Bedeutung', *Zeitschrift für Philosophie und Philosophische Kritik* 100 (1892), 25–50 (= [21], 143–62).

——[7] 'Über Begriff und Gegenstand', *Vierteljahresschrift für wissenschaftliche Philosophie* 16 (1892), 192–205 (= [21], 167–78).

——[8] 'Rezension von Georg Cantor, Zur Lehre vom Transfiniten', *Zeitschrift für Philosophie und philosophische Kritik* 100 (1892), 269–72 (= [21], 163–6).

——[9] 'Rezension von Husserl, *Philosophie der Arithmetik*', *Zeitschrift für Philosophie und philosophische Kritik* 103 (1894), 313–32 (= [21], 179–92).

——[10] *Grundgesetze der Arithmetik*, 2 vols. (Hildesheim: Olms, 1998; repr. of the 1893/1903 Jena edns.).

——[11] 'Kritische Beleuchtung einiger Punkte in E. Schröders Vorlesungen über die Algebra der Logik', *Archiv für systematische Philosophie* 1 (1895), 433–56 (= [21], 193–210).

——[12] *Über die Zahlen des Herrn Schubert* (Jena: Pohle, 1899; = [21], 241–61).

——[13] 'Über die Grundlagen der Geometrie' (1st ser.), *Jahresbericht der deutschen Mathematiker-Vereinigung* 12 (1903), 319–24, 368–75 (= [21], 262–72).

——[14] 'Was ist eine Funktion?', *Festschrift Ludwig Boltzmann* (Leipzig: Barth, 1904; = [21], 273–80).

——[15] 'Über die Grundlagen der Geometrie' (2nd ser.), *Jahresbericht der deutschen Mathematiker-Vereinigung* 15 (1906), 293–309, 377–403, 423–30 (= [21], 281–323).

——[16] 'Anmerkungen Freges zu: Philip E. B. Jourdain, The Development of the Theories of Mathematical Logic and the Principles of Mathematics', *Quarterly Journal of Pure and Applied Mathematics* 43 (1912), 237–69 (= [21], 334–41).

——[17] 'Der Gedanke: eine logische Untersuchung', *Beiträge zur Philosophie des deutschen Idealismus* 2 (1918–19), 58–77 (= [21], 342–62).

——[18] 'Die Verneinung', *Beiträge zur Philosophie des deutschen Idealismus* 1 (1918–19), 143–57 (= [21], 362–78).

____ [19] 'Gedankengefüge', *Beiträge zur Philosophie des deutschen Idealismus* 3 (1923–6), 36–51 (= [21], 378–94).

____ [20] *Translations from the Philosophical Writings of Gottlob Frege*, 3rd edn., ed. P. T. Geach and M. Black (Oxford: Blackwell, 1952).

____ [21] *Kleine Schriften*, ed. I. Angelelli (Hildesheim: Olms, 1967).

____ [22] *Wissenschaftlicher Briefwechsel*, ed. G. Gabriel *et al.* (Hamburg: Felix Meiner, 1976).

____ [23] *Gottlob Frege: Posthumous Writings*, ed. H. Hermes *et al.*, tr. P. Long and R. White (Oxford: Blackwell, 1979).

____ [24] *The Foundations of Arithmetic*, 2nd edn., tr. J. L. Austin (Oxford: Blackwell, 1980).

____ [25] *Funktion, Begriff, Bedeutung*, ed. G. Patzig (Göttingen: Vandenhoek & Ruprecht, 1980).

____ [26] *Nachgelassene Schriften*, ed. H. Hermes *et al.* (Hamburg: Felix Meiner, 1983).

____ [27] 'Vorlesungen über Begriffsschrift', *History and Philosophy of Logic* 17 (1996), 1–48.

Funke, O., *Englische Sprachphilosophie im späteren 18. Jahrhundert* (Berne: Franke, 1934).

Gabriel, G., 'Fregean Connection: *Bedeutung*, Value, and Truth-Value', in C. Wright (ed.), *Frege: Tradition and Influence* (Oxford: Blackwell, 1984), 188–93.

Gaskin, R., [1] 'Bradley's Regress, the Copula, and the Unity of the Proposition', *Philosophical Quarterly* 45 (1995), 161–80.

____ [2] *The Sea Battle and the Master Argument: Aristotle and Diodorus Cronus on the Metaphysics of the Future* (Berlin: Walter de Gruyter, 1995).

____ [3] ' "Kein Etwas, aber auch nicht ein Nichts!": Kann die Grammatik tatsächlich täuschen?', *Grazer Philosophische Studien* 51 (1996), 85–104.

____ [4] 'Fregean Sense and Russellian Propositions', *Philosophical Studies* 86 (1997), 131–54.

____ [5] 'Überlegungen zur Identitätstheorie der Prädikation', *Wissenschaft und Weisheit* 60 (1997), 87–103.

____ [6] 'Russell and Richard Brinkley on the Unity of the Proposition', *History and Philosophy of Logic* 18 (1997), 139–50.

____ [7] 'The Stoics on Cases, Predicates, and the Unity of the Proposition', in R. Sorabji (ed.), *Aristotle and After* (London: Institute of Classical Studies, 1997), 91–108.

____ [8] 'The Unity of the Declarative Sentence', *Philosophy* 73 (1998), 21–45.

____ [9] 'Tense Logic and the Master Argument', *Philosophiegeschichte und logische Analyse* 2 (1999), 202–24.

____ [10] 'Die Einheit der Aussage', in U. Meixner (ed.), *Metaphysik im postmetaphysischen Zeitalter* (Vienna: öbv & hpt, 2001), 305–10.

____ [11] 'Nonsense and Necessity in Wittgenstein's Mature Philosophy', in R. Gaskin (ed.), *Grammar in Early Twentieth-Century Philosophy* (London: Routledge, 2001), 199–217.

Gaskin, R., [12] 'Ockham's Mental Language, Connotation, and the Inherence Regress', in D. Perler (ed.), *Theories of Intentionality in Ancient and Medieval Thought* (Leiden: Brill, 2001), 227–63.

——[13] '*Complexe Significabilia* and Aristotle's *Categories*', in J. Biard and I. Rosier-Catach (eds.), *La Tradition médiévale des catégories (XIIe–XVe siècles)* (Louvain and Paris: Éditions Peeters, 2003), 187–205.

——[14] '*Complexe Significabilia* and the Formal Distinction', in A. Maierù and L. Valente (eds.), *Medieval Theories of Assertive and Non-Assertive Language* (Rome: Olschki, 2004), 495–516.

——[15] *Experience and the World's Own Language: A Critique of John McDowell's Empiricism* (Oxford: Clarendon, 2006).

Gauss, C. F., *Werke*, viii. (Leipzig: Teubner, 1900).

Geach, P. T., [1] 'Subject and Predicate', *Mind* 59 (1950), 461–82.

——[2] 'Form and Existence', *Proceedings of the Aristotelian Society* 55 (1954–5), 251–72.

——[3] *Reference and Generality* (Ithaca, NY: Cornell University Press, 1962).

——[4] 'Frege', in G. E. M. Anscombe and P. Geach, *Three Philosophers* (Oxford: Blackwell, 1963), 131–62.

——[5] 'Infinity in Scholastic Philosophy', in I. Lakatos (ed.), *Problems in the Philosophy of Mathematics* (Amsterdam: North Holland, 1967), 41–2.

——[6] *Mental Acts* (Bristol: Thoemmes, 1992; repr. of the 1971 edn.).

——[7] *Logic Matters* (Oxford: Blackwell, 1972).

——[8] 'Names and Identity', in S. Guttenplan (ed.), *Mind and Language* (Oxford: Clarendon, 1975), 139–58.

——[9] 'Critical Notice of Dummett's *Frege: Philosophy of Language*', *Mind* 85 (1976), 436–49.

——[10] 'Strawson on Subject and Predicate', in Z. van Straaten (ed.), *Philosophical Subjects* (Oxford: Clarendon, 1980), 174–88.

——[11] 'A Program for Syntax', in W. Buszkowski, W. Marciszewski, and J. van Benthem (eds.), *Categorial Grammar* (Amsterdam and Philadelphia: John Benjamins, 1988), 127–40.

Gelber, H., 'I Cannot Tell a Lie: Hugh of Lawton's Critique of William of Ockham on Mental Language', *Franciscan Studies* 44 (1984), 141–79.

Geulincx, A., [1] *Logica Fundamentis Suis a quibus Hactenus Collapsa Fuerat Restituta*, in *Opera Philosophica*, i, ed. J. Land (The Hague: Nijhoff, 1891), 165–454.

——[2] *Metaphysica ad Mentem Peripateticam*, in *Opera Philosophica*, ii, ed. J. Land (The Hague: Nijhoff, 1892), 199–310.

Giaquinto, M., *The Search for Certainty: A Philosophical Account of the Foundations of Mathematics* (Oxford: Clarendon, 2002).

Gibson, M., *From Naming to Saying: The Unity of the Proposition* (Oxford: Blackwell, 2004).

Gochet, P., 'The Syncategorematic Treatment of Predicates', in B. K. Matilal and J. L. Shaw (eds.), *Analytical Philosophy in Comparative Perspective* (Dordrecht: Reidel, 1985), 61–80.

Goddard, L., and Judge, B., 'The Metaphysics of Wittgenstein's *Tractatus*', *Australasian Journal of Philosophy*, monograph 1, 1982.

Gödel, K., *Collected Works*, 5 vols., ed. S. Feferman (Oxford: Clarendon, 1986–2003).

Goldfarb, W., [1] 'Russell's Reasons for Ramification', in C. Wade Savage and C. Anthony Anderson (eds.), *Rereading Russell: Essays on Bertrand Russell's Metaphysics and Epistemology* (Minneapolis: University of Minnesota, 1989), 24–40.

——— [2] 'Wittgenstein's Understanding of Frege: The Pre-Tractarian Evidence', in E. Reck (ed.), *From Frege to Wittgenstein: Perspectives on Early Analytic Philosophy* (Oxford: OUP, 2002), 185–200.

Goodman, N., and Quine, W., 'Steps towards a Constructive Nominalism', *Journal of Symbolic Logic* 12 (1947), 105–22.

Grandy, R., 'An Ockhamite Criticism of Church Semantics', *Monist* 61 (1978), 401–7.

Grattan-Guinness, I., *The Search for Mathematical Roots 1870–1940: Logics, Set Theories and the Foundations of Mathematics from Cantor through Russell to Gödel* (Princeton: Princeton University Press, 2000).

Gregory of Rimini, [1] *Lectura Super Primum et Secundum Sententiarum*, i. *Prologus et Dist. 1–6*, ed. A. Trapp and V. Marcolino (Berlin: Walter de Gruyter, 1981).

——— [2] *Lectura Super Primum et Secundum Sententiarum*, iii. *Dist. 19–48*, ed. A. Trapp and V. Marcolino (Berlin: Walter de Gruyter, 1984).

Griffin, J., *Wittgenstein's Logical Atomism* (Oxford: Clarendon, 1964).

Griffin, N., [1] 'Russell's Multiple Relation Theory of Judgment', *Philosophical Studies* 47 (1985), 213–47.

——— [2] 'Wittgenstein's Criticism of Russell's Theory of Judgement', *Russell* 4 (1986), 132–45.

——— [3] *Russell's Idealist Apprenticeship* (Oxford: Clarendon, 1991).

——— [4] 'Terms, Relations, Complexes', in A. Irvine and G. Wedeking (eds.), *Russell and Analytic Philosophy* (Toronto: University of Toronto, 1993), 159–92.

——— [5] 'Denoting Concepts in *The Principles of Mathematics*', in R. Monk and A. Palmer (eds.), *Bertrand Russell and the Origins of Analytical Philosophy* (Bristol: Thoemmes, 1996), 23–64.

Grimm, R., 'Names and Predicables', *Analysis* 26 (1966), 138–46.

Grossmann, R., [1] *Reflections on Frege's Philosophy* (Evanston, Ill.: Northwestern University Press, 1969).

——— [2] 'Structures, Functions, and Forms', in M. Schirn (ed.), *Studien zu Frege*, ii. (Stuttgart: Frommann-Holzboog, 1976), 11–32.

Hale, B., [1] 'Strawson, Geach, and Dummett on Singular Terms and Predicates', *Synthese* 42 (1979), 275–95.

——— [2] *Abstract Objects* (Oxford: Blackwell, 1987).

——— [3] 'Singular Terms (1)' and 'Singular Terms (2)', in B. Hale and C. Wright, *The Reason's Proper Study: Essays towards a Neo-Fregean Philosophy of Mathematics* (Oxford: Clarendon, 2001), 31–71.

——— [4] 'Universals and Particulars: Ramsey's Scepticism', in P. F. Strawson and A. Chakrabarti (eds.), *Universals, Concepts, and Qualities: New Essays on the Meaning of Predicates* (Aldershot: Ashgate, 2006), 177–203.

Haller, R., 'Untersuchungen zum Bedeutungsproblem in der antiken und mittelalter-lichen Philosophie', *Archiv für Begriffsgeschichte* 7 (1962), 57–119.

Hallett, M., [1] *Cantorian Set Theory and Limitation of Size* (Oxford: Clarendon, 1984).

——[2] 'Ernst Friedrich Ferdinand Zermelo (1871–1953)', in W. Ewald, *From Kant to Hilbert: A Sourcebook in the Foundations of Mathematics*, 2 vols. (Oxford: Clarendon, 1996), 1208–18.

Hamacher-Hermes, A., *Inhalts- oder Umfangslogik?* (Freiburg: Alber, 1994).

Hanks, P., [1] 'The Content–Force Distinction', *Philosophical Studies* 134 (2007), 141–64.

——[2] 'How Wittgenstein Defeated Russell's Multiple Relation Theory of Judgment', *Synthese* 154 (2007), 121–46.

Harris, J., *Hermes: Or, a Philosophical Inquiry Concerning Language and Universal Grammar* (London: Woodfall, 1751; repr. Menston, Ill.: Scolar, 1968).

Harris, Z., *Mathematical Structures of Language* (New York: Krieger, 1979).

Hausdorff, F., *Gesammelte Werke*, ii. *Grundzüge der Mengenlehre*, ed. E. Brieskorn *et al.* (Berlin: Springer, 2002).

Heijenoort, J. van, [1] 'Logic as Calculus and Logic as Language', *Boston Studies in the Philosophy of Science* 3 (1967), 440–6.

——[2] 'Sense in Frege' and 'Frege on Sense Identity', *Journal of Philosophical Logic* 6 (1977), 93–108.

Heim, I., and Kratzer, A., *Semantics in Generative Grammar* (Oxford: Blackwell, 1998).

Henninger, M., 'Aquinas on the Ontological Status of Relations', *Journal of the History of Philosophy* 25 (1987), 491–515.

Henry, D. P., *Medieval Logic and Metaphysics* (London: Hutchinson, 1972).

Hilbert, D., *Natur und mathematisches Erkennen*, ed. D. Rowe (Basel: Birkhäuser, 1992).

Hintikka, J., 'Standard vs. Nonstandard Distinction: A Watershed in the Foundations of Mathematics', in J. Hintikka (ed.), *From Dedekind to Gödel: Essays on the Development of the Foundations of Mathematics* (Dordrecht: Kluwer, 1995), 21–44.

——and Hintikka, M., *Understanding Wittgenstein* (Oxford: Blackwell, 1986).

——and Sandu, G., 'The Skeleton in Frege's Cupboard: The Standard versus Nonstandard Distinction', *Journal of Philosophy* 89 (1992), 290–315.

Hobbes, T., [1] *Computatio sive Logica*, part 1 of *De Corpore*, ed. I. Hungerland and G. Vick (New York: Abaris, 1981; Latin text reproduced from 1839 edn.).

——[2] *Leviathan* (London: Penguin, 1985).

Hochberg, H., [1] 'Nominalism, General Terms, and Predication', *Monist* 61 (1978), 460–75.

——[2] 'Logical Form, Existence, and Relational Predication', in P. French, T. Uehling, and H. Wettstein (eds.), *Midwest Studies in Philosophy*, vi (Minneapolis: University of Minnesota, 1981), 215–37.

——[3] 'The Wiener–Kuratowski Procedure and the Analysis of Order', *Analysis* 41 (1981), 161–3.

——[4] 'Russell, Ramsey, and Wittgenstein on Ramification and Quantification', *Erkenntnis* 27 (1987), 257–81.

_____ [5] 'A Refutation of Moderate Nominalism', *Australasian Journal of Philosophy* 66 (1988), 188–207.

_____ [6] 'Russell's Paradox, Russellian Relations, and the Problems of Predication and Impredicativity', in C. Wade Savage and C. Anthony Anderson (eds.), *Rereading Russell: Essays on Bertrand Russell's Metaphysics and Epistemology* (Minneapolis: University of Minnesota, 1989), 63–87.

_____ [7] 'Facts and Classes as Complexes and as Truth-Makers', *Monist* 77 (1994), 170–91.

_____ [8] 'Propositions, Truth and Belief: the Wittgenstein–Russell Dispute', *Theoria* 66 (2000), 3–40.

_____ [9] 'Relations, Properties, and Particulars', in H. Hochberg and K. Mulligan (eds.), *Relations and Predicates* (Frankfurt and Lancaster: Ontos, 2004), 17–53.

_____ [10] 'Russell and Ramsey on Distinguishing between Particulars and Universals', *Grazer Philosophische Studien* 67 (2004), 195–207.

Hodes, H., 'The Composition of Fregean Thoughts', *Philosophical Studies* 41 (1982), 161–78.

Hodges, W., [1] 'An Editor Recalls Some Hopeless Papers', *Bulletin of Symbolic Logic* 4 (1998), 1–16.

_____ [2] 'Elementary Predicate Logic', in D. Gabbay and F. Guenther (eds.), *Handbook of Philosophical Logic*, 2nd edn., i (Dordrecht: Kluwer, 2001), 1–129.

Horne Tooke, J., ΕΠΕΑ ΠΤΕΡΟΕΝΤΑ, *or The Diversions of Purley*, 2 vols., ed. R. Taylor (London: Thomas Tegg, 1829).

Hornsby, J., 'Truth: The Identity Theory', *Proceedings of the Aristotelian Society* 97 (1997), 1–24.

Horstmann, R.-P., *Ontologie und Relationen: Hegel, Bradley, Russell und die Kontroverse über interne und externe Beziehungen* (Königstein: Athenäum, 1984).

Hossack, K., 'Plurals and Complexes', *British Journal for the Philosophy of Science* 51 (2000), 411–43.

Hudson, R., *Word Grammar* (Oxford: Blackwell, 1984).

Humberstone, L., 'What *Fa* says about *a*', *Dialectica* 54 (2000), 3–28.

Hume, D., *A Treatise of Human Nature*, ed. P. H. Nidditch (Oxford: Clarendon, 1978).

Husserl, E., [1] *Philosophie der Arithmetik*, ed. L. Eley (The Hague: Nijhoff, 1970).

_____ [2] *Logische Untersuchungen* (Tübingen: Niemeyer, 1993).

Hutcheson, F., [1] *Metaphysicae Synopsis: Ontologiam et Pneumatologiam Complectens* (Glasgow: Foulis, 1742).

_____ [2] *Logicae Compendium* (Glasgow: Foulis, 1756).

_____ [3] *Logic, Metaphysics, and Natural Sociability of Mankind*, ed. J. Moore and M. Silverthorne (Indianapolis: Liberty Fund, 2006).

Hylton, P., [1] *Russell, Idealism, and the Emergence of Analytic Philosophy* (Oxford: Clarendon, 1990).

_____ [2] *Propositions, Functions, and Analysis: Selected Essays on Russell's Philosophy* (Oxford: Clarendon, 2005).

Imaguire, G., *Russells Frühphilosophie: Propositionen, Realismus und die sprachontologische Wende* (Hildesheim: Olms, 2001).

Jackson, F., 'Statements about Universals', *Mind* 86 (1977), 427–9.

Jacobi, K., [1] 'Diskussionen über Prädikationstheorie in den logischen Schriften des Petrus Abailardus', in R. Thomas and J. Jolivet (eds.), *Petrus Abaelardus: Person, Werk und Wirkung* (Trier: Paulinus, 1980), 165–79.

—— [2] 'Abelard and Frege: the Semantics of Words and Propositions', *Atti del Convegno Internazionale di Storia della Logica* (Bologna: Clueb, 1983), 81–96.

—— [3] 'Peter Abelard's Investigations into the Meaning and Function of the Speech Sign "Est"', in S. Knuuttila and J. Hintikka (eds.), *The Logic of Being* (Dordrecht: Reidel, 1986), 145–80.

—— [4] 'Philosophy of Language', in J. Brower and K. Guilfoy (eds.), *The Cambridge Companion to Abelard* (Cambridge: CUP, 2004), 126–57.

Jané, I., 'The Role of the Absolute Infinite in Cantor's Conception of Set', *Erkenntnis* 42 (1995), 375–402.

Johnson, W. E., *Logic* (Cambridge: CUP, 1921).

Johnston, C., 'The Unity of a Tractarian Fact', *Synthese* 156 (2007), 231–51.

Jubien, M., [1] 'Straight Talk about Sets', *Philosophical Topics* 17 (1989), 91–107.

—— [2], 'Propositions and the Objects of Thought', *Philosophical Studies* 104 (2001), 47–62.

Kanamori, A., 'The Empty Set, the Singleton, and the Ordered Pair', *Bulletin of Symbolic Logic* 9 (2003), 273–98.

Kant, I., *Kritik der reinen Vernunft* (Hamburg: Felix Meiner, 1998).

Kaplan, D., [1] 'How to Russell a Frege–Church', *Journal of Philosophy* 72 (1975), 716–29.

—— [2] 'Demonstratives', in J. Almog *et al.* (eds.), *Themes from Kaplan* (Oxford: OUP, 1989), 481–563.

Karger, E., [1] 'Théories de la pensée, de ses objets et de son discours chez Guillaume d'Occam', *Dialogue* 33 (1994), 437–56.

—— [2] 'William of Ockham, Walter Chatton, and Adam Wodeham on the Objects of Knowledge and Belief', *Vivarium* 33 (1995), 171–96.

—— [3] 'Mental Sentences According to Burley and the Early Ockham', *Vivarium* 34 (1996), 192–230.

Kaufmann, F., *Das Unendliche in der Mathematik und seine Ausschaltung* (Vienna: Franz Deuticke, 1930).

Kemmerling, A., [1] 'Gedanken und ihre Teile', *Grazer Philosophische Studien* 37 (1990), 1–30.

—— [2] 'Freges Begriffslehre, ohne ihr angebliches Paradox', in M. Siebel and M. Textor (eds.), *Semantik und Ontologie* (Frankfurt and Lancaster: Ontos, 2004), 39–62.

Keyt, D., 'Wittgenstein's Picture Theory of Language', in I. Copi and R. Beard (eds.), *Essays on Wittgenstein's Tractatus* (London: Routledge, 1966), 377–92.

Kienzler, W., *Wittgensteins Wende zu seiner Spätphilosophie, 1930–1932: Eine historische und systematische Darstellung* (Frankfurt: Suhrkamp, 1997).

Kimball, J., *The Formal Theory of Grammar* (Englewood Cliffs, NJ: Prentice-Hall, 1973).

King, J., [1] 'Structured Propositions and Complex Predicates', *Noûs* 29 (1995), 516–35.

_____ [2] 'Structured Propositions and Sentence Structure', *Journal of Philosophical Logic* 25 (1996), 495–521.

_____ [3] 'Designating Propositions', *Philosophical Review* 111 (2002), 341–71.

_____ [4] 'Formal Semantics', in E. Lepore and B. Smith (eds.), *The Oxford Handbook of Philosophy of Language* (Oxford: Clarendon, 2006), 557–73.

_____ [5] *The Nature and Structure of Content* (Oxford: OUP, 2007).

Kleemeier, U., *Gottlob Frege: Kontext-Prinzip und Ontologie* (Freiburg: Alber, 1997).

Kleene, S., *Introduction to Metamathematics* (Amsterdam: North Holland, 1952).

Klein, P., [1] 'Foundationalism and the Infinite Regress of Reasons', *Philosophy and Phenomenological Research* 58 (1998), 919–25.

_____ [2] 'Human Knowledge and the Infinite Regress of Reasons', *Philosophical Perspectives* 13 (1999), 297–325.

_____ [3] 'When Infinite Regresses are Not Vicious', *Philosophy and Phenomenological Research* 66 (2003), 718–29.

_____ and Ginet, C., 'Is Infinitism the Solution to the Regress Problem?', in M. Steup and E. Sosa (eds.), *Contemporary Debates in Epistemology* (Oxford: Blackwell, 2005), 131–55.

Kneale, W., and Kneale, M., *The Development of Logic* (Oxford: Clarendon, 1962).

Kreiser, L., *Gottlob Frege: Leben— Werk— Zeit* (Hamburg: Felix Meiner, 2001).

Krempel, A., *La Doctrine de la relation chez Saint Thomas* (Paris: Vrin, 1952).

Kretzmann, N., 'Medieval Logicians on the Meaning of the *Propositio*', *Journal of Philosophy* 67 (1970), 767–87.

Kripke, S., [1], 'Semantical Considerations on Modal Logic', in L. Linsky (ed.), *Reference and Modality* (Oxford: OUP, 1971), 63–72.

_____ [2] 'Is there a Problem about Substitutional Quantification?', in G. Evans and J. McDowell (eds.), *Truth and Meaning: Essays in Semantics* (Oxford: Clarendon, 1976), 324–419.

_____ [3] 'A Puzzle about Belief', in N. Salmon and S. Soames (eds.), *Propositions and Attitudes* (Oxford: OUP, 1988), 102–48.

_____ [4] *Wittgenstein on Rules and Private Language* (Oxford: Blackwell, 1982).

Küng, G., *Ontology and the Logistic Analysis of Language* (Dordrecht: Reidel, 1967).

Künne, W., [1] *Abstrakte Gegenstände: Semantik und Ontologie* (Frankfurt: Suhrkamp, 1983).

_____ [2] 'Propositions in Bolzano and Frege', in M. Beaney and E. Reck (eds.), *Gottlob Frege: Critical Assessments of Leading Philosophers*, i (London: Routledge, 2005), 124–53.

Kuratowski, C., 'Sur la notion de l'ordre dans la théorie des ensembles', *Fundamenta Mathematicae* 2 (1921), 161–71.

Kutschera, F. von, [1] *Gottlob Frege: Eine Einführung in sein Werk* (Berlin: Walter de Gruyter, 1989).

Kutschera, F. von, [2] 'Concepts of a Set', in A. Newen, U. Nortmann, and R. Stuhlmann-Laeisz (eds.), *Building on Frege: New Essays on Sense, Content, and Concept* (Stanford, Calif.: CSLI, 2002), 319–27.

Land, S., *From Signs to Propositions: The Concept of Form in Eighteenth-Century Semantic Theory* (London: Longman, 1974).

Landini, G., 'Russell's Substitutional Theory', in N. Griffin (ed.), *The Cambridge Companion to Bertrand Russell* (Cambridge: CUP, 2003), 241–85.

Langendoen, D., and Postal, P., *The Vastness of Natural Languages* (Oxford: Black-well, 1984).

Larkin, P., *Collected Poems*, ed. A. Thwaite (London: Marvell and Faber, 1988).

Larson, R., and Segal, G., *Knowledge of Meaning* (Cambridge, Mass.: MIT, 1995).

Leibniz, G. W., [1] *Die philosophischen Schriften von Gottfried Wilhelm Leibniz*, 7 vols., ed. C. Gerhardt (Berlin: Weidmann, 1875–90).

—— [2] *Logical Papers*, tr. and ed. G. Parkinson (Oxford: Clarendon, 1966).

—— [3] *New Essays on Human Understanding*, tr. and ed. P. Remnant and J. Bennett (Cambridge: CUP, 1981).

—— [4] *De Summa Rerum, Metaphysical Papers 1675–76*, tr. G. R. Parkinson (London: Yale University Press, 1992).

—— [5] *Schriften zur Logik und zur philosophischen Grundlegung von Mathematik und Naturwissenschaft* (Frankfurt: Suhrkamp, 1996).

—— [6] *The Labyrinth of the Continuum, Writings on the Continuum Problem, 1672–1686*, ed. R. Arthur (London: Yale University Press, 2001).

Lejewski, C., 'A Re-examination of the Russellian Theory of Descriptions', *Philosophy* 35 (1960), 14–29.

Lemmon, E. J., 'Sentences, Statements, and Propositions', in B. Williams and A. Montefiore (eds.), *British Analytical Philosophy* (London: RKP, 1966).

Lenders, W., *Die analytische Begriffs- und Urteilstheorie von G. W. Leibniz und Chr. Wolff* (Hildesheim: Olms, 1971).

Leonard, H., and Goodman, N., 'The Calculus of Individuals and its Uses', *Journal of Symbolic Logic* 5 (1940), 45–55.

Leonard, S., 'The Philosophical Basis of Eighteenth-Century Language Theories', in D. Hayden, G. Tate, and E. Alworth (eds.), *Classics in Linguistics* (London: Owen, 1968), 28–41.

Leppin, V., *Wilhelm von Ockham: Gelehrter, Streiter, Bettelmönch* (Darmstadt: Wissenschaftliche Buchgesellschaft, 2003).

Levine, J., [1] 'Logical Form, General Sentences, and Russell's Path to "On Denoting"', in R. Gaskin (ed.), *Grammar in Early Twentieth-Century Philosophy* (London: Routledge, 2001), 74–115.

—— [2] 'Analysis and Decomposition in Frege and Russell', *Philosophical Quarterly* 52 (2002), 195–216.

Lewis, D., [1] 'General Semantics', in B. Partee (ed.), *Montague Grammar* (San Diego, Calif.: Academic, 1976), 1–50.

—— [2] *Philosophical Papers*, i (Oxford: OUP, 1983).

_____ [3] *On the Plurality of Worlds* (Oxford: Blackwell, 1986).

_____ [4] *Counterfactuals* (Oxford: Blackwell, 1986).

_____ [5] *Parts of Classes* (Oxford: Blackwell, 1991).

_____ [6] *Papers in Philosophical Logic* (Cambridge: CUP, 1998).

_____ [7] *Papers in Metaphysics and Epistemology* (Cambridge: CUP, 1999).

_____ [8] 'Tensing the Copula', *Mind* 111 (2002), 1–13.

Libera, A. de, [1] 'Abélard et le dictisme', *Cahiers de la revue de théologie et de philosophie* 6 (Neuchâtel: Université de Neuchâtel, 1981), 59–97.

_____ [2] *La Référence vide: Théories de la proposition* (Paris: Presses Universitaires de France, 2002).

Linsky, B., [1] 'Why Russell Abandoned Russellian Propositions', in A. Irvine and G. Wedeking (eds.), *Russell and Analytic Philosophy* (Toronto: University of Toronto, 1993), 193–209.

_____ [2] *Russell's Metaphysical Logic* (Stanford, Calif.: CSLI, 1999).

_____ [3] 'The Metaphysics of Logical Atomism', in N. Griffin (ed.), *The Cambridge Companion to Bertrand Russell* (Cambridge: CUP, 2003), 371–91.

Linsky, L., [1] 'Terms and Propositions in Russell's *Principles of Mathematics*', *Journal of the History of Philosophy* 26 (1988), 621–42.

_____ [2] 'The Unity of the Proposition', *Journal of the History of Philosophy* 30 (1992), 243–73.

Locke, J., *An Essay Concerning Human Understanding*, ed. P. H. Nidditch (Oxford: Clarendon, 1975).

Long, P., 'Are Predicates and Relational Expressions Incomplete?', *Philosophical Review* 78 (1969), 90–8.

Loux, M., *Metaphysics: A Contemporary Introduction*, 2nd edn. (London: Routledge, 2002).

MacBride, F., [1] 'On How we Know What there is', *Analysis* 58 (1998), 27–37.

_____ [2] 'Whence the Particular–Universal Distinction?', *Grazer Philosophische Studien* 67 (2004), 181–94.

_____ [3] 'Negation and Predication: A Defence of Ramsey's Thesis', in A.-S. Maurin and N.-E. Sahlin (eds.), *Ramsey's Ontology: Metaphysica*, special issue 3 (2005), 61–87.

_____ [4] 'The Particular–Universal Distinction: A Dogma of Metaphysics?', *Mind* 114 (2005), 565–614.

_____ [5] 'Ramsey on Universals', in H. Lillehammer and D. H. Mellor (eds.), *Ramsey's Legacy* (Oxford: Clarendon, 2005), 83–104.

_____ [6] 'Predicate Reference', in E. Lepore and B. Smith (eds.), *The Oxford Handbook of Philosophy of Language* (Oxford: Clarendon, 2006), 422–75.

_____ [7] 'Neutral Relations Revisited', *Dialectica* 61 (2007), 25–56.

McDowell, J., [1] *Mind and World* (Cambridge, Mass.: Harvard University Press, 1994).

_____ [2] 'Having the World in View: Sellars, Kant, and Intentionality', *Journal of Philosophy* 95 (1998), 431–91.

_____ [3] *Meaning, Knowledge, and Reality* (Cambridge, Mass.: Harvard University Press, 1998).

_____ [4] *Mind, Value, and Reality* (Cambridge, Mass.: Harvard University Press, 1998).

McDowell, J., [5] 'Gadamer and Davidson on Understanding and Relativism', in J. Malpas, U. Arnswald, and J. Kertscher (eds.), *Gadamer's Century* (Cambridge, Mass.: MIT, 2002), 173–93.

——[6] 'Evans's Frege', in J. Bermúdez (ed.), *Thought, Reference, and Experience: Themes from the Philosophy of Gareth Evans* (Oxford: Clarendon, 2005), 42–65.

McGinn, C., *Logical Properties: Identity, Existence, Predication, Necessity, Truth* (Oxford: Clarendon, 2000).

McGuinness, B., 'Pictures and Form in Wittgenstein's *Tractatus*', in I. Copi and R. Beard (eds.), *Essays on Wittgenstein's Tractatus* (London: Routledge, 1966), 137–56.

McGuire, J., 'Phenomenalism, Relations, and Monadic Representation: Leibniz on Predicate Levels', in J. Bogen and J. McGuire (eds.), *How Things Are* (Dordrecht: Reidel, 1985), 205–33.

McTaggart, J., *The Nature of Existence*, 2 vols. (Cambridge: CUP, 1927).

Maddy, P., 'Proper Classes', *Journal of Symbolic Logic* 48 (1983), 113–39.

Maier, A., *Ausgehendes Mittelalter: Gesammelte Aufsätze zur Geistesgeschichte des 14. Jahrhunderts*, 2 vols. (Rome: Edizioni di Storia e Letteratura, 1964/67).

Makin, G., *The Metaphysicians of Meaning: Russell and Frege on Sense and Denotation* (London: Routledge, 2000).

Malcolm, J., 'A Reconsideration of the Identity and Inherence Theories of the Copula', *Journal of the History of Philosophy* 17 (1979), 383–400.

Marciszewski, W., 'A Chronicle of Categorial Grammar', in W. Buszkowski, W. Marciszewski, and J. van Benthem (eds.), *Categorial Grammar* (Amsterdam: John Benjamins, 1988), 7–21.

Marcus, R., *Modalities: Philosophical Essays* (Oxford: OUP, 1993).

Marenbon, J., *The Philosophy of Peter Abelard* (Cambridge: CUP, 1997).

Marion, M., 'Wittgenstein and Ramsey on Identity', in J. Hintikka (ed.), *From Dedekind to Gödel: Essays on the Development of the Foundations of Mathematics* (Dordrecht: Kluwer, 1995), 343–71.

Martin, R., *Truth and Denotation: A Study in Semantical Theory* (Chicago: Chicago University Press, 1958).

Martin of Dacia, *Modi Significandi*, in *Martini de Dacia Opera*, ed. H. Roos (Copenhagen: Bagge, 1961), 1–117.

Mates, B., [1] 'Synonymity', *University of California Publications in Philosophy* 25 (1950), 201–26.

——[2] *Stoic Logic* (Berkeley, Calif.: University of California Press, 1961).

Matilal, B. K., and Sen, P. K., 'The Context Principle and Some Indian Controversies over Meaning', *Mind* 97 (1988), 73–97.

Matthews, P., 'Greek and Latin Linguistics', in G. Lepschy (ed.), *History of Linguistics*, ii (London: Longman, 1994), 1–133.

Maurin, A.-S., *If Tropes* (Dordrecht: Kluwer, 2002).

——and Sahlin, N.-E., 'Some Ontological Speculations: Ramsey on Universals, Particulars, and Facts', in A.-S. Maurin and N.-E. Sahlin (eds.), *Ramsey's Ontology: Metaphysica*, special issue 3 (2005), 7–28.

Meinong, A., [1] 'Über Gegenstände höherer Ordnung und deren Verhältnis zur inneren Wahrnehmung', in R. Haller (ed.), *Abhandlungen zur Erkenntnistheorie und Gegenstandstheorie* (Graz: Akademische Druck- & Verlagsanstalt, 1971), 379–480.

———[2] *Über Annahmen*, ed. R. Haller (Graz: Akademische Druck- & Verlagsanstalt, 1977).

Meirav, A., *Wholes, Sums, and Unities* (Dordrecht: Kluwer, 2003).

Mellor, D. H., 'Properties and Predicates', in J. Bacon, K. Campbell, and L. Reinhardt (eds.), *Ontology, Causality, and Mind* (Cambridge: CUP, 1993), 101–18.

Mendelsohn, R., 'Frege on Predication', in P. French, T. Uehling, and H. Wettstein (eds.), *Midwest Studies in Philosophy*, vi (Minneapolis: University of Minnesota, 1981), 69–82.

Menzel, C., 'The Proper Treatment of Predication in Fine-Grained Intensional Logic', *Philosophical Perspectives* 7 (1993), 61–87.

Mertz, D., 'Objects as Hierarchical Structures: A Comprehensive Ontology', in H. Hochberg and K. Mulligan (eds.), *Relations and Predicates* (Frankfurt and Lancaster: Ontos, 2004), 113–48.

Meschkowski, H., *Probleme des Unendlichen: Werk und Leben Georg Cantors* (Brunswick: Vieweg, 1967).

Michon, C., 'Asymétries: Thomas d'Aquin et Guillaume d'Occam précurseurs de Frege', *Les Études philosophiques* 3 (1996), 307–21.

Mill, J. S., *A System of Logic* (London: Routledge, 1886).

Milne, P., [1] 'Frege's Context Principle', *Mind* 95 (1986), 491–5.

———[2] 'Reply to Currie', *Mind* 97 (1988), 457–60.

Monboddo [James Burnet], *Of the Origins and Progress of Language*, 6 vols. (Edinburgh: Kincaid & Creech, 1773–92; repr. Hildesheim: Olms, 1974).

Monk, R., *Bertrand Russell: The Spirit of Solitude* (London: Vintage, 1997).

Montague, R., *Formal Philosophy*, ed. R. Thomason (London: Yale University Press, 1974).

Moore, A., [1] 'Set Theory, Skolem's Paradox and the *Tractatus*', *Analysis* 45 (1985), 13–20.

———[2] *The Infinite* (London: Routledge, 1990).

Moore, G. E., [1] *Some Main Problems of Philosophy* (London: Allen & Unwin, 1953).

———[2] *Selected Writings*, ed. T. Baldwin (London: Routledge, 1993).

Moore, G. H., 'Beyond First-Order Logic: The Historical Interplay between Mathematical Logic and Axiomatic Set Theory', *History and Philosophy of Logic* 1 (1980), 95–137.

Moore, J., [1] 'Propositions, Numbers, and the Problem of Arbitrary Identification', *Synthese* 120 (1999), 229–63.

———[2] 'Propositions without Identity', *Noûs* 33 (1999), 1–29.

Mugnai, M., *Leibniz's Theory of Relations* (Stuttgart: Franz Steiner, 1992).

Muller, F. A., 'The Implicit Definition of the Set Concept', *Synthese* 138 (2004), 417–51.

Mulligan, K., Simons, P., and Smith, B., 'Truth-Makers', *Philosophy and Phenomenological Research* 44 (1984), 287–321.

Murdoch, J., [1] 'The "Equality" of Infinities in the Middle Ages', *Actes du XIe Congrès International d'Histoire des Sciences* (1968), 171–4.

——[2] 'Infinity and Continuity', in N. Kretzmann, A. Kenny, and J. Pinborg (eds.), *The Cambridge History of Later Medieval Philosophy* (Cambridge: CUP, 1982), 564–91.

Myhill, J., 'Problems Arising in the Formalization of Intensional Logic', *Logique et analyse* 1 (1958), 78–83.

Neale, S., [1] *Descriptions* (Cambridge, Mass.: MIT, 1990).

——[2] 'The Philosophical Significance of Gödel's Slingshot', *Mind* 104 (1995), 761–825.

Nemirov, L., 'No Argument Against Ramsey', *Analysis* 39 (1979), 201–9.

Neumann, J. von, 'Eine Axiomatisierung der Mengenlehre', *Journal für die reine und angewandte Mathematik* 154 (1925), 219–40.

Nidditch, P., *The Development of Mathematical Logic* (London: RKP, 1962).

Nolan, D., 'What's Wrong with Infinite Regresses?', *Metaphilosophy* 32 (2001), 523–38.

Noonan, H., 'The Concept Horse', in P. F. Strawson and A. Chakrabarti (eds.), *Universals, Concepts, and Qualities: New Essays on the Meaning of Predicates* (Aldershot: Ashgate, 2006), 155–76.

Norman, A., 'Regress and the Doctrine of Epistemic Original Sin', *Philosophical Quarterly* 47 (1997), 477–94.

Normore, C., 'Buridan's Ontology', in J. Bogen and J. McGuire (eds.), *How Things Are* (Dordrecht: Reidel, 1985), 189–203.

Nuchelmans, G., [1] *Theories of the Proposition: Ancient and Medieval Conceptions of the Bearers of Truth and Falsity* (Amsterdam: North Holland, 1973).

——[2] 'Adam Wodeham on the Meaning of Declarative Sentences', *Historiographia Linguistica* 7 (1980), 177–87.

——[3] *Late Scholastic and Humanist Theories of the Proposition* (Amsterdam: North Holland, 1980).

——[4] 'The Semantics of Propositions', in N. Kretzmann, A. Kenny, and J. Pinborg (eds.), *The Cambridge History of Later Medieval Philosophy* (Cambridge: CUP, 1982), 197–210.

——[5] *Judgment and Proposition: From Descartes to Kant* (Amsterdam: North Holland, 1983).

——[6] *Secundum/Tertium Adiacens: Vicissitudes of a Logical Distinction* (Amsterdam: Koninklijke Nederlandse Akademie van Wetenschappen, 1992).

Ockham, W., [1] *Summa Logicae*, ed. P. Boehner *et al.* (St Bonaventura, NY: Franciscan Institute, 1974).

——[2] *Expositio in Librum Perihermeneias Aristotelis*, etc., ed. A. Gambatese *et al.* (St Bonaventura, NY: Franciscan Institute, 1978).

——[3] *Quodlibeta Septem*, ed. J. C. Wey (St Bonaventura, NY: Franciscan Institute, 1980).

—— [4] *Scriptum in Librum Primum Sententiarum Ordinatio*, dd. xix–xlviii, ed. G. Etzkorn and F. Kelley (St Bonaventura, NY: Franciscan Institute, 2000).

Oliver, A., [1] 'Could there be Conjunctive Universals?', *Analysis* 52 (1992), 88–103.

—— [2] 'Frege and Dummett are Two', *Philosophical Quarterly* 44 (1994), 74–82.

—— [3] 'Some More Remarks on Logical Form', in R. Gaskin (ed.), *Grammar in Early Twentieth-Century Philosophy* (London: Routledge, 2001), 142–62.

—— [4] 'The Reference Principle', *Analysis* 65 (2005), 177–87.

—— and Smiley, T., [1] 'Strategies for a Logic of Plurals', *Philosophical Quarterly* 51 (2001), 289–306.

—— [2] 'Multigrade Predicates', *Mind* 113 (2004), 609–81.

—— [3] 'Plural Descriptions and Many-Valued Functions', *Mind* 114 (2005), 1039–68.

Olson, K., *An Essay on Facts* (Stanford, Calif.: CSLI, 1987).

Orenstein, A., 'What Makes Substitutional Quantification Different?', in R. Haller and W. Grassl (eds.), *Language, Logic, and Philosophy* (Vienna: Hölder-Pichler-Tempsky, 1980), 346–9.

Orilia, F., [1] 'Type-Free Property Theory, Bradley's Regress, and Meinong and Russell Reconciled', *Grazer Philosophische Studien* 39 (1991), 103–25.

—— [2] 'States of Affairs: Bradley vs. Meinong', *Meinongian Studies* 2 (2006), 213–38.

Owen, G. E. L., *Logic, Science, and Dialectic* (London: Duckworth, 1986).

Palmer, A., *Concept and Object: The Unity of the Proposition in Logic and Psychology* (London: Routledge, 1988).

Panaccio, C., [1], 'Guillaume d'Occam: Signification et Supposition', in E. Vance and L. Brind'Amour (eds.), *Archéologie du signe* (Toronto: Pontifical Institute of Medieval Studies, 1982), 265–86.

—— [2] 'Propositionalism and Atomism in Ockham's Semantics', *Franciscan Studies* 44 (1984), 61–70.

—— [3] 'From Mental Word to Mental Language', *Philosphical Topics* 20 (1992), 125–47.

—— [4] *Le Discours intérieur de Platon à Guillaume d'Ockham* (Paris: Seuil, 1999).

—— [5] *Ockham on Concepts* (Aldershot: Ashgate, 2004).

Pap, A., 'Types and Meaninglessness', *Mind* 69 (1960), 41–54.

Paqué, R., *Das Pariser Nominalistenstatut: Zur Entscheidung des Realitätsbegriffs der neuzeitlichen Naturwissenschaft* (Berlin: Walter de Gruyter, 1970).

Parsons, C., [1] 'Some Remarks on Frege's Conception of Extension', in M. Schirn (ed.), *Studien zu Frege*, i (Stuttgart: Frommann-Holzboog, 1976), 265–77.

—— [2] *Mathematics in Philosophy* (Ithaca, NY: Cornell University Press, 1983).

Parsons, T., [1] 'Criticism of "Are Predicates and Relational Expressions Incomplete?" ', *Philosophical Review* 79 (1970), 240–5.

—— [2] 'Why Frege should Not have Said "The Concept *Horse* is Not a Concept" ', *History of Philosophy Quarterly* 3 (1986), 449–65.

Partee, B., [1] 'Some Transformational Extensions of Montague Grammar', in B. Partee (ed.), *Montague Grammar* (San Diego, Calif.: Academic, 1976), 51–76.

—— [2] *Compositionality in Formal Semantics* (Oxford: Blackwell, 2004).

Partee, B., ter Meulen, A., and Wall, R., *Mathematical Methods in Linguistics* (Dordrecht: Kluwer, 1990).

—— and Rooth, M., 'Generalized Conjunction and Type Ambiguity', in P. Porter and B. Partee (eds.), *Formal Semantics: The Essential Readings* (Oxford: Blackwell, 2002), 334–56.

Pears, D., [1] 'Universals', in M. Loux (ed.), *Universals and Particulars* (New York: Doubleday, 1970), 35–49.

—— [2] 'The Relation between Wittgenstein's Picture Theory of Propositions and Russell's Theories of Judgment', *Philosophical Review* 86 (1977), 177–96.

Pelham, J., and Urquhart, A., 'Russellian Propositions', in D. Prawitz, B. Skyrms, and D. Westerståhl (eds.), *Logic, Methodology and Philosophy of Science* 9 (1994), 307–26.

Perler, D., *Der propositionale Wahrheitsbegriff im 14. Jahrhundert* (Berlin: Walter de Gruyter, 1990).

Phemister, P., *Leibniz and the Natural World: Activity, Passivity, and Corporeal Substances in Leibniz's Philosophy* (Dordrecht: Springer, 2005).

Pinborg, J., [1] *Die Entwicklung der Sprachtheorie im Mittelalter* (Münster: Aschendorff, 1967).

—— [2] 'Walter Burleigh on the Meaning of Propositions', *Classica et Mediaevalia* 28 (1967), 394–404.

—— [3] *Logik und Semantik im Mittelalter* (Stuttgart: Frommann-Holzboog, 1972).

Poincaré, H., 'Les Mathématiques et la logique', *Revue de métaphysique et de morale* 14 (1906), 294–317.

Poole, G., *Syntactic Theory* (Basingstoke: Palgrave, 2002).

Potter, M., [1] *Reason's Nearest Kin: Philosophies of Arithmetic from Kant to Carnap* (Oxford: OUP, 2000).

—— [2] *Set Theory and its Philosophy* (Oxford: OUP, 2004).

—— [3] 'Ramsey's Transcendental Argument', in H. Lillehammer and D. H. Mellor (eds.), *Ramsey's Legacy* (Oxford: Clarendon, 2005), 71–82.

Priest, G., [1] *Beyond the Limits of Thought*, 2nd edn. (Oxford: Clarendon, 2002).

—— [2] *In Contradiction: A Study of the Transconsistent*, 2nd edn. (Oxford: Clarendon, 2006).

Priestley, J., *A Course of Lectures on the Theory of Language and Universal Grammar* (Warrington: Eyres, 1762; repr. Menston, Ill.: Scolar, 1970).

Prior, A., [1] *Time and Modality* (Oxford: Clarendon, 1957).

—— [2] 'Entities', in *Papers in Logic and Ethics* (London: Duckworth, 1976), 25–32.

—— [3] *The Doctrine of Propositions and Terms*, ed. P. T. Geach and A. Kenny (London: Duckworth, 1976).

Putnam, H., [1] *Mathematics, Matter and Method* (Cambridge: CUP, 1975).

—— [2] *Reason, Truth, and History* (Cambridge: CUP, 1981).

Quine, W. V., [1] 'Designation and Existence', *Journal of Philosophy* 36 (1939), 701–9.

—— [2] *From a Logical Point of View* (Cambridge, Mass.: Harvard University Press, 1953).

—— [3] *Word and Object* (Cambridge, Mass.: MIT, 1960).

—— [4] *Ontological Relativity and Other Essays* (New York: Columbia University Press, 1969).

_____ [5] *The Roots of Reference* (La Salle, Ill.: Open Court, 1973).

_____ [6] *The Ways of Paradox and Other Essays*, rev. edn. (Cambridge, Mass.: Harvard University Press, 1976).

_____ [7] 'The Variable and its Place in Reference', in Z. van Straaten (ed.), *Philosophical Subjects* (Oxford: Clarendon, 1980), 164–73.

_____ [8] *Theories and Things* (Cambridge, Mass.: Harvard University Press, 1981).

_____ [9] *Methods of Logic*, 4th edn. (Cambridge, Mass.: Harvard University Press, 1982).

_____ [10] *Philosophy of Logic*, 2nd edn. (Cambridge, Mass.: Harvard University Press, 1986).

_____ [11] *Selected Logic Papers*, enlarged edn. (Cambridge, Mass.: Harvard University Press, 1995).

Ramachandran, M., 'A Strawsonian Objection to Russell's Theory of Descriptions', *Analysis* 53 (1993), 209–12.

Ramsey, F. P., [1] 'Universals and the Method of Analysis', *Proceedings of the Aristotelian Society*, supp. vol. 6 (1926), 17–26.

_____ [2] *The Foundations of Mathematics*, ed. R. Braithwaite (London: RKP, 1931).

_____ [3] *Notes on Philosophy, Probability and Mathematics*, ed. M. Galavotti (Naples: Bibliopolis, 1991).

Read, S., 'The Unity of the Fact', *Philosophy* 80 (2005), 317–42.

Resnik, M., [1] 'Frege's Theory of Incomplete Entities', *Philosophy of Science* 32 (1965), 329–41.

_____ [2] 'The Context Principle in Frege's Philosophy', *Philosophy and Phenomenological Research* 27 (1967), 356–65.

_____ [3] 'Frege's Context Principle Revisited', in M. Schirn (ed.), *Studien zu Frege*, iii (Stuttgart: Frommann-Holzboog, 1976), 35–49.

_____ [4] 'Frege and Analytic Philosophy: Facts and Speculations', in P. French, T. Uehling, and H. Wettstein (eds.), *Midwest Studies in Philosophy*, vi (Minneapolis: University of Minnesota, 1981), 83–103.

Ricketts, T., [1] 'Frege, the *Tractatus*, and the Logocentric Predicament', *Noûs* 19 (1985), 3–15.

_____ [2] 'Objectivity and Objecthood: Frege's Metaphysics of Judgment', in L. Haaparanta and J. Hintikka (eds.), *Frege Synthesized: Essays on the Philosophical and Foundational Work of Gottlob Frege* (Dordrecht: Reidel, 1986), 65–95.

_____ [3] 'Generality, Meaning, and Sense in Frege', *Pacific Philosophical Quarterly* 67 (1986), 172–95.

_____ [4] 'Truth and Propositional Unity in Early Russell', in J. Floyd and S. Shieh (eds.), *Future Pasts: The Analytic Tradition in Twentieth-Century Philosophy* (Oxford: OUP, 2001), 101–21.

_____ [5] 'Wittgenstein against Frege and Russell', in E. Reck (ed.), *From Frege to Wittgenstein: Perspectives on Early Analytic Philosophy* (Oxford: OUP, 2002), 227–51.

Rijk, L. M. de, [1] *Logica Modernorum*, ii/2 (Assen: Van Gorcum, 1967).

_____ [2] 'La Signification de la proposition (dictum propositionis) chez Abélard', *Studia Mediewistyczne* 16 (1975), 155–61.

Rijk, L. M. de, [3] 'Die Wirkung der neuplatonischen Semantik auf das mittelalterliche Denken über das Sein', in J. Beckmann *et al.* (eds.), *Sprache und Erkenntnis im Mittelalter* (Berlin: Walter de Gruyter, 1981), 19–35.

——[4] 'Peter Abelard's Semantics and his Doctrine of Being', *Vivarium* 24 (1986), 85–127.

Ross, W. D., *Aristotle's Metaphysics*, 2 vols. (Oxford: Clarendon, 1924).

Rumfitt, I., [1] 'Frege's Theory of Predication: An Elaboration and Defence, with Some New Applications', *Philosophical Review* 103 (1994), 599–637.

——[2] 'Sentences, Names, and Semantic Values', *Philosophical Quarterly* 46 (1996), 66–72.

——[3] 'Singular Terms and Arithmetical Logicism', *Philosophical Books* 44 (2003), 193–219.

——[4] 'Plural Terms: Another Variety of Reference?', in J. Bermúdez (ed.), *Thought, Reference, and Experience: Themes from the Philosophy of Gareth Evans* (Oxford: Clarendon, 2005), 84–123.

Russell, B., [1] *An Essay on the Foundations of Geometry* (London: Routledge, 1996).

——[2] *A Critical Exposition of the Philosophy of Leibniz*, 2nd edn. (London: Allen & Unwin, 1937).

——[3] *The Principles of Mathematics*, 2nd edn. (London: Allen & Unwin, 1937).

——[4] 'The Nature of Truth', *Proceedings of the Aristotelian Society* 7 (1906–7), 28–49.

——[5] 'Knowledge by Acquaintance and Knowledge by Description', in his *Mysticism and Logic* (London: Unwin, 1959), 200–21.

——[6] *Philosophical Essays* (London: Routledge, 1994).

——[7] 'Some Explanations in Reply to Mr. Bradley', *Mind* 19 (1910), 373–8.

——[8] *The Problems of Philosophy* (Oxford: OUP, 1967).

——[9] *Theory of Knowledge: The 1913 Manuscript* (London: Routledge, 1992).

——[10] *Our Knowledge of the External World* (London: Allen & Unwin, 1926).

——[11] *Introduction to Mathematical Philosophy* (London: Allen & Unwin, 1919).

——[12] *An Outline of Philosophy* (London: Routledge, 1993).

——[13] *Logic and Knowledge*, ed. R. C. Marsh (London: Allen & Unwin, 1956).

——[14] *My Philosophical Development* (London: Routledge, 1993).

——[15] *Essays in Analysis*, ed. D. Lackey (London: Allen & Unwin, 1973).

——[16] *The Collected Papers of Bertrand Russell*, ii. *Philosophical Papers 1896–99*, ed. N. Griffin and A. Lewis (London: Unwin Hyman, 1990).

——[17] *The Selected Letters of Bertrand Russell: The Private Years, 1884–1914*, ed. N. Griffin (London: Routledge, 1992).

——[18] *The Collected Papers of Bertrand Russell*, iv. *Foundations of Logic 1903–05*, ed. A. Urquhart and A. Lewis (London: Routledge, 1994).

Ryle, G., *Collected Papers*, 2 vols. (London: Hutchinson, 1971).

Sainsbury, R. M., [1] *Russell* (London: Routledge, 1979).

——[2] *Paradoxes*, 2nd edn. (Cambridge: CUP, 1995).

——[3] 'How Can we Say Something?', in R. Monk and A. Palmer (eds.), *Bertrand Russell and the Origins of Analytical Philosophy* (Bristol: Thoemmes, 1996), 137–53.

_____[4] 'Sense without Reference', in A. Newen, U. Nortmann, and R. Stuhlmann-Laeisz (eds.), *Building on Frege: New Essays on Sense, Content, and Concept* (Stanford, Calif.: CSLI, 2002), 211–30.

_____[5] *Reference without Referents* (Oxford: Clarendon, 2005).

Salmon, N., *Frege's Puzzle* (Cambridge, Mass.: MIT, 1986).

Schiffer, S., *The Things we Mean* (Oxford: Clarendon, 2003).

Schlick, M., *Die Probleme der Philosophie in ihrem Zusammenhang* (Frankfurt: Suhrkamp, 1986).

Schnieder, B., [1] 'Once More: Bradleyan Regresses', in H. Hochberg and K. Mulligan (eds.), *Relations and Predicates* (Frankfurt and Lancaster: Ontos, 2004), 219–56.

_____[2] 'The Importance of "Being Earnest"', *Philosophical Quarterly* 57 (2007), 40–55.

Schönfinkel, M., 'Über die Bausteine der mathematischen Logik', *Mathematische Annalen* 92 (1924), 305–16.

Schoenflies, A., 'Über die logischen Paradoxen der Mengenlehre', *Jahresbericht der deutschen Mathematiker-Vereinigung* 15 (1906), 19–25.

Schubert, A., *Untersuchungen zur stoischen Bedeutungslehre* (Göttingen: Vandenhoek & Ruprecht, 1994).

Scotus, J. D., *Opera Omnia*, vii, ed. P. Koser (Vatican City: Typis Polyglottis Vaticanis, 1973).

Seargent, D., *Plurality and Continuity: An Essay in G. F. Stout's Theory of Universals* (Dordrecht: Nijhoff, 1985).

Searle, J., [1] *Speech Acts: An Essay in the Philosophy of Language* (Cambridge: CUP, 1970).

_____[2] 'What is a Speech-Act?', in J. Searle (ed.), *The Philosophy of Language* (Oxford: OUP, 1971), 39–53.

Sellars, W., [1] *Science, Perception, and Reality* (New York: Humanities, 1963).

_____[2] 'Towards a Theory of Predication', in J. Bogen and J. McGuire (eds.), *How Things Are* (Dordrecht: Reidel, 1985), 285–322.

Shaftesbury [Anthony Ashley Cooper], *Characteristicks of Men, Manners, Opinions, Times*, 3 vols. (Indianapolis: Liberty Fund, 2001).

Sherwood, W., [1] *Syncategoremata*, in J. R. O'Donnell (ed.), 'The Syncategoremata of William of Sherwood', *Medieval Studies* 3 (1941), 46–93.

_____[2] *William of Sherwood's Treatise on Syncategorematic Words*, ed. and tr. N. Kretzmann (Minneapolis: Minnesota University Press, 1968).

Siderits, M., [1] 'Word Meaning, Sentence Meaning, and *Apoha*', *Journal of Indian Philosophy* 13 (1985), 133–51.

_____[2] 'The Prābhākara Mimāmsā Theory of Related Designation', in B. K. Matilal and J. L. Shaw (eds.), *Analytical Philosophy in Comparative Perspective* (Dordrecht: Reidel, 1985), 253–97.

_____[3] *Indian Philosophy of Language* (Dordrecht: Kluwer, 1991).

Simons, P., [1] 'Logic and Common Nouns', *Analysis* 38 (1978), 161–7.

_____[2] 'Individuals, Groups, and Manifolds', in R. Haller and W. Grassl (eds.), *Logic, Language, and Philosophy* (Vienna: Hölder-Pichler-Tempsky, 1980), 483–6.

Simons, P., [3] 'Unsaturatedness', *Grazer Philosophische Studien* 14 (1981), 73–96.

——[4] 'On Understanding Leśniewski', *History and Philosophy of Logic* 3 (1982), 165–91.

——[5] 'Token Resistance', *Analysis* 42 (1982), 195–203.

——[6] 'Function and Predicate', *Conceptus* 17 (1983), 75–89.

——[7] 'The Old Problem of Complex and Fact', *Teoria* 5 (1985), 205–25.

——[8] *Parts: A Study in Ontology* (Oxford: Clarendon, 1987).

——[9] 'Ramsey, Particulars, and Universals', *Theoria* 57 (1991), 150–61.

——[10] 'Bolzano on Collections', in W. Künne *et al.* (eds.), *Bolzano and Analytic Philosophy* (*Grazer Philosophische Studien* 53, 1997), 87–115.

——[11] 'Higher-Order Quantification and Ontological Commitment', *Dialectica* 51 (1997), 255–71.

Simplicius, *In Aristotelis Categorias Commentarium*, ed. C. Kalbfleisch (Berlin: Königl. Preuß. Akademie der Wissenschaften, 1907).

Sinisi, V., [1] 'Nominalism and Common Names', *Philosophical Review* 71 (1962), 230–5.

——[2] 'Discussion: "∈" and common names', *Philosophy of Science* 32 (1965), 281–6.

Sluga, H., [1] 'Frege und die Typentheorie', in M. Käsbauer (ed.), *Logik und Logikkalkül* (Munich: Alber, 1962), 195–209.

——[2] 'Review of *Frege: Nachgelassene Schriften*', *Journal of Philosophy* 68 (1971), 265–72.

Słupecki, J., 'St. Leśniewski's Protothetics', *Studia Logica* 1 (1953), 44–112.

Smith, A., *Considerations Concerning the First Formation of Languages*, in J. Bryce (ed.), *Adam Smith: Lectures on Rhetoric and Belles Lettres* (Indianapolis: Liberty Fund, 1985), 203–26.

Smith, B., 'An Essay in Formal Ontology', *Grazer Philosophische Studien* 6 (1978), 39–62.

Smith, N., 'Frege's Judgement Stroke', *Australasian Journal of Philosophy* 78 (2000), 153–75.

Smith, Q., 'The Infinite Regress of Temporal Attributions', *Southern Journal of Philosophy* 24 (1986), 383–95.

Soames, S., 'Direct Reference, Propositional Attitudes, and Semantic Content', in N. Salmon and S. Soames (eds.), *Propositions and Attitudes* (Oxford: OUP, 1988), 197–239.

Sommers, F., 'Types and Ontology', in P. F. Strawson (ed.), *Philosophical Logic* (Oxford: OUP, 1967), 138–69.

Sommerville, S., 'Wittgenstein to Russell (July, 1913). "I am very sorry to hear . . . my objection paralyses you"', in R. Haller and W. Grassl (eds.), *Language, Logic, and Philosophy* (Vienna: Hölder-Pichler-Tempsky, 1980), 182–8.

Soto, D. de, *Summulae* (Salamanca, 1554; repr. Hildesheim: Olms, 1980).

Spade, P. V., [1] 'Ockham's Distinction[s] between Absolute and Connotative Terms', *Vivarium* 13 (1975), 55–76.

——[2] 'The Semantics of Terms', in N. Kretzmann, A. Kenny, and J. Pinborg (eds.), *The Cambridge History of Later Medieval Philosophy* (Cambridge: CUP, 1982), 188–96.

Stalnaker, R., [1] 'Propositions', in A. MacKay and D. Merrill (eds.), *Issues in the Philosophy of Language* (London: Yale University Press, 1976), 79–91.

——[2] *Context and Content* (Oxford: OUP, 1999).

Stenius, E., [1] *Wittgenstein's Tractatus: A Critical Exposition of the Main Lines of Thought* (Oxford: Blackwell, 1960).

——[2] 'Sets', *Synthese* 27 (1974), 161–88.

Sterne, L., *The Life and Opinions of Tristram Shandy* (Harmondsworth: Penguin, 1967).

Stevens, G., [1] 'The Truth and Nothing But the Truth, Yet Never the Whole Truth: Frege, Russell, and the Analysis of Unities', *History and Philosophy of Logic* 24 (2003), 221–40.

——[2] 'From Russell's Paradox to the Theory of Judgement: Wittgenstein and Russell on the Unity of the Proposition', *Theoria* 70 (2004), 28–61.

——[3] *The Russellian Origins of Analytical Philosophy: Bertrand Russell and the Unity of the Proposition* (London: Routledge, 2005).

Stevenson, L., 'Frege's Two Definitions of Quantification', *Philosophical Quarterly* 23 (1973), 207–23.

Stirton, W., [1] 'A Problem Concerning the Definition of "Proper Name" ', *Philosophical Quarterly* 44 (1994), 83–9.

——[2] 'Singular Term, Subject, and Predicate', *Philosophical Quarterly* 50 (2000), 191–207.

Strawson, P. F., [1] *Individuals* (London: Methuen, 1959).

——[2] *Logico-Linguistic Papers* (London: Methuen, 1971).

——[3] 'Replies', in Z. van Straaten (ed.), *Philosophical Subjects* (Oxford: Clarendon, 1980), 260–96.

——[4] 'Concepts and Properties or Predication and Copulation', *Philosophical Quarterly* 37 (1987), 402–6.

——[5] 'My Philosophy', in P. K. Sen and R. R. Verma (eds.), *The Philosophy of P. F. Strawson* (New Delhi: Indian Council of Philosophical Research, 1995), 1–18.

——[6] *Subject and Predicate in Logic and Grammar*, 2nd edn. (Aldershot: Ashgate, 2004).

Stuhlmann-Laeisz, R., 'Das Kontextprinzip', in G. Gabriel and U. Dathe (eds.), *Gottlob Frege: Werk und Wirkung* (Paderborn: Mentis, 2000), 91–101.

Suarez, F., *Disputationes Metaphysicae*, in *Opera Omnia*, xxv and xxvi (Paris: Vivès, 1856–66; repr. Hildesheim: Olms, 1998).

Sullivan, P., [1] 'The Functional Model of Sentential Complexity', *Journal of Philosophical Logic* 21 (1992), 91–108.

——[2] 'The Sense of "A Name of a Truth-Value" ', *Philosophical Quarterly* 44 (1994), 476–81.

——[3] 'Wittgenstein on "The Foundations of Mathematics", June 1927', *Theoria* 61 (1995), 105–42.

——[4] 'Wittgenstein's Context Principle', in W. Vossenkuhl (ed.), *Ludwig Wittgenstein: Tractatus Logico-Philosophicus* (Berlin: Akademie, 2001), 65–88.

——[5] 'A Version of the Picture Theory', in W. Vossenkuhl (ed.), *Ludwig Wittgenstein: Tractatus Logico-Philosophicus* (Berlin: Akademie, 2001), 89–110.

Sullivan, P., [6] ' "The General Propositional Form is a Variable" (*Tractatus* 4.53)', *Mind* 113 (2004), 43–56.

Süssmilch, J., *Versuch eines Beweises, daß die erste Sprache ihren Urprung nicht vom Menschen, sondern allein vom Schöpfer erhalten habe* (Berlin: Königl. Preuß. Akademie der Wissenschaften, 1766; repr. Cologne: themen, 1998).

Swift, J., *Gulliver's Travels* (Harmondsworth: Penguin, 1985).

Tarski, A., [1] 'Der Wahrheitsbegriff in den formalisierten Sprachen', *Studia Philosophica* 1 (1935), 261–405, tr. as [2].

———[2] 'The Concept of Truth in Formalized Languages', tr. J. Woodger, in J. Corcoran (ed.), *Logic, Semantics, Metamathematics*, 2nd edn. (Indianapolis: Hackett, 1956), 152–278.

Textor, M., [1] *Bolzanos Propositionalismus* (Berlin: Walter de Gruyter, 1996).

———[2] 'Bolzano's Sententialism', in W. Künne *et al.* (eds.), *Bolzano and Analytic Philosophy* (*Grazer Philosophische Studien* 53, 1997), 181–202.

Thiel, C., *Sinn und Bedeutung in der Logik Gottlob Freges* (Meisenheim: Hain, 1965).

Tiles, M., *The Philosophy of Set Theory: A Historical Introduction to Cantor's Paradise* (Mineola, NY: Dover, 1989).

Trentman, J., [1] 'Predication and Universals in Vincent Ferrer's Logic', *Franciscan Studies* 28 (1964), 47–62.

———[2] 'Leśniewski's Ontology and Some Medieval Logicians', *Notre Dame Journal of Formal Logic* 7 (1966), 361–4.

Trettin, K., 'Tropes and Relations', in H. Hochberg and K. Mulligan (eds.), *Relations and Predicates* (Frankfurt and Lancaster: Ontos, 2004), 203–18.

Tugendhat, E., [1] 'Die Bedeutung des Ausdrucks "Bedeutung" bei Frege', in M. Schirn (ed.), *Studien zu Frege*, iii (Stuttgart: Frommann-Holzboog, 1976), 51–69.

———[2] *Vorlesungen zur Einführung in die sprachanalytische Philosophie* (Frankfurt: Suhrkamp, 1976).

Tweedale, M., *Abailard on Universals* (Amsterdam: North Holland, 1976).

Urmson, J., *Philosophical Analysis* (Oxford: Clarendon, 1956).

Urquhart, A., 'The Theory of Types', in N. Griffin (ed.), *The Cambridge Companion to Bertrand Russell* (Cambridge: CUP, 2003), 286–309.

Vallicella, W., [1] 'Three Conceptions of States of Affairs', *Noûs* 34 (2000), 237–59.

———[2] *A Paradigm Theory of Existence: Onto-Theology Vindicated* (Dordrecht: Kluwer, 2002).

———[3] 'Relations, Monism, and the Vindication of Bradley's Regress', *Dialectica* 56 (2002), 3–35.

———[4] 'Bradley's Regress and Relation-Instances', *Modern Schoolman* 81 (2004), 159–83.

Waim, G., *Tractatus Noticiarum* (Paris, 1528).

Wallace, J., 'On the Frame of Reference', *Synthese* 22 (1970), 117–50.

Wang, H., [1] *From Mathematics to Philosophy* (London: RKP, 1974).

———[2] 'Large Sets', in R. Butts and J. Hintikka (eds.), *Logic, Foundations of Mathematics, and Computability Theory* (Dordrecht: Reidel, 1977), 309–33.

———[3] *A Logical Journey from Gödel to Philosophy* (Cambridge, Mass.: MIT, 1996).

Watts, I., *Logic or the Right Use of Reason in the Inquiry after Truth* (London: Dove, 1825; repr. Elibron Classics, 2005).

Weidemann, H., *Aristoteles Peri Hermeneias* (Berlin: Akademie, 1994).

Weinberg, J., *Abstraction, Relation, and Induction: Three Essays in the History of Thought* (Madison: University of Wisconsin, 1965).

Weiner, J., [1] *Frege Explained: From Arithmetic to Analytic Philosophy* (Chicago and La Salle, Ill.: Open Court, 2004).

———[2] 'Semantic Descent', *Mind* 114 (2005), 321–54.

Weir, A., 'Naïve Set Theory is Innocent!', *Mind* 107 (1998), 763–98.

Weiss, B., 'On the Demise of Russell's Multiple Relations Theory of Judgement', *Theoria* 61 (1995), 261–82.

Wendland, V., 'Die Wissenschaftslehre Gregors von Rimini in der Diskussion', in H. Oberman (ed.), *Gregor von Rimini: Werk und Wirkung bis zur Reformation* (Berlin: Walter de Gruyter, 1981).

Whately, R., *Elements of Logic* (Boston and Cambridge: James Munroe, 1848).

Whitehead, A., and Russell, B., *Principia Mathematica*, 2nd edn., 3 vols. (Cambridge: CUP, 1925).

Wiggins, D., [1] 'On Sentence-Sense, Word-Sense and Difference of Word-Sense: Towards a Philosophical Theory of Dictionaries', in D. Steinberg and L. Jakobovits (eds.), *Semantics: An Interdisciplinary Reader in Philosophy, Linguistics, and Psychology* (Cambridge: CUP, 1971), 14–34.

———[2] *Sameness and Substance* (Oxford: Blackwell, 1980).

———[3] 'The Sense and Reference of Predicates: A Running Repair to Frege's Doctrine and a Plea for the Copula', in C. Wright (ed.), *Frege: Tradition and Influence* (Oxford: Blackwell, 1984), 126–43.

———[4] 'Meaning and Truth Conditions: From Frege's Grand Design to Davidson's', in B. Hale and C. Wright (eds.), *A Companion to the Philosophy of Language* (Oxford: Blackwell, 1997), 3–28.

Williamson, T., 'Converse Relations', *Philosophical Review* 94 (1985), 249–62.

Wilson, F., 'Burgersdijk, Bradley, Russell, Bergmann: Four Philosophers on the Ontology of Relations', *Modern Schoolman* 72 (1995), 283–310.

Winch, P., *Trying to Make Sense* (Oxford: Blackwell, 1987).

Wittgenstein, L., [1] *Tractatus Logico-Philosophicus* (London: RKP, 1922).

———[2] *Philosophical Investigations*, tr. G. E. M. Anscombe (Oxford: Blackwell, 1958).

———[3] *Philosophische Grammatik*, ed. R. Rhees (Frankfurt: Suhrkamp, 1973).

———[4] *Letters to C. K. Ogden* (Oxford: Blackwell, 1973).

———[5] *Philosophische Untersuchungen* (Frankfurt: Suhrkamp, 1977).

———[6] *Notebooks 1914–1916*, 2nd edn., ed. G. E. M. Anscombe and G. H. von Wright (Oxford: Blackwell, 1979).

———[7] *Über Gewissheit/On Certainty*, ed. G. E. M. Anscombe (Oxford: Blackwell, 1979).

———[8] *Vermischte Bemerkungen/Culture and Value*, ed. G. H. von Wright (Oxford: Blackwell, 1980).

Wittgenstein, L., [9] *Briefe: Briefwechsel mit B. Russell, G. E. Moore, J. M. Keynes, F. P. Ramsey, W. Eccles, P. Engelmann, und L. von Ficker* (Frankfurt: Suhrkamp, 1980).

_____ [10] *Wittgenstein's Lectures: Cambridge 1930–1932*, ed. D. Lee (Totowa, NJ: Rowman & Littlefield, 1980).

_____ [11] *Geheime Tagebücher*, 3rd edn., ed. W. Baum (Vienna: Turia & Kant, 1992).

Wodeham, A., *Lectura Secunda in Primum Sententiarum: Prologus et Distinctio Prima* eds. R. Wood and G. Gal (St Bonaventura, NY: Franciscan Institute, 1990).

Wolff, C., *Philosophia Rationalis sive Logica* (Frankfurt and Leipzig: Renger, 1732).

Wood, M., *Categorial Grammars* (London: Routledge, 1993).

Woodcock, E. C., *A New Latin Syntax* (London: Methuen, 1959).

Wright, C., [1] *Frege's Conception of Numbers as Objects* (Aberdeen: Aberdeen University Press, 1983).

_____ [2] 'Truth: A Traditional Debate Reviewed', in S. Blackburn and K. Simmons (eds.), *Truth* (Oxford: OUP, 1999), 203–38.

_____ [3] 'Why Frege does Not Deserve his Grain of Salt', in B. Hale and C. Wright, *The Reason's Proper Study: Essays towards a Neo-Fregean Philosophy of Mathematics* (Oxford: Clarendon, 2001), 72–90.

_____ [4] *Rails to Infinity: Essays on Themes from Wittgenstein's Philosophical Investigations* (Cambridge, Mass.: Harvard University Press, 2001).

Zalta, E., [1] *Intensional Logic and the Metaphysics of Intensionality* (Cambridge, Mass.: MIT, 1988).

_____ [2] 'Singular Propositions, Abstract Constituents, and Propositional Attitudes', in J. Almog, J. Perry, and H. Wettstein (eds.), *Themes from Kaplan* (Oxford: OUP, 1989), 455–78.

Zermelo, E., [1] 'Untersuchungen über die Grundlagen der Mengenlehre I', *Mathematische Annalen* 65 (1908), 261–81.

_____ [2] 'Neuer Beweis für die Möglichkeit einer Wohlordnung', *Mathematische Annalen* 65 (1908), 107–28.

_____ [3] 'Über den Begriff der Definitheit in der Axiomatik', *Fundamenta Mathematicae* 14 (1929), 339–44.

_____ [4] 'Über Grenzzahlen und Mengenbereiche', *Fundamenta Mathematicae* 16 (1930), 29–47.

Zimmerman, A., ' "Ipsum enim <'est'> nihil est" (Aristoteles, Periherm. I, c. 3): Thomas von Aquin über die Bedeutung der Kopula', in A. Zimmermann (ed.), *Der Begriff der Repraesentatio im Mittelalter* (Berlin: Walter de Gruyter, 1971), 282–95.

Index